Reading for Thinking

Third Edition

Laraine E. Flemming

HOUGHTON MIFFLIN COMPANY
Boston   New York

Senior Sponsoring Editor: Mary Jo Southern
Senior Associate Editor: Ellen Darion
Editorial Assistant: Danielle Richardson
Senior Project Editor: Kathryn Dinovo
Manufacturing Manager: Florence Cadran
Senior Marketing Manager: Nancy Lyman

Cover design: Harold Burch, Harold Burch Design, New York City
Cover image: Tim Lewis

Acknowledgments: Copyrights and acknowledgments appear on page 604, which constitutes an extension of the copyright page.

Printed in the U.S.A.

Library of Congress Catalog Card Number: 99-72008

ISBN: 0-395-95833-4

23456789-CS-03 02 01 00 99

As part of Houghton Mifflin's ongoing
commitment to the environment, this text
has been printed on recycled paper.

CONTENTS

Chapter 2   Reviewing Paragraph Essentials   *48*

Chapter 3   Power Tools for Learning: Paraphrasing and Annotating   *91*

Chapter 4   Beyond Paragraphs: Understanding and Outlining Longer Readings   *135*

Chapter 5   Summarizing and Synthesizing: Two More Strategies for In-Depth Learning   *173*

Chapter 8 Identifying Purpose and Tone 274

 Chapter 9 Understanding Figurative Language 315

 Chapter 10 Recognizing and Responding to Bias 338

Chapter 11   Understanding and Evaluating Arguments   *376*

Chapter 12   Reading and Responding to Essay Questions   *432*

TO THE INSTRUCTOR

For those of you who have successfully used *Reading for Thinking* in the past and intend to use it again in the future, rest assured: *Reading for Thinking*, 3rd Edition, still takes students step by step through the basics of reading comprehension and brings them—almost without their knowing it—into the realm of critical reading. Although the explanations of key terms like **main idea, thesis statement, argument,** and **tone** have all been revised, they retain the clarity and brevity praised by both teachers and students. The number and variety of the exercises have been increased, rather than decreased, so that student readers still have numerous chances to review every skill and concept.

As in the two previous editions, the readings were chosen based on two criteria: They had to be both stimulating and informative. Perhaps most significant for those who liked the previous editions, this third edition retains the crucial premise of earlier ones. Critical reading is not presented as an unrelated series of skills to be pursued for their own sake but rather as a coherent body of intellectual tools that can help students evaluate arguments, compare opposing points of view, and ultimately develop their own perspectives on current or controversial issues.

Having pointed out the many ways that this edition is similar to previous ones, let me say at the same time that *Reading for Thinking* has been extensively revised. There is much here that is altogether new.

New to the Third Edition

A New Chapter on Reading and Responding to Essay Questions

Reading for Thinking now ends with a chapter on how to read and respond to essay questions. The placement of this chapter is entirely intentional. Chapter 12 brings together everything students have learned in previous chapters, and they get to see, in practical terms, the way comprehension and critical reading skills go hand in hand. For example, in learning how to break an essay question into its basic parts—topic and requirements—students review what they already know about topics and main ideas. When called upon to evaluate essay answers—some of them their own—they bring into play what they have learned about good and bad arguments. Chapter 12 brings home a basic principle of this book: To get the most out of any text, readers need to use both comprehension and critical reading skills. The two are not separate entities; they are inextricably intertwined.

A New Chapter on Figurative Language

Chapter 9, *Understanding Figurative Language,* disproves what many students mistakenly believe—that figurative language is the province of poetry. The figures of speech covered in this chapter— similes, metaphors, and allusions—appear in all kinds of writing, and they are particularly present in writing meant to persuade. In addition to explanations guaranteed to demystify the function of figurative language in writing, this chapter also offers a series of inventive exercises that teach students how to recognize and interpret all three figures of speech.

A New Sample Chapter on Memory

The third edition of *Reading for Thinking* includes a sample chapter that allows for immediate practice of the SQ3R sequence of skills introduced in Chapter 1, *Getting a Head Start: Strategies for Academic Achievement.* The sample chapter, however, does more than give students a chance to practice surveying and reciting. It also offers clear explanations of how human memory works as well as practical tips on memory improvement.

A Brand New Chapter on Paraphrasing and Annotating

Students who consistently paraphrase and annotate are bound to see an improvement in concentration, comprehension, and memory. Because paraphrasing and annotating are essential to academic success, this edition of *Reading for Thinking* has given them a chapter all their own, *Power Tools for Learning: Paraphrasing and Annotating.*

A New Section on Reading Multiple-Choice Questions

Knowing how to correctly interpret multiple-choice questions is a special reading skill all its own, and it's not one that college students necessarily come by naturally. It seemed important, therefore, to include in this edition a thorough discussion of how to read and respond to multiple-choice questions.

Two End-of-Chapter Tests

Every chapter now ends with a new, double-test feature. The first test functions as a review quiz that helps students monitor their understanding of the chapter. Based on how well they do on the quiz, students can decide which portions of the chapter they need to review. Once they complete their review, they are ready for the chapter test that covers the same skills but uses different content.

This double-test feature has two benefits. First, it makes students assume responsibility for their performance on the chapter test. Based on the review quiz, they know full well whether or not they need additional review in order to be prepared for the chapter test. Second, the review quiz functions as a practice test and helps alleviate some of the anxiety students feel about taking the end-of-chapter test.

Word Notes

As before, potentially difficult words are defined throughout the chapter, and teachers who want to give students more practice with these words will find additional exercises in the manual. In this edition, there is also a new end-of-chapter feature called *Word Notes.* Each of these notes focuses on a word introduced in the chapter, using it to make a point about language in general. While some *Word Notes* examine how context alters meaning, others offer a range of possible synonyms or an insight into the word's history.

An Expanded Discussion of Synthesizing

The ability to synthesize is central to reading, writing, and critical thinking. We use it to make meaning out of separate words, sentences, and paragraphs. We use it to generalize, draw inferences, compare arguments, and develop our own point of view. In its third edition, *Reading for Thinking* more fully acknowledges the importance of synthesizing by tripling its original coverage.

A Revised Chapter on Analyzing Arguments

The chapter on arguments has been revised from beginning to end. The point of this extensive revision is to give students more practice analyzing extended arguments. The newly revised chapter also pays more detailed attention to the individual elements of an argument. Students learn about the three kinds of statements most likely to lie at the heart of a written argument: statements of condition, value, and policy. They also learn how to recognize the most common types of support used in an argument—reasons, examples, expert opinion, and research results. The chapter now ends with a discussion of the errors in logic frequently linked to each kind of support: irrelevant or circular reasoning, hasty generalization, inappropriate or unidentified experts, and dated research.

A Revised Chapter on Identifying Purpose and Tone

The new chapter on purpose now offers students more practice with longer readings. But here, too, the emphasis is on giving students more concrete tips for inferring a writer's purpose. Students learn how the title, source, tone, and thesis statement of a reading all combine to reveal the author's intention.

A Revised Chapter on Bias

The chapter on bias now includes an increased number of longer readings. It also includes more specific instruction on how to evaluate bias in the light of an author's purpose. Particular attention is paid to the way bias can intrude itself even into writing meant to inform, and students see specific examples of biased writing drawn from textbooks and reference works.

A New Aid to Comprehension

To help students monitor their comprehension of key concepts and terms, chapter sections are now followed by *Check Your Understanding* boxes that ask students to review what they have learned before going on to the next section. This particular feature is designed to reiterate a point already made in the book's opening chapter: Immediate review is the key to understanding and remembering.

A New Version of "Putting It All Together"

Users of *Reading for Thinking* have been particularly enthusiastic about the book's third and final part, which contains a series of thematically linked readings, each one followed by two sets of questions, one set testing comprehension, the other critical reading. Because this section of the book has been so popular, the key elements remain. The readings are still linked, either to one another or to issues raised in previous chapters, and each one is followed by the double set of questions along with a writing assignment and a critical thinking question. The difference is that the readings are no longer tightly tied into neat groups of four. The looser organization allows the reading topics to range more widely. For example, the selection titled "The Tragedy of Japanese Internment" reappears in this edition. However, it is now accompanied not just by other readings focusing on World War II, but also by a light-hearted essay about speaking Japanese from a Western perspective. Overall, most of the readings in Part III are new, and they cover a variety of topics, ranging from home schooling and the complex nature of heroism to feminism's new wave and the possible link between violence and pornography.

Creating the third edition of *Reading for Thinking* has been both hard work and fun. From my point of view, I like to think I have come up with a winning combination of great readings, solid explanations, and inventive exercises. But, ultimately, only you and your students can be the judge of this new edition.

Also Available

Teachers who feel their students need a more intensive review of basic comprehension skills than *Reading for Thinking* offers might find its precursor, *Reading for Results*, more appropriate to their needs. Unlike *Reading for Thinking*, which emphasizes critical reading a bit more heavily than comprehension, *Reading for Results* concentrates mainly on improving comprehension skills and includes only one chapter on critical reading. Students who have to struggle a little with the reading level of *Reading for Thinking* might be better off with *Reading for Success*, the first book in what is essentially a three-book series. Like *Reading for Results*, *Reading for Success* concentrates on improving comprehension, but it puts a good deal more emphasis on motivation, vocabulary, and single paragraphs. Although all three books work well together, they can certainly be used individually.

To My Reviewers

All the reviewers of *Reading for Thinking* did a terrific job. They not only gave me many useful general suggestions, but also a good many specific ones, which helped me fine-tune individual paragraphs and even sentences. I rely on my reviewers to tell me what to keep, revise, or eliminate, and the current group proved to be extremely astute guides in the revision process. My thanks go to Lynn Anderson of Navarro College; Barbara Bretcko of Raritan Valley Community College; Helen Carr of San Antonio College; Linda Clegg of Cerritos Community College; Eva Pena of Del Mar College; Diana Reeder of Santa Rose Junior College; and Louise Rice of Augusta State College. I would also like to add a special note of thanks to Joan Hellman of Catonsville Community College, Jane Centanni of Camden Community College, and Barbara Radigan of Community College of Allegheny County, three reviewers who have seen me through many editions and whose comments I value more highly than I can express in this short note.

To My Editors

I cannot possibly wrap up this preface without a special thanks to the gifted editors who have made working on *Reading for Thinking* a true pleasure. Just as she did with *Reading for Results,* Harriett Prentiss inspired me to work overtime creating just the right exercise to build or test a particular reading skill. She is a gifted editor, and I am so lucky to have her. As always, Ellen Darion, my senior associate editor, kept me posted, kept me on time, and just generally made me laugh when I needed it most. She really is a treasure. Speaking of treasures, there is no finer sponsoring editor than Mary Jo Southern (and over the years, I have worked with quite a few). Like all the authors she sponsors, I am her devoted fan. To this terrific threesome, I want to add the name of Bryna Fischer, a copyeditor nonpareil. Bryna is so good I expect that some day she will be writing her own books; I just hope she writes them in some other field than mine. And finally, many thanks to Nancy Benjamin and her very competent staff at Books By Design. They do a wonderful job of turning my tattered manuscript into a real, honest-to-goodness book.

Laraine Flemming

Becoming a Successful Student

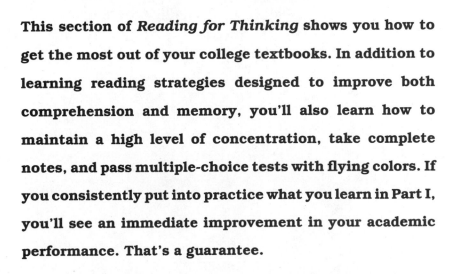

This section of *Reading for Thinking* shows you how to get the most out of your college textbooks. In addition to learning reading strategies designed to improve both comprehension and memory, you'll also learn how to maintain a high level of concentration, take complete notes, and pass multiple-choice tests with flying colors. If you consistently put into practice what you learn in Part I, you'll see an immediate improvement in your academic performance. That's a guarantee.

| **CHAPTER 1**

Getting a Head Start: Strategies for Academic Achievement

In this chapter you'll learn

- how to use a study technique called *SQ3R*.

- how to use context clues to figure out the meaning of unfamiliar words.

- how to recognize the specialized vocabulary of your courses.

- how to improve your concentration.

- how to mark textbook pages.

- how to take multiple-choice exams.

By the time you finish this book, you'll possess all the reading skills necessary to achieve academic success.

Still, like most students, you probably want to improve your academic performance immediately. The good news is that you can. If you put into practice all the pointers and tips introduced in Chapter 1, you'll be a better student in just a few weeks.

 # SQ3R: A System for Reading Textbooks

Textbooks aren't the same as novels. You can't just open up your textbook and start reading. Well, technically you can. But if you do, you won't understand and remember as much as you could if you used a study system like *SQ3R*.

Developed over fifty years ago by teacher and researcher Francis Robinson, *SQ3R* has stood the test of time, with numerous studies indicating that it improves comprehension. The letters *S-Q-R-R-R* stand for *survey, question, read, recite,* and *review.* Following each of these five steps when you read your textbooks will help you learn with greater speed and efficiency. So, without further ado, here's a brief explanation of each step.

S: Survey Before You Begin Reading

Survey a chapter before you begin reading it. Read only the title, the introduction, and the last page. Look carefully at all headings, captions, illustrations, and anything printed in the margins. Pay special attention to words printed in boldface or italics. Use this step to get a general sense of the chapter's content and to gauge how long it should take you to read it.

Q: Questions Help You Get Focused

To give your reading focus or purpose, use words like *why, what,* and *how* to transform headings into questions, such as "Why do glaciers grow and then retreat?" or "How do fossils of sea creatures end up on mountaintops?"

In addition to turning headings into questions, be sure to draw on your own personal knowledge and ask questions like "What do I know about this topic?" and "Do I agree with the author's point of view?" Questions like these also will help you focus your attention while you read and help you maintain concentration.

Raising and answering questions strengthens your motivation. Each time you can answer one of your own questions, you'll feel a sense of accomplishment. The more successful you feel, the more likely you are to keep reading.

R-1: Read the Chapter Section by Section

As you might expect, the first *R* in *SQ3R* stands for *read.* But here again you need to be systematic. Don't just read a chapter straight through from beginning to end. Instead, read it in sections or in bites, going from chapter section to chapter section and pausing to review after each one.

Each time you begin a chapter section, raise questions based on the heading. Whenever possible, predict how you think the author's train of thought will develop. For example, if you see the heading *Differences Between Broadcast and Print Media,* mentally make a prediction and pose a question like the following: "The author will probably point out several differences between television journalists and newspaper journalists. What exactly could those differences be?"

Even if you have to revise your questions and predictions when you finish reading a chapter section, those questions and predictions will still serve their purpose. They will keep you focused on the material and alert you to differences between what you expected to read and what the author actually said.

R-2: Recite at the End of Each Chapter Section

Each time you finish a chapter section, your goal is to monitor, or check, your understanding of what you've read and decide if you need to reread it. Try to answer the questions you posed about the heading, or simply ask yourself, "What were the key points in this reading?" Then see if you can recite some or all of those points. If you can't answer your own questions, you should reread the entire chapter section immediately or mark it for a later rereading with the letters *RR.*

If the reading assignment is particularly difficult or particularly important, it's a good idea to write out the answers to your questions. When you write your answers, you can't fool yourself into thinking you've understood material that is actually vague or unclear in your mind.

R-3: Review After You Finish Reading the Chapter

When you finish your assignment, go back over the chapter and look at the headings. For each heading, try to mentally recite a few of the author's key points. Even better, ask a friend to quiz you on each of the headings.

Yes, using *SQ3R* will take extra time. Simply reading a chapter straight through without surveying or reciting, for example, is a quicker method of studying. Unfortunately, it's not particularly effective. Thus, it's very much worth your while to make *SQ3R*—or some similar method—a regular study habit.

CHECK YOUR UNDERSTANDING

Test your understanding of what you've read by briefly naming and describing each step in *SQ3R* without looking back at the chapter. When you finish, compare what you've written with the actual chapter section to see how complete your answers are. *Note:* You probably won't remember all of the steps, but don't get discouraged. You will in time.

s. _____

_____

_____

_____

_____

g. _____

_____

_____

_____

_____

R. _____

_____

_____

_____

_____

R. _____

_____

_____

_____

_____

R. _____

_____

_____

_____

_____

_____

■ EXERCISE 1

DIRECTIONS Survey the sample chapter on pages 581–603. Then answer the questions that follow by circling the correct answer or filling in the blanks.

1. Based on your survey, which of the following do you think will *not* be covered in the chapter?

　a. Research on memory loss and Alzheimer's disease

　b. Long-term memory

　c. Short-term memory

　d. Memory improvement

2. What devices does the author use to highlight specialized vocabulary?

_____

3. Based on the headings, which one of the following questions do you think would help focus your reading?

   a. Can people with Alzheimer's use techniques to make themselves remember?

   b. What is the difference between short-term and long-term memory?

   c. Do childhood memories forever shape our adult lives?

4. Identify at least three questions you could use to guide your reading.

   a. _____

   b. _____

   c. _____

5. *True* or *False*. According to the chapter, having a good memory is pure luck. You either have one or you don't. _____

EXERCISE 2

DIRECTIONS Read the following selection drawn from the sample chapter on pages 589–591. Use the questions below to focus your reading. Then, when you finish the excerpt, check your understanding by seeing how well you can answer those same questions.

Getting Focused

1. In the context of memory, what does it mean to *recall* information?
2. What is the *serial position effect*?
3. Explain how the term *recognition* relates to memory.
4. What are *distractors*?
5. What is a *savings score*?

Measuring Memory—The Answer Is on the Tip of My Tongue

 Because memory is not an all-or-nothing event, there are several ways of measuring it. Three commonly used **memory tasks** are *recall, recognition,* and *relearning.* Let's see how they differ.

Recall

What is the name of the first song on your favorite record album? Who won the World Series last year? Who wrote the Gettysburg Address? If you can answer these questions you are demonstrating recall. To recall means to supply or reproduce facts or information. Tests of recall often require *verbatim* (word-for-word) memory. If you study a poem or a speech until you can recite it without looking, you are recalling it. If you complete a fill-in-the-blank question, you are using recall. When you take an *essay* exam and provide facts and ideas without prompting you are also using recall, even though you didn't learn your essay verbatim. Essay tests tend to be difficult because they offer few cues to aid memory.

Memory task Any task designed to test or assess memory.

Recall To supply or reproduce memorized information with a minimum of external cues.

The order in which information is memorized has an interesting effect on recall. To experience it, try to memorize the following list, reading it only once:

> BREAD, APPLES, SODA, HAM, COOKIES,
> RICE, LETTUCE, BEETS, MUSTARD, CHEESE,
> ORANGES, ICE CREAM, CRACKERS, FLOUR, EGGS.

Serial position effect The tendency to make the most errors in remembering the middle items of an ordered list of information.

If you are like most people, you will have the most difficulty recalling items from the middle of the list. This is called the **serial position effect.** The last items on a list appear to be remembered best because they are still in STM. The first items are also remembered because they entered an "empty" short-term memory where they could be rehearsed and moved to long-term memory (Medin & Ross, 1992). The middle items are neither held in STM nor moved to LTM, so they are often lost.

Recognition

If you tried to write down all the facts you could remember from a class taken last year, you might conclude that you learned very little. However, a more sensitive test based on **recognition** could be used. For instance, you could be given a *multiple-choice* test on facts and ideas from the course. Since multiple-choice tests only require you to recognize the correct answer, we would probably find evidence of considerable learning.

Recognition Memory in which previously learned material is correctly identified as that which was seen before.

Recognition memory can be amazingly accurate for pictures, photographs, or other visual input. One investigator showed subjects 2560 photographs at a rate of one every 10 seconds. Subjects were then shown 280 pairs of photographs. One in each pair was from the first set of photos and the other was similar but new. Subjects could tell with 85 to 95 percent accuracy which photograph they had seen before (Haber, 1970). This finding may explain why people so often say, "I may forget a name, but I never forget a face."

Recognition is usually superior to recall. This is why police departments use photographs or a lineup to identify criminal suspects. Witnesses who disagree in their recall of a suspect's height, weight, age, or eye color often agree completely when recognition is all that is required. Identification is even more accurate when witnesses are allowed to hear suspects' voices as well as see them (Melara, DeWitt-Rickards, & O'Brien, 1989).

Question: Is recognition always superior?

Distractors False items included with a correct item to form a test of recognition memory (for example, the wrong answers on a multiple-choice test).

False positive A false sense of recognition.

It depends greatly on the kind of **distractors** used. These are false items included with an item to be recognized. If the distractors are very similar to the correct item, memory may be poor. A reverse problem sometimes occurs when only one choice looks like it could be correct. This can produce a **false positive,** or false sense of recognition. For example, there have been instances in which witnesses described a criminal as black, tall, or young. Then a lineup was held in which a suspect was the only African American among whites, the only tall suspect, or the only young person (Loftus, 1980). Under such circumstances a false identification is very likely.

Relearning

In a classic experiment on memory, a psychologist read a short passage in Greek to his son. This was done daily when the boy was between 15 months and 3 years of age. At age 8, the boy was asked if he remembered the Greek passage. He showed no evidence of recall. He was then given selections from the passage he heard and selections from other Greek passages. Could he recognize the one he heard as an infant? "It's all Greek to me!" he said, indicating no recognition (and drawing a frown from everyone in the room).

Had the psychologist stopped, he might have concluded that no memory of the Greek remained. However, the child was then asked to memorize the original quotation and others of equal difficulty. This time his earlier learning became evident. The boy memorized the passage he had heard in childhood 25 percent faster than the others (Burtt, 1941). As this experiment suggests, relearning is typically the most sensitive measure of memory.

Relearning Learning again something that was previously learned. Used to measure memory of prior learning.

Savings score If relearning takes less time than original learning, the amount of time saved (expressed as a percentage) is a savings score.

When a person is tested by **relearning,** how do we know a memory still exists? As with the boy described, relearning is measured by a **savings score.** Let's say it takes you one hour to memorize all the names in a telephone book. (It's a small town.) Two years later you relearn them in 45 minutes. Because you "saved" 15 minutes, your savings score would be 25 percent (15 divided by 60 times 100). Savings like this are a good reason for studying a wide range of subjects. It may seem that it's a waste to learn algebra, history, or a foreign language because so much is lost within a year or two. But if you ever need such information, you will find you can relearn it in far less time. (Dennis Coon, *Essentials of Psychology.* St. Paul, Minn.: West Publishing, 1993.)

Questions

Here are the same questions you used to guide your readings. See how well you can answer them without looking back at the text.

1. In the context of memory, what does it mean to *recall* information?

_____

_____

2. What is the *serial position effect*?

_____

_____

3. Explain how the term *recognition* relates to memory.

_____

_____

4. What are *distractors?*

_____

_____

5. What is a *savings score?*

_____

_____

Exercise 3

DIRECTIONS Read the entire sample chapter on pages 581–603. Be sure to recite while you read and to review once you finish. Then see how well you can answer the following questions without looking back at the chapter. Circle the letter of the correct answer.

1. Selective attention

   a. controls concentration.

   b. is responsible for forgetting.

   c. determines which information moves on to long-term memory.

2. Chunking

   a. recodes information into larger units.

   b. recodes information into smaller units.

   c. can be used only for numbers.

3. Information that makes its way into long-term memory

   a. remains forever unchanged.

   b. is relatively permanent.

   c. lasts for no more than thirty years.

4. The serial position effect refers to

   a. changes in memory that take place over time.

   b. the difficulty we have remembering items from the middle of a list.

   c. the way important pieces of information crowd out of memory information of lesser importance.

5. Distractors are

   a. damaged brain cells.

   b. pieces of information that never found their way into long-term memory.

   c. false items included along with correct items that are to be recognized.

6. Ebbinghaus is famous for

   a. discovering the effects of chunking.

   b. identifying the role of distractors in remembering.

   c. plotting the curve of forgetting.

7. The most obvious cause of forgetting is

   a. insufficient brain cells.

   b. failure to encode.

   c. information overload.

8. According to the theory of state-dependent learning,

   a. we are more likely to remember information in situations that recreate the original learning conditions.

   b. we are more likely to remember information in a state of hypnosis.

   c. we are more likely to remember information if we put ourselves into a state of relaxation brought on by the use of meditation or drugs.

9. Learning proceeds best

   a. when the learner gets immediate feedback.

   b. when we work with others who have similar goals.

   c. when we are praised for our efforts.

10. Overlearning encourages

    a. forgetting.

    b. remembering.

    c. mental fatigue.

 # Using Context Clues

Having a systematic method for reading textbooks is essential to being a successful student. However, as you may already know, some textbooks seem to be filled with unfamiliar words. To master the material in those textbooks, you need more than a good study method. You also need to know how context clues can help you determine word meaning.

The **context** of a word is the sentence or passage in which the word appears. Fortunately, context can often help you figure out an *approximate meaning* of unfamiliar words. Although that meaning may not be exactly the same as the one that you'll find in the dictionary, it will be close enough so that you can continue reading without interruption. The following pages illustrate four of the most common context clues.

Contrast Clues

Sentences containing contrast clues include **antonyms,** words or phrases opposite in meaning to the words you don't know. For example, suppose you were asked what the word *ostentatious* meant. You might not be able to define it. After all, the word doesn't turn up that often in everyday conversation. But suppose that word had a context, or setting, as in the following passage:

> Contrary to what many of us assume, the very rich are seldom *ostentatious* in their dress; they do not need to wear showy clothes to impress others. Secure in their wealth, they can afford to look plain and unimpressive.

In this case, the context of the word *ostentatious* provides contrast clues to its meaning. The words *plain* and *unimpressive* are antonyms for *ostentatious.* Using those contrast clues, you could **infer,** or read between the lines and figure out, that *ostentatious* means being showy or trying to impress.

Restatement Clues

For emphasis, authors sometimes deliberately say the same thing two different ways. Look, for example, at the following passage:

> Caffeine may well be bad for you. But without a cup of coffee in the morning, I get very *cantankerous.* My son says that on coffeeless days, I give new meaning to the words *cranky* and *ill-tempered.*

Here, the author announces that she becomes *cantankerous* in the morning if she doesn't have a cup of coffee. Then, to emphasize that point, she offers a restatement clue—two **synonyms,** or words similar in meaning, to the word *cantankerous: cranky* and *ill-tempered.* Thanks to that restatement, you can easily infer the meaning of *cantankerous*—"to be cranky and ill-tempered."

Example Clues

Be alert to passages in which the author supplies an example or an illustration of an unfamiliar word. Examples of the behavior or thinking associated with a word can often give you enough information to infer a good approximate definition.

The captain had a *dour* personality. He never laughed or smiled. He always prepared for the worst and seemed disappointed if the worst didn't happen.

You might infer from the examples in the above passage that *dour* means "gloomy and depressed," and you would be absolutely correct.

General Knowledge Clues

Although contrast, restatement, and examples are common context clues, not all context clues are so obvious. Sometimes you have to base your inference solely on your familiarity with the experience or situation described in the text, as in the following example:

As soon as I asked Magdalena to drive, I knew I had made a mistake. She was an excellent driver but always took the most *circuitous* route in order to enjoy the scenery. By the time we arrived at the restaurant, waiters were clearing the tables, and the restaurant was closed until dinnertime.

This passage does not contain any contrasts, restatements, or examples. But you can still figure out that *circuitous* means "indirect or roundabout." After all, the driver *chose* to take the route, so *circuitous* cannot mean "wrong." Because they arrived too late for lunch, the word must mean that the route was not direct.

Turning to the Dictionary

As the examples show, it's possible to infer a definition of an unfamiliar word from its context. Sometimes, however, context does not give you a definition that seems appropriate, and you won't be able to make sense of the passage without knowing what the word means. In a case like this, you should look up the word before you continue reading.

Using context to derive meaning is valuable because it allows you to read without constantly referring to a dictionary. However, after you finish reading, you should still compare the definitions you inferred with those in the dictionary. That way, you will be sure your definitions are correct.

■ EXERCISE 4

DIRECTIONS Use context to define the italicized words in the following sentences. Then identify the type of context clue that helped you infer your definition: *C* (contrast), *R* (restatement), *E* (example), or *G* (general knowledge).

EXAMPLE In *flagrant* disregard of the rules, she passed on the right and exceeded the speed limit by at least twenty miles an hour.

Definition *open, obvious*

Type of Clue *E*

EXPLANATION The examples of flagrant disregard—speeding, passing on the right—both suggest definitions like "open" and "obvious."

1. The surprise party was a complete *fiasco;* she had never before given a party that was such a failure.

Definition _____

Type of Clue _____

2. As a child he had been the most *gregarious* kid on the block, but as an adult he became a loner who found it difficult to bear the company of others.

Definition _____

Type of Clue _____

3. When the author stood at the podium to speak, there were no signs of her previous *trepidation.* In contrast to her earlier mood, she was remarkably relaxed and calm. Her voice did not break, her hands did not shake, and she seemed totally in command of the situation.

Definition _____

Type of Clue _____

4. Before her death, the witch screamed out a *malediction* on the heads of her accusers, and more than one was terrified by the curse.

Definition _____

Type of Clue _____

5. When it comes to publicity, the *incumbent* president obviously has more access to the press than other candidates. As the person already holding the office, the president is automatically followed everywhere by the press.

Definition _____

Type of Clue _____

6. He had come from an extremely *affluent* home where money was no object. But he gave it all up to live a life of poverty and serve those needier than himself.

Definition _____

Type of Clue _____

7. Although she wanted to, there was no way to *mitigate* the harshness of her criticism.

Definition _____

Type of Clue _____

8. The bulldog was remarkably *tenacious*. He wouldn't let go of the robber's leg even when the man rained blows down on his head. He only let go when his master yelled, "Stop!"

Definition _____

Type of Clue _____

9. Books on time management are popular primarily because *procrastination* is so common. After all, how many of us can honestly say we have never put off or postponed something we didn't want to do— washing the dog, writing a paper, cleaning the house—until the very last possible minute?

Definition _____

Type of Clue _____

10. After saving his mother from drowning, the twelve-year-old boy was *inundated* with letters praising him for his heroism.

Definition _____

Type of Clue _____

Context and Meaning

Keep in mind that *context affects word meaning.* For example, based on context, you probably correctly inferred that the word *incumbent* in the previous exercise means "holding or being in office." But the definition of that word can change with the context. Look, for example, at the following sentence: "It was *incumbent* on her to provide a sense of direction because she was the leader of the party." In this sentence, *incumbent* means "required" or "obligated." Many words have more than one meaning, and changing the context of a word can dramatically change its meaning.

 # Recognizing and Mastering Specialized Vocabulary

Most academic subjects have a specialized vocabulary all their own. Words like *utility* in economics (the satisfaction received from consuming a service or product) and *exogamy* in anthropology (marriage outside of one's tribe, group, or family) are examples of the specialized vocabulary you need to know in order to master either of these subjects.

Anxious for you to learn the specialized vocabulary of their subject matter, authors of textbooks usually provide an explicit definition right before or right after they introduce a key term. Thus, you need to pay close attention to any words that are highlighted in boldface, italics, or colored ink *and* followed by a definition. Such words are bound to belong to the specialized vocabulary of the subject you're studying. Look, for example, at the way the author of a textbook on management defines the term *corporate culture.*

 Organizations develop unique internal cultures. Within the last decade, much attention has been focused on the relationship between a corporation's culture and its success. **Corporate culture** consists of the shared values, symbols, stories or myths, rituals, and language that shape an organization's work patterns. (Judith G. Bulin, *Supervision,* Boston: Houghton Mifflin, 1995, p. 5.)

With a passage like this one, you should pause a moment to study the boldface term and its definition. You should also write the word and definition on an index card or in a vocabulary notebook so you can file it away for later review. The more familiar you become with the specialized vocabulary of each subject, the easier it will be to read and understand your reading assignment.

If you don't completely understand the definition of a specialized term that you find in your textbook chapter, check for a **glossary** in the back of the book that lists specialized vocabulary words along with their definitions. If the glossary doesn't answer your questions, ask your instructor about the word or term causing you difficulty. Whatever you do, don't let specialized vocabulary remain vague or unclear in your mind. Take the time to learn and understand those definitions so that you don't have to puzzle over specialized vocabulary every time you read.

◾ EXERCISE 5

DIRECTIONS In your next study session, make at least three index cards recording the specialized vocabulary words you encounter in your reading. Write the word on one side and the definition on the other; that way, you can quiz yourself anytime you have a few spare moments.

 # Improving Your Concentration

Improving your reading skills is certainly central to successfully completing your assignments and passing exams. But research has also shown that good readers know how to focus their attention and concentration while they read.[1] If you are one of those students whose mind wanders while reading, the following pages will show you how to stay focused on the task at hand.

Getting Focused

There are lots of things you can do to improve your concentration. Where you study and with whom you study are just two of the factors that can affect your ability to concentrate.

[1]Sharon L. Smith, "Learning Strategies of Mature College Learners," *Journal of Reading* 26 (1982): 5–12.

Find a Quiet Place

When it's time to study, search out a place that is fairly free of distractions. If your home or the dorm is too noisy, go to a public or school library.

Study at the Same Time

Like most of us, you are probably a creature of habit. Thus, if you consistently study at the same time and in the same location, your response to that time and place will become automatic. You'll no sooner sit down at your regular time and in your designated study area than you'll be ready to start working.

Be Prepared

Before you even open your textbook, make sure you have everything you need—your pen, notebook, calculator, eraser, and so on. Whatever you do, don't give yourself built-in excuses for breaking your concentration. You don't want to be searching for your favorite pen when you should be studying.

Turn Off the Music

Many students insist that listening to music while studying doesn't disturb their concentration. However, research on effective learning conditions does not support their point of view. Most of those studies show that students who listen to music while studying have lower comprehension levels than those who read in a quiet setting.[2] So think about turning off the music whenever you're ready to study.

Look for the Right Study Companions

Studying with other people can be a great way to learn. In a study group, you can talk over the material, quiz one another, and compare notes. However, if you're forming a study group, choose your study companions carefully. Avoid anybody who whines about working or is easily distracted. Choose instead people who want to

---

[2]See Virginia Voeks, *On Becoming an Educated Person.* Philadelphia: W. B. Saunders, 1979.

do well in school and who accept the fact that they have to work hard to achieve their goals.

Set Time Limits for Each Assignment

Every time you begin a study session, try to determine exactly how much time you want to spend on each assignment. For example, tell yourself that in one hour you're going to read ten to fifteen pages of your psychology text. Knowing exactly how much you want to accomplish in one hour will make you more conscious of how effectively you're using your allotted time. In particular, you'll become more aware of how minor distractions can eat away at your study time. As a result, you'll be less likely to make a quick phone call or stare out the window during the time you've allotted for completing an assignment. An added bonus is that whenever you complete an assignment on time, you'll feel a sense of accomplishment.

Staying Focused

The appropriate physical setting, regular study times, and the right study companions can get you off to a good start. However, staying mentally focused also depends a lot on how you approach your assignments as well as on your study techniques.

Underline and Annotate

Underlining key words is a wonderful strategy for maintaining concentration. It forces you to pay close attention to the material in order to decide which words are essential to expressing the author's ideas. Just as valuable are **annotations,** or marginal notes, that list key points, identify potential test questions, and record personal comments. The rate of forgetting is highest right after you finish reading. If you review what you've read by taking notes in the margins or jotting down potential test questions, you can slow down the rate of forgetting and improve your ability to remember. (You'll learn more about annotation in Chapter 3.)

Be a Critical Reader

When you're studying, don't limit yourself to simply understanding an author's ideas. Instead, be a **critical reader**—someone who analyzes, evaluates, and judges an author's content and style. Critical readers **analyze,** or break the author's message down into its individual parts, in order to see how well those parts fit together. They also check to see if the author's ideas are clearly illustrated or explained. Above all, critical readers consider what they might already know about the subject under discussion and try to determine if their knowledge and experience confirm or contradict the author's point of view.

Vary Your Assignments

Varying your assignments is an excellent way to combat mental fatigue and the resulting loss of concentration. If, for example, you've spent an hour doing math problems and you are feeling tired, don't just keep plugging away at those problems. Instead, shift to a radically different assignment, like reading a short story for your English class.

Vary Your Learning Strategies

In the same way that varying your assignments can help you stay focused, varying your learning strategies can also help keep you sharp and alert for long periods of time. Thus, if you've been reading and taking notes for an hour and are feeling tired, try switching to a different learning technique. Ask a friend to quiz you on your notes. If you're working alone, make a list of **recall clues**—words or phrases that represent a larger set of ideas. Then quiz yourself by looking at the recall clues and trying to remember the ideas they represent.

There are many different ways to master new material. For example, if you're reading in your biology text about the parts of a flower, you could mark key passages, try to visualize the flower's parts, or sketch and label the parts. Any one of these techniques will help you absorb the material, and you don't have to rely on just one or the other. You can switch back and forth as you see fit.

Maintain a Positive Attitude

If a course doesn't grab your attention immediately, don't sit back and decide to be bored. Instead, tell yourself that every course can teach you something of value, and it's up to you to find that something. Being bored is pointless and self-defeating. Even more important, it hinders concentration. If a course does not immediately excite you, you need to ask questions, do some outside reading, or create a study group that can generate enthusiasm.

Take Breaks

If you work straight through for two hours, your concentration is bound to suffer because your eyes and your brain get tired. The trick is to not let yourself reach the point of exhaustion. Instead, give yourself a ten- to fifteen-minute break for every hour you study. That's time enough to prevent eye strain and mental fatigue from setting in.

CHECK YOUR UNDERSTANDING

See if you can list the six different techniques described under the heading **Staying Focused.**

1. _____

_____

2. _____

_____

3. _____

_____

4. _____

_____

5. _____

_____

6. _____

_____

◄■ **EXERCISE 6**

DIRECTIONS The following page introduces a concentration checklist. Make two copies. Fill one out now and the other a month from now. Your goal is to turn every *no* into a *yes*.

CONCENTRATION CHECKLIST

	Yes	No
1. Do you specify how many pages you intend to cover before you begin an assignment?	☐	☐
2. Do you generally study at the same time and in the same place?	☐	☐
3. Are you always on the lookout for good study companions?	☐	☐
4. While you study, do you constantly make decisions about what is important and what is not?	☐	☐
5. Do you underline selectively and annotate, or write, in the margins?	☐	☐
6. Are you careful to vary the kinds of tasks you do?	☐	☐
7. Do you vary your learning strategies?	☐	☐
8. Do you periodically look up and mentally review key points from your reading?	☐	☐
9. Do you try to connect what you are learning with what you already know?	☐	☐
10. Are you a critical reader who evaluates the author's ideas and agrees or disagrees with the author's arguments?	☐	☐
11. If you find a passage you don't understand, do you write down your questions and plan to ask for help later?	☐	☐
12. Do you give yourself a ten-minute break for each hour of study?	☐	☐
13. If you have a lapse of concentration, do you immediately try to get back on track?	☐	☐
14. Do you congratulate or reward yourself when you finish your work within the time limits you set?	☐	☐
15. Do you try hard to maintain a positive attitude and develop an interest in each of your courses?	☐	☐

Mastering the Art of Underlining

If you are trying to improve your concentration, underlining while you read can play a key role. Underlining will help you concentrate and think more deeply about the author's ideas. As a result, you'll remember more of the material. Yet despite the obvious benefits of underlining, many students don't know how to do it effectively. Afraid of leaving out something important or just because they aren't paying enough attention, many students underline too much. Although underlining too little can be a problem, it's much less common than underlining too much. As a result, when exams roll around, students find themselves reviewing entire chapters rather than selected portions. To underline effectively, keep the following pointers in mind. (Note: To be completely effective, underlining should be combined with annotating, which is covered on pages 99–118.)

Be Selective

Instead of underlining each and every word in every sentence, underline only the words necessary to explain the central or main point of the paragraph. You can figure out which words are necessary by asking yourself, What words are essential to the author's meaning? The answer to that question tells you the words that need to be underlined.

Here is a sample passage in which only the key words are underlined. Read just the underlined words, and see how they convey the message of the paragraph.

Tornadoes

A **tornado** is a storm with a very intense low-pressure center. Tornadoes are short-lived and local in extent, but they can be extremely violent. They typically follow a very narrow, sharply defined path, usually in the range of 300–400 m wide. U.S. National Weather Service records show that tornadoes have the strength to drive 2 × 4 wooden boards through brick walls, lift an 83-ton railroad car, and carry a home freezer over a distance of 2 km. (Barbara W. Murck, Brian J. Skinner, and Stephen C. Porter, *Environmental Geology.* New York: John Wiley & Sons, 1996, p. 238.)

If you read just the underlined words in this passage, you can still re-create most of the original meaning. That's the true test of effective underlining.

You may be wondering why we underlined only one of the examples in the last sentence. Although all three are helpful in describing the intensity of a tornado, with a series like this it's usually a good idea to underline the first item and then annotate the others in the margin, using words like *examples, reasons, consequences,* and so on.

Find a Balance Between Underlining Too Much and Underlining Too Little

Here are two more underlined passages. In the first one, the reader has underlined too much; in the second, too little.

Adaptive strategies are the <u>unique cultural patterns ethnic minorities use to promote the survival and well-being of the community, families, and individual members of the group.</u> Adaptive strategies help them <u>gain access to educational, medical, political, and legal services, employment, housing, and other important resources and services. These strategies are reflected in the childrearing goals and practices found in these groups (Harrison et al., 1990). Three of the most important adaptive strategies are (1) the extended family, (2) biculturalism, and (3) ancestral world views.</u> (Kelvin L. Seifert, Robert J. Hoffnung, and Michelle Hoffnung, *Lifespan Development,* Boston: Houghton Mifflin, 1997, p. 390.)

If you buy your textbooks in a used-book store, you'll notice that the excessive underlining shown above is very typical in used textbooks—at least in the first chapter. After that opening chapter, the underlining usually dribbles off to nothing. Students who underline every sentence often realize they are wasting their time and stop doing it. Unfortunately, they don't always take the time to figure out what they were doing wrong. Instead, they give up on underlining altogether.

Just as ineffective as too much underlining is underlining too little. To understand why, read just the underlined words in the following passage. See if you can figure out what the paragraph is about. Don't be surprised if you can't.

The *extended family* includes parents, children, and other relatives such as aunts, uncles, grandparents, and cousins, as well as some individuals not biologically related. In <u>African-American extended families</u>, for example, the high degree of interdependence among three or more generations of kin (child, parent, grandparent), as well as nonbiological family members, helps to provide the material aid such as food, shelter, clothing, money, child care, household maintenance, and social and emotional support that are <u>critical for effective family functioning</u> (Harrison et al., 1990; Stack, 1981). <u>Hispanic-American families</u> also show high degrees of connectedness, loyalty, and solidarity with parents and other relatives and of interdependence and mutual support (McGoldrick et al., 1982). (Seifert et al., *Lifespan Development*, p. 390.)

The person who underlined this passage correctly understood that the term *extended family* was important. But beyond underlining that term, the reader hasn't even tried to highlight the definition or indicate its relationship to the two minority groups mentioned. As a result, the phrases that are underlined are all but useless for later reviews.

Use Pencil Rather Than Pen

While you are still learning how to underline efficiently, use a pencil rather than a pen or a felt-tip marker. That way, if you change your mind, you can always erase. After you review and further refine your understanding of what's essential, you can go back and underline again, this time with a pen or marker.

Check for Accuracy

Every once in a while, test your underlining to see if it makes sense. When you read over the underlined words, you should be able to fill in the gaps and come up with the general meaning of the passage. If reading only the underlined words doesn't make any sense, erase and start over.

EXERCISE 7

DIRECTIONS Circle the letter of the passage that best fits the guidelines for selective underlining described on pages 25–26.

EXAMPLE

a. **Participative Leadership Style**

Participative leaders share <u>decision making</u> with group members. <u>Participative leadership encompasses so many behaviors that it can be divided into three subtypes:</u> <u>consultative, consen-</u>

sus, and democratic. **Consultative leaders** confer with group members before making a decision. However, they retain the final authority to make decisions. **Consensus leaders** are called that because they strive for consensus. They encourage group discussion about an issue and then make a decision that reflects general agreement and will be supported by group members. All workers who will be involved in the consequences of a decision have an opportunity to provide input. A decision is not considered final until all parties involved agree with the decision. Another criterion of consensus is that the group members are willing to support the final decision even if they do not agree with it totally. **Democratic leaders** confer final authority on the group. They function as collectors of group opinion and take a vote before making a decision. Some observers see very little differentiation between democratic leadership and free-rein leadership. (Adapted from Andrew J. DuBrin, *Leadership.* Boston: Houghton Mifflin, 1998, p. 110.)

b. **Participative Leadership Style**

Participative leaders share decision making with group members. Participative leadership encompasses so many behaviors that it can be divided into three subtypes: consultative, consensus, and democratic. **Consultative leaders** confer with group members before making a decision. However, they retain the final authority to make decisions. **Consensus leaders** are called that because they strive for consensus: They encourage group discussion about an issue and then make a decision that reflects general agreement and will be supported by group members. All workers who will be involved in the consequences of a decision have an opportunity to provide input. A decision is not considered final until all parties involved agree with the decision. Another criterion of consensus is that the group members are willing to support the final decision even if they do not agree with it totally. **Democratic leaders** confer final authority on the group. They function as collectors of group opinion and take a vote before making a decision. Some observers see very little differentiation between democratic leadership and free-rein leadership. (Adapted from DuBrin, *Leadership,* p. 110.)

c. **Participative Leadership Style**

Participative leaders share decision making with group members. Participative leadership encompasses so many behaviors that it can be divided into three subtypes: consultative, consensus, and democratic. **Consultative leaders** confer with group members before making a decision. However, they retain the final authority to make decisions. **Consensus leaders** are called that because they strive for consensus. They encourage group discussion about an issue and then make a decision that reflects general agreement and will be supported by group members. All workers who will be involved in the consequences of a decision have an opportunity to provide input. A decision is not considered final until all parties involved agree with the decision. Another criterion of consensus is that the group members are willing to support the final decision even if they do not agree with it totally. **Democratic leaders** confer final authority on the group. They function as collectors of group opinion and take a vote before making a decision. Some observers see very little differentiation between democratic leadership and free-rein leadership. (Adapted from DuBrin, *Leadership,* p. 110.)

EXPLANATION The correct answer is *b.* If you read over only the underlined words, you can still make sense of the paragraph without feeling that something crucial has been left out or that too much has been left in, forcing you to reread the entire paragraph.

a. Hispanic Americans

A new minority group has emerged in the United States—Hispanic Americans, also called Latinos. Today the category actually includes several groups. Besides Mexican Americans and Puerto Ricans, there are Cuban immigrants who began to flock to the Miami area when their country became communist in 1959. There are also the "other Hispanics"—immigrants from other Central and South American countries who have come here as political refugees and job seekers. By 1996, the members of all these groups totaled about 28 million, constituting nearly 11 percent of the U.S. population, the second largest minority. Because of high birth rates and the continuing influx of immigrants, Hispanic Americans are expected to outnumber African Americans in the next decade.

The Spanish language is the unifying force among Hispanic Americans. Another source of common identity is religion: at least 85 percent are Roman Catholic. There are, however, significant differences within the Hispanic community. Mexican Americans are by far the largest group, accounting for 64 percent of Hispanics. They are heavily concentrated in the Southwest and West. Puerto Ricans make up 11 percent and live mostly in the Northeast, especially in New York City. . . . Cubans constitute 5 percent of the U.S. Hispanic population. (Alex Thio, *Sociology.* New York: Addison & Longman, 1997, p. 299.)

b. **Hispanic Americans**

A new minority group has emerged in the United States—Hispanic Americans, also called Latinos. Today the category actually includes several groups. Besides Mexican Americans and Puerto Ricans, there are Cuban immigrants who began to flock to the Miami area when their country became communist in 1959. There are also the "other Hispanics"—immigrants from other Central and South American countries who have come here as political refugees and job seekers. By 1996, the members of all these groups totaled about 28 million, constituting nearly 11 percent of the U.S. population, the second largest minority. Because of high birth rates and the continuing influx of immigrants, Hispanic Americans are expected to outnumber African Americans in the next decade.

The Spanish language is the unifying force among Hispanic Americans. Another source of common identity is religion: at least 85 percent are Roman Catholic. There are, however, significant differences within the Hispanic community. Mexican Americans are by far the largest group, accounting for 64 percent of Hispanics. They are heavily concentrated in the Southwest and West. Puerto Ricans make up 11 percent and live mostly in the Northeast, especially in New York City. . . . Cubans constitute 5 percent of the U.S. Hispanic population. (Thio, *Sociology*, p. 299.)

c. **Hispanic Americans**

A new minority group has emerged in the United States—Hispanic Americans, also called Latinos. Today the category actually includes several groups. Besides Mexican Americans and Puerto Ricans, there are Cuban immigrants who began to flock to the Miami area when their country became communist in 1959. There are also the "other Hispanics"—immigrants from other Central and South American countries who have come here as political refugees and job seekers. By 1996, the members of all these groups totaled about 28 million, constituting nearly 11 percent of the U.S. population, the second largest minority. Because of high birth rates and the continuing influx of immigrants, Hispanic Americans are expected to outnumber African Americans in the next decade.

The Spanish language is the unifying force among Hispanic Americans. Another source of common identity is religion: at least 85 percent are Roman Catholic. There are, however, significant differences within the Hispanic community. Mexican Americans are by far the largest group, accounting for 64 percent of Hispanics. They are heavily concentrated in the Southwest and West. Puerto Ricans make up 11 percent and live mostly in the Northeast, especially in New York City. . . . <u>Cubans</u> constitute <u>5 percent of</u> the <u>U.S.</u> Hispanic <u>population</u>. (Thio, *Sociology*, p. 299.)

◢◣◢◖ Reading and Responding to Multiple Choice

Currently, multiple-choice questions are the most popular type of test question. Easy to correct, they also let teachers test a wide range of knowledge. It makes sense, therefore, for you to learn how skillful test-takers read and respond to multiple-choice questions.

Understand the Purpose and Prepare Accordingly

For the most part, multiple-choice questions directly or indirectly rely on seven words: *who, what, where, why, when, which,* and *how.* These words readily lend themselves to brief questions that can be easily incorporated into multiple-choice answers, or options, like the ones listed below:

1. Which of the following British colonies was founded last?

  a. Plymouth

  b. Pennsylvania

  c. Georgia

  d. Massachusetts Bay Colony

  e. Jamestown, Virginia

2. Who discovered the law of universal gravitation?

  a. Johannes Kepler

  b. Sir Isaac Newton

  c. Galileo

  d. Aristotle

  e. Tycho Brahe

To study for multiple-choice tests, scour your textbook and lecture notes for references to famous figures, significant dates, crucial events, and major theories. Then review and reduce your notes until

_____

(*Answers:* 1.*c* 2.*b*)

you have a collection of 3×5 index cards that show the name, date, event, or theory on one side with a brief description or explanation on the other. In the last day or two before the exam, rely primarily on your index cards for reviews.

Be Familiar with the Format

Just as understanding the structure of a paragraph makes you a better reader, understanding how multiple-choice questions are set up can make you a better test-taker.

Type 1: Incomplete Sentence

The most common type of multiple-choice question starts with a partial or incomplete statement called the "stem." The test-taker's job is to circle the letter of the ending that correctly completes the stem. Here's an example:

One of the chief reasons Americans were willing to join the peacetime North Atlantic Treaty Organization was because of the

a. Cuban Missile Crisis.
b. Hungarian Revolution.
c. Berlin Blockade.
d. Berlin Wall.
e. Bay of Pigs.

From a test-taking perspective, multiple-choice questions that open with an incomplete sentence can sometimes help you eliminate an option. When you're stuck on a multiple-choice question, you should always read the stem followed by each possible answer. If you're lucky, one or even two options might not grammatically fit the opening portion of the sentence as well as the other answers, and you can cross them out as potential answers. Look, for example, at the following:

Johannes Kepler was an

a. astronomer.
b. astrologer.
c. physicist.

d. anthropologist.

e. paleontologist.

In this case, you could immediately eliminate options *c* and *e* because the article *an* is almost always followed by words beginning with the vowels *a, e, i, o, u.* Although grammatical errors that make an option and the stem incompatible are not likely to appear in standardized tests created by an organization, they are possible in teacher-made tests. Your poor, overworked instructor has to create three different exams in one week. Under this type of pressure, it's easy for grammatical incompatibility to creep into a multiple-choice question and answer.

Type 2: Complete Sentence

Less common but still popular is a complete question followed by several answers:

From what source did the American Transcendentalists* find inspiration?[3]

a. the Bible

b. political leaders

c. nature

d. Buddhism

If you're stuck on a multiple-choice question with this format, start by reading the question with each separate answer. Sometimes one of the answers will jog your memory and help you make the correct choice.

Do the Easy Ones First

Whatever the format used on a multiple-choice exam, your first response should be to quickly read through all the questions, looking for those you can answer immediately. But even this first quick reading needs a method, so here's one that works for many successful test-takers.

---

*transcendentalists: People like Henry David Thoreau, Margaret Fuller, and Ralph Waldo Emerson who turned to nature for inspiration.
[3]Adapted from William O. Kellogg, *AP United States History.* New York: Barron's Educational Service, 1996, p. 198.

Anticipate the Answer, Then Read the Options

In your first reading of the whole exam, read each stem or question and see if an answer comes to mind. Then quickly skim the options, checking to see if an answer that closely resembles yours is there. *Make sure you read all the options.* You don't want to circle *a* without looking at *b* and then discover when you get the test back that *b* was really the better answer.

At this stage, it's important not to dawdle. If the options provided don't resemble the answer you came up with, don't try to make one fit by reading into the question and forcing words to assume meanings they don't normally possess. Instead, mark the question and go back to it once you have looked over the entire exam. After you have circled the answers you knew immediately, it's time to return to those questions that weren't quite as easy to answer.

Look for Key Words

If, on your second reading of a multiple-choice question, the answer still doesn't spring to mind, try to identify the names, events, or terms that are essential to the meaning of the stem or question. Then underline or circle them. Often, these key words or phrases will help you eliminate wrong answers and make it easier for you to determine the right one. Take, for example, the following test question. What word or phrase do you think might help you select an answer? Put a circle around it.

In what century did the Protestant Reformation begin?

a. sixteenth

b. nineteenth

c. eighteenth

d. seventeenth

If you circled the phrase "Protestant Reformation," you are on the right track and ready to start the process of elimination.

Use What You Know to Eliminate Wrong Answers

Let's say you studied hard but still drew a blank on the above question about the Protestant Reformation. Is it time to give up and go on to the next question? Absolutely not. Instead, try to call up what you know about the Protestant Reformation and test each option in the light of that knowledge.

For example, you may not know exactly when the Protestant Reformation began. However, when you look at each possible answer, you might know immediately that it occurred way before the eighteenth or nineteenth centuries. Good, now there are only two answers to choose from.

At this point, you may remember that Martin Luther, the leader of the Protestant Reformation, was born in 1483. Based on common sense, you wouldn't assume that Luther led a religious revolution before the 1500s. After all, he was still a teenager. And if Luther led the Reformation as an older adult, then—thanks to the process of elimination—you have your answer: The Protestant Reformation began in the sixteenth century, also known as the 1500s.

Look for the Option "All of the Above"

Sometimes when you look over the options, you'll notice that two or even three answers seem to be correct. Study those choices carefully to see if there is a word or phrase that might eliminate one of them. If there isn't and one option says "all of the above," that's probably the correct answer.

Watch Out for the Words *Not* and *Except*

Whenever you see the words *not* or *except* in the stem of a question, circle them to make them stand out. That way you'll be sure to take the words into consideration when choosing your answers. Consider, for example, the following question. Ignore the word *not* and you are bound to choose the wrong answer.

Which scientist was not involved in the making of the hydrogen bomb?

a. J. Robert Oppenheimer

b. Edward Teller

c. Werner von Braun

d. John von Neumann

Be Willing to Guess

Unless there's a penalty for a wrong answer, don't be afraid to guess as a last resort. If you are really stumped and just aren't sure which answer is right, circle the one you think most plausible, keeping in mind the following pointers. They sometimes apply and can help you make an "educated" guess.

Making an Educated Guess

1. The correct answer is sometimes longer and more detailed than the wrong answer.

2. The incorrect options are sometimes very similar and the correct answer is the one option that is quite different.

3. Words like *all*, *never*, and *always* frequently signal wrong answers, whereas words like *sometimes*, *usually*, and *generally* are more likely to be included in correct answers.

4. If two options seem equally correct and there's no option for "all of the above," choose the option that comes later in the list of answers. Test makers frequently put the wrong answer first because they know that some students are quick to choose the first seemingly correct answer they see.

5. Silly or foolish answers are not there to trick you. They really are wrong.

Don't Get Bogged Down

When you get your test, figure out generally how much time you can spend on each question. If you don't know the answer to a question and find yourself going way over your time limit, circle the question number and go back to it after you have answered all the other questions.

Avoid Overanalyzing

When answering multiple-choice questions, don't overinterpret or overanalyze either the stem or the options. Assign words their conventional, or common, meanings, and don't assume unlikely or rare meanings in an effort to discover where the instructor is trying to dupe you into choosing the wrong answer. Yes, your instructor wants to test your knowledge *and* your ability to read closely and carefully. But he or she does not want to mislead you with impossibly tricky questions or answers. So relax and take the language of the exam at its face value. There are no complicated, hidden meanings requiring you to wrench the language from its usual context.

EXERCISE 8

DIRECTIONS For each question, circle the letter of the correct answer.

1. Multiple-choice questions are
   a. used primarily in science and history tests.
   b. not as popular as they once were.
   c. inferior to essay questions.
   d. the most popular type of test question.
   e. never used to test mathematical knowledge.

2. Multiple-choice questions rely heavily on the
   a. words *define, explain,* and *illustrate.*
   b. reader's ability to read between the lines.
   c. words *who, what, why, where, when, which,* and *how.*
   d. test-taker's vocabulary.
   e. words *analyze, evaluate, annotate, synthesize, compare,* and *contrast.*

3. The incomplete portion of a multiple-choice test is called the
   a. stalk.
   b. stem.
   c. base.
   d. root.
   e. core.

4. When you first read the exam questions, you should read
   a. every second question.
   b. only the options.
   c. only the ones that look hard.
   d. all the questions.
   e. only the ones that look easy.

5. Identifying key words in a multiple-choice question will help you to do what?

_____

WORD NOTES

Chapter 1 introduced the word *malediction,* meaning "curse." You are more likely to remember the meaning of this word if you keep in mind the meanings of its parts. *Mal* is a prefix meaning "bad" or "badly"; the root *dict* means "to say" or "to speak." Combine knowledge of these word parts with context, and you should have no trouble defining the italicized words in the sentences that follow:

1. In an attempt to win the election, each opponent *maligned* the other.

Maligned means _____

2. Before he could become a news anchorman, he needed *diction* lessons; he looked fabulous, but he had a tendency to slur his words.

Diction means _____

3. The vampire's *malevolent* smile sent chills up and down her spine; she felt as if she had looked into the face of evil.

Malevolent means _____

4. The priest had a favorite *dictum*: "If you understand it, it is not God."

Dictum means _____

Summing Up

Listed below are the most important points in Chapter 1. Put a check mark in the box if you think the point is clear in your mind. Leave the box blank if you need to review the material one more time. The page numbers in parentheses tell you where to look to review each point on the list.

☐ **1.** The letters in *SQ3R* stand for *survey, question, read, recite, recall.* Each of these five steps serves a different purpose, and each of the five will aid your understanding of textbooks. (pp. 4–6)

☐ **2.** Having a systematic method for reading textbooks is important. However, you also need to use context clues such as *contrast, restatement, example,* and *general knowledge* to determine the meaning of unfamiliar words. (pp. 13–15)

☐ **3.** Because they want you to know the specialized vocabulary essential to their subject, textbook authors use several different techniques to make specialized words and terms stand out from the text. Skillful readers are aware of these techniques and use them to identify specialized vocabulary. (pp. 18–19)

☐ **4.** The ability to concentrate isn't a matter of luck. On the contrary, you can use specific techniques to maintain concentration. (pp. 19–23)

☐ **5.** Despite the benefits of underlining while reading, many students don't know how to underline effectively. The key to underlining is finding a balance between underlining too much and too little. (pp. 25–27)

☐ **6.** Multiple-choice questions are currently the most popular kind of test question. Thus, it pays for students to know how to read and respond to multiple-choice questions. (pp. 31–37)

TEST YOUR UNDERSTANDING

To see how well you have understood this chapter, take the following review quiz. Then use the answer key provided by your instructor to correct it. If you score 80 percent or above, you're ready to take the end-of-chapter exam. However, if you score below 80 percent, look over the quiz carefully to see what kinds of questions you missed. Use the **Summing Up** section to find out which pages you should review before taking the chapter exam.

◢◣◯ Chapter 1: Review Quiz

DIRECTIONS Answer the following questions by circling the appropriate letter or filling in the blanks.

1. Name and describe each step in *SQ3R*.

S: _____

_____

Q: _____

_____

R: _____

_____

R: _____

_____

R: _____

_____

2. Use context to define the italicized word in each sentence. Then circle the letter of the context clue you used to derive your definition.

a. When the storm began, we decided to wait for a more *auspicious* moment; no one in the group wanted to go on a picnic under such unfavorable conditions.
The word *auspicious* means _____

_____.

Context Clue   a. contrast
b. example
c. restatement
d. general knowledge

b. I can't accept that *spurious* hundred dollar bill; it has George Washington's face where Benjamin Franklin's should be.
The word *spurious* means _____

_____.

Context Clue   a. contrast
b. example
c. restatement
d. general knowledge

c. Because of its harsh policies, the government is in a very *precarious* position; and because it is so insecure, the World Bank is unwilling to extend the term of the country's loans.
The word *precarious* means _____

_____.

Context Clue   a. contrast

b. example

c. restatement

d. general knowledge

d. The expression "Have a nice day" has been repeated so often, it has become *perfunctory*.
The word *perfunctory* means _____

_____.

Context Clue   a. contrast

b. example

c. restatement

d. general knowledge

3. The Latin prefix *mal* means _____.

4. Experienced readers know that definitions of words can change with _____.

5. Words like *utility* and *exogamy* are examples of what?

_____

6. To improve your concentration, you should

a. find a quiet place.

b. study at the same time every day.

c. be prepared.

d. turn off the music.

e. do all of the above.

7. To stay focused while you read, which of the following is *not* essential?

a. listening to music

b. underlining and annotating

c. reading critically

d. varying your assignments

e. varying your learning strategies

8. Define the term *critical reader.*

_____

_____

9. Based on what you have learned from Chapter 1, which passage is more effectively underlined?

a. Canada: A Harm-Based Approach to Obscenity

In February 1992, the Supreme Court of Canada <u>ruled that obscenity was to be defined by the harm it does to women's pursuit of equality</u>. In *Butler v. Her Majesty the Queen,* the Court unanimously <u>redefined obscenity</u> as sexually <u>explicit material that involves violence or degradation</u>.* According to the Canadian Court, <u>violent and degrading sexual material will almost always constitute an undue exploitation of sex</u> and <u>interferes with progress</u> toward gender equality.

    <u>The Court's ruling sets out clear guidelines. Adult erotica,</u>* no matter how explicit, <u>is</u> not <u>considered obscene</u>. Erotic material that <u>contains violence, degradation, bondage,</u> or <u>children is considered illicit obscenity</u>. In effect, the Court decided that a threat to <u>women's equality is an acceptable ground</u> for some limitation of free speech. <u>As of this writing, Canada is</u> the only nation that has redefined obscenity in terms of <u>harm to women rather than as material that offends moral values</u>. (Albert Richard Allgeier and Elizabeth Rice Allgeier, *Sexual Interactions.* Boston: Houghton Mifflin, 1995, p. 530.)

b. Canada: A Harm-Based Approach to Obscenity

In February <u>1992</u>, the <u>Supreme Court of Canada</u> <u>ruled</u> that <u>obscenity</u> was to be <u>defined</u> by the <u>harm</u> it does <u>to women's pursuit</u> of equality. In *Butler v. Her Majesty the Queen,* the <u>Court</u> unanimously <u>redefined obscenity as sexually explicit material</u> that <u>involves violence</u> or <u>degradation</u>. According to the Canadian Court, violent and <u>degrading</u> sexual material will almost always constitute an undue <u>exploitation of sex</u> and <u>interferes with progress</u> toward <u>gender equality</u>.

    The Court's ruling sets out clear guidelines. Adult erotica, no matter how explicit, is not considered obscene. Erotic material

_____

*degradation: the act of reducing to a lower condition.
*erotica: literature or art that focuses on sexual desire.

that contains violence, degradation, bondage, or children is considered illicit obscenity. In effect, the Court decided that a threat to women's equality is an acceptable ground for some limitation of free speech. As of this writing, Canada is the only nation that has redefined obscenity in terms of harm to women rather than as material that offends moral values. (Allgeier et al., *Sexual Interactions*, p. 530.)

10. When you underline a passage, what question should you **ask?**

     _____.

11. To underline effectively, readers need to find a balance between

     _____.

12. Describe the two kinds of multiple-choice formats.

     a. _____

     b. _____

13. In your first reading of all the multiple-choice questions, you

     should begin by _____

     _____.

14. On your second reading of the questions, you should use key words

     to help you _____

     _____.

15. If you are really stumped on a multiple-choice question, you

     should _____, unless there is _____.

> Use the answer key provided by your instructor to correct your quiz. If you score 80 percent or above, you are ready for the chapter exam. If you score below 80 percent, look carefully at the questions you answered incorrectly. Then use the **Summing Up** section to decide which pages you need to review.

Chapter Test 1

DIRECTIONS Answer the following questions by circling the appropriate letter or filling in the blanks.

1. What is the purpose of surveying before you read?

_____

2. Why should you pose questions and make predictions before you begin to read?

_____

3. How can reciting after reading be helpful?

_____

4. *True* or *False.* You should read a chapter in sections, pausing after each one to review what you've read. _____

5. Use context to define the italicized word in each sentence. Then circle the letter of the context clue you used to derive your definition.

a. Because of the high altitude, his brain had been deprived of oxygen and he was *incoherent.* Because he wasn't making any sense, his fellow climbers couldn't understand his warnings.

The word *incoherent* means _____

_____.

Context Clue
    a. contrast
    b. general knowledge
    c. example
    d. restatement

b. The snowstorm *obliterated* all traces of the wolf's tracks.

The word *obliterated* means _____

_____.

Context Clue
    a. contrast
    b. general knowledge
    c. example
    d. restatement

c. President Truman spoke little and to the point, unlike President Eisenhower, who was more *loquacious* by nature.

The word *loquacious* means _____

_____.

Context Clue   a. contrast

b. general knowledge

c. example

d. restatement

d. The discussion leader tried hard to *facilitate* the discussion between the opposing parties. If one side made a muddled statement, she would immediately try to clarify to avoid disagreement or confusion.

The word *facilitate* means _____

_____.

Context Clue   a. contrast

b. general knowledge

c. example

d. restatement

6. Most academic subjects have a _____ all their own.

7. Why is it a good idea to regularly study at the same time and in the same location?

_____

8. Define the term *critical reader.* _____

_____.

9. The key role of underlining is to _____.

10. What question should you ask when you want to decide how much to underline in a passage?

_____

11. Which of the following passages is more effectively underlined?

a. Within each region of the United States, there are many unique influences and variations too numerous to mention. The key point, however, is that these **regional differences** may <u>affect</u>

consumption patterns. To illustrate, due to a strong Mexican in-fluence, consumers in the Southwest have a stronger preference for spicy foods as well as for foods such as tortillas, salsa, and pinto beans. Beef barbecue is particularly popular in Texas due to a large cattle industry, whereas parts of the Deep South lean toward pork barbecue. California has developed a reputation for health consciousness and health foods. There are even regional differences in the type of stuffing used at Thanksgiving. Corn-bread stuffing tends to be more popular in the South, in contrast to oyster stuffing in the North. Asian families on the West Coast, on the other hand, are more likely to substitute rice for stuffing.

Styles of music may also differ across regions. The Deep South developed a distinct style of southern rock (e.g., the Allman Brothers and Lynyrd Skynrd). Nashville and Texas have tradi-tionally been strongholds of country music, and Kentucky is known as the home of bluegrass. More recently, Seattle has been recognized as the capital of the "grunge sound," with bands such as Pearl Jam, Soundgarden, and Nirvana.

b. Within each region of the United States, there are many unique influences and variations too numerous to mention. The key point, however, is that these **regional differences** may affect consumption patterns. To illustrate, due to a strong Mexican in-fluence, consumers in the Southwest have a stronger preference for spicy foods as well as for foods such as tortillas, salsa, and pinto beans. Beef barbecue is particularly popular in Texas due to a large cattle industry, whereas parts of the Deep South lean toward pork barbecue. California has developed a reputation for health consciousness and health foods. There are even regional differences in the type of stuffing used at Thanksgiving. Corn-bread stuffing tends to be more popular in the South, in contrast to oyster stuffing in the North. Asian families on the West Coast, on the other hand, are more likely to substitute rice for stuffing.

Styles of music may also differ across regions. The Deep South developed a distinct style of southern rock (e.g., the Allman Brothers and Lynyrd Skynrd). Nashville and Texas have tradi-tionally been strongholds of country music, and Kentucky is known as the home of bluegrass. More recently, Seattle has been recognized as the capital of the "grunge sound," with bands such as Pearl Jam, Soundgarden, and Nirvana.

12. When you underline, look for a balance between _____

_____.

13. When you take a multiple-choice test, you should
    a. read all the questions through once.
    b. answer first all of the questions you know immediately.
    c. use the process of elimination.
    d. guess if you are completely stumped.
    e. do all of the above.

14. If you are really stumped on a question, you should
    a. stay with it until you get the answer, no matter how long it takes.
    b. forget about it and go on to the other questions.
    c. mark it so that you can return to it when you have answered the other questions.
    d. ask your instructor for assistance.
    e. do all of the above.

15. If you absolutely have to guess, which of the following pointers would *not* apply?
    a. The correct answer is sometimes longer and more detailed than the wrong answers.
    b. The incorrect answers are sometimes very similar, and the correct answer is the one that's quite different.
    c. Words like *all, never,* and *always* frequently signal wrong answers.
    d. The first answer in the list of options is usually the correct one.
    e. If two options seem equally correct, and there is no option that says "all of the above," choose the option that appears later in the list.

C H A P T E R 2

Reviewing Paragraph Essentials

In this chapter, you'll learn

- **how to identify topics.**
- **how to recognize main ideas.**
- **how to locate topic sentences.**
- **how to separate major and minor details.**

Part I of *Reading for Thinking* relies heavily on your ability to identify the essential elements in a paragraph: *topic*, *main idea*, and *supporting details*. To make sure that these three terms are clear in your mind, Chapter 2 offers a quick review of all three.

 ## Starting with the Topic

Finding the topic is the first step toward discovering the main idea of a paragraph. The **topic** of a paragraph is the subject the author chooses to discuss or explore. It's the person, place, object, event, or idea most frequently mentioned or referred to by the author. Usually, you can find the topic by posing one key question: Who or what is most frequently mentioned or referred to in the paragraph? To illustrate, let's use the following example:

The use of animals in scientific research is a controversial subject that provokes strong emotions on both sides. Animal rights activists define animals as sentient* beings who can think, feel, and suffer. They insist, therefore, that the rights of animals be acknowledged and respected. The more conservative animal rights activists argue that the use of animals in research should be strictly monitored while the more radical activists insist that research using animals should be banned altogether. In response to these objections, research scientists who experiment on animals have reorganized their research to take better care of the animals involved. They argue, however, that research on animals is ethical and necessary because it saves human lives and alleviates* human suffering.

What's the topic of this paragraph? Is it "animal rights activists" or the "use of animals in research,"? If you said it was the "use of animals in research" you are right on target. That is, indeed, the subject most frequently mentioned or referred to in the paragraph. The phrase "animal rights activists" is mentioned or referred to several times but not as frequently as the phrase "use of animals in research."

Another thing you should notice about the topic of the above paragraph is the number of words needed to express it; five, to be exact. Occasionally, you will be able to express the topic of a paragraph in a single word. However, much of the time you will need a phrase of two or more words to zero in on the precise topic. Look, for example, at the following paragraph. What's the topic?

Although the fighting took place far from the United States, the Vietnam War deeply affected the way Americans lived their lives. Military service became an important, life-changing experience for over 2 million Americans. In the typical tour of duty, they encountered racial tensions, boredom, drugs, and a widespread brutality against the Vietnamese. Even those Americans who did not fight were changed by the war. Millions of young men spent a substantial part of their late adolescence or young adulthood wondering whether they would be drafted or seeking ways to avoid participation in the fighting. Far more men did not go to Vietnam than went, but the war created deep

*sentient: aware, possessed of consciousness.
*alleviates: relieves, eliminates.

divisions among people of an entire generation. Those who fought in the war often resented those who did not, and people who did not go to Vietnam sometimes treated those who did with scorn, pity, or condescension. (Michael Schaller, Virginia Scharf, and Robert Schulzinger, *Present Tense.* Boston: Houghton Mifflin, 1992, p. 301.)

Here again, no one single word could effectively sum up the topic. The word *Americans* won't do. Nor will the phrase "Vietnam War." To express the focus of the paragraph, we need a phrase like "the effect of the Vietnam War on American life." Note, too, that the words in the topic don't appear next to each other. This topic was created by combining words from different parts of the paragraph and adding the word *life.* The point here is that identifying the topic often requires you to do a good deal more than simply look for a word or two. On the contrary, frequently you have to figure out how to piece together a topic that will most effectively help you unlock paragraph meaning. To be effective, the topic you create should be general enough to include everything discussed in the paragraph and specific enough to exclude what isn't.

◾ EXERCISE 1

DIRECTIONS Read each paragraph. Then circle the letter of the correct topic.

EXAMPLE According to the attachment theory of love, adults are characterized, in their romantic relationships, by one of three styles. *Secure lovers* are happy when others feel close to them. Mutual dependency in a relationship (depending on the partner and the partner's depending on you) feels right to them. Secure lovers do not fear abandonment. In contrast, *avoidant lovers* are uncomfortable feeling close to another person or having that person feel close to them. It is difficult for avoidant lovers to trust or depend on a partner. The third type, *anxious-ambivalent lovers*, want desperately to get close to a partner but often find that the partner does not reciprocate the feeling, perhaps because anxious-ambivalent lovers scare away others. They are insecure in the relationship, worrying that the partner does not really love them. Research on the attachment theory shows that about 53 percent of adults are secure, 26 percent are avoidant, and 20 percent are anxious-ambivalent.

Topic a. mutual dependency in a relationship
b. attachment theory of love
c. secure lovers

EXPLANATION In this paragraph, almost every sentence mentions or refers to the attachment theory of love. Therefore, the "attachment theory of love" is the topic. "Secure lovers" are the focus of only three sentences and "mutual dependency in a relationship" is mentioned only once.

1. Among the explanations of our nation's high divorce rate and high degree of dissatisfaction in many marriages is that we have such strong expectations of marriage. We expect our spouse to simultaneously be a lover, a friend, a confidant, a counselor, a career person, and a parent, for example. In one research investigation, unhappily married couples expressed unrealistic expectations about marriage (Epstein and Eidelson, 1981). Underlying unrealistic expectations about marriage are numerous myths about marriage. A myth is a widely held belief unsupported by facts. (John W. Santrock, *Life-Span Development*. Madison, Wis.: Brown and Benchmark, 1995, p. 445.)

Topic a. marriage

b. expectations about marriage

c. myths about marriage

2. Surveys show that about three out of four U.S. corporations have **ethics codes**. The purpose of these codes is to provide guidance to manager and employees when they encounter an ethical dilemma. A typical code discusses conflicts of interest that can harm the company (for example, guidelines for accepting or refusing gifts from suppliers, hiring relatives, or having an interest in a competitor's firm). Rules for complying with various laws, such as antitrust, environmental, and consumer protection laws, also are popular code provisions. The most effective codes are those drawn up with the cooperation and widespread participation of employees. An internal enforcement mechanism, including penalties for violating the code, puts teeth into the code. A shortcoming of many codes is that they tend to provide more protection for the company than for employees and the general public. They do so by emphasizing narrow legal compliance*—rather than taking a positive and broad view of ethical responsibility toward all company stockholders—and by focusing on conflicts of interest that will harm the company. (William C. Frederick, James E. Post, and Keith Davis, *Business and Society*. New York: McGraw-Hill, 1992, p. 94.)

---

*compliance: obedience.

Topic a. U.S. corporations

b. ethics codes

c. penalties for violations of ethics codes

3. Matthew failed the first grade. His handwriting was messy. He did not know the alphabet and never attended very well to the lessons the teacher taught. Matthew is almost always in motion. He can't sit still for more than a few minutes at a time. His mother describes him as very fidgety. Matthew has attention-deficit* hyperactivity disorder. Attention-deficit disorder, as it is commonly called, is characterized by a short attention span, distractibility, and high levels of physical activity (Barkley, 1989; Berman, 1992; O'Connor, Crowell, and Sprafkin, 1993). In short, children with this disorder do not pay attention and have difficulty concentrating on what they are doing. Estimates of the number of children with attention-deficit hyperactivity disorder vary from less than 1 percent to 5 percent. While young children or even infants may show characteristics of this disorder, the vast majority of hyperactive children are identified in the first three grades of elementary school. This is the point at which teachers are likely to recognize that children have great difficulty paying attention, sitting still, and concentrating on their schoolwork. (Adapted from Santrock, *Life-Span Development*, p. 281.)

Topic a. learning disorders

b. attention-deficit disorder

c. the first three grades of elementary school

4. From the 1960s to the 1980s, inflation was the single most critical issue facing the world's economies. A high level of inflation creates so much instability and social unrest that it restricts business's capacity to operate successfully and a society's ability to function. In some countries, the value of local money has been cut to one-hundredth or even one-thousandth of its value. What formerly cost one unit of currency now costs 1,000 or more: in other words, an ice cream cone that originally cost 20 cents would now cost 20,000 cents, or $200! (Frederick et al., *Business and Society*, p. 196.)

Topic a. society's ability to function

b. world economies

c. inflation

---

*deficit: lack, loss.

5. Throughout the seventeenth and eighteenth centuries, the rulers of Russia allowed most Russians to live in miserable poverty. But in 1855 a new emperor, Alexander II, came to the throne and, unlike his predecessors, he was determined to improve the lot of the Russian people. Alexander II relaxed press censorship and permitted the Russians to travel abroad more freely. Under his rule, minorities in the empire were treated better, and the courts were reorganized so that criminals might have a trial by jury. Alexander's greatest achievement was his decision to free the serfs, the poor men and women who had been the slaves of the rich landowners.

Topic   a. the suffering of the Russian people

       b. the achievements of Alexander II

       c. the rulers of Russia

 # From Topic to Main Idea

Once you know the topic of a paragraph, the next logical step is to determine the main idea. The **main idea** is the central point or message of the paragraph. The main idea is what unites, or ties together, all the sentences in the paragraph.

To discover the main idea of a paragraph, you need to ask two key questions: (1) What does the author want to say *about* the topic? and (2) What idea or thought is developed throughout most of the paragraph?

To illustrate how these questions can help you determine the main idea, let's look at two different paragraphs. Here's the first one.

> For a period of about seventy-five years (1765–1840), the Gothic novel, an early relative of the modern horror story, was popular throughout Europe. Many of the most popular novels—those written by Horace Walpole, Ann Radcliffe, and Monk Lewis—were sold by the thousands, quickly translated, and frequently plagiarized. The stories were the object of fascination because they described a world where mysterious happenings were a matter of course, and ghostly, hooded figures flitted through the night. Gothic novels were read and discussed by men and women of the upper classes, and publishers, ever alert to a ready market, made sure that copies of the books were available at bargain prices. Thus, even the poorest members of the working class could afford to pay a penny to enter the Gothic world of terror, and they paid their pennies in astonishing numbers.

In this example, the opening sentence announces that the Gothic novel enjoyed great popularity for almost a century. The remaining sentences either give specific examples of how popular the novels were or explain the source of their popularity. Because the author repeatedly returns to the idea that the Gothic novel was very popular, we can say that this is the main idea of the paragraph.

Now, try to determine the main idea in another paragraph. As you read the following example, look for the topic—the subject repeatedly mentioned or referred to—and keep asking yourself, "What does the author want to say about that topic?" and "What one idea is developed throughout most of the paragraph?"

Well before the middle of the next century, the world faces an energy shortage of extraordinary proportions. By the year 2040, the total population on earth is expected to double to about 10 billion people. With the continued industrialization of Asia, Africa, and the Americas, world energy consumption is expected to triple. At that rate of consumption, the world's known oil supply will be depleted in about sixty years. The supply of gas will be depleted in about 100 years. If we are to maintain an acceptable quality of life, we must find new sources of energy that will make up for the shortages that are bound to occur in the coming decades.

The topic of this paragraph is "the energy shortage." That's the subject repeatedly mentioned or referred to. However, we still need to figure out what the author wants to say about that topic. We need to discover the one idea that is developed, not just in a single sentence, but throughout the paragraph.

If you go through the paragraph sentence by sentence, you'll see that each one further develops the point made in the first sentence: We're facing an energy shortage that's likely to arrive very soon. This main idea is developed not just in the opening sentence but throughout the entire paragraph.

CHECK YOUR UNDERSTANDING

Explain the difference between the topic and the main idea of a paragraph.

_____

_____

_____

EXERCISE 2

DIRECTIONS Read each paragraph. Then circle the appropriate letter to identify the topic and the main idea.

EXAMPLE Impatient for victory as World War II dragged on, American leaders began to plan a fall invasion of the Japanese islands, an expedition that was sure to incur high casualties. But the successful development of an atomic bomb by American scientists provided another route to victory in World War II. The secret atomic program, known as the Manhattan Project, began in August 1942 and cost $2 billion. The first bomb was exploded in the desert near Alamogordo, New Mexico, on July 16, 1945. Only three weeks later, on August 6, the Japanese city of Hiroshima was destroyed by a bomb dropped from an American B-29 airplane called the *Enola Gay*. A flash of dazzling light shot across the sky; then, a huge purplish mushroom cloud boiled 40,000 feet into the atmosphere. Dense smoke, swirling fires, and suffocating dust soon engulfed the ground for miles. Much of the city was leveled almost instantly. Approximately 130,000 people were killed; tens of thousands more suffered severe burns and nuclear poisoning. On August 9, another atomic bomb flattened the city of Nagasaki, killing at least 60,000 people. Four days later, the Japanese, who had been sending out peace feelers since June, surrendered. Formal surrender ceremonies were held September 2 on the battleship *Missouri*. (Mary Beth Norton et al., *A People and a Nation*. Boston: Houghton Mifflin, 1994, p. 827.)

Topic a. the invasion of Japan

(b.) the atomic bomb

c. World War II

Main Idea a. Desperate for a victory, American leaders planned an invasion of the Japanese islands.

(b.) The atomic bomb gave the American forces another way to bring World War II to an end.

EXPLANATION Most of the sentences in the sample paragraph explain how the atomic bomb helped end World War II. That makes *b* the best answer for both the topic and the main idea.

1. People have many different reasons for wanting children. Some really like children and want an opportunity to be involved with their care. Some women strongly desire the experience of pregnancy and childbirth. Many young adults see parenthood as a way to demonstrate their adult status. For people coming from happy families, having children is a means of recreating their earlier happiness. For those from unhappy families, it can be a means of doing better than their parents did. Some people have children simply because it's expected of them. Because society places so much emphasis on the fulfillment motherhood is supposed to bring, some women who are unsure of what they want to do with their lives use having a child as a way to create an identity. (Seifert et al., *Lifespan Development,* p. 484.)

Topic a. childhood

b. reasons for having children

c. parenting and past experience

Main Idea a. Some people have children in order to recreate the happiness they themselves experienced growing up.

b. There are many different reasons why people have children.

2. *Fiber* is generally defined as that part of plants (cell wall material) that is essentially indigestible. Though not a direct source of nutrition, dietary fiber serves at least two vital functions in the body. It speeds the passage of food waste through the colon, allowing less time for absorption of dietary cholesterol and less tissue exposure to potential cancer-producing substances in the feces. In addition, some high-fiber foods (especially vegetables such as cabbage, cauliflower, and broccoli) may stimulate the production of cancer-fighting enzymes in the intestinal tract. (Robert L. Williams and James D. Long, *Manage Your Life.* Boston: Houghton Mifflin, 1991, p. 70.)

Topic a. nutrition

b. cancer-producing substances

c. fiber

Main Idea a. Fiber is the indigestible portion of plants.

b. Fiber serves the body in two important ways.

3. The U.S. government has a real interest in knowing what types of products U.S. businesses are exporting to the rest of the world. The federal government is understandably concerned that products that say "Made in America" are of good quality. U.S. companies have sometimes exported products to other nations that were banned from sale at home because of safety concerns. In addition, the government is concerned that U.S. companies not sell military technology to unfriendly nations. In the 1980s, a number of cases arose in which U.S. and West German businesses illegally sold sophisticated technology with potential military applications to Libya, Iran, and Iraq. These transactions violated U.S. laws that restrict the sale of classified military technology to only those customers approved by the Department of Defense. (Adapted from Frederick et al., *Business and Society,* p. 252.)

Topic a. federal regulations

     b. the export of American products

     c. the weapons industry

Main Idea a. The U.S. government needs to be sure that U.S. companies are not selling weapons to unfriendly governments.

     b. The U.S. government needs to be informed about the products that U.S. businesses export to other countries.

4. One important line of thinking about stress focuses on the differences between Type A and Type B personalities. Type A individuals are extremely competitive, are very devoted to work, and have a strong sense of time urgency. They are likely to be aggressive, impatient, and very work-oriented. They have a lot of drive and want to accomplish as much as possible as quickly as possible. Type B individuals are less competitive, less devoted to work, and have a weaker sense of time urgency. Such individuals are less likely to experience conflict with other people and more likely to have a balanced, relaxed approach to life. They are able to work at a constant pace without time urgency. Type B people are not necessarily more or less successful than are Type A people. But they are less likely to experience stress. (David Van Fleet and Tim Peterson, *Contemporary Management.* Boston: Houghton Mifflin, 1994, p. 349.)

Topic a. stress reduction for Type A individuals

     b. the differences between Type A and Type B people

     c. the personality traits of Type B individuals

Main Idea a. Type A people are likely to experience a high degree of stress.

     b. One theory about stress divides people into two different kinds of personalities, Type A and Type B.

5. Sports have become an increasingly integral part of American culture. Thus, it is not surprising that more and more children become involved in sports every year. Yet participation in sports can have both positive and negative consequences for children. Children's participation in sports can provide exercise, opportunities to learn how to compete, increased self-esteem, and a setting for developing peer relations and friendships. However, sports can also have negative consequences for children: Too much pressure to achieve and win, physical injuries, a distraction from academic work, and unrealistic expectations for an athlete. Few people challenge the value of sports for children when conducted as part of a school education or intramural program, but some question the appropriateness of highly competitive, win-oriented sports teams in schools. (Adapted from Santrock, *Life-Span Development,* p. 276.)

Topic a. sports and self-esteem

b. the benefits of school intramural sports programs

c. positive and negative effects of sports in schools

Main Idea a. For children, participating in sports can have both drawbacks and advantages.

b. School sports programs should not put so much emphasis on competition.

 # Recognizing Topic Sentences

Topic sentences are general sentences that put into words the main idea or central thought of a paragraph. If someone were to ask you what a paragraph was about, you could use the topic sentence as explanation. Although not all paragraphs contain topic sentences, a good many do. Particularly in textbooks, writers favor topic sentences because they speed up communication between reader and writer, making it easier for the reader to follow the writer's train of thought without getting confused.

As you might guess, experienced readers are always on the lookout for topic sentences. They consciously search, that is, for general sentences that (1) are explained in more specific detail and (2) could be used to sum up the paragraph. Be forewarned, however: The first sentence of a paragraph is not always the topic sentence. Yes, topic sentences are more likely to open than to close a paragraph, but they can and do appear anywhere—beginning, middle, or end.

Topic Sentence in First Position

Authors often like to begin a paragraph with a topic sentence that sums up the main idea. The sentences that follow then go on to develop or prove the main idea expressed in the opening topic sentence. Here's an example of a paragraph with the topic sentence in first position:

Topic Sentence <u>In the last few years, Judge Howard Broadman has become the center of controversy over what supporters and critics alike have come to call "creative sentencing."</u> The term refers to the judge's penchant* for offering defendants what he considers acceptable alternatives to a jail sentence. For example, one defendant had to wear a T-shirt that announced his status as a criminal on probation. In another case, an abusive husband had to donate his car to a shelter for battered women. In perhaps his most publicized case, Judge Broadman gave a woman found guilty of child abuse a chance to avoid four years in jail if she would voluntarily allow Norplant, a form of birth control, to be implanted in her arm.

In this example, the topic sentence introduces the term "creative sentencing," and the rest of the paragraph explains what that means.

Topic Sentence in Second Position

Sometimes an author will begin a paragraph with one or two introductory sentences and then follow with a topic sentence. For an illustration, read the following paragraph.

Topic Sentence [1]The letters and journals of America's early Pilgrims are filled with complaints about food or, more precisely, about the lack of it. [2]<u>The first settlers, so adventurous when it came to travel, were amazingly slow to recognize that seventeenth-century America offered almost every kind of food imaginable; it just wasn't the exact same food they were used to eating at home.</u> [3]No, there wasn't much mutton, or lamb, to be had, but there were lobsters in abundance, along with oysters, duck, salmon, scallops, clams, and mussels. [4]There were also sweet and white potatoes, peanuts, squash, green beans, strawberries, and tomatoes. [5]Luckily for the settlers, the Indians in the New World grew and relished all of these foods, and they taught the Pilgrims to do the same. [6]But it took a while for the Pilgrims to catch on. [7]For example, during their first years in New

*penchant: leaning, tendency.

England, the English settlers refused to eat clams or mussels. [8]They hadn't eaten them in the Old World, so in the new one, they fed them to the pigs. [9]No wonder their Indian neighbors often looked on in amazement or maybe even amusement.

In this paragraph, the first sentence is an **introductory sentence.** The sentence is not developed in the remainder of the paragraph. Instead, it offers a partial introduction to the topic: the early Pilgrims and their attitude toward food in the New World. The real point of the paragraph comes in the second sentence, where we learn that the early Pilgrims took an incredibly long time to recognize the wonderful selection of foods at their disposal. The second sentence is the topic sentence because it expresses an idea developed by the remaining sentences in the paragraph.

Here now is a variation on paragraphs that open with an introductory sentence or two. Once again, the introductory sentence helps introduce the topic but is not developed by any of the remaining sentences. The main difference between the paragraph that follows and the previous one is that the topic sentence begins with the contrast transition *however.*

Topic Sentence

[1]Most of us, males and females alike, love weddings. [2]<u>However, a good deal of evidence in the English language implies that weddings are more important to women than to men.</u> [3]A woman cherishes the wedding and is considered a bride for a whole year, but a man is referred to as a groom only on the day of the wedding. [4]The word *bride* appears in *bridal attendant, bridal gown, bridesmaid, bridal shower,* and even *bridegroom.* [5]Groom comes from the Middle English *grom,* meaning "man," but that meaning of the word is seldom used outside of the context of the wedding. [6]With most pairs of male/female words, people habitually put the masculine word first—*Mr. and Mrs., his and hers, boys and girls, men and women, kings and queens, brothers and sisters, guys and dolls,* and *host and hostess*—but it is the *bride and groom* who are talked about, not the *groom and bride.* (Adapted from Alice Pace Nilsen, "Sexism in English," *About Language.* Boston: Houghton Mifflin, 1994, p. 251.)

As you probably guessed, **contrast transitions** are words and phrases such as *but, however,* and *yet in reality.* These transitions signal to the reader that the author is about to contradict or modify a point previously made. Although contrast transitions don't always introduce topic sentences that follow on the heels of introductory sentences, they are quite common in this type of paragraph. As a matter of fact, if you spot one of the transitions listed below opening the second or third sentence of a paragraph, check to see if the next sentence and the topic sentence aren't one and the same.

Common Contrast Transitions	
however	in opposition
unfortunately	in contradiction
but	on the other hand
even so	nevertheless
yet	despite the fact
still	nonetheless
on the contrary	yet in fact
just the opposite	yet in reality

Topic Sentence in the Middle

Sometimes authors postpone the topic sentence until the middle of the paragraph. Look, for instance, at the paragraph that follows. The topic sentence appears smack in the middle. Notice, too, the use of a contrast transition. Here again, the transition signals that the author is about to change direction.

Topic Sentence

[1]In general, bats have a varied diet. [2]Flowers, insects, and fish are among their favorite foods. [3]Some bats, however, really are like the bats in horror movies. [4]They do, indeed, dine on blood. [5]<u>Contrary to their on-screen image, however, these so-called vampire bats don't attack and kill humans.</u> [6]They get their dinner from sleeping livestock. [7]Under the cover of darkness, they make small, pinprick incisions with their razor-sharp teeth. [8]Then they drink their fill from their sleeping prey. [9]Vampire bats are so skillful at getting their dinner they usually don't even wake the sleeping animals.

In this paragraph, the author uses several sentences to introduce the topic—vampire bats—and the real point of the paragraph comes in the fifth sentence.

Topic Sentence at the End

Sometimes authors develop a paragraph with a series of specific facts, examples, or studies. Then, in the last sentence, they state the main idea. To be sure, it's not the most common pattern, but it certainly does exist, as the following paragraph illustrates.

Topic Sentence

Advised about the sad plight of pandas who have been driven out of their homes, thousands of people will contribute money to save the pandas' natural habitat.* Similarly, "Save the Whale" campaigns have been in progress for years, and millions of dollars have been spent to help ailing or hunted whales. Currently, in many areas, bats are endangered, but don't expect a campaign to save them from extinction. Bats just don't have the appeal of ancient whales and cuddly pandas. <u>Most people are so repulsed by bats that wildlife organizations have been reluctant to mount a campaign to help them; they are convinced that no one would be interested.</u>

Topic Sentence in Two Steps

Much of the time, the main idea in a paragraph can be summed up in a single sentence. Still, you need to be prepared for a fairly common alternative: the two-step topic sentence. Here's an illustration of one.

[1]Movie director George Romero has made a number of horror films. [2]But none of his films has ever matched the fame won by *The Night of the Living Dead*. [3]Made on a low budget with inexperienced actors, the film tells the story of technology gone wrong. [4]Radiation in the atmosphere has caused the dead to come back to life and attack the living. [5]Not only have the dead come back to life, they have become cannibals as well. [6]Even worse, the living corpses are practically indestructible. [7]Only a bullet through the head can stop them, a discovery not made until the film is half over and the audience has been properly horrified. [8]Not surprisingly, Romero's film has become a cult classic, and true horror fans know the dialogue by heart.

In this paragraph, sentences 3 through 8 tell readers more about a film called *The Night of the Living Dead*. So at first glance, it would seem likely that sentence 2 is the topic sentence. But sentence 2, with its reference to "his films," requires sentence 1 to make complete sense: "None of movie director George Romero's films has ever matched the fame won by his classic horror film, *The Night of the Living Dead*." Yes, writers do usually sum up main ideas in a single sentence, but not always. So be prepared to give them a little help

_____

*habitat: living environment.

by **synthesizing,*** or combining, two sentences into one complete topic sentence.

Question-and-Answer Topic Sentence

Particularly in textbooks, authors are likely to make the first or second sentence the topic sentence. However, they are also fond of opening a paragraph with a question. The answer that follows is usually the topic sentence.

Topic Sentence

What is genetics? In its simplest form, genetics is the study of heredity. It explains how certain characteristics are passed on from parents to children. Much of what we know about genetics was discovered by the monk Gregor Mendel in the nineteenth century. Since then, the field of genetics has vastly expanded. As scientists study the workings of genetics, they've developed new ways of manipulating genes. For example, scientists have isolated the gene that makes insulin, a human hormone, and now use bacteria to make quantities of it. (Kim Magliore, *Cracking the AP Biology Exam.* New York: Random House, 1998, p. 105.)

Questions for Analyzing Paragraphs

1. **To find the topic,** ask "Who or what is repeatedly mentioned or referred to here?"

2. **To discover the main idea,** ask "What does the author want to say *about* the topic? What idea is developed throughout most of the paragraph?"

3. **To locate the topic sentence,** ask "Which sentence or sentences could I use to sum up, in general terms, the contents of the paragraph?"

 EXERCISE 3

DIRECTIONS In the blank following each paragraph, write the number (or numbers) of the topic sentence.

EXAMPLE [1]Compared with a corporate executive or a military officer, a teacher may not appear to have a great deal of power. [2]But

---

*For more on synthesizing, see pp. 187–195.

teachers have a special type of power. [3]Henry Adams* caught the sense of the teacher's *long-term* power in the words "A teacher affects eternity: no one can tell where his influence stops." [4]The teacher's powerful influence arises from the fact that he or she has an impact on people when they are still at a very impressionable stage. [5]Teachers take "a piece of living clay and gently form it, day by day." [6]Many careers are open to you, but few offer such truly inspiring power. (Adapted from Kevin Ryan and James M. Cooper, *Those Who Can, Teach.* Boston: Houghton Mifflin, 1992, p. 148.)

Topic Sentence _2_

> **EXPLANATION** Sentence 1 is an introductory sentence, while sentences 3 through 6 all explain the second sentence of the paragraph. Sentence 2 sums up the point of the entire paragraph, making it the topic sentence of the paragraph.

1. [1]Before the collapse of the Communist party in Eastern Europe, the East German secret police, the *Staatsicherheit* (or Stasi), was an enormous bureaucracy that reached into every part of society. [2]It had 85,000 full-time employees, including 6,000 people whose sole task was to listen in on telephone conversations. [3]Another 2,000 steamed open mail, read it, resealed the letters, and sent them on to the intended recipients. [4]The Stasi also employed 150,000 active informers and hundreds of thousands of part-time snitches. [5]Files were kept on an estimated 4 to 5 million people in a country that had a total population, including children, of just 17 million. [6]Although East Germany had a large standing army, the Stasi kept its own arsenal of 250,000 weapons. (Adapted from Kenneth Janda, Jeffrey M. Berry, and Jerry Goldman, *The Challenge of Democracy.* Boston: Houghton Mifflin, 1995, p. 452.)

Topic Sentence _____

2. [1]What causes plants to bloom? [2]Although you may think that plants flower based on the amount of sunlight they receive, they actually bloom according to the amount of uninterrupted darkness; this principle of plant bloom is called *photoperiodism*. [3]Plants that bloom in late summer and fall, like asters and sedum, are called short-day plants. [4]They require long periods of darkness and only short periods of light. [5]Plants that flower in late spring and early summer, such as daisies and poppies, are called long-day plants. [6]They need only short periods of darkness to blossom.

---

*Henry Adams: (1838–1918) American historian.

Topic Sentence _____

3. ¹As the twenty-first century nears, some people believe that the earth is now fully explored, and they turn their gaze skyward seeking new frontiers. ²Ocean scientists, however, believe that the earth's oceans are ripe for exploration. ³In fact, it was only in the nineteenth century that new technology made ocean exploration possible. ⁴One hundred fifty years ago, diving bells enabled a few brave explorers to make brief descents underwater to more than 30 meters, and, holding their breath, divers sometimes went to twice that depth—but only for a minute or so at a time. ⁵Even earlier, by 1800, several experimental diving suits had been designed and tested; a clever Englishman named John Lethbridge had invented a diving barrel equipped with a small glass viewport, and Robert Fulton had successfully launched the *Nautilus*, the first working submarine. (Adapted from *Scientific American: Triumph of Discovery*. New York: Henry Holt Company, 1995, p. 155.)

Topic Sentence _____

4. ¹On the surface, effective listening might seem to require little more than an acute sense of hearing. ²But, in fact, there's a big difference between hearing and listening. ³*Hearing* occurs when sound waves travel through the air, enter your ears, and are transmitted by the auditory nerve to your brain. ⁴As long as neither your brain nor your ears are impaired, hearing is involuntary. ⁵It occurs spontaneously with little conscious effort on your part. ⁶*Listening*, in contrast, is a voluntary act that includes attending to, understanding, and evaluating the words or sounds you hear. ⁷If you sit through a lecture without making an effort to listen, there's a good chance that the speaker's words will become just so much background noise. (Laraine Flemming and Judith Leet, *Becoming a Successful Student*. New York: HarperCollins, 1994, p. 93.)

Topic Sentence _____

5. ¹When we are extremely fearful or angry, our heartbeat speeds up, our pulse races, and our breathing rate tends to increase. ²The body's metabolism accelerates, burning up sugar in the bloodstream and fats in the tissues at a faster rate. ³The salivary glands become less active, making the mouth feel dry. ⁴The sweat glands may overreact, producing a dripping forehead, clammy hands, and "cold sweat." ⁵Finally, the pupils may enlarge, producing the wide-eyed look that is characteristic of both terror and rage. ⁶In effect, strong emotions are not without consequences. ⁷They bring about

powerful changes in our bodies. (Zick Rubin, Letitia Anne Peplau, and Peter Salovey, *Psychology*. Boston: Houghton Mifflin, 1993, p. 370.)

Topic Sentence _____

6. [1]Every human body ages over time. [2]Scientists believe that the probable maximum human life span is about 150 years; the record of the oldest person to date is Shigechiyo lzumi (1865–1986) of Japan, who lived to be 120 years and 237 days. [3]There are two theories as to why all living things grow old and die. [4]The *free-radical theory* states that free radicals, certain chemicals produced as a by-product of biological activity, are particularly harmful to healthy cells. [5]As a person ages, free radicals gradually destroy cells until they can no longer function properly, causing the entire body (especially whole organ systems such as the kidneys or heart) to break down and die. [6]The *programmed senescence theory* suggests that the rate at which we age is predetermined, and that our genetic makeup controls the aging and death of the cells. [7]After enough of the cells die, the organs cease to function and death occurs. (Patricia Barnes-Svarney, ed., "Theories on Aging," *New York Public Library Science Desk Reference*. New York: Macmillan, 1995, p. 161.)

Topic Sentence _____

7. [1]On May 28, 1934, Elzire Dionne gave birth to five daughters who became famous as the Dionne Quintuplets. [2]Their birth made immediate headlines and was celebrated as a medical and maternal miracle. [3]Unfortunately, the little girls' fame was their downfall; almost from the moment of their birth, they were exploited by everyone around them. [4]Their parents were poor and didn't know how to support their family, which already included six children. [5]Confused and desperate, they agreed to put their five daughters on display at the Chicago World's Fair. [6]For a brief moment, it seemed as if the girls were saved from a miserable fate when the family physician, Dr. Allan Roy Dafoe, stepped in and insisted the girls were too frail to be on exhibit. [7]But when Dafoe took control of the girls' lives, he made himself rich by displaying the quintuplets to tourists and collecting fees for product endorsements.

Topic Sentence _____

 8. [1]Whereas race is based on popularly perceived physical traits, ethnicity is based on cultural characteristics. [2]An **ethnic group,** then,

is a collection of people who share a distinctive cultural heritage. [3]Members of an ethnic group may share a language, religion, history, or national origin. [4]They always share a feeling that they are a distinct people. [5]In the United States, members of an ethnic group typically have the same national origin. [6]As a result, they are named after the countries from which they or their ancestors came. [7]Examples are Polish Americans, Italian Americans, or Irish Americans. (Thio, *Sociology*, p. 294.)

Topic Sentence _____

9. [1]In the Islamic faith, a *jihad* is a holy war undertaken either to expand the rule of Islam or to defend it against its enemies. [2]Because the group that calls itself the Islamic Jihad has been in the news a good deal over the past decade, many people are under the false impression that the jihad is a frequent occurrence. [3]It is not. [4]In fact, it is anything but common, and there are very strict rules about when and how a jihad can be conducted. [5]First, there must be a reasonable chance that the jihad will be successful; otherwise, it should not be undertaken. [6]Second, a jihad must bring nonbelievers into the fold, and it must cease once they have accepted the faith. [7]By the same token, if the jihad begins in response to a threat, it must end as soon as the threat disappears. [8]Judged according to these criteria,* there hasn't been a jihad in hundreds of years.

Topic Sentence _____

10. [1]In 1543, the scientist Andreas Vesalius made a shocking admission. [2]To create his new anatomy book with its detailed descriptions and drawings of the human body, he had flouted* religious laws and dissected human corpses. [3]At the time, all three major religions—Judaism, Christianity, and Islam—forbade the dissection of human bodies. [4]As a result, physicians and scientists had based all of their conclusions about the human body on the dissection of animals. [5]Although they were outraged at Vesalius's challenge to religious law, his colleagues could not ignore the visual accuracy of his drawings. [6]In the end they had to reevaluate their own conclusions about the workings of the human body.

Topic Sentence _____

———————
*criteria: standards.
*flouted: showed contempt for.

CHECK YOUR UNDERSTANDING
Define the terms *topic, main idea,* and *topic sentence.*

Topic: _____

Main idea: _____

_____

Topic sentence: _____

_____

 # The Function of Supporting Details

Once you've found the main idea of a paragraph, you've identified the author's purpose or reason for writing the paragraph. However, there's more to a paragraph than the main idea. To clarify their ideas and make them convincing, authors use major and minor supporting details. The **major supporting details** are the examples, reasons, studies, statistics, facts, and figures that explain, develop, or prove an author's main idea or point. **Minor supporting details** further develop major details, add an interesting fact or story, or provide repetition for emphasis.

Because topic sentences are general sentences that sum up or interpret a variety of events, facts, examples, or experiences, they cover a good deal of ground and thus are subject to misunderstanding. Authors, therefore, use supporting details to avoid being misinterpreted, or misunderstood. Supporting details are the author's way of saying to readers, "I mean this, not that."

For an illustration of supporting details at work, look at the following sentence: "Most people who have survived near-fatal automobile accidents tend to behave in the same fashion." Given only this one sentence, could you be sure you understood the author's message? After all, that sentence could mean different things to different people. Perhaps survivors have nightmares, or fears about their health. Maybe they are just very slow and careful drivers.

Look now at the following paragraph. Note how the addition of supporting details clarifies the author's meaning.

Most people who have survived near-fatal automobile accidents tend to behave in the same fashion. They are fearful about driving even a mile or two over the speed limit and flatly refuse to go faster than the law allows. If they are not at the wheel, their terror increases. As passengers, they are extremely anxious and are prone to offering advice about how to take a curve or when to stop for a light.

In this instance, the supporting details illustrate the three types of behavior that the author has in mind. Those illustrations are the author's way of answering questions such as "What does 'behave in the same fashion' mean?"

Supporting details can range from reasons and examples to statistics and definitions. The form they take all depends on the main idea they serve. Look, for example, at the following paragraph. Here the writer wants to convince readers that a book defending the right to be fat is very much worth reading:

> [1]Marilyn Wann's book *Fat! So?* deserves a large and appreciative audience, one that does not consist solely of those who are overweight. [2]For starters, Wann is refreshingly unembarrassed about being fat (she tips the scales at 270), and that takes courage in a culture as obsessed as ours is with being thin. [3]If anything, the author encourages her readers—in the chapter titled "You, Too, Can Be Flabulous"—to embrace the word *fat* and use it in favorable contexts, such as "You're getting fat; you look great." [4]Still, despite her lively, and often humorous, style, Wann is good at describing the real misery our society inflicts on fat people. [5]Her chapters on the suffering endured by overweight teenagers are particularly moving, and they make a strong case for the need to attack, and attack hard, the tendency to treat the overweight as second-class citizens. [6]The book is also filled with sound advice about healthy eating habits. [7]Clearly, the author is not encouraging her readers to go out and gorge themselves on pizza and beer. [8]What she is suggesting is that they eat right in order to get fit, rather than thin. [9]Insisting that some people can, because of heredity, never be anything but overweight, Wann argues that they should not suffer for the genetic hand they've been dealt. [10]On the contrary, they should learn how to flaunt* their excess poundage and make society accept them just as they are.

In this paragraph, the major details all give reasons why Marilyn Wann's book deserves a wide audience. The minor details, in turn, flesh out and emphasize the major ones. Note, too, that at least two of the minor details are as important as the major detail they de-

---

*flaunt: to show off.

velop. In sentence 6, the author suggests that Wann's book is good because it offers sound advice about healthy eating. But without the presence of the minor details that follow, it would be hard to understand how a book celebrating fat could also provide tips on healthy eating. Minor details 7 and 8 help explain this seeming contradiction: Wann's advice focuses on eating to be fit rather than thin.

This illustration of major and minor details working together raises a key point: Don't be fooled by the labels *major* and *minor.* Sometimes minor details can be as meaningful as major ones, so you need to judge them in terms of what they contribute to the major details they modify. If a minor detail simply adds a personal note or provides repetition for emphasis, you don't need to think about it much, and you certainly don't need to include it in your notes. But if a major detail doesn't make much sense without the minor one that follows, then both details are equally important.

CHECK YOUR UNDERSTANDING

Explain the relationship between major and minor details.

_____

_____

EXERCISE 4

DIRECTIONS Read each paragraph and fill in the first blank with the number (or numbers) of the topic sentence. Answer the questions that follow by circling the correct answer or filling in the blanks.

EXAMPLE

¹What makes an effective leader? ²To be sure, no one characteristic or trait defines an effective leader. ³It is true, however, that the most effective leaders hold group members to very high standards of performance. ⁴Setting such standards increases productivity because people tend to live up to the expectations set for them by superiors. ⁵This is called the *Pygmalion* effect*, and it works in a subtle, almost unconscious way. ⁶When a managerial leader believes that a group

---

*Pygmalion: According to myth, Pygmalion, the king of Cyprus, carved and then fell in love with the statue of a woman who was transformed into a human being. The phrase *Pygmalion effect* reflects the myth's suggestion that wishing or believing something can make it happen.

member will succeed, the manager communicates this belief without realizing that he or she is doing so. [7]Conversely, when a leader expects a group member to fail, that person will not disappoint the manager. [8]The manager's expectation of success or failure becomes a self-fulfilling prophecy. [9]The manager's perceptions contribute to the success or failure. (DuBrin, *Leadership*, p. 85.)

a. Topic sentence: *3*

b. The major details help answer what question or questions about the topic sentence? *Why do effective leaders set such high standards?*

c. *True* or *False:* Sentence 5 is a major supporting detail. Explain your answer. *This supporting detail further explains the previous one, making it a minor but far from unimportant detail.*

d. *True* or *False:* Sentence 9 is also a major supporting detail. Explain your answer. *The point made in Sentence 9 was already clear from previous statements in the paragraph, so the supporting detail adds little more than repetition.*

EXPLANATION Sentence 3 is the only sentence that can effectively sum up the paragraph. Explanations for the *true* and *false* answers already appear in the blanks above.

1. [1]Despite its rapid spread, Islam is not a religion for those who are casual about regulations. [2]On the contrary, adhering to its rules takes effort and discipline. [3]One must rise before dawn to observe the first of five prayers required daily, none of which can take place without first ritually cleansing oneself. [4]Sleep, work, and recreational activities take second place to prayer. [5]Fasting for the month of Ramadan,* undertaking the pilgrimage to Mecca at least once in a lifetime, paying tax for relief of the Muslim poor, and accepting Islam's creed require a serious and energetic commitment. [6]On the whole, the vast majority of Muslims worldwide do observe those

*Ramadan: Muslim holy month.

tenets.* (Adapted from Jan Goodwin, *Price of Honor*. New York: Penguin Books, 1994, p. 29.)

a. Topic sentence: _____

b. The major details help answer what question or questions about the topic sentence?

_____

_____

c. *True* or *False:* Sentence 4 is a major supporting detail.

Explain your answer. _____

_____

d. *True* or *False:* Sentence 5 is also a major supporting detail.

Explain your answer. _____

_____

2. [1]The orchestra conductor Arturo Toscanini was born with a phenomenal memory that served him well throughout his career. [2]For example, Toscanini could remember every single note of every musical score he had ever studied. [3]Once, when he couldn't find a musical score for a performance, he simply wrote it down from memory. [4]When the score was finally found, it was clear that Toscanini had not made one single error. [5]When late in life his eyesight failed him, Toscanini conducted all of his concerts from memory. [6]Audiences agreed that his blindness did not in any way hinder the conductor's performance.

a. Topic sentence: _____

b. The major details help answer what question or questions about the topic sentence?

_____

_____

c. *True* or *False:* Sentence 3 is a major detail.

Explain your answer. _____

_____

———————
*tenets: rules; principles.

d. *True* or *False:* Sentence 6 is a minor detail.

Explain your answer. _____

_____

3. ¹Those cuddly toys known as teddy bears seem to have been around forever. ²But actually the first teddy bears came into being when President Theodore "Teddy" Roosevelt showed himself too much of a sportsman to shoot a staked bear cub. ³In 1902 Roosevelt visited Mississippi to settle a border dispute, and his hosts organized a hunting expedition. ⁴To make sure that the president would remain in a good mood, they staked a bear cub to the ground so that Roosevelt couldn't miss. ⁵To his credit, Roosevelt declined the offer to shoot the bear. ⁶When the incident was publicized, largely through a political cartoon by cartoonist Clifford Berryman, a Russian candy store owner named Morris Mitchom made up a toy bear out of soft, fuzzy cloth and placed it in his shop window with a sign reading "Teddy's Bear." ⁷The bear was a hit with passersby, and teddy bear mania spread rapidly throughout the country.

a. Topic sentence: _____

b. The major details help answer what question or questions about the topic sentence?

_____

_____

c. *True* or *False:* Sentence 4 is a minor detail.

Explain your answer. _____

_____

d. *True* or *False:* Sentence 6 is a major detail.

Explain your answer. _____

_____

4. ¹Did you ever ask yourself just how much truth there is to the eerie legend of Count Dracula? ²You may be surprised to discover that centuries ago there did exist a Prince Vlad, said to be the source of the Dracula legends. ³Prince Vlad, however, did not spend his time seeking out fresh young victims; instead, he had disobedient members of the villages he ruled brought to his castle, where they would be executed before his eyes. ⁴On one occasion, Vlad became furious because some visiting Turkish diplomats failed to remove their turbans. [5]They meant no disobedience; it was simply not their custom to do so. [6]As punishment for this supposed insult, Vlad had the turbans nailed to their heads.

a. Topic sentence: _____

b. The major details help answer what question or questions about the topic sentence?

_____

_____

c. *True* or *False:* Sentence 4 is a minor detail.

Explain your answer. _____

_____

d. *True* or *False:* Sentence 5 is a major detail.

Explain your answer. _____

_____

5. [1]Many people don't know the difference between a patent and a trademark. [2]But there is a difference. [3]Usually granted for seventeen years, a patent protects both the name of a product and its method of manufacture. [4]In 1928, for example, Jacob Schick invented and then patented the electric razor in an effort to have complete control over his creation. [5]Similarly, between 1895 and 1912, no one but the Shredded Wheat company could make shredded wheat, because the company had the patent. [6]A trademark is a name, symbol, or other device that identifies a product and makes it memorable in the minds of consumers. [7]*Kleenex, Jell-O,* and *Sanka* are all examples of trademarks, as is the lion that introduces MGM pictures. [8]Aware of the power that trademarks possess, companies fight to protect them and do not allow anyone else to use one without permission. [9]Occasionally, however, a company gets careless and loses control of a trademark. [10]*Aspirin,* for example, is no longer considered a trademark, and any company can call a pain-reducing tablet an aspirin.

a. Topic sentence: _____

b. The major details help answer what question or questions about the topic sentence?

_____

_____

c. *True* or *False:* Sentence 3 is a minor detail.

Explain your answer. _____

_____

d. *True* or *False:* Sentence 5 is a major detail.

Explain your answer. _____

_____

WORD NOTES

Page 67 introduced the word *flouted*, meaning "showed contempt for" while page 69 introduced the word *flaunt*, meaning "to show off." Because these two words sound alike, they are often confused with one another. Test your understanding of what each one means by first filling in the blanks. Then use each one in a sentence.

1. Eager to _____ tradition, he decided to wear a sweatshirt to his class reunion, even though he knew everyone else would dress up rather than down.

2. People who are really wealthy don't usually _____ their riches.

Now it's your turn:

Flout: _____

_____

Flaunt: _____

_____

Summing Up

Listed below are the most important points in Chapter 2. Put a check mark in the box if you think the point is clear in your mind. Leave the box blank if you need to review the material one more time. The page numbers in parentheses tell you where to look to review each point on the list.

1. The topic is the person, place, or event most frequently mentioned in the paragraph. It's also the starting point for analyzing a paragraph. Usually you can find the topic by posing one question: Who or what is most frequently mentioned or referred to in the paragraph? (pp. 48–50)

2. Once you know the topic, the next step is to determine the main idea that is the central message or point of the paragraph. The main idea unites all the sentences in the paragraph. To discover the main idea, ask two questions: (1) What does the author want to say about the topic? and (2) What idea or thought is developed throughout most of the paragraph? (pp. 53–54)

3. Particularly in textbooks, the main idea is likely to be expressed in a topic sentence. Topic sentences are general sentences that sum up paragraphs and are explained in more specific details. (p. 58)

4. Although the opening of a paragraph is the most likely place for a topic sentence, topic sentences can and do appear anywhere in a paragraph. (pp. 59–62)

5. Sometimes writers use two sentences to express the main idea, and it's up to the reader to synthesize them into one complete topic sentence that sums up the paragraph. (pp. 62–63)

6. Writers also like to use a question to introduce the topic sentence. If a question opens a paragraph, it's quite possible that the answer is the topic sentence. (p. 63)

7. Major and minor details anticipate and answer questions readers might have. Major details are the examples, definitions, reasons, studies, statistics, facts, and figures that explain, develop, or prove the author's point. Minor details flesh out major ones, add lively or colorful facts, and repeat key points for emphasis. (pp. 68–70)

TEST YOUR UNDERSTANDING

To see how well you have understood this chapter, take the following review quiz. Then correct it using the answer key provided by your instructor. If you score 80 percent or above, you're ready to take the end-of-chapter exam. However, if you score below 80 percent, look over the quiz carefully to see what kinds of questions you missed. Then use the **Summing Up** section of the chapter to find out which pages you should review before taking the chapter exam.

◢◣◆ Chapter 2: Review Quiz

Part A

DIRECTIONS Write the number (or numbers) of the topic sentence in the accompanying blank.

1. [1]Throughout the 1950s, repeated attempts were made to unionize migrant farm workers, but because the workers had to follow the crops they picked, they were hard to organize. [2]They were never in one place for very long. [3]However, in the 1960s, a Mexican-American farm worker named Cesar Chavez succeeded against all odds, at unionizing agricultural workers. [4]Using the donations he had gathered from friends and supporters, Chavez traveled from farm to farm speaking to California's migrant workers, most of whom were Mexican-Americans like himself. [5]Used to union activists who came to their fields and talked down to them, the farm workers knew immediately that Chavez understood and respected them in a way other union organizers had not. [6]One by one, they joined his organization, the National Farm Workers' Association. [7]In 1965, recognizing the power in numbers, Chavez persuaded union members to take part in a strike initiated by Filipino grape pickers. [8]Then he went to the media and told the country that no one should eat grapes picked by people who were paid starvation wages and denied the right to toilet facilities while they worked in the fields. [9]To the amazement of the grape growers, millions of people listened. [10]The boycott lasted until 1970, and cost the growers millions of dollars. [11]Cesar Chavez's National Farm Workers' Association had become a force to be reckoned with. [12]Farm owners had to recognize the union, which was renamed the United Farm Workers.

Topic Sentence _____

2. [1]The sinking of the luxury liner *Lusitania* by a German submarine helped propel the United States into World War I. [2]Although initially it was claimed that the ship had been torpedoed for no reason except German viciousness, later evidence contradicted that story. [3]In fact, the boat's cargo was almost completely contraband.* [4]It was carrying fifty-one tons of shrapnel shells and five thousand boxes of bullets. [5]Within eighteen minutes of being hit at 2:10 P.M. on the afternoon of May 6, 1915, the *Lusitania* sunk beneath three hundred feet of water. [6]Because there weren't enough crew members to man the forty-eight lifeboats, panic reigned and hundreds of people died—1,195 to be ex-

---

*contraband: goods prohibited by law or treaty from being imported.

act. [7]Furious at what was perceived to be German treachery, the American public began to support the idea of going to war against Germany.

Topic Sentence ____

3. [1]In 1987, Brazilian labor leader and environmentalist Francisco "Chico" Mendes was awarded the United Nations Global 500 Prize, along with a medal from the Society for a Better World. [2]Sadly, medals couldn't save his life when he took on a group of cattle ranchers in Acre, Brazil. [3]Determined to drive out rubber workers like the ones Mendes represented, the ranchers openly used threats and violence to do it. [4]Mendes, who had a public name and the respect of his fellow workers, was a special thorn in the ranchers' side, and they threatened his life. [5]Mendes took their death threats seriously but refused to give up his labor activities. [6]On December 15, 1988, he told a friend, "I don't think I'm going to live." [7]One week later, Mendes was shot in the chest as he stepped out of his house.

Topic Sentence ____

Part B

DIRECTIONS Read each paragraph and write the number (or numbers) of the topic sentence in the blank. Then answer the questions by circling the correct answer or writing in the blanks.

4. [1]The history of television goes a lot further back than many people suppose. [2]In fact, in 1884, a German experimenter, Paul Nipkow, developed a rotating disk that became the central technology for transmitting images by wire and radiowaves. [3]Then, early in the 1920s, companies such as General Electric and RCA began experiments with television, and other corporations soon followed. [4]But the person who played the key role in developing television was not part of a corporation. [5]In 1922, a skinny teenager named Philo T. Farnsworth astonished his high school teacher by making diagrams of electronic circuits that could transmit moving pictures through air. [6]Farnsworth eventually patented his system and, by 1927, a picture of Herbert Hoover appeared on an experimental TV. (Adapted from Melvin L. DeFleur and Everette E. Dennis, *Understanding Mass Communication.* Boston: Houghton Mifflin, 1996, p. 216.)

  a. Topic sentence: ____

  b. What question or questions about the topic sentence do the major details help answer?

  _____

  _____

c. *True* or *False:* Sentence 5 is a major detail.

Explain your answer. _____

_____

d. *True* or *False:* Sentence 6 is a minor detail.

Explain your answer. _____

_____

5. [1]Just as important as taking steps to keep burglars outside is planning what to do if one of them makes it inside. [2]Start by making a "safe haven." [3]This is a room—ideally a bathroom or a bedroom—that has a window or other means of escape. [4]The room should also have a telephone and a list of emergency numbers. [5]Make sure, too, that you have an escape plan, and that the windows and doors involved in that plan can be easily opened. [6]If you do come face to face with an intruder in your home, try not to panic. [7]The more level-headed you are, the more likely you'll be able to think of a way to defuse the situation. [8]Most burglars just want to get out of the house once they've been detected, so don't attack or try to hold the intruder until police arrive. [9]The general rule is simple: Fight only if you have to. (Adapted from Richard L. Bloom, "What to Do If There's a Burglar in the House," *Bottom Line Personal Book of Bests*. New York: St. Martin's Press, 1992, p. 144.)

a. Topic sentence: _____

b. What question or questions about the topic sentence do the major details help answer?

_____

_____

c. *True* or *False:* Sentence 3 is a minor detail.

Explain your answer. _____

_____

d. *True* or *False:* Sentence 4 is a major detail.

Explain your answer. _____

_____

6. [1]Just as we have been taught to believe that getting married is part of being an adult, we've also been taught to believe that having children is part of being married. [2]We have come to think that children are a sign of the love between a woman and a man and that therefore children make the couple happier. [3]But some research suggests the opposite is true: Although having children may increase personal happiness (particularly the wife's), children tend to decrease marital happiness. [4]In a study comparing couples who intentionally had children with those who intentionally were child-free, the latter reported having more "positive marital interactions" such as fun away from home, working together on a project, and having sexual relations (Feldman, 1981, p. 597). [5]According to another study, spouses are happiest before children come and after they leave home. [6]This negative effect of children on marriage appears to be true for both spouses of all races, major religious preferences, educational levels, and employment status (Glenn & McLanahan, 1992). (Adapted from David Knox, *Choices in Relationships*. St Paul, Minn.: West Publishing, 1985, p. 299.)

   a. Topic sentence: _____

   b. What question or questions about the topic sentence do the major details help answer?

   _____

   _____

   c. *True* or *False:* Sentence 4 is a minor detail.

   Explain your answer. _____

   _____

   d. *True* or *False:* Sentence 5 is also a minor detail.

   Explain your answer. _____

   _____

7. [1]Throughout the sixteenth and seventeenth centuries, Native Americans relied on fire to alter and control their environment. [2]Cabeza de Vaca, the Spanish explorer who crossed much of the Southeast during the 1530s, noted that the Ignaces Indians of Texas went about "with a firebrand, setting fire to the plains and timber so as to drive off the mosquitoes, and also to get lizards and similar things which they eat, to come out of the soil." [3]Plains Indians used fires for communication: to report a herd of buffalo or warn of danger, as well as to drive off enemies in war. [4]In California, Indians burned fields annually to remove old seed stocks and prepare the soil for new growth. [5]In 1602, the Spanish explorer Vizcaino reported that near San Diego, the Indians "made so many columns of smoke on the mainland that at night it looked like a procession and in the daytime the sky was overcast."

a. Topic sentence: _____

b. What question or questions about the topic sentence do the major details help answer?

_____

_____

c. *True* or *False:* Sentence 3 is a major detail.

Explain your answer. _____

_____

d. *True* or *False:* Sentence 5 is also a major detail.

Explain your answer. _____

_____

8. [1]What causes someone to be shy? [2]There's no one simple answer to that question; on the contrary, people seem to suffer from shyness for a number of reasons. [3]To begin with, shy persons often lack social skills. [4]They aren't sure how to meet and greet or how to start a conversation and keep it going. [5]Shy people are also afflicted by evaluation fears. [6]They are terrified that, in some way, they will be ridiculed or rejected for being inadequate. [7]A third problem for shy people is the self-defeating bias in their thinking. [8]Shy people believe that social encounters are going to go wrong, and naturally they always blame themselves if things don't go well. (Adapted from Coon, *Essentials of Psychology*, p. 484.)

a. Topic sentence: _____

b. What question or questions about the topic sentence do the major details help answer?

_____

_____

c. *True* or *False:* Sentence 4 is a major detail.

Explain your answer. _____

_____

d. *True* or *False:* Sentence 6 is also a major detail.

Explain your answer. _____

_____

9. ¹Agoraphobia is an intense fear of being in public places where escape or help might not be readily available. ²Victims fear that panic-like symptoms will occur and incapacitate them, causing them to behave in an embarrassing manner, such as fainting, losing bowel control, or displaying excessive fear in public. ³Ultimately, the anxiety over showing these symptoms can prevent agoraphobics from leaving their homes. ⁴Agoraphobia has a lifetime prevalence* rate of approximately 3.5 percent for males and 7 percent for females. ⁵A nationwide survey of more than nine hundred persons with agoraphobia disclosed that nearly 75 percent of all sufferers remember a particular event that seemed to bring on the disorder. ⁶In some instances, that event was the death of a family member; in others, it was a serious illness or the first sign of marital difficulties.

a. Topic sentence: _____

b. What question or questions about the topic sentence do the major details help answer?

_____

_____

c. *True* or *False:* Sentence 2 is a major detail.

Explain your answer. _____

_____

d. *True* or *False:* Sentence 6 is a minor detail.

Explain your answer. _____

_____

 10. ¹According to David Halberstam, who won a Pulitzer Prize for his work as a war correspondent in Vietnam, television had a decisive

_____

*prevalence: the number of cases of a disease in a given population at a specific time.

impact on the Vietnam War* and its outcome. [2]In total, this longest war in United States history played in living rooms for fifteen years. [3]CBS sent its first combat news team to Vietnam in 1961, and the station was also there for the final evacuation of U.S. troops in 1975. [4]At first, Vietnam coverage tended to be "sanitized," stressing U.S. efficiency and military might, but the 1968 Tet offensive brought the war to the Saigon hotels where journalists had once stayed in relative safety. [5]As a result, war in all its blood and violence burst on to America's television screens and entered America's living rooms— a fact that undermined support for the war. (Adapted from Sydney W. Head, Christopher H. Sterling, and Lemuel B. Schofield, *Broadcasting in America.* Boston: Houghton Mifflin, 1994, pp. 430–431.)

a. Topic sentence: _____

b. What question or questions about the topic sentence do the major details help answer?

_____

_____

c. *True* or *False:* Sentence 3 is a major detail.

Explain your answer. _____

_____

d. *True* or *False:* Sentence 4 is a minor detail.

Explain your answer. _____

_____

> Use the answer key provided by your instructor to correct your quiz. If you score 80 percent or above, you are ready for the chapter exam. If you score below 80 percent, look carefully at the questions you answered incorrectly. Then use the **Summing Up** section to decide which pages you need to review.

---

*Vietnam War: Vietnam, a country in Southeast Asia, was the scene of a civil war between 1954 and 1975. In an effort to ward off a communist takeover, the United States, like France before it, entered into that civil war on the side of South Vietnam.

Chapter Test 2

Part A

DIRECTIONS Write the number (or numbers) of the topic sentence in the accompanying blank.

1. [1]The largest demographic* group in the United States, called "baby boomers," consists of those born between 1946 and 1964. [2]Because baby boomers are presently the segment with the greatest economic impact, they are the target for numerous products and services. [3]This includes cars, housing, foreign travel, and recreational equipment. [4]Boomers are also heavy consumers of banking and investment services. [5]They are the heaviest users of frozen dinners and are a growing market for movies, especially highly original ones with adult themes. [6]They are also the target of marketing efforts for children's products and services. (Wayne D. Hoyer and Deborah J. MacInnis, *Consumer Behavior.* Boston: Houghton Mifflin, 1997, p. 357.)

Topic Sentence _____

2. [1]Beavers, North America's largest rodents (they grow to more than two feet long), are delightful to watch for their industry and their family affection. [2]Yet few animals have been so relentlessly exploited as the beaver. [3]In the eighteenth and nineteenth centuries, beaver pelts were worth their weight in gold. [4]As a result, by 1896, at least fourteen American states—Massachusetts, Vermont, New Hampshire, New York, Rhode Island, Connecticut, Pennsylvania, New Jersey, Delaware, Maryland, Illinois, Indiana, West Virginia, and Ohio—had announced that all of their beavers had been killed. [5]By the beginning of the twentieth century, it looked as if the beaver was about to disappear from the face of the earth. [6]But thanks to a beaver recovery program, which included trapping and relocating to protected areas, beavers have made an impressive comeback throughout the country. (Adapted from Sy Montgomery, *Nature's Everyday Mysteries,* p. 99.)

Topic Sentence _____

3. [1]Coral reefs are extremely important to the environment, and they perform many useful functions; above all, they provide a habitat for organisms that cannot survive elsewhere. [2]Yet coral reefs all over

---

*demographic: related to the characteristics of a population.

the world are being threatened by human activities. [3]Logging near the waters of Bascuit Bay in the Philippines has destroyed 5 percent of the coral reefs in the bay. [4]Dynamite fishing around the world has not only killed large numbers of fish, it has also blown apart a significant number of coral reefs in Kenya, Tanzania, and Mauritania. [5]Coral reefs have also fallen victim to the tourist industry. [6]Coral and shells are hot tourist commodities, and they have been collected in large quantities for sale to souvenir-hungry tourists. [7]Undoubtedly, the most violent assault on the reefs has come from nuclear testing. [8]France, for example, has detonated* more than 100 nuclear devices in Polynesian waters once rich with coral reefs that are rapidly disappearing.

Topic Sentence _____

4. [1]Where can you exchange messages with the president, find ten people interested in full-body tattoos, or assume an entirely new personality? [2]Yes, it's the Internet. [3]Unless you happen to have just emerged from a years-long stay in a cave, you have probably heard of this network of computers and their users, but you may not be aware of the wealth of information that it can provide *anyone*. [4]The most basic Internet service is electronic mail or **E-mail.** [5]This service allows you to contact other Internet users at their Internet address. [6]Next up the line in netdom is the **newsgroup,** a computerized discussion group. [7]The Internet is currently running over 5,000 newsgroups on just about every imaginable topic—from whale watching to kick boxing. [8]With a **browser,** a software program that allows you to view documents on the World Wide Web,* you can find information about any topic that strikes your fancy just by typing keywords into a box labeled *search*. [9]Want to download, or copy onto your computer, the information you find? [10]No problem. [11]With **FTP,** file transfer protocol, you can load up on free data and software. (Adapted from *Culturescope: Guide to an Informed Mind.* Ed. Staff of Princeton Review. New York: Random House, 1995, p. 348.)

Topic Sentence _____

5. [1]Around 1950 agriculture in the United States underwent a profound change. [2]For one thing, agriculture became energy intensive, or, more specifically, fossil-fuel intensive. [3]In 1950, an amount of energy equal to less than half a barrel of oil was used to produce a

---

*detonated: set off, caused to explode.
*World Wide Web: A system of electronic documents linked together to make up a network of information resources.

ton of grain. [4]By 1985, the amount of energy needed to produce a ton of grain had more than doubled. [5]Searching for ways to increase the yield of the lands already in use, farmers also began to rely heavily on inputs of water, on inputs of chemical fertilizers and pesticides (many of which are petroleum-derived products), and on high-yield strains of crops. [6]In some areas, especially the drier regions of the Southwest, irrigation projects allowed dry lands to be cultivated. [7]In contrast to past agricultural practice, farmers began to concentrate on producing only one or two profitable crops as opposed to a variety of crops. (Adapted from Donald G. Kaufman and Cecilia M. Franz, *Biosphere 2000*. New York: HarperCollins, 1993, p. 182.)

Topic Sentence _____

Part B

DIRECTIONS Read each paragraph and write the number (or numbers) of the topic sentence in the blank. Then answer the questions that follow by circling the correct answer or writing it in the blanks.

6. [1]The term **bilingual education** refers to programs designed to instruct nonnative speakers of English who have not yet mastered English as their second language. [2]For the most part, bilingual programs are considered purely transitional, providing support to students in their native language until they can speak English well enough to function in classrooms where only English is spoken. [3]A typical bilingual program begins by teaching kindergarten students in their primary language and translating key words into English. [4]However, by the end of first or second grade, English is the primary language, with words only occasionally being translated into the students' native tongue. [5]For a while now, bilingual education has been a controversial topic, with critics arguing that the native language should be eliminated from the classroom as early as possible because it interferes with the learning of English. [6]But research does not support this claim (Hakuta & Garcia, 1989). [7]On the contrary, bilingualism seems to improve the thinking abilities of children. (Adapted from Santrock, *Life-Span Development*, p. 301.)

a. Topic sentence: _____

b. What question or questions about the topic sentence do the major details help answer?

_____

_____

c. *True* or *False:* Sentence 3 is a major detail.

Explain your answer. _____

_____

d. *True* or *False:* Sentence 4 is a minor detail.

Explain your answer. _____

_____

7. [1]Analyses of non-Western cultures suggest that beliefs about maintaining ties with those who have died vary from culture to culture. [2]In contrast with Western beliefs, maintaining ties with the deceased is accepted and sustained in the religious rituals of Japan. [3]Yet among the Hopi Indians of Arizona, the deceased are forgotten as quickly as possible and life is carried on as usual. [4]In fact, the Hopi funeral ritual concludes with a break-off between mortals and spirits. [5]The diversity of grieving is nowhere clearer than in two Muslim societies—one in Egypt, the other in Bali. [6]Among Muslims in Egypt, the bereaved* are encouraged to dwell at length on their grief, surrounded by others who relate similarly tragic accounts and express their own sorrow. [7]By contrast, in Bali, bereaved Muslims are encouraged to laugh and be joyful rather than be sad. (Santrock, *Life-Span Development*, p. 301.)

a. Topic sentence: _____

b. What question or questions about the topic sentence do the major details help answer?

_____

_____

c. *True* or *False:* Sentence 2 is a major detail.

Explain your answer. _____

_____

d. *True* or *False:* Sentence 4 is a minor detail.

Explain your answer. _____

_____

*bereaved: those suffering the loss of a loved one.

8. [1]Even more than had been the case with Vietnam, Operation Desert Storm*—thanks to time-zone difference and satellite relays, as well as around-the-clock reporting—was a televised "living room war" on American prime time. [2]But it was a far more *controlled* television war than Vietnam had been, the result of tight Pentagon* limits on media access to troops and events and of censorship. [3]Television showcased military successes, highlighting exotic hardware through the use of Pentagon-released videos and making widespread use of on-air expert commentators—many of them retired military officers. [4]There was little or no analysis or criticism of the military effort or of diplomatic efforts immediately before or after—instead, the emphasis was on live-action shots of American technological superiority. [5]Later, in mid-1991, television covered victory parades in Washington, New York, and elsewhere. [6]These programs projected an America throwing off old self-doubts that had lingered since the loss in Vietnam nearly two decades before. [7]Only months after the war was over did disquieting television reports about Iraqi civilian losses, allied soldiers killed by "friendly fire," and attempted cover-ups of other military mistakes become widely reported—but by then few were paying attention. (Head, Sterling, and Schofield, *Broadcasting in America*, p. 434.)

a. Topic sentence: _____

b. What question or questions about the topic sentence do the major details help answer?

_____

_____

c. *True* or *False:* Sentence 3 is a major detail.

   Explain your answer. _____

_____

d. *True* or *False:* Sentence 4 is also a major detail.

   Explain your answer. _____

_____

9. [1]Research on attitude change suggests that people pay attention to messages that fit their established opinions and ignore those that don't. [2]Thus, media such as radio, television, and newspapers tend

_____

*Desert Storm: a 1990 war waged to get Iraqi troops out of Kuwait.
*Pentagon: the United States military establishment.

to reinforce existing views rather than changing them. [3]Faced with a message that challenges their beliefs, the listener, viewer, or reader often ignores anything that doesn't fit his or her existing world view; this kind of selective perception* also accounts for what's called the *boomerang effect*. [4]Experiments have shown that those with strong beliefs are likely to misinterpret messages that challenge their opinions. [5]In other words, people will ignore or distort evidence rather than be challenged by it. [6]The classic example of the boomerang effect was the popular television show *All in the Family*. [7]The show was meant—in the person of the lead character, Archie Bunker—to make bigotry* look laughable and silly. [8]Yet viewer surveys consistently discovered that those who shared Archie Bunker's wide-ranging prejudices thought of the character as a role model who helped confirm the rightness of their opinions.

a. Topic sentence: _____

b. What question or questions about the topic sentence do the major details help answer?

_____

_____

c. *True* or *False:* Sentence 4 is a major detail.

Explain your answer. _____

_____

d. *True* or *False:* Sentence 5 is a minor detail.

Explain your answer. _____

_____

10. [1]**Trichotillomania** is a disorder characterized by an inability to resist the impulse to pull out one's own hair. [2]Although trichotillomania principally involves the hairs in the scalp, a person with this disorder may pull hair from other parts of the body, such as eyelashes, beard, or eyebrows. [3]The hair pulling is not provoked by skin inflammation, itch, or other physical condition. [4]Rather, the person simply cannot resist the impulse, which begins with a feeling of tension that is replaced by a feeling of release or gratification* after the hair is pulled. [5]Initially, the hair pulling may not disturb the follicles,

_____

*perception: way of seeing.
*bigotry: prejudice.
*gratification: pleasure.

and new hair will grow. [6]In severe cases, new growth is compromised and permanent balding results. [7]One thirty-five-year-old woman entered therapy saying that she had a compulsion to pull the hairs from her head. [8]When asked to reveal the extent of her hair pulling, the woman took off her wig. [9]She was completely bald except for a few strands of hair at the back of her head. [10]There is no information on the prevalence of trichotillomania, although it is probably more common than currently believed and more common among women than men (Meyer, 1989). [11]About 1 to 2 percent of college students appear to have a past or current history of this disorder (American Psychiatric Association, 1994). (David Sue, Derald Sue, and Stanley Sue, *Understanding Abnormal Behavior*. Boston: Houghton Mifflin, 1997, p. 247.)

a. Topic sentence: _____

b. What question or questions about the topic sentence do the major details help answer?

_____

_____

c. *True* or *False:* Sentence 3 is a minor detail.

Explain your answer. _____

_____

d. *True* or *False:* Sentence 4 is also a minor detail.

Explain your answer. _____

_____

CHAPTER 3

Power Tools for Learning: Paraphrasing and Annotating

 In this chapter, you'll learn

- **how to monitor, or check, your understanding of a difficult passage by** *paraphrasing.*

- **how to** *annotate* **pages by jotting down key points, personal comments, and potential test questions in the margins.**

- **how to use paragraph patterns to predict test questions.**

Paraphrasing and annotating are two essential learning strategies that can markedly improve both concentration and comprehension. As an added bonus, they can also aid remembering. So crucial are these strategies to academic

**success, they deserve—and, in this case, receive—a chapter
all their own.**

 # The Purpose of Paraphrasing

The goal of **paraphrasing** is to retain the original meaning of a passage while finding new words to express it. In the two-step process of discovering meaning and finding new words to re-create it, you force yourself to pull the author's ideas apart and put them back together again—only in a different form. Is it any wonder, then, that paraphrasing encourages a deeper level of learning than reading without paraphrasing?

Here is an example of good paraphrasing.

Original   Video rental stores started out in the 1970s as locally owned mom-and-pop stores. But their prosperity lasted just a few years until big national chains emerged to gobble up the local markets.

Paraphrase   In the 1970s, video rental stores were frequently small and locally owned. But many of these stores lost their market when the huge national chains came to town.

The meaning of both passages is similar. The difference is in the language. Although the ideas remain the same in the paraphrase, most of the words are new. This example illustrates the key rule of accurate paraphrasing: *Change the words, never the meaning.*

The following paraphrase is far from accurate. Look it over carefully. Can you figure out the ways in which this paraphrase distorts the original meaning?

Paraphrase   In the late 1970s, video rental stores were wildly successful as small, locally owned businesses, but they couldn't compete with the huge national chains that charged less and drove the smaller stores out of business.

In this case, the paraphrase adds two elements that don't appear in the original. The original passage does not describe the degree of success experienced by the early video stores. They may or may not have been "wildly successful." We just don't know. The original passage also doesn't say exactly why the locally owned video stores went out of business. Yet the paraphrase assumes that price cutting was involved. Here again, the paraphrase distorts the original meaning.

Paraphrasing encourages in-depth learning because it forces you to closely study the author's original words and search your mind for another way to express the same idea. However, when you paraphrase you must stay as close as possible to the author's original meaning. Tamper with the meaning and you defeat your purpose.

EXERCISE 1

DIRECTIONS Identify the more accurate paraphrase by circling the appropriate letter.

Original **EXAMPLE** Political campaigns vary in the effectiveness with which they transmit their messages via the news media. Effective tactics recognize the limitations of both the audience and the media. The typical voter is not deeply interested in politics and has trouble keeping track of multiple themes supported with details. By the same token, television is not willing to air lengthy statements from candidates. (Janda et al., *The Challenge of Democracy*, p. 305.)

Paraphrase a. Most political campaigns simply do not take into account voter limitations. Instead, candidates assume that the typical voter is deeply interested in political issues. The truth is that the typical voter cares more about a candidate's image than about the candidate's political positions.

b. Not all political campaigns use the news media with equal effectiveness. Those that are successful recognize that television is not willing to air long, detailed explanations and that the typical voter neither understands nor cares much about political issues.

EXPLANATION In this case, paraphrase *a* is not correct. It says candidates assume that the typical voter is deeply interested in political issues. Yet the original says only that the typical voter is not deeply interested in politics. It makes no mention of what candidates do or do not assume. Paraphrase *a* also leaves out a key component, or element, of the original, which points out that "television is not willing to air lengthy statements." *Remember:* Accurate paraphrases retain all parts of the original meaning without adding new information.

Original 1. Most Americans were taken by surprise when the second wave* of feminism swept the nation in the 1960s. Women's rights had been considered a dead issue—in the words of *Life* magazine, feminism

---

*wave: new trend or movement.

seemed "as quaint as linen dusters* and high-button shoes." Supposedly, it lost its relevance once women won the vote. (Flora Davis, *Moving the Mountain.* New York: Simon & Schuster, 1991, p. 26.)

Paraphrase a. By the 1960s, feminism was again a hot topic, and most people were taken by surprise. Many people thought that the battle for women's rights was over when women won the right to vote.

b. In the 1960s, to almost everyone's surprise, the feminist movement reappeared and became a force to be reckoned with. Surprisingly, no one realized at the time what consequences would result from the second wave of feminism.

Original **2.** You may have heard that colds come from being chilled, from getting your feet wet, from sleeping in a draft, or from not wearing a hat on cold, rainy, or windy days. Sound familiar? In fact, these so-called mechanisms do not explain the acquisition of colds whatsoever. (Kathleen D. Mullen et al., *Connections for Health.* Boston: WCB/McGraw-Hill, 1996, p. 403.)

Paraphrase a. The old myths about catching colds are untrue. People catch colds from coming into contact with one of the two hundred different viruses that cause colds.

b. Claims that catching colds from getting chilled or wet are not based on fact.

■ EXERCISE 2

DIRECTIONS Paraphrase each of the following statements.

Original **EXAMPLE** About 25 percent of people are primarily *auditory*, learning and thinking through hearing; another 15 percent are primarily *kinesthetic*, learning by feeling, touch, and movement. (Adapted from Donald J. Lofland, *Powerlearning*, p. 13.)

Paraphrase *Around 25 percent of the population learns mainly through listening, whereas another 15 percent learns largely by touch or movement.*

EXPLANATION As it should, the paraphrase replaces most of the original language but retains the original meaning. *Note:* There may

---

*dusters: long coats worn around the turn of the century.

be times when there is no substitute for the original language; for example, in this case, *percent* would be a difficult word to replace.

Original 1. Divorce lawyers all over the country are noticing a brand-new phenomenon: Internet-sparked divorces. In other words, marriages are breaking up when one spouse or the other meets someone online in a chatroom and decides that that someone is a true soulmate. There actually have been cases of spouses abandoning their marriage and running off with people they had met only online and never even seen.

Paraphrase _____

_____

_____

Original 2. University of Tulsa psychologist Judy Berry studied seventy-three Oklahoma eighth graders who had taken a parenting course. For ten days, the children had to take care of a ten-pound sack of flour as if it were a baby. Berry's research on her young subjects suggests the course worked: The teenagers in the study had a sounder sense of parental responsibility than they did before they took the course.

Paraphrase _____

_____

_____

CHECK YOUR UNDERSTANDING

What is the key rule of accurate paraphrasing?

_____

_____

_____

▰▰◉ When Should You Paraphrase?

At this point, you know the purpose of paraphrasing. However, you may not be quite sure *when* to paraphrase. Actually, the answer to that question varies. If, for example, you are reading material that is both difficult and unfamiliar—say, chemistry or philosophy—then paraphrasing the key points of every paragraph—the main idea and major supporting details—may be your best bet. It will be slow going, but there's a bonus. You will probably need to read the material only once rather than over and over again.

If you are reading a sociology or health textbook, where you are familiar with some of the concepts, or ideas, then paraphrase only the passages you don't readily understand. If you finish a paragraph and aren't quite sure of the author's meaning, it's the time to check your understanding by paraphrasing. If you can't paraphrase, mark the paragraph for rereading (RR). Paraphrasing chapter sections when you finish them is also an excellent way to test your understanding and ensure long-term remembering.

■ EXERCISE 3

DIRECTIONS Read each paragraph. Identify the topic sentence by writing the number (or numbers) in the blank. Then paraphrase the topic sentence on the lines that follow.

EXAMPLE [1]The shortages of the 1970s forced the United States to think more seriously about its reliance on oil. [2]At the national level, the energy crisis raised concerns over national security, trade losses, and environmental damage. [3]Closer to home, oil shortages and rising energy costs resulted in worries about the effect on the family budget, transportation to and from school, and the heating and cooling of homes, schools, and offices. [4]For the first time in peacetime, Americans were forced to curb their energy consumption, and it was a sobering experience. (Kaufman and Franz, *Biosphere 2000*, 1993, p. 218.)

Topic Sentence _1_

Paraphrase *Due to the oil shortages in the seventies, the United States had to reconsider the role oil would play in its future.*

EXPLANATION Only sentence 1 effectively sums up the paragraph, which details how the United States reconsidered the consequences of relying on oil. As it should, the paraphrase changes the language but leaves the meaning in place.

1. [1]In 1936, the German dictator Adolf Hitler did everything possible to showcase the Olympic games held in Berlin, Germany. [2]Hitler had a lot riding on the games; they were supposed to prove that the Germans were members of a master race or, at the very least, prove the superiority of white skin. [3]But Hitler hadn't reckoned with the talent of Jesse Owens, the black track star from Ohio State, who stormed the Olympics and walked away with four gold medals. [4]Owens's athletic performance was so stunning that a largely German audience cheered him lustily as he won the 100 and 200 meter races, cleared the long jump, and ran his heart out in relay races. [5]Hitler was so upset, he left the stadium when Owens received his gold medals. [6]Hitler's departure was a relief to Owens, who had been worrying that he might have to shake the hand of a man who considered him subhuman. [7]Fortunately for Owens, famous for his polite and humble manner, Hitler spared him that unpleasant task.

Topic Sentence _____

Paraphrase _____

_____

_____

2. [1]American men used to be the tallest people on the planet, but not anymore. [2]According to anthropologist Barry Bogin, the Americans have slipped to fourth place. [3]In first place are the Dutch, who look down from an average height of five feet, ten inches, up six inches from an earlier average of five feet, four inches in 1850. [4]Next come the Swedes and Danes who average around five feet, nine inches. [5]At five feet, eight inches, the American male is a good deal taller than his counterpart of 1850, who averaged five feet, six inches, but he is still considerably shorter than his European counterparts. [6]According to Bogin, the undernourishment of American children has quite literally stunted their growth and accounts for the loss of height.[1]

Topic Sentence _____

_____
[1]*Utne Reader*, May–June 98, p. 16.

Paraphrase _____

_____

_____

3. [1]By most accounts, the first gush of an American oil well occurred in New York in the year 1627 when two men dug a hole and something black and sticky came spurting out. [2]Calling the sticky mess "the Devil's tar," the two men plugged the hole and directed the oil into a nearby river, where it formed a 35-mile-long oil slick.[2] [3]It wasn't until 1859 that someone officially went looking for oil and found it. [4]This was the year Colonel Edwin L. Drake became the first person to tap an oil well in the United States. [5]Drilling in Titusville, Pennsylvania, Drake used parts of a steam machine to drill only sixty feet beneath the surface of the earth. [6]To his surprise and delight, Drake struck oil even though he had not penetrated the earth's surface by much. [7]In a short time, the well was pumping over twenty barrels of oil a day. [8]By 1862 a full-scale oil rush was in progress as others tried to follow in the footsteps of the fortunate Col. Drake.

Topic Sentence _____

Paraphrase _____

_____

_____

4. [1]In many Western societies, an increasing number of individuals are either delaying or avoiding getting married. [2]As evidence, the proportion of Americans aged thirty to thirty-four who have never married has risen 9.4 percent for men and 6.2 percent for women since 1970, and the proportion of married couples under the age of twenty-five has decreased in the United States by over a third since 1980. [3]For many, careers have become more important than marriage. [4]Also, because it is now more acceptable for a man and woman to live together before marriage, many do not see an immediate need to enter into a long-term commitment. [5]Thus, over 23 million people currently live alone, and the 2000s will see rapid growth in the number of singles and roommates. (Hoyer and MacInnis, *Consumer Behavior,* p. 367.)

---

[2]Michael Sims, *Darwin's Orchestra.* New York: Henry Holt, 1997, p. 296.

Topic Sentence ——————

Paraphrase ————————————————————

————————————————————

————————————————————

CHECK YOUR UNDERSTANDING
Describe three different ways to use paraphrasing.
————————————————————
————————————————————
————————————————————
————————————————————

Annotating Pages

Annotating pages while you read helps concentration, comprehension, and memory. But as a learning technique, annotating pages is useful only if you make the right kind of marginal notes. A comment like "Boy, this is boring" is not going to improve your concentration or your comprehension, and it certainly won't aid remembering. To be effective, marginal annotations should (1) paraphrase key points, (2) make connections between the author's thoughts and your own experience, and (3) predict possible test questions.

Identify Key Points

The space in the margins of your textbook is limited. That means you need to develop a system that helps you identify the main idea and supporting details without cluttering up the margins so much you can't read what you've written. Your system may not be like anyone else's. That's not important. What matters is that you annotate to highlight what's essential in the passage. Compare the following selections. Both have been underlined and annotated, but not in the same way. Yet each set of annotations makes the main idea and supporting details stand out.

Long Prison Terms

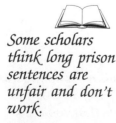

Some scholars think long prison sentences aren't effective or fair.

reasons why

How many times have you heard the expression, "Lock 'em up and throw away the key"? It captures the frustration law-abiding people feel about the problem of crime in America. It reflects a belief that society is best off when criminals are housed in prisons for long periods. This strategy has an obvious appeal—locking up offenders prevents them from committing additional crimes in the community, at least during the course of their confinement. Yet, according to some scholars, long prison sentences may be unjust, unnecessary, counterproductive,* and inappropriate.

- Unjust if other offenders who have committed the same crime receive shorter sentences.
- Unnecessary if the offender is not likely to offend again.
- Counterproductive whenever prison increases the risk of subsequent or habitual criminal behavior.
- Inappropriate if the offender has committed an offense entailing insignificant harm to the community. (Freda Adler, Gerhard O. W. Mueller, and William S. Laufer, *Criminal Justice.* New York: McGraw-Hill, 1994, p. 349.)

In this case, the main idea—"Some scholars think long prison sentences aren't effective or fair"—is identified in the margin. The major details—the reasons why scholars don't think long sentences are effective—are highlighted by means of an arrow and the annotation "reasons why." The key words in each reason are also underlined, paving the way for later note taking.

Look now at another example of how the passage might be annotated.

Long Prison Terms

Some scholars think long prison sentences are unfair and don't work.

How many times have you heard the expression, "Lock 'em up and throw away the key"? It captures the frustration law-abiding people feel about the problem of crime in America. It reflects a belief that society is best off when criminals are housed in prisons for long periods. This strategy has an obvious appeal—locking up offenders prevents them from committing additional crimes in the community, at least during the course of their confinement. Yet, according to some scholars, long prison sentences may be unjust, unnecessary, counterproductive, and inappropriate.

---

*counterproductive: tending to hurt rather than help.

4 reasons

① • <u>Unjust</u> if <u>other offenders</u> who have <u>committed</u> the <u>same crime</u> <u>receive shorter sentences</u>.

② • Unnecessary <u>if</u> the <u>offender</u> is <u>not likely</u> to <u>offend again</u>.

③ • Counterproductive <u>whenever prison increases</u> the risk of subsequent or habitual <u>criminal behavior</u>.

④ • Inappropriate <u>if</u> the <u>offender</u> has committed an offense entailing <u>insignificant harm</u> to the community. (Adler, Mueller, and Laufer, *Criminal Justice*, p. 349.)

In this instance, a slightly different paraphrase of the topic sentence appears in the margin, and the four reasons get both a label and numbered arrows.

Exactly how you annotate is up to you. Each person has his or her own method. Also, different kinds of textbook material require different kinds of annotations. You might use more arrows in a science text or circle more dates in a history book. What's important is that you make annotating a habit. Once you do, you'll be surprised at your increased ability to concentrate, understand, and remember.

The following chart identifies several symbols you can use to underline and annotate pages. Feel free, however, to make up your own symbols or to adapt the ones listed here to suit your particular needs. Whatever symbols you decide on, just be sure to use them consistently, so you know exactly what each one represents.

Symbols for Underlining and Annotating Pages	
═ ═ ═	**Double underlining** to highlight the main idea of the entire reading
▁ ▁ ▁	**Single underlining** to highlight main ideas in paragraphs
=	**Equal sign** used to signal a definition
1, 2, 3, 4	**Numbers** to itemize and separate a series of supporting details

(1830)	**Circles** to highlight key points, specialized vocabulary, key terms, statistics, and dates
?	**Question marks** to indicate confusion
!	**Exclamation points** to indicate your surprise at the author's statements
∿∿∿	**Squiggly lines** under words you need to look up in a dictionary
↗	**Arrows** to identify cause and effect relationships
‖	**Vertical lines** to emphasize passages longer than a sentence or two
:	**Colon** to signal restatement
★★★	**Stars** to identify a crucial piece of information
RR	Symbol to indicate passages in need of a second reading
RP	Symbol to identify ideas for research papers
TQ	Symbol to identify the possible source of a test question
See p. 27 or Compare p. 27	**Cross-reference notes** to compare closely related statements in the text
Charles Darwin	**Boxes** to highlight names you need to remember

Make Connections

Research on learning shows that reading scores improve when students can make connections between what they already know and what they read. For an illustration of how to create such links, look at the following passage. Yes, the paraphrased main idea appears in the margin along with one or two supporting details, but so too do some comments based on the reader's personal experience. Those comments appear in boldface.

Cancer Quackery

When cancer attacks, people do risky things like turn to quacks—multimillion dollar business.

Aunt Mary

May be prof. educated, but also may not.

Quack treatments are particularly risky in cancer's early stages.

Aunt Mary almost died because she went to a quack who treated her with apricot pits.

Quacks aren't easy to recognize.

Aunt Mary's doctor seemed like an old sweetheart—Ha!

Cancer quackery is a multimillion-dollar industry in the U.S. alone each year. When cancer strikes, many people do foolish, irresponsible, or dangerous things. One of the things they do is turn to "quacks." These practitioners offer the cancer patient friendly attentiveness, hope, or "secret" cures. The person with cancer may be desperate, so the practitioner who can make these offers has appeal. Quacks may be professionally educated physicians; however, many times they have no degree and no medical education whatsoever.

Responsible physicians do not offer secret cures or make guarantees about treatment interventions. Quack treatments can be especially dangerous to the patient who has cancer in its early stages. Trying useless gadgets or therapeutically worthless drugs is costly and wastes valuable time. Quacks may have no conscience about telling patients that they have cancer when in fact they do not. After a series of worthless but expensive "treatments," the patient is declared "cured." The practitioner takes the credit, which opens the door for the testimonial and exploitation of more people. Quacks cannot be recognized by their appearance alone. They are smart, friendly, and impressively attired. They provide warmth, act concerned, and give assurance to patients who are filled with anxiety. (Mullen et al., *Connections for Health*, p. 380.)

As the example shows, this reader does not confine her marginal annotations to rephrasing the author's main idea and supporting details. She also includes personal comments that echo the author's thoughts. These comments anchor the author's ideas in her memory by connecting them to the reader's personal experience.

Record Potential Test Questions

In addition to taking notes and jotting comments in the margins of your text, you should also jot down possible test questions.

As you read, give special attention to words and sentences that stand out because of repetition, italics, boldface, or colored ink. All of these devices are used to emphasize key points and essential vocabulary. This is the kind of material likely to make its way into an exam. Once you've identified potentially test-rich material, use the words introduced in Chapter 1—*how, why, when, where, which,* and *what*—to formulate possible test questions. If you happen to know that your instructor favors essay exams, become familiar with the words likely to be used in essay exams (see the chart on pp. 435–436). Then you can use them to create test questions.

To illustrate, here's a sample passage accompanied by two test questions.

TQ: What is the function of the sympathetic nervous system?

TQ: Explain how the sympathetic nervous system prepares the body for fight or flight.

The <u>sympathetic nervous system</u> <u>prepares</u> the <u>body to deal</u> with <u>emergency situations</u>. It prepares us for "fight or flight." The system <u>speeds up</u> the <u>heart</u>, <u>sends blood</u> to the <u>muscles</u>, and <u>releases sugar</u> from the liver for <u>quick energy.</u> It can be activated by threat or by sexual arousal. (Allgeier and Allgeier, *Sexual Interactions,* p. 143.)

The test questions you predict may well appear on the exam. Even if they don't, writing potential exam questions in the margins is always worth the effort. When you finish a chapter section, you can test your understanding and review what you've read by trying to answer your own questions. When you try to answer potential test questions, you are simultaneously checking comprehension, aiding memory, and reviewing for exams—all of which make jotting test questions in the margins a highly effective study strategy.

◼ EXERCISE 4

DIRECTIONS Read, underline, and annotate the following passage. *Note:* Try your hand at using some of the symbols introduced on pages 101–102 and make sure to pose at least one test question.

Rebellion in a Small Texas Town

The Mexican-American movement was a local one, born of poverty and oppressive segregation. Reflecting the grassroots character of the movement was the important role that youths played. Many Mexican-American teens and young adults adopted the term **Chicano** to stress their unwillingness to accept the dictates of Anglo society and to distinguish themselves from the more **accommodationist*** Mexican-Americans they called *Tio Tacos.*

In the small south Texas town of Ed Couch-Elsa, where the aver-

---

*accommodationist: adapting to the viewpoint of those with more power.

age education level for Mexican-Americans was 3.5 years of schooling, Mexican-American students walked out of the high school in November 1968. Supported by their parents and most of the Mexican-American community, the students demanded dignity, respect, and an end to "blatant discrimination against Mexican-American students in the schools." For one thing, corporal punishment in the form of spankings was common for speaking Spanish on school grounds outside of Spanish class, and students wanted it stopped. The school board, blaming "outside agitators" for the unrest, suspended over 150 students and finally expelled 20. But changes took place. The board agreed not to discourage the speaking of Spanish and to incorporate a Mexican-American heritage program into the curriculum.

An extremely poor school district, Ed Couch-Elsa was limited in its efforts to improve the curriculum or educational environment, but under pressure from the Mexican-American community, other school districts, including Los Angeles, implemented Mexican-American studies and bilingual programs, hired more Mexican-American teachers and counselors, and adopted programs to meet the special needs of migrant farm worker children who moved from one school to another during picking season. By the 1970s, calls for bilingual education had become an important educational reform focus for the Latino community. (Carol Berkin et al., *Making America: A History of the United States.* Boston: Houghton Mifflin, 1995, p. 945.)

 # Using Paragraph Patterns to Predict Test Questions

Paying close attention to highlighting devices like boldface, italics, and colored ink is a good way to predict test questions. However, recognizing the pattern of organization used in a paragraph can also help you zero in on the type of question your instructor is likely to pose. True, teachers don't limit themselves to test questions based on paragraph patterns, but they do rely on them rather heavily. That's one reason why it pays to familiarize yourself with the six patterns commonly used to organize, or structure, paragraphs.

Pattern 1: Definition

Textbook authors know full well that students must master the specialized vocabulary of their academic subjects. Thus, it's not surprising that they frequently devote whole paragraphs to explaining what a key term means. Usually those paragraphs introduce the term in boldface, colored ink, or italics; define it; and then provide an example or detail that further clarifies its meaning. Here's an example of a definition paragraph. In addition to the potential test questions written in the margins, pay attention to how the passage is marked to make key points stand out.

TQ: What is product modification?

TQ: What conditions must be met for product modification to take place?

Product modification refers to changing one or more of a product's characteristics. For this approach to be effective, several conditions must be met. First, the product must be modifiable. Second, existing customers must be able to perceive that a modification has been made. Third, the modification should make the product more consistent with customers' desires. (William A. Pride, Robert J. Hughes, and Jack R. Kapoor, *Business.* Boston: Houghton Mifflin, 1997, p. 396.)

When you see an entire paragraph devoted to defining a key term, your best bet is a test question that asks you to recall some aspect of the definition. As you can see, that's the focus of the test questions shown above.

Pattern 2: Classification

Particularly in business and science textbooks, authors frequently explain a system of classification. They begin by explaining how some large group can be divided into smaller categories or subgroups. Then they describe the specific characteristics of each subgroup. Here's an example. Again, check out the underlining and annotations that accompany the paragraph.

Hippocrates classified people according to the four fluids in their body.

TQ: Explain Hippocrates' system of classification.

Like his contemporaries,* the Greek physician Hippocrates believed that the human body consisted of four *humors,* or fluids: black bile, yellow bile, blood, and phlegm. Hippocrates' contribution was to classify human beings according to the fluid that predominated in their bodies. Persons with an excess of black bile were classified as *melancholic* and were presumed to be depressed and pessimistic. The *choleric,* possessing excess yellow bile, were considered quick-tempered and irritable. Persons with a predominance of blood were *sanguine.* They were usually cheerful and optimistic. The *phlegmatic,* possessing excess phlegm, were thought to be slow, unemotional, and uninvolved with the world at large.

*contemporaries: people living at the same time.

While the <u>theory</u> has long since been <u>discarded</u>, the meanings of some of these <u>terms persist</u>.

As soon as you realize that an author is intent on outlining a system of classification, jot a test question like the one above in the margin.

Pattern 3: Process

Like the classification paragraph, the process paragraph frequently turns up in both business and science texts, where authors need to explain, step by step, how something works or develops: Here, for example, is a paragraph that outlines the stages in digestion.

Digestive system prepares food to be turned into energy.

TQ: *Explain the process of digestion.*

In the human body, the (digestive system) breaks down <u>food</u> so it can be used <u>for energy</u>. As <u>food enters</u> the <u>mouth</u>, <u>chewing</u>, along with <u>enzymes</u> in the saliva, <u>break it down</u> into small pieces. Next the <u>esophagus contracts</u> and <u>pushes</u> the <u>food into</u> the <u>stomach</u>, where muscles, enzymes, and digestive acids <u>turn</u> the <u>food into</u> a thick <u>liquid</u>. That <u>liquid</u> is <u>emptied</u> into the <u>small intestine</u>, where most of its <u>nutrients are absorbed</u>. <u>What remains</u> travels <u>to</u> the <u>large intestine</u>, where <u>water</u> is <u>removed</u> from <u>digested food</u> and turned <u>into waste</u>. (Adapted from Barnes-Svarney, *The New York Public Library Science Desk Reference*, p. 166.)

Anytime you recognize the process pattern, you would do well to jot down a test question that asks you to remember the sequence of stages or steps in the process described. Not only is this a likely test question, but answering it is also a sure-fire means of review.

Words like *steps, stages, phases*, and *process* are all signs that you are reading a process paragraph, but so too are the transitions listed below:

Transitions That Identify a Sequence of Steps	
First, second, third	Toward the end
Finally	By the time
Then	At this point
Next	In this stage
Afterward	In the final stage

Pattern 4: Sequence of Dates and Events

Authors who write about history and government frequently use a **sequence of dates and events** to explain or argue their claims. In this pattern, the supporting details present a series of dates and events listed according to the order in which they occurred. Here's an example:

TQ: What are the dates of the Mexican-American War?

The Democrat James Polk became president of the United States in (1844) From the very beginning of his presidency, Polk made it clear that he intended to expand the boundaries of the United States. In (1846) he ordered General Zachary Taylor to take troops into Mexican territory. On (April 25) of the same year, the Mexican military fired on Taylor's troops and war between the United States and Mexico began, even though Congress had not yet officially declared it. By (1847) U.S. troops had arrived in Mexico City and were claiming victory. (The opening phrase in the Marines' anthem— "From the Halls of Montezuma"—is a reference to the arrival of those troops in Mexico's capital.) In (1848) Mexico and the United States signed the Treaty of Guadalupe Hidalgo, which ceded a portion of Mexican land that today includes Arizona, Utah, Nevada, and New Mexico to the United States. Polk had his wish: He had expanded and redefined U.S. borders. But in an effort to assuage* the war's critics—and there were many who considered the war with Mexico unjust—the United States government paid the Mexican government $15 million.

TQ: What was the name of the treaty that ended the Mexican-American War?

If you recognize a sequence of dates and events pattern in a paragraph, use your knowledge of the pattern to create test questions that focus on the significance of particular dates or the sequence of events that led up to some important happening or achievement.

Although the presence of several dates and events organized in a sequence is an obvious clue to this pattern, so too are the following transitions:

Transitions That Mark Dates and Events

After	Then
From ____ to ____	Finally
In ____	Before

---

*assuage: calm, soothe.

In the years	Previously
During the years	A year later
In the years that followed	Following
In the following years	At that point
Between the years _____ and _____	

Pattern 5: Comparison and Contrast

In all kinds of textbooks, authors are likely to compare (mention similarities) and contrast (cite differences). Sometimes they devote an entire chapter section to pointing out the similarities and differences between two topics, but they are more likely to confine the comparison and contrast pattern to a single paragraph. Here is an example.

TQ: Explain the difference between assertive and aggressive behavior. Give examples for each type.

My uncle Ralph always keeps cool.

My ex-wife is a good example.

Assertive behavior involves standing up for your rights and expressing your thoughts and feelings in a direct, appropriate way that does not violate the rights of others. It is a matter of getting the other person to understand your viewpoint. People who exhibit assertive behavior skills are able to handle their conflict situations with ease and assurance while maintaining good interpersonal relations. In contrast, aggressive behavior involves expressing your thoughts and feelings and defending your rights in a way that openly violates the rights of others. Those exhibiting aggressive behavior believe that others' rights must be subservient to theirs, and they have a difficult time maintaining good interpersonal relations. They are likely to interrupt, talk fast, ignore others, and use sarcasm or other forms of verbal abuse to maintain control. (Adapted from Barry L. Reece and Rhonda Brandt, *Effective Human Relations in Organizations.* Boston: Houghton Mifflin, 1996, pp. 350–353.)

A paragraph like the above with its two topics—assertive and aggressive behavior—and its emphasis on the differences between them has comparison and contrast written all over it. Thus, it all but cries out for you to predict a test question that asks for a description of how the two topics are similar or different.

Topic sentences such as "Spartan society was very different from the society of Athens" or "In the old West, there wasn't all that much difference between cowboys and cowgirls" are strong indications of the comparison and contrast pattern of development, particularly if they are accompanied by transitions like those listed below:

Transitions That Signal Comparison or Similarity

Similarly	In the same manner
Likewise	In like manner
In much the same vein	Along the same lines
By the same token	Just like

Transitions That Signal Contrast or Difference

However	Nevertheless	In reality
But	Unfortunately	On the contrary
And yet	Whereas	In opposition
On the one hand	In contrast	Conversely
On the other hand	Nonetheless	
Still	Despite that fact	

Pattern 6: Cause and Effect

Because relating cause to effect is so basic to our thinking, you will encounter cause and effect paragraphs in every type of textbook. No matter what the discipline, or subject matter, authors need to explain how one event (the cause) produced another event (the effect).

The <u>ultraviolet radiation</u> from the sun that reaches the earth's sur-face <u>is a health threat</u>. At the very least, it causes <u>aging</u>[①] and <u>wrin-</u>

Ultraviolet radiation is harmful.

TG: Describe the effects of ultraviolet radiation.

Effects

kling of the skin. At the very worst, it is responsible for ②cataracts, ③sunburn, ④snowblindness, and ⑤skin cancer, which claims around 15,000 lives each year in the United States alone. Exposure to UV radiation also ⑥suppresses the immune system, enabling cancers to become established and grow. In addition, ⑦radiation slows plant growth, ⑧delays seed germination, and ⑨interferes with photosynthe-sis.* (Adapted from Kaufman and Franz, *Biosphere 2000*, p. 266.)

Cause and effect paragraphs are a likely source of test questions. When you encounter them in your reading, make sure you can easily identify both cause (or causes) and effect (or effects). Then turn that information into a question like the one that appears above.

Transitions That Signal Cause and Effect

Consequently	Therefore
As a result	Thus
In response	In the aftermath
In reaction	Hence

Verbs That Connect Cause and Effect

Produces	Engenders
Brings about	Creates
Generates	Sets off
Initiates	Leads to
Causes	Results in
Fosters	Stimulates

Mixed Patterns

As you might expect, writers don't restrict themselves to a single paragraph pattern. If their material calls for it, they combine patterns. When you recognize two or more patterns in a paragraph or reading, see if you can generate a test question for each pattern. For an illustration, see the annotations that follow.

---

*photosynthesis: process by which plants use sunlight to create food.

TG: Define the term "scientific method."

TG: Explain each step in the scientific method.

Examples of research questions.

Example of hypothesis.

All research studies of human development follow some form of **scientific method,** or set of procedures designed to ensure objective observations and interpretations of observations. Even though it is not always possible to follow these procedures perfectly, they form an ideal to which psychological research tends to aspire (Cherry, 1995; Levine & Parkinson, 1994). The procedures or steps in the scientific method are as follows: (1) *Formulating research questions.* Sometimes these questions refer to previous studies, such as when a developmental psychologist asks, "Are Professor Deepthought's studies of thinking consistent with studies of thinking from less developed countries?" Other times they refer to issues important to society, such as "Does preschool education make children more socially skilled later in childhood?" (2) *Stating questions as hypotheses.* A **hypothesis** is a statement that expresses a research question precisely. In making a hypothesis out of the preschool education question above, a psychologist would further define the terms *preschool education* and *socially skilled:* "Do children in day care learn to share toys with other children at an earlier age than children cared for at home?" (3) *Testing the hypothesis.* Having phrased a research question as a hypothesis, researchers can conduct an actual study of it. The choice of study method usually depends on convenience, ethics, and scientific appropriateness. (Seifert and Hoffnung, *Child and Adolescent Development,* pp. 16–17.)

In this paragraph, the authors combine two patterns—definition and process—to make their point. What are two likely test questions based on this passage? Well, the two in the margins are definite possibilities.

CHECK YOUR UNDERSTANDING

Name and describe each of the patterns introduced on pages 105–111.

1. _____

2. _____

3. _____

4. _____

5. _____

6. _____

■ EXERCISE 5

DIRECTIONS Identify the paragraph pattern or patterns by circling the appropriate letter or letters. Then identify the one test question you would *not* be likely to predict given the paragraph.

 EXAMPLE Two small lakes in a remote part of Cameroon, a small country in central Africa, made international news in the mid-1980s when deadly clouds of carbon dioxide (CO_2) gas from deep beneath the surface of the lakes escaped into the surrounding atmosphere, killing animal and human populations far downwind. The first gas discharge, which occurred at Lake Monoun in 1984, asphyxiated* 37 people. The second, which occurred at Lake Nyos in 1986, released a highly concentrated cloud of CO_2 that killed more than 1700 people. The two events have similarities other than location: both occurred at night during the rainy season; both involved volcanic crater lakes; and both are likely to recur unless there is some type of technologic intervention.* (Murck et al., *Environmental Geology*, p. 121.)

Patterns a. definition

b. process

c. sequence of dates and events

d. classification

(e.) comparison and contrast

(f.) cause and effect

Test Questions a. What caused the two disasters at Lake Monoun and Lake Nyos?

b. In what ways were the disasters at Lake Monoun and Lake Nyos similar?

(c.) How did the people of Cameroon react to the disasters at Lake Monoun and Lake Nyos?

EXPLANATION In this case, there are two patterns at work: one is cause and effect; the other, comparison and contrast. The paragraph tells us what caused the two disasters and how they were similar. Thus, it is the source of two possible questions: (1) What caused the two disasters at Lake Monoun and Lake Nyos? (2) How were the disasters at Lake Monoun and Lake Nyos similar? However, the paragraph tells us nothing about the public's reaction. Thus, question *c* is *not* suggested by the paragraph.

---

*asphyxiated: killed by loss of air.
*intervention: interference.

1. In 1862 Congress passed the **Homestead Act.** This measure offered 160 acres of land free to any American citizen who was a family head and over twenty-one. The only conditions were that the settler live on the land for five years and make improvements to it. In the well-watered East, 160 acres was a sizable farm. Yet in the semi-arid West, it was barely enough to support a family. To prosper, a farmer needed at least twice that amount. Despite these risks, the Homestead Act produced an explosion of settlement. Within a half century after the passage, all western territories had gained enough settlers— at least 60,000—to become states. As a result of the Homestead Act, most western areas experienced enormous population growth. (Thomas V. DiBacco, Lorna C. Mason, and Christian G. Appy, *History of the United States.* Boston: Houghton Mifflin, 1991, p. 315.)

Patterns a. definition

b. process

c. sequence of dates and events

d. classification

e. comparison and contrast

f. cause and effect

Test Questions a. In what year did Congress pass the Homestead Act?

b. What was the Homestead Act and what effect did it have?

c. Explain why the Homestead Act was considered a failure.

2. A **tsunami** is a very long ocean wave that is generated by a sudden displacement of the sea floor. The term is derived from a Japanese word meaning "harbor wave." Tsunamis are sometimes referred to as **seismic sea waves** because submarine and near-coast earthquakes are their primary cause. They are also popularly called "tidal waves," but this is a misnomer*; tsunamis have nothing to do with tides. Tsunamis can occur with little or no warning, bringing death and massive destruction to coastal communities. (Murck et al., *Environmental Geology*, p. 131.)

Patterns a. definition

b. process

c. sequence of dates and events

d. classification

e. comparison and contrast

f. cause and effect

---

*misnomer: inappropriate name.

Test Questions   a. Tsunamis are caused by _____.

                 b. Describe how a tsunami affects ocean life.

                 c. What is the meaning of the word *tsunami* and what is its origin?

3. Watergate,* the scandal that rocked the nation, began on June 17, 1972, when five men were caught trying to burglarize the offices of the Democratic National Committee. The arrest of the five men led to an investigation that uncovered a White House plan of systematic espionage* against political opponents. Deeply involved in that plan were the two top aides to President Richard Nixon, John Erlichman and H. R. Haldeman. On April 30, 1973, Attorney General Elliot Richardson appointed a special prosecutor, Harvard Law School professor Archibald Cox, to conduct a full-scale investigation of the Watergate break-in. On May 20, 1973, the Senate Committee on Presidential Activities opened hearings, and on July 16 White House aide Alexander Butterfield told the committee that President Nixon had taped all the conversations that occurred in his office. However, President Nixon refused to turn the tapes over to the investigating committee, and on October 20 he ordered the dismissal of prosecutor Cox. After a storm of public protest, Nixon agreed in June of 1974 to turn over the tapes. Once members of the committee had examined the tapes closely, they discovered that eighteen-and-one-half minutes had been mysteriously erased. By July 30 the House Judiciary Committee had approved three articles of impeachment. Rather than face almost certain disgrace, Richard Milhous Nixon resigned as president on August 9, 1974.

Patterns   a. definition

         b. process

         c. sequence of dates and events

         d. classification

         e. comparison and contrast

         f. cause and effect

Test Questions   a. What was the public's response to the resignation of Richard Nixon?

                 b. Outline the chain of events that began with the break-in at the Watergate and ended with the resignation of Richard Nixon.

                 c. How did the scandal known as Watergate affect the U.S. government?

---

*The Watergate is a hotel-apartment-office complex in Washington, D.C., where the committee's offices were located.
*espionage: spying.

4. Manners and morals are terms that overlap, sometimes confusingly, but here I am using the two words in senses that are easier to distinguish. *Manners* would be the standards of conduct that prevail in a group, large or small, and hence they would change from group to group and year to year. *Morals* would be defined as the standards that determine the relations of individuals with other individuals, one with one—a child with each of its parents, a husband with his wife, a rich man with a poor man (not *the* rich with *the* poor)—and also the relations of any man with himself, his destiny, and his God. They are answers found by individuals to the old problems of faith, hope, charity or love, art, duty, submission to one's fate . . . and hence they are relatively universal; they can be illustrated from the lives of any individuals, in any place, at any time since the beginning of time. (Malcolm Cowley, *New England Writers and Writing.* Hanover, NH: University Press of New England, 1996, p. 238.)

Patterns a. definition

    b. process

    c. sequence of dates and events

    d. classification

    e. comparison and contrast

    f. cause and effect

Test Questions a. How does Malcolm Cowley apply the distinction between manners and morals to the work of Nathaniel Hawthorne?

      b. According to Malcolm Cowley, morals are _____.

      c. Explain the difference between manners and morals.

5. During the process of labor, the mother's uterus contracts rhythmically and automatically to force the baby downward through the vaginal canal. The contractions occur in a relatively predictable sequence of stages. The **first stage of labor** usually begins with relatively mild and irregular contractions of the uterus. As contractions become stronger and more regular, the cervix (the opening of the uterus) dilates, or widens, enough for the baby's head to fit through. Toward the end of this stage, which may take from eight to twenty-four hours for a first-time mother, a period of **transition** begins. The cervix nears full dilation, contractions become more rapid, and the baby's head begins to move into the birth canal. Although this period generally lasts for only a few minutes, it can be extremely painful because of the increasing pressure of the contractions. The **second stage of labor** is from complete dilation of the cervix to birth. It usually lasts between one and one-and-one-half hours. During the **third stage of labor,** which lasts only a few minutes, the afterbirth (the placenta and umbilical cord) is expelled. (Adapted from Seifert and Hoffnung, *Childhood and Adolescent Development,* pp. 131–132.)

Patterns   a. definition

b. process

c. sequence of dates and events

d. classification

e. comparison and contrast

f. cause and effect

Test Questions   a. Describe the three stages of labor in the process of birth.

b. For a first-time mother, the first stage of labor takes anywhere from ————————— to —————————.

c. What complications are likely to occur during the third stage of labor?

WORD NOTES

Remember the word *counterproductive* from page 100? It meant tending to hurt a cause or goal rather than help it. Most words that begin with the prefix *counter-* also suggest a sense of opposition or contradiction, and for good reason. The prefix *counter-* comes from the Latin word *contra*, meaning, in most cases, "contrary," "opposing," or "opposite."

Using context and what you know about the prefix *counter-*, write definitions for each of the italicized words below.

1. As a young man, he had been part of the *counterculture*, but as he grew older, he found himself accepting rather than rejecting society's established values and traditions.

————————————————————————————

2. She had no *counterargument* when her supporters accused her of running an uninspired campaign.

————————————————————————————

3. When the president's actions were questioned, his supporters *counterattacked* by threatening to investigate those who
questioned his behavior.

_____

4. The corporal did not have the rank to *countermand* the ser-
geant's order to march even though he knew it was a terrible
mistake.

_____

Look up *counter-* in a dictionary. What is its second, less common meaning?

_____

Summing Up

Listed below are the most important points in Chapter 3. Put a check
mark in the box if you think the point is clear in your mind. Leave
the box blank if you need to review the material one more time. The
page numbers in parentheses tell you where to look to review each
point on the list.

☐ **1.** The goal of paraphrasing is to retain the original meaning of a
passage while at the same time finding new words to express it.
(pp. 92–93)

☐ **2.** There are three different ways to use paraphrasing. If you are
reading dense and difficult material, it pays to paraphrase often,
maybe even every other paragraph. If the material is familiar,
however, save paraphrasing for hard-to-understand passages
that confused you. A third use for paraphrasing is at the end of
a chapter section in order to test your understanding. (pp. 95–
96)

☐ **3.** Annotations, or marginal jottings, are an excellent way to ensure
in-depth learning. But not just any jotting will do. Concentrate
on (1) identifying the main idea and supporting details, (2) making personal connections, and (3) recording potential test questions. (pp. 99–104)

☐ **4.** Recognizing the pattern of organization used in a paragraph can aid in predicting test questions. Often, the pattern signals the type of question likely to be asked. Six different patterns are commonly used in textbooks: (1) definition, (2) process, (3) sequence of dates and events, (4) classification, (5) comparison and contrast, and (6) cause and effect. (pp. 105–111)

TEST YOUR UNDERSTANDING

To see how well you have understood this chapter, take the following review quiz. Then correct it using the answer key provided by your instructor. If you score 80 percent or above, you're ready to take the end-of-chapter exam. However, if you score below 80 percent, look over the quiz carefully to see what kinds of questions you missed. Use the **Summing Up** pages of the chapter to find out which pages you should review before taking the chapter exam.

Chapter 3: Review Quiz

Part A

DIRECTIONS Identify the more accurate paraphrase by circling the appropriate letter.

1. Because China has banned them from selling their products door-to-door, vendors* for companies like Amway, Mary Kay, and Avon are not very happy with China at the moment. According to the Chinese press, such door-to-door marketing tends to foster "excess hugging" and "weird cults."[3]

Paraphrase a. The Chinese government has given an odd reason for its ban on door-to-door salespeople for companies like Avon and Amway: they give rise to "weird cults" and "excess hugging."

b. Amway, Mary Kay, and Avon have decided to stop selling their products in China because their salespeople have become the victims of too much hugging.

2. During World War II, movies about Japan made little effort to develop a Japanese character or explain what Japan hoped to accomplish in the war. The Japanese remained nameless, faceless, and almost totally speechless. No attempt was made to show a Japanese soldier trapped by circumstances beyond his control, or a family man who longed for home, or an officer who despised the militarists* even if he supported the military campaign. This stands in sharp contrast to the portrayal of the German soldiers, who were often shown as decent human beings distinct from the Nazis. (Adapted from Clayton R. Koppes and Gregory D. Black, *Hollywood Goes to War.* Berkeley: University of California Press, 1998, p. 254.)

Paraphrase a. During World War II, Hollywood filmmakers were applauded for engaging in propaganda that was openly racist. The 1942 film *Wake Island,* for example, with its story of 377 marines who resisted Japanese invasion, was a smash hit despite its use of racial stereotypes to characterize Japanese soldiers. Today, however, such cinematic practices, even during wartime, would be sharply criticized.

---

*vendors: people who sell products.
*militarists: people devoted to war.
[3]"China Slams the Door on the Avon Lady," *Newsweek,* May 4, 1998, p. 49.

b. During World War II, Hollywood filmmakers made propaganda movies that failed to distinguish between the Japanese government's war machine and the Japanese soldier caught up in that machine. Oddly enough, they did not do the same in propaganda films about Germany. In these films, they made a distinction between the Nazi government and the German people.

3. Disco became the biggest commercial pop genre* of the 1970s— actually, the biggest pop music movement of all time—and in the end, its single-minded, booming beat proved to be the most resilient and enduring stylistic breakthrough of the last twenty years or so. (Mikal Gilmore, *Night Beat.* New York: Doubleday, 1998, p. 241.)

Paraphrase a. In the 1970s, disco challenged rock and roll's position as the music of the young. But thankfully, following the success of *Saturday Night Fever,* disco died a fast and well-deserved death.

b. In the 1970s, disco was the hottest dance music around; over the last two decades, its pulsing beat has proved to have real staying power.

4. In the nineteenth and early twentieth centuries, the South American countries of Argentina, Uruguay, and Brazil had their own home-grown cowboys, called gauchos. Derived from the Spanish word *wáhcha,* the word *gaucho* usually referred to cowhands or horse handlers, but it could also refer to horse thieves and mercenaries.*

Paraphrase a. In the South American countries of Argentina, Uruguay, and Brazil, gauchos were considered romantic figures, and much like America's cowboys, they were the heroes of countless movies and novels. Among the most famous of these novels was *The Four Horsemen of the Apocalypse,* which also became a movie.

b. During the nineteenth and beginning of the twentieth centuries, American-like cowboys called gauchos worked the ranches of Uruguay, Argentina, and Brazil. Although the term *gaucho*— which comes from the Spanish word *wáhcha*—meant "cowboy" or "horse handler," it could also be a negative term that referred to horse thieves and soldiers of fortune.

---

*genre: type or class; a category of literature, music, or art.
*mercenaries: soldiers for hire, soldiers of fortune.

Part B

DIRECTIONS Choose the passage that is most effectively underlined and annotated.

5. a. **What Is the Internet?**

Changing and growing every day The Internet is a huge international computer network made up of other computer networks. It is changing and growing every day, as new networks and users plug into it. The Internet is an important part of the Information Superhighway that Vice President Al Gore popularized. It connects people all over the globe; it's on twenty-four hours a day; it's uncensored.

Began in 1969 The Net, as it's called, began in 1969 as a U.S. government experiment. The goal was to enable academic and military researchers around the country and the world to communicate with one *Cold War fears* another. Part of the motive for developing the Net had to do with Cold War fears: It was designed to keep working in the event of nuclear attack. That meant the system had to be decentralized, so that there was no Internet "headquarters" that could be bombed, thus disabling the system. (Lynette Padwa, *Everything You Pretend to Know and Are Afraid to Ask*, p. 82.)

b. **What Is the Internet?**

So what! The Internet is a huge international computer network made up of other computer networks. It is changing and growing every day, as new networks and users plug into it. The Internet is an *He's a real stiff.* important part of the Information Superhighway that Vice President Al Gore popularized. It connects people all over the globe; it's on twenty-four hours a day; it's uncensored.

The Net, as it's called, began in 1969 as a U.S. government experiment. The goal was to enable academic and military research- *I don't understand.* ers around the country and the world to communicate with one another. Part of the motive for developing the Net had to do with Cold War fears: It was designed to keep working in the event of nuclear attack. That meant the system had to be decentralized, so that there was no Internet "headquarters" that could be bombed, thus disabling the system. (Padwa, *Everything You Pretend to Know and Are Afraid to Ask,* p. 82.)

c. **What Is the Internet?**

Def: Internet is large computer network linking nations. The Internet is a huge international computer network made up of other computer networks. It is changing and growing every day, as new networks plug into it. The Internet is an important part of the Information Superhighway that Vice President Al Gore popularized. It <u>connects people all over the globe</u>; it's on <u>twenty-four hours</u> a day; it's <u>uncensored</u>.

My roommate is on it 24 hrs a day.

The Net, as it's called, <u>began in 1969 as a U.S. government experiment</u>. The goal was <u>to enable academic</u> and <u>military research-ers</u> around the country and the world <u>to communicate</u> with one another. Part of the <u>motive for developing</u> the Net had to do with <u>Cold War fears</u>: It was <u>designed to keep working</u> in the event of <u>nuclear attack</u>. That meant the system had to be decentralized, so that there was <u>no Internet "headquarters" that could be bombed</u>, thus disabling the system. (Padwa, *Everything You Pretend to Know and Are Afraid to Ask*, p. 82.)

Net started in 1969

for this reason:

TQ: What is the Internet and how did it originate?

Part C

DIRECTIONS Identify the paragraph pattern (or patterns) by circling the appropriate letter (or letters). Then, circle the letter of the test question you think would *not* appear on an exam.

6. *Chaos* is the scientific term for the complex, unpredictable order that underlies the natural world. Chaos theory holds that systems are predictable at first, but can be thrown off course by very small events. The typical example is smoke, which may flow upward from a flame in a single plume but quickly billows and changes shape at the slightest breeze. Although the original scheme has changed, the billowing smoke does follow a pattern—an extremely complex, unpredictable pattern that is, in fact, the pattern of chaos. (Padwa, *Everything You Pretend to Know and Are Afraid to Ask,* p. 176.)

Patterns a. definition

b. process

c. sequence of dates and events

d. classification

e. comparison and contrast

f. cause and effect

Test Questions a. Define the term *chaos* when it's used in the context of science.

b. Give an example of chaos theory in action.

c. Who first outlined chaos theory?

7. The Central Intelligence Agency, or CIA, has a long but not necessarily distinguished history. Established in 1947, under the same act that created the National Security Council, the purpose of the CIA was to collect, combine, and analyze information about the activities of foreign governments. This information was considered necessary to conduct foreign policy and protect U.S. interests abroad. Although the CIA started out as a rather small agency, its power was enormously expanded during the 1950s under the leadership of its director, Allen Dulles, the brother of Secretary of State John Foster Dulles. The fifties were the time of the Cold War, when it was assumed that the communists were ready and willing to take over the United States. Thus the CIA was allowed to conduct covert* operations both in and outside of America. Unfortunately, the fifties were not the CIA's finest hour. In 1953, in an effort to protect America's oil interests, it helped bring down the government of Iranian leader Mohammed Mossadegh. The following year it toppled the government of Guatemala's democratically elected president, Jacobo Arbenz, largely because he was pursuing land reform that threatened the interests of America's United Fruit Company. At home the agency infiltrated* religious and cultural groups in an effort to root out alleged spies. The right of the CIA to conduct such operations went unchallenged until the mid-1970s, when congressional investigations revealed that it had attempted to assassinate several foreign leaders, among them Cuba's Fidel Castro. The agency's reputation was further damaged in 1994 when it was discovered that one of its career officers, Aldrich Ames, had been spying for the Soviet Union for decades. In 1996 a Senate committee recommended that the CIA confine its efforts to hunting down terrorists and eliminating drug traffic.

Patterns a. definition

        b. process

        c. sequence of dates and events

        d. classification

        e. comparison and contrast

        f. cause and effect

Test Questions a. How did John Foster Dulles help shape the CIA's role in foreign affairs?

        b. In the mid-seventies, what was revealed about the CIA's activities?

        c. Why did the CIA help topple the government of Jacobo Arbenz in 1954?

---

*covert: secret.
*infiltrated: entered into for purposes of spying.

8. Most exams in college rely on two types of remembering, *recall* and *recognition*. Recall refers to the ability to supply or reproduce facts or information acquired some time in the past. When you remember the lines of your favorite song, the dates of the Korean War, or the year John F. Kennedy died, you are using recall. Recall is also at work when you complete fill-in-the-blank questions on a mid-term or final. Recognition comes into play when you only have to recognize some previously acquired knowledge or experience. For example, if you had to pick a suspect out of a police lineup, you would be using recognition rather than recall. Recognition is also at the heart of multiple-choice tests, where you have to recognize and select the correct answer. Not surprisingly, recall is the more difficult memory task, and it is usually harder to recall information than it is to simply recognize it when you see it.

Patterns
  a. definition
  b. process
  c. sequence of dates and events
  d. classification
  e. comparison and contrast
  f. cause and effect

Test Questions
  a. Explain the difference between recognition and recall.
  b. What do the terms *recall* and *recognition* mean in the context of remembering?
  c. Describe the limitations of multiple-choice exams when they are used to measure learning.

9. The changes that come with sleep can be measured with an **electro-encephalograph** (e-LEK-tro-en-SEF-uh-lo-graf), or brain-wave machine, commonly called an **EEG.** The brain gives off tiny electrical signals that can be amplified and recorded. With the help of an EEG, researchers have identified four different sleep stages. **Stage 1:** As you lose consciousness and enter **light sleep,** your heart rate slows down. Breathing becomes irregular; the muscles of your body relax. In stage 1 sleep, the EEG is made up mainly of small, irregular waves. Persons awakened at this time may or may not be aware that they were asleep. **Stage 2:** As sleep deepens, the EEG begins to show short bursts of activity called **sleep spindles,** and body temperature drops. Sleep spindles seem to mark the true boundary of sleep. Within four minutes after spindles appear, the majority of persons who are awakened recognize that they had been asleep (Bonnet & Moore, 1982). **Stage 3:** In stage 3, new brain waves called **delta**

waves begin to appear. Delta waves signal deeper sleep and a further loss of consciousness. **Stage 4:** In stage 4, the brain-wave pattern becomes almost pure delta waves, and the sleeper is in a state of oblivion.* If you sound a loud noise during stage 4, the sleeper will awaken in confusion and may not remember the noise. (Adapted from Coon, *Essentials of Psychology*, p. 228.)

Patterns a. definition

b. process

c. sequence of dates and events

d. classification

e. comparison and contrast

f. cause and effect

Test Questions a. Name and describe each of the stages in sleep.

b. What is the relationship between dreams and *sleep spindles?*

c. Describe what happens during stage 2 of sleep.

10. In studying marriage in the United States, researchers have defined three different types or patterns of marital relations. In the *equal partnership marriage,* everything is open to negotiation (who works, who cooks, who pays the bills, and so on), and there is no preset assignment of roles and responsibilities. In the *conventional marriage,* in contrast, the man is the undisputed head of the household and the sole economic provider. The woman is the mother and homemaker responsible for all domestic tasks. The conventional marriage pattern used to be the dominant pattern but not any longer. A third pattern of marital relations is the *junior partner* relationship. The junior partner, typically the wife, brings in some of the income and takes some decision-making responsibilities. The senior partner, usually the husband, often helps the wife at home, but he does not share equally the family responsibilities such as cooking and child care. This is the most common form of marriage today.

Patterns a. definition

b. process

c. sequence of dates and events

d. classification

e. comparison and contrast

f. cause and effect

---

*oblivion: unconsciousness.

Test Questions a. Identify and describe the three types of marital relations described by researchers.

b. In what ways are junior partner and equal partner relationships similar?

c. Why has the conventional marriage begun to decline?

> Use the answer key provided by your instructor to correct your quiz. If you score 80 percent or above, you are ready for the chapter exam. If you score below 80 percent, look carefully at the questions you answered incorrectly. Then use the **Summing Up** section to decide which pages you need to review.

Chapter Test 3

Part A

DIRECTIONS Identify the more accurate paraphrase by circling the appropriate letter.

1. Folk wisdom has it that animals can predict earthquakes. Over the years, there have been many reports of livestock busting out of their barns or household pets pacing in a frenzy before an earthquake. Actually, there may be something to this old wives' tale. According to Helmut Tributsch of the Free University of Berlin, an animal's skin is much drier than a human's. There is a lot of electromagnetic upset just before an earthquake, and this increase in electromagnetic activity makes an animal's hair stand up. Naturally, the animal is not pleased and shows it.

Paraphrase **a.** For years people have noticed that animals seem to know in advance when an earthquake will hit. Right before a tremor, cattle have been known to crash from their barns and pets to pace about nervously. Well, in fact, this animal behavior may well be an accurate prediction of earthquake activity. According to Helmut Tributsch of the Free University of Berlin, an animal's skin is a lot drier than a human's. Thus animals may be responding to the static electricity that is in the air right before an earthquake.

  b. Like so much other folk wisdom, the notion that animals can predict earthquakes seems to be accurate. According to Helmut Tributsch, a German earthquake expert, animals do know when an earthquake is about to hit. That's why cats howl, dogs pace, and cattle bolt right before an earthquake.

 2. A *dialect* is a language use—including vocabulary, grammar, and pronunciation—unique to a particular group or region. Audiences sometimes make negative judgments about a speaker based on his or her dialect. Such negative judgments are called *vocal stereotypes.* (Gronbeck et al., *Principles of Speech Communication,* 1995, p. 100.)

Paraphrase **a.** A dialect is a particular way of speaking. Unfortunately, people sometimes judge others based on the way they speak. Southerners, for example, rightfully complain about being stereotyped because of their accent.

  b. The term *vocal stereotypes* refers to the negative judgments people sometimes make based on a person's particular dialect. A dialect is speech unique to a group or region, and it includes vocabulary, grammar, and pronunciation.

3. Psychological research generally indicates that pornography has little long-term effect on people's sexual behavior, but that violent pornography can increase men's aggression toward women, as well as create more tolerant attitudes toward violence against women. (Janet Shibley Hyde, *Understanding Human Sexuality.* New York: McGraw-Hill, 1994, p. 528.)

Paraphrase a. Overall psychological studies do not suggest a link between pornography and changes in sexual behavior. However, they do suggest that violent pornography increases the possibility of aggression against women.

b. Some feminists object to pornography on the grounds that it humiliates women and increases the chance of sexual harassment, but no studies indicate that there is a connection between sexual harassment and the reading or viewing of pornography.

4. Once dogs were befriended by humans, they generally became much-loved, but obedient, companions. Cats, in contrast, were immediately worshipped as gods, which may explain the origin of the rhyme "Dogs drool but cats rule."

Paraphrase a. Once dogs entered human society, they became treasured companions who, nevertheless, knew their place. Cats, however, didn't worry about being obedient because they were worshipped as gods. Maybe that's where the saying "Dogs drool but cats rule" came from.

b. In ancient Egypt, cats were held in such high esteem, they were protected by law from mistreatment. Dogs, admired for their hunting skills, nonetheless never earned legal protection. Perhaps that's why cat lovers like to say "Dogs drool but cats rule."

Part B

DIRECTIONS Circle the letter of the passage that is most effectively underlined and annotated.

5. a. **TV as Habit**

Long-term trends aside, <u>people tend to turn on their television sets day after day in the same overall numbers</u>, with no apparent
?? regard for the particular programs that may be scheduled. <u>Expressed in terms made famous by Marshall McLuhan, the *medium* matters more than the message</u>.
★★

Paul Klein, former CBS programming chief, has proposed a theory similar to McLuhan's. Klein theorizes that people stay with the same station until they are driven to another station by an objectionable program. But even if they find *all* programs objectionable, according to the Least Objectionable Program theory (LOP), they will stay tuned to the one *least* objectionable rather than turning off the set entirely.

I don't get it.

This accounted, wrote Klein, for the steady 90 percent of the prime-time audience gathered in by the three television broadcast networks until the 1980s. It also explained why seemingly excellent programs sometimes failed (because they were scheduled against even better programs), and why seemingly mediocre programs sometimes succeeded (because they opposed even more objectionable mediocrities). (Head et al., *Broadcasting in America*, p. 409.)

b. **TV as Habit**

Long-term trends aside, people tend to turn on their television sets day after day in the same overall numbers, with no apparent regard for the particular programs that may be scheduled. Expressed in terms made famous by Marshall McLuhan, the *medium* matters more than the message.

Paul Klein's theory: people stay with the Least Objectionable Program (LOP).

Paul Klein, former CBS programming chief, has proposed a theory similar to McLuhan's. Klein theorizes that people stay with the same station until they are driven to another station by an

I actually do this.

objectionable program. But even if they find *all* programs objectionable, according to the Least Objectionable Program theory (LOP), they will stay tuned to the one *least* objectionable rather than turning off the set entirely.

TQ: Explain Paul Klein's theory of TV viewing.

This accounted, wrote Klein, for the steady 90 percent of the prime-time audience gathered in by the three television broadcast networks until the 1980s. It also explained why seemingly excellent

LOP in action

programs sometimes failed (because they were scheduled against even better programs), and why seemingly mediocre programs sometimes succeeded (because they opposed even more objectionable mediocrities). (Head et al., *Broadcasting in America*, p. 409.)

c. **TV as Habit**

Long-term trends aside, people tend to turn on their television sets day after day in the same overall numbers, with no apparent

People are addicted to television.

regard for the particular programs that may be scheduled. Expressed in terms made famous by Marshall McLuhan, the *me-*

Marshall McLuhan

dium matters more than the message.

Paul Klein

Paul Klein, former CBS programming chief, has proposed a theory similar to McLuhan's. Klein theorizes that people stay with the same station until they are driven to another station by an objectionable program. But even if they find *all* programs objectionable, according to the Least Objectionable Program theory (LOP), they will stay tuned to the one *least* objectionable rather than turning off the set entirely.

90 percent of the prime-time audience gathered in by the 3 networks.

This accounted, wrote Klein, for the steady 90 percent of the prime-time audience gathered in by the three television broadcast networks until the 1980s. It also explained why seemingly excellent programs sometimes failed (because they were scheduled against even better programs), and why seemingly mediocre programs sometimes succeeded (because they opposed even more objectionable mediocrities). (Head et al., *Broadcasting in America*, p. 409.)

Part C

DIRECTIONS Identify the paragraph type (or types) by circling the appropriate letter (or letters). Then, circle the letter of the test question you think would *not* appear on the exam.

6. *El Niño* is a seasonal ocean current flowing along the coast of northern Peru. Between January and March, the current reaches its highest peak. It is warm, nutrient poor, and low in salinity.* Normally, El Niño travels a few degrees south of the equator before converging with the north-flowing Peru current. However, in some years, a weakening of the normally strong southeast trade winds allows El Niño to extend further south and the temperature in the current rises, which results in increased rainfall in some areas. This affects the patterns of ocean currents and can cause floods and droughts in some areas of the world.

Patterns
a. definition

b. process

c. sequence of dates and events

d. classification

e. comparison and contrast

f. cause and effect

---

*salinity: salt level.

Test Questions a. How did El Niño affect North America in 1999?

b. What is El Niño?

c. When does El Niño normally reach its highest peak?

7. The American College of Sports Medicine has described four major categories of fitness: (1) cardiorespiratory endurance, (2) muscular fitness, (3) flexibility, and (4) body composition. *Cardiorespiratory endurance* refers to the body's ability to sustain strenuous activity for long periods of time. *Muscular fitness* includes both the strength and endurance capability of your muscles. *Flexibility* refers to the ability of a specific joint to move through its entire range of motion without pain. *Body composition* refers to the amount of your body that is fat versus fat-free tissues. Each of these four elements is important to your overall level of fitness. (Mullen et al., *Connections for Health*, p. 171.)

Patterns a. definition

b. process

c. sequence of dates and events

d. classification

e. comparison and contrast

f. cause and effect

Test Questions a. What is cardiorespiratory endurance?

b. Why is flexibility the most important category of fitness?

c. Name and describe the four categories of fitness.

8. A computer with a virus is a bit like a human with a cold: A "foreign body" (in the form of a hidden code attached to a program) "infects" the computer. But this virus can do more than cause sniffles and sneezing—it can cause the loss of irreplaceable data. Computer viruses enter computers, either on an infected diskette or downloaded from another computer. Once inside the computer, the virus can multiply, infecting other programs on the computer's hard disk. Some viruses perform seemingly "innocent" actions such as flashing "Happy Birthday, Columbus" on Columbus Day. Other viruses are more insidious,* and after being triggered by a certain keystroke, can wipe out whole files of data. (Barnes-Svarney, ed., *New York Public Library Science Desk Reference*, p. 199.)

---

*insidious: harmful.

Patterns a. definition

    b. process

    c. sequence of dates and events

    d. classification

    e. comparison and contrast

    f. cause and effect

Test Questions a. What can you do to protect your computer against viruses?

    b. How is a virus like a cold?

    c. How does a virus enter a computer?

9. In 1800 the intense and handsome attorney Aaron Burr almost beat Thomas Jefferson in his campaign for president, but scandal quickly destroyed Burr's potentially promising career. In 1804, when Burr ran for governor of New York, he made a deal to support the Southern Confederacy,* but when his political supporters found out, they were furious, and he lost the election. Burr blamed his loss on his long-time rival, Alexander Hamilton, and challenged Hamilton to a duel, which took place on July 11, 1804. Hamilton was mortally wounded and died a lingering death, for which Burr was held responsible. To escape his disgrace, Burr went West late in 1805, and by 1806 there were rumors that he was trying to take control of Louisiana. When attempts were made to arrest him, Burr tried to flee to Florida, but he was captured and put on trial for treason. Acquitted in September of 1807, Burr's career was, nevertheless, finished.

Patterns a. definition

    b. process

    c. sequence of dates and events

    d. classification

    e. comparison and contrast

    f. cause and effect

Test Questions a. In what year was Aaron Burr acquitted of treason?

    b. Why was Aaron Burr put on trial for treason?

    c. What position did Alexander Hamilton hold in the U.S. government?

---

*Confederacy: The Southern states that wanted to leave the Union in order to preserve the institution of slavery.

10. In some South American tribes, men and women speak different languages. The men cannot understand the women's language, but the women can understand the men's. On the surface, at least, American men and women appear to speak a common language, but, in fact, some evidence suggests that we are not so different from those South American tribes. Here too the sexes sometimes seem to speak two different languages. As the linguist Robin Lakoff has shown in a study of speech differences, women use more questions than men. They interrupt less frequently and are more likely to suggest than assert. Women also make greater use of qualifiers like *might, could*, and *probably*. Men are far more likely to state their opinions as facts, and they are more likely to interrupt than women.

Patterns a. definition

b. process

c. sequence of dates and events

d. classification

e. comparison and contrast

f. cause and effect

Test Questions a. Briefly describe the results of Robin Lakoff's study of speech differences.

b. *True* or *False:* Research on speech differences shows that women ask more questions than men.

c. How does occupation affect gender differences in speech?

C H A P T E R 4

Beyond Paragraphs: Understanding and Outlining Longer Readings

In this chapter you'll learn

- **how to identify main ideas in longer readings.**

- **how to recognize the *thesis statements* that sum up main ideas.**

- **how to evaluate supporting details.**

- **how to create informal outlines.**

In Chapter 4, you'll be making use of the same skills you polished in Chapter 2, *Reviewing Paragraph Essen-*

135

tials. **Only this time, you will be applying those skills, with some modification, to readings a good deal longer than a paragraph.**

 # Understanding Longer Readings

To really understand a paragraph, you need to answer three questions:

1. What's the topic?
2. What's the main idea?
3. Which supporting details are essential to understanding that main idea?

Fortunately, those same questions also apply to readings much longer than a single paragraph. Still, that's not to say there are no differences between reading a single paragraph and reading longer selections. There are, in fact, five crucial differences you need to take into account.

The Main Idea Controls More Than a Paragraph

In longer readings, the main idea unifies not just a single paragraph but all or most of the paragraphs in the reading. Because it controls the content of all the other paragraphs, think of the main idea in a longer reading as the **controlling idea.** The controlling idea gives all the other paragraphs a purpose: They are there to explain its meaning and answer any questions it might raise in the minds of readers.

The Main Idea Might Well Be Expressed in Several Sentences

The main idea of a reading can often be summed up in a single sentence. But sometimes it requires several sentences, maybe even a paragraph. For that reason, many composition textbooks use the term **thesis statement** to talk about the main idea of a research paper or essay, and we'll use the same term here. For practical purposes, the change in terms means you shouldn't always expect to find the main idea of a reading summed up in one sentence.

Thesis Statements Don't Wander Quite So Much

Topic sentences can appear anywhere in a paragraph—at the beginning, middle, or end. Thesis statements, in contrast, are more fixed in their location. Yes, an author will occasionally build up to the main idea and put the thesis statement at the very end of a reading. But that's not typical. Far more likely is the appearance of the thesis statement at the beginning of a reading. Thus, the opening paragraphs deserve particularly close attention.

Supporting Details Take Up More Space

In longer readings, one supporting detail essential to the main idea can take up an entire paragraph. Thus, longer readings require you to do a good deal more sifting and sorting of information as you decide which individual statements are essential to your understanding of a major detail.

Minor Details Can Also Occupy an Entire Paragraph

As they do in paragraphs, minor details in longer readings further explain major ones, add colorful facts, or use repetition for emphasis. However, like major details, minor details can also occupy an entire paragraph, and just as in paragraphs, they may or may not be important. Sometimes minor supporting details supply the examples or explanations necessary for a clear understanding of a major detail. When this is the case, the minor details should be considered essential. But if they simply add a colorful anecdote, or story, or else provide repetition for emphasis, you need not store them away in your long-term memory, and you certainly don't need to include them in your notes.

Now that you know how reading a paragraph is different from reading a more extended piece of writing, it's time to put what you have learned into practice. Read the following selection.

Research on Leadership

Thesis Statement

1 In business, managers have to be leaders. Thus, it comes as no surprise that researchers have been studying the nature of leadership in business. At the University of Michigan, researchers have found that leadership behavior among managers can be divided into two categories. Whereas some managers are job-centered, others tend to be employee-centered.

Topic Sentence 2 Leaders who practice job-centered behavior closely supervise their employees in an effort to monitor and control their performance. They are primarily concerned with getting a job done and less concerned with the feelings or attitudes of their employees— unless those attitudes and feelings affect the task at hand. In general, they don't encourage employees to express their opinions on how best to accomplish a task.

Topic Sentence 3 In contrast, leaders who practice employee-centered behavior focus on reaching goals by building a sense of team spirit. An employee-centered leader is concerned with subordinates' job satisfaction and group unity. Employee-centered leaders are also more willing to let employees have a voice in how they do their jobs.

Topic Sentence 4 The Michigan researchers also investigated which kind of leadership is more effective. They concluded that managers whose leadership was employee-centered were generally more effective than managers who were primarily job-centered. That is, their employees performed at higher levels and were more satisfied. (Adapted from Van Fleet and Peterson, *Contemporary Management,* p. 332.)

Having read "Research on Leadership," look closely at the two sentences that make up the thesis statement. Now look at the topic sentences of the remaining paragraphs. Can you see how those topic sentences serve to clarify the thesis statement? This reading illustrates how thesis statements and topic sentences work together. The thesis statement introduces the author's general point. Then the topic sentences of each paragraph serve as supporting details that flesh out and clarify that point. Within each paragraph, the major details should always clarify the topic sentence; however, they may or may not directly support the thesis statement.

The following diagram expresses the relationship between thesis and topic sentences within a reading or essay.

Thesis Statement

> At the University of Michigan, researchers found that leadership behavior among managers can be divided into two categories. Whereas some managers are job-centered, others tend to be employee-centered.

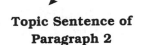
Topic Sentence of Paragraph 2

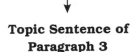
Topic Sentence of Paragraph 3

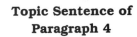
Topic Sentence of Paragraph 4

> Leaders who practice job-centered behavior closely supervise their employees in an effort to monitor and control their performance.

> Leaders who practice employee-centered behavior focus on reaching goals by building team spirit.

> Michigan researchers also investigated which kind of leadership is more effective.

Before going on to Exercise 1, read the following selection and underline the thesis statement. Remember, the thesis statement shouldn't unify just one paragraph. It should unify the entire reading.

Looking Back at the Death Penalty

1 Today the penalty of death is reserved for "serious" crimes such as murder, treason, espionage, and rape. And when it is actually carried out (as it is in only one of every thirty death sentencings in the United States), the means of execution in Western countries are by firing squad, hanging, gas chamber, electric chair, and lethal injection—all relatively fast ways to go.

2 In ancient and medieval times, however, death was handed out for many more offenses, some trivial by modern standards. In India, you could have been sentenced to death for spreading falsehoods, killing a cow, or stealing a royal elephant. In Egypt, during the peak of feline worship, death was the punishment for injuring

a cat (even if it recovered). Judeans imposed the death penalty for cursing; the Babylonians for selling bad beer; the Assyrians for giving a bad haircut, since stylish coiffures were signs of class.

3 In parts of the Middle East, perjurers were executed by being intravenously embalmed while still alive. The embalming solution replaced the victim's blood and quickly caused cardiac arrest, and in that regard the mode of execution was a forerunner of the modern lethal injection.

4 The oldest reference to a death sentence dates back to 1500 B.C. The criminal was a teenage male, and his crime was recorded simply as "magic." The mode of death was left to his choosing (poisoning or stabbing), and the executioner was to be himself.

5 In Rome during the same period, a citizen could be executed for many serious offenses, but also for trivial matters, as prescribed by law: for "publishing lies," for singing "insulting songs" about high-ranking officials, for "cheating by a patron of his client," and for "making disturbances in the city at night." (Adapted from Charles Panati, *Extraordinary Endings*. New York: Harper & Row, 1989, pp. 136–137.)

Tempting as it might be to assume that the first paragraph of the reading contains the thesis statement, that assumption would lead you astray in this instance. None of the sentences in paragraph 1 is developed beyond the first paragraph. Thus, the first paragraph cannot possibly contain the thesis statement.

Look now at paragraph 2. The first sentence is the topic sentence. All of the sentences after the first one serve to illustrate the rather "trivial" offenses that once earned the death sentence. However, the topic sentence of paragraph 2 also expresses the main idea of the entire reading. As a matter of fact, the topic sentence in paragraph 2 is also the thesis statement of the entire reading. If you look at paragraphs 3, 4, and 5, you'll see that all three—like the individual sentences in paragraph 2—serve to identify the trivial offenses mentioned in paragraph 2.

CHECK YOUR UNDERSTANDING

Describe how single paragraphs differ from longer readings.

1. _____

   _____

2. _____

_____

3. _____

_____

4. _____

_____

5. _____

_____

EXERCISE 1

DIRECTIONS Underline the thesis statement of each reading.

EXAMPLE

The Trail of Tears

Thesis 1 Throughout the nineteenth century, the Cherokee Indians proved
Statement   themselves to be highly inventive and enterprising. They also
showed a willingness to adapt and excel at whatever they learned
from white settlers. Unfortunately, their success did not save
them from being evicted from their tribal lands.

2 In 1820, the tribe established a system of government modeled
on that of the United States. It elected a principal chief, a senate,
and a house of representatives. In 1821, Sequoya, a Cherokee
warrior who had been crippled in a hunting accident, produced a
workable alphabet of Cherokee characters. The Cherokees studied
the alphabet enthusiastically, and within months thousands
could read and write the new alphabet. By 1828, the Cherokees
were producing their own weekly newspaper, and the paper's read-
ership was growing faster than the papers could be produced.

3 Unfortunately, in the same year, the Georgia legislature outlawed the Cherokee government. Gold had been discovered on
tribal lands almost ten years before, and greedy land speculators*
were determined to take control of those lands, even if it meant il-

---

*speculators: people who engage in risky financial dealings in order to gain high
profits.

legally evicting the Cherokee people. In 1832, the U.S. Supreme Court ruled in favor of the Cherokees' right to their lands. But that decision was ignored by federal authorities, and, in 1838, federal troops drove about 20,000 Cherokees west on a forced march for three hundred miles. During the march so many Cherokees died from hunger, disease, and exposure that the route they followed came to be called the "Trail of Tears."

EXPLANATION In this reading, the thesis statement consists of three sentences rather than one. The thesis statement tells readers that the author intends to explore two related points: (1) The Cherokees were highly enterprising and inventive and (2) their achievements did not save them from being evicted from their tribal lands. Paragraphs 2 and 3 then provide the supporting details that clarify both parts of this thesis statement.

1. Altering Consciousness

1 People throughout history have sought ways to alter consciousness. A dramatic example is the sweat lodge ritual of the Sioux Indians. During the ritual, several men sit in total darkness inside a small chamber heated by a bed of coals. Cedar smoke, bursts of steam, and the aroma of sage fill the air. The men chant rhythmically. The heat builds. At last, they can stand it no more. The door is thrown open. Cooling night breezes rush in. And then? The cycle begins again—often to be repeated four or five times more. Among the Sioux, this ritual is viewed as a cleansing of mind and body. When the experience becomes especially intense, it brings altered awareness and personal revelation.*

2 Some altered states of consciousness are sought primarily for pleasure, as is often true of drug intoxication. Yet, as the Sioux example illustrates, many cultures regard changes in consciousness as pathways to enlightenment. Almost every known religion has accepted at least some altered states as a source of mystical experience. Accepted avenues have ranged from fasting, meditation, prayer, isolation, sleep loss, whirling, and chanting, to self-inflicted pain and mind-altering substances.

3 In many cultures, the special powers attributed to medicine men, shamans, or healers are believed to come from an ability to enter a trance and communicate with spirits. Often, rituals that help form tribal bonds among community members are accentuated by altered states of consciousness.

4 In short, all cultures recognize and accept some alterations of

------

*revelation: sudden insight or understanding.

consciousness. However, the meanings given various states vary greatly—from signs of "madness" and "possession" by spirits to life-enhancing breakthroughs. Thus, cultural conditioning greatly affects what altered states a person recognizes, seeks, considers normal, and attains (Ward, 1989). (Coon, *Essentials of Psychology*, p. 222.)

2. Our Oldest Enemy: The Locust

1   On July 28, 1962, radar operators at the Indian National Physical Laboratory in Delhi sounded the alarm. They had spotted a gigantic airborne invasion in progress, and the enemy was already only sixty miles south of the city.

2   Specialized emergency teams were instantly alerted. India and her traditionally hostile neighbor, Pakistan, joined forces: Aircraft from both countries roared into action, flying only sixty-five feet above the ground in a skillful counterattack. The initial battle raged for a week; sporadic fighting continued until December, when the two countries declared themselves victorious. The enemy dead numbered more than one-hundred *billion.*

3   It had been no human invasion but a far more fearsome and rapacious* threat: locusts. Using chemicals sprayed from aircraft, humans wreaked havoc on these prodigiously* destructive pests. Nevertheless, throughout most of history, the reverse has been true. When a plague of locusts arrives, it has been people who have suffered more than the locusts.

4   The earliest written record of a locust plague is probably in the Book of Exodus, which describes an attack that took place in Egypt in about 3500 B.C.: "They covered the face of the whole earth, so that the land was darkened . . . and there remained not any green in the trees, or in the herbs of the field, through all the land of Egypt." Another biblical account, in the Book of Job, describes trees "made white" as locusts even stripped the bark from the branches.

5   Locusts have always spelled disaster. In 125 B.C., they destroyed the grain crop in northern Africa; 80,000 people died of starvation. In A.D. 591, a plague of locusts in Italy caused the deaths of more than a million people and animals. In 1613, disaster struck the French region of La Camargue when locusts ate enough grass in a single day to feed 4,000 cattle for a year. The Nile Valley suffered in 1889 when locusts so thoroughly destroyed crops that even the mice starved in their wake. Between 1949

---

*rapacious: greedy.
*prodigiously: enormously.

and 1963 locust swarms in Africa caused an estimated $100 million worth of damage annually. In 1988, the Ethiopian cereal crop was laid waste, leaving a million people without food. (Simon Adams and Lesley Riley, eds., "The Ravenous Millions," *Facts and Fallacies.* Pleasantville, N.Y.: Readers Digest, 1988, p. 50.)

3. Killer Bees

1 Although their name makes them sound like something out of a horror film, killer bees really do exist. And while they are not quite so terrifying as their name implies, they are definitely not an insect—like the ladybug—that one should invite into the garden. On the contrary, both animals and humans would do well to avoid these sometimes ferociously angry bees.

2 Killer bees (officially called Africanized honeybees) originated in Brazil in 1956 as an experiment in mating the African honeybee with local bees. The breeders were hoping to get bees that would produce more honey. Instead, they produced extremely aggressive bees that have attacked—and in some cases killed—both people and animals. Each year the bees move about 350 miles (563 kilometers) north; in 1990, they crossed the U.S. border into Hidalgo, Texas.

3 Similar to the rumors that surround sharks, myths about African bees abound.* For example, it's not true that they fly faster than domestic honeybees. On the contrary, both types of bees average between 12 and 15 miles per hour. Also, the sting of the African bee actually has less, not more, venom than that of domestic honeybees. African bees are also a good deal smaller than domestic honeybees, not gigantic in size as has been rumored.

4 Still, African bees do have some features that make them an insect to avoid. When an African bee's body is crushed—from a swat, for example—it releases an odor that incites nearby bees to attack. Also, African bees vigorously and aggressively protect their hives. About ten times as many African bees as European bees will sting when their colonies are invaded. The good news is that scientists believe the African bees' aggressiveness will eventually diminish as they interbreed with the more peaceful European bees to the north.

4. Eat Garlic for Your Health

1 The ancient Egyptians believed that garlic could cure a wide variety of ills. In fact, early writings on the medical uses of herbs record close to thirty uses for the plant that the Romans used to

---

*abound: exist in great supply.

call "the stinking rose." For example, it was claimed that garlic could heal wounds, cure stomach cramps, and chase away common colds. What's surprising about these claims is that modern science actually bears many of them out, and eating garlic seems to be remarkably good for your health.

2   In 1858 Louis Pasteur* discovered that garlic could kill bacteria. Since Pasteur's time, researchers have found that garlic also inhibits the growth of bacteria in the stomach. A diet rich in garlic actually inhibits the growth of the bacteria that cause ulcers. Some studies have also suggested that eating garlic can slow the growth of cancers in the colon, breast, and skin. Although research still needs to be done to prove conclusively* that garlic can help prevent or cure cancer, existing evidence does suggest it may well help us fight this deadly disease.

3   There are also indications that garlic can help prevent heart disease. A diet high in garlic consumption seems to reduce the chance of blood clots. In addition, garlic may reduce hardening of the arteries, another heavy contributor to heart problems.

4   Because garlic has such a powerful—some would even say unpleasant—smell, many people are loath* to eat it. Instead, they consume deodorized garlic pills. Unfortunately, though the pills do confer some health benefits, they aren't as effective as the raw garlic cloves. So if you want to eat garlic for your health, you might consider stocking up on breath mints as well.

 ## Major and Minor Details

Major details in longer readings directly explain the thesis statement. They answer potential questions readers might raise; further define any general words or terms; and, when necessary, offer proof of an author's claim. While major details in a paragraph consist of single sentences, in longer readings you may find that an entire paragraph is devoted to explaining one major detail. When this happens, you'll have to decide how much of the paragraph is essential to your understanding of that one detail.

As they do in paragraphs, minor details in longer readings further explain or flesh out major details; they also provide color or emphasis. But here again, you can't assume that minor details are auto-

---

*Louis Pasteur: (1822–1895) French microbiologist who invented pasteurization and developed a vaccine for rabies.
*conclusively: without a doubt.
*loath: unwilling.

matically not essential to your understanding of the thesis statement. It all depends on what they contribute to your understanding of the major details they modify.

Read the following selection. As you do, think about which supporting details are essential to your understanding of the underlined thesis statement.

Defining Love

1   What is love? No one knows for sure. However, researcher R. J. Sternberg has a theory. <u>According to Sternberg, love consists of three separate ingredients, and each one is crucial either to falling in love or to staying in love.</u>

Thesis Statement

2   Passion is a feeling of heightened sexual arousal, and it's usually accompanied by a strong, romantic attraction. In the throes* of passion, each lover feels that life is barely worth living unless the other is present. Unfortunately, passionate feelings almost always diminish over time, although they are still essential to initiating the love relationship. Luckily, if there's a strong sense of intimacy between the partners, the loss or decrease of passion can be accepted and the love maintained.

3   Intimacy—feelings of closeness, sharing, and affection—is essential to staying in love. Both partners need to feel that they view the world in similar ways and can turn to one another in times of great sadness or joy. If the one you love is not the one you feel particularly close to, you may find that, over time, love doesn't last. Typically in a relationship, intimacy grows steadily at first and then levels off.

4   Commitment refers to a conscious decision to stay with a person both in good times and in bad. Like intimacy, a sense of commitment is essential to staying in love over time. But unlike intimacy, commitment frequently requires some hard work and a determined effort. It seldom comes without effort.

While reading the thesis statement in this selection, you probably wondered what three ingredients the author had in mind. Anticipating that question, the author defines all three. Those definitions are the major details that refer directly to the thesis statement. However, the minor details that expand upon those major details cannot simply be ignored—not if you want to understand Sternberg's theory. Minor detail or not, it is important to remember that if intimacy is lacking, love doesn't last—at least from R. J. Sternberg's point of view.

---

*throes: pangs, spasms.

▄ EXERCISE 2

DIRECTIONS Read each selection and look carefully at the underlined thesis statement. Then answer the questions that follow by filling in the blanks or circling the correct letter.

EXAMPLE

The Ancient Roman Circus

Thesis
Statement

1 Although nowadays we think of the circus as an amusing entertainment for kids, originally it was not quite such a harmless event. To be sure, the first circus, like its twentieth-century counterpart, included death-defying events. But there was one big difference. In the early Roman circus, death was a very real possibility, and circus spectators were accustomed to—and expected—bloodshed.

2 The Roman Circus Maximus began under the rule of Julius Caesar, and it specialized in two big events—brutal fights between gladiators (or between gladiators and animals) and equally bloody chariot races. In most cases, both events ended in the death of either a person or an animal. If nobody died, the audience was likely to be disappointed. Even worse, the emperor would be displeased.

3 Not surprisingly, the circus event that was in fashion usually reflected the taste of the man in power. Julius Caesar, for example, favored aggressive chariot races. Because the charioteers were usually slaves racing to win their freedom, they drove their horses unmercifully, and serious accidents were an exciting possibility. In the hopes of surviving, the charioteers wore helmets and wrapped the chariot reins around their bodies. They also carried knives to cut themselves free if necessary. Spills occurred more often than not, and the charioteers would be thrown from the chariot and dragged repeatedly around the ring by runaway horses. Knives and helmets not withstanding, most did not survive, not that the screaming crowd cared.

4 During the reign of Augustus, from 27 B.C. to A.D. 14, a fight to the death between man and beast was the favored circus event, and more than 3,500 lions and tigers perished in the circus arena, taking with them hundreds of gladiators. Under the half-mad Emperor Nero, who ruled in the first century A.D., the most popular circus spectacle was lion versus Christian, with the Christians the guaranteed losers. Fortunately for both Christians and

the slaves who followed in their wake, this savage circus practice was outlawed in A.D. 326 by the Emperor Constantine.

5   Although the pitting of Christians against lions was staged in a special arena, most of the circus events that took place in Rome were staged in the largest arena of them all—the Colosseum. The capacity of this great stadium, completed in A.D. 79, was enormous. It seated close to fifty thousand people. In one Colosseum season alone, 2,000 gladiators went to their deaths, all in the name of circus fun.[1]

1. How would you paraphrase the thesis statement?

Unlike the modern circus, the ancient Roman circus was a good deal more deadly.

2. Which question about the thesis statement do the major supporting details help to answer?

   a. What are the similarities between ancient and modern circuses?

   (b.) How did early circus events all but guarantee death?

EXPLANATION As it should, the paraphrase restates the point of the thesis statement but alters the words. The most likely question raised by the thesis statement is *b*. The main idea of the entire reading is that ancient circuses were often deadly, and the reader needs to know why this was so.

1. The Police Personality

Thesis Statement

1 In *Justice Without Trial*, sociologist Jerome Skolnick argues that in the same way doctors, janitors, lawyers, and industrial workers develop unique ways of looking at, and responding to, their work environment, so too do police officers. This effect of work on a person's world outlook Skolnick calls the **working personality.** Not surprisingly, the working personality of the police officer is molded by the dangerous conditions in which police work.

2   Police work is potentially dangerous, so officers need to be constantly aware of what is happening around them. It's not surprising, then, that suspicion is a key element of the police officer's working personality. At the academy, trainees are warned about what happens to officers who are too trusting. They also learn

---

[1](Based on the figures cited by Charles Panati, *Browser's Book of Beginnings.* Boston: Houghton Mifflin, 1984, pp. 262–264.)

about the many officers who have died in the line of duty because they did not exercise proper caution. On the street they need to stay alert for signals that crimes may be in progress: an unfamiliar noise, someone "checking into" an alleyway, a secret exchange of goods. Under these conditions, it would be surprising if officers did *not* become suspicious. As George Kirkham, police officer and professor, argues: "Chronic suspiciousness is something that a good cop cultivates in the interest of going home to his family each evening."

3   The environment in which they work demands that police officers gain immediate control of potentially dangerous situations. Because the police are routinely called upon to demonstrate authority, the need to be in authority also becomes a crucial element of the officer's working personality. However, that authority is often challenged by a hostile public, and in some cases the police have overreacted to what they see as challenges to their authority.

4   Public hostility, coupled with other factors—a belief that courts are too lenient on criminals; the realization that it is often wiser to "look the other way" if they become aware of corrupt practices by their peers; the part that favoritism may play in promotions—leads to yet another trait that characterizes the police officer's working personality: cynicism.*

5   In a study of 220 New York City police officers, Professor Arthur Niederhoffer, himself a former police officer, found that 80 percent of the new recruits believed that the department was a smoothly operating, effective organization. Within a couple of months on the job, fewer than one-third still held that belief. They had become cynical about police work, supervisors, and the operating policies of the department. Moreover, cynicism increased with length of service and among the more highly educated who were not promoted. Researchers Robert Regoli and Eric Poole argue that cynicism increases police officers' desire to exert authority over ordinary citizens. As the use of authority increases, citizens become more hostile, making police feel even more threatened, and the cycle continues. (Adapted from Adler et al., *Criminal Justice*, p. 237.)

1. How would you paraphrase the thesis statement?

_____

_____

---

*cynicism: a tendency to believe the worst.

2. Which question about the thesis statement do the major supporting details help to answer?

    a. How is the working personality of police officers affected by the conditions in which they work?

    b. How does the working personality of the police officer differ from that of the doctor?

2. Inhalants

Thesis Statement

1 The use of inhalants—gases that can be breathed into the lungs—appears to be on the rise, especially among young adolescents. One recent survey found that almost 20 percent of eighth-grade students reported that they had used an inhalant at some time in their lives. While among college-age adults the use of inhalants is reported to be less, it is currently estimated that 13.9 percent of young adults have used inhalants at some time in their lives, at least 3.1 percent having used them in the last year.

2 Glue, solvents,* and aerosols from paints, hair spray, nail polish remover, and the like are the most common substances inhaled. These substances are not considered drugs by society. Thus they are not regulated. Their availability helps explain why inhalants are so popular with young adolescents, who can purchase them at any drug or paint store.

3 When inhalants are breathed into the lungs they are quickly absorbed into the bloodstream and travel to the brain. In low doses these chemicals cause lightheadedness and dizziness, and provide a temporary high. In higher doses, depression of the central nervous system can lead to sleep or coma. The effects of inhalants can be poisonous to the body, resulting in heart rhythm disturbances and even death. Permanent brain damage affecting memory and reasoning abilities are often the effects of long-term inhalant abuse. (Adapted from Mullen et al., *Connections for Health*, p. 477.)

1. How would you paraphrase the thesis statement?

_____

_____

2. Which question about the thesis statement do the major supporting details help to answer?

    a. Why is inhalant use among adolescents currently on the rise?

    b. What kind of legislation do we need to curb the use of inhalants?

_____

*solvents: liquids used to dissolve other materials.

Outlining Longer Readings

For reading assignments that cover fairly familiar or uncomplicated material, you can probably prepare for class discussions or exams simply by reviewing your underlining and your annotations. However, if the material is at all complicated, you may want to take notes using an **informal outline.**

Like a formal outline, an informal outline signals relationships by aligning or indenting sentences, words, or phrases. However, you needn't worry about using *all* sentences or *all* phrases, and you don't have to fuss over capital or lowercase letters. You can also use whatever symbols seem appropriate to the material, combining letters, numbers, abbreviations, dashes, and so on, as you need them. In other words, informal outlines are not governed by a fixed set of rules. The main thing to keep in mind is the goal of your informal outline: to develop a clear blueprint of the author's ideas and their relationship to one another.

Here are some pointers for creating informal outlines that are clear, concise, and complete.

Start with the Title

The title of an essay, article, or chapter section usually identifies the topic being discussed. Sometimes it will identify the main idea of the entire reading. Thus, your outline should usually open with the title.

Follow with the Thesis Statement

After the title comes the paraphrase of the thesis statement. Because indenting to show relationships is crucial to outlining, put your paraphrase at the left-most margin of your notepaper.

List the Major Details

Now's the time to look over the supporting paragraphs and sift out the major details. At this point, keep in mind that the major details you select have to be carefully evaluated in relation to the thesis statement, and minor details in a paragraph should only be included if they are essential to the major ones. Outlining, like underlining, requires conscious and consistent selectivity. Here's an outline of the reading from pages 147–148.

The Ancient Roman Circus

The first circus began in ancient Rome, but it was much bloodier than the circus we know today.

1. The first circus, Circus Maximus, originated under Julius Caesar.
2. Ancient circuses specialized in bloody events; emperor and spectators were upset if no one died.
3. Which event was featured depended on the emperor in power.
   a. Julius Caesar liked chariot races: slaves raced for their freedom and risked their lives, often dying in the process.
      —dragged around the ring when they couldn't cut themselves free
   b. During reign of Augustus, more than 3,500 lions and tigers died in the circus arena, taking with them hundreds of gladiators.
      —fight to the death
   c. Under Nero, Christians were thrown to the lions.
4. Colosseum in Rome staged biggest circuses.
   a. It held 50,000 people.
   b. In one season, 2,000 gladiators went to their death.

Always Indent

As the sample outline illustrates, an outline is not the same as a list. When you make an outline, you have to indent to indicate whether different ideas carry equal weight. Major details, for example, should all be aligned in the same position to indicate their relationship to one another. Similarly, if you are summarizing several different chapter sections, then the main ideas of each section should be aligned one underneath the other.

Be Consistent

Letters, numbers, dashes (—), stars (☆☆☆), or asterisks (∗∗) can help you separate major and minor details. Whichever symbols you use, be sure to use them consistently within the outline. Don't switch back and forth, sometimes using numbers for major details and sometimes using letters. In the long run, this kind of inconsistency will only confuse you.

Be Selective

When you outline, reduce the original text as much as possible, retaining essential details and eliminating nonessential details. When adding supporting details to your outline, always decide what you need to include and what you can safely leave out.

■ EXERCISE 3

DIRECTIONS Read the following selection. Underline and annotate it. Then make an outline that is both concise and complete.

EXAMPLE

World War II: Interning Japanese-Americans

1 Compared with previous wars, the nation's wartime civil liberties record during World War II showed some improvement, particularly where African-Americans and women were concerned. But there was one enormous exception: the internment* of 120,000 Japanese-Americans. The internment of Japanese-Americans was based not on suspicion or evidence of treason; their crime was solely their race—the fact that they were of Japanese descent.

2 Popular racial stereotypes used to fuel the war effort held that Japanese people abroad and at home were sneaky and evil, and the American people generally regarded Japan as the United States's chief enemy. Moreover, the feeling was widespread that the Japanese had to be repaid for Pearl Harbor. Thus, with a few notable exceptions, there was no public outcry over the relocation and internment of Japanese-Americans.

3 Yet there were two obvious reasons why the internment of Japanese-Americans was completely unnecessary. First and foremost, there was absolutely no evidence of any attempt by Japanese-Americans to hurt the American war effort. The government's own studies proved that fact beyond question. Thus it's not surprising that in places where racism was not a factor, in Hawaii for example, the public outcry for internment was much more muted.

4 Secondly, Japanese-American soldiers fought valiantly for the

*internment: imprisonment.

United States. The all Japanese-American 442nd Combat Team—drawn heavily from young men in internment camps—was the most decorated unit of its size in the armed forces. Suffering heavy casualties in Italy and France, members of the 442nd were awarded a Congressional Medal of Honor, several Distinguished Service Crosses, 350 Silver Stars, and more than 3,600 Purple Hearts. (Adapted from Norton et al., *A People and a Nation*, p. 795.)

Title *World War II: Interning Japanese-Americans*

Thesis Statement *In World War II, the imprisonment of Japanese-Americans spoiled an otherwise creditable civil rights record.*

Supporting Details
1. *Racial stereotypes used to power the war effort encouraged people to see Japanese-Americans as the enemy.*

2. *There was also a general belief that the Japanese had to be paid back for bombing Pearl Harbor.*

3. *Two reasons why internment unnecessary*

   1) *Absolutely no evidence of wrongdoing, a fact proven by government studies*

   2) *Japanese-American soldiers fought bravely to defend the U.S. —The all Japanese-American combat team was drawn largely from internment camps, and it was the most decorated of its size.*

EXPLANATION Your outline of the same reading might have used letters instead of numbers and avoided dashes altogether. Still the content would have been fairly similar. Given the thesis statement, you need to include the causes of internment as well as the reasons why the authors consider it an "enormous exception" to an otherwise creditable record.

1. The Gains and Losses of Beauty

1 No doubt about it, extremely good-looking people have a significant social edge. They are less lonely, less socially anxious (espe-

cially about interactions with the opposite sex), more popular, more sexually experienced, and, as we noted earlier, more socially skilled (Feingold, 1992b). The social rewards for physical attractiveness appear to get off to an early start. Mothers of highly attractive newborns engage in more affectionate interactions with their babies than do mothers of less attractive infants (Langlois et al., 1995). Given such benefits, one would expect that the beautiful would also have a significant psychological advantage. But they don't. Physical attractiveness (as rated by judges) has little if any association with self-esteem, mental health, personality traits, or intelligence (Feingold, 1992b).

2   One possible reason why beauty doesn't affect psychological well-being is that *actual* physical attractiveness, as evaluated by others, may have less impact than *self-perceived* physical attractiveness. People who view themselves as physically attractive do report higher self-esteem and better mental health than those who believe they are unattractive (Feingold, 1992b). But judges' ratings of physical attractiveness are only modestly correlated* with self-perceived attractiveness. When real beauties do not see themselves as beautiful, their appearance may not be psychologically valuable.

3   Physically attractive individuals may also fail to benefit from the social bias for beauty because of pressures they experience to maintain their appearance. In contemporary American society, such pressures are particularly strong in regard to the body. Although both facial and bodily appearance contribute to perceived attractiveness, an unattractive body appears to be a greater liability than an unattractive face (Alicke et al., 1986). Such a "body bias" can produce a healthy emphasis on nutrition and exercise. But it can sometimes lead to distinctly unhealthy consequences. For example, men may pop steroids in order to build up impressive muscles. Among women, the desire for a beautiful body often takes a different form.

4   Women are more likely than men to suffer from what Janet Polivy and her colleagues (1986) call the "modern mania for slenderness." This zeal* for thinness is promoted by the mass media. Roseanne aside, popular female characters in TV shows are more likely than popular male characters to be exceedingly thin; women's magazines stress the need to maintain a slender body more than do men's magazines (Silverstein et al., 1986b). (Sharon S. Brehm and Saul M. Kassin, *Social Psychology*. Boston: Houghton Mifflin, 1996, p. 180.)

*correlated: related to.
*zeal: strong desire.

Title _____

Thesis Statement _____

_____

_____

Supporting Details _____

_____

_____

_____

_____

_____

_____

_____

_____

_____

_____

_____

_____

2. The Value of Social Diversity

1 Some groups are more diverse than others, with a greater number of members differing in ethnicity, gender, personality, skill, or other qualities. Generally, the more diverse a group, the more effective it is in achieving its goal. Research has found, for example, that athletic teams with a wide range of different skills among their members often outperform teams with less diverse skills, and that the more heterogeneous* the personnel of a bank, the more likely the bank will adopt innovative practices, make high-

_____

*heterogeneous: varied, different.

quality decisions, and become successful (Johnson and Johnson, 1997).

2   Why is diversity so useful? Because diverse groups have more ways of solving a problem than less diverse ones. Suppose each member of any group has only one way of solving a problem. Now, a group of, say, five people who think differently and see the world differently will come out with five different ways of solving a problem, while a group of five people who think alike and see the world the same may have only one same way of solving the problem. A diverse group, then, can draw on an ample supply of ideas and data, but a homogeneous* group is more likely to suffer a shortage of ideas and data.

3   A diverse group is also unlikely to have the problems that a homogeneous group often has, such as the tendency to engage in groupthink and the difficulty in adapting to changing conditions (Johnson and Johnson, 1997). Diversity can have problems, though, if people are prejudiced, intolerant, or closed-minded against fellow group members who are different. (Thio, *Sociology*, pp. 103–104.)

Title _____

Thesis Statement _____

_____

_____

Supporting Details _____

_____

_____

_____

_____

_____

_____

_____

_____

_____

*homogeneous: uniform, similar.

_____

_____

_____

| CHECK YOUR UNDERSTANDING |

Describe the main goal of an effective informal outline.

_____

_____

_____

WORD NOTES

Recall that on page 145 some people were loath, or reluctant, to eat garlic because of the effect on their breath. Now that you know the adjective *loath*, you should also learn the related and commonly misused verb *loathe*, meaning "to hate or dislike." Although both *loath* and *loathe* are based on an Old English root *lath*, meaning "hateful," the two words are different in meaning and function. To show that you understand those differences, fill in the blanks left in the following sentences. Then write two sentences of your own, using *loathe* or *loath*.

1. The people of Chile quickly learned to _____ the policies of the military government.

2. Although she detested his behavior, the secretary of health and human services was _____ to openly defy someone so powerful.

loathe: _____

_____

loath: _____

_____

Summing Up

Listed below are the most important points in Chapter 4. Put a check mark in the box if you think the point is clear in your mind. Leave the box blank if you need to review the material one more time. The page numbers in parentheses tell you where to look to review each point on the list.

☐ **1.** Although there are similarities, reading a paragraph is not exactly the same as reading an article, essay, or chapter section. There are five differences you need to keep in mind when reading longer selections: (1) the main idea governs a good deal more than a single paragraph, (2) the main idea is likely to be expressed in several sentences called the *thesis statement,* (3) the thesis statement is more fixed in location, (4) the major details take up more space and require readers to spend more time sifting out essential information and (5) the same is true for minor details. (pp. 136–137)

☐ **2.** *Major details* in longer readings answer questions about the thesis statement; further define general words or terms used in that statement; and, when necessary, they help prove the author's claim. *Minor details* help explain major details. They can also provide emphasis or add an interesting fact or anecdote. They may or may not be essential to your understanding of the reading. It all depends on how necessary minor details are to explaining a major detail. (pp. 145–146)

☐ **3.** Except for the use of indentation, informal outlines do not follow the strict rules applied to formal outlines. The goal of an informal outline is to create a clear and detailed blueprint of the author's ideas, one that shows the relationship between those ideas by indicating which details are major and which are minor. (pp. 151–153)

TEST YOUR UNDERSTANDING

To see how well you have understood this chapter, take the following review quiz. Then correct it using the answer key provided by your instructor. If you score 80 percent or above, you're ready to take the end-of-chapter exam. However, if you score below 80 percent, look over the quiz carefully to see what kinds of questions you missed. Then use the **Summing Up** pages of the chapter to find out which pages you should review before taking the chapter exam.

Chapter 4: Review Quiz

Part A

DIRECTIONS Underline the thesis statement in each selection.

1. Marital Satisfaction in New Families

1   Almost all studies that measure marital satisfaction before and after the birth of the first child have found that the birth of a child is a mixed marital blessing (Cowan & Cowan, 1988). Jay Belsky and Michael Rovine (1990) found that couples who were least satisfied with their marriages before the birth were most likely to report decline in satisfaction after, since problems that existed before were likely to have been magnified by the additional stresses brought on by the birth.

2   Babies do not appear to create severe marital distress where none existed before; nor do they bring couples with distressed marriages closer together. Rather, the early postpartum* months bring on a period of disorganization and change. The leading conflict in these first months of parenthood is division of labor in the family. Couples may regain their sense of equilibrium in marriage by successfully negotiating how they will divide the new family responsibilities. Husbands' participation in child and home care seems to be positively related to marital satisfaction after the birth. One study found that the more the men shared in doing family tasks, the more satisfied were the wives at six and eighteen months postpartum and the husbands at eighteen months postpartum (Cowan & Cowan, 1988).

3   While many couples experience a difficult transition to parenthood, they also find it rewarding. Children affect parents in ways that lead to personal growth, enable reworking of childhood conflicts, build flexibility and empathy, and provide intimate, loving human connections. They also give a lot of pleasure. In follow-up interviews of new parents when their children were eighteen months old, Philip Cowan and Carolyn Cowan (1988) found that almost every man and woman spoke of the delight they felt from knowing their child and watching the child develop. They reported feeling pride for and closeness to their spouses, more adult with their own parents, and a renewed sense of purpose

---

*postpartum: following a birth.

at work. (Adapted from Seifert et al., *Lifespan Development,*
p. 488.)

2. Partner Selection

1   What characteristics do men and women look for in a potential romantic partner? According to the research of psychologist David
Buss, men and women often look for similar characteristics, most
importantly kindness, understanding, and intelligence.

2   Although we have all heard the old saying "opposites attract,"
this does not appear to be the case when it comes to selecting a
romantic partner for a long-term committed relationship. In his research, Buss studied similarities and differences between spouses
and found that the similarities were indeed striking. Couples in
Buss's study were similar in age, race, religion, ethnic background, and socioeconomic status. They often grew up within driving distance of each other. Additionally, Buss also found that attitudes, opinions, and worldviews were also very much alike among
the couples.

3   As couples live together, over time certain compatibilities become more important. Sharing values, a willingness to tolerate
flaws and to make changes in response to each other, communicating effectively, and sharing religious beliefs seem to be especially important in the long run.

4   The results of a nationally representative study of sexual practices in the United States, reported in 1994, has confirmed Buss's
findings. Robert Michael and his colleagues state that "on every
measure except religion [including race/ethnicity, age, and educational level], people who are in any stage of a sexual relationship
are remarkably similar to each other. And married people are
even very likely to have the same religion." Michael and his colleagues point out that some individuals do have successful romantic relationships with people who are very different from themselves, but this is an exception—not the rule. Additionally,
Michael and his colleagues believe the pattern of "like attracts
like" holds true for homosexuals as well as heterosexuals.

5   Michael and his colleagues propose that it is easier for individuals in a romantic relationship to share their lives with each other
when they have similar backgrounds and interests. Additionally,
they believe that social networks, consisting of family, friends,
and business associates, exert subtle and not so subtle influences on individuals to select a romantic partner that will fit into
these social groups. (Mullen et al., *Connections for Health,*
pp. 212–213.)

Part B

DIRECTIONS Underline the thesis statement. Then answer the questions by filling in the blanks or circling the correct letter.

3. Feminist Objections to Pornography

1 Beginning around 1978, some—though not all—feminists became very critical of pornography (e.g., Griffin, 1981; Lederer, 1980; Morgan, 1978). Why would feminists be opposed to pornography? In general, there are three basic reasons for their objections.

2 First, they argue that pornography debases women. In the milder, soft-core versions, it portrays women as sex objects whose breasts, legs, and buttocks can be purchased and then ogled.* This scarcely represents a respectful attitude toward women. Second, pornography associates sex with violence toward women. As such, it contributes to rape and other forms of violence against women and girls. Robin Morgan put it bluntly: "Pornography is the theory and rape is the practice" (Morgan, 1980, p. 139). Third, pornography shows, indeed glamorizes, unequal power relationships between women and men. A common theme in pornography is men forcing women to have sex, and so the power of men and subordination of women is emphasized. Consistent with this point, feminists do not object to sexual materials that portray women and men in equal, humanized relationships—what we would term *erotica*.

3 Feminists also note the intimate relationship between pornography and traditional gender roles. They argue that pornography may serve to perpetuate traditional gender roles. By seeing or reading about dominant males and submissive,* dehumanized females, each new generation of adolescent boys is socialized to accept these roles. (Adapted from Hyde, *Understanding Human Sexuality,* p. 524.)

1. What question or questions about the thesis statement are the supporting details meant to answer?

_____

_____

2. Which of the following is *not* a major detail?

    a. Feminists argue that pornography debases women.

---

*ogled: stared at.
*submissive: obedient.

b. Pornography associates sex with violence toward women.

c. Feminists do not object to sexual materials that portray women and men in equal, humanized relationships.

4. Clinton's First Step Toward a "Newly Inclusive America"

1   One of the first campaign pledges President Clinton addressed on his arrival at the White House was the lifting of the fifty-year-old ban on gays in America's military services. Though the Pentagon brass and conservative members of both houses of Congress had already indicated their concerns on this issue, Clinton made it clear that this was one campaign promise he intended to keep. Those close to the president pointed out that the lifting of the ban fit in with his notion of "a newly inclusive America."

2   After a tumultuous* week of public scrutiny, Clinton announced a two-step plan that involved a delay for at least six months, during which time Defense Secretary Les Aspin could consult with the Joint Chiefs of Staff on how best to proceed with the details of lifting the ban. Only after the practical questions were discussed would Clinton issue the executive order banning discrimination based on sexual preference. Soon after Clinton's announcement, both officers and rank-and-file military personnel voiced their opposition to the lifting of the ban. Many in the military were concerned about living arrangements and conduct—and the effect on other service personnel of having openly gay colleagues living in their midst.

3   Among others, General Colin Powell, chairman of the Joint Chiefs of Staff, downplayed the connection between the military's policy toward homosexuals and its one-time policy toward blacks. But as many observers pointed out, there are some distinct similarities. Until President Truman's 1948 executive order directing "equality of treatment" for all members of the armed forces, the military justified a racially discriminatory policy on the grounds of morale and discipline—the same arguments used to defend the ban on gays. Though at first slow to implement changes that would end discrimination, the military found that its sudden need for additional personnel during the Korean War was solved by admitting blacks into the armed services in integrated units. Gradually, segregated facilities and troubled expectations gave way to a fully integrated army—in the name of efficiency.

---

*tumultuous: excited, full of upheaval.

4   It remains to be seen whether the military may once again act as an agency of social reform when it publicly opens the doors of the armed services to gay and lesbian Americans. Such a change will certainly not come without a struggle. As soon as Clinton's intentions were evident, conservative activists like Patrick Buchanan, candidate for the Republican presidential nomination in 1992, and William Kristol, former chief of staff for Vice President Dan Quayle, jumped headlong into the fray. Arguing that the public was not convinced that lifting the ban was a good idea, they and other conservatives tried to stem this and other gay rights initiatives* while increasing their own bases of power. As the battle over gay rights intensifies, many Americans may be forced to decide between their own opinions regarding sexual behavior and their beliefs in protecting equal rights for all. (Adapted from Paul E. Johnson et al., *American Government.* Boston: Houghton Mifflin, 1994, pp. 174–175.)

1. What question or questions about the thesis statement are the supporting details meant to answer?

_____

_____

2. Which of the following details is *not* a major one?

 a. Clinton announced a two-step plan that involved a delay for at least six months during which time Defense Secretary Les Aspin could consult with the Joint Chiefs of Staff on how best to proceed with the details of lifting the ban.

 b. Many in the military were concerned about living arrangements and conduct.

 c. Among others, General Colin Powell, Chairman of the Joint Chiefs of Staff, downplayed the connection between the military's policy toward homosexuals and its one-time policy toward blacks.

Part C

DIRECTIONS Read and outline the following selection.

5. Conspicuous Consumption

1 Formally defined, *conspicuous consumption* is the acquisition and visible display of luxury goods and services to demonstrate one's

_____

*initiatives: opening moves, introductory steps.

ability to afford them. Thus, conspicuously consumed items are important to their owner because of what they say to others. The visibility of these goods and services is critical because the message will not be communicated if others cannot see them.

2   Initially, the concept of conspicuous consumption was used to describe the behavior of the upper classes who would buy and display very expensive items in order to communicate their wealth and power. For example, in the 1890s William H. Vanderbilt's private railway car was designed to be more expensive than his rival's, Leland Stanford, and his third yacht had to be bigger and better than anyone else's.

3   Today, however, conspicuous consumption can be observed in most social classes. In other words, individuals at all levels can "keep up with the Joneses"—acquiring and displaying the trappings that are characteristic of a respected member of their class. For example, a middle-class family might buy a personal computer, showing their neighbors that they can afford it and that they want their children to get ahead. Going to Europe or Vail* could be a way for a consumer to tell others that she has "made it." Or a working-class man might buy a new motorboat or stereo to show off to his peers.

4   In the Arab world, the newly rich upper classes engage in the conspicuous consumption of items such as cars, planes, and other technologically advanced products. Even in former communist countries, consumers now show consumption competitiveness. The idea is that one might be the "shame of the village" if one cannot keep up with others.

5   As another way of showing status, some consumers engage in conspicuous waste. Those proud of their wealth may buy houses they never use, pianos that no one plays, and cars that no one drives. The once struggling singer Engelbert Humperdinck owns a fleet of Rolls-Royces and five mansions in the United States and Europe. (Adapted from Hoyer and MacInnis, *Consumer Behavior,* pp. 335–337.)

Title _____

Thesis Statement _____

_____

_____

_____

*Vail: Vail, Colorado—a ski resort for the rich and famous.

Supporting Details _____

_____

_____

_____

_____

_____

_____

_____

_____

_____

_____

_____

_____

_____

> Use the answer key provided by your instructor to correct your quiz. If you score 80 percent or above, you are ready for the chapter exam. If you score below 80 percent, look carefully at the questions you answered incorrectly. Then use the **Summing Up** section to decide which pages you need to review.

⟩⟨● Chapter Test 4

Part A

DIRECTIONS Underline the thesis statement in each selection.

1. Touching and Being Touched

1 Touching and being touched is an essential part of being human. However, the amount and meaning of touch changes with age, purpose and location. Infants and their parents, for example, engage in extensive touching behavior, but this decreases during adolescence. The amount of touching behavior increases after adolescence as young people begin to establish romantic relationships. No matter how much we are touched, however, most of us want to be touched more than we are (Mosby, 1978).

2 There are different types of touches: positive affective touches, playful touches, control touches, ritualistic touches, and task-related touches (Jones & Yarbrough, 1985). *Positive affective touches* transmit messages of support, appreciation, affection, or sexual intent. *Playful touches* lighten our interactions with others. *Control touches* are used to get other people's attention and to gain their compliance. *Ritualistic touches* are those we use during communication rituals such as greeting others and saying good-bye. *Task-related touches* are those that are necessary for us to complete tasks on which we are working. Touches also can fit into more than one category at a time. We can, for example, touch others as part of a ritual to express positive affection.

3 Age, sex, and region of the country also influence the amount people touch. To illustrate, people between eighteen and twenty-five and between thirty and forty report the most touching, while old people report the least (Mosby, 1978). Women find touching more pleasant than men, as long as the other person is not a stranger (Heslin, 1978). Finally, people who live in the South touch more than people who live in the North (Howard, 1985).

4 The United States is generally a noncontact culture. People do not engage in a great deal of touching. There are, however, situations in which people are likely to touch (Henley, 1977). People are more likely to touch, for example, when giving information or advice than when receiving information or advice. People are more likely to touch others when giving orders than when receiving orders, when asking for a favor than when granting a favor, or

when trying to persuade others than when being persuaded. (Adapted from William B. Gudykunst et al., *Building Bridges*, Boston: Houghton Mifflin, 1995, pp. 319–320.)

2. Twelve-Step Programs

1 Over the years we have seen a growing number of people turn to twelve-step programs for help with drug and alcohol abuse, eating disorders, or emotional disabilities. It has been estimated that 3 million people attend one of the hundreds of different twelve-step programs every week. Most of these programs rely on the fundamentals that have guided Alcoholics Anonymous (AA) for several decades. The format of all twelve-step programs is very similar and consists of two general aspects.

- *Working the steps.* This means admitting the problem, recognizing that life has become unmanageable, and turning life over to a higher power. Six of the steps included in the AA program mention a higher power.

- *Attending meetings.* Members of twelve-step programs meet in church basements, community centers, centers on college campuses, and other locations to share their experiences and seek support from the group. It is this voluntary "community" that becomes an important healing influence on many twelve-step members. They describe their own problems and listen to others who have experienced similar problems. In most cases, strong bonding develops among group members.

2 Do twelve-step programs such as Narcotics Anonymous, Overeaters Anonymous, Schizophrenics Anonymous, and Codependents Anonymous have a lasting impact on members? Do the programs really work? A few critics say these programs simply replace one form of addiction with an addiction to group support. Instead, these critics advocate treatment programs that help people take control of their own lives and learn how to solve their own problems. Those who support twelve-step programs say that the emphasis on the connection to a higher power is the opposite of the isolated, unworthy feeling experienced by people who display addictive behaviors. Joan Borysenko, author of *Guilt Is the Teacher, Love Is the Lesson*, states that twelve-step programs are "psychologically sophisticated" and are "a potent force for healing shame and addiction."

3 There is no doubt that we do not fully understand all the factors that contribute to the apparent success of twelve-step programs. One therapist says that researchers may never fully understand the

"richness and complexity" of these voluntary groups of people who share a common problem. (Reece and Brandt, *Effective Human Relations in Organizations,* p. 402.)

Part B

DIRECTIONS Answer the questions by filling in the blanks or circling the correct letter.

3. Telecommunication* and the World Wide Web

1   **Telecommunication** tools allow users to expand the boundaries of communication well beyond the walls of the local classroom. Imagine giving a student access to the very limits of human knowledge—experts in every field of endeavor and interactive databases with links to many others. This is what telecommunication offers education. We believe students need to have skill in intelligently navigating this electronic world.

2   The **Internet** is a patchwork of computer networks that span the globe. Computers communicate with one another on this patchwork using an international electronic language. Once this language is installed on a computer, it can be used with a variety of tools to transfer information over the Internet.

3   **E-mail** (electronic mail) is one of the most basic and useful communication tools enabled by networking technologies. E-mail is not encumbered by distance/cost factors associated with other forms of communication, and an e-mail message can be delivered across the hall or across the world in minutes. Students can write and respond to messages within the course of a day, even with "key pals" (e-mail pen pals) in other states or other countries. Its convenience, accessibility, and low cost give e-mail a great advantage over standard mail, phone, and fax. Additionally, an e-mail message can be quoted for reply, forwarded to others, stored for future use, deleted, or printed—all quickly and easily.

4   E-mail communication, like all forms of communication, can break down cultural barriers and stereotypes. For example, when one elementary class in Charlottesville, Virginia, communicates with another class in an Alaskan Eskimo village, they can learn about each other and their cultures. Suppose that Mrs. Johnson's class in Charlottesville is studying Inuit cultures. She might ask her students, "What do you think kids your age in Alaska like to eat?" Some of the students, remembering pictures and facts about the agricultural aspects of the region, respond, "I bet they

---

*telecommunication: communication by electronic transmission.

like to eat fish." The class composes a quick question to the Alaskan class, whose members write back that they indeed like fish but would rather eat pizza! Similarly, students in foreign language classes can converse with native speakers through e-mail. E-mail is an excellent way to encourage students to write and to learn about different cultures from other students in those cultures.

5   The Internet also enables students to telnet to libraries around the world. Telnet is a standard Internet application that allows a user to "log in" on other computers. Many students may not have access to a large metropolitan or university library in their local area, but through telecommunication a student can access almost any major metropolitan or university library in the world. (Ryan and Cooper, *Those Who Can, Teach,* pp. 210–211.)

1. How would you paraphrase the thesis statement?

_____

_____

2. What question or questions about the thesis statement do the supporting details help answer?

_____

_____

4. Cultural Definitions of the Family

1 To accurately understand and assess the families they treat, mental health professionals and social workers cannot afford to make judgments solely on the basis of standards derived, or drawn from, European-American, middle-class families. In point of fact, there are a number of major differences between European-American family values and those of other ethnic groups. If mental health professionals and social workers fail to recognize those differences, they can make inappropriate diagnoses and decisions.

2   Most middle-class European-Americans stress individuality and independence. In contrast, many ethnic minority families emphasize family unity over individual identity. Viewed from this perspective, an Asian-American college student who can't make a job decision without asking parental advice is not unusually immature or dependent. Within the framework of Asian-American family values, he or she is acting appropriately.

3   In Asian and Hispanic families, the parents are expected to be in charge of the children. In these cultures, a child speaks when

spoken to and is discouraged from interrupting if adults are speaking. Thus, traditional family therapy, with its emphasis on everyone participating equally, could well be considered a violation of cultural norms, and therapists would need to find another way for family members to interact.

4   Hispanic, Native-American, and African-American families operate out of a communal family system that includes aunts, uncles, and close family friends. Within these ethnic groups, parents are likely to transfer children from one group of relatives to another. Therapists not aware of this practice are inclined to view it as a form of neglect.

5   In fact in 1987, a Native-American child was taken away from his parents for precisely this reason. A social worker had observed the child in question being transferred from one family to another and had drawn the wrong conclusion. This case and others like it confirm how important it is for mental health professionals and social workers to be aware of cultural differences. (Based on information in Sue et al., *Understanding Abnormal Behavior,* pp. 60–66.)

1. How would you paraphrase the thesis statement?

_____

_____

2. What question or questions about the thesis statement do the supporting details help answer?

_____

_____

Part C

DIRECTIONS Read and then outline the following selection.

5. Striving for Superiority

1   Psychologist Alfred Adler suggested that the primary goal of the psyche* was superiority. Although initially he believed that individuals struggled to achieve superiority over others, Adler eventually developed a more complex definition of the drive for superiority.

2   Adler's concept of striving for superiority does not refer to the everyday meaning of the word *superiority.* He did not mean that we

_____

*psyche: mind, spirit.

innately seek to surpass one another in rank or position, nor did he mean that we seek to maintain an attitude of exaggerated importance over our peers. Rather, Adler's drive for superiority involves the desire to be competent and effective, complete and thorough, in whatever one strives to do.

3   Striving for superiority occasionally takes the form of an exaggerated lust for power. An individual may seek to play god and exercise control over objects and people. The goal may introduce a hostile tendency into our lives, in which we play games of "dog eat dog." But such expressions of the desire for superiority do not reflect its more positive, constructive* nature.

4   According to Adler, striving for superiority is innate and is part of the struggle for survival that human beings share with other species in the process of evolution. From this perspective, life is not motivated by the need to reduce tension or restore equilibrium, as Sigmund Freud tended to think; instead, life is encouraged by the desire to move from below to above, from minus to plus, from inferior to superior. The particular ways in which individuals undertake their quest for superiority are determined by their culture, their unique history, and their style of life. (Adapted from Barbara Engler, *Personality Theories*. Boston: Houghton Mifflin. 1995, p. 101.)

Title _____

Thesis Statement _____

_____

Supporting Details _____

_____

_____

_____

_____

_____

_____

_____

_____

*constructive: useful.

C H A P T E R   5

Summarizing and Synthesizing: Two More Strategies for In-Depth Learning

> **In this chapter you'll learn**
>
> • how to *summarize* information, reducing it to one-third or one-quarter of its original length.
>
> • how to *synthesize* different points of view into one coherent, or connected, whole.

Now that you know how to analyze both single paragraphs and longer, multiparagraph selections, you're ready to master summarizing and synthesizing—two learning techniques essential to college success. Summarizing a

173

difficult paragraph is a good way to make sure you understand it. Then, too, many of the courses you take in college will require some summary writing. Synthesizing will help you connect the different sources of information that make up your courses—lecture notes, textbook assignments, and outside readings. It's also essential to developing original topics for research.

 # Writing Effective Summaries

The goal of an effective summary is to reduce the author's original words to a bare minimum, yet still retain the main idea and a few of the *most essential* details. This means that evaluating each and every sentence in terms of its importance to the passage is critical to writing an effective summary. Let's use the following passage as an example:

 [1]On January 28, 1986, the American space program suffered the worst disaster in its more than thirty-year history. [2]The entire world was shocked when the space shuttle *Challenger* exploded seconds after lift-off, claiming the lives of seven brave astronauts and crippling our entire space agenda. [3]I suppose the oldest cliché in our culture, spoken on battlegrounds and indeed virtually anywhere Americans die, is "We must press forward so we can say they did not die in vain." [4]Rest assured. [5]They didn't. [6]The deaths of our seven *Challenger* astronauts probably saved the lives of untold thousands of Americans. [7]For, you see, if the O-rings had not failed on January 28, 1986, but rather on May 20, 1987, the next scheduled shuttle launch, in the words of Dr. John Gofman, professor emeritus at the University of California at Berkeley, you could have "kissed Florida good-bye." [8]Because the next shuttle, the one that was to have explored the atmosphere of Jupiter, was to carry forty-seven pounds of plutonium 238, which is, again, according to Dr. Gofman, the most toxic substance on the face of the earth. [9]Dr. Helen Caldicott corroborates Dr. Gofman's claim in her book, *Nuclear Madness,* when she cites studies estimating one ounce of widely dispersed plutonium 238 particles as having the toxicity to induce lung cancer in every person on Earth. (Gronbeck et al., *Principles of Speech Communication,* p. 275.)

To summarize this passage effectively, the first question we need to ask is "What's the main idea?" As you know from Chapters 2 and 4, the main idea is the central thought that recurs throughout a paragraph or reading. It's what knits together all the sentences in the passage. In this case, the main idea appears in sentence 6, which is the topic sentence of the entire paragraph. According to that sentence, the seven *Challenger* astronauts did not die in vain. From the author's point of view, their deaths saved the lives of thousands. This is the main idea of the paragraph, and it will also be the main idea of our summary, which opens with this sentence: "The seven astronauts aboard the *Challenger* did not die a pointless death; they saved the lives of thousands."

Although the summary of a paragraph might indeed be a single sentence, that's not possible here. In this case, we need at least one more sentence to answer the question so obviously raised by the opening line of our summary. How did the astronauts' deaths save the lives of thousands? Look now at our completed summary and see how that question gets answered.

> The seven astronauts aboard the *Challenger* did not die a pointless death on January 28, 1986; they saved the lives of thousands. The next scheduled launch was to carry forty-seven pounds of plutonium 238, a poisonous substance. If the O-rings had failed on that mission rather than the *Challenger*'s, thousands would have died.

The original passage has nine sentences. Our summary has three. Since the goal of a summary to to reduce a passage to about one-third or one-quarter of its original length, that's just about right. Because the summary paraphrases the topic sentence of the entire passage and answers, in general terms, the question raised by that topic sentence, we can be satisfied that this is indeed an effective summary.

Summarizing Longer Readings

To summarize a reading longer than a paragraph, you need to start by posing much the same question as the one you use to summarize paragraphs. Only in this instance, you're not looking for the main idea of a single paragraph. You want the main, or controlling, idea of the entire reading.

Once you've established the main idea that focuses or controls the entire reading, you need to locate the topic sentences of all the remaining paragraphs and decide if they need to be included—paraphrased, of course—in your summary.

If you're writing a summary as part of a formal assignment, you also might want to begin by underlining and annotating the reading before summarizing it. Then you will be in a better position to make sure that your summary retains only the most essential parts of the reading—the controlling main idea and just those supporting details needed to answer any questions it might raise in a reader's mind.

Here to illustrate is an annotated three-paragraph passage followed by a one-paragraph summary.

Can We Trust You?

"integrity tests"

More and more employers are using written psychological tests to screen job applicants. The exams, often dubbed honesty or integrity tests, are supposed to predict tendencies toward theft and a range of potentially troublesome behaviors, including lateness, abuse of sick leave, even an inclination to participate in strikes. Since the 1988 federal ban on polygraphs, or lie detectors, the government's Office of Technology Assessment (OTA) estimates that as many as 6,000 companies give the tests to about 5 million people per year, most of them applicants for low-skilled jobs such as shop clerks. One type of test asks direct questions, such as "How honest are you?" and "Do you think it's stealing to take small items home from work?" Other tests are subtle: "How often do you blush?" and "Do you make your bed?"

tests supposedly predict lateness, abuse of sick leave, strike participation

6,000 companies use tests

Types of questions → Why would blushing or not blushing predict honesty?

★★

Most experts say the tests' value is questionable at best, and the American Psychological Association recently joined the OTA in issuing a warning of their potential misuse. Much of the problem centers around the interpretation of the results. Paul Sackett, a professor of industrial relations at the University of Minnesota, says the tests can be useful but the results, usually summarized in a simple comment such as "recommended" or "not acceptable," are gross oversimplifications of a complex psychological exam.

one of experts

Reason why questionable

good!

Some states have already taken steps to prevent discrimination based on the new tests. Massachusetts has outlawed them, and Rhode Island prohibits their use as the only hiring criterion. (Adapted from Billy Allstetter, "Can We Trust You?" *American Health*, November 1991, p. 27.)

prohibit use as only criterion

Sample Summary

A number of employers, perhaps as many as 6,000 per year, have started using exams, nicknamed "honesty tests," to screen employees. The tests ask questions like "How honest are you?" and "Do you make your bed?" The answers to these questions are supposed to reveal potentially troublesome employees. However, many experts say the tests may be less useful than some employers think. According to Paul Sackett, a professor of industrial relations, interpretation of the tests cannot be so easily reduced to simple labels like "recommended" or "not recommended." Several states have tried to prevent discrimination based on the tests. Massachusetts and Rhode Island do not accept them as the only standard for hiring people.

As it should, our summary opens with a paraphrase of the thesis statement. That paraphrase is followed by just enough supporting details to clarify exactly what "integrity tests" are and explain the controversy surrounding them.

Pointers for Summary Writing

Writing summaries is not hard. Just follow these basic principles:

Make Your First Sentence Count

The first sentence of your summary should paraphrase the main idea of the paragraph or of the entire reading. It should also include any significant background information that might have been given in the introduction.

Paraphrase with Care

When you summarize, you can eliminate everything but the main idea and most essential details. However, you must still remember the first rule of paraphrasing: Change the form but never the meaning. When you finish your summary, check to see that you have stayed true to the original text.

Make Distinctions Between the Essential and the Absolutely Essential

If an author explains a main idea with three separate examples, you should decide which of those examples *best* illustrates the author's point and answers any questions raised by the topic sentence. That's the one to include in your summary. Leave out the other two. A good summary always reduces the original text to its barest and most essential bones, so be selective when you write one.

Don't Interpret or Evaluate

Next to "be selective," this is probably the most crucial piece of advice for writing summaries. The goal of summary writing is to reduce a passage to its briefest form while still retaining its essential meaning. A summary does *not* evaluate or judge the author's ideas. For example, you may think the passage on page 174 about the deaths of the *Challenger* astronauts is flat-out nonsense. Nevertheless, that opinion should not make its way into your summary. Even if you're summarizing a paragraph just for your own research, keep your opinions in the margins. If you cite an author's ideas in your term paper, you don't want to mistakenly include a judgment that was yours, not the author's.

Make Connections Between Sentences

Writing summaries requires you to combine information from different parts of the original text. As a result, the original connections between sentences can get lost. For that reason, it's important to read your summary aloud and check to hear how your sentences flow together. If they don't flow easily and you can't figure out why one sentence follows another, you may need to add some transitions to connect the ideas. As you know from Chapter 2, transitions are verbal bridges that help readers move easily from one thought to another. For a list of the most common transitions, see the following chart:

Common Transitional Signals

Transitions indicating an addition to the original train of thought:

also, in addition, further, furthermore, lastly, moreover, first, second, secondly, too

Transitions indicating that the author is changing, challenging, or contradicting the original train of thought:

although, after all, but, by (in) contrast, however, nevertheless, on the contrary, yet, still, despite that fact, rather

Transitions signaling that the author is pointing out similarities:

similarly, likewise, by the same token, in the same vein

Transitions that introduce examples and illustrations:

for example, for instance, specifically, in other words, that is

> **Transitions that introduce the effects of some cause:**
>
> as a result, consequently, thus, therefore, hence, in response
>
> **Transitions that help readers follow a sequence in time:**
>
> in the meantime, next, soon, after a while, in time, of late, thereafter, afterward, finally, then
>
> **Transitions that repeat a point already made:**
>
> in short, in brief, in conclusion, in other words, on the whole, in summary, to reiterate, to sum up

Revise If Necessary

If the summary you're writing is to be handed in for an assignment, then you probably should prepare another draft in order to double-check your word choice, grammar, and punctuation.

Don't Forget the Author and Title

If you are turning in your summary, make sure that you add the author and title of the selection. Sometimes instructors want that information in a heading or a footnote, but often you'll be expected to weave it into the opening sentence. When you are assigned to write a summary, always check with your instructor to find out how he or she wants you to handle the author and title.

> ### CHECK YOUR UNDERSTANDING
>
> Write down as many pointers for effective summary writing as you can remember. There are seven in all.
>
> 1. _____
>
> 2. _____
>
> 3. _____
>
> 4. _____
>
> 5. _____
>
> 6. _____
>
> 7. _____

◆ **EXERCISE 1**

DIRECTIONS Read the following selection. Then circle the letter of the more effective summary.

EXAMPLE

Erich Fromm's Theory of Human Nature

1 The psychologist Erich Fromm was born in Frankfurt, Germany, in 1900, the only child of a deeply Orthodox Jewish* family. At the age of thirteen, Fromm began to study the Talmud,* beginning an interest in religious literature and an admiration of the German mystic* "Meister" Eckhart (1260?–1327?) that remained throughout his life. In his later years, Fromm did not formally practice religion, but he referred to himself as an "atheistic mystic," and it is clear that Fromm's early religious experiences left a distinct mark on his personality and work. The moral and committed tone of his writings has a quality that has been described as reminiscent of the Old Testament prophets. He was deeply interested in religion, and both his earlier and later writings reflect this concern.

2 Erich Fromm began with the thesis (1941) that *freedom* is a basic human condition that poses a "psychological problem." As the human race has gained more freedom by transcending* nature and other animals, people have become increasingly characterized by feelings of separation and isolation. Thus, a major theme of Fromm's writings is the concept of loneliness. To be human is to be isolated and lonely, because one is distinct from nature and others, and it is loneliness, according to Fromm, that radically separates human nature from animal nature. Unlike other animals, we know we are going to die, and this knowledge leads to feelings of despair.

3 Fromm believed that human beings have two ways to respond to the problem of freedom. They can work with one another in a spirit of love to create a society that will optimally fulfill their needs, or they can "escape from the burden" of freedom into "new dependencies and submission" by giving themselves over to a strong leader. From Fromm's perspective, relying on a leader helps the individual escape feelings of isolation, but it does not

---

*Orthodox Jewish: following to the letter the tenets of Judaism.
*Talmud: collection of ancient Jewish writings on which Jewish law is based.
*mystic: a person who enters a trancelike state in order to become more spiritual.
*transcending: overcoming.

creatively meet the needs of humanity or lead to optimum* personality development.

Summary a. **Erich Fromm's Theory of Human Nature**

For psychologist Eric Fromm, freedom is part of being human, but it is also a source of anxiety. In exercising our freedom, we often end up lonely and respond by forming communities based on affection or else giving ourselves over to some higher authority.

(b.) **Erich Fromm's Theory of Human Nature**

The psychologist Erich Fromm believed that a sense of freedom is essential to the human condition and the source of a profound psychological problem. As human beings have gained more freedom by overcoming their animal nature, they have become increasingly isolated and lonely. The feeling of loneliness finds its fullest expression in the problem of death because, unlike other animals, we know that we're going to die, and that knowledge leads to despair. From Fromm's point of view, there were two possible responses to the problem of loneliness. Human beings can work together in a spirit of love to create a society that would fulfill their needs, or they can escape into "new dependencies and submission" by giving themselves over to the control of a powerful leader who dominates their lives. The problem with this response is that it eliminates loneliness at the expense of personal development.

c. **Erich Fromm's Theory of Human Nature**

Born in Frankfurt, Germany, and the only child of a deeply Orthodox Jewish family, the psychologist Erich Fromm studied the Talmud and early on showed an interest in religious mysticism. That religious mysticism made a profound mark on his work. Fromm developed the thesis that freedom is a basic condition of human nature. To be human is to be isolated and therefore in despair. Unlike the animals, we know that we are going to die. The more we separate ourselves from the world of nature and identify ourselves as free beings, the more likely we are to experience feelings of loneliness and separation. These feelings of loneliness and separation are most powerfully expressed in our despair at the thought of death. Human beings can resolve this problem in two ways: (1) They can work together in a spirit of love and create a society that meets their needs, or (2) They can escape from freedom by giving themselves over to the control of a powerful leader.

*optimum: the highest or most favorable level of function or condition.

EXPLANATION Answer *b* is the only one that fits the guidelines for summary writing on pages 177–179. Answer *a* doesn't explain the source of the anxiety, and answer *c* contains some unnecessary details and leaves out a necessary one: Fromm's cautionary note about choosing a powerful leader. It also fails to make effective connections between sentences.

1. Illusion of the Perfect Mate

1   The illusion that you have found the perfect partner—one who will be all things to you and vice versa—will carry you through courtship. But the reality is very different. You have not found the perfect mate—there isn't one. Anyone you marry will come with a minus quality, and the one quality that is lacking may become the only one you regard as important (Sammons, 1984).

2   Columnist Ann Landers once asked her readers, "If you had it to do over again, would you marry the same person?" She received fifty thousand responses. Fifty-two percent replied "no," and 48 percent said "yes." Marital happiness is hard to predict because the drug of the premarital period—love—alters your view of the partner; but this view is only an illusion.

3   Your illusion of the perfect mate is helped along by some deception on the part of your partner, who is showing you only his or her best side. At the same time, you are presenting only favorable aspects of yourself to the other person. Such deceptions are usually not deliberate but are an attempt to withhold undesirable aspects of one's self for fear that the partner may not like them.

4   For example, one male student said he knew he drank too much but that if his date found out, she would be disappointed and maybe drop him. He kept his drinking hidden throughout their courtship. They married and are now divorced. She said of him, "I never knew he drank whiskey until our honeymoon. He never drank like this before we were married." (Adapted from Knox, *Choices in Relationships,* pp. 230, 234.)

Summary   a.   **Illusion of the Perfect Mate**

When Ann Landers asked the question "If you had it to do over again, would you marry the same person?" she got 50,000 responses, and 52 percent of her readers said they would not choose the same mate.

b.   **Illusion of the Perfect Mate**

It doesn't pay to put only your best foot forward on a date. Because you have presented only favorable aspects of yourself, you and your date may be misled into thinking that you are right for one another when, in fact, you have nothing in common. Too many people make this mistake when they would be far better off just being themselves.

c. **Illusion of the Perfect Mate**

There's no such thing as the perfect mate, which may be one reason why Ann Landers got so many nos when she asked this question: "If you had it to do over again, would you marry the same person?" Out of 50,000 responses, 52 percent said "no." No matter who your mate is, he or she will always be lacking something.

2. **Hardship on the Plains**

1   In America in the nineteenth century, most migrants went west because opportunities there seemed to promise a better life. Railroad expansion made remote farming regions accessible, and the construction of grain elevators eased problems of shipping and storage. As a result of population growth, the demand for farm products grew rapidly, and the prospects for commercial agriculture—growing crops for profit—became more favorable than ever.

2   Life on the farm, however, was much harder than the advertisements and railroad agents suggested. Migrants often encountered scarcities of essentials they had once taken for granted. The open prairies contained little lumber for housing and fuel. Pioneer families were forced to build houses of sod and to burn manure for heat. Water was sometimes as scarce as timber. Few families were lucky or wealthy enough to buy land near a stream that did not dry up summer and freeze in winter. Machinery for drilling wells was scarce until the 1880s, and even then it was very expensive.

3   Weather seldom followed predictable cycles. In summer, weeks of torrid* heat and parching winds suddenly gave way to violent storms that washed away crops and property. The wind and cold of winter blizzards piled up mountainous snowdrifts that halted all outdoor movement. During the Great Blizzard that struck Nebraska and the Dakota Territory in January 1888, the temperature plunged to 36 degrees below zero, and the wind blew at 56 miles per hour. The storm stranded schoolchildren and killed several parents who ventured out to rescue their children. In the spring, melting snow swelled streams, and floods threatened millions of acres. In the fall, a week without rain could turn dry grasslands into tinder, and the slightest spark could ignite a raging prairie fire.

---

*torrid: intensely hot.

4   Nature could be cruel even under good conditions. Weather that was favorable for crops was also good for breeding insects. Worms and flying pests ravaged corn and wheat. In the 1870s and 1880s swarms of grasshoppers virtually ate up entire farms. Heralded only by the din of buzzing wings, a mile-long cloud of insects would smother the land and devour everything: plants, tree bark, and clothes. As one farmer lamented, the "hoppers left behind nothing but the mortgage." (Norton et al., *A People and a Nation,* pp. 492–493.)

Summary a. During the nineteenth century, countless men and women went west in the belief that farming was a way to make money and improve their lot in life. Life on the farm, however, proved to be much harder and more rigorous than most expected. Essentials like lumber and water were hard to come by, and the weather was both harsh and unpredictable. In winter, the temperature might plunge as low as 36 degrees below zero while the wind could blow at 56 miles per hour. In summer, scorching heat and drought would suddenly be followed by slashing rain storms. Insects were an additional problem and plagues of grasshoppers could devour entire farms.

b. In the nineteenth century, the American West seemed to be the land of opportunity. Many were convinced that farming was the way to make a fortune, but they were deeply disappointed upon their arrival. Lumber and water were hard to obtain. People were forced to build their houses out of sod and burn manure to stay warm. Machinery was scarce and expensive, making farm labor backbreaking and discouraging. If that weren't enough, there was the weather to contend with, and the heat and cold were intolerable. During the Great Blizzard that struck Nebraska and the Dakota Territory in January of 1888, the temperature plunged to 36 degrees below zero and the wind blew at 56 miles per hour. The storm stranded schoolchildren and killed several parents who ventured out to rescue their children. And in the spring, when streams melted, there were floods to contend with. It was a no-win situation, and it is not surprising that so many people gave up and went back east.

c. Throughout the nineteenth century, thousands of men and women decided to make their way west and try their hand at farming in the hopes of earning a fortune. But those hopes were quickly dashed upon their arrival. Life was hard in the west and it was easy to get discouraged and give up, particularly given the weather, which alternated between torrid heat and freezing cold. As if the unpredictable weather were not bad enough, there were floods and fires to contend with, along with plagues of locusts and bees. People who migrated west in the nineteenth century were badly fooled by the railroad agents who promised a land of milk and honey in exchange for the price of a ticket.

◼ EXERCISE 2

DIRECTIONS Read and summarize the following passages.

EXAMPLE The search for a cheap, quick, and long-lasting insecticide was finally successful in 1939, when a Swiss chemist, Paul Müller, confirmed the bug-killing properties of dichlorodiphenyltrichloroethane (DDT). Used on everything from the potato beetle to disease-bearing lice and fleas (as well as in World War II to fumigate troops' bedding and clothing), DDT was heralded as a huge success for twentieth-century agriculture. But within twenty years, many insects developed strains resistant to the poison. Meanwhile, it wreaked havoc on the food chain by killing off insects beneficial to the environment. In the end, DDT was not a boon to the human race. If anything, it proved a disaster, the proportions of which are still becoming known.

Summary *When it was first introduced, DDT was considered a miracle chemical that could destroy pesky insects like lice, fleas, and beetles, but within twenty years it proved to be more disaster than miracle. Unfortunately, it killed off valuable insects as well as those that did harm.*

EXPLANATION As it should, our summary begins with the main idea of the original passage. In addition to the main idea, the sample summary also adds just enough supporting details to answer the potential question: How did the supposed miracle turn into a disaster?

1. Religion and Politics

 1 The family forms and transmits political beliefs according to its religious tradition. In general, Catholic families are somewhat more liberal on economic issues than Protestant ones, while Jewish families are much more liberal on both economic and social is-

sues than families of either Catholics or Protestants. There are two theories as to why this should be so.

2   The first has to do with the social status of religious groups in America. When they immigrated to this country, Catholics and Jews were often poor and the object of discrimination. As a result they often affiliated* themselves with whichever party and social doctrine seemed most sympathetic to their plight. In many places the Democratic party and a liberal social doctrine seemed to offer the most support. Today Catholics and Jews enjoy greater economic prosperity and face much less discrimination, and so their support for Democrats and liberal candidates has weakened.

3   The second theory emphasizes the content of the religious tradition more than the social status of its adherents.* In this view the Jewish religion has always emphasized social justice as much as personal rectitude.* By contrast evangelical* Protestant denominations emphasize personal salvation (becoming "born again") more than questions of social policy. This difference in teachings has led Jews to be disproportionately liberal and fundamentalist Protestants to be disproportionately conservative on many social issues. (Adapted from James Q. Wilson and John Dilulio, *American Government*. Boston: Houghton Mifflin, 1998, p. 117.)

Summary _____

_____

_____

_____

_____

_____

2. The Conquest of Peru

1 The conquest of Mexico in 1519 by Hernando Cortés and a small band of Spanish explorers produced huge quantities of gold and silver, more than Europe had ever seen. Inspired by dreams of winning the same wealth and glory, another Spanish explorer,

---

*affiliated: connected or associated.
*adherents: followers.
*rectitude: integrity, honesty.
*evangelical: intent on spreading the gospel.

Francisco Pizarro, decided to conquer the Incan empire of Peru. Pizarro fulfilled his dreams, but at a tragic cost to the Incan people.

2   In 1529, Charles I, king of Spain, granted Pizarro the right to conquer and rule Peru, allowing him to raise a small Spanish military force. In 1531, Pizarro set sail for Peru with a force of about 180 men. Upon arrival in 1532, Pizarro's small band was able to land unopposed because the Incas assumed that the fair-skinned Spaniards were returning Incan deities, or gods. In less than a year, Pizarro quickly took control of the Incan empire and imprisoned Atahualpa, the Incan emperor. Atahualpa tried to negotiate his freedom by offering the Spaniards a ransom in gold, but in 1533, while the gold was being collected, Pizarro had Atahualpa strangled to death. With the loss of its leader, the Incan empire was engulfed in civil war by 1537; by 1538 the empire lay in ruins.

Summary _____

_____

_____

_____

_____

_____

Learning How to Synthesize

The prefix *syn-* means "together," "with," or "united." As it so often is, that prefix is a clue to meaning: when you synthesize ideas, you bring them together and combine them into a new whole. Imagine, for example, that your American history book contained the following passage about President Harry Truman's decision to drop the atomic bomb:

When told that the military had followed his orders to drop the atomic bomb on the city of Hiroshima, President Harry S. Truman did not seem deeply disturbed by the news. According to all accounts, Truman announced to a group of sailors that dropping the bomb was "the greatest thing in history." He then went off to see a comedy revue aboard the ship he was traveling on and laughed heartily throughout the show.

This passage suggests that Truman was not especially concerned about his decision to drop the atomic bomb. Imagine, however, that in another reading assignment you encountered a passage with a slightly different perspective, or point of view:

On July 31, President Harry S. Truman gave the order to bomb the city of Hiroshima as soon as the weather cleared. Shortly after, in his diary, Truman somberly noted that "we have discovered the most terrible bomb in the history of the world." Following the actual bombing of both Hiroshima and Nagasaki, Truman began to complain of excruciating headaches. Asked if the headaches had a physical or psychological origin, the president replied with a one-word answer—"both."

To synthesize these two passages, you'd need to figure out the relationship between them.

To Discover Underlying Connections, Ask Questions Like These:

1. Do the authors express similar points of view on the same issue?
2. Do the authors express different points of view or perspectives on the same issue?
3. Do they describe the same situation as it appeared during different stages or times?
4. Does one author make a point that is contradicted by the other author or authors?
5. Does one author make a general point that the others disagree with or illustrate through an example?
6. Does one author describe the cause of a particular event or situation while the other analyzes the effect?

In the case of our sample passage, the authors describe Truman's reaction to dropping the bomb from different perspectives. Whereas one author concentrates on Truman's public statements, the other looks at his private musings. That means our synthesis statement needs to connect two different perspectives on the same issue: "In public, Harry Truman generally appeared to have no worries about dropping the atomic bomb; but in private, he may well have had his doubts." This is the kind of marginal note that can help you tie together textbook and lecture notes or make connections between different articles on the same subject.

All too often, students listen to lectures, complete reading assignments, and review handouts without taking the time to figure out how they connect. The result is a jumble of facts with no overall point and no pattern that supports long-term remembering. If you want to make sure this doesn't happen to you, take the time to create synthesis statements.

Just as important, synthesis statements can eliminate forever a question that plagues so many college students: "What do I write about for my research paper—it's supposed to be original research, but I don't have anything original to say." Well, in point of fact, you do too have something to say, once you know how to synthesize. The whole point of synthesizing is to combine different pieces of information into a new (read "original") whole.

Here are three views of Lady Bird Johnson, the wife of former president Lyndon Baines Johnson. How might you create a synthesis statement that links them together?

a. A significant change in the role of the first lady came with Lady Bird Johnson. Her predecessor, the youthful Jackie Kennedy, had captivated the American public with her beauty, charm, and elegance. Lady Bird Johnson shrewdly staked out her own territory, choosing an issue with which to identify herself (beautification of America) and playing a visible role in working for relevant policy changes. (Janda et al., *The Challenge of Democracy*, p. 416.)

b. During Johnson's tenure* in the White House, Lady Bird Johnson was always at his side offering him advice about how to conduct the presidency. Few people, however, realized the extent of Lady Bird's influence. When Lady Bird talked, Lyndon listened. Many believe that it was Lady Bird who convinced Johnson to drop out of the presidential race in 1968, a decision that stunned the nation.

c. Although her campaign to beautify America was often derided, Lady Bird Johnson should be viewed as one of America's first environmentalists. In her own gentle way, she made people realize that America the beautiful would never stay that way unless people took action to preserve it.

*tenure: the period of time during which something—usually an office—is held.

All three passages focus on Lady Bird Johnson, each one from a slightly different perspective. Passage *a* tells us that Lady Bird differed from Jackie Kennedy and staked out her own territory by working to beautify America. Passage *b* explains that Lady Bird had a strong political influence on her president-husband. Passage *c* insists that Lady Bird Johnson's campaign to beautify America was not always taken seriously but should have been. Here's one way to synthesize all three statements:

> Lady Bird Johnson may not have had Jackie Kennedy's youthful beauty and charm, but in her role as presidential wife, she had an important and long-lasting effect on American society.

The above synthesis statement finds a common thread in all three passages: Lady Bird did a great deal of good. But note, too, how the synthesis statement incorporates the opening point of passage *a:* Lady Bird couldn't rely on beauty or personal charm as did Jackie Kennedy. In the synthesis statement, that difference becomes an introduction to the common point of our three selections.

CHECK YOUR UNDERSTANDING

Explain the difference between a summary and a synthesis statement.

_____

_____

◼– EXERCISE 3

DIRECTIONS Read each group of passages. Then circle the number of the statement that more effectively synthesizes all three passages. *Note:* Keep in mind that an effective synthesis statement should not in any way contradict the passages it combines.

EXAMPLE

a. John Steinbeck's *Grapes of Wrath* movingly conveys the misery facing the migrant workers who, throughout the depression, traveled Route 66 across the country, searching for work. As Steinbeck writes, "Route 66 is the path of people in flight, refugees from dust and shrinking land, from the thunder of tractors and shrinking ownership, from the twisting winds that howl up out of Texas, from the foods that bring no richness to the land and steal what little richness is there."

b. Statistics suggest the magnitude of the Great Depression's effect on the business world. The stock market crash in October 1929 shocked investors and caused a financial panic. Between 1929 and 1933, one hundred thousand businesses failed; corporate profits fell from $10 billion to $1 billion; and the gross national product was cut in half. Banks failed by the thousands. (Adapted from Norton et al., *A People and a Nation,* p. 754.)

c. As unemployment soared during the Great Depression, both men and women suffered homelessness. In 1932, a squad of New York City police officers arrested twenty-five in "Hoover Valley," the village of tents and crates constructed in Central Park. All over the country, people were so poor they lived in miserable little camps called "Hoovervilles," named in sarcastic honor of President Herbert Hoover, whose policy on the depression was to pretend it didn't exist.

***Synthesis
Statement*** 1. During the Great Depression, no one suffered more than the men and women who earned their living as migrant workers.

②. The Great Depression took a terrible toll on people from all walks of life.

EXPLANATION Passages *a, b,* and *c* all give specific examples of different groups that suffered as a result of the Great Depression. Statement 1 is incorrect because it puts the suffering of migrant workers above the suffering of the other groups, and none of the passages makes that point. Sentence 2 is a better synthesis statement because it combines the ideas in all three passages without adding any ideas that weren't there in the first place.

1. a. When World War II broke out in Europe on September 1, 1939, the United States was the only world power without a propaganda agency. Ever since World War I, Americans had been suspicious of the claim that propaganda could be used to good effect. Many believed that British propaganda had helped maneuver the United States into World War I. They had also not forgotten the bloody anti-German riots that had been touched off by movies like America's own *Beast of Berlin* (1919). To most Americans, *propaganda* was simply a dirty word, no matter what its purpose.

    b. In 1939, as the world began to career into World War II, the president of the United States, Franklin Delano Roosevelt, applied pressure on Hollywood to make feature films that were little more than propaganda vehicles, but Hollywood producers were not so ready to give in. Committed to the doctrine of pure entertainment, pure profit, and above all to the need for America to stay out of the war, most balked at making films that reflected the horror engulfing Europe.

    c. The Japanese bombed Pearl Harbor on December 7, 1941. Astonished and outraged, the United States entered World War II. On December 17 of the same year, President Roosevelt appointed Lowell Mellett as head of the Hollywood propaganda office. Mellett's job was to make sure that Hollywood films aided the war effort, and for the most part, Hollywood was happy to cooperate by making films that celebrated the war effort and castigated* America's enemies.

Synthesis Statement 1. Up until the bombing of Pearl Harbor, the United States did not have an official propaganda office, a terrible mistake that produced unexpected and horrifying consequences.

    2. Before the bombing of Pearl Harbor, Hollywood, like most of America, mistrusted propaganda. But after the bombing, propaganda became an acceptable part of the war effort and Hollywood embraced it.

2. a. The Egyptians revered Maat as the goddess of justice who weighed the hearts of the dead on a scale. The right balance guaranteed a happy afterlife; the wrong one promised torment.

    b. The ancient Greeks worshipped Dike as the goddess of justice. When the Romans inherited her, they renamed her Justitia and represented her with a blindfold around her eyes to symbolize her lack of bias.*

    c. With the arrival of Christianity and the rejection of the ancient gods, the goddess of justice was demoted to a saint and people apparently became suspicious of her ability to fairly deal out justice. Santa Justitia was often depicted holding an unevenly balanced scale. The implication was that the rich got different justice than the poor.

---

*castigated: harshly criticized or punished.
*bias: prejudice in favor of one side or another (for more on this subject, see Chapter 10).

Synthesis 1. Whereas the ancient Greeks and Romans held the goddess of
Statement justice in great respect, the early Christians seem to have been
a bit more suspicious of how justice was meted* out.

2. The Christians refused to accept all of the ancient gods and god-
desses, including Justitia, the goddess of justice.

3. a. In the 1992 election, political action committees (PACs) contributed over $50 million to the various campaigns. The 1996 elec-
tion saw even greater amounts of PAC money pour into campaign
coffers. This sort of funding of the presidency puts a price tag on
democracy: whoever contributes the most money has the most
access to the president.

b. In the name of campaign reform, there are those who would make
illegal the contributions of political action committees (PACs). Yet
these contributions, no matter how high the sums, are nothing
more than a legitimate form of free speech. Any group who wants
to contribute to a political campaign as a show of support should
have the right to do so.

c. Given the millions of dollars that were contributed to campaign
funds in the 1992 and 1996 elections, it's not hard to understand
why enthusiasm for campaign reform has never been higher. Yet,
while outlawing all contributions by political action committees
(PACs) seems extreme, it's clear that they have to be more closely
monitored and accounted for.

Synthesis 1. When it comes to the campaign contributions of political action
Statement committees, or PACs, there's a good deal of disagreement. But
on one point, no one disagrees: PACs contributed huge sums to
the presidential campaigns of 1992 and 1996.

2. Political action committees (PACs) and their contributions to political campaigns may be controversial, but there is no proof of
the claim that has so often been made—that they weaken the
democratic process.

4. a. In 1998, many people objected to President Clinton's proposed
plan to bomb Iraq, and they made their feelings known by send-
ing e-mail to the president.

*meted: distributed.

b. In the campaign against the elimination of land mines* around the world, computers played a key role. Those who supported the elimination of the mines kept in touch and up-to-date via e-mail.

c. In 1998, activists fighting to make insurers extend hospital stays for breast cancer patients used the Internet to publicize their fight and collect signatures for petitions.

Synthesis 1. Because of the Internet, people who never found the time to write
Statement letters are managing to stay in touch.

2. Thanks to the Internet, it's become easier for political activists around the world to stay in touch.

5. a. With its brilliant and innovative techniques, D. W. Griffith's *The Birth of a Nation* dramatically changed the face of American movies forever. Before Griffith, movies contained neither close-ups nor fade-outs. It was Griffith who brought those two techniques to the screen. With the exception of Orson Welles and *Citizen Kane*, no other director and no other film have been as influential as Griffith and *The Birth of a Nation*.

 b. By 1910, motion pictures had become an art form, thanks to creative directors like D. W. Griffith. Griffith's most famous work, *The Birth of a Nation* (1915), an epic film about the Civil War and Reconstruction, used innovative techniques—close-ups, fade-outs, and battle scenes—that gave viewers heightened drama and excitement. Unfortunately, the film fanned racial prejudice by depicting African-Americans as a threat to white moral values. An organized black protest against it was led by the infant National Association for the Advancement of Colored People (NAACP). (Norton et al., *A People and a Nation,* p. 583.)

c. Despite the film's famed innovations, it's nearly impossible for moviegoers to take pleasure in D. W. Griffith's *The Birth of a Nation.* Powered by racism, the film enrages more than it entertains, and it's no wonder that the NAACP picketed the film when it first appeared.

Synthesis 1. D. W. Griffith was a famous film director who profoundly influ-
Statement enced the American film industry; in fact, Griffith changed the face of American film.

---

*land mines: explosive devices, usually laid below the surface of the ground; they explode if stepped on.

2. Although no one can deny the contribution that D. W. Griffith's *The Birth of a Nation* made to film history, many find it hard to overlook the racism that runs through the film.

-▪ EXERCISE 4

DIRECTIONS Read each set of statements. Then, in the blank lines that follow, write a synthesis statement that links them together.

EXAMPLE

a. Even before the war, Nazi officials had targeted Jews throughout Europe for extermination. By war's end, about 6 million Jews had been forced into concentration camps and had been systematically killed by firing squads, unspeakable tortures, and gas chambers. (Norton et al., *A People and a Nation,* p. 843.)

b. To protest Hitler's treatment of the Jews during World War II, the philosopher Simone Weil went on a prolonged hunger strike. In the end, the fabulously gifted Weil starved to death rather than take food while the prisoners of concentration camps were being reduced to walking skeletons.

c. Born to a wealthy Swedish family, Raoul Wallenberg could easily have ignored the horror Adolf Hitler unleashed on the world. But he chose not to. Using his considerable daring, charm, and brains, Wallenberg saved the lives of thousands of Jewish refugees who would have died a horrible death without his help.

Synthesis Statement *During World War II, the plight of the Jews stirred people like Simone Weil and Raoul Wallenberg to extraordinary acts of heroism.*

EXPLANATION All three passages focus on the plight of the Jews in World War II, and two of the passages describe how some people tried to stop or hinder what was happening. As you can see, the synthesis statement weaves together those two threads of thought.

1. a. Having studied the meditative states of monks and yogis,* researcher Elmer Green advocates and practices meditation. For him, it is a way of making the mind enter a deeper state of consciousness.

---

*yogis: people versed in meditation and focused more on the spirit than on the body.

b. In the 1960s and 1970s, the Essalen Institute at Big Sur was the center of what was then called the "human potential movement." At the heart of Essalen and the movement in general was Michael Murphy, who had co-founded the institute with his former classmate Richard Price. Although Murphy eventually moved away from the anti-intellectualism of Essalen's teachers, he has remained committed to the daily practice of meditation. For him, the meditative state is a way to unlock human creativity.

c. Although many exaggerated claims have been made for the benefits of meditation, the research supporting those claims has not always been forthcoming. Much of the existing research consists of personal anecdotes, or stories, and many of the studies designed to test the effects of meditation have been poorly designed.

Synthesis Statement

_____

_____

_____

2. a. Every society is concerned with the socialization of its children— that is, with making sure that children learn early on what is considered socially correct and morally ethical behavior.

b. In Asian societies, the family is considered the most important agent of socialization.

c. In the last decade, a number of studies have suggested that in the United States, a child's peer group may be overtaking the family as the most powerful agent of socialization.

Synthesis Statement

_____

_____

_____

3. a. No matter how far back in history we look, we find human beings making and listening to music. . . . At some point in our past, it was important enough that all human beings born, no matter whether Bengalese, Cruit, or Quechua, no matter whether blind, left-handed, or freckled, were not merely *capable* of making music; they *required* music to add meaning to their lives. (Diane Ackerman, *A Natural History of the Senses.* New York: Vintage Books, 1991, p. 210.)

b. The little girl would take no notice of anyone who entered the room. She seemed locked inside her own private world, unable or unwilling to leave it. But if her uncle played the piano, she would sit next to the piano bench, listening raptly,* a smile playing around her lips. As far as anyone knew, the music of the piano was the only sound that reached her.

c. Music doesn't just seem to soothe the spirit, it also appears to have a powerful effect on the body. In two different studies conducted at the University of Wisconsin, patients suffering from high blood pressure experienced a five- to ten-point decrease in their blood pressure readings after listening to the music of Mozart for a half hour.

Synthesis Statement

_____

_____

_____

4. a. Anne Frank was a German-Jewish girl who hid from the Nazis with her parents, their friends, and some other fugitives in an Amsterdam attic from 1942 to 1944. Her diary covering the years of hiding was found by friends and published in 1947. Against the background of the mass murder of European Jewry, the book presents an impressive picture of how a group of hunted people found a way to live together in almost intolerable proximity.* It is also a stirring portrait of a young girl whose youthful spirit triumphs over the misery of her surroundings.

b. _The Diary of Anne Frank_ has been read by millions. It has been both a successful play and film. People are drawn to the story of Anne and her family because it reminds us that the human spirit has enormous resiliency* even in the face of terrifying evil.

c. In _Surviving and Other Essays,_ psychologist and concentration camp survivor Bruno Bettelheim argued that the world had embraced Anne Frank's story too uncritically. For Bettelheim, Anne's fate demonstrated "how efforts at disregarding in private life what goes on around one in society can hasten one's destruction."

---

*raptly: intently.
*proximity: closeness.
*resiliency: the ability to respond or spring back.

Synthesis
Statement   _____

_____

_____

WORD NOTES

Page 181 introduced the word *optimum,* meaning "at the highest or most favorable level of function or condition." The English word *optimum* is derived from the Latin word *optimus,* meaning "best." Use your knowledge of word history and context clues to define the words italicized in the following sentences:

1. When she saw the look on his face, she knew immediately it was the *optimal* moment to propose.

Optimal means _____.

2. Despite the harsh conditions of his childhood, he was a terrific *optimist,* always looking on the bright side of things.

Optimist means _____.

3. To succeed, the scientists knew they had to *optimize* the conditions for the experiment.

Optimize means _____.

Check your definitions in the dictionary. Then answer these two questions:

4. In the context of philosophy, what is *optimism*?

_____

5. In the context of biology, what does *optimum* mean?

_____

Summing Up

Listed below are the most important points in Chapter 5. Put a check mark in the box if you think the point is clear in your mind. Leave the box blank if you need to review the material one more time. The page numbers in parentheses tell you where to look to review each point on the list.

1. Summaries reduce a passage to about one-third or one-quarter of its original length. The goal of a summary is to retain the main idea and only those supporting details essential to answering questions readers might have about the main idea. (pp. 174–177)

2. Summaries do not interpret the author's words. The goal of a summary is to condense, or reduce, the original text without passing any judgment on it. (pp. 177–179)

3. When you synthesize different readings on the same subject, you try to identify the relationship between them. They may, for example, all share a similar point of view; or else the author of one source may disagree with the other authors. In some instances, one author may identify the cause of an event while two others look at the effects. The goal of synthesizing is to find a way to link or pull together different readings that share a common thread. (pp. 187–190)

4. Synthesizing ensures long-term remembering and understanding and provides you with topics for research papers. (p. 189)

TEST YOUR UNDERSTANDING

To see how well you have understood this chapter, take the following review quiz. Then correct it using the answer key provided by your instructor. If you score 80 percent or above, you're ready to take the end-of-chapter exam. However, if you score below 80 percent, look over the quiz carefully to see what kinds of questions you missed. Then use the **Summing Up** pages of the chapter to find out which pages you should review before taking the chapter exam.

Chapter 5: Review Quiz

Part A

DIRECTIONS Read the following selections. For each one, circle the letter of the more effective summary.

1. The Triumph of American Movies

1 Moving pictures in America got their start in carnivals and side-shows. Cheap amusements, they were the poor person's substitute for live theater. Popular almost from the beginning, movies were still not considered quite legitimate in the early years between 1896 and 1910, and "nice" people didn't always admit to watching them. However, by the 1920s, the "picture shows" had become a popular and accepted form of entertainment. American movies had begun to take over the foreign market, and movies were America's fifth-biggest industry.

2   It was in the twenties that American director Mack Sennett brought the Keystone Cops to the silver screen. Wildly popular with audiences, the Keystone Cops specialized in endless chases, scantily clad young women, and slapstick comedy of the pie-in-your-face variety. The 1920s also saw the rise of screen idols such as Mary Pickford and Rudolph Valentino. While Pickford played roles that celebrated the power of little-girl innocence, Valentino specialized in Latin lovers, whose handsome face and burning eyes made women swoon. Actors like Pickford and Valentino were the first movie stars to be so popular they actually had fan clubs, a common enough occurrence now but not then.

3   However, it was the British-born Charlie Chaplin, in his role as "The Little Tramp," who truly won the world's heart. With his cane, bowler hat, and ragged, baggy pants, Chaplin breathed life into corny stories about a young man whose aspirations never matched his abilities and who rarely if ever won the heart of the girl he loved. Chaplin's genius was to make his audiences laugh and cry at the same time, and they loved him for it—not just in his adopted American home but abroad as well. Almost single-handedly, Chaplin won for the American movie industry an unrivaled mass audience that spanned the continents.

4   Only German movie makers briefly competed with the Americans in the twenties. In films like *The Cabinet of Dr. Caligari*, German directors such as F. W. Murnau produced highly acclaimed Expressionist* dramas that specialized in heightened emotional

---

*Expressionist: a movement in the arts that focused on extreme states of mind.

states of horror and madness. But it wasn't long before American money had beckoned the Germans to Hollywood and consolidated America's domination of the picture industry.

Summary a. American movies started out in carnivals and sideshows. Movies were what poor people watched because they couldn't afford a ticket to the theater. But by the 1920s, the American movie industry was a virtual blockbuster: It was the fifth largest industry in the country. In the 1920s, America was also in heated competition with Germany for dominance over the world movie industry, but it wasn't long before the Germans were won over by American money, leaving the field clear for American domination. In addition the Germans never produced movie stars as popular as Mary Pickford, Rudolph Valentino, and Charlie Chaplin. It was this trio that made the American film industry a powerhouse at home and abroad.

b. By the 1920s, the American movie industry was garnering huge profits both at home and abroad. While stars like Mary Pickford and Rudolph Valentino were widely popular at home, it was Charlie Chaplin who really captured the international market with his portrayal of "The Little Tramp." True, the German movie industry briefly rivaled the American, but that rivalry didn't last long as the more gifted German directors, like F. W. Murnau, were lured to Hollywood by the promise of huge salaries.

2. **Disappearing Species**

1 On several occasions in the earth's history, large numbers of species have become extinct, perhaps because of the impact of comets and asteroids. Ecologists believe that the earth is currently experiencing an extinction catastrophe as large as the ancient geological ones, but in this case, the catastrophe will not be the result of a comet or asteroid.

2 Instead, scientists point the accusing finger at our own human species: The problem is our success. From Africa, we have spread over Europe and Asia, then Australia, into the Americas (probably within the last 10,000 years or so), and, even more recently, across the remote islands of the Pacific. We are one of the most abundant species on the planet, and our numbers are rapidly increasing. Each year we consume about 40 percent of the world's total plant growth on land. (Some of this consumption is what we and our domestic animals eat; some is the wood we burn or use for other purposes.) In the oceans, we have repeatedly taken out more than the annual growth—the "interest" in our ecological sav-

ings account—and the balance has shrunken accordingly. Many once-profitable fisheries, such as herring and cod, are now virtually depleted and dozens of species of birds are dying or are near death. (Adapted from Stuart L. Pimm, *Triumph of Discovery*. New York: Henry Holt, 1995, p. 39.)

Summary a. Thanks to the successful spread of the human race, the earth may be experiencing an extinction catastrophe. Herring and cod are almost extinct, and many species of birds are dead or dying, because of humanity's march across the globe.

      b. Throughout history the earth has experienced large-scale species extinction, and now is no exception. Herring and cod are almost extinct, as are many species of birds. This is simply what's known as survival of the fittest.

Part B

DIRECTIONS Read and summarize the following passage.

3. Interpreting Your Dreams

In an effort to understand and analyze dreams, Sigmund Freud identified four ways in which dreams disguised their meaning. According to Freud, the first disguise is **condensation.** Through condensation, a single character in a dream may represent several people at once. A character in a dream who looks like a teacher, acts like your father, talks like your mother, and is dressed like your employer might be a condensation of all the authority figures in your life. A second way of disguising dream content is **displacement.** Displacement may cause the most important emotions or actions of a dream to be redirected toward safe or seemingly unimportant targets. Thus, a student angry at his parents might dream of accidentally wrecking their car instead of directly attacking them. A third dream process is **symbolization.** Freud believed that dreams are often expressed in images that are symbolic rather than literal* in their meanings. To uncover the meaning of dreams, it helps to ask what feelings or ideas a dream image might symbolize. Let's say, for example, that a student dreams of coming to class naked. A literal interpretation would be that the student is an exhibitionist.* A more likely symbolic meaning might be that the student feels vulnerable in the class or is

---

*literal: based on reality.
*exhibitionist: a person who will do anything for attention.

unprepared for a test. A process called **secondary elaboration** is the fourth method by which the meaning of dreams is disguised. Secondary elaboration is the tendency to make a dream more logical, and to add details when remembering it. (Adapted from Coon, *Essentials of Psychology,* p. 256.)

Summary _____

_____

_____

_____

_____

_____

_____

_____

Part C

DIRECTIONS Read each group of passages. Then circle the number of the statement that more effectively synthesizes all three passages.

4. a. Sigmund Freud, the founder of psychoanalysis,* insisted that a child's relationship to his or her mother determined behavior even in adult life. For Freudians, then, therapy needs to focus on childhood patterns and their reemergence in adult life.

b. Initially a follower of Sigmund Freud, Carl Jung broke with Freud over Jung's belief that the human psyche was deeply influenced by unconscious *archetypes,* patterns of behavior that had been part of humanity for centuries but were called forth only under certain conditions. For Jung and those who followed him, understanding the effect of ancient archetypes on behavior was a crucial part of therapy—more important, in fact, than the analysis of early childhood behavioral patterns.

c. For the philosopher Jean-Paul Sartre, behavior is not a product of the past. Rather it is the end result of conscious choices on the part of the individual. For the followers of Sartre—called *existentialists*—the individual is free to make and remake the pattern of his or her own life.

---

*psychoanalysis: a theory of the human mind and its ills.

Synthesis Statement 1. Freud and Jung both believed that human behavior was the product of the past. However, they disagreed profoundly about what in the past most profoundly shapes human behavior.

2. In contrast to Freud and Jung, who believed that human behavior was fixed on patterns from the past, Jean-Paul Sartre believed that each individual was responsible for the shape of his or her existence.

5. a. Albert Einstein, the most influential scientist of the twentieth century, was considered by his parents to be retarded. He spoke slowly and haltingly and never answered questions quickly or without thinking. Even in high school, he was considered one of the slower students, and his teachers were unimpressed by his performance.

b. Pablo Picasso, whom many consider the twentieth century's greatest painter, was a failure at school. He did so badly that his father hired a special tutor for him, but the tutor quit because he considered Picasso a dunce.*

c. Early on, Wolfgang Amadeus Mozart was considered a musical prodigy,* and his father knew immediately that his son would accomplish great things. By the age of seven, Mozart was already writing and performing his own music, and his musical genius burned brightly until his death at the age of thirty-seven.

Synthesis Statement 1. Although some geniuses are like Mozart and reveal their talent as children, others are like Picasso and Einstein—slow to reveal their extraordinary gifts.

2. Already in childhood, it's usually clear which children are destined for genius. Mozart is a good example of this general rule.

Use the answer key provided by your instructor to correct your quiz. If you score 80 percent or above, you are ready for the chapter exam. If you score below 80 percent, look carefully at the questions you answered incorrectly. Then use the **Summing Up** section to decide which pages you need to review.

---

*dunce: a person with no brains.
*prodigy: person, often a child, with exceptional talents or powers.

Chapter Test 5

Part A

DIRECTIONS Read the following selections. For each one, circle the letter of the more effective summary.

1. Risk-Taking Behavior

1 Why are some individuals willing to take risks that can be a real threat to life and health whereas others prefer to play it safe? There are at least two reasons for the differences in risk-taking behavior. Although the risk of danger may be real, perceptions of that risk can vary from person to person, or from time to time. Two people, for example, may have very different ideas about a situation's risk potential. Whereas one person might conclude that there is very little risk involved, another might think that the risk to health or well-being is quite high. For example, how many among us would walk a tightrope strung one thousand feet above the ground? Yet some people do it on an almost daily basis and think nothing of it. Then, too, most people will not take the same risks at forty as they did at twenty. Age tends to convince most of us that death is a reality while the young are likely to think it will happen to someone else.

2 A second reason why we vary in our willingness to take risks is that the vision of future rewards can cloud our assessment of danger. Some people might be willing to work in very hazardous environments (e.g., the clean-up following a nuclear accident in a reactor) for a high salary, while others would not consider it at any price. Money, however, is only one form of reward that modifies our evaluation of risk. Taking risks in return for potential social admiration is another circumstance in which there is a potential for reward—one that is particularly prevalent among young adults. For example, driving a car very fast may be the result of a desire for social admiration.

3 In such a case, risk is evaluated by balancing the rewards and the potential dangers. When the potential rewards are larger than the perceived risk, some individuals may fail to take any actions that reduce the threat of injury. Eyes on the prize, they choose to ignore the threat of danger. (Adapted from Mullen et al., *Connections for Health*, p. 317.)

Summary a. Why are some individuals willing to take a risk that others would never even consider? There are two different answers to that one question. First of all, people evaluate risk in different ways. A twenty-year-old may well perceive little risk in driving too fast while under the influence of alcohol, whereas a forty-year-old may determine that the same situation is fraught* with danger. Then, too, some people place little value on a human life, even when it's their own.

b. Why are some people willing to take risks that endanger both life and limb? There are two different answers to that seemingly simple question. One answer is that we don't all define risk in the same way. Risky behavior for one person may not be considered risky for another. A second reason is that the promise of a reward can help disguise the threat of risk. Money and social admiration are powerful rewards that can cloud the amount of risk involved in a particular activity such as working in a hazardous environment or driving too fast.

2. Faces and First Impressions

1 People may not measure each other by bumps on the head, as phrenologists* used to do, but first impressions are influenced in subtle ways by a person's height, weight, skin color, hair color, eyeglasses, and other aspects of appearance (Alley, 1988; Bull & Rumsey, 1988; Herman et al., 1986). As social perceivers, we are even influenced by a person's name. For example, Robert Young and his colleagues (1993) found that fictional characters with "older generation" names such as Harry, Walter, Dorothy, and Edith are judged less popular and less intelligent than those with "younger generation" names such as Kevin, Michael, Lisa, and Michelle.

2 The human face in particular attracts more than its share of attention. For example, Diane Berry and Leslie Zebrowitz-McArthur (1986) have found that adults who have baby-faced features— large round eyes, high eyebrows, round cheeks, a large forehead, smooth skin, and a rounded chin—are seen as warm, kind, naive, weak, honest, and submissive. In contrast, adults with mature features—small eyes, low brows and a small forehead, wrinkled skin, and an angular chin—are seen as stronger, more dominant, and less naive. Thus, in small claims court, judges are more likely to favor baby-faced defendants accused of intentional wrongdoing, but they tend to rule against baby-faced defendants accused of negligence (Zebrowitz & McDonald, 1991). And in the workplace, baby-faced job applicants are more likely to be recom-

---

*fraught: heavy, filled with.
*phrenologists: people who claim to analyze character by touching the bumps on their subjects' heads.

mended for employment as daycare teachers, whereas mature-faced adults are considered to be better suited for work as bankers (Zebrowitz et al., 1991).

3   What accounts for these findings? There are three possible explanations. One is that human beings are genetically programmed to respond gently to infantile features so that real babies are treated with tender loving care. Another possibility is that we simply learn to associate infantile features with helplessness and then generalize this expectation to baby-faced adults. Third, maybe there is an actual link between appearance and behavior—a possibility suggested by the fact that subjects exposed only to photos or brief videotapes of strangers formed impressions that correlated with the self-descriptions of these same strangers (Berry, 1990; Kenny et al., 1992). Whatever the explanation, the perceived link between appearance and behavior may account for the shock that we sometimes experience when our expectations based on appearance are not confirmed. (Adapted from Brehm and Kassin, *Social Psychology*, pp. 83–84.)

Summary a. Like our names, our faces play an important role in making a first impression. Researchers Diane Berry and Leslie Zebrowitz-McArthur have shown, for example, that people with baby faces are frequently perceived, at first sight, to be innocent, naive, and helpless. In contrast, people with sharper, more mature and more angular faces are often thought to be strong and domineering. No one really knows why this is so, but there are three theories. One theory is that human beings are genetically programmed to treat with care those who have childlike faces. Another theory says that we are used to treating babies in a certain way, and we then apply that same behavior to grownups who happen to have baby faces. And finally, there really may be a connection between how people look and how they behave.

b. We may no longer try to determine people's character by the bumps on their head—the way phrenologists used to do—but we are still influenced, it turns out, by a person's name. In 1993, researcher Robert Young found that characters with old-fashioned names like Harry, Dorothy, and Edith were assumed to be less popular and less intelligent than characters with more modern names like Kevin, Lisa, and Michelle. Our sense that appearance and behavior must be a match is probably one reason why we are so shocked when a person's behavior doesn't fit his or her appearance. We never seem to expect, for example, someone with a baby face to commit a violent crime. That's the kind of thing we would expect of someone who had a more mature and more angular face.

Part B

DIRECTIONS Read and summarize the following selection.

3. Term Limits

1 One illustration of Americans' antagonism toward legislators is the movement toward **term limits.** Fifteen states have passed laws that place a limit on the number of years legislators can serve in office. Those laws are aimed at both state legislatures and Congress. The length of term limits varies from state to state, but typically members of a state house of representatives can serve eight years, and a member of a state senate can serve eight to twelve years.

2 Despite overwhelming support from voters, term limits for members of Congress may never take effect. The Supreme Court has yet to make a final ruling, but a lower federal court has determined that it is unconstitutional for a state to place term limits on members of Congress. The legal reasoning is simple: The Constitution specifically sets qualifications for representatives and senators. (A representative must be at least twenty-five years old and a citizen for at least seven years; a senator must be at least thirty years old and a citizen for nine years. Both must be residents of the state in which they are elected.) Accordingly, if a state sets a term limit for members of Congress, it is in effect amending the Constitution on its own by adding qualifications. The Supreme Court has, however, ruled term limits on state legislators to be constitutional. (Adapted from Janda et al., *The Challenge of Democracy*, p. 366.)

_____

_____

_____

_____

_____

_____

Part C

DIRECTIONS Read each group of passages. Circle the number of the statement that more effectively synthesizes all three passages.

4. a. For Freud, the father of psychoanalysis, therapy did not promise happiness. His patients, Freud said, could expect only to change "misery into common unhappiness." To ask for more was, in his opinion, a naive notion based on an unrealistic worldview.

b. From Freud's perspective, human nature would always be plagued by a death instinct that would undermine all attempts to live fully, productively, and happily. The best he could promise from therapy was that the patient would learn how to make unconscious and destructive desires more conscious and thereby control them, but the struggle to do so would never end.

c. Whereas Freud anchored his therapy firmly in the unconscious, the psychologist Carl Rogers, born when Freud was first formulating his theory of the unconscious in 1902, concentrated on the conscious. More optimistic than Freud ever dreamed of being, Rogers believed that clients—he disliked the term *patients*—could discover solutions to life's problems and become happier people.

Synthesis Statement 1. For the European temperament, Freudian psychology and its strain of pessimism may have been appropriate, particularly in the early part of the twentieth century when the world was racked by war. But Americans did not take kindly to Freud's bleak worldview.

2. Unlike Sigmund Freud, who considered unhappiness a natural and normal part of life, Carl Rogers insisted that successful therapy could solve life's problems and make happiness a realistic goal.

5. a. In *Gridlock'd,* the ill-fated rap singer Tupac Shakur combined a magnetic screen presence with the ability to create a believable and sympathetic film character. Up against one of the most gifted actors working today, Tim Roth, Shakur more than held his own. Whatever one might think of his music, there's no denying that Shakur could act.

b. Tupac Shakur was a man who seemed to be beset by demons, and his music reflected his personal conflicts. At one moment, he could sing with tenderness and compassion about the strength and determination of women, as in "Brenda's Got a

Baby" and "Keep Ya Head Up"; in the next, in songs like "Hit 'Em Up," he would switch to a mean-spirited gangster persona* who considered women little more than sexual prizes to be won or lost in brutal male rivalries.

c. I don't know whether to mourn Tupac Shakur or to rail against all the terrible forces—including the artist's own self-destructive temperament—that have resulted in such a wasteful, unjustifiable end. I do know this, though: Whatever its causes, the murder of Shakur, at age twenty-four, has robbed us of one of the most talented and compelling voices of recent years. He embodied just as much for his audience as Kurt Cobain did for his. That is, Tupac Shakur spoke to and for many who had grown up within (and maybe never quite left) hard realities—realities that mainstream culture and media are loath to understand or respect—and his death has left his fans feeling a doubly-sharp pain. (Gilmore, "Tupac Shakur: Easy Target," *Night Beat,* p. 386.)

Synthesis 1. Like rapper Biggie Smalls, the violence of Tupac Shakur's music
Statement spilled over into his personal life and ultimately destroyed him.

2. Like his music, Tupac Shakur's personal life was filled with self-destructive violence, but there is no denying that he was a man of extraordinary gifts.

---

*persona: mask.

Becoming a More Critical Reader

Part I of *Reading for Thinking* concentrated on strategies for improving reading comprehension and long-term remembering. Part II of *Reading for Thinking* takes you into the realm of critical reading, where you go beyond just understanding the author's words. Now you will learn how to read between the lines in order to create meaning and evaluate the author's point of view.

C H A P T E R   6

Reading Between the Lines: Drawing the Right Inferences

 In this chapter, you'll learn

- **how to draw inferences about main ideas in paragraphs.**

- **how to infer the appropriate thesis statement for a longer reading.**

- **how to evaluate your inferences.**

- **how to infer supporting details.**

Chapter 6 shows you how to find words for what the author suggests but never says outright. In short, it teaches you the art of drawing inferences. By the way, it's no accident that Chapter 6 bridges the gap between Parts I and II. Essential to understanding an author's meaning, draw-

213

**ing the appropriate inferences also lies at the heart of critical
reading.**

 # Inferring Main Ideas in Paragraphs

Although many paragraphs contain topic sentences, not all of them
do. Sometimes authors choose to imply, or suggest, the main idea.
Instead of stating the point of the paragraph in a sentence, they offer
specific statements designed to help their readers draw the appropriate inference, or conclusion. Here's an example:

> The philosopher Arthur Schopenhauer lived most of his life com-
> pletely alone; separated from his family and distrustful of women,
> he had neither wife nor children. Irrationally afraid of thieves, he
> kept his belongings carefully locked away and was said to keep
> loaded pistols near him while he slept. His sole companion was a
> poodle called *Atma* (a word that means "world soul"), but even Atma
> occasionally disturbed his peace of mind. Whenever she was both-
> ersome or barked too much, her master would grow irritated and
> call her *mensch*, the German word for "human being."

In this paragraph the author makes specific statements about
Schopenhauer's character and behavior: (1) he lived most of his life
alone, (2) he distrusted women, (3) he always thought he was going
to be robbed, (4) his only companion was a dog, and (5) he would
call his dog a "human being" if she irritated him. However, none of
those statements sums up the point of the paragraph. That means
the paragraph lacks a topic sentence.

Nevertheless, the paragraph does imply, or suggest, a main idea
like the following: Schopenhauer did not care for his fellow human
beings. This inference follows quite naturally from statements made
in the paragraph. We can say, then, that it's an appropriate inference.

Appropriate and Inappropriate Inferences

Experienced readers know that authors do not always state their
main ideas in a sentence. Thus, if readers can't find a sentence that
sums up the paragraph, they read between the lines and infer a topic
sentence that fits the paragraph. However, they are always careful
to draw an **appropriate inference,** an inference solidly based on
statements made by the author.

To recognize the difference between an appropriate and an inappropriate inference, imagine that we had inferred this topic sentence from the sample paragraph about Schopenhauer:

Schopenhauer's miserable childhood made it impossible for him to have a healthy relationship with other people.

Although the paragraph offers plenty of evidence that Schopenhauer did not have a healthy relationship with people, it does not discuss his childhood. Because our inference is not based on information drawn from the paragraph, it is inappropriate. Although personal experience and general knowledge do suggest that an adult who has problems may have had a troubled childhood, we cannot rely solely on personal experience or knowledge to draw inferences. To be useful, *inferences in reading must combine what the reader already knows with what the author explicitly says*. Inferences that do not combine the two can produce misreadings that distort the author's intended meaning.

To judge your ability to distinguish, or see the difference, between appropriate and inappropriate inferences, read the following paragraph. When you finish, look over the two inferences that follow and decide which one is appropriate and which one is not.

In the West, the Middle Eastern country of Kuwait has a reputation for being more liberal than other Middle Eastern countries where women's rights are concerned. Yet the majority of female students are not permitted to study abroad, no matter how good their grades. Similarly, female students almost never receive funding for international athletic competitions. Although the Kuwaiti government promised to give women the right to vote once the Gulf War was over, the women of Kuwait are still not allowed to participate in elections. Kuwaiti feminists, however, still hope that the government will one day keep its promise.

Based on this paragraph, which of the following topic sentences do you think is appropriate?

1. The government of Kuwait will never honor its promise to let women vote.
2. Despite Kuwait's liberal reputation, in many key areas women are not treated as the equals of men.

If you chose inference 2, you've grasped the difference between appropriate and inappropriate inferences. Inference 2 is solidly backed by statements in the paragraph, statements that support the idea that women lack equality in key areas. In addition, inference 2 is not contradicted by any statements in the paragraph.

The same cannot be said, however, for inference 1, which is contradicted by the last sentence in the paragraph. If Kuwaiti feminists still have hope, there's no reason to infer that the Kuwaiti government will *never* honor its promise to give women the vote.

Another problem with inference 1 is that the paragraph does not focus solely on voting rights. The paragraph also addresses funding for female athletes and travel privileges for female students. None of the statements addressing these issues can be used as the basis for inference 1, making it clear that the inference is inappropriate.

Appropriate inferences are solidly based on—or follow from—statements made in the paragraph, and they are not contradicted by any statements in the paragraph.

Inappropriate inferences do not follow from statements made in the paragraph, and they are likely to be contradicted by the author's actual words. Overall, they tend to rely too heavily on the reader's personal experience or general knowledge rather than on the author's statements.

EXERCISE 1

DIRECTIONS After reading each paragraph, circle the letter of the topic sentence that more effectively sums up the implied main idea.

EXAMPLE In the past twenty years, countless numbers of men and women have paid large sums of money for a treatment commonly known as *cell therapy*. Their reason was simple: They believed that the injection of cells taken from lambs could help them maintain their youth. They either did not know or did not choose to believe what any doctor would tell them: Animal cells, when injected into the body of a human being, are treated like any other foreign substance. The body gathers its defenses to reject the cells, and within three or four days they are destroyed.

Topic Sentence (a.) Cell therapy is both expensive and useless.

  b. Cell therapy should be available for everyone, not just for the rich.

EXPLANATION Nothing in the paragraph suggests that cell therapy should be made available to everyone. On the contrary, most of the statements in the paragraph suggest that cell therapy is useless against aging, making inference *a* the better choice for an implied main idea.

1. Meet Rebecca. She's three years old, and both her parents have full-time jobs. Every evening, Rebecca's father makes dinner for the family—Rebecca's mother rarely cooks. But when it's dinnertime in Rebecca's dollhouse, she invariably chooses the mommy doll and puts her to work in the kitchen. Now meet George. He's four, and his parents are still loyal to the values of the sixties. He was never taught the word *gun,* much less given a war toy of any sort. On his own, however, he picked up the word *shoot.* Thereafter he would grab a stick from the park, brandish* it about and call it his "shooter." (Adapted from Laura Shapiro. "Guns and Dolls," *Newsweek,* May 28, 1990, p. 56.)

Topic Sentence a. Despite parental example or training, many children still embrace traditional roles for girls and boys.

b. Girls are born with an instinct to mother while boys are born with an instinct for aggression.

2. According to Dr. Susan Love, women behave in a doctor's office much as they do in social settings. "Women want a relationship with their doctors," says Dr. Love. "They want the doctor to talk to them, to explain things."[1] Men, in contrast, aren't all that interested in a relationship with their physicians. When something is wrong, they want it fixed, and friendly chitchat is pretty irrelevant. Studies suggest, too, that men don't get as much routine health care as women do, and they generally try to escape the doctor's office as quickly as possible.

Topic Sentence a. Men and women behave differently with their doctors.

b. Physicians like their female patients more than they like their male ones.

 3. On the one hand (if you can forgive the pun*), left-handers have often demonstrated special talents. Left-handers have been great painters (Leonardo da Vinci, Picasso), outstanding performers (Marilyn Monroe, Jimi Hendrix), and even presidents (Ronald Reagan,

---

*brandish: display, wave.
[1]Abigail Zieger, "What Doctors of Both Sexes Think of Patients of Both Sexes," *New York Times,* June 2, 1998, p. 20.
*pun: play on words.

George Bush). (As these examples suggest, left-handedness is considerably more common among males than among females.) And left-handedness has been reported to be twice as common among children who are mathematical prodigies as it is in the overall population (Benbow, 1988). On the other hand, left-handers have often been viewed as clumsy and accident-prone. They "flounder about like seals out of water," wrote one British psychologist (Burt, 1937, p. 287). The very word for "left-handed" in French—*gauche*—also means "clumsy." Because of such negative attitudes toward left-handedness, in previous decades parents and teachers often encouraged children who showed signs of being left-handed to write with their right hands. (Rubin et al., *Psychology*, p. 59.)

Topic Sentence a. Left-handed people tend to be more creative than right-handed people; nevertheless, the world has been organized to suit right-handers rather than left-handers.

          b. Although some very gifted people have been left-handers, left-handed people have a reputation for being clumsy or awkward.

4. The topaz, a yellow gemstone, is the birthstone of those born in November. It is said to be under the influence of the planets Saturn and Mars. In the twelfth century, the stone was used as a charm against evil spirits, and it was claimed that a person could drive off evil powers by hanging a topaz over his or her left arm. According to Hindu tradition, the stone is bitter and cold. If worn above the heart, it is said to keep away thirst. Christian tradition viewed the topaz as a symbol of honor, while the fifteenth-century Romans thought the stone could calm the winds and destroy evil spirits.

Topic Sentence a. There are many superstitions associated with the topaz.

          b. The superstitions surrounding the topaz are yet another example of human stupidity.

5. For the record, no mushroom has ever attacked a person, even when provoked. Touching mushrooms does not produce poisoning, rashes, or warts. And of the thousands of North American mushroom species, only six are known to be deadly. Many dozens are edible, and many thousands are strikingly beautiful. All are ecologically* important, giving back nutrients to the earth and enhancing the lives of trees, herbs, and flowers. (Montgomery, *Nature's Everyday Mysteries*, pp. 81–82.)

---

*ecologically: having to do with the relationship between organisms and their environment.

Topic Sentence a. For the most part, mushrooms are both beautiful and beneficial.

b. Most people are afraid of eating wild mushrooms, but they shouldn't be.

■ EXERCISE 2

DIRECTIONS Read each paragraph. On the blank lines that follow, write a topic sentence that sums up the main idea implied by the paragraph.

EXAMPLE The plant known as Kudzu was introduced to the South in the 1920s. At the time, it promised to be a boon* to farmers who needed a cheap and abundant food crop for pigs, goats, and cattle. However, within half a century, kudzu had overrun seven million acres of land, and many patches of the plant had developed root systems weighing up to three hundred pounds. Currently, no one really knows how to keep kudzu under control, and it's creating problems for everyone from boaters to farmers.

Topic Sentence *Intended to help farmers, kudzu has proven to be more harmful than beneficial.*

EXPLANATION At the beginning of the paragraph, the author tells readers that in the 1920s kudzu was viewed as a help to farmers. However, by the end of the paragraph, the author tells us what a pest the plant has become. Thus, it makes sense that the implied main idea unites these two different perspectives on kudzu.

1. For football and baseball players, the mid-twenties are usually the years of peak performance. Professional bowlers, however, are in their prime in their mid-thirties. Writers tend to do their best work in their forties and fifties, while philosophers and politicians seem to reach their peak even later, after their early sixties. (Adapted from Coon, *Essentials of Psychology*, p. 139.)

Topic Sentence _____

_____

2. The webs of some spiders contain drops of glue that hold the spiders' prey fast. Other webs contain a kind of natural Velcro that tangles and grabs the legs of insects. Then, too, spiderwebs don't always

---

*boon: benefit, favor.

function simply as traps. Some webs also act as lures. Garden spiders use a special silk that makes their intricate decorations stand out, and experiments have shown that the decorated parts attract more insects. Other kinds of spiders, like the spitting spider, use their webs as weapons. The web is pulled taut to snap shut when a fly enters.

Topic Sentence _____

_____

3. The day you learned of your acceptance to college was probably filled with great excitement. No doubt you shared the good news and your future plans with family and friends. Your thoughts may have turned to being on your own, making new friends, and developing new skills. Indeed, most people view college as a major pathway to fulfilling their highest aspirations. However, getting accepted may have caused you to wonder: What will I study? How will I decide on a major? Will I do the amount of studying that college requires? Will I be able to earn acceptable grades? (Adapted from Williams and Long, *Manage Your Life*, p. 157.)

Topic Sentence _____

_____

4. Every year the scene is so unchanging I could act it out in my sleep. In front of the Hayden Planetarium on a muggy Saturday morning, several dozen parents gather to wave goodbye to their boys as the bus ferries them off for eight weeks of camp. First-time campers are clutchy. Old-timers are cocky. My own sons fret at length about carsickness. Then the parents give the kids a final hug and shuffle sullenly back to their depopulated urban nests. But not this year. When the bus pushed out of the planetarium's circular driveway four Saturdays ago, at last removing the waving boys at the tinted windows completely from our view, one parent interrupted the usual hush by very tentatively* starting to clap. Then other parents joined in, first clapping and finally laughing uproariously. (Frank Rich, "Back to Camp," *New York Times,* July 22, 1995, p. 19.)

Topic Sentence _____

_____

_____
*tentatively: hesitantly, shyly.

5. In the nineteenth century, when white settlers moved into territory inhabited by Navajo and other tribal peoples, the settlers took much more than they needed simply to survive. They cut open the earth to remove tons of minerals, cut down forests for lumber to build homes, dammed the rivers, and plowed the soil to grow crops to sell at distant markets. The Navajo did not understand why white people urged them to adopt these practices and improve their lives by creating material wealth. When told he must grow crops for profit, a member of the Comanche tribe (who, like the Navajo, believed in the order of the natural environment) replied, "The earth is my mother. Do you give me an iron plow to wound my mother's breast? Shall I take a scythe* and cut my mother's hair?" (Norton et al., *A People and a Nation*, p. 499.)

Topic Sentence _____

_____

CHECK YOUR UNDERSTANDING

Explain the difference between an appropriate and an inappropriate inference.

_____

_____

_____

Inferring the Main Idea in Longer Readings

Longer readings, particularly those in textbooks, generally include thesis statements that express in words the main idea or thought of the entire reading. However, even writers of textbooks occasionally imply a thesis statement rather than explicitly stating it. When this happens, you need to respond much as you did to paragraphs without a topic sentence. Look at what the author actually says and ask what inference can be drawn from those statements. That inference is your *implied thesis statement.*

---

*scythe: a sharp curved knife used to cut wheat.

To illustrate, here's a reading that lacks a thesis statement, yet still suggests a main idea:

J. Edgar Hoover and the FBI

1 Established in 1908, the Federal Bureau of Investigation (FBI) was initially quite restricted in its ability to fight crime. It could investigate only a few offenses like bankruptcy fraud and antitrust violations, and it could not cross state lines in pursuit of felons. It was the passage of the Mann Act in 1910 that began the Bureau's rise to real power. According to the Mann Act, the Bureau could now cross state lines in pursuit of women being used for "immoral purposes" such as prostitution. Prior to the Mann Act, the Bureau had been powerless once a felon crossed a state line; now at least the FBI could pursue those engaged in immoral acts.

2 It was, however, the appointment of J. Edgar Hoover in 1924 that truly transformed the Bureau. Hoover insisted that all FBI agents had to have college degrees and undergo intensive training at a special school for FBI agents. He also lobbied* long and hard for legislation that would allow the Bureau to cross state lines in pursuit of all criminals. He got his wish in 1934 with the Fugitive Felon Act, which made it illegal for a felon to escape by crossing state lines. Thanks to Hoover's intensive efforts, the way was now open for the FBI to become a crack crime-fighting force with real power.

3 And fight crime the agency did. Its agents played key roles in the investigation and capture of notorious criminals from the thirties, among them John Dillinger, Clyde Barrow, Bonnie Parker, Baby Face Nelson, Pretty Boy Floyd, and the boss of all bosses— Al Capone.

4 In 1939, impressed by the FBI's performance under Hoover, President Franklin D. Roosevelt assigned the FBI full responsibility for investigating matters related to the possibility of espionage by the German government. In effect, Roosevelt gave Hoover a mandate* to investigate any groups he considered suspicious. This new responsibility led to the investigation and arrest of several spies. Unfortunately, J. Edgar Hoover did not limit himself to wartime spying activities. Instead, he continued his investigations long after World War II had ended and Germany had been defeated.

5 Suspicious by nature, Hoover saw enemies of the United States everywhere, and his investigations cast a wide net. In secret, the

*lobbied: worked to influence government officials.
*mandate: legal right.

agency went after the leaders of student and civil rights groups. Even esteemed civil rights leader Martin Luther King Jr. was under constant surveillance by the FBI. FBI investigation techniques during this period included forging documents, burglarizing offices, opening private mail, conducting illegal wire taps, and spreading false rumors about sexual or political misconduct. It wasn't until Hoover's death in 1972 that the FBI's secret files on America's supposed "enemies" were made public and these investigations shut down.[2]

Look for a sentence or group of sentences that sum up this reading, and you're not going to find them. There is no one thesis statement that sums up J. Edgar Hoover's positive *and* negative effect on the FBI. It's up to the reader to infer one like the following: "J. Edgar Hoover was a powerful influence on the FBI. Although he did some good, he also tarnished the agency's reputation and image." This implied thesis statement neatly fits the contents of the reading without relying on any outside information not supplied by the author. It is also not contradicted by anything said in the reading itself. In short, it meets the criteria of an appropriate inference.

Exercise 3

DIRECTIONS Read the following selections. Then circle the letter of the thesis statement that more effectively sums up the implied main idea of the entire reading.

The Hermits of Harlem

1 On March 21, 1947, a man called the 122nd Street police station in New York City and claimed that there was a dead body at 2078 Fifth Avenue. The police were familiar with the house, a decaying three-story brownstone in a run-down part of Harlem. It was the home of Langley and Homer Collyer, two lonely recluses* famous in the neighborhood for their odd but seemingly harmless ways.

2 Homer was blind and crippled by rheumatism. Distrustful of doctors, he wouldn't let anybody but Langley come near him. Using his dead father's medical books, Langley devised a number of odd cures for his brother's ailments, including massive doses of orange juice and peanut butter. When he wasn't dabbling in medicine, Langley liked to invent things, like machines to clean the inside of pianos or intricately wired burglar alarms.

---

[2](Information drawn from Adler, Mueller, and Laufer, *Criminal Justice*, pp. 146–147.)
*recluses: people who live alone, cut off from others.

3   When the police responded to the call by breaking into the Collyers' home, they were astonished and horrified. The room was filled from floor to ceiling with objects of every shape, size, and kind. It took them several hours to cross the few feet to where the dead body of Homer lay, shrouded in an ancient checkered bathrobe. There was no sign of Langley, and the authorities began to search for him.

4   When they found him, he was wearing a strange collection of clothes that included an old jacket, a red flannel bathrobe, several pairs of trousers, and blue overalls. An onion sack was tied around his neck; another was draped over his shoulders. Langley had died some time *before* his brother. He had suffocated under a huge pile of garbage that had cascaded down upon him.

5   On several occasions, thieves had tried to break in to steal the fortune that was rumored to be kept in the house. Langley had responded by building booby traps, intricate systems of trip wires and ropes that would bring tons of rubbish crashing down on any unwary intruder. But in the dim light of his junk-filled home, he had sprung one of his own traps and died some days before his brother. Homer, blind, paralyzed, and totally dependent on Langley, had starved to death.[3]

Thesis Statement (a.) In the end, the Collyer brothers' eccentric and reclusive ways led to their death.

b. The Collyer brothers' deaths were probably suicides.

EXPLANATION In this case, *a* is the more appropriate inference because statements in the reading suggest that the brothers' eccentricity contributed to their deaths. It was, for example, a trap of Langley's own devising that killed him. However, there is no evidence that either of the brothers chose to die.

1. Frustration

1 **External frustrations** are based on conditions outside of the individual that impede progress toward a goal. All of the following are external frustrations: getting stuck with a flat tire, having a marriage proposal rejected, finding the cupboard bare when you go to get your poor dog a bone, finding the refrigerator bare when you go to get your poor tummy a T-bone, finding the refrigerator gone when you return home, being chased out of the house by your

---

[3]Adams and Riley, "Hermits of Harlem," *Facts and Fallacies*. Pleasantville, N.Y.: Reader's Digest Association, 1988, p. 226.

starving dog. In other words, external frustrations are based on *delay, failure, rejection, loss,* and other direct blocking of motives.

2   **Personal frustrations** are based on personal characteristics. If you are four feet tall and aspire to be a professional basketball player, you very likely will be frustrated. If you want to go to medical school, but can earn only D grades, you will likewise be frustrated. In both examples, frustration is actually based on personal limitations. Yet, failure may be *perceived* as externally caused.

3   Whatever the type of frustration, if it persists over time, it's likely to lead to aggression. The frustration-aggression link is so common, in fact, that experiments are hardly necessary to show it. A glance at almost any newspaper will provide examples such as the following:

> **Justifiable Autocide**
>
> BURIEN, Washington (AP)—Barbara Smith committed the assault, but police aren't likely to press charges. Her victim was a 1964 Oldsmobile that failed to start once too often.
>
> When Officer Jim Fuda arrived at the scene, he found one beat-up car, a broken baseball bat, and a satisfied 23-year-old Seattle woman.
>
> "I feel good," Ms. Smith reportedly told the officer. "That car's been giving me misery for years and I killed it."
>
> (As quoted in Coon, *Essentials of Psychology,* p. 419.)

Thesis Statement   a.   External frustration is the more painful type of frustration, and it frequently leads to aggressive feelings and actions.

b.   Although there are two different types of frustration, both can, if they persist, lead to aggressive behavior.

2. Children Having Children

1   Like other sixteen-year-olds, Gail thinks about her clothes, her friends, and getting her homework done. But Gail has to think about something else that most sixteen-year-olds do not: her six-month-old daughter. Gail is one of more than a million teenagers in the United States who get pregnant each year. Many of these girls will raise their baby as a single parent (Children's Defense Fund, 1989).

2   Today, few pregnant teenagers opt for adoption, in part because of greater acceptance of single parents (Rickel, 1989). For a girl uncertain about her identity and future, a baby can seem a "solution" to teenage dilemmas. "I want to have the baby," said one teenage mother. "It would be my own. Something that was mine and would love me" (Kaser, Kolb, & Shephard, 1988). The

girls most likely to become single parents are those who are doing poorly in school, have low self-esteem and aspirations, and grow up in poor single-parent families (Furstenberg, Brooks-Gunn, & Chase-Lansdale, 1989).

3   The teen mother is thrust prematurely into adult responsibilities. "This is harder than I thought it would be," a fifteen-year-old confided. "My mother can't always take care of [the baby], and my friends don't want him around" (Kaser, Kolb, & Shephard, 1989). Compared to their peers who delay parenthood, teenage girls who become pregnant are more likely to drop out of school, to require public assistance, to have more children, and to have poor job prospects.

4   The children of the young single mothers often have problems in school, in their social relationships, and with the law (Furstenberg, Brooks-Gunn, & Chase-Lansdale, 1989). The mother's lack of education, low income, and inexperience as a parent can cause difficulties. For example, adolescent mothers tend to talk to their infants less than older mothers do—perhaps because they don't know that infants benefit from such stimulation.

5   For children to be successful parents, they must grow up a lot faster than their peers. Recently, social programs have been developed to help teenagers—and more are needed. Family-planning and sex-education programs aim at preventing pregnancy. Counseling programs help pregnant teenagers think about their options, which include adoption, abortion, and keeping the baby. Comprehensive programs help teenage mothers stay in school by providing daycare and teaching effective parenting skills. (Rubin et al., *Psychology,* p. 242.)

Thesis Statement a. With the help of new social programs, most teenage mothers are avoiding the problems that plagued them in the past.

  b. Most teenage mothers have a difficult time raising their children.

▱◖◗ **Inferring Details**

In addition to main ideas, writers also expect their readers to read between the lines and infer supporting details. For an illustration, read the following paragraph. Then decide which inference sums up a supporting detail that is suggested but never explicitly stated.

The buzz echoed faintly at first, a tentative, conversational hum vibrating on the back channels of the Internet: "Is it true?" asked a message posted to a public discussion group. "Did the FBI really nail Kevin Mitnick?" It did indeed. In February of 1995, federal law authorities knocked on Mitnick's Raleigh, North Carolina, apartment door at 1:30 in the morning, interrupting his long career as America's most sought after computer bad boy. "The Condor is extinct," moaned another message. The reference is to Mitnick's favorite film, *Three Days of the Condor,* a 1975 Robert Redford movie about a CIA analyst on the run from shadowy forces within the government. The evil at play in Mitnick's case, alleges the FBI, is the thirty-one-year-old hacker's total obsession with burrowing his way into the most secret nerve centers of telephone companies and corporate computer systems. (Vic Sussman, "Gotcha! A Hard-core Hacker Is Nabbed," *U.S. News and World Report,* February 27, 1995, p. 66.)

1. Although he was hunted by the FBI, Kevin Mitnick apparently had at least one fan.

2. When he got caught, Kevin Mitnick was deeply apologetic for all the trouble he had caused.

If you look back at the paragraph, it should be clear that the first inference is appropriate, whereas the second one is not. Support for inference 1 comes from the sentence that tells us that one message "moaned," "The Condor is extinct." The use of the word *moaned* and the word *extinct*—as if Mitnick belonged to an endangered species—suggests that someone felt unhappiness at his capture. However, none of the statements in the paragraph suggests that Mitnick was apologetic for his actions. Because no support for inference 2 can be found, it's not appropriate.

■ EXERCISE 4

DIRECTIONS After reading each paragraph, circle the letter of the implied supporting detail that readers are expected to supply.

EXAMPLE The incidence* of melanoma, the most dangerous and the deadliest form of skin cancer, has nearly doubled in the past ten years. That increase may be due to many factors, including lifestyle changes, migration to the Sunbelt, and better detection, but the depleted ozone layer may also be partly to blame. While it's not clear how much ozone depletion has been responsible for current melanoma cases, there's no doubt that the thinning ozone layer raises

---

*incidence: the extent, or frequency, of an occurrence.

the future risk of skin cancer. (Adapted from *Consumer Reports,* 1991, p. 51.)

Implied (a.) It's generally believed that the ozone layer will continue to be de-
Supporting Detail pleted.

b. The use of pesticides and industrial pollution will further damage the ozone layer.

EXPLANATION The words *thinning* and *future risk* suggest that the decrease in the ozone layer is an ongoing process that will continue into the future, making *a* the better answer.

1. If we're really interested in saving the environment, and therefore ourselves, there are some not-so-easy things we can and must do. About population: On the personal level, we can stop at two, or one, or none—and learn to love other people's children. On the government level, we can give every couple the knowledge and technology to choose the number of their children, and then give them straight, honest reasons why they should choose no more than two. The U.S. government, which used to be foremost in this field, has essentially stopped funding family planning and population education both domestically and internationally. We need to lean hard on our leaders to reverse that policy. (Donella Meadows, "Four Not-So-Easy Things You Can Do to Save the Planet," *In Context,* No. 26, Summer 1990, p. 9.)

Implied a. Big families are no longer popular in America.
Supporting Detail b. Earth is in danger of being overpopulated.

2. Dr. C. James Mahoney seemed incredulous* as he sat cuddling a four-month-old chimpanzee named Cory. But the reports were true: The highly regarded New York University primate research center* at which the veterinarian had worked for eighteen years was being taken over by a New Mexico foundation charged by federal officials with a long list of violations of animal-welfare laws. The primate center and its 225 chimpanzees were added last week to the holdings of the Coulston Foundation, a research group that already owns or leases 540 other chimpanzees for medical tests. The foundation, based in Alamogordo, New Mexico, now has control of well over half of the chimpanzees used in medical research in the United States. Critics, including Dr. Jane Goodall, who pioneered studies of the

---

*incredulous: stunned, disbelieving.
*primate research center: center that studies the behavior of animals closely related to humans.

endangered species in the wild, claim that the foundation, already cited for the deaths of at least five chimpanzees, cannot possibly care for more. (Andrew C. Revkin, "A Furor over Chimps," *New York Times,* August 13, 1995, p. 2.)

Implied Supporting Detail

a. Dr. C. James Mahoney was stunned at learning that he would soon be out of a job.

b. Dr. C. James Mahoney was stunned by the news that the chimps he had cared for would be turned over to the Coulston Foundation.

3. In the nineteenth century, questions about natural resources caught Americans between the desire for progress and the fear of spoiling the land. By the late 1870s and early 1880s, people eager to protect the natural landscape began to coalesce* into a conservation* movement. Prominent* among them was western naturalist John Muir, who helped establish Yosemite National Park in 1890. The next year, under pressure from Muir and others, Congress authorized President Benjamin Harrison to create forest reserves—public land protected from cutting by private interests. Such policies met with strong objections. Lumber companies, lumber dealers, and railroads were joined in their opposition by householders accustomed to cutting timber freely for fuel and building material. Public opinion on conservation also split along sectional lines. Most supporters of regulation came from the eastern states, where resources had already become less plentiful; opposition was loudest in the West, where people were still eager to take advantage of nature's bounty.* (Norton et al., *A People and a Nation,* p. 509.)

Implied Supporting Detail

a. Because the early conservation movement was led by Easterners, many Westerners did not support it.

b. In the East, the early conservation movement caught on quickly because people there had begun to see firsthand that the country's resources were not endless.

4. Although his armies were all defeated by April of 1865, Jefferson Davis, the leader of the Southern Confederacy, remained in hiding and called for guerrilla* warfare and continued resistance. But one by one, the Confederate officers surrendered to their opponents. On

---

*coalesce: to come or grow together.
*conservation: the act of protecting or preserving.
*prominent: famous.
*bounty: goodness, riches.
*guerrilla: used to characterize warfare waged by small, informal bands of soldiers.

May 10, Davis and the Confederate postmaster were captured near Irwinville, Georgia, and placed in prison. Andrew Johnson, who had assumed the presidency upon Lincoln's death, issued a statement to the American people that armed rebellion against legitimate authority could be considered "virtually at an end." The last Confederate general to lay down his arms was Cherokee leader Stand Watie, who surrendered on June 23, 1865. (Berkin et al., *Making America*, p. 439.)

Implied Supporting Detail
a. Because he did not know his armies were all defeated, Jefferson Davis continued to fight.

b. In the face of defeat, Jefferson Davis would not abandon the Confederate cause.

WORD NOTES

Page 228 introduced the word *incredulous*, meaning "disbelieving," as in "Her story about being abducted by Martians left him *incredulous*." You'll have an easy time remembering this word if you keep in mind that its root, *cred*, means belief. Remember, too, that the prefix *in-* means "not," and the chance of your forgetting the meaning of *incredulous* is slim.

Use context and your knowledge of what the root *cred* means to define the italicized words in the following sentences:

1. Please don't give any *credence* to his claims that ginseng tea can cure cancer.

Credence means: _____

2. The actor gave a very *credible* performance as a man with only a week to live.

Credible means: _____

3. The Amish *creed* is very strict and many young people are rebelling against it, to the great sorrow of their parents.

Creed means: _____

4. Her extraordinary *credulity* cost her dearly when she invested in a diamond mine said to be located in Cleveland.

Credulity means: _____

SUMMING UP ■ **231**

5. Don't be so *credulous;* you will end up losing all your hard-earned savings.

Credulous means: _____

Summing Up

Listed below are the most important points in Chapter 6. Put a check mark in the box if you think the point is clear in your mind. Leave the box blank if you think you need to review the material one more time. The page numbers in parentheses tell you where to look in order to review each point on the list.

☐ **1.** Authors don't always put main ideas of paragraphs into topic sentences. Sometimes they expect readers to read between the lines and infer a topic sentence that sums up the main idea. (p. 214)

☐ **2.** Appropriate inferences are based more on what the author says than on the reader's personal experience or knowledge. Inappropriate inferences do not follow from the author's words and they rely too heavily on the reader's experience and background. (pp. 214–216)

☐ **3.** Authors don't always use thesis statements to express main ideas in longer readings. Sometimes they expect readers to infer a thesis statement that sums up the main idea of the entire reading. (pp. 221–223)

☐ **4.** Like main ideas, supporting details sometimes need to be inferred by the reader. (pp. 226–227)

TEST YOUR UNDERSTANDING

To see how well you have understood this chapter, take the following review quiz. Then correct it using the answer key provided by your instructor. If you score 80 percent or above, you're ready to take the end-of-chapter exam. However, if you score below 80 percent, look over the quiz carefully to see what kinds of questions you missed. Then use the **Summing Up** pages of the chapter to find out which pages you should review before taking the chapter exam.

Copyright © Laraine Flemming. All rights reserved.

Chapter 6: Review Quiz

Part A

DIRECTIONS For each passage, choose the topic sentence that more effectively sums up the implied main idea.

1. Every year desperate, distraught cancer victims travel to the Philippines in the hopes of being cured by people who call themselves "psychic surgeons." These so-called surgeons claim to heal the sick without the use of a knife or anesthesia, and many victims of serious illness look to them for a cure. But curing the sick is not what these surgeons are about. When they operate, they palm* bits of chicken and goat hearts, then they pretend to pull a piece of disease-ridden tissue out of the patient's body. If a crowd is present, and it usually is, the surgeons briefly display the lump of animal tissue and pronounce the poor patient cured. Not surprisingly, psychic surgeons cannot point to many real cures; nevertheless, the desperate and dying still seek them out.

Topic Sentence   a. More people than ever before are flocking to psychic surgeons.

        b. Psychic surgeons are complete frauds.

2. Do you like to watch colorful birds? Then keep your eyes peeled for the gorgeous indigo bunting, with its marbled mix of green, yellow, and blue feathers. Well, at least the male is a fabulous creature; the female is a rather drab brown. If your tastes run to splashes of pure brilliant color, then scan the woods for the scarlet tanager, whose fire-engine-red color is interrupted only by pure black wings. Unless, of course, you're looking at a female, who's a bit on the dowdy side. If you prefer your birds even more flamboyant,* then keep your eyes peeled for the Halloween-colored Baltimore oriole, who likes to hang out around swampy areas. The female is a bit bolder and more inclined to appear at bird feeders. Unfortunately, she's—you guessed it—a drab brown.

Topic Sentence   a. Bird watching has become a more popular hobby than ever before, but unfortunately, it still has a nerdy image.

        b. Among certain birds, only the males are colorful.

3. For a long time, scientists have speculated that birds might actually be descended from dinosaurs; but they haven't had any proof, at

*palm: conceal in one's hand.
*flamboyant: showy, outrageous.

least not until recently. In 1998, diggers in China's fossil-rich earth found dinosaur bones bearing what appeared to be featherlike markings. According to paleontologist Philip Currie, the fossils are the evidence needed to prove the dinosaur-bird connection. However, Larry Martin, a paleontologist at the University of Kansas, is less convinced that the impressions on the bones came from feathers. Still, he, like almost everyone else who tries to reconstruct the past, is anxious to see the new fossils when they go on display. From his point of view, seeing just may be believing.

Topic Sentence a. Although not everyone is convinced, there is now some real evidence suggesting that birds descended from dinosaurs.

  b. Thanks to the discovery of dinosaur bones in China, it's now definite that birds descended from dinosaurs.

4. In the sixties, with the coming of feminism's second wave, many women refused to shave their legs or wear makeup. They were tired, they said, of being valued for their looks. Like men, they wanted to be esteemed* for what they could accomplish. In the nineties, feminism continues its march toward equality, but modern feminists, advocates of what's called "girl power," proudly wear makeup and paint their fingernails. For them, being different from men by being more intensely feminine is their badge of a proud feminist consciousness. Nowadays, the pronouncements of the Spice Girls carry more weight than those of old-time feminist Gloria Steinem.

Topic Sentence a. Feminists in the nineties don't necessarily share the same goals as those of the sixties.

  b. Compared to feminists in the sixties, feminists in the nineties have been much more successful.

5. Between 1845 and 1846, Ireland was hit by a blight that attacked its staple crop, potatoes. As the potatoes rotted in the fields, close to one million people died from starvation, malnutrition, and disease, and an additional million were forced to flee their starving country. Between 1847 and 1854, the United States opened its doors to 1.2 million Irish immigrants. Yet, fearful of this large, new population, many Americans looked to the suffering Irish arrivals with suspicion. All too often, Irish immigrants were confronted by signs that read "No Irish Need Apply," and many wondered if they hadn't made a terrible mistake.

---

*esteemed: respected.

Topic Sentence a. When Irish immigrants arrived in America between 1847 and 1854, they were blamed for everything from poverty to unemployment.

b. Fleeing the catastrophic effects of the potato blight, many Irish immigrants entered the United States between 1847 and 1854, but they did not receive an especially warm welcome.

Part B

DIRECTIONS Read each passage and answer the accompanying questions. To do so, you will need to draw the appropriate inferences.

6. Particular essays and books that contain sexually explicit material or even words that are offensive to certain members of a community have been a great source of legal controversy in schools. In one important case, *Keefe v. Geanakos* (1969), a Massachusetts English teacher, Robert Keefe, assigned his students an article from the well-respected *Atlantic Monthly*. The article contained a particular offensive word. (Hint: The word was *not* "mother beater.") Mr. Keefe's assignment caused a storm, and he was eventually fired for refusing to agree that he would not assign the article again. Subsequently, he was reinstated by a 1969 circuit court decision because the offending word existed in a number of books already in the school library; because the school board had not notified him that such material was prohibited; and, finally, because that court believed that the word was not all that shocking to the students. As the decision stated, "With the greatest respect to such parents, their sensibilities are not the full measure of what is proper education." (Ryan and Cooper, *Those Who Can, Teach,* pp. 166–167.)

a. Who raised a storm of controversy about the article? _____

b. Did the school administration support Mr. Keefe in his choice of

reading matter? _____

Explain your answer: _____

_____

c. Did Mr. Keefe agree that he had made a mistake? _____

Explain your answer: _____

_____

7. Though it is a mere 3 to 5 percent of the population, the upper class possesses at least 25 percent of the nation's wealth. This class has two segments: upper-upper and lower-upper. Basically, the upper-upper class is the "old rich"—families that have been wealthy for several generations—an aristocracy of birth and wealth. Their names are in the *Social Register,* a listing of acceptable members of high society. A few are known across the nation, such as the Rockefellers, Roosevelts, Vanderbilts, and du Ponts. Most are not visible to the general public. They live in grand seclusion, drawing their incomes from the investment of their inherited wealth. In contrast, the lower-upper class is the "new rich," including Bill Gates of Microsoft, Ted Turner of CNN, and Michael Eisner of Disney. Although some of them are wealthier than the old rich, the new rich generally have less prestige because they have hustled to make their money, like everybody else beneath their class. The old rich, who have not found it necessary to "lift a finger" to make their money, tend to look down on the new rich. But the new rich continue to work extremely hard. Bill Gates, for example, puts in seventy-two hours of work a week (Lewis, 1995). (Thio, *Sociology,* p. 228.)

a. How do the old rich feel about mingling with those who are not as rich? _____ _____

Explain your answer: _____

_____

b. Are the old rich ready and willing to welcome the newly rich into their world? _____

Explain your answer: _____

_____

c. Is Bill Gates anxious to enter the world of the old rich? _____

Explain your answer: _____

_____

8. In 1940, a group of Jehovah's Witnesses challenged the law that required compulsory saluting of the flag in public schools. Arguing for the right to religious freedom, they insisted that saluting the flag forced them to worship graven* images and sued the Minersville School District (*Minersville School District v. Gobitis*). Ultimately,

_____

*graven: sculpted or carved.

the case went before the Supreme Court, and the Witnesses lost. The reaction in Minersville and elsewhere was both swift and brutal: The Gobitises were jeered at on the street, their children were beaten up at school, and local churches led a boycott of the family business. In other communities, the Jehovah's Witnesses fared even worse. They were forced to swallow castor oil; others were tarred, feathered, and even castrated for following the dictates of their faith.

a. Why were the Gobitis children beaten?

_____

b. Once they lost their case, did the Jehovah's Witnesses in and around Minersville begin saluting the flag? _____

Explain your answer: _____

_____

c. Did the local churches sympathize with the Gobitis's religious beliefs? _____

Explain your answer: _____

_____

Part C

DIRECTIONS Circle the letter of the thesis statement that sums up the implied main idea of the entire reading.

9. Explaining the Growth of the Bureaucracy*

1 What accounts for the growth of bureaucracies and bureaucrats since the late 1800s? Was all this growth the result of bureaucratic incompetence and unresponsiveness? Many observers believe that the growth can be attributed directly to the expansion of the nation itself. There are a great many more of us—more than 248 million in 1990, compared with fewer than 5 million in the 1790s—and we are living closer together. Not only do the residents of cities and suburbs require many more services than did the predominantly rural dwellers of the early 1800s, but the challenges of urban and industrial life have intensified and outstripped the capacity of families or local and state governments to cope with them. Thus the American people have increasingly turned to their national government for help.

_____

*bureaucracy: management of a government through bureaus or departments staffed by nonelected officials.

2   There is considerable evidence that the growth of bureaucracies is "of our own making." Public opinion polls indicate widespread public support for expanding federal involvement in a variety of areas. Even when public support for new programs is low, pollsters find Americans unwilling to eliminate or reduce existing programs. Furthermore, the public's expectations about the quality of service it should receive are constantly rising. The public wants government to be more responsive, responsible, and compassionate in administering public programs. Officials have reacted to these pressures by establishing new programs and maintaining and improving existing ones.

3   The federal bureaucracy has also expanded in response to sudden changes in economic, social, cultural, and political conditions. During the Great Depression and World War II, for example, the federal bureaucracy grew to meet the challenges these situations created. Washington became more and more involved in programs providing financial aid and employment to the poor. It increased its regulation of important industries and during the war imposed controls over much of the American economy. As part of the general war effort, the federal government also built roads and hospitals and mobilized the entire population. When these crises ended, the public was reluctant to give up many of the federal welfare and economic programs implemented during the time of emergency. (Alan R. Gitelson, Robert L. Dudley, and Melvin J. Dubrick, *American Government*. Boston: Houghton Mifflin, 1998, p. 358.)

Thesis Statement   a. Bureaucracies are simply a fact of modern life, and there is no escaping them.

b. At least three different factors account for the growth of bureaucracies.

10. **Holiday Cheer**

1 The observance of public school holidays began around the turn of the century. The goal of school holidays, at that time at least, was to bring people together. Holiday celebrations in the schools—particularly Christmas—were meant to unite a nation of immigrants. But as Bob Dylan would say, "The Times They Are a-Changin'."

2   In Chicago, the principal of the Walt Disney Magnet School saw his attempt at holiday harmony backfire. This elementary school has a mix of students, including black, Asian, Muslim, Hispanic, Yugoslavian, Romanian, and Jewish children, so the principal

tried to tone down Christmas by issuing a ban on Santa Claus and any other symbols or activities associated with "a specific religious tradition." Teachers protested—one gave the principal a copy of *How the Grinch Stole Christmas*—and the head of the school board overturned the ban. With Christmas parties, decorations, and carols in full swing throughout the school, Essam Ammar, a Muslim parent, asked, "How am I going to raise my children as proud Muslims with all this going on?"

3   As passions intensify over how to celebrate the holiday season, some parents are demanding that a wide variety of other religious and ethnic holidays, including the Hindu Diwali festival, Hanukkah, and Kwanzaa, get equal time with Christmas. Others protest any diminution* of Christmas traditions, such as bans on trees and Santa Claus in some communities. At the moment, there seems to be no resolution in sight.

Thesis Statement a. Celebrating the holiday season in public schools began as an effort to bring together people who might otherwise stay separated.

b. Observing the holidays in public schools has become far more complicated than it once was as different ethnic groups compete to celebrate their particular holiday.

Use the answer key provided by your instructor to correct your quiz. If you score 80 percent or above, you are ready to do the chapter exam. If you score below 80 percent, look carefully at the questions you answered incorrectly. Then use the **Summing Up** section to decide which pages you need to review.

---

*diminution: act of decreasing.

⚡ Chapter Test 6

Part A

DIRECTIONS After reading each paragraph, circle the letter of the topic sentence that more effectively expresses the implied main idea.

 1. In one study, done in the early 1970s when young people tended to dress in either "hippie" or "straight" fashion, experimenters donned hippie or straight attire and asked college students on campus for a dime to make a phone call. When the experimenter was dressed in the same way as the student, the request was granted in more than two-thirds of the instances; when the student and requester were dissimilarly dressed, the dime was provided less than half the time (Emswiller, Deaux, & Willits, 1971). In another experiment, marchers in an antiwar demonstration were found to be more likely to sign the petition of a similarly dressed requester *and* to do so without bothering to read it first. (Cialdini, *Influence*, p. 164.)

Topic Sentence a. The results of two different studies suggest that people don't necessarily read the petitions they sign.

b. The results of two different studies suggest that we are more likely to help those who dress the way we do.

 2. Some people choose to handle conflict by engaging in **avoidance,** or not confronting the conflict at all. They simply put up with the situation, no matter how unpleasant it may be. While seemingly unproductive, avoidance may actually be useful if the situation is short-term or of minor importance. If, however, the problem is really bothering you or is persistent, then it should be dealt with. Avoiding the issue often uses up a great deal of energy without resolving the aggravating situation. Very seldom do avoiders feel that they have been in a win-win situation. Avoiders usually lose a chunk of their self-respect since they so clearly downplay their own concerns in favor of the other person's. (Roy Berko, Andrew D. Wolvin, and Darlyn Wolvin, *Communicating*. Boston: Houghton Mifflin, 1992, p. 248.)

Topic Sentence a. Avoiding conflict is a bad strategy for dealing with life's problems; it's often better to meet problems head-on.

b. Although avoiding conflict can be effective in some situations, it's an ineffective strategy when the problem is persistent.

 3. To be a compelling speaker, you must work to be vivid in your presentation. Good descriptions, a colorful choice of language, and a lively style can all encourage listeners to pay attention to your message. For example, a speaker addressing a group of potential airline flight attendants can stress the importance of cabin safety with some vivid descriptions of past accidents. Humor is another useful speaking strategy. If relevant and in good taste, humor can gain and keep the listeners' attention. It may also allow them to relax. Humor was creatively used by a minister who was asked how long a good sermon should be: "I use one rule," he said. "The mind can only absorb what the seat can endure." In trying to keep your audience's attention, you may also wish to use the device of novelty—treating a subject in a unique fashion. One speaker, for instance, used novelty when he started a speech by saying, "I'm much like you in many ways. I have two arms, two legs, two hands, two eyes, and two ears. I'm different from you, however, because I'm on methadone. You see, I'm a heroin addict." (Berko et al., *Communicating*, p. 387.)

Topic Sentence a. Good speakers use a variety of techniques to keep their listeners' attention.

b. Good speakers are hard to find, and it's unusual to hear a speech that isn't boring.

4. The first thing any potential candidate for president must achieve is name recognition. This was certainly the task facing Jimmy Carter in 1976. Carter was so little known that he referred to himself as "Jimmy Who." Almost twenty years later, an Arkansas governor named William Jefferson Clinton had the same problem and managed to overcome it. But once a presidential candidate solves the name-recognition problem, he still has to establish his credibility as a contender. This was the task of Republican John Connally of Texas in 1980 and of Democrat John Glenn in 1984. And yes, Bill Clinton ran up against the same obstacle in 1992. Ultimately, Clinton managed to make himself a credible contender, whereas Connally and Glenn could not.

Topic Sentence a. Bill Clinton managed to overcome the two obstacles facing any presidential candidate.

b. Like Jimmy Carter, Bill Clinton began his campaign for president as a relative unknown.

Part B

DIRECTIONS After reading each passage, identify the supporting details the writer expects readers to infer.

5. Debates about human nature are always fascinating. But what initially inspired social psychologists to study the nature of helping were hair-raising stories about bystanders who fail to take action even when someone else's life is in danger. The problem first made headlines in March 1964. Kitty Genovese was walking home from work in Queens, New York, at 3:20 in the morning. As she crossed the street from her car to her apartment, a man with a knife appeared. She ran, but he caught up and stabbed her. Genovese cried frantically for help and screamed, "Oh my God, he stabbed me! . . . I'm dying, I'm dying!"—but to no avail. The man fled but then returned, raped her, and stabbed her eight more times, until she was dead. In the still of the night, the attack lasted for over half an hour. Thirty-eight neighbors heard the screams, turned lights on, and came to their windows. One couple even pulled chairs up to their window and turned out the light to see better. Yet nobody came down to help. Until it was over, nobody even called the police. (Kassin, *Social Psychology,* pp. 509–510.)

The author expects readers to infer that the story of Kitty Genovese

illustrates the problem of _____

_____

6. In 1963, Martin Luther King Jr. sought to increase the support of the movement for civil rights. In May, he helped organize demonstrations for the end of segregation in Birmingham, Alabama. The protesters found the perfect enemy in Birmingham's police commissioner, Eugene "Bull" Connor, whose beefy features and snarling demeanor made him a living symbol of everything evil. Connor's police used clubs, dogs, and fire hoses to chase and arrest the demonstrators. President John F. Kennedy watched the police dogs in action on television with the rest of the country and confessed that the brutality made him sick. He later observed that "the civil rights movement should thank God for Bull Connor. He's helped it as much as Abraham Lincoln." As a result of the demonstrations, the president sent the head of the Justice Department's civil rights division to Birmingham to try to work out an arrangement between King's demonstrators and business leaders that would permit desegregation of lunch counters, drinking fountains, and bathrooms.

The president also made several calls to the business leaders himself, and they finally agreed to his terms. (Schaller et al., *Present Tense*, p. 235.)

The authors never explain why President Kennedy thought Bull Connor actually helped the civil rights movement. Instead, they expect you to infer that Connor helped the movement by _____

_____

7. During a national address focusing on civil rights, President John F. Kennedy acknowledged that the nation faced a moral crisis. He rejected the notion that the United States could be the land of the free "except for the Negroes." Reversing his earlier reluctance to request civil rights legislation, he announced that he would send Congress a major civil rights bill. The law would guarantee service to all Americans regardless of race in public accommodations—hotels, restaurants, theaters, retail stores, and similar establishments. Moreover, it would grant the federal government greater authority to pursue lawsuits against segregation in public education and increase the Justice Department's powers to protect the voting rights of racial minorities. (Schaller et al., *Present Tense*, p. 236.)

The authors do not specifically define the moral crisis facing the nation. Instead they expect you to infer that _____

_____

was the cause of a moral crisis in America.

8. On Christmas Day, 1859, the ship HMS *Lightning* arrived at Melbourne, Australia, with about a dozen wild European rabbits bound for an estate in western Victoria. Within three years, the rabbits had started to spread, after a bushfire destroyed the fences enclosing one colony. From a slow start at first, the spread of the rabbits picked up speed during the 1870s, and by 1900 the rabbit was the most serious agricultural pest ever known in Australia. Rabbits eat grass, the same grass used by sheep and cattle, and so quickly the cry went up: "Get rid of the rabbit!" The subsequent history of control attempts in Australia is a sad tale of ecological ignorance. Millions of rabbits were poisoned and shot at great expense with absolutely no effect on their numbers. Nowhere else has the introduction of an exotic species had such an enormous impact and spotlighted the folly of the introduction experiment. *Act in haste, and repent at leisure.* (Adapted from Krebs, *The Message of Ecology*, p. 8.)

Although the author does not specifically say how the rabbits got off the estate, he expects you to infer that they _____

_____

Part C

DIRECTIONS Circle the letter of the thesis statement that sums up the implied main idea of the entire reading.

9. **Improving Your Memory**

1 Do you, like just about everyone else, want to improve your memory? Well, the good news is that you can. All you have to do is put the following advice into practice, and you'll see immediate results.

2   For example, remembering when Christopher Columbus discovered America is easy enough if you use visualization. You could, for example, imagine Columbus standing on the beach with his ships in the harbor in the background. Fortunately, unrealistic images work just as well or better, and you could imagine Columbus's boat having the large numerals *1492* printed on its side, or Columbus reviewing his account books after the trip and seeing in dismay that the trip cost him $1,492. You could even envisage something still more fanciful: Since 1492 sounds like the phrase "for tea, nightie two," you might imagine Columbus serving tea in his nightie to two Indians on the beach. A weird image like this is often easier to remember than a realistic one because its silliness makes it more distinct (Levin, 1985).

3   Visual imagery also works well for remembering single terms, such as unfamiliar words in a foreign language. The French word for snail, *l'escargot,* can be remembered easily if you form an image of what the word sounds like in English—"less cargo"—and picture an event related to this English equivalent, such as workmen dumping snails overboard to achieve "less cargo" on a boat. The biological term *mitosis* (which refers to cell division) sounds like the phrase "my toes itch," so it is easier to remember if you picture a single cell dividing while scratching its imaginary toes.

4   Another device for memory improvement is called the method of loci, or locations. With this method, you purposely associate objects or terms with a highly familiar place or building. Suppose you have to remember the names of all of the instruments in a standard symphony orchestra. Using the method of loci, choose a familiar place, such as the neighborhood in which you live, and

imagine leaving one of the instruments at the doorstep of each house or business in the neighborhood. To remember the instruments, simply take an imaginary walk through the neighborhood, mentally picking up each instrument as you come upon it.

5   Research on loci has found the method effective for remembering a wide variety of information (Christen and Bjork, 1976). The same loci, or locations, can work repeatedly on many sets of terms or objects without one set interfering with another. After memorizing the musical instruments in the above example, you could still use your neighborhood to remember the names of exotic fruit, without fear of accidentally "seeing" a musical instrument by mistake. Loci can also help in recalling terms that are not physical objects, such as scientific concepts. Simply imagine the terms in some visual form, such as written on cards, or, better yet, visualize concrete objects that rhyme with each term and leave these around the mental neighborhood.

6   Imagery and visual loci work for two reasons (Pressley and McDaniel, 1988). First, they force you to organize new information, even if the organization is self-imposed. Second, they encourage you to elaborate mentally on new information. In "placing" musical instruments around the neighborhood, you have to think about what each instrument looks like and how it relates to the others in a symphony. These mental processes are essential for moving information into long-term memory. (Adapted from Kevin L. Seifert, *Educational Psychology*. Boston: Houghton Mifflin, 1991, pp. 199–201.)

Thesis Statement a. Visual imagery and the method of loci are two strategies for improving memory.

   b. Visual imagery is the most effective method available for remembering new words from a foreign language.

10. **Remembrance of Things Past**

1 A whiff of perfume, the top of a baby's head, freshly cut grass, a locker room, the musty odor of a basement, the floury aroma of a bakery, the smell of mothballs in the attic, and the leathery scent of a new car—each may trigger what Diane Ackerman (1990) has called "aromatic memories." Frank Schab (1990) tested this theory in a series of experiments. In one, subjects were given a list of adjectives and instructed to write an antonym, or word opposite in meaning, for each adjective. In half of the sessions, the sweet smell of chocolate was blown into the room. The next day, subjects were asked to list as many of the antonyms as they could—

again, in the presence or absence of the chocolate aroma. As it turned out, the most words were recalled when the smell of chocolate was present at both the learning and the recall sessions. The reason? The smell was stored in the memory right along with the words, so it later served as a retrieval cue.

2 The retrieval of memories is influenced by factors other than smell. In an unusual study, Duncan Godden and Alan Baddeley (1975) presented deep-sea divers with a list of words in one of two settings: fifteen feet underwater or on the beach. Then they tested the divers' recall in the same or another setting. Illustrating what is called *context-dependent memory*, the divers recalled 40 percent more words when the material was learned and retrieved in the same context. The practical implications are intriguing. For example, recall may be improved if material is retrieved in the same room in which it was initially learned (Smith, 1979).

3 Indeed, context seems to activate memory even in three-month-old infants. In a series of studies, Carolyn Rovee-Collier and her colleagues (1992) trained infants to shake an overhead mobile equipped with colorful blocks and bells by kicking a leg that was attached to the mobile by a ribbon. The infants were later more likely to recall what they learned (in other words, to kick) when tested in the same crib and looking at the same visual cues than when there were differences. Apparently, it is possible to jog one's memory by reinstating the initial context of an experience. This explains why I will often march into my secretary's office for something, go blank, forget why I was there, return in defeat to my office, look around, and ZAP!, suddenly recall what it was I needed.

4 Studies also reveal that it is often easier to recall something when our state of mind is the same at testing as it was while we were learning. If information is acquired when you are happy, sad, drunk, sober, calm, or aroused, that information is more likely to be retrieved under the same conditions (Bower, 1981; Eich, 1980; Eich et al., 1994). The one key complicating factor is that the mood we're in leads us to evoke memories that fit our current mood. When we are happy, the good times are most easy to recall; but when we feel depressed or anxious, our minds become flooded with negative events of the past (Blaney, 1986; Ucros, 1989). (Adapted from Kassin, *Social Psychology*, p. 231.)

Thesis Statement a. Research shows that smell is one of the most important factors affecting the retrieval of information from memory.

       b. The retrieval of memories is influenced by at least three different factors: smell, context, and state of mind.

CHAPTER 7

Defining the Terms *Fact* and *Opinion*

In this chapter you'll learn

- **how to tell the difference between** *fact* **and** *opinion.*

- **how to recognize statements that stir opinion into fact.**

- **how to distinguish between** *informed* **and** *uninformed* **opinions.**

- **how to identify opinions backed by** *circular reasoning* **and** *irrelevant facts.*

- **how to determine the right balance of fact and opinion in textbooks.**

The goal of Chapter 7 is to ensure that you have a clear understanding of the terms *fact* and *opinion.* Once you understand exactly what these two terms mean, you'll be in

a better position to evaluate how well or poorly an author uses facts to buttress, or support, opinions readers might question.

Distinguishing Between Fact and Opinion

Statements of **fact** provide information about people, places, events, and ideas that can be **verified,** or checked, for accuracy. Facts do not reveal the author's personal **perspective,** or point of view. The following are all statements of fact:

- American Samoa consists of seven islands in the South Pacific.
- The Treaty of Versailles ended World War I.
- For his work on atomic structure, scientist Niels Bohr was awarded the Nobel Prize in physics in 1922.
- John Wilkes Booth assassinated Abraham Lincoln on April 14, 1865.

These facts can be checked in encyclopedias or other reference books in libraries anywhere in the world and they will always be the same. Facts do not vary with place or person. Whether you live in Dayton, Ohio, or Fairbanks, Alaska, if you look up Martin Luther King Jr.'s date of birth, it will always be the same: January 15, 1929.

Troubling Facts

Because facts can be checked, they are generally not subject to question or argument. However, statements of fact can be questioned if they are not widely known. For example, it's a fact that the Native-American leader Black Elk publicly criticized the book bearing his name, *Black Elk Speaks.* But that fact is not generally known and therefore could be questioned, particularly by those who admired the book.

Then, too, facts can and do change over a period of time as new discoveries or methods of research come to light. This is especially true in fields like science, history, and medicine, where information is considered factual only insofar as it is based on existing levels of knowledge. As scientists and historians gain a more precise knowledge of the world, the facts on which they base their theories sometimes undergo a dramatic change.

For example, it was once considered a fact that the Sun revolved around Earth. But in the sixteenth century, a Polish astronomer named Nicolaus Copernicus used the laws of planetary motion to challenge that "fact." Copernicus proved that, *in fact*, Earth revolves around the Sun.

Generally, however, facts are fixed pieces of information. They often consist of dates, names, and statistics, and thus cannot be affected by the writer's background or training. Facts can be **verified**, or checked, and *proved* accurate or inaccurate, true or false, to the satisfaction of most people. Thus, unless they are newly discovered, they are not often the subject of disagreement.

Statements of Fact

- can be checked for accuracy or correctness.
- can be proved true or false.
- are not affected by the writer's background or training.
- rely heavily on names, dates, and statistics.
- are not usually the subject of argument.

Calling It a Fact Doesn't Necessarily Make It One

Because people tend to accept facts without giving them too much thought, some writers and speakers preface opinions with the phrase "the fact is," as in the following sentence: "*The fact is* that Richard Nixon, had he not resigned, would have been impeached." Despite the opening phrase, this statement really is an opinion, and not everyone would agree with it. In effect, what the author tries to do is bully you into agreeing that the statement is an indisputable, or unquestionable, fact when it's anything but. Similarly, beware of the phrase "it's a fact that." This phrase is often used to discourage readers or listeners from thinking critically about a writer's or speaker's claims.

Opinions

Statements of **opinion** reflect the writer's perspective on the subject discussed. Shaped by an author's personal experience, training, and background, opinions on the same subject can vary from person to person, group to group, and place to place. For an illustration, ask a group of teenagers how they feel about high school dress codes. Then ask their parents. Don't be surprised if you uncover a marked difference of opinion.

Unlike facts, opinions cannot be verified with outside sources.

They are too **subjective**—too personal—to be checked in reference books or historical records. The following are all statements of opinion:

- Babyface is an artist of extraordinary talent.
- Thanks to cellist Yo-Yo Ma, the glorious music of Argentinian Astor Piazzolla is now more widely known.
- Killing animals for sport is wrong, and hunters should be ashamed of themselves.
- This country needs stricter gun control laws.

Because opinions are so heavily influenced by one's training, knowledge, and experience, it's impossible to talk about them as accurate or inaccurate, right or wrong. For example, if you own a dog and firmly believe that dogs are more desirable pets than cats, no cat lover can prove you wrong. That's your opinion, and you have a right to it.

Still, that doesn't mean that opinions cannot be judged or evaluated. They most certainly can. Critical readers want and need to distinguish between informed and uninformed opinions. **Informed opinions** are backed by evidence; **uninformed opinions** lack adequate evidence. Once you can distinguish between the two, you'll be surprised at how often writers give their opinions without bothering to support them. So yes, the old saying is true: Everyone has the right to an opinion. But it's also true that every opinion does not deserve the same consideration or respect. (For more on informed and uninformed opinions, see pp. 255–261.)

Statements of Opinion

- can be evaluated but cannot be verified for accuracy or correctness.
- cannot be proved true or false.
- are shaped by the writer's background or training.
- often communicate value judgments, indicating that the author thinks something is right or wrong, good or bad.

In addition to the characteristics listed in the box, the language a writer uses is another important clue to the presence of opinions.

The Language of Opinions

- Statements of opinion often include verbs or adverbs such as *appears, seems, possibly, probably, likely,* and *presumably.*

- Statements of opinion often make comparisons using words such as *more, most, better, best, greatest,* and *finest.*

- Statements of opinion include words that make value judgments: *beautiful, perfect, significant, interesting,* and *crucial.*

- Opinions are frequently prefaced, or introduced, with phrases like *one interpretation of, another possibility is, this study suggests, in all likelihood,* and *it would seem.*

◼ EXERCISE 1

DIRECTIONS Label each statement *F* for fact or *O* for opinion.

F   **EXAMPLE** The first commercially printed Christmas cards were produced in London in 1843.

EXPLANATION Because this statement can be readily verified, it is clearly a fact rather than an opinion.

_____ **1.** All this uproar about animal rights is nonsense. Animals don't have rights.

_____ **2.** In 1909, Ernest Rutherford showed that atoms were mostly space.

_____ **3.** When it was under Spanish control, the city of Los Angeles was called *El Pueblo de Nuestra Señora la Reina de Los Angeles del Río Porciúncula,* which means "The Town of Our Lady the Queen of the Angels by the Little Portion River."[1]

_____ **4.** People who refuse to believe in alien abduction* are simply afraid to face the truth.

---

[1]Bill Bryson, *Made in America.* New York: William Morrow and Company, 1994, p. 106.
*abduction: kidnapping.

_____ **5.** Martin Luther King Jr.'s "Letter from Birmingham Jail" was published in 1963 by the American Friends Service Committee, a Quaker organization.

_____ **6.** Teenagers today are obsessed with money and success. They don't care about making the world a better place.

_____ **7.** The atomic weight of carbon is closer to 12 than to 14.

_____ **8.** Women's stomachs are less effective than men's when it comes to absorbing alcohol and neutralizing* its effects.

_____ **9.** Rap music is here to stay.

_____ **10.** Queen Victoria of England died on January 22, 1901; at her death, she had been queen for almost sixty-four years.

Blending Fact and Opinion

Reading critically would probably be a good deal easier if authors kept statements of fact and opinion neatly divided. But they don't. Whether consciously or unconsciously, writers of all kinds—and textbook authors are no exception—can't always avoid coloring a fact with an opinion. Your job as a critical reader is to make sure you recognize when and where fact and opinion blend together. That way, you won't mistakenly accept as fact an opinion you haven't consciously thought through or considered. Take, for example, the following sentence:

> At least thirty-eight states have sensibly decided to give terminally ill patients the right to refuse medical treatment.

At a quick glance, this sentence might appear to be a statement of fact. After all, it's easy enough to verify how many states have given terminally ill patients the right to reject medical treatment. But think again about the author's use of the word *sensibly.* This is a word with positive **connotations,** or associations. Use it to describe someone, and chances are he or she would be pleased. What the author has done in the above sentence is to include her opinion of the action that these thirty-eight states have taken. That makes the statement neither fact nor opinion. Instead, it's a blend of both.

Now what about the next sentence? How would you label it—fact, opinion, or a blend of both?

---

*neutralizing: making harmless or without effect.

> In 1944, Russian troops entered eastern Czechoslovakia, and the nightmare of life under Communist rule began.

The first part of this sentence is a fairly obvious statement of fact. Any encyclopedia can tell you when Russian troops entered Czechoslovakia. But what about the phrase *nightmare of life under Communist rule?* Do you detect any trace of opinion in those words? If you said yes, you're well on your way to being a critical reader. People who took part in or supported the Communist regime in Czechoslovakia would probably not agree that life under Communist rule was a nightmare. What we have here is another example of a statement that blends fact and opinion.

To discover when writers have mixed a pinch of opinion in with their facts, you'll need to be alert to **charged,** or **connotative, language**—language that carries with it strong positive or negative connotations. Writers dealing in pure fact tend to rely heavily on **denotative language.** They employ words that suggest little more than their **denotation,** or dictionary definitions. Words like *table, chair,* and *rock,* for example, carry little or no emotional impact. Thus, they are considered far more denotative than connotative.

Changing the Connotation with the Context

Change the **context,** or setting, of a word, and it can become more connotative than denotative. For example, the word *stories* in the following sentence evokes little more than its denotation.

> *Aesop's Fables* is a collection of *stories* written by a Greek storyteller.

However, look what happens when the context of the word *stories* changes:

> In an effort to deny Jean a promotion, a jealous coworker spread *stories* about her character.

With this change in context, the word *stories* no longer refers to "an account of events"; instead, it becomes a synonym for *lies* and takes on a negative connotation. This example illustrates a key point about labeling language connotative or denotative: *Context is crucial.* Don't assume that a word that is denotative in one sentence is always lacking an emotional charge. A word can be connotative or denotative, depending on the setting in which it appears.

CHECK YOUR UNDERSTANDING
Explain how an author can mix an opinion in with a fact.
_____
_____

EXERCISE 2

DIRECTIONS Read each sentence and look carefully at the italicized word or words. Then fill in the blank with one of the following letters:

D for dictionary meaning only

C+ for positive connotation

C− for negative connotation

_*D*_   **EXAMPLE** Gertrude Stein was a *twentieth-century author* who spent most of her life in France.

EXPLANATION The phrase *twentieth-century author* does not carry with it any positive or negative associations. It simply identifies the time in which Stein lived.

_____ **1.** Woodstock is a village in New York State that was the scene of the *greatest rock music festival* in the history of rock and roll.

_____ **2.** "Zulu" is a *general name* for some 2.5 million Bantu-speaking peoples who live in South Africa.

_____ **3.** The Amazon River is the *second longest river* after the Nile.

_____ **4.** Nuclear weapons are the *plague of the twentieth century.*

_____ **5.** In the nineteenth century, Marshall "Wild Bill" Hickok was *fearless* in his pursuit of outlaws.

_____ **6.** *Famed revolutionary hero* Emiliano Zapata was *beloved* by the poor of Mexico.

_____ **7.** Gospel music is the kind of *intense joyful music* that *makes the spirit sing.*

_____ **8.** Francisco Goya was a Spanish painter of the *late eighteenth and nineteenth centuries.*

_____ **9.** John James Audubon was a nineteenth-century *painter and naturalist.**

_____ **10.** John D. Rockefeller, founder of the Standard Oil Company, was famous for his charity work, but he was also known as a *robber baron* whose business methods were remarkably *ruthless.*

◼ EXERCISE 3

DIRECTIONS Some of the following statements are purely factual. Others blend fact and opinion. Label the statements that are pure fact with an *F*. For the statements that blend fact and opinion, put a *B* in the blanks. For those sentences you mark with a *B*, underline the word or words that led you to your conclusion.

B

EXAMPLE Leslie Marmon Silko's *Ceremony* is the <u>deeply moving</u> story of a young Native American held prisoner during World War II.

EXPLANATION In this statement, the author provides factual information about the book's plot. The words *deeply moving* convey the author's opinion of the book.

_____ **1.** According to the Television Advertising Bureau, an extraordinary 98.2 percent of all American households have a television set.

_____ **2.** Psychiatrist Bruno Bettelheim spent many years studying fairy tales and their effect on children.

_____ **3.** An astounding number of people have tattoos covering 98 percent of their body.

_____ **4.** Amazingly, Diane Nash was only twenty-two years old when she led the campaign to desegregate the lunch counters in Nashville, Tennessee.

_____ **5.** Jerry Garcia, the long-time lead singer for the Grateful Dead, died on August 5, 1995.

_____ **6.** Juan Rodríguez Cabrillo explored the coast of California in 1542.

_____ **7.** After World War I, victorious Britain and France greedily divided up the Turkish Empire.

---

*naturalist: person who studies the natural world.

_____ **8.** Surprisingly, Muhammad, the founder of Islam, devoted a number of his sermons to the subject of women's rights.

_____ **9.** After World War II, Great Britain turned Palestine over to the United Nations, which in November 1947 voted to create the state of Israel.

_____ **10.** In 1908, the phenomenal Jack Johnson became the first African American to win the world heavyweight championship.

Informed vs. Uninformed Opinions

While everybody has a right to an opinion, it doesn't follow that every opinion deserves the same degree of attention or respect. Imagine, for example, that a friend saw you taking an aspirin for a headache and told you that chewing a clove of garlic was a far better remedy. When you asked why, he shrugged and said: "I don't know. I heard it someplace." Given this lack of explanation, not to speak of evidence, it's unlikely that you would start chewing garlic cloves to rid yourself of headaches. Uninformed opinions—opinions lacking any sufficient reasons or evidence—usually do fail to persuade.

More likely to convince are informed opinions backed by logic or evidence. For an example, look at this paragraph, which opens by expressing an opinion about the Ford Motor Company in its early years:

When Henry Ford organized the Ford Motor Company in 1903, his relationships with government were relatively simple. There was only one important antitrust law on the books, and his business was not large enough to be affected by it. The federal government did not tax the income of his company or its employees. No unions were permitted in the Ford plant, and government regulations concerning wages, hours, working conditions, and safety and health were unheard of. The government exacted no payments from the company for employee retirement and pension plans for the simple reason that none existed. Nor was the fledgling* automaker plagued with problems of a polluted environment, an energy shortage, or consumer complaints about auto safety, all of which in later years would bring the wrath of the government down on the Ford company. Ford's main legal worry in those early years was a patent infringement suit brought against him by competitors, but he eventually won the suit in the courts. (Frederick et al., *Business and Society*, p. 207.)

---

*fledgling: just starting out.

In this case, the authors effectively blend fact with opinion. The year when Ford organized the motor company bearing his name is a matter of fact. It can be readily checked in reference books. But saying that Ford's relationship to the government was "relatively simple" is a matter of opinion. After all, people differ widely in their interpretation of broad, general words like *simple* or *complicated.*

Aware that they need to supply their readers with a solid basis for their opinion, the authors note there was only one "important" antitrust law on the books. Although the word *important* makes this statement more opinion than fact—people differ on what's important—it still provides a more specific explanation for these opening claims, and we begin to understand why the authors use the word *simple.* Further explanation comes in the form of factual statements that tell us the federal government did not tax the company's income or employees. In addition, we learn that unions were not permitted in the plant, and there were no regulations governing safety, health, and working conditions. By the time we reach the last sentence of the paragraph, it's clear that we are dealing with an informed opinion, solidly based on both reason and fact.

Recognizing Circular Reasoning

The paragraph on Ford offers a good example of an informed opinion. Would you say the same about the next passage?

> We Americans like to brag about progress, but, in fact, life was better in the nineteenth century than in the twentieth. People were happier and more at peace with themselves. There just wasn't the same kind of anxiety and tension that there is today. If we had a chance, we would probably all get into a time machine and go backward, rather than forward. All of our highly touted technological progress has not brought us an increased measure of contentment.

The author of this paragraph believes life was better a century ago. However, she—like our friend who prescribes garlic for headaches—offers no solid evidence to support that opinion. She could have quoted from journals, letters, or interviews; cited statistics; or even mentioned that there was hardly any divorce a century ago. But instead of offering support that might justify her opinion, the author simply makes the same claim over and over again in different words. This tactic, called **circular reasoning,** is typical of writers given to promoting uninformed opinions. In response to circular reasoning, critical readers rightly become skeptical, or suspicious, of the opinion expressed.

CHECK YOUR UNDERSTANDING

Explain and give an example of circular reasoning.

_____

_____

_____

Identifying Irrelevant Facts

Authors who haven't completely thought out the basis for their opinions are also given to supplying **irrelevant,** or unrelated, facts. Look, for example, at the following example.

> Health care workers must be tested for the virus that causes AIDS. To date, more than 100,000 people have died from AIDS-related illnesses. In addition, current figures from the national Centers for Disease Control show that thousands more are already infected with HIV, the virus that causes AIDS, and will probably develop full-blown AIDS.

To make her opinion about AIDS testing convincing, the author needs factual statements that support a cause and effect connection between infected health care workers and the spread of the virus that causes AIDS. Those facts would be relevant and would help justify her opinion.

But those are not the facts the author supplies. Instead, she offers two facts proving that AIDS is a serious epidemic. Unfortunately, these facts are irrelevant to her opinion about mandatory testing. Critical readers would not be convinced.

Looking for Relevant Facts

In judging opinions, critical readers are always on the lookout for **relevant facts** that have a direct connection to the opinion being expressed. Consider, for example, the following passage.

> The Italian government takes excellent care of Italy's mothers. Pregnant women in Italy are guaranteed paid leaves, combined with free medical care. According to a 1971 law, pregnant women must be allowed to stay at home during the last two months of

pregnancy, and new mothers can stay at home for the first three months following their baby's birth. During this five-month period, the government guarantees women who worked before their pregnancy 80 percent of their former salary.

In this passage, the author offers readers an opinion about how the Italian government treats mothers. (Note the connotations of the word *excellent*.) In support of this point of view, the passage supplies specific facts describing the financial and medical aid offered to mothers by the Italian government. Unlike the facts in the earlier paragraph on testing health care workers, the facts in this passage are relevant, or related, to the author's claim.

CHECK YOUR UNDERSTANDING

Explain the difference between relevant and irrelevant facts.

_____

_____

■ EXERCISE 4

DIRECTIONS Read each statement of opinion. Then look carefully at the two statements meant to provide support. Only one will be relevant; the other will be either irrelevant or circular. Put an *R* in the blank following the relevant statement. Mark the remaining statement with either a *C* (circular) or an *I* (irrelevant).

Opinion **EXAMPLE** Radon gas is a serious health hazard, one that can no longer be ignored.

Support a. A 1997 study by the federal government confirmed what other studies have found: there is a connection between radon gas in the home and the occurrence of lung cancer.

  R

b. When it comes to radon gas, Americans are like ostriches. They refuse to acknowledge the threat, preferring to stick their heads in the sand and pretend it doesn't exist.

  C

EXPLANATION Statement *a* is relevant because it cites a study supporting the author's claim that radon gas is a serious threat that must be recognized. Statement *b*, however, goes around in circles, repeating the opening opinion in different words.

Opinion **1.** All too often, doctors aren't sensitive to their patients' emotional needs.

Support a. When Francine Vogler suffered a neck injury, her physician told her she might die or become a quadriplegic. Then he walked out of the room.[2]

_____

b. A bedside manner is crucial to being an effective physician, but many doctors today lack the skills to provide their patient with the emotional comfort so essential to healing.

_____

Opinion **2.** Canadian health care is a far cry from what it used to be.

Support a. Historically, Canadians have been proud of their health care system. But currently that system is undergoing some profound changes, and few of those changes are improvements.

_____

b. The Canadian government has reduced its contributions to the health care system by 30 percent, and doctors have begun refusing to see patients if they think they will not be paid.

_____

Opinion **3.** Internet Web sites are a terrific source of information for news-hungry Americans.

Support a. One house in five relies on the Internet for news.

_____

b. At the Web site called Newshub, the leading headline stories are updated every fifteen minutes, so that Web users can get a quick update in a minimal amount of time.

_____

Opinion **4.** The past five years have seen some amazing archeological discoveries.

Support a. Archaeologists have found the cave where the Greek playwright

_____
[2]Thio, *Sociology*, p. 466.

Euripides wrote at least one of his plays more than 2500 years ago.

_____

b. Euripides is believed to have written at least ninety-two plays; among the most famous are *Medea* and *The Bacchants*.

_____

Opinion **5.** It's becoming increasingly clear that there must be life on Jupiter.

Support   a. According to new images of Jupiter, there appears to be a warm sea in which heat and moisture may well have encouraged the formation of life.

_____

b. Skeptics may doubt it, but all the signs lead to one conclusion: life exists on Jupiter.

_____

Opinion **6.** Currently, trampolines are popular toys for kids, but they shouldn't be. Trampolines are dangerous.

Support   a. Every year, trampoline jumping produces more than sixty thousand injuries, including fractures and dislocations.[3]

_____

b. Trampolines are not toys, and they shouldn't be treated as such.

_____

Opinion **7.** On June 23, 1972, President Richard Nixon signed Title IX into law, making gender discrimination in education illegal. Thanks to Title IX, women's sports would never be the same.

Support   a. When Title IX was enacted, little more than 30,000 women participated in college athletics; today there are more than 120,000 female athletes on college campuses.

_____

b. When Richard Nixon signed Title IX into law, neither he nor anyone else realized what a profound impact it would have on women's sports.

_____

_____
[3]*Time*, March 16, 1998, p. 22.

Opinion **8.** Vitamin E just may be the most beneficial vitamin a person can take in an effort to ensure a healthy old age.

Support a. A report published in 1997 in the *New England Journal of Medicine* shows that the mental deterioration caused by Alzheimer's disease can be dramatically slowed by taking vitamin E.

——

b. High doses of a mineral called selegiline also appear to slow down the mental deterioration caused by Alzheimer's disease.

——

Opinion **9.** Read Sebastian Junger's *The Perfect Storm,* and you may never set foot on a boat again.

Support a. *The Perfect Storm* describes in terrifying detail the destruction of the *Andrea Gail,* a fishing boat that sank during a 1991 storm, taking with it all six crew members.

——

b. Sebastian Junger's *The Perfect Storm* stayed on the bestseller list for months, earning him a good deal of money and several lawsuits.

——

Opinion **10.** At present, English dominates on the Internet, but it may not dominate for long.

Support a. Usenet, the bulletin board system for the Internet, is where one can find messages on just about any topic.

——

b. Many non-English-speaking people are creating Web sites in their own languages and efforts are under way to develop software that provides immediate translations.

——

▶◗ Fact and Opinion in Textbooks

Many students assume that textbook writers restrict themselves to facts and avoid presenting opinions. Although that may be true for some science texts, it's not true for textbooks in general, particularly in the areas of psychology, history, and government. Look, for example, at the following passage. Do you detect the presence of an opinion?

Presidents are not just celebrities, they are the American version of royalty. Lacking a royal family, Americans look to the president to symbolize the uniqueness of their government. (Gitelson et al., *American Government*, p. 311.)

If you said the entire passage was an opinion, you'd be right. There's no way to verify how *all* Americans feel about the role of the president. And a good many may have no use for the notion of royalty, so why would they look for a substitute?

As the excerpt illustrates, textbooks do, indeed, offer opinions along with facts. However, that's not a failing as long as the authors offer support for the opinions they convey in their writing.

Here, for example, is another textbook excerpt. The authors open with an opinion about the American military's attempt to manage news during the Gulf War. Note, however, that the opinion is not left unsupported. On the contrary, a specific example follows right on its heels.

Opinion

Example offered as support

Part of the strategy [during the Gulf War] was to "spin" the news, so that U.S. successes were emphasized and losses minimized. When announcing that eleven marines had been killed in action, for example, the military first showed twenty minutes of footage on Iraqi bridges and buildings being blown up, and the American deaths were treated virtually as an afterthought. The strategy, which worked, was to force nightly news programs to divide their attention between the bad news—eleven killed at the outset of a potentially difficult ground war—and the good news—visually spectacular footage of a truck traveling across a bridge seconds before the bridge blew up. (Paul E. Johnson et al., *American Government*. Boston: Houghton Mifflin, 1994, p. 354.)

The two examples cited here should make it clear that you can't reserve critical reading skills for newspapers and magazines. You also have to apply them to textbooks. In short, be on the alert for the presence of personal opinions in your textbooks and check to see that those opinions are followed by relevant supporting details.

WORD NOTES

The discussion of fact and opinion on page 247 introduced the word *verify*, meaning to prove true. *Verify* is an important word to add to your vocabulary. However, you should also consider learning some of its synonyms. Learning groups of words related in meaning is a good way to rapidly enlarge your vocabulary.

1. **Confirm:** to remove all doubts, as in "Can you *confirm* the receipt of my proposal?"

2. **Corroborate:** to strengthen through statements supplied by another, as in "No one was alive to *corroborate* the testimony of the accused."

3. **Substantiate:** to establish something by means of factual evidence, as in "The historian's position had now been firmly *substantiated* by the discovery of both diaries and letters."

4. **Authenticate:** to prove genuine, as in "The museum was swindled when it paid for the sculpture before it was *authenticated.*"

Now fill in the blanks with one of the four words defined above.

1. Because the professor's long-time assistant was able to

   _____ his statements, the police were willing to let him go.

2. The art historian was unable to ___ _____ the painting as a genuine Picasso.

3. The secretary called to _____ the arrival of the package.

4. Researchers have been able to _____ long-standing rumors about Thomas Jefferson's affair with his slave, Sally Hemmings.

Summing Up

Listed below are the most important points in Chapter 7. Put a check mark in the box if you think the point is clear in your mind. Leave the box blank if you need to review the material one more time. The page numbers in parentheses tell you where to look to review each point on the list.

☐ 1. Statements of fact provide information about people, places, events, and ideas that can be verified or checked for accuracy. (pp. 247–248)

☐ **2.** Statements of opinion are shaped by the author's personal experience, training, or background. They cannot be labeled true or false. However, they can be evaluated as informed or uninformed. (pp. 248–249)

☐ **3.** Many statements mix fact with opinion. The presence of connotative language is a strong clue to the presence of an opinion in what, at first glance, appears to be a statement of fact. (pp. 251–252)

☐ **4.** Informed opinions are backed by supporting reasons or evidence. Uninformed opinions lack both, often relying instead on circular reasoning or irrelevant facts. (pp. 255–258)

TEST YOUR UNDERSTANDING

To see how well you have understood this chapter, take the following review quiz. Then correct it using the answer key provided by your instructor. If you score 80 percent or above, you're ready to take the end-of-chapter exam. However, if you score below 80 percent, look over the quiz carefully to see what kinds of questions you missed. Then use the **Summing Up** pages of the chapter to find out which pages you should review before taking the chapter exam.

◢◣◯ **Chapter 7: Review Quiz**

Part A

DIRECTIONS Label each of the following statements *F* for fact, *O* for opinion, or *B* for both.

_____ **1.** Michael Jordan was the greatest athlete in the history of basketball.

_____ **2.** Among people suffering from depression, one portion of the brain is significantly smaller than the other.

_____ **3.** The planet Neptune was discovered in 1846 by the German astronomer Johann G. Galle.

_____ **4.** The murder in Dallas, Texas, of John Fitzgerald Kennedy, the thirty-fifth president of the United States, proved to be one of the most profound acts of the twentieth century. (David Wallechinsky, *The Twentieth Century.* Boston: Little, Brown, 1995, p. 147.)

_____ **5.** Cholera cases in the United States have increased fivefold since the 1980s.

_____ **6.** Louise Brown, the world's first test-tube baby, was born on July 25, 1978.

_____ **7.** More films should be made in black and white rather than in color.

_____ **8.** For decades, it's been painfully clear that our water resources are limited, and we must pay more attention to water conservation.

_____ **9.** Physical competence produces psychological competence. (M. Burch Tracy Ford, head of Miss Porter's School in Farmington, Conn.)

_____ **10.** Eggs contaminated by salmonella bacteria are the number one cause of food poisoning outbreaks in the United States.

Part B

DIRECTIONS Label each passage with either an *I* for informed opinion or a *U* for uninformed opinion.

11. Although most people over the age of three love firework displays, they probably don't realize that fireworks are big business, and a highly creative and competitive one at that. A few family-owned companies, such as Zambelli International, Sunset Fireworks, and Pyro Spectacular compete fiercely for a chance at the big Fourth of July displays. To make sure they have an edge, each company closely guards its recipes for spectacular effects. No one really knows, for example, how Zambelli International creates its gorgeous floral bouquet of red camellias and gold chrysanthemums. And if it's up to the owners, no one ever will.

———

12. Even though Elvis Presley died on August 6, 1977, he is certainly not forgotten. On the contrary, the legend of Elvis lives on. To honor the twentieth anniversary of his death, RCA released a four-volume CD, *Elvis Presley Platinum: A Life in Music.* It was so popular that record stores couldn't keep it on the shelves. In honor of that same anniversary, over fifty thousand fans descended on Graceland, Elvis's former home in Tennessee. In 1997 and 1998, the San Jose Ballet toured the country with a ballet performed in the singer's honor. It was called *Blue Suede Shoes.*

———

13. It shouldn't have taken the murder of a tiny beauty queen to make parents question the value of beauty pageants for children. These pageants were always a disgrace. They do nothing but harm to both parents and children alike. Beauty pageants for grown-up women are bad enough, but beauty pageants for children are simply disgusting. They should be sharply criticized by the media and, if possible, banned by state legislatures.

———

14. Hunters like to claim that they were among the first environmentalists, but nothing could be further from the truth. Hunting benefits only those men and women who like to kill living creatures for sport. Oddly enough, environmental groups like the National Audubon Society and the Sierra Club support hunting, but that should not encourage anyone else to do so. The only way animals should be hunted is with a camera, never with a gun.

———

15. The label *organic* doesn't necessarily mean that food has been grown or raised without pesticides and man-made fertilizers. Currently, what's considered organic in one state may not be in another. Some states' certification programs allow organic produce to be grown with certain fertilizers and insecticides that other states specifically prohibit. Moreover, twenty states have no rules whatsoever governing organic food. "As it now stands, in an unregulated state there's nothing to stop some farmers from just sticking an organic label on their tomatoes, say, and putting them out for sale without ever hav-

ing followed any organic principles," observes Katherine DiMatteo, executive director of the national Organic Trade Association. (Adapted from Jennifer Reid Holman, "Can You Trust Organic?" *Self,* November 1997, p. 163.)

_____

Part C

DIRECTIONS Label each supporting statement with one of these three letters: *R* (relevant), *I* (irrelevant) or *C* (circular).

Opinion **16.** The Internet certainly can't replace the family doctor, but, now more than ever, it is possible to get accurate medical information online.

Support a. To ensure that citizens get accurate medical information, the U.S. government has created the Healthfinder Web site (www.healthfinder.gov), which evaluates all health-related Web sites for accuracy.

_____

b. More and more Americans are becoming dissatisfied with traditional medical care and are turning to alternative medical treatments like acupuncture and herbal remedies; in fact, one out of three Americans now seeks medical care from a person not in possession of a conventional medical degree.

_____

Opinion **17.** Almost single-handedly, Roger Tory Peterson (1908–1996) made bird watching a hobby anyone could pursue.

Support a. Before Peterson, there was no pocket-size guidebook that birders could use for identifying the birds they saw. Peterson's guidebook was the first that could be carried in a pocket for ease of identification.

_____

b. Birds are more than beautiful; they are early indicators of what's right or wrong with the planet.

_____

Opinion **18.** The American economy may be booming, but not everyone is benefiting from that boom.

Support   a. While some Americans are making more money than ever before, others are not doing so well.

_____

          b. In 1997 alone, more than twenty-six million Americans turned to local charities because they didn't have enough to eat.

_____

Opinion **19.** New York City's rent control program may not be as beneficial as many people seem to think.

Support   a. Rent control discourages home ownership, which is probably one reason why New York's home ownership rate is less than half of the average for other large American cities.

_____

          b. Rent control was first introduced in 1943. It was one of the federal government's many wartime regulations.

_____

Opinion **20.** Greek New Age composer Yanni Hrisomallis is enormously popular.

Support   a. The composer Yanni has millions of fans.

_____

          b. Yanni's 1997 CD of his concert at the Greek Acropolis* sold seven million copies.

_____

> Use the answer key provided by your instructor to correct your quiz. If you score 80 percent or above, you are ready for the chapter exam. If you score below 80 percent, look carefully at the questions you answered incorrectly. Then use the **Summing Up** section to decide which pages you need to review.

_____

*Acropolis: an old and famous building in Athens, Greece.

◢◣◉ Chapter Test 7

Part A

DIRECTIONS Label each of the following statements *F* for fact, *O* for opinion, or *B* for both.

_____ **1.** E-mail filters are software packages that can screen out specific senders or subjects from a person's e-mail.

_____ **2.** In 1996, snowfalls and floods caused $78 million dollars worth of damage in Yosemite National Park.

_____ **3.** On February 1, 1960, four black college students staged the first sit-in at a segregated lunch counter.

_____ **4.** Surprisingly, thalidomide, the drug that caused such horrifying birth defects in the 1960s, is now being used in the treatment of both cancer and leprosy.

_____ **5.** Chris Rock just may be the most talented comedian in show business today.

_____ **6.** Unbelievable as it may seem, President Harry Truman claimed that he never lost a moment's sleep over his horrifying decision to drop the atomic bomb.

_____ **7.** Alexander Graham Bell, the inventor of the telephone, was born in Scotland.

_____ **8.** The chemical symbol for water is H_2O.

_____ **9.** The brilliant revolutionary leader Emiliano Zapata lived as an outlaw for many years until he was killed in 1919.

_____ **10.** The opening and closing lines of Lincoln's Gettysburg Address are especially memorable.

Part B

DIRECTIONS Label each passage with either an *I* for informed opinion or a *U* for an uninformed opinion.

11. In the forties and fifties, saxophonist Charlie Parker was the most influential musician in the world of jazz. Parker toured with various bands, but he really made his name after hours in New York clubs like Minton's Playhouse and Monroe's Uptown. There he played in informal jazz sessions and began developing the distinctive bebop sound that won him the admiration of other musicians. By the mid-forties, Parker had formed his own group and was recording some of his most famous pieces, like "Now's the Time" and "Scrapple from the Apple." Many of his compositions* from this period became jazz favorites and made Charlie "Bird" Parker an idol to his fellow musicians.

———

12. Normally a peaceful people, the Pueblo Indians of New Mexico rebelled violently against the cruel and inhuman treatment of the Spanish explorers who colonized New Mexico in 1542. Disdainful* of Pueblo customs, the Spanish forced the Indians to convert to Catholicism. At the same time, the underground *kivas,* or chambers, where the Indians normally worshipped were destroyed, as were all ceremonial masks. Indians suspected of practicing their own religion were cruelly punished—forced to become slaves, whipped, imprisoned, even hanged simply for clinging to their beliefs. Outraged by the treatment of his people, Popé, a Pueblo medicine man, organized a revolt and persuaded nearly every member of the Pueblo tribe to participate. On August 10, 1680, the Pueblos swept into the city of Santa Fe and killed more than four hundred of their Spanish oppressors. Those who survived fled New Mexico, leaving it in the hands of the victorious Pueblo rebels.

———

13. The punk rock groups popular between 1976 and 1983 truly lived up to the self-reliant, do-it-yourself ethic* of their songs. Bands like the Stooges, the Ramones, and the New York Dolls prided themselves on avoiding or eliminating the control of the big record companies, preferring instead to put out their own records. Rather than hiring a talent agency to promote them, punk bands relied on newspapers and magazines called fanzines, which they published themselves. Groups like Kleenez and X-Ray Spex distributed their records through small record shops and almost totally avoided the mass-marketing techniques employed by big record companies. In effect, they opened up the world of music to groups that did not have wide commercial appeal.

———

14. Writer, social critic, and Trappist monk Thomas Merton is one of the most heroic figures of the twentieth century. Great men like Merton come along all too infrequently, and few men or women are pos-

—————
*compositions: musical pieces.
*disdainful: disrespectful.
*ethic: belief.

sessed of his virtues. Those lucky enough to know Merton while he lived were among the fortunate few. Sadly, Merton died in a freak accident. While on a monastic convention in Thailand, he was electrocuted by faulty wiring in a fan.

———

15. Companies marketing television directly linked to the Internet are convinced that Net TV will be a profit blockbuster. But there are at least three reasons why their optimism may not be justified. Unfortunately, it takes a long time for Web pages to appear on the screen, and TV has taught us that the desire to be entertained can be instantly gratified by switching the channel. Few people will be patient enough to wait for slow-moving Web pages to come up on the television screen. And what about eye strain? Most people sit around two to three feet away from the TV. That's not a good distance for reading screens full of text and pictures. Yet that's exactly what people will be doing with Net TV. Then, too, it's not at all clear that Web sites designed to function with computer software can be so readily adapted to television. All in all, it's better to have a wait-and-see attitude about the effects of Net TV.

———

Part C

DIRECTIONS Label each supporting statement with one of these three letters: *R* (relevant), *I* (irrelevant), or *C* (circular).

Opinion 16. It seems clear that young children benefit from learning to play music.

Support   a. In a 1997 study, researchers at the University of California in Irvine found that musical instruction markedly increased the ability of three- and four-year-old children to think accurately about relationships in both time and space.

———

     b. In a 1994 study, college students who listened to a half hour of Mozart before taking exams received higher scores than students who sat in a quiet room.

———

Opinion 17. There have been many good baseball players, even a few great ones, but there was only one Mickey Mantle.

Support
    a. In an effort to keep him alive, doctors gave Mickey Mantle a liver transplant, but the transplant couldn't save his life when lung cancer ravaged his body.

———

    b. In 1953 Mantle hit the longest home run ever measured, and in 1956 he won baseball's Triple Crown for his batting average (.353), number of homers (52), and runs batted in (130).

———

Opinion **18.** Women in the military should be allowed to engage in combat alongside men.

Support
    a. If women do not engage in combat, then Americans have to answer the question raised by Lieutenant General Claudia Kennedy: "Why do you value the daughters of America more than the sons?"[4]

———

    b. According to Fred C. Ikle, who was undersecretary of defense in the Reagan administration, the military cannot "cultivate the necessary commitment to physical violence and fully protect [women] against the risk of harassment."[5]

———

Opinion **19.** In our public schools, girls and boys don't necessarily receive the same treatment.

Support
    a. In high school, girls would be better off if they didn't have to compete with boys.

———

    b. A 1998 report by the American Association of University Women, "Gender Gaps: Where Schools Still Fail Our Children," suggested that girls were not encouraged to master computers in the same way boys were.

———

Opinion **20.** The Americans with Disabilities Act (ADA) has done a lot to improve the lives of the disabled, but much more needs to be done in order to bring people with disabilities into the mainstream of life.

---

[4]Richard Raynor, "Women in the Warrior Culture," *New York Times*, June 22, 1977, p. 40.
[5]Ibid., p. 29.

Support

a. Although the ADA has made public buildings and transit systems more accessible, the percentage of small businesses hiring the disabled has slipped from 54 percent to 48 percent; thus, two-thirds of all working-age disabled people are unemployed.

————

b. Writer Nancy Mars, who suffers from multiple sclerosis, cautions those without any physical disability to think of themselves as "temporarily" abled, since no one is ever immune from the ravages of time and disease.

————

CHAPTER 8

Identifying Purpose and Tone

 In this chapter, you'll learn

- how *informative* and *persuasive* writing differ from one another.

- why discovering the author's purpose is essential to critical reading.

- how the title and source of a reading help you predict its purpose.

- how thesis statements help you confirm or revise your prediction.

- how tone relates to purpose.

- how to recognize an ironic tone.

Most writing falls into three categories: (1) writing meant to inform, (2) writing designed to persuade, and

(3) writing intended purely to entertain. Because we're focusing on critical reading issues, such as evaluating evidence and separating fact from opinion, this chapter is solely concerned with writing meant to inform or persuade. Determining whether a writer intends to inform or persuade can sometimes be difficult. However, writing bent on entertaining is pretty easy to recognize. The only possible complication or difficulty might be that you don't share the author's sense of humor.

 ## Understanding the Difference Between Informative and Persuasive Writing

To be a good critical reader, you need a clear understanding of how informative and persuasive writing differ.

Informative Writing

The goal of **informative writing** is to make the audience more knowledgeable about a particular subject. Informative writing usually leans heavily on factual information and doesn't promote any one opinion. If anything, informative writing is likely to offer competing opinions on the same subject while the author remains objective, or impartial, refusing to champion one opinion over another.

Here's a good example of writing meant primarily to inform:

 Two factors in the development of obesity in children are beyond human control. These two factors are heredity and age. Like it or not, thinness and fatness do run in families. Overweight children tend to have overweight parents and underweight parents tend to have underweight children (LeBow, 1984). In addition, most people inevitably put on fat more during certain periods of life than during others. Late childhood and early puberty form one of these periods; at this time, most children gain fat tissue out of proportion to increases in other tissues, such as muscle and bone. (Adapted from Seifert and Hoffnung, *Child and Adolescent Development,* p. 390.)

In this example, the topic is obesity in children, and the authors briefly describe two of its causes: heredity and age. Notice, however, that they themselves do not express a point of view about their subject. Nor do the authors suggest that readers should adopt a particular point of view. Their primary purpose is dispensing information. It is not persuasion.

Persuasive Writing

Persuasive writing promotes one particular opinion. Its goal is to make readers share or at least seriously consider the author's point of view. Although writers intent on persuasion certainly use facts, those facts are carefully chosen to make their case convincing. And when they present opposing points of view, it is only to disprove them. Unlike authors of informative writing, authors of persuasive writing are not objective. Even if they try to keep an open mind, they remain *subjective.* That means they are committed to their point of view and hope you will share it. Here, to illustrate, is a passage written with a persuasive intent.

> The notion that strangers must be feared is not only lamentable* but also wrong. The media have documented the crimes of psychopathic rapists, kidnappers, child snatchers, and criminals. Such monsters exist. But the harsh truth is that more people are hurt by those they know than they are by those whom they don't. Women are more likely to be battered by their husbands and lovers than by strangers. They are more likely to be raped by someone they know. Social workers and physicians frequently find that when the elderly are neglected and abused, the perpetrators are spouses and children and not paid caretakers. And when children are abducted, sexually molested, and/or abused, the culprit is most often a parent, a stepparent, or a trusted relative. (Joan Retsinas, "Don't Speak to Strangers," *Newsweek,* October 31, 1988, p. 10.)

In this case the author has a definite point of view she wants readers to share: Encouraging the notion that strangers are automatically dangerous is a mistake. She then goes on to offer evidence for her position in the hope that readers will share it.

---

*lamentable: sad.

CHECK YOUR UNDERSTANDING

See how well you can sum up the differences between informative and persuasive writing.

Informative Writing	Persuasive Writing

The Importance of Purpose

Identifying an author's primary **purpose,** or reason for writing, is important because the author's purpose determines how critically you need to read. After all, your time is limited. You can't possibly check every source or ponder everything you read. With informational writing, you can relax and read to understand the author's message. You can safely assume that the writer is objectively describing events or ideas without telling you how to interpret or view them. In fact, a writer whose primary purpose is to inform is very likely to give you different explanations of the same events so that you can develop your own opinions.

However, the more an author leans toward persuasion, the more you must *evaluate* what you read, considering the amount and kind of evidence offered. Because persuasive writing tries to affect how you think, feel, and believe, you need to look for reasons, check facts, and consider the effect of word choice before you let yourself be influenced.

In a very real way, the author's purpose shapes or determines your reading response. The clearer it becomes that an author is intent on persuasion, the more willing you must be to do a close and critical reading.

Determining the Primary Purpose

To be sure, a good deal of writing blends information and persuasion. For example, a writer who wants to inform her readers about changes that have taken place in Berlin, Germany, since the Berlin Wall* came down also needs to persuade her readers that her account is accurate and trustworthy. Similarly, an author may wish to convince his readers that they should give more money to AIDS research. But to make that position persuasive, he will probably inform them about current funding.

As a critical reader, you should always try to determine an author's primary, or major, purpose. Be aware, however, that it's not always possible to claim with absolute certainty whether a writer meant to inform *or* persuade. Some writers inform and persuade in equal measure.

CHECK YOUR UNDERSTANDING

In your own words, why is knowing the author's purpose important?

_____

_____

_____

_____

Predicting Purpose

The only way to truly identify an author's purpose is to read what he or she has to say. However, even before you begin reading, there are two very important clues you can use to predict the author's purpose—the source of the reading and the author's background.

The Source Is a Clue to Purpose

The source or location of a reading is often a solid clue to purpose. Technical manuals, guide books, science texts and journals, refer-

---

*Berlin Wall: the wall that divided East and West Germany. It was erected by the Communist government to keep East Germans from fleeing to democratic West Germany.

ence books, dictionaries, reports of scientific experiments, and newspaper accounts of current events are usually written primarily to inform. Writing drawn from these sources usually does not promote any one particular point of view, but instead offers an *objective*, or impersonal, account of both people and events.

Unlike the above sources, editorials, opinion pieces, letters to the editor, and book, movie, and theater reviews in both newspapers and magazines are all likely to promote one particular point of view over other, competing points of view. The same applies to pamphlets published by political parties or special interest groups, books and articles challenging or revising commonly held beliefs or theories, biographies of famous people, and journals promoting particular causes. All of these sources are likely to feature persuasive writing.

Check the Author's Background

Information about the author's background is not always available to you. But when it is, it can be a useful clue to purpose. For example, a government official who represents the U.S. Department of Health and Human Services and reports on the use of antibiotics in poultry raising is less likely to have a persuasive intent than the president of the New England Poultry Association. If a writer represents a group that could benefit from what he or she claims, then you should suspect a persuasive purpose. You might be wrong, but the chances are good that you will be right.

EXERCISE 1

DIRECTIONS What follows is a list of possible sources for written material. Next to each item on the list is a blank. Put a *P* in the blank if you think the source is likely to contain persuasive writing. If you think it's likely to contain informative writing, put an *I* in the blank.

P   **EXAMPLE** A letter to the editor on the subject of gun control, taken from the *Pittsburgh Post-Gazette*

EXPLANATION In contrast to other newspaper writing, letters to the editor—like editorials—are a strong clue to persuasive writing.

_____ **1.** An article about Cuban leader Fidel Castro appearing in the *Encyclopaedia Britannica*

_____ **2.** An article about Fidel Castro appearing on the front page of the *New York Times*

_____ **3.** A biography of Fidel Castro titled *The Man Who Destroyed Cuba*

_____ **4.** A book titled *A Field Guide to American Houses*

_____ **5.** A government pamphlet titled *Historic Buildings in the Southern States*

_____ **6.** A book review of a work titled *The Triumph of American Architecture*

_____ **7.** A government report on global warming

_____ **8.** A letter about global warming written to the editor of the *Atlanta Times*

_____ **9.** A book titled *The Field Guide to North American Birds*

_____ **10.** An article about the disappearance of songbirds appearing in a journal titled *Save the Earth Now*

Titles Also Provide Clues

Another clue to purpose is the title of a reading. Titles that simply describe a state of affairs—"Teamwork Used to Teach Math"—usually signal that the writer simply wants to inform readers without necessarily persuading them. Titles that express an opinion are quite a different matter. A title like "Teamwork and Mathematics Don't Mix" should immediately suggest to you that the author's primary purpose is persuasion.

Sometimes, of course, the title is no help whatsoever in determining the author's purpose. So be prepared for titles like "A Noble Nation" or "Family Affairs." They attract your attention but don't reveal the author's purpose.

■— **EXERCISE 2**

DIRECTIONS Read each pair of titles. If the title suggests the writer wants mainly to inform, put an *I* in the blank. If it suggests persuasion, fill in the blank with a *P*.

EXAMPLE

a. Bilingual Education Is on the Rise ___*I*___

b. Congress Should Pass "English Only" Legislation ___*P*___

EXPLANATION The first title simply describes a state of affairs without passing any judgment. The second title takes a definite stand, indicating that the writer wants readers to be persuaded.

1. a. Against Assisted Death _____

    b. Assisted Death in the Netherlands _____

2. a. Support for Same-sex Schools Is Increasing _____

    b. It Will Take More Than Same-sex Schools to Get Rid of Gender Bias _____

3. a. Women Don't Belong in the Military _____

    b. Women in the Military _____

4. a. Astrology: The Science of Crackpots* _____

    b. Understanding Astrology _____

5. a. The Science of Cloning _____

    b. Let's Be Cautious About Cloning _____

EXERCISE 3

DIRECTIONS Try your hand at creating titles that express your intent. Make title *a* a statement that suggests your purpose is to inform. Title *b* should be a statement that shows your intention to persuade.

EXAMPLE

Topic Animal Rights

a. *The History of the Animal Rights Movement in America*

b. *Animals Don't Have Rights; People Do*

EXPLANATION Title *a* suggests the writer is intent on describing the animal rights movement whereas title *b* suggests the author wants to discourage support for the movement.

1. Topic The Super Bowl

    a. _____

    b. _____

—————

*crackpots: persons with odd ideas.

2. **Topic**   School Prayer

   a. _____

   b. _____

3. **Topic**   Censorship and the Internet

   a. _____

   b. _____

4. **Topic**   Divorce

   a. _____

   b. _____

5. **Topic**   Daycare

   a. _____

   b. _____

 # The Thesis Statement Is the Clincher

The title, source, and any available information about the author's background can frequently suggest the author's purpose. But it's the author's stated or implied thesis statement that is the clincher, or deciding factor. It will tell you whether your initial prediction about purpose is accurate or in need of revision.

Thesis Statements in Informative Writing

Thesis statements in informative writing describe but do not judge events, people, or ideas. Here, for example, the writer describes an author's beliefs about Greek culture.

> In *Black Athena*, Charles Bernal argues that the Greeks were deeply indebted to the Egyptians for almost every aspect of their culture.

Based on this thesis statement, which does not in any way evaluate Bernal's work, experienced critical readers would assume the author intends to describe Charles Bernal's book without making any claims about its value. While the remainder of the reading could prove them wrong—critical readers continuously test and revise their expectations—it's more than likely that their first response will prove correct.

Thesis Statements in Persuasive Writing

Writers intent on persuasion will usually introduce or imply a thesis statement that identifies some action that needs to be taken, some belief that should be held, or some value judgment that should be shared. Here is an example.

> Charles Bernal has expended enormous energy on *Black Athena*, but he is absolutely wrong to assert, as he does, that he has rewritten the history of the eastern Mediterranean. (Emily Vermeale, "The World Turned Upside Down," *New York Review of Books*, March 26, 1992, p. 43.)

Faced with this thesis statement, most critical readers would correctly assume that the author wants readers to share her opinion of *Black Athena*.

Look now at the next two thesis statements. Which one do you think suggests that the author's goal is to persuade? Put a *P* in the blank next to that statement.

_____ **1.** A number of factors cause children to become obese, or seriously overweight.

_____ **2.** Because obesity is a serious health problem, parents need to pay close attention to what their children eat.

If you filled in the blank next to statement 2, you correctly recognized that the first statement did not encourage readers to pass any judgment or take any action. Statement 2, in contrast, strongly suggests that readers should share the author's feelings about obesity in children—it's a serious health problem. It also encourages parents to act on those feelings by keeping a close watch on their children's diet. This is the kind of thesis statement that tells readers to look for and evaluate the author's evidence for such a claim.

◄■ EXERCISE 4

DIRECTIONS Read each pair of thesis statements. Write an *I* in the blank if the writer intends mainly to inform. Write a *P* if the statement encourages readers to share the writer's point of view.

EXAMPLE

a. In 1998, five U.S. sites were listed on the one hundred most endangered historic spots in the world; all are threatened by housing developments, industry, or simple neglect.

   I

b. In 1998, Mesa Verde National Park in Colorado landed on the
   list of one hundred most endangered historic spots. Mesa Verde
   is the site of eight-hundred-year-old cliff dwellings built by the
   Anasazi, Native Americans who inhabited Colorado and Utah
   about A.D. 100. Given its historical significance, we must do everything possible to save the park.

   P

EXPLANATION Statement *a* simply identifies an existing state of
affairs, while statement *b* calls readers to action.

1. a. Nothing could be more wrong-headed than San Francisco's decision to make smoking marijuana legal for medical purposes.

   _____

   b. In 1991, San Franciscans approved the use of marijuana for
   medical purposes.

   _____

2. a. In 1996, Buck and Luther, two Atlantic bottlenose dolphins,
   were retired from Navy service with full honors. To prepare them
   for a return to the sea, the Navy sent them to a retraining center
   in Florida. But some person or group set the dolphins free before
   retraining was completed, and the two dolphins barely survived
   their punishing first few weeks at sea.

   _____

   b. It's sad but true that we humans often hurt wild animals in our
   attempts to help them. When two Atlantic bottlenose dolphins
   were retired from Navy service, they were sent to a retraining center in preparation for their return to the ocean and life on their
   own. Unfortunately, some misguided animal lovers decided to
   speed up the process and liberated the dolphins before they
   were ready. Buck and Luther barely survived their newfound
   freedom.

   _____

3. a. The Tuskegee Study of Untreated Syphilis in the Negro Male was begun in 1932, when the United States Public Health Service began tracking 399 black men with syphilis. The study's stated purpose was to chart the natural history of the disease without treatment, but the men recruited for the study were never told its purpose.

———

b. In May of 1997, President Clinton apologized on behalf of the nation to the survivors of the Tuskegee Study of Untreated Syphilis in the Negro Male. But his apology can never erase the horrible stain that experiment left on America's history.

———

4. a. The research of sociologists Elaine Wethington and Ronald Kessler is too flawed to be taken seriously. It brings little or nothing to the debate about women and work.

———

b. Sociologists Elaine Wethington of Cornell University and Ronald Kessler of the University of Michigan found that women who worked at low-wage, part-time jobs were more stressed than women who worked full time.

———

5. a. Radon, particularly in combination with smoking, poses an important public health risk and it should be recognized as such.

———

b. Research strongly suggests that radon, a naturally occurring radioactive gas, which collects in many homes, is linked to over 20,000 deaths from lung cancer.[1]

———

6. a. Now that scientists have found the hormone that triggers hunger, they need to take the next step and discover how this hormone can be controlled. Such a discovery would be an enormous advance in the war against obesity.

———

b. Based on research at the University of Texas Southwestern Medi-

———

[1]"Researcher Links Radon to 21,000 Deaths a Year," *New Haven Register,* February 20, 1998, p. F1.

cal Center, scientists believe they have found the hormone that triggers feelings of hunger.

_____

7. a. On any given day at least ten Americans will die waiting for an organ transplant.

_____

b. There are at least two relatively easy ways we can increase the number of organs available and thereby save thousands of lives. First, we need a strong public relations campaign that encourages people to become potential donors and carry donor cards with them. Second, when performing routine medical checkups, doctors should ask healthy patients if they would consider identifying themselves as organ donors. If these two simple steps are taken, thousands of lives could be saved.

_____

8. a. Scientists have found seven fossil ants encased in chunks of amber that are almost one hundred million years old.

_____

b. The discovery of seven ants encased in amber millions of years old proves that ants had a complex social system of behavior much earlier than anyone previously realized.

_____

9. a. The ease and immediacy of e-mail are forcing those who rely on it to consider something many have not thought about in years— grammatical correctness.

_____

b. A quick glance at almost any electronic bulletin board suggests that grammar is no longer being taught in our schools.

_____

10. a. The bald eagle, a scavenger* and carrion* eater, is not fit to be America's national emblem.

_____

b. Once an endangered species, the bald eagle is making a comeback.

_____

_____
*scavenger: one who feeds on dead or decaying material.
*carrion: dead and decaying flesh.

EXERCISE 5

DIRECTIONS Write two paired thesis statements about the same topic. Statement *a* should suggest you want to inform; statement *b* that you want to persuade. *Note:* If possible, write statements that are factually accurate. But if you don't have the facts, you can, for the sake of this exercise, invent them.

EXAMPLE

Topic   Beta-Carotene Pills and Cancer

a. *In the fight against cancer, the World Health Organization recommends eating fresh fruit and vegetables rather than relying on beta-carotene pills, which have been promoted as a nutritional weapon against the war on cancer.*

b. *Thanks to the stand taken by the World Health Organization, it's now abundantly clear that beta-carotene pills are useless in the fight against cancer.*

EXPLANATION As it should, statement *a* simply describes a state of affairs—the World Health Organization's stand on beta-carotene pills. Statement *b*, however, uses the World Health Organization's position to make a value judgment about beta-carotene pills: They're useless in the war against cancer.

1. Topic   Body Piercing

a. _____

_____

_____

b. _____

_____

_____

2. Topic   Children Who Commit Violent Crimes

a. _____

   _____

   _____

b. _____

   _____

   _____

3. Topic   School Uniforms

a. _____

   _____

   _____

b. _____

   _____

   _____

4. Topic   Fertility Treatments

a. _____

   _____

   _____

b. _____

   _____

   _____

Purpose Affects Tone

Tone in writing is much like tone of voice in speech. It's the emotion or attitude that emerges from the author's choice of both language and content. For an illustration of how tone can vary from author to author, read the following excerpts.

I am a lawyer. I have practiced law for more than thirty years. I think it is an honorable profession. And yet lawyers are the target of the most demeaning* (and immensely popular) jokes in our society. At a time when ethnic, gender, and racial jokes are considered politically incorrect, lawyer bashing has become the great American pastime. (Gerald D. Skoning, "Lawyer Jokes Are No Joke," *Chicago Tribune,* March 6, 1998, p. 23.)

As a lawyer myself, I would like to say just how annoyed and insulted I am by the current popularity of lawyer jokes. I think I do a good job for my clients and that I am appropriately paid for the long hours I put in service to their interests. But somehow being well paid for work well done is considered bad form, and I and other members of my profession would apparently be better liked if we were willing to work for nothing. Fortunately, all those lawyer bashers out there (who can't resist a cheap shot) have not made me hate myself or my profession.

Both of these passages are about lawyer bashing, and both express resentment that it exists. Note, however, the difference in tone. While the first author uses a reasonable tone that expresses his dislike of lawyer jokes without anger, the second author employs an insulted tone that makes his annoyance hard to miss.

The ability to create tone is an important writing skill. However, it's just as important for readers to recognize how tone can help identify purpose.

Tone in Informative Writing

Critical readers are alert to the relationship between tone and purpose. They know, for example, that informative writing is likely to have a cool, unemotional, neutral tone. A neutral tone relies heavily on denotative language and doesn't try to affect readers' emotions. In informative writing, the tone is unlikely to betray the author's personal feelings about the topic discussed.

Look, for example, at the following passage from pages 275–276, written solely to inform. Note the absence of charged language. Note, too, that the authors' personal feelings are not revealed.

Two factors in the development of obesity in children are beyond human control. These two factors are heredity and age. Like it or not, thinness and fatness do run in families. Overweight children tend to have overweight parents, and underweight children tend to

*demeaning: undignified, humiliating.

have underweight parents (LeBow, 1984). And most people inevitably put on fat more during some periods of life than others. Late childhood and early puberty form one of these periods; at this time, most children gain fat tissue out of proportion to increases in other tissues, such as muscle and bone. (Seifert and Hoffnung, *Child and Adolescent Development*, p. 390.)

In the passage above, the authors simply want to tell readers about the two factors in obesity that are beyond human control, and their tone matches their purpose—objective and direct.

Tone in Persuasive Writing

In persuasive writing, tone can vary enormously. Although it can be cool and reserved, it's more likely to express some kind of emotion. The tone in persuasive writing can be coaxing, admiring, enthusiastic, rude, even sarcastic. How, for example, would you describe the tone of the following passage?

I have been fat all of my life and I am thoroughly sick of apologizing for it. This is my declaration of independence from all you skinny people out there who have insisted how much better off I would be if I lost a few pounds. Tragically, we live in a culture that celebrates the thin and denigrates* the fat. This state of affairs leads to the kind of desperate and dangerous dieting I have engaged in for most of my adult life. And I am not alone in this obsession with losing weight. At some time in their lives, at least 80 percent of the American population has dieted to lose weight, even though studies show the majority of diets fail (Fett and Dick, 91). We would probably all be a lot better off if we spent time improving our souls instead of our bodies. No matter what we do, our bodies will decay; our souls will not.

At the beginning of the paragraph, judging by the words alone, it appears that the author wants only to inform readers about his own miserable dieting experience. He seems to focus solely on himself. He doesn't express any wish to affect other peoples' lives. But the passionate and angry tone is a dead giveaway to the author's real purpose, which is more persuasive than informative. By the end of the passage, it's clear the author wants us to believe that we should stop thinking so much about dieting and instead spend more time concentrating on our souls.

Checking the match between tone and purpose is important. In-

---

*denigrates: criticizes, demeans.

formative writing that suddenly becomes angry and emotional in tone may be more persuasive in intent than you initially realized. Or, it may be that the writer honestly intends to inform, but his or her bias interferes with the writer's ability to stay fair and balanced. Whatever you do, *don't think of tone as verbal decoration.* For writers, it's a tool to create meaning. For readers, it's a crucial clue to the author's primary purpose. Tone also tells you how willing the author might be to at least acknowledge another point of view.

Words Useful for Describing Tone

admiring	insulted
amused	insulting
annoyed	ironic (saying the opposite of
angry	what is intended)
appalled	joyful
astonished	nostalgic (looking fondly to-
awed (filled with wonder)	ward the past)
cautious	outraged
critical	passionate
disgusted	regretful
disrespectful	sad
dumbfounded (very sur-	sarcastic
prised)	shocked
embarrassed	solemn
enthusiastic	sorrowful
horrified	surprised
humorous	

■ EXAMPLE 6

DIRECTIONS After reading each selection, identify the author's purpose. Then circle the letter of the word or phrase that best fits the author's tone.

EXAMPLE Jazz singer Ella Fitzgerald was a quiet and humble woman who experienced little of the love she sang about so exquisitely for more than fifty years. Her voice, even in later years when she suffered from crippling arthritis, was always filled with a clear, light energy that could set the toes of even the stodgiest* listeners tapping. Although Fitzgerald, an African American, came of age in

---

*stodgiest: lacking in life, without energy.

an era when racism was rampant, whatever bitterness she felt never spilled over into her music. She sang the lyrics of a white Cole Porter or a black Duke Ellington with the same impossible-to-imitate ease and grace, earning every one of the awards that were heaped upon her in her later years. When she performed with Duke Ellington at Carnegie Hall in 1958, critics called Fitzgerald "The First Lady of Jazz." Although she died in 1996, no one has come along to challenge her title, and Ella Fitzgerald is still jazz's First Lady.

Purpose   a. to inform

(b.) to persuade

Tone   a. coolly annoyed

(b.) enthusiastic and admiring

c. emotionally neutral

EXPLANATION Throughout the passage, the author describes Ella Fitzgerald in strong, positively charged language, thereby creating an enthusiastic and admiring tone that encourages readers to share the admiration. The purpose is therefore persuasive.

1. As a mail carrier for over twenty years, I can tell you firsthand that we are much maligned members of the population. Customers see only the flaws in mail delivery. They never appreciate the huge effort that makes service both speedy and efficient. For 33 cents, you can send mail anywhere in the country, from Hawaii to Alaska. You'd think this would impress most people, but no. Instead of thanking us for services rendered, they whine and complain about the few times mail gets lost. And just because a few members of the postal service have engaged in violent behavior, people now use the insulting term *going postal* to refer to unexpected outbreaks of violence brought on by stress. This expression unfairly insults the rest of us hardworking employees who do our jobs without complaint day in and day out.

Purpose   a. to inform

b. to persuade

Tone   a. comical

b. insulted

c. emotionally neutral

2. In his book *An Anthropologist on Mars*, the renowned neurologist* Dr. Oliver Sacks gives readers an important and insightful perspec-

_____
*neurologist: a doctor who specializes in the workings and diseases of the nervous system.

tive on injuries and disorders of the brain. According to Dr. Sacks, some injuries and disorders result in greater creativity and achievement. With compassionate insight, Dr. Sacks describes, for example, a painter who becomes colorblind through a car accident. Initially in despair, the painter eventually started painting stunning black-and-white canvases that won him more critical acclaim than he had received before his mishap.

As in his previous works, Dr. Sacks gives readers an unexpected perspective on disease and injury. In *An Anthropologist on Mars*, he once again makes us rethink and reconsider our most cherished beliefs about health and illness. His book should be required reading for anyone interested in the power of human beings to adapt to and ultimately overcome loss.

Purpose   a. to inform

           b. to persuade

Tone   a. admiring

       b. cautious

       c. emotionally neutral

3. The National Panhellenic Conference passed a resolution last month endorsing substance-free fraternities and encouraging their twenty-six member sororities to participate in alcohol-free events with them. "The conduct, scholastic performance, and health and welfare of students are being adversely affected by the alcohol-dominated culture of many college campuses," the resolution stated. "Substance-free housing will result in a higher quality fraternity experience and improved health and safety among collegiate members." The resolution by the National Panhellenic Conference was the most recent by a Greek organization to support substance-free living. Several national fraternities have already decided to eliminate alcohol in their chapter houses, and many more will soon follow, said national Greek leaders. (Greg Johnson, "Banning Booze," *The Daily Northwestern*, Vol. 119, No. 32, November 3, 1997, p. 1.)

Purpose   a. to inform

           b. to persuade

Tone   a. outraged

       b. relaxed and friendly

       c. emotionally neutral

4. Jazz pianist Michel Petrucciani, who died in 1999 at the age of thirty-one, was only about four feet tall. But he was a giant when he sat in front of a piano. The childhood victim of a disease that turned his bones so brittle they could barely support his tiny body, Petrucciani couldn't go out and play like other kids. Instead, he stayed home, played the piano and listened to the music of jazz and swing greats like Dexter Gordon, Benny Goodman, and Miles Davis. For Petrucciani—who stayed upbeat, determined, and feisty* until the day of his death—disease had forced him to turn to music. Ironically, he was grateful for that. The world, in turn, should be grateful for the music this young man produced. Although Petrucciani's music never quite loses its jazz edge, it's also lush and lyrical, filled with a sense of passionate longing. Michel Petrucciani died with a small but loyal following, yet if there is any justice in the world, that following will grow. One only has to listen to the artist play songs like "Miles Davis Licks" and "Bimini" to know immediately that his talent was both rare and great.

Purpose a. to inform

b. to persuade

Tone a. solemn and serious

b. emotionally neutral

c. enthusiastic and admiring

CHECK YOUR UNDERSTANDING

Define the term *tone* and explain its relationship to purpose.

_____

_____

_____

 # Learning to Recognize Irony

No discussion of tone would be complete without some mention of **irony**—the practice of saying one thing while implying exactly the opposite. This might sound confusing at first, but like most of us, you've probably used irony more than once in your life. Haven't you ever had a really horrible day and said to someone, "Boy, what a

---

*feisty: combative.

great day this was!" Or, seeing a friend wearing a sad expression, maybe you said, "Gee, you look happy."

If either of these examples sounds familiar, then you know more about irony than you think, and you're prepared for writers who assume an ironic tone like the one used in the following example:

> The school board has decided to reduce the school budget once again. But why take half measures? Why not eliminate the budget altogether and close our schools? After all, a little learning is a dangerous thing, or so they say. Better to keep our children totally ignorant and out of harm's way.

The author of this paragraph doesn't want his readers to take what he says *literally,* or at face value. After all, who would seriously suggest that keeping children ignorant is a good idea? The author's point is just the opposite of what he actually says. He doesn't want the school budget further reduced. But instead of saying that directly, he makes an outrageous suggestion that draws attention to where the cuts could lead.

When writers present what seems to be an outrageous or impossible opinion as if it were obvious common sense, critical readers assume the writer is being ironic, and they respond by inferring a message directly opposed to the author's actual words. As you might expect, *an ironic tone is a good indicator of a persuasive purpose.*

CHECK YOUR UNDERSTANDING
What is irony?
_____
_____
_____

EXERCISE 7

DIRECTIONS Read each passage and circle the letter that best identifies the author's tone.

EXAMPLE According to the American Association of Furriers, wearing fur coats is once again back in fashion. Well, isn't that good news for the thousands of mink, rabbits, foxes, and raccoons that are brutally slaughtered so that fashionable men and women can sport a trendy fur coat or hat. No doubt these animals are honored to suffer and die for the sake of making humans feel well dressed.

Tone (a.) ironic

    b. comical

    c. emotionally neutral

    EXPLANATION Someone who uses the phrase "brutally slaughtered" to describe the killing of animals for their fur is unlikely to mean it when she says that the return of fur is good news for animals. This is a clear case of an ironic tone that suggests the author means the exact opposite of what she says.

1. When the voters of Michigan sent Charles Diggs Jr. to the United States House of Representatives in 1954, he became the first black congressman in the state's history. He was not, however, the first black congressman in the United States. During the period of Reconstruction, from 1865 to 1877, the United States government tried to rebuild the South after the political and economic devastation of the Civil War. Black citizens held prominent government positions throughout the nation, including the posts of mayor, governor, lieutenant governor, state supreme court justice, U.S. senator, and U.S. congressman. (Juan Williams, *Eyes on the Prize.* New York: Penguin, 1987, p. 49.)

Tone a. outraged

    b. lighthearted

    c. emotionally neutral

2. It is refreshing to note that many right-thinking citizens are calling for a ban on the celebration of Halloween because the holiday encourages devil worship. Hallelujah? It doesn't take the intellect of a TV evangelist to see that the wearing of "Casper the Friendly Ghost" costumes leads children to the wanton embrace of Beelzebub.* And it is a known fact that candy corn is the first step toward addiction. Only the devil (or an underemployed dentist) would knowingly offer popcorn balls to innocent children. But why stop at Halloween? Many other holidays conceal wickedness behind a vicious veil of greeting cards and Bob Hope TV specials. (Steve Ruebal, "Toss Out Halloween? Let's Not Stop There," *USA Today,* October 29, 1991, p. 11A.)

Tone a. confident

    b. enthusiastic

    c. ironic

---

*Beelzebub: another name for the devil.

3. I prefer the scruffy feel of the dog to the putting-green smoothness of the cat, a tail that wags happily to a tail that curls and uncurls like a cobra, an exuberant* bark to a maddeningly complacent* purr—"the most hideous of all the sounds in the world," according to the English man of letters Hilaire Belloc. Dogs lick you as if you were an ice cream cone, with grateful, life-affirming slurps; cats perform exploratory, clinical swabs with their tiny, pink, emery-board tongues. Before choosing a pet, consider a few chapter titles from Desmond Morris's book *Dogwatching:* "Why Does a Dog Wag Its Tail?" "Do Dogs Show Remorse?" and "Why Do Male Dogs Like Having Their Chests Scratched?" Now compare those with a few from Morris's *Catwatching:* "Why Does a Tomcat Tear at the Fabric of Your Favorite Chair?" "Why Does a Cat Spray Urine on the Garden Wall?" (George Howe Cott, "Why We Love Dogs," *Life,* October, 1994, p. 9.)

Tone a. humorous

 b. outraged

 c. emotionally neutral

4. According to one of your readers, insufficient attention has been paid to the possibility that men are also victims of domestic violence. It is his opinion that men are, in fact, just as likely to be victimized by women as women are by men. The difference is that men, for fear of looking unmasculine, fail to report it. Well, I'm just all broken up at the thought of this new social problem. I can imagine how horrible it is for a 220-pound male to be terrorized by a 120-pound female. The poor thing must live in terror at the thought of her menacing approach. A man like that is certainly as much in need of our sympathy as are the women who end up hospitalized or worse in the wake of a domestic dispute.

Tone a. ironic

 b. friendly

 c. emotionally neutral

5. On December 1, 1955, Rosa Parks left the Montgomery Fair department store late in the afternoon for her regular bus ride home. All thirty-six seats of the bus she boarded were soon filled, with twenty-two Negroes seated from the rear and fourteen whites from the front. Driver J. P. Blake, seeing a white man standing in front of the bus,

---

*exuberant: excited, happy.
*complacent: self-satisfied.

called out for the four passengers on the row just behind the whites to stand up and move to the back. Nothing happened. Blake finally had to get out of the driver's seat to speak more firmly to the four Negroes. "You better make it light on yourselves and let me have those seats," he said. At this, three of the Negroes moved to stand in the back of the bus, but Parks responded that she was not in the white section and didn't think she ought to move. She was in no-man's-land. Blake said that the white section was where he said it was, and he was telling Parks that she was in it. As he saw the law, the whole idea of no-man's-land was to give the driver some discretion* to keep the races out of each other's way. He was doing just that. When Parks refused again, he advised her that the same city law that allowed him to regulate no-man's-land also gave him emergency police power to enforce the segregation codes. He would arrest Parks himself if he had to. Parks replied that he should do what he had to do; she was not moving. She spoke so softly that Blake would not have been able to hear her above the drone of normal bus noise. But the bus was silent. Blake notified Parks that she was officially under arrest. (Taylor Branch, *Parting the Waters*. New York: Simon & Schuster, 1988, p. 128.)

Tone   a. ironic

      b. admiring

      c. emotionally neutral

Clues to Purpose

Informative Writing

- appears in textbooks, newspapers, lab reports, research findings, case studies, and reference works.
- employs a title that simply names or describes a topic.
- states or suggests a main idea that describes a situation, event, person, concept, or experience without making any judgment.
- relies more on denotative than connotative language.
- employs more statements of fact than statements of opinion.
- takes an emotionally neutral tone.
- remains objective and reveals little or nothing about the author's personal feelings.

---

*discretion: ability or power to decide.

Persuasive Writing

- appears in newspaper editorials, political pamphlets, opinion pieces, and articles or books written to explain the author's position on current or past events.
- states or suggests a controlling idea identifying an action that needs to be taken or a belief that should be held, or at the very least considered.
- may lean heavily on connotative language.
- relies a good deal on opinion and uses facts mainly to serve opinions.
- often expresses a strong emotional tone that reveals the author's personal feelings.
- can employ irony.

WORD NOTES

The word *irony*, defined on page 294, is a widely used term. Like so many other words, its meaning can vary with context. For example, how would you define the word *ironic* when it appears in the following sentence: "Isn't it a bit ironic for you to simultaneously imitate and criticize your best friend's behavior?" In this example, the word *ironic* indicates that a particular action is the opposite of what one would expect. This is another commonly used meaning for the words *irony* or *ironic*.

The word *irony* is closely related in meaning to *sarcasm*. However, there is a difference. In both irony and sarcasm, what is said is actually the opposite of what is meant. The difference is that irony is used to make a point whereas sarcasm is used strictly to insult or hurt (which may be one good reason why sarcastic people don't have a lot of friends).

In your literature or drama classes, you may also be introduced to the phrase *dramatic irony*. The phrase refers to a device playwrights use when they create characters who know less than their audience. All through the famous play *Oedipus Rex*, for example, the audience knows that disaster will strike when King Oedipus finds out the truth about his birth, but the king himself remains completely unaware until it's too late.

Take a philosophy course and you could be introduced to the term *Socratic irony*. According to the Greek philosopher Plato, his teacher, Socrates, would first claim ignorance and then ask a series of questions that would lead his students to the point he wanted to make: "I know nothing of it, but I wonder 'what is the nature of love?'" This method is called Socratic irony, in part because it is based—like irony in general—on a contradiction. Socrates always claimed not to know anything but was, in fact, leading his students toward the point he wanted to make.

Summing Up

Listed below are the most important points in Chapter 8. Put a check mark in the box if you think the point is clear in your mind. Leave the box blank if you need to review the material one more time. The page numbers in parentheses tell you where to look to review each point on the list.

☐ **1.** To be an effective critical reader, you need to understand the difference between *informative* and *persuasive* writing. Informative writing provides the audience with information and doesn't promote any one opinion. Persuasive writing, on the other hand, tries to make readers share or at least consider the author's point of view. (pp. 275–276)

☐ **2.** Detecting a writer's purpose is important because the author's purpose determines how critically you need to read. (p. 277)

☐ **3.** To predict the author's purpose, look at the source of the writing and the title, and pay attention to any information about the author's background. (pp. 278–283)

☐ **4.** Test your initial predictions about the author's purpose against the stated or implied thesis statement. In informative writing, the thesis statement is likely to describe people and events without judging them. The thesis statement in persuasive writing usually suggests an action or a belief that the author wants to share. (p. 283)

☐ **5.** In the context of writing, *tone* refers to the emotion or attitude suggested by the author's choice of language and content. (p. 288)

☐ **6.** Purpose affects tone. Writers who want mainly to inform tend to use an emotionally neutral tone, whereas writers intent on persuasion are likely to employ a tone that reveals some emotion or feeling. (pp. 289–291)

☐ **7.** Writers who assume an ironic tone say one thing but imply another. If you detect irony in an author's tone, he or she is probably intent on persuasion. (pp. 294–295)

TEST YOUR UNDERSTANDING

To see how well you have understood this chapter, take the following review quiz. Then correct it using the answer key provided by your instructor. If you score 80 percent or above, you're ready to take the end-of-chapter exam. However, if you score below 80 percent, look over the quiz carefully to see what kind of questions you missed. Then use the **Summing Up** section to find out which pages you should review before taking the chapter exam.

Chapter 8: Review Quiz

DIRECTIONS Read each passage. Then answer the accompanying questions by circling the appropriate letter or letters.

1. Navajo Skinwalkers

Among the Navajo of the southwestern United States, it is said that no human being is all good or all evil. In the Navajo view, human beings have both qualities or, more accurately, the capacity to do both good and evil. According to Witherspoon (1977), the goal of Navajo life is to bring one's impulses under control so that one grows and develops through a complete life in a condition of *hozho*—the state of beauty, harmony, good, and happiness—and then dies naturally of old age and becomes one with the universal beauty, harmony, and happiness that make up the ideal positive environment.

A person's *ch'indi*, or potential for evil, can be controlled by rituals that restore one to a state of *hozho*. Although the state of inward beauty achieved through living in outward harmony with the ideal environment can be disrupted by contact with dangerous (*bahadzid*) things or by the sorcery* of others, perhaps leading to illness or death, such states can be countered by a traditional ritual chant, or "sing," of which there are over sixty. Rituals channel supernatural power by reenacting the Navajo creation myths, which relate the deeds of the gods, both good and evil. (Richley Crapo, *Cultural Anthropology*. Guilford, CT: Dushkin Publishing, 1987, p. 211.)

1. What is the primary purpose of this reading?
   a. to inform
   b. to persuade

2. Which of the following helped you determine the author's purpose?
   a. title
   b. thesis statement
   c. source of the selection
   d. tone

3. How would you describe the author's tone?
   a. admiring
   b. critical
   c. emotionally neutral

---

*sorcery: witchcraft.

2. You Either Have Free Speech or You Don't

A controversial issue for many Americans is whether people who are known to be racist or to have other destructive views should be allowed to speak at public places like state universities. Even those who cherish the American Constitution and its guarantee of free speech have difficulty supporting free speech for bigots.* However, painful as it may be to accept, freedom of speech is an all-or-nothing proposition.* You can't have freedom of speech for some people and not for others. If you ban unpopular people from speaking, you no longer have freedom of speech. In short, you no longer have a democracy.

At a state university in California recently, David Duke, once identified as a Ku Klux Klan grand wizard, was invited by students to speak in a debate on the subject of affirmative action.* The invitation itself caused an uproar in both the university and the community. One local editorial labeled Duke's views beyond the limits of legitimate discussion. Even the governor of the state agreed that Duke's invitation should be withdrawn. However, the president of the university correctly argued that public institutions must be places where *all* ideas can be explored. In addition, members of African-American and gay organizations argued that Duke should be allowed to speak because they wanted the opportunity to challenge him in person.

As a result of those arguments, the debate took place. Even more importantly, it took place peacefully, with only a few incidents involving protesters taking place outside the auditorium. The president of the university courageously held her ground in refusing to interfere with the students' decision to invite Duke to speak and thus refusing to limit one of the most precious rights we Americans possess. After all, once one speaker is banned, it becomes a little too easy to ban another one. Hard as it is to accept, it's still true that "you either have free speech or you don't."

1. What is the primary purpose of this reading?

    a. to inform

    b. to persuade

---

*bigots: people who consider other people to be inferior because of their race, gender, religion, or sexual orientation.
*proposition: a statement put forth for acceptance.
*affirmative action: a federally supported plan to make sure that women and minorities have access to jobs and education.

2. Which of the following helped you determine the author's purpose?

    a. title

    b. thesis statement

    c. source of the selection

    d. tone

3. How would you describe the author's tone?

    a. concerned

    b. humorous

    c. emotionally neutral

3. New Ideas in Education

In the early 1800s, school curricula had consisted chiefly of moral-istic pieties.* *McGuffey's Reader,* used throughout the nation, taught homilies* such as "By virtue we secure happiness" and "One deed of shame is succeeded by years of penitence." But in the late nineteenth century, psychologist G. Stanley Hall and edu-cational philosopher John Dewey asserted that modern education ought to prepare children differently. They insisted that personal development, not subject matter, should be the focus of the curric-ulum. Education, argued Dewey, must relate directly to experi-ence; children should be encouraged to discover knowledge for themselves. Learning relevant to students' lives should replace rote memorization and outdated subjects.

Progressive education, based on Dewey's *The School and Soci-ety* (1899) and *Democracy and Education* (1916), was a uniquely American phenomenon. Dewey believed that learning should fo-cus on real-life problems and that children should be taught to use their intelligence and ingenuity as instruments for controlling their environment. From kindergarten through high school, Dewey asserted, children should learn through direct experience. Dewey and his wife Alice put these ideas into practice in the Labo-ratory School that they directed at the University of Chicago.

Personal growth became the driving principle behind higher ed-ucation as well. Previously, the purpose of American colleges and universities had been that of their European counterparts: to train a select few for the professions of law, medicine, teaching, and religion. But in the late 1800s, institutions of higher educa-tion multiplied, aided by land grants and by an increase in the number of people who could afford tuition. Between 1870 and

*pieties: statements suggesting the value of virtuous behavior.
*homilies: statements with a moral message.

1910 the number of colleges and universities in the United States grew from 563 to nearly 1,000. Curricula expanded as educators sought to make learning more appealing and to keep up with technological and social changes. (Norton et al., *A People and a Nation*, pp. 609–610.)

1. What is the primary purpose of this reading?

    a. to inform

    b. to persuade

2. Which of the following helped you determine the author's purpose?

    a. title

    b. thesis statement

    c. source of the selection

    d. tone

3. How would you describe the author's tone?

    a. sarcastic

    b. lighthearted

    c. emotionally neutral

4. *Juku*, **Japanese for "Cram School"**

On a brisk Saturday morning, while most of their friends were relaxing at home, sixteen-year-old Jerry Lee and eight other Asian teenagers huddled over their notebooks and calculators for a full day of math and English lessons.

During the week they all attend public schools in the city. But every Saturday, they go to a Korean *hagwon*, or cram school, to spend up to seven hours immersed in the finer points of linear algebra or Raymond Chandler.*

"I complain, but my mom says I have to go," said Jerry, a Stuyvesant High School student from Sunnyside, Queens, who has already scored a 1520 on the Scholastic Aptitude Test for college but is shooting for a perfect 1600. "It's like a habit now."

Long a tradition in the Far East, where the competition to get into a top university borders on the fanatic, the cram schools of Asia have begun to appear in this country too, in Queens and New Jersey and Los Angeles and elsewhere, following the migration of many Koreans, Japanese, and Chinese over the last two decades.

---

*Raymond Chandler (1888–1959): considered by many to be the finest mystery writer of all time; the creator of fictional detective Philip Marlowe.

In the last ten years, the cram schools—called *juku* in Japanese and *buxiban* in Chinese—have become a flourishing industry, thriving on immigrant parents' determination to have their children succeed. Only a handful of cram schools existed here when the *hagwon* that Jerry attends, the Elite Academy, opened in 1986. Today, the Korean-language yellow pages list about three dozen Asian cram schools in the New York area. In Los Angeles, the Chinese yellow pages list about forty.

While the pressure to get into a good school is not nearly so extreme in the United States, the cram schools, such as the ambitiously named Nobel Education Institute in Arcadia, a heavily Asian suburb of Los Angeles, have nonetheless found a burgeoning niche in Asian communities. Chinese and Korean newspapers bulge with cram school advertisements. Some schools simply print lists of their graduates who have been accepted to New York City's specialized high schools, as well as to Harvard, Stanford, and MIT.

For many busy parents, the schools have become a kind of academic baby-sitting service. But most see them as a way of ensuring that their children excel in spite of the public schools that they perceive as lax* and unchallenging compared with those in Asia. (Ashley Dunn, "Cram Schools: Immigrants' Tools for Success," *New York Times*, January 28, 1995, p. 1.)

1. What is the primary purpose of this reading?

   a. to inform

   b. to persuade

2. Which of the following helped you determine the author's purpose?

   a. title

   b. thesis statement

   c. source of the selection

   d. tone

3. How would you describe the author's tone?

   a. admiring

   b. critical

   c. emotionally neutral

5. And They Call This Mercy?

The word *euthanasia* means "good death" or "mercy killing." But the name does not fit with the act. When one person assumes the

---

*lax: lacking in strictness or firmness.

right to take the life of another, there is no goodness or mercy involved. No one has the right to decide when a life should end.

Life is our most precious gift and we cannot just fling that gift away when it suits us. Refusing to accept assistance from machinery that maintains respiration is one thing, but asking to die is another. That's why the book *Final Exit* is such a disgrace to the publishing industry. The book suggests that we as individuals have the right to plan our own death; to decide, in effect, that we are tired of living. Yet that decision—to decide when life ends—lies in God's hands, not in ours.

Jack Kevorkian, the man who has championed an individual's right to take his or her own life, has not done the public a service by making headlines aiding and abetting suicide. Instead, he has encouraged others to believe that they too can choose when to die. That choice, however, is not ours to make. (Dale Matthews, "And They Call This Mercy?" *Moral Matters,* April 12, 1999, p. 20.)

1. What is the primary purpose of this reading?

    a. to inform

    b. to persuade

2. Which of the following helped you determine the author's purpose?

    a. title

    b. thesis statement

    c. source of the selection

    d. tone

3. How would you describe the author's tone?

    a. outraged

    b. astonished

    c. emotionally neutral

> Use the answer key supplied by your instructor to correct your quiz. If you score 80 percent or above, you are ready for the chapter exam. If you score below 80 percent, look carefully at the questions you answered incorrectly. Then use the **Summing Up** section to decide which pages you need to review.

Chapter Test 8

DIRECTIONS Read each passage. Then answer the accompanying questions by circling the correct letter or letters.

1. The Ritual Slaves of Ghana

Just twelve years old, with a shy smile, bare feet, and simple printed cloth that serves as her only clothing, Abla Kotor has begun a life of servitude* and atonement* for a crime she did not commit.

For now her duties mostly involve sweeping the dirt courtyard of a local fetish priest, a spiritual intermediary* between worshippers and deities of the area's traditional religion, juju.* But her responsibilities will grow to include providing sexual favors to the priest who has become her master. In the meantime, she must learn to cook and to farm, serving long hours weeding fields where there are crops of yam, manioc, and corn. And servants like her are typically denied the fruits of their hard labor. Instead, their families, often wretchedly poor, are expected to send food to feed them.

Miss Kotor has little idea of why she was sent to the shrine here by her family four months ago, or, for that matter, what the future holds. Without even knowing it, she has joined a community of several thousand female ritual slaves in the corner of southeastern Ghana. Here, girls known as *trocosi,* or slaves of the gods, are routinely given by their families to work as slaves in religious shrines as a way of appeasing the gods for crimes committed by relatives.

Once given to a priest, a girl is considered his property, and can be freed only by the priest, in which case her family must replace her with a new young girl. To ensure that the gods remain appeased, this process is repeated for a serious crime, with families giving up generation after generation of girls in perpetual atonement. . . . (Excerpted from Howard W. French, "The Ritual Slaves of Ghana: Young and Female," *New York Times,* January 20, 1997, pp. A1, A4.)

1. How would you describe the author's primary purpose?

    a. to inform

    b. to persuade

---

*servitude: slavery.
*atonement: repayment for a crime.
*intermediary: person in the middle; a go-between.
*juju: the giving of supernatural powers to an object.

2. Which of the following helped you determine the author's purpose?

    a. title

    b. thesis statement

    c. source of the selection

    d. tone

3. How would you describe the author's tone?

    a. sad

    b. disgusted

    c. emotionally neutral

2. Pornography

Pornography has become an enormous industry today. A major reason is that the demand for sexually explicit materials has soared over the last decade. The number of hard-core video rentals, for example, skyrocketed from only 75 million in 1985 to 665 million in 1996. Today, the United States has become by far the world's leading producer of hard-core videos, churning them out at the astonishing rate of about 150 new titles a week. Pornography has also gone online; whatever X-rated, hard-core material that is available in adult bookstores can be accessed via the Internet (Schlosser, 1997; Weber, 1997). But is pornography harmful?

According to some conservatives, pornography is harmful to society. The studies most often cited to support this view, conducted in laboratories, suggest that exposure to pornography increases aggression. In these studies, male subjects were first made to feel irritated, angry, or ready to behave aggressively. Then they were exposed to pornographic materials. Mostly their level of aggression increased significantly (Soble, 1996; Linz & Malamuth, 1993). However, the artificial laboratory setting is quite different from the real world outside.

According to some liberals, pornography is harmless. To support this view, studies that fail to show a connection between pornography and rape are often cited. Cities with high circulation of sexually oriented magazines, for example, have largely the same rates of rape as cities with low circulation. But the pornography in such studies is mostly *nonviolent,* depicting merely nudity and consensual sex (Strossen, 1996; Linz & Malamuth, 1993).

Other studies suggest that *violent* pornography is harmful, as some feminists assert. For example, research often finds that men who see slasher movies, in which a female rape victim is cut up, show less sympathy for rape victims in general. Studies on rapists suggest that men who lack rape sympathy are more likely to assault women (Kipnis, 1996; Cole, 1995; Linz & Malamuth, 1993). (Adapted from Thio, *Sociology,* p. 174.)

1. How would you describe the author's primary purpose?

    a. to inform

    b. to persuade

2. Which of the following helped you determine the author's purpose?

    a. title

    b. thesis statement

    c. source of the selection

    d. tone

3. How would you describe the author's tone?

    a. outraged

    b. sad

    c. emotionally neutral

3. Make It Illegal to Be a Bad Samaritan*

On May 25, 1997, twenty-two-year-old Jeremy Strohmeyer chased seven-year-old Sherrice Iverson into the stall of a public bathroom, where he molested and then strangled her. At one point, his friend David Cash looked over the door of the stall and saw Strohmeyer struggling with the little girl. Cash, however, didn't intervene to help Sherrice. Instead, he told his friend they had to get going and left the little girl alone with her killer.

Although Jeremy Strohmeyer is now serving a life sentence without parole, David Cash is a free man. In Las Vegas, where the crime was committed, there's no law saying a bystander has to come to the aid of a crime victim, even if the victim is in danger of being murdered. Yet as the case of Sherrice Iverson suggests, we need a Good Samaritan law. We need a law that says bystanders can't simply watch or walk away while someone is being brutally attacked. They don't have to intervene physically, but they must

*Samaritan: A Samaritan is someone from Samaria, but in the Bible, the Good Samaritan selflessly helps someone who has been hurt.

call for help. If they don't, they should be fined and sentenced to spend some time in jail. In states where they already have a Good Samaritan law, the penalties for breaking that law should be made much, much tougher. In Vermont, for example, failure to help someone being attacked only results in a hundred-dollar fine. The fine should be a hundred times that amount.

Although many European countries do have Good Samaritan laws, American individualism seems to have interfered with the court's willingness to make protecting others part of our legal code. According to UCLA law professor Peter Arnella, "The criminal law in this country tends to overvalue the notion of individual rights . . . even when the person is risking a serious social harm."

A famous turn-of-the-century case often cited by legal scholars certainly supports Arnella's position. During a couple's weekend vacation, one member fell into a drug-induced coma. The man's partner responded by going home and leaving him to die. The case ultimately went all the way to the Michigan Supreme Court, where the court found that the partner who left had no legal duty to intervene and offer aid.

Legal or not, most people would argue that there was a moral duty at stake in the Michigan case and certainly in the case of Sherrice Iverson. We need a Good Samaritan law on the books, and we need it now. (Helen Robeson, "Make It Illegal to Be a Bad Samaritan," *Modern Moral Choices*, June 1, 1999, p. 25.)

1. How would you describe the author's primary purpose?

   a. to inform

   b. to persuade

2. Which of the following helped you determine the author's purpose?

   a. title

   b. thesis statement

   c. source of the selection

   d. tone

3. How would you describe the author's tone?

   a. confident

   b. angry

   c. emotionally neutral

4. Hyphenated America

In the nineteenth century, most **old-stock Americans*** assumed that immigrants should quickly learn English, become citizens, and restructure their lives and values to resemble those of old-stock Americans. Immigrants from Britain were often rapid assimilators,* for they already spoke English and their religious values were similar to those of major old-stock Protestant denominations.* Most immigrants, however, resisted rapid assimilation.

For most immigrants, assimilation took place over a lifetime or over generations. Most held fast to customs in their own culture at the same time that they took up a new life in America. Their sense of identity drew on two elements: where they came from and where they were now. Being conscious of their new identity as a German in America, or an Italian in America, they often came to think of themselves as **hyphenated Americans:** German-American, Italian-American, Polish-American.

On arriving in America, with its strange language and unfamiliar customs, many immigrants reacted by seeking out people who shared their cultural values, practiced their religion, and, especially, spoke their language. Ethnic communities emerged throughout regions with large numbers of immigrants. These communities played significant roles in newcomers' transition from the old country to America. They gave immigrants a chance to learn about their new home with the assistance of those who had come before. At the same time, they could retain the values and behavior from their old country that they found most important without awkwardness.

Hyphenated America developed a unique blend of ethnic institutions, often unlike anything in the old country but also unlike those of old-stock America. Fraternal lodges based on ethnicity sprang up, and often provided not only social ties but also benefits in case of illness or death. Among these lodges were the Ancient Order of Hibernians (Irish), the Sons of Hermann (German), and the Sons of Italy. Social groups often included singing societies devoted to the music of the old country. Foreign-language newspapers were vital in developing a sense of identity that connected the old country to the new, for they provided news from the old country as well as from other similar communities in the United States. (Berkin et al., *Making America*, p. 557.)

---

*old-stock Americans: term used by the Census Bureau to describe people who were born in the United States.
*assimilators: people who readily fit into a new way of life.
*denominations: religious groups.

1. How would you describe the author's purpose?

   a. to inform

   b. to persuade

2. Which of the following helped you determine the author's purpose?

   a. title

   b. thesis statement

   c. source of the selection

   d. tone

3. How would you describe the author's tone?

   a. disgusted

   b. astonished

   c. emotionally neutral

5. We Need Less Hysteria and More Common Sense

In the fall of 1997, a young man named Ross Vollbrecht from Nashville, Indiana, was barred from playing in his school's final game of football. What did the young man do to merit such a punishment? Surely he must have stolen from a classmate, sworn at a teacher, or cheated on an exam. These are the kinds of student infractions* one expects to hear about if a boy or girl is forbidden to participate in a crucial high school ritual. Ross Vollbrecht, however, did none of these things. His mistake was to take up chewing tobacco and get caught with the tobacco on his person. Yes, Ross was eighteen and had a legal right to chew tobacco if he wanted to, but school policy forbids the use of drugs, and tobacco is, after all, a drug. The young man had to be punished and punished severely.

When I read Ross's story, my first response was, "Well, so is coffee. Why didn't they penalize every player who had a cup of java during the semester?" Does this make me sound unsympathetic to the school's position? If so, good; I am unsympathetic. Actually, I am outraged because this case reminds me of an earlier one, where a young girl almost got suspended for bringing Advil on campus. It, too, is a drug you see. And while we are citing the sins of today's youth, let's not forget the seven-year-old boy who got suspended from school for stealing a kiss from one of his female classmates. We'll teach him to harass helpless females.

---

*infractions: violations of rules.

Now I know full well that we need to have our young people follow rules and regulations, but the application of those rules and regulations needs to be tempered by common sense. Schools do need to guard against drug use and sexual harassment, but school administrators need not go on witch hunts looking for these twin evils where they don't exist. If a drug is legal off of school grounds, then the administration has to think twice before penalizing a student for its possession. And come on, a six-year-old who steals a kiss from a classmate is not exactly in the same position as the owner of a computer company who thinks his or her secretary should pay for a promotion with sexual favors. Again, each case has to be considered in its proper context. Above all, the people in charge of our schools need to apply more reason and less hysteria when monitoring the behavior of their young charges. (A letter to the editor of the *Carson City Flyer* from Ellen Niemand, a high school teacher.)

1. How would you describe the author's primary purpose?

   a. to inform

   b. to persuade

2. Which of the following helped you determine the author's purpose?

   a. title

   b. thesis statement

   c. source of the selection

   d. tone

3. How would you describe the author's tone?

   a. angry and ironic

   b. amused and humorous

   c. emotionally neutral

CHAPTER 9

Understanding Figurative Language

In this chapter, you'll learn

- the meaning of figurative language.

- how to recognize and make sense out of similes.

- how to recognize and interpret metaphors.

- how to recognize and respond to allusions.

Like understanding the difference between fact and opinion, knowing how to interpret *figurative language*—language that makes sense in imaginative rather than realistic terms—is essential to reading in general and critical reading in particular. Once you become familiar with the three kinds of figurative language introduced in this chapter, you

315

will be in a better position to determine meaning, identify tone, and even detect bias.

 # What Is Figurative Language?

Figurative language is language that encourages the comparison or association of two seemingly unlike things or ideas. Although figurative language works in imaginative terms, it makes little sense in literal, or real, terms. For example, if a friend tells you that his uncle is "a bear of a man," you don't—if introduced—expect to see a grizzly with a human head. You know right off that your friend is making an imaginative comparison between his uncle and a creature similar in stature and strength, maybe even in temperament. Your friend is speaking figuratively, not literally.

CHECK YOUR UNDERSTANDING

Define the term *figurative language:* _____

_____

_____

 # Types of Figurative Language

Figurative language can be broken down into various **figures of speech.** These are special types of verbal expression, all of which employ some kind of comparison or association between people, events, objects, or ideas. The following pages introduce three of the most important figures of speech used in writing: similes, metaphors, and allusions.

Similes

Similes are comparisons that use the words *like* or *as* to create meaning by revealing an unexpected connection or likeness. For example, in his famous "Letter from Birmingham Jail," Martin Luther

King Jr. argued that racial tension was "like a boil that can never be cured as long as it is covered up." The purpose of this simile was to help readers vividly imagine how dangerous it was for racial tension to fester without ever being acknowledged. The simile also helped create the intensely serious tone of King's letter.

Now look at the next simile, drawn from a book review. What does it tell you and what kind of tone does it help create?

> Reading Alice Mattison's novel *Hilda and Pearl* is like eating a DoveBar. It's so rich and delicious, one can't help wishing it would never end.

In this instance, the simile tells you that reading Mattison's novel is a delightful experience; it also helps create the author's admiring tone.

Similes can also use the word *as*. For example, Raymond Chandler, a mystery writer whose mastery of clever similes contributed to his fame, described one character with an unforgettable simile. In Chandler's words, the man was "as crazy as two waltzing mice"—a phrase that perfectly expressed the character's oddball disposition and at the same time contributed to the smart-alecky tone Chandler used for his crime stories.

CHECK YOUR UNDERSTANDING

What is a simile? _____

_____

Create a simile that describes a friend, family member, or classmate.

_____

_____

EXERCISE 1

DIRECTIONS Read each passage. Then identify and explain the simile.

EXAMPLE Talking to General Dunlop is always an unsettling experience. To me, it's like hitting a tennis ball over the net only to have a pineapple lobbed back at you. The only thing you know for sure is that you'd better expect the unexpected.

a. What two things are compared in the author's simile?

Talking to General Dunlop is compared to playing tennis with someone who returns a pineapple instead of a tennis ball.

b. What point does that comparison help to make?

When you talk to General Dunlop, you never know what to expect.

EXPLANATION The simile in this passage illustrates just how unsettling conversations with General Dunlop really are. When talking to the general, you can expect a response as surprising as a pineapple being returned to you in a tennis game.

1. When he was a Harvard professor, the philosopher and psychologist William James would think aloud in front of his students, letting his ideas flow like a "rambling, sparkling stream." (David S. Reynolds, "Radical Pragmatist," *New York Times Book Review*, March 15, 1998, p. 11.)

a. What two things are compared in the author's simile?

_____

_____

b. What point does that simile help to make?

_____

_____

2. Many parents complain that bringing home their first baby is like walking around with a dozen eggs on their head. They're afraid to make one false move for fear of disaster.

a. What two things are compared in the author's simile?

_____

_____

b. What point does that simile help to make?

_____

_____

3. Jazz singer Billie Holiday lived a rough-and-tumble life that left her a legacy of despair. But when she went on stage before an audience, the past was forgotten. She was like a queen totally in command of her awestruck subjects, none of whom dared make a sound.

a. What two things are compared in the author's simile?

_____

_____

b. What point does that simile help to make?

_____

_____

4. Writing about a computer hacker who invaded his privacy, author Joshua Quittner claimed, "I remember feeling as powerless as a minnow in a flash flood. Someone was invading my private space—my family's private space—and there was nothing I or the authorities could do."[1]

a. What two things are compared in the author's simile?

_____

_____

b. What point does that simile help to make?

_____

_____

5. In praise of Quentin Tarantino's film *Pulp Fiction*, Elizabeth Brand wrote that the film "towers over other movies as menacingly as a gang lord at a preschool."[2]

a. What two things are compared in the author's simile?

_____

_____

b. What point does that simile help to make?

_____

_____

---

[1]Joshua Quittner, "Invasion of Privacy," *Time*, August 25, 1997, p. 30.
[2]*Time*, October 10, 1994, p. 78.

Metaphors

Metaphors also make unexpected comparisons that contribute to both meaning and tone. They aren't, however, as easy to spot as similes because they don't use the words *like* or *as*. Note the absence of either word in the following passage, where the author compares family conversations to volcanic eruptions.

> The voices of my world were seldom tender and unquestioning. Conversations . . . among members of my . . . family were . . . eruptions. (W. S. DiPiero, "Gots Is What You Got," in *The Best American Essays 1995,* ed. Jamaica Kincaid. Boston: Houghton Mifflin, 1995, p. 84.)

When the passage is presented in a more expanded form, you can also see more clearly how the author's use of metaphor contributes to his angry, bitter tone.

> The voices of my world were seldom tender and unquestioning. Conversations, especially among members of my mother's family, were choleric* eruptions. If by some accident a rational argument took place, defeat was registered not by words or acknowledgment but by a sardonic,* defiant sneer. Anger, impatience, and dismissive ridicule of the unfamiliar were the most familiar moods. Everyone around me, it seemed, except for my father's side of the family, spoke in brittle, pugnacious* tones that I still hear when my own voice comes snarling out of its vinegary corner. (W. S. DiPiero, "Gots Is What You Got," in *The Best American Essays 1995,* p. 84.)

Did you spot the other metaphors in the passage? Did you notice, for example, that by using the word *snarling,* the author compares himself to an angry animal. Or perhaps you noticed the word *vinegary,* which implies that the author's corner of the room was sour and bitter, like the taste of vinegar.

If you picked up on either one of these metaphors, you are well on your way to understanding the power of figurative language. Now look at the next passage. The author uses a metaphor to express the degree of her pain. Can you find that metaphor?

> Twenty years ago, when I was nine and living in America, I came home from school one day with a toothache. Several weeks

---

*choleric: excitable, easily ignited or set off.
*sardonic: mocking, scornful.
*pugnacious: ready to fight.

and misdiagnoses later, surgeons removed most of the right side of my jaw in an attempt to prevent the cancer they found there from spreading. No one properly explained the operation to me, and I awoke in a cocoon of pain that prevented me from moving or speaking. (Lucy Grealy, "Mirrorings," in *The Best American Essays 1994* (ed. Tracy Kidder). Boston: Houghton Mifflin, 1994, p. 183.)

Up until the last sentence, the language is more or less denotative (see page 252). But in the last sentence the author compares herself to an infant moth or butterfly wrapped in a cocoon, only her cocoon is made out of pain, not silk.* By means of that comparison, the author helps readers imagine the extent of her pain: It covered her entire body and allowed her no escape. The cocoon image also reinforces the author's bewildered tone.

Be Aware of Submerged Metaphors

In your reading, you are bound to notice that some metaphors are more explicit, or more obviously expressed, than others. "A bear of a man," for example, is a pretty clear-cut metaphor. But some metaphors have been in use for so long it's easy to forget that a comparison is at work; that's why some people refer to them as *submerged.* Consider the expression "to round everybody up," as in the following sentence: "Try to round everybody up before the meeting." In this case, gathering people together is implicitly compared to a cattle roundup. Yet, because the phrase has been used so often, it's easy to forget its metaphorical basis. Still, it pays to be alert to such submerged metaphors rather than letting them unconsciously influence your thinking. Consider, for example, the following:

> Our troops have gone into the infested area. With enough firepower, exterminating the enemy will not be difficult.

The submerged, or underlying, metaphor used here suggests that the enemy forces are bugs rather than people and helps to cover up the reality of what's being discussed—killing human beings, not bugs. Critical readers would "think through" the metaphor to decide if they actually support the action described.

---

*The cocoons of some moths and butterflies are spun from silk.

CHECK YOUR UNDERSTANDING

Explain the difference between a metaphor and a simile.

_____

_____

You have already used a simile to describe a friend or class-mate. Now use a metaphor to describe the same person.

_____

_____

EXERCISE 2

DIRECTIONS Underline the submerged metaphor in each sentence.

EXAMPLE "Don't tell me what to do," she <u>shot</u> back.

EXPLANATION We have been comparing a harsh verbal retort to shooting a gun off for so long, it's easy to forget that there is actually a metaphor in play in that expression.

1. That kind of monotonous work grinds you down after a while.
2. When he asked a rude question, she slapped him down hard.
3. They had just met, but he was already head over heels in love.
4. Her spiteful attitude was poisoning the atmosphere of the meeting.
5. After working the night shift, he fell into a dead sleep.

EXERCISE 3

DIRECTIONS Identify and explain each metaphor.

EXAMPLE If as many people died in plane crashes annually as do in smoking-related deaths, the government would spend millions investigating and correcting the problems. Instead, the votes from a sympathetic Congress give tobacco farms and companies the protection to thrive as though the tobacco industry was a rare species near extinction. (Susan Gilbert McGuire, "The Cost of Smoking," *Chicago Tribune*, March 28, 1996, p. 20.)

a. In this passage, the author uses a metaphor to compare

the tobacco industry to *a rare species near extinction.*

b. That comparison helps to make what point?

It suggests that both the rare species and the tobacco industry are being taken care of although the tobacco industry is hardly in danger.

1. During the second round, Gogarty caught the 135-pound Martin flush on the nose, opening a spigot of blood. After the round as cornermen tried to stop the flow, Jim asked Christy if she wanted to continue. "I was concerned because she's my wife first, my fighter second," he says. "She told me, 'Don't you dare stop this fight!'" (Steve Wulf, "Belle of the Brawl," *Time*, April 1, 1996, p. 20.)

a. In this passage, the author uses a metaphor to compare

_____ to _____.

b. That comparison helps to make what point?

_____

_____

2. English was the ticket to success in the United States, perhaps even more for Latinos than Asians. Ninety-two percent of Mexican-origin Americans and 90.2 percent of Puerto Ricans who took the SATs for college entrance in 1984 said English was their best language. . . . One study concluded that Puerto Rican men with fluency in English may have raised their wages by as much as 20 percent. (Lawrence Fuchs, "Respecting Diversity, Promoting Unity," in *About Language*, ed. William H. Roberts and Gregoire Turgeon, p. 153.)

a. In this passage, the author uses a metaphor to compare

_____ to _____.

b. That comparison helps to make what point?

_____

_____

3. When he [Elvis Presley] died, he was reading *The Scientific Search for the Face of Jesus.* He liked books about the promises of other worlds, alien existence, predestination, and the afterlife. . . . He had become a beloved national ruin. (Julie Baumgold, "Midnight in the Garden of Good and Elvis," in *The Best American Essays 1995,* pp. 50–51.)

    a. In this passage, the author uses a metaphor to compare

    _____ to _____.

    b. That comparison helps to make what point?

    _____

    _____

4. If your sentences are carelessly formed, not only will the summary be unreadable, you will also lose the connection among the pieces of information in the summary. You could simply wind up with tossed word salad. (Charles Bazerman, *The Informed Writer.* Boston: Houghton Mifflin, 1995, p. 79.)

    a. In this passage, the author uses a metaphor to compare

    _____ to _____.

    b. That comparison helps to make what point?

    _____

    _____

5. To paraphrase famed French critic Roland Barthes, moviegoers all too often lie prone and receive their cinematic nourishment in the same way that hospital patients get fed intravenously.

    a. In this passage, the author uses a metaphor to compare

    _____ to _____.

    b. That comparison helps to make what point?

    _____

    _____

Allusions

Allusions are brief references to historical events, mythological figures, and famous people—both real and fictional. In an earlier time, allusions functioned mainly to display a writer's learning, but nowadays their role is more complex. Allusions are a form of verbal short-hand meant to call up a whole chain of associations in readers. They help writers explain or prove a point; they also contribute to tone and reveal bias. For an illustration, look at the following example. Do you recognize the allusion?

> Undoubtedly, an increasing number of men have rejected the traditional male-role imperatives.* "Be the breadwinner," "Push your way to the top," "Stick in there and fight," "Men don't cry." Indeed, there is a life after Rambo. (Alex Thio, *Sociology,* p. 292.)

Did you recognize the allusion to Rambo, the fictional character created by actor Sylvester Stallone in a series of highly successful action films? In these films, the character of Rambo is icily independent. With much bloodshed, he single-handedly lays to rest his many enemies, apparently without remorse or anxiety. Relying on readers to recognize the allusion, the author uses it to define the phrase "male-role imperatives"—to be tough, strong, and unemotional. At the same time, the allusion helps maintain the relaxed, informal tone of his writing.

Note how the same passage, with a different allusion, takes on a slightly more formal, more academic tone.

> Undoubtedly, an increasing number of men have rejected the traditional male-role imperatives. "Be the breadwinner," "Push your way to the top," "Stick in there and fight," "Men don't cry." As the poet Robert Bly has suggested, men are exhausted by the effort of trying to be the invincible warrior.

What about the next passage? Can you find an allusion that helps the author define for readers the power of gossip columnist Walter Winchell?

> In the thirties and forties, the slogan on Walter Winchell's newspaper column read: "He sees all, he knows all." No wonder Winchell was known as the Big Brother of gossip columnists.

If you've read George Orwell's book *1984,* you know already that the allusion in the above passage is to Big Brother, a character in that famous novel. In the novel, Big Brother uses a network of spies to gather information about the populace under his control. No wonder Winchell was once widely feared. If his name could be linked to Big Brother, he too must have had access to even the best-kept secrets.

---

*imperatives: commands.

Enlarging Your Store of Allusions

Allusions can help you determine meaning and identify tone. But they are only useful if you recognize them when you see them. Consider, for example, the following italicized allusion to a famous female character.

Following in the tragic footsteps of Tolstoy's *Anna Karenina,* too many women still seem to believe that sacrificing all for love is a worthwhile choice to make. It appears, in fact, that on the romance front, feminists have not made much progress. Women, unlike men, still seem to believe that romance is what gives life meaning.

If you know that Anna Karenina, the heroine of Tolstoy's novel by the same name, gave up her marriage, her children, and ultimately her life for the love of a man who abandoned her, you immediately grasp the author's point. But if you don't, your understanding of the passage is probably a little vague.

This is just one instance in which an allusion is central to the author's meaning. But it's not atypical. The more you read, the more likely you are to encounter numerous allusions from science, the arts, and popular culture. While popular culture references, like the one to Rambo, will be readily at your disposal, you may have to work at developing a vocabulary of allusions that extend beyond those from TV and movies. Anytime you encounter an allusion you don't know, make a note of it and look it up when you get a chance. Paperback dictionaries don't usually include names of people and places, but hardbound desk dictionaries usually do. In addition, there are some very good reference works that have compiled long lists of our culture's common allusions. *The Dictionary of Cultural Literacy* and *The Dictionary of Global Culture* are two of the best. If you have access to a computer with a modem, you're really in luck because there are numerous Web sites that can give you the information you need. Try, for example, http://www.accurate-eye.com.au/800.htm for allusions to myths, legends, and folklore or http://www.accurate-eye.com.au/820.htm for literary allusions.

CHECK YOUR UNDERSTANDING

When they were first used, what was the purpose of allusions? _____

What is their purpose now? _____

_____

EXERCISE 4

DIRECTIONS Read each sentence or passage and look at the italicized allusion. Then read the explanation of that allusion. When you finish, circle the letter of the statement that best explains the purpose of the allusion.

EXAMPLE In Ken Burns, the creator of the acclaimed PBS series *The Civil War*, America has finally found its *Homer*. A television blockbuster today, *The Civil War* will still be watched and talked about years from now.

> Homer was an ancient Greek poet said to have written *The Iliad*, a long poem that recorded the events of the Trojan War. Homer's description of the war between the Greeks and the Trojans was so powerful, translations of *The Iliad* are still read today.

The author alludes to Homer in order to

a. suggest that Ken Burns is also a great poet who will be read for centuries.

b. suggest the extraordinary nature of Ken Burns's achievement.

EXPLANATION Since Homer was a famous poet who made the ancient Trojan War live on in history, using his name in reference to Ken Burns, who is not a poet, is a compliment to the filmmaker's ability to make the war come alive more than a century after it ended.

1. I was thirty years old when I had my right nostril pierced, and back home friends fell speechless at the news, lapsing into long telephone pauses of the sort that *June Cleaver* would employ if the *Beave* had ever called to report, "Mom, I'm married. His name's Eddie." (Natalie Kusz, "Ring Leader," in *The Best American Essays 1997*, pp. 70–71.)

> June Cleaver was a character in a famous situation comedy called *Leave It to Beaver*. On the show, she was the perfect mother who never had a hair out of place, never raised her voice, and never ever made a mistake. To many, she was the symbol of the perfect suburban mom. "The Beave" was a nickname for her mischievous young son.

The author alludes to June Cleaver and the Beave to suggest

a. that her friends admired her daring and were envious of it.

b. the degree of shock her friends experienced at her news.

2. Waiting for the judge to arrive, I had the feeling that I was a character in Beckett's *Waiting for Godot,* and messages from the bailiff that the judge was on her way did little to cheer me up.

> *Waiting for Godot* is a play about two tramps, Vladimir and Estragon, who wait for a man called Godot. Each day a boy comes to tell them Godot will be there tomorrow, but as the play ends, Vladimir and Estragon are still waiting.

The author alludes to *Waiting for Godot* to suggest that

a. She no longer believes the judge will appear.

b. She is too bored to pay attention to the bailiff's words.

3. When it comes to talent, the young dancer is another *Nijinsky.* Yet given his odd behavior, even his most devoted admirers fear that he has more in common with Nijinsky that just talent.

> Vaslav Nijinsky (1890–1950) was a Russian ballet dancer whose phenomenal ability made him a world-famous star. In 1919 Nijinsky was diagnosed with schizophrenia and spent the rest of his life in treatment for the devastating disease.

The author alludes to Nijinsky to suggest that

a. the young dancer will eventually alienate all of his admirers because he is so demanding and ill-tempered.

b. the young dancer is extremely talented but may also be suffering from a serious psychological disorder.

4. Watching the couple as they eyed the menu suspiciously, I couldn't help but think of Grant Wood's *American Gothic.* The two seemed a throwback to another, sterner time, when dinner out was not part of the weekly—or for that matter, the yearly—routine. For these two, dinner out seemed to be another chore to be finished as quickly as possible.

> The painting *American Gothic* (1930) by Grant Wood shows an unsmiling, middle-aged couple from the nineteenth century. The man holds a pitchfork and looks solemn. The woman, dressed in black, stares into space with pursed lips and a pinched face.

The author alludes to *American Gothic* to suggest that

a. the two people are quarreling with one another.

b. the two people don't appear to be enjoying themselves.

5. According to direct-marketing mogul* Ben Suarez, businesspeople today need *Machiavellian* techniques to fight the "criminal element" in government. One of Suarez's latest enterprises involved his selling of necklaces like the one in the 1997 blockbuster movie *Titanic*. Intent on stopping him, Twentieth Century Fox, the maker of the film, went to court, but Suarez is still selling the necklaces. Whatever techniques Ben Suarez learned from Machiavelli, they seem to work.

> Niccolo Machiavelli was a Renaissance political philosopher whose book *The Prince* advised rulers to be ruthless and cunning if they wanted to hold on to their power.

The author alludes to Machiavelli to suggest that

a. Suarez behaves like a man from another century.

b. Suarez is wily* and determined in pursuit of his goals.

WORD NOTES

Now that you are skilled at recognizing and interpreting metaphors, you might choose to use them more in your own writing, as well you should. However, if you do, take care to avoid "worn out" or "dead" metaphors. These are metaphors that have been used so often they no longer make ideas clearer or more vivid. If anything, they make even fresh ideas seem stale and old. Three such metaphors appear in the following sentences. Put a circle around each one.

---

*mogul: a very rich and powerful person.
*wily: clever, tricky.

1. Those old conflicts are all water over the dam.
2. The attorney decided to burn her bridges and abandon the firm.
3. He turned out to be such a scoundrel; it's really true that you can't tell a book by its cover.

Cliché is another word for dead metaphor, and you can use the two terms interchangeably. We all use clichés, or dead metaphors, in conversation. In general we don't have the time to ponder every word for originality. But for the most part, writers do have the time, and dead metaphors like those shown above should be avoided.

Give three examples of dead metaphors:

_____

_____

_____

Summing Up

Listed below are the most important points in Chapter 9. Put a check mark in the box if you think the point is clear in your mind. Leave the box blank if you need to review the material one more time. The page numbers in parentheses tell you where to look to review each point on the list.

1. Figurative language is language that makes sense in the world of the imagination but can't be translated into realistic action. The large category of figurative language can be subdivided into different figures of speech. (p. 316)

2. Similes use the words *like* and *as* to compare two seemingly unlike things that actually share an unexpected connection. Similes help create both tone and meaning. (pp. 316–317)

3. Metaphors don't use the words *like* or *as*, but they too implicitly compare two seemingly unlike things in order to help the reader better understand an experience or idea. (pp. 320–321)

4. Allusions are references to people, places, or events meant to call up a chain of associations in the reader's mind and thereby help clarify an author's ideas. Allusions also have a powerful effect on tone. (pp. 324–325)

TEST YOUR UNDERSTANDING

To see how well you have understood this chapter, take the following review quiz. Then correct it using the answer key provided by your instructor. If you score 80 percent or above, you're ready to take the end-of-chapter exam. However, if you score below 80 percent, look over the quiz carefully to see what kind of questions you missed. Then use the **Summing Up** section to find out which pages you should review before taking the chapter exam.

◢◣◯ Chapter 9: Review Quiz

DIRECTIONS Answer the following questions by filling in the blanks or underlining the appropriate word.

1. Explain the simile used in the following sentence: "Propaganda is a bit like pornography—hard to define but most people think they will know it when they see it." (Koppes and Black, *Hollywood Goes to War,* p. 49.)

   a. In this sentence, the author uses a simile that compares

   _____ to _____.

   b. What point does that simile help to make?

   _____

   _____

2. In 1997, Susan Charlé of the *New York Times* wrote an article about bear thievery in Yosemite. Charlé describes how the bears, lusting for cookies and such, broke into hundreds of cars to steal food. She titled the article "To the Bears of Yosemite, Cars Are Like Cookie Jars." Explain the simile at work in that title. Cars are like cookie jars

   because _____

   _____.

3. Read the following passage and underline the submerged metaphor the author uses to describe Homer's great work *The Iliad.*

   Homer, in his terrifying exactness, tells us where the spear comes in and goes out, what limbs are severed; he tells us that the dead will not return to rich soil, that they will not take care of parents, receive pleasure from their young wives. . . . In the end, the war (promoted by the gods) will consume almost all of them, Greeks and Trojans alike. (David Denby, "Does Homer Have Legs?" in *The Best American Essays 1994,* p. 58.)

4. Underline the submerged metaphor used in the following sentence: The committee is trying to bulldoze the president into signing the bill, but they cannot be allowed to succeed.

5. Explain the metaphor in the following passage:

   In casual conversation, the research leader flits from topic to topic and never comes to rest on any one. But in the laboratory, he's quite different. He is famous for his ability to focus on the topic under discussion without ever becoming distracted.

a. In this passage, the research leader's conversational style is compared to _____.

b. What does the author suggest by means of that metaphor?

_____

_____

6. Explain the metaphor in the following passage:

> In North Korea, starvation is everywhere, and, as usual, the hardest hit are the children. They sit quietly in schools and museums, speaking little and playing not at all. Their arms and legs are twigs. The U.S. government should put politics aside and offer North Korea aid immediately.

In this passage, what metaphor does the author use to bring home to readers the suffering of starving children?

_____

7. Identify the metaphor in the following sentence: "Time is the worst kind of thief, greedy and invisible." (Christina Garcia, "Thou Shalt Not Steal," *Self*, December 1997, p. 140.)

In this sentence, the author uses a metaphor that compares

_____ to _____.

8. Underline the metaphor in the following passage:

> When Heinrich Schliemann set out to find the site of the Trojan War and prove that the people, places, and events in *The Iliad* really existed, he told the Turkish government that he would split what he found with the Turks.* But when Schliemann discovered his Trojan treasures he did nothing of the kind, and Turkey is still smoldering over Schliemann's trickery.

9. Explain the allusion in the following sentence: It was a *Gone With the Wind* kind of romance and their timing had always been off. Thus, none of their friends was surprised when they split up.

> *Gone With the Wind* is a famous novel that became an even more famous movie. By the time the novel's heroine, Scarlett O'Hara, finally decides she loves its hero, Rhett Butler, he is no longer in love with her.

---

*In the 1870s, Schliemann was digging on Turkish soil.

What does the allusion in this passage help to explain?

_____

_____

10. That newspaper is a piece of trash and the editor makes William Randolph Hearst seem scrupulous* by comparison.

> William Randolph Hearst was a newspaper publisher in the late nineteenth and early twentieth centuries. In the 1890s, his newspapers whipped up public hostility toward Spain, often printing false stories about Spanish mistreatment of Cuba. But Hearst didn't care as long as newspaper sales increased.

In this passage, the allusion to Hearst helps make what point?

_____

_____

> Use the answer key supplied by your instructor to correct your quiz. If you score 80 percent or above, you are ready for the chapter exam. If you score below 80 percent, look carefully at the questions you answered incorrectly. Then use the **Summing Up** section to decide which pages you need to review.

*scrupulous: conscientious and exact.

◣◗ Chapter Test 9

DIRECTIONS Answer the following questions by filling in the blanks or underlining the appropriate word.

1. The Dutch scholar Erasmus said that a good memory should be like a fish net. It should keep all the big fish and let the little ones escape. What point about memory was Erasmus trying to make by means of this simile?

    _____

    _____

2. Identify the metaphor in the following passage.

    The Japanese health care system is remarkably democratic. Thanks to a national health insurance system, few are left outside the umbrella.

    a. In this passage, the author compares _____

       to _____.

    b. What is the point of the metaphor?

       _____

3. Identify the metaphors in the following passage.

    Unexpectedly, I turned inward. I encircled myself in solitude. I didn't know it at the time, but it was kind of a cloak around me. (Mary Morris, *Nothing to Declare*. New York: Penguin Books, 1988, p. 180.)

    a. In this passage, the author compares solitude to _____

       and to _____.

    b. What is the point of those metaphors?

       _____

4. Identify the simile in the following sentence: The point you are making is about as useful as a pair of high heels at a relay race.

    a. In this passage, the author compares _____

       to _____.

    b. What is the point of the simile? _____

5. Identify and explain the following metaphor: Currently the debate over how the U.S. government should handle China is at high boil.

a. In this sentence, the author compares _____

  to _____.

b. The use of this metaphor helps make what point? _____

_____

6. Explain the italicized allusion in the following passage.

Feminism didn't start in the factory. It started in wood-paneled salons, spread to suburban living rooms, with their consciousness-raising sessions,* and eventually ended up with *Norma Rae*. (Gina Bellafante, "It's All About Me," *Time*, June 29, 1998, p. 5.)

> *Norma Rae* was a 1979 movie starring Sally Field in the title role. As Norma Rae, Field plays a working class woman who learns to believe in her ability to change the world by successfully bringing a union into her factory.

What point does the allusion in this passage help to make?

_____

_____

7. Underline the simile in the following sentence:

She finally found the right places and we sat in them. I'd never seen a flip-up theater seat, and my weight would barely hold it down. I let it fold me up, knees to chin. . . . Then the lights went down and the curtains opened like a huge chenille bathrobe. (Shirley Abbott, *Love's Apprentice*. New York: Houghton Mifflin, 1998, p. 8.)

8. What point does the author want to make through the allusion to Moby Dick?

For the senator, national health care had become his Moby Dick. He was determined, no matter what the cost, to make the issue come to a vote in the Senate, and he didn't care if he offended both his friends and his enemies to do it.

_____

*consciousness-raising sessions: group meetings in which women got together to discuss their concerns. Such meetings were popular in the 1960s and 1970s.

> *Moby Dick, or The Whale* (1851) is a book by American writer Herman Melville. In it the main character, the one-legged Captain Ahab, is intent on finding and killing Moby Dick, the great white whale who cost him his leg. To that end, he sacrifices his life and the lives of most of his crew.

What point does the allusion in this passage help to make?

_____

_____

9. Identify and explain the simile in the following sentence.

> Day after day, the heat in Dallas seems to build like a Gulf hurricane growing in force. (National Public Radio, *Morning Edition*, July 16, 1998)

a. In this simile, the author compares _____

  to _____.

b. The point of the simile is that _____

_____

10. What point does the author want to make through the allusion to Spike Lee's first film?

> Native-American writer Sherman Alexie is hoping that his first movie, *Smoke Signals*, which he wrote and directed, will do for him what *She's Gotta Have It* did for director Spike Lee.

> Spike Lee made his commercial film debut with *She's Gotta Have It* in 1986, when he was twenty-nine years old. The movie, made on a shoestring budget, was a surprise hit, and it launched Lee's career as a filmmaker.

What point does the allusion in this passage help to make?

_____

_____

C H A P T E R   1 0

Recognizing and Responding to Bias

 In this chapter you'll learn

- **how to recognize bias in informative writing.**

- **how to evaluate bias in persuasive writing.**

As the title suggests, Chapter 10 returns to the subject of *bias*. In this chapter, you'll learn more about how an author's personal feelings can intrude themselves into informative writing, despite the best efforts to remain objective. You'll also learn how to recognize when bias in persuasive writing has become excessive, or gone too far. While bias is a natural part of persuasive writing, it can sometimes interfere with an author's ability to treat opposing points of view

fairly. When that happens, critical readers take note and reserve judgment.

Bias Isn't Necessarily Bad

The word *bias* has a bad reputation. We frequently use it to suggest that someone has a closed mind and cannot or will not listen to opposing points of view. But *bias* merely refers to a point of view or personal leaning. In other words, expressing a bias isn't necessarily bad.

Because of our background, experience, and training, most of us have personal opinions that influence how we see and interpret the world around us. Thus, how critical readers react to or evaluate an expression of bias depends a good deal on context, on where that bias appears, and on the degree, or strength, of the bias expressed.

For example, unless they are writing for the editorial page, newspaper reporters are expected to report events as objectively as possible. If reporters describe those events in highly connotative or emotionally charged language that reveals their personal point of view, they are doing readers a disservice, and their biases are inappropriate in that context.

In contrast, editorials in newspapers are expected to express a bias. In fact, that's one of the reasons we read them. We want, for example, to get columnists Maureen Dowd's or Bob Herbert's perspective on some current issue. However, even writers determined to persuade should offer readers a fair and reasonable argument. If a writer is so committed to one point of view that he or she can't be logical or fair, then the degree of bias is excessive, and we need to be wary of accepting that writer's point of view.

In sum, then, all writers have biases, and there's nothing wrong with revealing them in the appropriate context. What's important is that writers not let bias interfere with their ability to be logical and fair.

Recognizing Bias in Informative Writing

Writers whose primary goal is to inform rather than persuade usually work hard to keep their biases to themselves. For example, the author of a textbook on modern American history might be a long-time Republican who considers Democrat Lyndon Baines Johnson one of history's worst presidents. Yet, in writing a chapter that covers Johnson's presidency, he should control his inclination to criticize Johnson's record. Like writers of reference works, authors of textbooks are expected to provide an impersonal and objective account of events and allow students to form their own opinions.

Still, writers are only human. Try as they might, they can't always eliminate every shred of personal bias from their writing. Although the overall tone of a passage may be emotionally neutral, the connotations of individual words or phrases can still suggest a personal bias or leaning. Note, for example, the italicized words in the following paragraph. These words have negative connotations and suggest that the authors do not admire the way former president Harry Truman handled foreign policy.

President Truman . . . had a personality that tended to increase international tensions. Whereas Roosevelt had been *ingratiating,** patient, and evasive, Truman was *brash,** *impatient,* and direct. *He seldom displayed the appreciation of subtleties so essential to successful diplomacy.* In his first meeting with V. M. Molotov, the Soviet commissar of foreign affairs, Truman sharply *berated** the Soviet Union* for violating the Yalta accords,* a charge Molotov denied. When Truman *shot back* that the Soviets should honor their agreements, Molotov stormed out of the room. The president was pleased with his "tough method." "I gave it to him straight 'one-two to the jaw.'" This *simplistic display of toughness* became a trademark of American Cold War* diplomacy.* (Norton et al., *A People and a Nation,* p. 488.)

The authors of this textbook passage are probably not fans of Harry Truman. But would you say the same about the author of the next passage?

On his first day in office, Harry Truman remarked to a newspaperman, "Did you ever have a bull or a load of hay fall on you? If you

---

*ingratiating: eager to please.
*brash: hasty and unthinking.
*berated: criticized harshly.
*Soviet Union: the former name of fifteen separate republics governed by the Communist party, also called "Soviet Russia."
*Yalta accords: agreements made at the end of World War II in the city of Yalta, located near the Black Sea.
*Cold War: a period of hostile rivalry between the United States and Communist Russia.
*diplomacy: the conduct by government officials of relations between nations.

ever did, you know how I felt last night." Yet President Truman's *native intelligence enabled him to grasp quickly the situation into which he was so suddenly thrown,* and on which he had not been briefed by Roosevelt. He had to have a few boon* companions from Missouri around the White House for relaxation, but *he won the friendship and respect of gentlemen in politics* such as Dean Acheson, soldiers such as General Marshall, and foreign statesmen such as Clement Attlee. He made good cabinet, judicial, and ambassadorial appointments; *he kept a firm hand* on the new Department of Defense and the foreign service; and, *with more fateful decisions than almost any president in our time, he made the fewest mistakes.* Truman was always folksy, always the politician, *but nobody can reasonably deny that he attained the stature of a statesman.* (Samuel Eliot Morison, *The Oxford History of the American People.* New York: Oxford University Press, 1965, p. 1051.)

Unlike the authors of the first passage, the author of this passage admires Harry Truman's record as president, and his choice of words encourages readers to do the same.

When they recognize bias in writing meant to inform, critical readers don't throw up their hands in horror and refuse to read further. Instead, they try to identify the author's particular leaning and make sure that they don't absorb it right along with the author's description of events or ideas.

What's Left Out *Is* Significant

Sometimes the intrusion of bias in informative writing is obvious in the author's choice of words. But bias can also be more subtle. Sometimes writers reveal bias not by what they say but by what they leave out. For example, a history writer who records only the successful or praiseworthy actions of President Franklin Delano Roosevelt but leaves out Roosevelt's order to intern, or imprison, Japanese Americans during World War II is showing a bias in favor of Roosevelt. Anytime an author describes a person or position where opposing points of view are possible without mentioning—or just barely acknowledging—the opposition, your critical antennae should go up. The writer's purpose may be informative, but you, the reader, are still not getting the whole story.

---

*boon: in this context, good-natured, jolly.

> *Informative Writing Lacking in Bias*
>
> - employs an emotionally neutral tone throughout.
> - describes both sides of an issue equally without evaluating or judging either side.
> - includes no personal opinions or value judgments from the author.
> - includes little or no connotative language.
>
> *Informative Writing That Reflects a Bias*
>
> - may use charged language that interrupts an emotionally neutral tone.
> - gives the author's personal opinion.
> - emphasizes either positive *or* negative views of a subject but doesn't give equal space to both sides.

EXERCISE 1

DIRECTIONS Each of the following passages comes from a source where one would expect the author *not* to reveal any evidence of bias. Read each passage. Then circle the appropriate letters to indicate whether or not the author or authors have eliminated all evidence of bias.

EXAMPLE

Trial Elements

A trial is often compared to a boxing match. Both are contests between *adversaries*, persons who oppose or fight one another. In a trial, the adversaries are called **litigants** and, rather than hitting each other, they challenge each other's evidence and testimony. For this reason, an American trial is often labeled an **adversary proceeding.** The judge acts as a referee and interprets the rules of the "match."

The person who files suit in a civil case is called a **plaintiff.** In a criminal trial, the prosecution brings the charges. The United States attorney is the prosecutor in federal cases. In state trials, the prosecutor may be known as the state's attorney, county prosecutor, or district attorney. The person being sued or charged with the crime is the **defendant.**

Every trial has two purposes: to establish the facts of the case, and to find the law that applies. The role of the jury is to decide questions of fact. (Adapted from Richard J. Hardy, *Government in America.* Boston: Houghton Mifflin, 1993, p. 502.)

Presence of Bias   a. The author is describing the elements of a trial and clearly favors our legal system.

b. The author is describing the elements of a trial and is clearly critical of our system.

(c.) It's impossible to determine the author's personal feelings.

EXPLANATION Drawn from a textbook, this selection does not reveal any bias for or against our legal system. The language remains almost completely denotative, and there is no evidence whatsoever of the author's personal opinion.

1. The Presidency of John F. Kennedy

1   John F. Kennedy's ambitious social program, the New Frontier, promised more than Kennedy could deliver: an end to racial discrimination, federal aid to education, medical care for the elderly, and government action to halt the recession* the country was suffering. Only eight months into his first year, it was evident that Kennedy lacked the ability to move Congress, which was dominated by conservative Republicans and southern Democrats. Long-time members of Congress saw him and his administration as publicity hungry. Some feared the president would seek federal aid to parochial schools. The result was the defeat of federal aid to education and of a Kennedy-sponsored boost in the minimum wage.

2   Still struggling to appease conservative members of Congress, the new president pursued civil rights with a notable lack of vigor. Kennedy did establish the President's Committee on Equal Employment Opportunity to eliminate racial discrimination in government hiring. But he waited until late 1962 before honoring a 1960 campaign pledge to issue an executive order forbidding segregation in federally subsidized housing. Meanwhile, he appointed five die-hard segregationists to the federal bench in the Deep South. The struggle for racial equality was the most important domestic issue of the time, and Kennedy's performance disheartened* civil rights advocates. (Adapted from Norton et al., *A People and a Nation,* p. 991.)

---

*recession: economic downturn.
*disheartened: disappointed.

Presence of Bias a. The authors are admirers of John F. Kennedy.

b. The authors are critical of John F. Kennedy.

c. It's impossible to determine the authors' personal feelings.

2. The Civil Rights Act of 1964

1   In 1961, a new administration, headed by President John F. Kennedy, came to power. At first Kennedy did not seem to be committed to civil rights. His stance changed as the movement gained momentum and as more and more whites became aware of the abuse being heaped on sit-in demonstrators, freedom riders (who tested unlawful segregation on interstate bus routes), and those who were trying to help blacks register to vote in southern states. Volunteers were being jailed, beaten, and killed for advocating activities among blacks that whites took for granted.

2   In late 1962, President Kennedy ordered federal troops to ensure the safety of James Meredith, the first black to attend the University of Mississippi. In early 1963, Kennedy enforced the desegregation of the University of Alabama. In April 1963, television viewers were shocked to see civil rights marchers in Birmingham, Alabama, attacked with dogs, fire hoses, and cattle prods. (The idea of the Birmingham march was to provoke confrontations with white officials in an effort to compel the national government to intervene on behalf of blacks.) Finally, in June 1963, Kennedy asked Congress for legislation that would outlaw segregation in public accommodations.

3   Two months later, Martin Luther King Jr., joined in a march on Washington, D.C. The organizers called the protest "A March for Jobs and Freedom," signaling the economic goals of black America. More than 250,000 people, black and white, gathered peaceably at the Lincoln Memorial to hear King speak. "I have a dream," the great preacher extemporized,* "that my little children will one day live in a nation where they will not be judged by the color of their skin but by the content of their character."

4   Congress had not yet enacted Kennedy's public accommodations bill when he was assassinated on November 22, 1963. His successor, Lyndon B. Johnson, considered civil rights his top legislative priority. Within months, Congress enacted the Civil Rights Act of 1964, which included a vital provision barring segregation in most public accommodations. This congressional action was, in part, a reaction to Kennedy's death. But it was also almost certainly a response to the brutal treatment of blacks

---

*extemporized: spoke without practice or preparation.

throughout the South. (Janda et al., *The Challenge of Democracy,* pp. 549–550.)

Presence of Bias a. The authors are admirers of John F. Kennedy.

b. The authors are critical of John F. Kennedy.

c. It's impossible to determine the authors' personal feelings.

3. **Lowell, Robert** (1917–1977)   American poet of famous aristocratic American family; regarded by most critics as the best English language poet of his generation and by certain readers as beyond criticism altogether. For better or for worse, Lowell was the modern poet-as-film-star: his private affairs were apparently carried out mainly in public (this is miscalled "confessionalism"): his themes included the personalities and behaviour of his relatives, his various marriages and liaisons,* the (presumably) affective disorder which landed him in hospital many times, and so on. Lowell was extremely gifted but the conventional view of his development, even where this judges the most recent poems as failures, is not quite correct, for it mistakes potential for achievement, and over-rates him. (Adapted from Martin Seymour-Smith, *Who's Who in Twentieth Century Literature.* New York: McGraw-Hill, 1976, p. 216.)

Presence of Bias a. The author admires Robert Lowell.

b. The author is critical of Robert Lowell.

c. It's impossible to determine the author's personal feelings.

4. **The Animal Rights Movement**

1   Opposition to animal research has a long history, going back at least as far as the antivivisectionist movement of the nineteenth century. In recent years the growth of the animal rights movement was spurred by a book called *Animal Liberation* (1975), by Australian philosopher Peter Singer. Singer argued that many uses of animals by humans—for food, for clothing, and as captive research subjects—reflected "speciesism": the exploitation of certain species (nonhuman animals) for the benefit of another (humans). Because animals, like humans, can feel pain, Singer argued, they are entitled to just as much consideration as humans are.

2   In Singer's view, speciesism is a form of discrimination that is just as evil as racism and sexism. "Would the experimenter be prepared to perform his experiment on a human infant?" Singer asks. "If not, then his readiness to use nonhumans is simple discrimination" (Singer, 1976, p. 156).

———

*liaisons: love affairs.

3   Many animal rights supporters have advanced their views in books and articles and have worked for laws and regulations that would ensure the humane treatment of animals. Others have resorted to acts of terrorism in the name of animal rights (Jasper & Nelkin, 1992). Some activists have invaded animal laboratories, destroyed equipment, stolen data, and let the animals out of their cages. Animal rights activists have also staged dramatic demonstrations . . . in an attempt to convince the public of what they see as the cruelty of animal research.

4   The animal rights movement has been accused by researchers of painting a distorted picture of animal research. In fact, most animal research is neither cruel nor painful, and the large majority of animal researchers are concerned about animal welfare (Novak, 1991). When researchers employ surgical procedures with animals, they almost always use anesthesia to eliminate pain. Many animal rights supporters acknowledge such humane practices but believe that animal research remains unnecessarily intrusive. But the moral fervor of other animal rights advocates has led them to engage in misleading portrayals of scientists as sadists and laboratories as torture chambers. (Rubin et al., *Psychology,* pp. 68–69.)

Presence of Bias   a. The authors support the animal rights movement.

b. The authors are critical of the animal rights movement.

c. It's impossible to determine the authors' personal feelings.

 # Responding to Bias in Persuasive Writing

We don't expect to find bias in informative writing, so encountering it usually comes as a surprise. Persuasive writing, in contrast, raises different expectations. We expect writers to be personally engaged—to tell us about the personal experiences or feelings that led them to their point of view. In short, we expect persuasive writing to express a bias. What we don't expect, even in persuasive writing, is that writers be imprisoned and blinded by their biases. In other words, we expect them to acknowledge opposing points of view and to treat these points of view fairly. A writer who fails to acknowledge opposing points of view or, even worse, responds to them with little more than insults or ridicule should not be completely trusted. Yes, the writer may sound confident and convincing, but you probably need to know a bit more before deciding to support or share the writer's point of view.

To understand the difference between appropriate and inappropriate bias in persuasive writing, compare the following passages.

> After reading about courses teaching television literacy,* I must say I am appalled by the sheer idiocy that abounds on so many college campuses today. What should instructors do if they discover that students have trouble reading their textbooks because they have spent too much time watching television? What else? Give those same students more television to watch. That way, teachers can avoid making demands on students *and* avoid doing their job. All they need to do is flip on the television set and call themselves "media specialists."

The author of this passage expresses a strong bias against courses in television literacy. But the problem with the passage is not the author's bias. The problem is that the author doesn't explain or defend those feelings. Instead, in a tone of outraged irony, he ridicules the opposing point of view. In this case, the author's bias interferes with his ability to be persuasive.

To see how an author can express a bias and still be persuasive, read the following passage. Although the author freely admits her bias, she still keeps an open mind and points out not just what's wrong about opposing points of view but also what's right.

> I must admit to being troubled by courses that make commercials and soap operas the focus of study. Although I agree that television programming plays a powerful role in most people's lives and that its influence over our minds and imaginations should be critically examined, I'm not sure courses in television literacy are the answer. A better alternative would be to make television viewing a small portion of a course on critical reading and thinking. Then students could apply their critical skills to both television scripts and images. This approach would eliminate what seems to be a legitimate objection to courses in television literacy—that they encourage students to do more of what they already do: Watch too much TV.

In this passage, the author expresses a definite bias: She is not in favor of courses "that make commercials and soap operas the focus of study." Still, that bias does not prevent her from giving the opposing point of view its due. She admits that the influence of television "should be critically examined," and she suggests an alternative to courses in television literacy: critical thinking or reading

---

*television literacy: the condition of being educated or knowledgeable on the subject of television.

courses that would examine the role of television without encouraging students to spend even more time watching TV.

To evaluate bias in persuasive writing, look over the following list. Anytime you encounter a writer intent on persuasion, make sure you can say no to these five questions.

Questions to Help Evaluate Bias in Persuasive Writing

1. Does the author use a tone that drips sarcasm or erupts in anger?

2. Does the author ignore the possibility that opposing points of view might exist?

3. Does the author rely more on insulting the opposition than on explaining the merits of his or her position?

4. Does the author insist that opposing points of view have no value or merit without explaining why those opposing points of view are mistaken or inaccurate?

5. Does the author make use of circular reasoning or irrelevant facts? (See Chapter 7.)

If you answer "yes" to even one of the above five questions, you need to find a more balanced discussion of the issue at hand before taking sides.

EXERCISE 2

DIRECTIONS Each selection expresses a bias, but only one expresses such a strong bias that critical readers would be suspicious of the author's ability to fairly evaluate opposing points of view. Put a check (√) in the blank if you think the author is biased but fair. Put a *B* in the blank if you think the author is too biased to be fair.

EXAMPLE

A Scientist: I Am the Enemy

1 I am the enemy! One of those vilified, inhumane physician-scientists involved in animal research. How strange, for I have never thought of myself as an evil person. I became a pediatrician because of my love for children and my desire to keep them healthy. During medical school and residency, however, I saw many children die of leukemia, prematurity and traumatic injury—circum-

stances against which medicine has made tremendous progress, but still has far to go. More important, I also saw children, alive and healthy, thanks to advances in medical science such as infant respirators, potent antibiotics, new surgical techniques, and the entire field of organ transplantation. My desire to tip the scales in favor of the healthy, happy children drew me to medical research.

2   My accusers claim that I inflict torture on animals for the sole purpose of career advancement. My experiments supposedly have no relevance to medicine and are easily replaced by computer simulation.* Meanwhile, an apathetic public barely watches, convinced that the issue has no significance, and publicity-conscious politicians increasingly give way to the demands of the activists.

3   We in medical research have also been unconscionably apathetic. We have allowed the most extreme animal rights protesters to seize the initiative and frame the issue as one of "animal fraud." We have been complacent in our belief that a knowledgeable public would sense the importance of animal research to the public health. Perhaps we have been mistaken in not responding to the emotional tone of the argument created by those sad posters of animals by waving equally sad posters of children dying of leukemia or cystic fibrosis.

4   Much is made of the pain inflicted on these animals in the name of medical science. The animal rights activists contend that this is evidence of our malevolent and sadistic nature. A more reasonable argument, however, can be advanced in our defense. Life is often cruel, both to animals and human beings. Teenagers get thrown from the back of a pickup truck and suffer severe head injuries. Toddlers, barely able to walk, find themselves at the bottom of a swimming pool while a parent checks the mail. Physicians hoping to alleviate the pain and suffering these tragedies cause have but three choices: Create an animal model of the injury or disease and use that model to understand the process and test new therapies; experiment on human beings—some experiments will succeed, most will fail—or finally, leave medical knowledge static, hoping that accidental discoveries will lead us to the advances.

5   Some animal rights activists would suggest a fourth choice, claiming that computer models can simulate animal experiments, thus making the actual experiments unnecessary. Computers can simulate, reasonably well, the effects of well-understood principles on complex systems, as in the application of the laws of physics to airplane and automobile design. However, when the principles themselves are in question, as is the case with the complex biological systems under study, computer modeling alone is of little value.

---

*simulation: imitation.

6   One of the terrifying effects of the effort to restrict the use of animals in medical research is that the impact will not be felt for years and decades: Drugs that might have been discovered will not be; surgical techniques that might have been developed will not be; and fundamental biological processes that might have been understood will remain mysteries. (Ron Kline, "A Scientist: I Am the Enemy," *Newsweek,* December 18, 1991, pp. 77–78.)

EXPLANATION The author of this reading openly expresses a bias in favor of using animals in research. However, his bias does not interfere with his ability to respond to an opposing point of view. He challenges those who disagree without insulting them, and his tone is passionate without becoming rude or angry.

1. Hunters Are Wildlife's Best Friends

1   I am a hunter. I feed my family with the game I kill. All Americans eat dead stuff, but our meat is better, and it is harvested with a responsible connection to the earth. This is true conservation—the wise use.

2   Our time-honored tradition continues because, in the face of global habitat destruction, those of us who cherish wildlife have demanded restrictions on its harvest, based on a sound and proven scientific equation of sustained-yield management.

3   We save and guard habitat and manage wildlife not for our freezers or shooting opportunities but rather for the future of this most valuable resource. The condition of wildlife and the ground that supports it are a barometer by which the quality of our lives is based.

4   Read this very carefully, because these game laws and restrictions are self-imposed, insisted upon, policed and financed by us hunters to the tune of billions of dollars a year.

5   The lies of the animal-rights freaks are perpetrated for the single cause of greed. They are to animals what Jim Bakker* was to religion. After deceiving millions of Americans out of millions of dollars, they have yet to save any animals.

6   Look closely at their shameful agenda and track record. These zealots* hate Americans who eat turkey on Thanksgiving. They are also extremely dangerous, having bombed medical-testing labs, destroyed family-run farms, and even been convicted of animal abuse on occasion, grandstanding their lies at the expense of real animals' welfare. They recently committed their most repulsive act yet when

---

*Jim Bakker: a television evangelist who served time in prison for improper use of funds collected for religious purposes.
*zealots: people so committed to a cause they lack all reason or compassion.

one group proclaimed that the heinous crimes charged to accused mass murderer Jeffrey Dahmer were the exact same crimes as the preparation of a chicken for the grill. No clear-thinking American could possibly stand behind such statements.

7   If you truly appreciate wild animals, these people must be stopped and hunters' dedicated efforts must be supported. Sure, we have bad guys. But those who conduct legal banking businesses should never be lumped together with bank robbers. Poachers are the bad guys, and hunters despise them as our number one enemy.

8   When responsible citizens are genuinely concerned about the well-being and future of wildlife, they do their homework and discover the truth. Our Ted Nugent World Bowhunters organization is dedicated to this truth and to sharing the wonderment of the great out-of-doors with our families and friends. (Ted Nugent, "Hunters Are Wildlife's Best Friends," *USA Today*, October 3, 1991.)

———

2. Living with Wildlife

1   Hunters tend to think of themselves as friends of wildlife. But I find the position hard to accept when I consider the harm hunting does to animals. The stress hunting inflicts on animals—the noise, the fear and the constant chase—severely restricts the ability to eat properly and store the fat and energy they need to survive the winter.

2   Hunting also disrupts migration and hibernation; and the campfires, recreational vehicles, trash, and other hunting side effects endanger the wildlife and the environment. For animals like wolves who mate for life and have close family units, hunting can severely harm entire animal communities.

3   Hunters claim that they pay for "conservation" by buying hunting licenses, duck stamps, etc., but the relatively small amount each hunter pays does not cover the cost of hunting programs or game warden services. The public lands many hunters use are supported by taxpayers, and the U.S. Fish and Wildlife service programs, which benefit hunters, get as much as 90 percent of their funds from fees. Funds benefiting "nongame" species are scarce.

4   Hunters kill more animals than recorded tallies indicate. It is estimated that for every animal a hunter kills and recovers, at least two wounded but unrecovered animals die slowly and painfully of blood loss, infection, or starvation. Those who don't die often suffer from disabling injuries. Because of carelessness, or the effects of alcohol, scores of horses, cows, dogs, cats, hikers and others are wounded or killed each year by hunters.

5   Before you support a "wildlife" or "conservation" group, ask if it supports hunting. Such groups as the National Wildlife Federation, The National Audubon Society, The Sierra Club, the Izaak Walton League, The Wilderness Society and many others are prohunting.

6   To combat hunting in your area, post "No Hunting" signs on your land, join or form a local antihunting organization, protest organized hunts, play loud radios and spread deer repellant or human hair (from barber shops) near hunting areas, tell others the facts about hunting, and encourage your legislators to enact or enforce wildlife protection laws.

7   As the actor Jimmy Stewart put it, "Animals give me more pleasure through the viewfinder of a camera than they ever did in the cross hairs of a shotgun. And after I've finished 'shooting,' my unharmed victims are still around for others to enjoy." (Excerpted from "People for the Ethical Treatment of Animals," PETA.)

___

 ## Bias and Careless Thinking

Writers whose bias keeps them from considering opposing points of view are inclined to use circular reasoning and irrelevant facts (see pages 256–257). They don't do this because they're dishonest. They are just so certain of their own rightness they don't always think about convincing others. Sure that they—and only they—are right, they fail to thoroughly explain their position.

In addition to using circular reasoning and irrelevant facts, writers blinded by bias also tend to engage in two other kinds of careless thinking—*slippery slope* and *personal attack.*

Slippery Slope

Writers who engage in *slippery slope* thinking insist that taking even one step in a particular direction will invariably lead to another even more undesirable step or series of steps that will end in disaster. Here's an example:

> If we ban handguns, the next step will be the banning of rifles, and then people who hunt for food will no longer be able to feed their families.

Writers who use slippery slope thinking assume that events similar in nature follow one another without reference to any specific conditions. They ignore the fact that events rise from a particular circumstance. For example, many people want to ban handguns because statistics show a connection between handguns in the home and violent crime, both in and outside the home. That same connection does not exist between hunting rifles and crime. Thus, it makes no sense to claim that banning handguns will automatically lead to banning rifles. Handguns and rifles are similar kinds of weapons, but they are used in very different ways and in very different circumstances.

Personal Attacks

Be wary of a writer who substitutes personal attacks for relevant facts or reasons. In the following passage, for example, the author attacks her opponent's character rather than objectively evaluating his point of view.

> Once again, David DeGrecco, columnist for the *New Jersey Sun*, has presented his tired old case for gun control. As usual, DeGrecco serves up the argument that gun control laws can help eliminate some of the violence plaguing city streets across the country. Outspoken as usual, DeGrecco is curiously silent about his own recent bout with criminal behavior. Less than two weeks ago, he and several others were arrested for demonstrating at the opening of a nuclear power plant. For one so determined to bring law and order to our streets, DeGrecco does not seem to mind breaking a few laws himself.

Here the author is obviously biased against the gun control laws championed by David DeGrecco. That's certainly her right. Still, to persuade critical readers, she needs to challenge what the columnist claims—that gun control laws can help eliminate violence. But instead of doing that, she attacks the man personally, pointing out that he was recently jailed. Yet DeGrecco's position on nuclear power has nothing to do with the issue at hand—gun control. This, then, is another instance of bias clouding the writer's ability to respond fairly and respectfully to opposing points of view.

EXERCISE 3

DIRECTIONS Each of the following passages expresses a strong bias for or against a particular position. But in a few cases the author has fallen victim to the two errors in reasoning described on pages 352–353. Identify these passages by putting an *S* (for slippery slope) or a *P* (for personal attack) in the blank. If the passage does not contain either error, put a check (√) in the blank.

EXAMPLE It doesn't take a genius to figure out that we need to find a way to make various kinds of education more affordable. President Clinton, who never once called himself the "Education President" but deserves that title more than any person who has sat in the Oval Office, has proposed a variety of measures. He would like to let middle-class families deduct up to $10,000 of the cost of tuition or training. He wants to combine seventy different job programs, almost all of which he inherited from the Bush administration, into a simple voucher* so people can pursue the training or education of their choice. He proposed expanding the college grant program to include 800,000 more students by the year 2002. He created an outstanding national service program that allows students to save up credits to pay for college at the same time they're helping neighborhoods and communities. And all that doesn't even count what he's done and will continue to do for elementary and high school education. Let nobody tell you that this man is not committted at his core to education. (James Carville, *We're Right, They're Wrong.* New York: Random House, 1996, p. 89.)

√

EXPLANATION In this passage, the author expresses a strong bias in favor of President Clinton and his stand on education. He consistently argues his case with facts and figures, and he does not resort either to the slippery slope or personal attack errors in reasoning.

1. Where Does It End?

1 Let me say right off that I don't smoke. I quit twenty-five years ago and don't have any plans to light up in this lifetime. Having offered my credentials as a non-smoker, let me also say that I am troubled by the war being waged against both smokers and tobacco companies.

2 All across the country smokers are being treated like second-class citizens. For example, smokers living in California or Maryland can't go out to a restaurant and expect to eat in the smokers' section. There isn't any. If they want to eat out, they have to leave their cigarettes at home. If they light up at the table, someone will show them the door. As of yet, most states are more liberal in their approach to smoking, but other states will no doubt follow the more radical lead of California and Maryland.

---

*voucher: a written certificate guaranteeing cash or credit.

3   Equally disturbing is the 1998 lawsuit filed by twenty-two states against the big tobacco companies. The goal of the suit is the recovery of Medicaid costs spent on those with smoking-related illnesses. Now this may sound like a righteous lawsuit, but consider the implications. What happens if those twenty-two states win? Whose head will turn up next on the chopping block? Maybe it will be time to sue the liquor companies. After all, state money must have been spent caring for patients suffering from cirrhosis of the liver, and heavy liquor consumption is a prime cause of that gruesome disease. By this time, we all know that a diet high in fat is linked to cancer and heart disease. If the tobacco companies can get sued, the beef industry will probably be next. Then it will be the sugar industry and who knows where it will all end.[1]

2. **Making Divorce Harder to Get for Others**

Recently, State Representative Michael D. Flink introduced into the state legislature* a bill that would dramatically alter our current divorce laws and make getting a divorce much more difficult. Representative Flink's support of this bill is ironic. Twice divorced and now married a third time, Representative Flink apparently feels he will have no further need for a divorce in the future. Thus, he can safely make divorce more difficult for others, claiming that both parties' consent and a one-year waiting period could help slow the rate of divorce and keep families intact.

3. **Unmarried But Promoting Daycare?**

Feminist Gloria Stanton has put her considerable powers of persuasion behind a bill requiring large corporations to institute daycare centers for employees with small children. According to Stanton, the daycare centers would quickly pay for themselves in increased productivity and decreased absenteeism. To prove her point, she cites an array of federally funded studies showing that corporations who provide daycare have a more stable work force. I must admit I find Ms. Stanton's position a bit laughable. After all, the woman is not married and has no children. What could she possibly know about the effects of daycare on company productivity?

---

[1]Modeled on an editorial by Adrian Pratt. "Cigarette Regulations Becoming Downright Un-American," *Online Athens* (www.onlineathens.com), January 4, 1998.
*A form of this bill was actually introduced into the Texas legislature in 1997.

4. Egg Donation May Not Be Such a Miracle for Donors

1 Because so many couples desperately want a child and can't have one, the search for women ready and willing to donate their eggs for in vitro fertilization* has become a big business. Although many people consider in vitro fertilization a wondrous miracle, I must admit to being skeptical about the use of egg donors. The couple who gains a child, thanks to a donor, may be rightly jubilant; the donor may be taking more risks than she realizes.

2 For starters, the egg donation process is not particularly pleasant. To prepare, women take daily hormone injections that force the maturation of ten to twenty eggs instead of the normal one or two. As a result of the injections, donors often suffer cramping and mood swings. Sometimes their ovaries become dangerously enlarged. At this time, there have been no signs of long-term side effects on donors, but it is possible that the injections may increase the possibility of ovarian cancer. No one really knows for sure what the long-term effects are mainly because in vitro fertilization hasn't been around for that long.

3 Those who favor the use of egg donors argue that the women are being well paid for the risks they take. Unfortunately, the issue of payment only raises another objection. Clinics and hospitals pay donors as much as five thousand dollars for their eggs. In the face of such a sum, women who are young or poor—or in many cases both—can be lured by the money into ignoring the risks. As Diana Aronson, the executive director of Resolve, the national support group for infertile couples, points out, the large sums of money offered donors can lead to what she calls "inappropriate assessment of risk. If you're a college student, four cycles at $5,000 each may pay for . . . college"[2] and if you're a poor, unmarried mother, $5,000 will pay the rent for months.

4 Yes, egg donation may well provide infertile couples with the baby they so desperately desire, but someone else may be paying a terrible price for their joy. Couples desiring the use of egg donation should ask themselves if they are willing to let another human being take serious health risks so that they can become parents.

_____

*in vitro fertilization: *in vitro* literally means "in glass"; the term refers to the process of creating life in an artificial setting outside the human body.
[2]Marie McCullough, "Life for Sale: Market for Women's Eggs Is Heating Up," *Philadelphia Inquirer,* March 8, 1998, pp. A-1 and 19.

5. In 1992, the American Association of University Women published the report *How Schools Shortchange Girls.* As the title indicates, the study strongly suggested that public schools were not doing enough to ensure that boys and girls were treated equally. The report made a great deal of the fact that teachers tend to call on boys more than on girls. As a result of that AAUW report, many educators have begun to sing the praises of single-sex schools. In fact, the pages of this newspaper recently featured letters from several educators who had gone to all-girl schools and were convinced that they were better off as a result. Still, no matter how trendy it may be to applaud same-sex schools, I beg to disagree.

2   Girls need to have boys in the classroom. If they don't learn how to work with and compete against boys while they are in school and the stakes aren't so high, how will they do it after graduation when they enter the world of work? Imagine, for example, that a young woman who has never been in intellectual competition with men enters a management meeting where only men are present. Is she going to hold her own, or is she going to become anxious and tongue-tied because her male colleagues don't use the "nurturing" style purportedly employed more by women than by men? I think the latter is a real possibility.

3   Then, too, where does this isolation by gender end? Can we expect women who have gone to same-sex schools to demand that the workplace also be segregated?* Probably. Once we agree that women should study only with one another, the segregated workplace can't be far behind.

WORD NOTES

On page 340, you learned the meaning of the word *berate*—to criticize harshly and at length. This is yet another word with some useful synonyms that you should add to your vocabulary.

1. **Upbraid:** to criticize or reproach with good reason, as in "The court *upbraided* her for fleeing the country after she had been allowed to go free on bail."
2. **Revile:** to criticize or reproach using abusive language, as

-----

*segregated: divided by sex or race.

in "Those who had collaborated with the Nazis were *reviled* by their neighbors after the war ended."

3. **Rail:** to criticize or reproach with language that is harsh but not necessarily abusive, as in "It does not pay to *rail* at one's fate; a better strategy is to do something that will change it."

4. **Vituperate:** to criticize with abusive language. *Note:* The word *vituperate* appears more frequently as an adjective or a noun than a verb, as in (1) "The king was not touched by the *vituperation* heaped on him by his hungry subjects" and (2) "In arguments, she tends to use the kind of *vituperative* language that only makes matters worse."

Pay attention to the subtle differences among these four words as you use them to fill in the blanks. *Note:* You will have to change the endings.

1. The young mother _____ her tiny daughter for running into the street.

2. There's really no point in _____ at the Internal Revenue Service. Taxes are like death; they are simply part of life.

3. When his neighbors found out he had been a member of the Ku Klux Klan, he was _____ for it.

4. The level of _____ in his speech was terrifying; it was hard to believe that one human being could be filled with so much hate.

Now it's your turn to use them in sentences.

1. **upbraid:** _____

_____

2. **revile:** _____

_____

3. **rail:** _____

_____

4. **vituperation:** _____

_____

Summing Up

Listed below are the most important points in Chapter 10. Put a check mark in the box if you think the point is clear in your mind. Leave the box blank if you need to review the material one more time. The page numbers in parentheses tell you where to look to review each point on the list.

☐ **1.** How critical readers respond to bias depends on the context in which that bias appears and the strength of the bias expressed. (p. 339)

☐ **2.** Although informative writing should keep bias at a minimum, writers may unconsciously reveal their personal feelings. Therefore, critical readers should be alert to the presence of bias even in writing intended solely to inform. (pp. 339–341)

☐ **3.** Emotionally charged language is a sign of bias in informative writing, but so, too, is the absence of opposing points of view. Sometimes what's been left out is a significant clue to the presence of bias. (p. 341)

☐ **4.** Bias in persuasive writing is to be expected. Nevertheless, even writers who express a strong bias should treat opposing points of view fairly. If an author doesn't, critical readers should become suspicious as to the soundness of the writer's position. (pp. 346–348)

TEST YOUR UNDERSTANDING

To see how well you have understood this chapter, take the following review quiz. Then correct it using the answer key provided by your instructor. If you score 80 percent or above, you're ready to take the end-of-chapter exam. However, if you score below 80 percent, look over the quiz carefully to see what kinds of questions you missed. Then use the **Summing Up** pages of the chapter to decide which pages you should review before taking the chapter exam.

Chapter 10: Review Quiz

Part A

DIRECTIONS Each of the following passages appears in a source where one would expect to find no evidence of bias. Read each passage. Then circle the appropriate letter to indicate whether or not the passage reveals a bias.

1. **Donoso, José (1924–)** Born in Santiago, Chile to a prominent family, José Donoso quit school at age nineteen and traveled in South America, where he worked on sheep farms and as a dockhand. Later, he went to school in the United States and received a B.A. from Princeton University in 1951. Donoso spent the next decade working as a teacher and journalist in Chile, writing profusely. In 1955, Donoso published his first book, *Veraneo y otros cuentos* (*Summer Vacation and Other Stories*), which received the Municipal Literary Prize; one year later, he published *Dos Cuentos* (1956; *Two Short Stories*), and in 1957 his first novel, *Coronación* (*Coronation*), appeared to much critical acclaim. *Coronación* describes the moral collapse of an aristocratic family, a recurrent theme in Donoso's work. Marrying Maria Pilar Serrano, a Bolivian painter, in 1961, Donoso began writing what is often considered his masterpiece, *El obsceno pájaro de la noche* (1970; *The Obscene Bird of Night*). He also renewed his friendship with Mexican novelist Carlos Fuentes, whom he had met in grade school. While spending some time at Fuentes's home, he completed *El lugar sin límites* (1966; *Hell Has No Limits*) and *Este Domingo* (1966; *This Sunday*), grim novels of psychological desolation and anguish. (Kwame Anthony Appiah and Henry Louis Gates Jr., *The Dictionary of Global Culture*. New York: Alfred Knopf, 1997, p. 185.)

   a. The authors admire Donoso's work.

   b. The authors are critical of Donoso's work.

   c. It's impossible to determine the author's personal feelings.

2. **Christoph Gottwald (1960–),** German Novelist and Poet.   Because he got his start writing mysteries popular with everyone but the critics, Gottwald's emergence as serious novelist has been shamelessly ignored. Yet his 1997 novel *End Station Palma,* reminiscent of Heinrich Böll's early work, is worthy of serious critical attention. Using themes he probed previously in novels like *Cologne Crackup* (1980) and *Lifelong Pizza* (1994), Gottwald again ex-

plores the inability of language to communicate our deepest
needs, often with tragic results. Abandoning the comic detach-
ment he used so brilliantly in his first two books, the novelist now
assumes the voice of a man passionately committed to his subject
and tortured by the strength of his own emotions. A conservative
voice in a literary world desperate to be trendy, Gottwald may not
get the audience he deserves, either in Germany or America. However, his fiction—in contrast to the work of his more highly
praised and less talented contemporaries—will be read by future
generations, long after more acclaimed novelists have been properly consigned to the trashbin of history. (Lawrence Wordsmith,
Twentieth Century Comparative Literature. Nanuet, NY: Bush-
whacked Press, 1999, p. 20.)

a. The author admires Gottwald's work.

b. The author is critical of Gottwald's work.

c. It's impossible to determine the author's personal feelings.

3. Magnet Schools

1   One alternative approach to school integration has gained some
advocates in recent years: *magnet schools.* These are schools, usually located in inner cities, with special academic programs.

2   The first magnet schools appeared in the early 1970s. By the
1980s, they were often used as the chief tool for achieving school
integration: Dallas, Houston, Los Angeles, Milwaukee, and San
Diego received court orders to found them; Chicago, Cincinnati,
Indianapolis, and Seattle set them up hoping to sidetrack legal
trouble; a few cities, including Cambridge, Massachusetts, even
set them up without threat of court order.

3   Despite the proliferation* of magnet schools across the country, they have their critics. One criticism is that they deliberately
skim off the brightest students and teachers in each district.
Moreover, they often cost more money to set up and run than ordinary schools do. In addition, some magnet schools are apparently special in name only. In the mid-seventies, an investigation
of twenty magnet schools in Berkeley, California, seemed to show
that all schools were pretty much the same. And in Boston most
principals of magnet schools were reported to "admit privately
that their magnet theme is grossly underdeveloped—or nonexistent" (Barr, 1982; see also U.S. Department of Education, 1984).

---

*proliferation: spread, increase.

(David Popanoe, *Sociology.* Upper Saddle River, N.J.: Prentice-Hall, 1989, p. 400.)

a. The author is a supporter of magnet schools.

b. The author is critical of magnet schools.

c. It's impossible to determine the author's personal feelings.

4. Sigmund Freud

1 Sigmund Freud (1885–1939), the father of psychoanalytic theory, grew up in a middle-class Jewish family in Vienna, Austria, where he spent most of his life. As a young man, Freud received a medical degree and opened a practice as a neurologist. Among his patients were many cases of *hysteria,* an emotional disorder characterized by physical symptoms such as twitches, paralysis, and even blindness without any discernible* physical basis. Freud's work with these patients gradually led him to conclude that repressed memories and wishes underlie emotional disorders and that personality involves a perpetual conflict among forces within ourselves.

2 Freud's early writings were denounced by other scientists. In his later years, however, Freud began to receive the recognition he deserved for his courageous exploration of the human mind. When the Nazis invaded Austria in 1938, Freud was persuaded to move to England. He died a year later. (Rubin et al., *Psychology,* p. 395.)

a. The authors admire the work of Sigmund Freud.

b. The authors are critical of Freud's work.

c. It's impossible to determine the authors' personal feelings about Freud's work.

5. Jewish Refugees from the Holocaust

By World War II's end, about six million Jews had been forced into concentration camps and had been systematically killed by firing squads, unspeakable tortures, and gas chambers. The Nazis also exterminated as many as 250,000 gypsies and about 60,000 gay men. During the depression, the United States and other nations had refused to relax their immigration restrictions to save Jews fleeing persecution. The American Federation of Labor and Senator William Borah of Idaho, among others, argued that new immigrants would compete with American workers for

*discernible: visible to the eye.

scarce jobs, and public opinion polls supported their position. This fear of economic competition was fed by anti-Semitism. Bureaucrats applied the rules so strictly—requiring legal documents that fleeing Jews could not possibly provide—that otherwise-qualified refugees were kept out of the country. From 1933 to 1945, less than 40 percent of the German-Austrian immigration quota was filled. (Norton et al., *A People and a Nation,* p. 543.)

a. The authors believe that World War II immigration restrictions were necessary at the time.

b. The authors are highly critical of World War II immigration restrictions.

c. It's impossible to determine the authors' personal feelings.

Part B

DIRECTIONS Each of the following selections expresses a bias, but only one expresses a bias so strongly that readers should be wary of the author's ability to be fair. Put a check (√) in the blank if the author is biased but fair. Put a *B* in the blank if you think the author's bias has clouded his or her judgment.

6. Movie critics, like politicians, should have a limited term in office. Over time, they become cynical, stupid, and self-serving. Keep in mind, after all, that movie critics loved Quentin Tarantino's movie *Pulp Fiction* and hated Kevin Costner's film *Waterworld.* Yet I really loved *Waterworld* and hated *Pulp Fiction.* The former had no foul language and no sex. It also had a happy ending. The latter, in contrast, had nothing but foul language, perverted sex, and gruesome violence. If so called "respected" critics can favor *Pulp Fiction* over *Waterworld,* then there's something wrong somewhere, and we need to get rid of all the old-timers and replace them with people who know how to tell a good movie from a bad one.

———

7. Without doubt, most of the people who favor assisted suicide are motivated by compassion and pity for those in pain. Still, those who support assisted suicide are making a false assumption. They assume that the men and women contemplating suicide are determined to die because life has become too hard, too difficult, and too pain-ridden for them. Yet, workers at suicide hotlines report that, apart from fearing unbearable pain, what the terminally

ill fear most is being a burden to their families.[3] Hence, their so-called choice is motivated more by a desire to help others than it is by a desire to help themselves. Before deciding that someone has the legal right to assist in a suicide, we need to know a good deal more about why a person chooses to die.

─────

Part C

DIRECTIONS At least two of the following selections use either the slippery slope or character attack to convince readers. Circle the appropriate letters to identify those selections.

8. Although it had previously permitted such actions, in 1997 Australia abolished all legal right for a person to assist at a suicide. Let us hope that the United States learns from Australia's mistake and never grants assisted suicide legal status. For if we say that it is acceptable for a friend or relative to help take the life of someone in pain, where do we draw the line? Will it be all right for parents to assist in the suicide of a child born deformed? Will it be acceptable to pull the plug on someone in a coma even when no one knows whether or not the patient wants to live? All that we hold dearest as human beings is based on the sanctity of life as the ultimate value.[4] Our horror at Hitler's* gas chambers, Stalin's purges, Mao's famines, and Pol Pot's killing fields stems not only from the enormity of the suffering involved. The truth is that when you extinguish life on that scale, a light goes out in all human souls. One could argue that the difference between those cases and assisted suicide is that the latter is entirely voluntary. However, once the right to die ascends to the same pedestal as the right to live, the pace of sanctioned killings, we suspect, will be no less horrifying. By stepping back, Australia has earned the thanks of a great many people.

   a. The author employs the slippery slope.

   b. The author relies on a character attack.

   c. There is no error in reasoning.

─────

[3]"Against Assisted Death," *Wall Street Journal,* April 1, 1997, p. A-18.
[4]From here on, the passage is a direct quote from "Against Assisted Death," p. A-18.
*Adolf Hitler, Joseph Stalin, Mao Zedong, and Pol Pot were all dictators responsible for the deaths of millions of people.

9. Forgetting Prison's Purpose

1 As the recent guest editorial André DeMarco makes abundantly clear, it's easy to forget what prisons are for: They were designed to punish, not reward, criminals for their crimes.

2 According to Mr. DeMarco, high-security prisons that keep criminals in what amounts to permanent isolation are barbaric.* They are a throwback to an earlier time before enlightened individuals like himself recognized that rehabilitation* was the true goal of a prison term.

3 Mr. DeMarco believes that sustained isolation and inactivity should be replaced by a more humane daily schedule that allows prisoners access to communal activities such as lifting weights and playing basketball. If we don't make such changes, Mr. DeMarco argues, then we are in the process of creating criminals who are more brutal when they come out of prison than when they entered.

4 But even if we do soften the current harshness of high-security prisons, will that satisfy bleeding heart liberals like Mr. DeMarco? Probably not. Next they will be demanding work release for dangerous felons, a trained chef in the prison kitchen, and a VCR in every prisoner's cell. People are in prison because they committed crimes. They should be punished for those crimes, not rewarded.

a. The author employs the slippery slope.

b. The author relies on a character attack.

c. There is no error in reasoning.

10. The Benefits of Granting Most-Favored-Nation Status to China

1 The granting of "most-favored-nation" status to China has been controversial for a while now because of that nation's harsh treatment of political dissidents.* Those who oppose giving China this economic benefit believe that China's human rights violations make it ineligible for any special favors from our government.

2 On a personal level, I too abhor China's treatment of political opposition. The Chinese government's willingness to imprison, even execute, those who disagree has been well documented. Still, it is important to consider whether or not granting most-favored-nation status can be used as a tool to encourage more democratic policies in China.

---

*barbaric: inhuman.
*rehabilitation: the act of restoring good behavior through reeducation.
*dissidents: people who disagree with their government.

3   For one thing, limited trade isolates a country, whereas encouraging trade exposes that country to customs and values outside their own. If U.S. companies gain increased access to China, the Chinese government, along with its people, will gain new insight into democratic standards and principles. As a result, China's leaders may well recognize that a more democratic form of government will help them stay in power by draining off the anger and rebellion still simmering beneath the surface of Chinese society.

4   In addition, China is a large country and a very attractive site for business investments of many other Western countries. If we reduce our economic contact with China, other countries will quickly take our place. Although the loss to our business communities is not a good reason for us to ignore our principles, it is also true that China would not suffer as a consequence and therefore would have no motivation to change.

a. The author employs the slippery slope.

b. The author relies on a character attack.

c. There is no error in reasoning.

Use the answer key provided by your instructor to correct your quiz. If you score 80 percent or above, you are ready for the chapter exam. If you score below 80 percent, look carefully at the questions you answered incorrectly. Then use the **Summing Up** section to decide which pages you need to review.

Chapter Test 10

Part A

DIRECTIONS Each of the following passages appears in a source where one would expect no evidence of bias. Read each selection. Then circle the appropriate letter to indicate whether or not the authors have actually eliminated all trace of bias.

1. Carl Rogers

1   Like [Sigmund] Freud, Carl Rogers (1902–1987) was a practicing psychotherapist. His theory, like Freud's, evolved from what he saw in his patients, but there the similarity ends. From the beginning, Rogers rejected most psychoanalytic assumptions about the importance of unconscious forces. Instead, he focused on each person's unique, conscious, and immediate experiences and each person's need for self-fulfillment. "At bottom," Rogers said, "each person is asking, 'Who am I, *really*? How can I get in touch with this real self, underlying all my surface behavior? How can I become myself?'" (Rogers, 1961, p. 108).

2   According to Rogers, we each try to maintain an organized, consistent image of ourselves, and it is this **self-concept** that directs our behavior and determines how we see reality. People's self-concepts may be influenced by the racial, religious, or national groups to which they belong.

3   Almost inevitably, conflicts arise between the values we have incorporated into our self-concept and our actual experiences. Chris may view himself as "a good student" (the self-concept) but discover that he does not enjoy his courses (the experience). Or there may be a conflict between a person's *real self* (the actual self-concept) and her *ideal self* (the self-concept she would like to have). For example, Marie sees herself as a friendly and popular person (her real self), but she would like to see herself as making a greater contribution to humanity (her ideal self). Such discrepancies*—or *incongruences*, in Rogers's terms—can lead to intense feelings of guilt or sadness (Higgins, 1987). They may also propel people to change either their behavior or their self-concept, in the service of personal growth. (Adapted from Rubin et al., *Psychology,* p. 403.)

a. The authors admire the work of Carl Rogers.

b. The authors are critical of Carl Rogers's work.

c. It's impossible to determine the authors' personal feelings.

*discrepancies: things that don't fit.

2. Sexual Harassment

1 Most sociologists define **sexual harassment** as an unwelcome act of a sexual nature. In 1993 the U.S. Supreme Court provided a more precise legal definition: Sexual harassment is any sexual conduct that makes the workplace environment so hostile or abusive to the victims that they find it hard to perform their job.

2 The Supreme Court's definition came with its ruling on the suit that Teresa Harris filed against her former boss, Charles Hardy. In 1987 Harris quit her job in despair because she felt she had been sexually harassed by Hardy. According to Harris, Hardy often asked her—and other female employees—to retrieve coins from the front pockets of his pants. He once asked Harris to go with him to a hotel room to negotiate her raise. And he routinely made such remarks to her as "You're a woman; what do you know?" She spent six years trying to convince judges that she was sexually harassed in violation of federal law, but to no avail. The judges found Hardy's conduct not severe enough to "seriously affect her psychological well-being." But Harris persisted, and finally the Supreme Court ruled that sexual harassment does not have to inflict "severe psychological injury" on the victim. As the Court says, federal law "comes into play before the harassing conduct leads to a nervous breakdown" (Sachs, 1993). (Thio, *Sociology,* 1998, p. 279.)

a. The author agrees with the sexual harassment ruling.

b. The author disagrees with the sexual harassment ruling.

c. It's impossible to determine the author's personal feelings.

3. America's Entry into the First World War

1 The outbreak of the Great War in Europe in 1914 at first stunned Americans. For years they had witnessed and participated in the international competition for colonies, markets, and weapons supremacy. But full-scale war seemed unthinkable in the modern age of progress. "Civilization is all gone, and barbarism come," moaned one social reformer. The French and Germans were using "huge death engines to mow down men and cities," observed *Harper's Weekly.* "We go about in a daze, hoping to awake from the most horrid of nightmares." Articulated by well-organized groups, peace sentiment in the United States strengthened with each grisly report from the European battlefield.

2 For almost three years President Wilson kept America out of the war. During this time, he sought to protect U.S. interests as a neutral trader and to improve the nation's military posture

should the United States ever decide to join the fight. He lectured the belligerents to rediscover their humanity and to respect international law. But American neutrality finally fell victim to German naval warfare like the sinking of the *Lusitania*. (Adapted from Norton et al., *A People and a Nation*, p. 98.)

a. The authors accept Wilson's reasons for entering the First World War.

b. The authors are critical of Wilson's reasons for entering the First World War.

c. It's impossible to determine the authors' personal feelings.

4. **America Enters World War I**

1 President Woodrow Wilson had promised that the United States would stay neutral in the war: "There is such a thing as a nation being too proud to fight." But in April of 1917, the Germans had announced they would have their submarines sink any ship bringing supplies to their enemies; and they had sunk a number of merchant vessels. Wilson now said he must stand by the right of Americans to travel on merchant ships in the war zone. "I cannot consent to any abridgement* of the rights of American citizens in any respect."

2 As Richard Hofstadter points out (*The American Political Tradition*): "This was rationalization* of the flimsiest sort." The British had also been intruding on the rights of American citizens on the high seas, but Wilson was not suggesting we go to war with them. Hofstadter says Wilson "was forced to find legal reasons for policies that were based not upon law but upon the balance of power and economic necessities."

3 It was unrealistic to expect that the Germans should treat the United States as neutral in the war when the United States had been shipping great amounts of war materials to Germany's enemies. In early 1915, the British liner *Lusitania* was torpedoed and sunk by a German submarine. She sank in eighteen minutes, and 1,198 people died, including 124 Americans. The United States claimed the *Lusitania* carried an innocent cargo, and therefore the torpedoing was a monstrous German atrocity. Actually, the *Lusitania* was heavily armed: it carried 1,248 cases of 3-inch shells, 4,927 boxes of cartridges (1,000 rounds in each box), and

---

*abridgement: the act of reducing.
*rationalization: an explanation that seems to be based on reason but really only serves someone's self-interest.

2,000 more cases of small-arms ammunition. Her manifests*
were falsified to hide this fact, and the British and American governments lied about the cargo. (Howard Zinn, *A People's History
of the United States.* New York: Harper Perennial, 1995, pp. 354–
355.)

a. The author accepts Wilson's reasons for entering the First World
   War.

b. The author is critical of Wilson's reasons for entering the First
   World War.

c. It's impossible to determine the author's personal feelings.

5. Men's Quiet Revolution

1 Along with the women's movement, a quiet revolution has been going on among some men who want to free themselves from the demands of the traditional male role. As we have observed, men are
expected to be tough, aggressive, and competitive and to suppress
their emotions even if they feel like crying when sad. It can be difficult for men to relate closely to their wives and children, because such a close relationship requires sensitivity, warmth, and
tenderness—the very qualities discouraged by the masculine role.
It also can be difficult to develop deep friendships with other men
because of the pressure to be competitive and to put up a tough,
impersonal front (Messner, 1997; Jesser, 1996).

2   Consequently, a growing number of men support gender equality. They can see how equality helps reduce the burden of being
male. They can also see the benefit of encouraging their wives to
pursue careers outside the home if that is their choice. Imprison-
ing a bored and frustrated wife in the homemaking role is believed by many to be likely to cause the marriage to fall apart.
Moreover, the working wife can boost the family income. A working wife makes it possible for men to change careers, if they wish,
rather than being trapped in the wrong job. The significant financial contributions from their working wives relieve the pressure
on men. If they do not have to work so hard to make a living, they
can take more time for their family and discover the joys of father-
hood (Messner, 1997; Jesser, 1996).

3   Many of these men, however, do not *totally* support equality between the sexes. They are what Kathleen Gerson (1993) calls "autonomous men." They like to enjoy freedom from the traditional
burden of being the family's sole breadwinner but refuse to share

---

*manifests: lists of cargo on board.

equally with their wives the responsibility of housework and childcare. As a result, while these autonomous men can *have* it all, their working wives tend to *do* it all, coming home after a day of work to a "second shift" of doing housework and caring for children (Hochschild, 1989). A more recent study found that working wives still do 87 percent of the shopping, 81 percent of the cooking, 78 percent of the cleaning, and 63 percent of the bill paying (Holmes, 1996b). The younger generation of men, though, are more inclined to do domestic chores. According to a survey, already nearly half of the young men—ages 18 to 24—interviewed said they would be interested in staying home with their young children so that their wives could succeed in their careers. (Thio, *Sociology*, 1998, pp. 286–287.)

a. The author admires the traditional male role.

b. The author is critical of the traditional male role.

c. It's impossible to determine the author's personal feelings.

Part B

DIRECTIONS Each of the following selections expresses a bias. Put a check (√) in the blank if you think the author is biased but fair. Put a *B* in the blank if you think the author has become too biased to treat the opposition fairly.

6. Draining the Glen Canyon Dam

1 Completed in 1963, the Glen Canyon Dam was part of a federal program created to control the flow of the Colorado River and irrigate the surrounding region. When the dam was built, it created the two-hundred-mile-long Lake Powell, one of the largest artificial bodies of water in the world. But the extraordinary beauty of Lake Powell aside, the Glen Canyon Dam has turned out to be a mistake. The dam should be dismantled and Lake Powell drained of its water.

2 As the Sierra Club leadership has effectively argued, Lake Powell is an inefficient reservoir. It loses almost an acre of water yearly. In addition, the West has no shortage of electrical power. Thus, the electric power generated by the dam is unnecessary.

3 To most people's surprise, even the two men most responsible for the dam's creation in the first place, former Arizona senator Barry Goldwater and former secretary of the interior Stewart Udall, agree with the Sierra Club's proposals. As G. Pascal Zachary has written, "big dams now symbolize waste, inefficiency, and

corruption."[5] The Glen Canyon Dam is no exception, and despite the controversy surrounding the Sierra Club's proposal, plans to dismantle the dam should go forward.

———

7. Classical Music's New Lease on Life

1 Walk through the classical section of almost any music store and you can tell there have been some dramatic changes in the classical music world. On one side of the aisle, you're likely to find a picture of jazz vocalist Bobby McFerrin singing with the St. Paul Chamber Orchestra. On the other, you might see a new recording by classical composer Arvo Part, with a cover quote from rock star Michael Stipe of the group R.E.M. declaring Part's music "a house on fire." No wonder, then, that some classical music lovers are up in arms and writing books with titles like *Who Killed Classical Music?*

2 In point of fact, long-time lovers of classical music are right to be anxious. In their efforts to attract more youthful consumers, record companies that market classical music are searching out what's hip or trendy and sometimes forgetting to ask a crucial question: Is the music any good?

3 Still, classical music purists who shudder at the sound of famed cellist Yo-Yo Ma playing the sexy tangos of jazz musician Astor Piazzolla are ignoring an important side effect of the music industry's feverish efforts to attract a younger audience. Those efforts, driven or not by the profit motive, may well be creating a new audience for classical music. For it is precisely the newer and flashier recordings that are encouraging people who have never before bought classical music to give it a try.

4 Take, for example, cellist Yo-Yo Ma's successful, jazz-oriented *Soul of the Tango* CD. Many fans of that work went out and purchased some of Ma's other classical recordings. Yet, most of these same fans had never before purchased a piece of classical music.

5 Similarly, Nadja Salerno-Sonnenberg's pop-sounding collection titled *It Ain't Necessarily So* won the violinist legions of new fans willing to buy her other titles, even if the CDs do mention the names of Bach, Beethoven, and Brahms. Instead of complaining that violinists who pose in black leather pants* are giving classical music a bad name, classical music lovers should be cheering:

———
[5]G. Pascal Zachary, "In These Times," *Utne Reader*, November 2, 1997, p. 20.
*Violinist Viktoria Mullova posed wearing black leather pants.

After years of declining numbers, the audience for classical music may just be on the rise.

_____

Part C

DIRECTIONS At least two of the following selections use either the slippery slope or character attack to convince readers. Circle the appropriate letters to identify those selections.

8. No Sexual Harassment Equals No Soldiers

1 Recently, there's been a good deal of attention focused on sexual harassment in the military, and rightly so. No one wants to see officers in charge of young female recruits abuse their power by sexually harassing those in their charge. However, supporters of women in the military are making a crucial mistake when they try to eliminate sexism in the military and at the same time insist that women should go into combat right alongside men.

2 To be a warrior means that a soldier has to revert to a more primitive mode of behavior and thought. It means that one has to assume a kill or be killed mentality that allows little room for compassion or thought. It is very hard, perhaps impossible, to encourage this mindset in men yet expect them to fight side by side with women without reverting to a more primitive mode of behavior. As Fred C. Ikle, an undersecretary of defense in the Reagan administration expressed it, "You can't cultivate the necessary commitment to physical violence and fully protect against the risk of harassment. Military life may . . . foster the attitudes that tend toward rape, such as aggression and single-minded assertion."[6]

3 Viewed from this perspective, efforts to eliminate sexual harassment could have disastrous consequences during wartime, particularly if women are allowed into combat. Committed to being respectful toward women, male soldiers will also feel that they cannot behave aggressively in the presence of women. As a result, they will hold back during combat training and eventually during combat itself. Our country will lose its military strength and its position as a world power.

    a. The author employs the slippery slope.

    b. The author relies on a character attack.

    c. There is no error in reasoning.

_____

[6]Richard Raynor, "The Warrior Besieged," *New York Times*, June 22, 1997, p. 29.

9. English Belongs to Everybody

1 This is a time of widespread anxiety about the language. Some Americans fear that English will be engulfed or diluted by Spanish and want to make it the official language. There is anxiety about a crisis of illiteracy, or a crisis of semiliteracy among high school, even college, graduates.

2 Anxiety, however, may have a perverse side effect: Experts who wish to "save" the language may only discourage pleasure in it. Some are good-humored and tolerant of change, others intolerant and snobbish. Language reinforces feelings of social superiority or inferiority; it creates insiders and outsiders; it is a prop to vanity or a source of anxiety, and on both emotions the language snobs play. Yet the changes and the errors that irritate them are no different in kind from those which have shaped our language for centuries. As Hugh Kenner wrote of certain British critics in *The Sinking Island,* "They took note of language only when it annoyed them." Such people are killjoys: They turn others away from an interest in the language, inhibit their use of it, and turn pleasure off.

3 Change is inevitable in a living language and is responsible for much of the vitality of English; it has prospered and grown because it was able to accept and absorb change. As people evolve and do new things, their language will evolve too. They will find ways to describe the new things and their changed perspective will give them new ways of talking about the old things. For example, electric light switches created a brilliant metaphor for the oldest of human experiences, being *turned on* or *turned off.* To language conservatives those expressions still have a slangy, low ring to them; to others they are vivid, fresh-minted currency, very spendable, very "with it." . . .

4 It might also be argued that more Americans hear more correct, even beautiful, English on television than was ever heard before. Through television more models of good usage reach more American homes than was ever possible in other times. Television gives them lots of colloquial English, too, some awful, some creative, but that is not new.

5 Hidden in this is a simple fact: Our language is not the special private property of the language police, or grammarians, or teachers, or even great writers. The genius of English is that it has always been the tongue of the common people, literate or not. English belongs to everybody: The funny turn of phrase that pops into the mind of a farmer telling a story; or the traveling salesman's dirty joke; or the teenager saying, "Gag me with a spoon"; or the pop lyric—all contribute, are all as valid as the tortured

image of the academic, or the line the poet sweats over for a week.

6   Through our collective language sense, some may be thought beautiful and some ugly, some may live and some may die; but it is all English and it belongs to everyone—to those of us who wish to be careful with it and those who don't care. (Excerpted from Robert MacNeil, *Wordstruck*. New York: Viking Books, 1989.)

a. The author employs the slippery slope.

b. The author relies on a character attack.

c. There is no error in reasoning.

10. **Whose Rights Matter More?**

1 For six months now, animal rights activists have been picketing the Taylor Medical Center, where chimpanzees are being used to develop a vaccine for AIDS. The demonstrators argue that the research must be stopped because the chimps are kept in isolation, and isolation is torture for animals as social as chimpanzees. The demonstrators insist that they do not want to stop the research altogether. They claim they simply want to stop it long enough so that appropriate living conditions for the chimps can be created.

2   But no one should let themselves be deceived by these seemingly reasonable demands. Animal rights activists have an agenda. They want to see all research using animals come to a halt, but they know this position is considered extreme by reasonable people. So they disguise their true goals by starting small and asking that research cease only long enough to make the animals being tested more comfortable.

3   Rest assured, however, this will never satisfy people who are, at the core of their being, seriously misguided, even disturbed. The world view of animal rights activists is so completely off kilter that they consider the lives of animals equal to the lives of human beings. People who think like this should spend their time in a psychiatrist's office, not demonstrating in front of research labs, where they interfere with important work that could one day save millions of lives.

a. The author employs the slippery slope.

b. The author relies on a character attack.

c. There is no error in reasoning.

CHAPTER 11

Understanding and Evaluating Arguments

In this chapter you'll learn

- why the ability to analyze arguments is a key critical reading skill.

- how to identify the essential elements of a written argument.

- how to recognize common errors that undermine or weaken an author's argument.

You may not be aware of it, but arguments are everywhere. The candidate who says "vote for me" gives you an argument explaining why. The salesperson who wants to sell you a new VCR is quick to describe the advantages of the latest models. Likewise, the newspaper columnist who thinks the president's foreign policy is a comedy of errors tries to convince you to think the same way.

The point of these examples is simple. Once you can analyze and evaluate the often competing arguments that confront you each and every day, you are in a better position to make informed decisions about which arguments are convincing and which ones are not. In other words, you are better able to decide whether or not you will share—or at least consider—the other person's point of view.

What's the Point of the Argument?

The starting point of an argument is the opinion, belief, or claim the author of the argument wants readers to accept or at least seriously consider. Whenever you encounter an argument in your reading, the first thing to do is decide what opinion, belief, or claim the author thinks you should share. In other words, you need to discover the central point of the author's argument. Discovering that point will be easier once you are familiar with the three kinds of statements— condition, value, and policy—likely to be at the heart of a written argument.

Statements of Condition

These statements assert that a particular condition or state of affairs exists or existed. Although these statements are based more on fact than opinion, they usually identify a state of affairs not likely to be well known by readers and thus in need of proof. The following would all be considered statements of condition.

1. Most of the great classical novels have not been turned into financially successful movies.
2. The family as we know it has not been in existence for very long.
3. Although Henry David Thoreau celebrated solitude in his now classic book, *Walden,* he actually spent very little time alone.
4. Romantic love is an altogether modern invention.

Although reasons are essential in any argument, statements of condition usually rely heavily on sound factual evidence.

Statements of Value

Statements of value express approval or disapproval. Frequently they contrast two people, ideas, or objects and suggest that one is better or worse than the other. The following are all statements of value.

1. Among all the sports, boxing is the most dehumanizing.
2. Cats are smarter than dogs.
3. The American educational system is in a serious state of decline.
4. Nowadays, movies rely too much on action and not enough on dialogue.

Although statements of value can and do require facts, they typically need examples and reasons as well. For example, to talk about the "state of decline" in American education, a writer would probably have to offer statistics proving an earlier superiority and more statistics or examples illustrating the current decline.

Statements of Policy

Statements of policy suggest that a particular action should or should not be taken. These opinion statements often include words like *must, need, should, would,* or *ought.* The following are all statements of policy.

1. The Internet needs to be censored so that children do not have access to pornographic material.
2. Shoeless Joe Jackson* should be admitted to the National Baseball Hall of Fame.
3. College athletes who do not maintain a B average should be prohibited from playing any team sports.
4. Consumers should have the right to take legal action against HMOs that provide inadequate medical care.

With statements of policy, factual evidence is important, but sound reasons that answer the question *why* are essential.

Can different types of argument statements be combined? The answer is most definitely yes. Here's an example: "Despite the cloud of shame surrounding his name, Shoeless Joe Jackson was never convicted of any crime. As one of the most talented players in the

---

*Shoeless Joe Jackson: a famous baseball player who many think was unfairly implicated in the Black Sox baseball scandal of 1919.

history of baseball, he should be admitted to the Baseball Hall of Fame." In this case, we have a statement of condition (Jackson was never convicted of a crime). But we also have a statement of value (he was one of the most talented players in the history of baseball), and a statement of policy (he should be admitted to the Baseball Hall of Fame).

In your analysis of an argument, be on the lookout for statements that describe an existing condition, assign value, or urge a policy or action. Such statements, separately or combined, are usually central to an author's argument.

CHECK YOUR UNDERSTANDING

Name and describe the three types of statements likely to be at the center of an argument.

1. _____

_____

2. _____

_____

3. _____

_____

EXERCISE 1

DIRECTIONS Read each statement. In the blank that follows, identify the type of statement by circling the correct letter or letters.

EXAMPLE

1. Every survey course in American literature should include several of the authors who emerged during the Harlem Renaissance.*

   a. statement of condition

   b. statement of value

   (c.) statement of policy

_____

*Harlem Renaissance: a period during the 1920s when Harlem was an intellectual and cultural capital.

2. Legalized gambling threatens community stability; therefore, it should be banned from our state.

a. statement of condition

(b.) statement of value

(c.) statement of policy

EXPLANATION The first sentence is a statement of policy. It clearly announces an action that *should* be taken. The second combines a statement of value—legalized gambling threatens the community— with a statement of policy—it should be banned.

1. Because pesticides are endangering our food supply, more should be done to increase public awareness concerning the dangers posed by pesticides.

a. statement of condition

b. statement of value

c. statement of policy

2. Eating garlic may not do a lot for your breath, but it can do wonders for your health.

a. statement of condition

b. statement of value

c. statement of policy

3. People who use marijuana solely for medicinal purposes should not be subject to persecution.

a. statement of condition

b. statement of value

c. statement of policy

4. Those of us who truly care about animals need to make a commitment to vegetarianism.

a. statement of condition

b. statement of value

c. statement of policy

5. Poet and philosopher Ralph Waldo Emerson had a gift for friendship: He brought out the best in everyone he met.

a. statement of condition

b. statement of value

c. statement of policy

6. Listening to music can sharpen and enhance a person's creative powers. Instead of being eliminated, music appreciation should be part of our elementary curriculum.

   a. statement of condition

   b. statement of value

   c. statement of policy

7. Snowboarding should not be considered an Olympic sport.

   a. statement of condition

   b. statement of value

   c. statement of policy

8. Mark Twain was a humorist whose writing had a serious social message.

   a. statement of condition

   b. statement of value

   c. statement of policy

9. Online magazines like *Salon* and *Feed* have an energy and bite not found in print magazines like *The Atlantic Monthly* and *The New Yorker.*

   a. statement of condition

   b. statement of value

   c. statement of policy

10. Parents should limit the amount of television preschool children are allowed to see.

   a. statement of condition

   b. statement of value

   c. statement of policy

EXERCISE 2

DIRECTIONS Make up three different statements you think you could effectively argue. One should be a statement of value; the other two should be statements of policy and condition.

Statement of value: _____

_____

Statement of policy: _____

_____

Statement of condition: _____

_____

_____

■ EXERCISE 3

DIRECTIONS Read each passage. At the end, paraphrase the main point of the argument and identify it as a statement of policy, value, or condition.

EXAMPLE

Banning Bathing Suits

1   After far too many years, critical attention has finally been paid to the portion of the Miss America pageant called the swimsuit competition. Thankfully, people are beginning to complain about this event. In 1996, a telephone poll was conducted on the night of the pageant to determine if the swimsuit competition should remain. Although the majority of callers voted to retain it, a good portion were critical and argued that the swimsuit segment should be eliminated. The question will undoubtedly be raised again, and the next time the answer may well be different. Let's hope so, because this portion of the pageant only serves to demean the women who participate in it.

2   It should be clear to everyone that there are women whose appearance and intellect make them likely candidates for the crown. Yet these same women might well be eliminated from the competition for some minor physical flaw, like bulging thighs. A woman who has the appropriate appearance and intellect should not be eliminated because she bulges in a bathing suit. Beauty and brains are infinitely more important criteria for choosing Miss America than are ten extra pounds of body fat.

a. What's the author's point?

   The swimsuit competition should be eliminated.

   _____

b. That point is expressed in a statement of

   a. condition.

   b. value.

   (c.) policy.

EXPLANATION Because the author supports a particular action—the eliminating of the swimsuit competition—statement of policy is the correct answer.

1. Americans should take a tip from the Japanese and rent dogs to lonely travelers. Silly as it sounds to non–dog owners, many dog lovers are soothed by the presence of a dog when they travel, even if it isn't their own. Aware of the problem of dog deprivation, some Japanese pet shops will, for a fee, supply the lonely traveler with a tail-wagging companion. The outings get the dog out of the kennel and help make the foreign visitor feel at home.

    a. What's the author's point?

    _____

    _____

    b. That point is expressed in a statement of

        a. condition.

        b. value.

        c. policy.

2. If you ask writers why they use word processing, they will tell you that it makes them write better. If you press them to explain how, they will say that the physical act of writing goes much faster on a keyboard, that word processing makes their writing look good, that revision is much easier on a word processor. Word processing offers powerful advantages, but the tool you use when you write is only a tool. Like all powerful tools, a computer can make writers more efficient than they are without it. It can do huge damage, however, in the hands of somebody who doesn't know how to use it: The same qualities that make it powerful also make it dangerous. (Adapted from Sharon Cogdell, "Computers and Writing," in *About Language,* p. 46.)

    a. What's the author's point?

    _____

    _____

    b. That point is expressed in a statement of

        a. condition.

        b. value.

        c. policy.

3. Parents anxious to screen what their children view on the Internet should know about software that can filter out objectionable material. There is, for example, software that can screen out anti-Semitic* Web sites. By next year, Catholics will also be able to purchase software that filters out material contradictory to Catholic teaching. Similarly, several software packages currently under development can filter out all sexually explicit Web sites. Parents cannot afford to simply turn their children loose in front of the computer screen. There are too many people intent on using the Internet to influence and control the minds of children. Parents need to be alert to that danger and protect their children by buying software designed to filter out harmful influences or experiences.

a. What's the author's point?

_____

_____

b. That point is expressed in a statement of

    a. condition.

    b. value.

    c. policy.

4. Having looked at a motley* assortment of documents, I have come to some understanding of why handwriting is important to us. Since the eighteenth century, I have found, handwriting has functioned as a way to define and reveal the self. In the ways that we have taught handwriting, practiced it, and perceived it, we have tried both to shape what we ought to be and to express what we hope to be. (Tamara Plakins Thornton, "Handwriting in America," *UB Today*, vol. 16 no. 2, Winter 1998, p. 13.)

a. What's the author's point?

_____

_____

b. That point is expressed in a statement of

    a. condition.

    b. value.

    c. policy.

---

*anti-Semitic: discriminating against people of the Jewish faith.
*motley: having many elements or parts that don't really fit together.

5. Most of us know about Rosa Parks and her decision, on December 1, 1955, not to move to the back of the bus. Parks's bravery sparked the historic bus boycott in Montgomery, Alabama, and her name entered the history books. What fewer people know is that almost ten years before, in 1946, a young black woman named Irene Morgan boarded a Greyhound bus to Gloucester County, Virginia. Weak from recent surgery, Morgan also refused to move to the back of the bus when told to do so. The police were called and she was placed under arrest. Convicted of her "crime," Morgan appealed her decision and made legal history when Thurgood Marshall argued her case before the Supreme Court and won.

    a. What's the author's point?

_____

_____

    b. That point is expressed in a statement of
       a. condition.
       b. value.
       c. policy.

 # Four Common Types of Support

Writers who want their arguments to be taken seriously know they have to do more than state their position. They also have to provide appropriate support. Critical readers, in response, need to recognize and evaluate that support, deciding if it is both relevant and up-to-date. Four common types of support are likely to be used in an argument: reasons, examples and illustrations, expert opinions, and research results.

Reasons

Reasons are probably the most common method of support used by authors who want to argue a point. In the following passage, the author hopes to persuade her readers that war is a curse and no cause for joy—no matter who wins or who loses. Aware that some readers may not agree, the author supplies reasons in support of her claim.

> How is it that anyone can be jubilant or joyous during wartime? For both winners and losers, war is a curse. It brings nothing but death and destruction. It destroys feelings of compassion and un-

derstanding, and it encourages aggression and brutality. Horrified by a human being who takes the life of another during peacetime, we pin medals on those who do it during wartime.

As a means of persuasion, the author offers three reasons: (1) war brings death and destruction; (2) war destroys feelings of compassion and understanding; and (3) war encourages aggression and brutality. The author hopes these three reasons will convince readers to share her point of view.

Examples and Illustrations

Particularly when arguing general statements of value—for example, boxing is dangerous, pesticides cause health problems, or Isaac Newton was an eccentric* genius—writers are likely to cite examples, illustrations, or even personal experience as proof of their point. Look at how the following author uses examples to persuade readers that plastic litter is not just unsightly, but also deadly.

> As litter, plastic is unsightly and deadly. Birds and small animals die after getting stuck in plastic six-pack beverage rings. Pelicans accidentally hang themselves with discarded plastic fishing line. Turtles choke on plastic bags or starve when their stomachs become clogged with hard-to-excrete crumbled plastic. Sea lions poke their heads into plastic rings and have their jaws locked permanently shut. Authorities estimate that plastic refuse annually kills up to two million birds and at least 100,000 mammals. (Gary Turbak, "60 Billion Pounds of Trouble," *American Legion Magazine.*[1])

In this case, the author piles example upon example in an effort to convince readers that plastic can be lethal.

Expert Opinion

In an effort to be persuasive, writers often call upon one or more experts who support their position. In the following passage, for instance, the author suggests that cloning geniuses may not be a good idea. To make her point, she gives a reason *and* cites an expert's opinion.

> With the birth of Dolly, the first successfully cloned sheep, some have suggested that we can now consider the human gene pool a

*eccentric: odd, weird.
[1]Also used in Rosen and Behrens, *The Allyn and Bacon Handbook.*

natural resource. We can clone a Nobel Prize–winning writer like Toni Morrison or a star athlete like Michael Jordan and thereby create a population of gifted and talented people. What could be wrong with that? Well, in the long run, probably a lot.

There's simply no guarantee that the cloned copies would be everything the originals were. After all, genes don't tell the whole story, and the clone of a prizewinning scientist, if neglected as a child, might well end up a disturbed genius, no matter what the original gene source. As John Paris, professor of bioethics at Boston College, so correctly says on the subject of cloning, "Choosing personal characteristics as if they were the options on a car is an invitation to misadventure."[2]

In this case, the author doesn't just let her argument rest solely on her own reasoning. She also makes it clear that at least one knowledgeable expert is very much on her side.

Research Results

In the same way they use experts, writers who want to persuade are likely to use the results of research—studies, polls, questionnaires, and surveys—to argue a point. In the following passage, for example, the author uses an expert and a study to support a statement of condition: There's a quiet revolution taking place among Amish women.

In a tiny shop built on the side of a farmhouse in Pennsylvania's Lancaster County, Katie Stoltzfus sells Amish* dolls, wooden toys, and quilts. Does she ever. Her shop had "a couple of hundred thousand" dollars in sales last year, says the forty-four-year-old Amish entrepreneur and mother of nine. Mrs. Stoltzfus's success underscores a quiet revolution taking place among the Amish. Amish women, despite their image as shy farm wives, now run about 20 percent of the one thousand businesses in Lancaster County, according to a study by Donald B. Kraybill, a professor of sociology at Elizabethtown College in Elizabethtown, Pennsylvania. "These women are interacting more with outsiders, assuming managerial functions they never had before, and gaining more power within their community because of their access to money," says Professor Kraybill, who recently wrote a book about Amish enterprises. (Tim-

---

[2]Jeffrey Kluger, "Will We Follow the Sheep?" *Time*, March 10, 1997, p. 71.
*Amish: a religious group that generally avoids contact with the modern world and its modern machinery.

othy Aeppel, "More Amish Women Are Tending to Business," *Wall Street Journal*, February 8, 1996, p. B1.)

To make sure that readers seriously consider his position, the author cites a study and identifies the person who conducted the study, making it clear that his opinion is grounded in solid research.

CHECK YOUR UNDERSTANDING

Name and describe the four types of support common to written arguments.

1. _____

_____

2. _____

_____

3. _____

_____

4. _____

_____

EXERCISE 4

DIRECTIONS Select one of the three statements you created for Exercise 2 on pages 381–382. Make an informal outline that shows, in rough detail, how you would support your point.

EXERCISE 5

DIRECTIONS Each group of statements opens with an opinion or claim that needs to be argued. Circle the letters of the two sentences that help argue that point.

EXAMPLE Eyewitness testimony is far from reliable.

(a.) The testimony of eyewitnesses can often be influenced by the desire to please those in authority.

(b.) Studies of eyewitness testimony reveal an astonishingly high number of errors.

c. Eyewitness testimony holds a great deal of weight with most juries.

EXPLANATION Statements *a* and *b* both undermine the reliability of eyewitnesses and thereby provide reasons why eyewitness testimony cannot always be considered reliable. Statement *c*, however, is not relevant, or related, to the claim made about eyewitness testimony.

1. Uniforms should be mandatory* for all high school students.

   a. Most students hate the idea of wearing a uniform.

   b. Parents on a strict budget would no longer have to worry about being able to provide expensive back-to-school wardrobes.

   c. If uniforms were mandatory in high school, students would not waste precious time worrying about something as unessential as fashion.

2. All zoos should be abolished.

   a. Zoos only encourage the notion that animals are on Earth for the amusement of humans.

   b. If all zoos were closed, no one has any idea what would happen to the animals now living in them.

   c. Although many zoos have improved the living conditions for the animals they possess, those animals still lack the freedom they have in the wild.

3. Incoming college freshmen should be required to take an introductory course in computer skills.

   a. Students who don't have access to a computer of their own can usually find one in the library or writing center.

   b. Many college instructors simply assume that students have a basic knowledge of how to use a computer, and their assignments reflect that assumption.

   c. Students who can't use a computer to do research are at a disadvantage; they don't have as many resources at their disposal.

4. Because the deer population is sky-high, hunters should be allowed to shoot more deer per season.

   a. Desperate for food, deer are foraging by the roadside, where many are hit by cars, another indication that their population has to be reduced.

   b. With the exception of hunting, there doesn't seem to be any practical way to slow down the growth in the deer population.

   c. Most hunters have a great respect for the animals they kill.

*mandatory: required or commanded by authority.

5. Parents need to limit the amount of television their children watch.

a. Unlike reading, watching television does not encourage a child to think imaginatively.

b. Children who watch a lot of television are consistently exposed to violence and can easily become too accepting of it.

c. Programs for children dominate Saturday morning television.

EXERCISE 6

DIRECTIONS Read each passage. Then answer the questions that follow.

EXAMPLE Unfortunately, some people still believe that African Americans endured slavery without protest. But nothing could be further from the truth. In 1800, for example, Gabriel Prosser organized an army of a thousand slaves to march on Richmond. However, a state militia had been alerted by a spy, and the rebellion was put down. Prosser was ultimately executed for refusing to give evidence against his co-conspirators. In 1822, Denmark Vesey plotted to march on Charleston, but he, too, was betrayed by an informer. Probably the most serious revolt occurred in 1831 under Nat Turner. It resulted in the execution of Turner and more than a hundred black rebels.

a. What is the point of the author's argument?

It's simply not true that African Americans endured slavery without protest.

b. Paraphrase the examples used to support that claim.

1. In 1800, Gabriel Prosser organized an army of slaves to march on Richmond.

2. In 1822, Denmark Vesey plotted to take over Charleston.

3. In 1831, Nat Turner and 100 rebels revolted.

EXPLANATION In this case, the author uses three examples to make her point: African Americans did not endure slavery without protest.

1. The fact that more women are lawfully arming themselves should be good news for everyone concerned with violence against women. Since the publication of Betty Friedan's *The Feminine Mystique*, feminists have been urging women to be independent and self-sufficient. What better evidence that women have "arrived" than that they no longer have to rely exclusively on police (still mostly male) for protection? Feminists should applaud every woman who is skilled in handgun use. (Talk about controlling your own body.) Liberation from fear when walking on a dark street, driving on a country road late at night, or withdrawing cash from a bank machine is more important on a daily basis to most women than smashing any glass ceiling in the workplace. (Laura Ingraham, "Armed and Empowered," *Pittsburgh Post-Gazette,* May 19, 1998, p. E-3.)

a. What is the point of the author's argument?

_____

_____

b. Paraphrase the reason she uses to support that claim.

_____

_____

2. Alfred Nobel, born in 1833, was the inventor of dynamite, but, ironically, he was also a committed promoter of peace. When a newspaper mistakenly printed the Swedish businessman's obituary, calling him a "merchant of death," Nobel grew obsessed with leaving behind a peaceful legacy that would help improve society. When he died in 1896, his relatives were outraged by his will: Ninety-four percent of his vast fortune was to be used for an annual award to a handful of people around the globe whose work—in physics, chemistry, medicine, literature, and peacemaking (the economics category was added in 1969)—had "conferred the greatest benefit on mankind." The will's wording was so vague, however, that its executors spent five years quarreling over what it meant. Thus, the first Nobel Prizes were not awarded until the fifth anniversary of Nobel's death.

a. What is the point of the author's argument?

_____

_____

b. How does the author illustrate that point?

_____

_____

_____

3. History classes in high school and college should pay more attention to the many groups and cultures that shaped America's past. Curriculums that take a multicultural approach would better prepare students to live in a diverse world. If children learn about different cultures early in life, they might be less likely as adults to apply negative labels to people different from themselves. In addition, there is some evidence that teaching students more about their own particular history can improve their self-esteem and ultimately their classroom performance. In one study, conducted in 1991 by the Science and Education Foundation, students at North Carolina State University improved their grade point average after enrolling in an Afrocentric educational program. Analysis of the test results suggests there was a cause and effect relationship between the improved grades and the changed curriculum, which stressed Africa's role in the creation of western culture.

a. What is the point of the author's argument?

_____

_____

b. Paraphrase one of the reasons used to support the author's point.

_____

_____

c. Who conducted the study used to support the author's claim?

_____

4. Anyone who's gone to college has experienced pre-finals terror—the horrible anxiety that puts your stomach on a roller coaster and your brain into a blender. Few college students escape those final-exam jitters because everyone knows just how much is riding on that one exam, often more than half of the course grade. Yet therein lies the crux* of the problem. Infrequent, high-stakes exams don't encourage students to do their best work. More frequent tests, given, say, every two or three weeks, would be a much more effective method of discovering how well students are or are not mastering course concepts. With more frequent testing, students would be less anxious when they take exams; thus anxiety would no longer interfere with exam performance. More frequent testing also encourages students to review on a regular basis, something that a one-shot final

_____

*crux: core, heart, key point.

exam does not do. Lots of tests also mean lots of feedback, and students would know early on in the course what terms or concepts required additional explanation and review. They wouldn't have to wait until the end of the semester to find out that they had misunderstood, or missed altogether, a critical point or theory.

a. What is the point of the author's argument?

_____

_____

b. Paraphrase the three reasons the author uses to support that claim.

_____

_____

_____

_____

_____

_____

_____

_____

_____

Flawed Arguments

The previous section of this chapter introduced four common types of support that you are likely to find in an argument. This section tells you what flaws you should check for in each one.

Irrelevant Reasons

In their haste to prove a point, authors sometimes include reasons that aren't truly relevant, or related, to their claim. Here, for example, is an argument flawed by an irrelevant reason.

The 1996 tragedy on Mount Everest in which eight people died in a single day is proof enough that amateurs should not be scaling the world's highest mountain. Even with the most skillful and reliable guides, amateurs with little or no mountaineering experience cannot possibly know how to respond to the sudden storms that strike the mountain without warning. Dependent upon their guides for every move they make, amateur climbers can easily lose sight of the guides when a heavy storm hits. Left to their own devices, they are more than likely to make a mistake that will harm themselves or others. And besides that, rich people—the climb can cost anywhere from $30,000 to $60,000—shouldn't be encouraged to think that money buys everything. As F. Scott Fitzgerald so powerfully illustrated in *The Great Gatsby*, it's precisely that attitude that often leads to tragedy and death.

The point of this passage is clear-cut: Amateurs should not be climbing Mount Everest. In support of that claim, the author does offer a relevant reason. Mount Everest can be the scene of sudden storms that leave amateur climbers stranded, separated from their guides, and likely to harm themselves or others. But tucked away in the passage is a far less relevant reason: Rich people should not be allowed to think money buys everything. Well, maybe they shouldn't. Still, that particular reason, along with the allusion to *The Great Gatsby*, is not especially related to the author's claim. Neither one clarifies why amateurs and the world's tallest mountain don't mix, which is the point that needs to be argued.

Circular Reasoning

As you know from Chapter 7, writers sometimes engage in circular reasoning. They offer an opinion and follow it with a reason that says the same thing in different words. Unfortunately, circular reasoning is not that unusual—particularly when an author is utterly convinced of his or her own rightness. In the following passage, for example, the writer believes that health care workers should be tested for AIDS. He's so convinced he's right, he's forgotten to give his readers a reason why the testing should be done. Instead, he repeats his opening point as if it were a supporting reason.

Health care workers, from hospital technicians to doctors, should be forced to undergo AIDS testing, and the results should be published. Although there has been much talk about this subject, too little has been done, and the public has suffered because of it. We need to institute a program of mandatory testing as soon as possible.

Hasty Generalizations

General statements by definition cover a lot of territory. They are meant to sum up and express a wide variety of individual events or experiences. When generalizations are used in arguments, the rule of thumb is simple: The broader and more wide ranging the generalization, the more examples writers need to supply in order to make their point convincing. If an author trics to provc a broad generalization about a large group by citing one or even two examples, you need to—metaphorically speaking—prick up your ears, because something is wrong.

In the following passage, the author makes a general statement about all HMOs. Unfortunately, that statement is based on one lone example, a fact that seriously weakens his argument.

> HMOs are not giving consumers adequate health care. Instead, budgeting considerations are consistently allowed to outweigh the patients need for treatment. In one case, a child with a horribly deformed cleft palate was denied adequate cosmetic surgery because the child's HMO considered the surgery unnecessary, yet the child had trouble eating and drinking.[3]

Unidentified or Inappropriate Experts

In the passage about cloning on pages 386–387, it makes sense for the author to quote a bioethicist in support of her opinion. After all, a bioethicist specializes in the study of moral and ethical issues that result from biological discoveries and applications. However, critical readers are rightly suspicious of allusions to unidentified experts who may or may not be qualified to offer an opinion. Consider, for example, the "expert" cited in the following passage:

> Despite the doom-and-gloom sayers who constantly worry about the state of the environment, the earth is actually in pretty good shape. As Dr. Paul Benjamin recently pointed out, "Nature is perfectly capable of taking care of herself; she's been doing it for hundreds of years."

The author uses Dr. Paul Benjamin to support her claim that environmentalists worried about the earth are dead wrong. However, for all we know, Dr. Benjamin might be a dentist, and his dental degree does not qualify him as an environmental expert. Without some knowledge of Dr. Benjamin's **credentials,** or qualifications,

---

[3]Howard Fineman, "HMOs Under the Knife," *Newsweek*, July 27, 1998, p. 21.

we shouldn't be swayed by his opinion. It also wouldn't hurt to know more about Dr. Benjamin's personal background and biases. If, for example, he's worked for a company cited for abuses to the environment, his ability to stay objective, or neutral, is suspect.

Occasionally, a writer might also attempt to support an argument by citing a famous person who doesn't truly qualify as an expert in the area under discussion.

> We should abolish NATO and end foreign aid. After all, didn't George Washington tell us to avoid entangling ourselves in the affairs of other nations? Even today, we should let his wisdom be our guide and steer clear of foreign involvements that drain our energy and our resources.

In the eighteenth century, George Washington may well have qualified as an expert in foreign affairs. But to cite him as an authority on modern problems is a mistake. It is doubtful that Washington could have imagined America's current status as an international power. Because his opinion could not be considered adequately informed, critical readers would not be impressed by references to his name and authority.

Unidentified or Dated Research

In the following passage, the author relies on some "studies" to prove a statement of policy: Pornography should be more strictly censored. But to be convincing as support, scientific research needs **attribution;** in short, we need to know who conducted it. References to unnamed studies like the one in the following passage would not arouse the confidence of critical readers.

> Pornography must be more strictly censored. It does, in fact, offer a clear and present danger to the lives of women. Studies have shown again and again that pornography is directly related to the number of rapes and assaults on women. As if that weren't enough, by repeatedly presenting women as sexual objects, pornography encourages sexual discrimination, a cause-and-effect relationship noted by several prominent researchers.

Authors may identify a study in the text itself or in a footnote that refers the reader to a list of sources in the back of the book. Where a study is identified doesn't matter. What matters is that the author provides readers with enough information to check the source of the supposed evidence.

It also helps to know when the study was conducted; a writer who uses out-of-date studies rightfully runs the risk of losing readers' confidence. Take, for example, the following passage.

> The threat of radon gas is not as serious as we have been led to believe. In 1954, a team of government researchers studying the effects of radon in the home found no relationship between high levels of the gas in private dwellings and the incidence of lung cancer.

Here we have an author trying to prove a point about radon gas with a study almost a half-century old. To be considered effective evidence for an opinion, scientific research should be considerably more up-to-date.

CHECK YOUR UNDERSTANDING

Complete the following chart by explaining each type of error that can occur in an argument.

Type of Support	Possible Error	Definition of Error
Reasons	Irrelevant Reasons	
	Circular Reasoning	
Examples and Illustrations	Hasty Generalizations	
Expert Opinion	Unidentified Experts	
	Inappropriate Experts	
Research Results	Unidentified Research	
	Dated Research	

EXERCISE 7

DIRECTIONS For this exercise, refer to the informal outline you prepared for Exercise 4 on page 388. Complete any research you might need to help make your point convincing. Then write a rough draft of the entire argument. Look the draft over to make sure your point is clearly stated and your support is free of the flaws discussed on pages 393–397.

EXERCISE 8

DIRECTIONS Read each selection and answer the questions that follow by circling the letter of the correct answer or filling in the blanks.

EXAMPLE

China Doesn't Deserve MFN Status

1 As he did in 1994, the president has again granted the People's Republic of China most-favored-nation (MFN) trading status. Without question, this is a mistake of almost catastrophic proportions.

2 The Chinese government has in no way earned the political approval suggested by MFN status. On the contrary, reports smuggled out of China by Amnesty International and Human Rights Watch indicate that the political repression that followed the 1989 massacre in Tiananmen Square* continues. In 1995, Human Rights Watch reported that a dozen Chinese intellectuals were thrown into jail simply for signing a petition that asked for democratic reforms. For much the same reason, the widely respected student leader Wang Dan languished for years in a Chinese jail. As dissident leader and Nobel Peace Prize nominee Wei Jingsheng describes in *The Courage to Stand Alone*—written while Jingsheng sat in a Chinese prison for fifteen years—political prisoners can expect little more than starvation, isolation, and torture.

3 How can our government pay lip service to the cause of human rights and, at the same time, grant China most-favored-nation status? When we grant China MFN status, we sanction* political repression in its severest form.

1. What is the author's point?
   Giving China MFN status is a terrible mistake.

———

*Tiananmen Square: place where men and women demonstrated for democratic reforms; many participants were beaten, killed, and imprisoned.
*sanction: approve.

2. What two reasons does the author give in support of that point?

a. *The Chinese government hasn't earned the political approval that status confers because political repression continues.*

b. *When we give China MFN status, we are approving political repression.*

3. In addition to those two reasons, does the author include any of the following?
   - (a.) examples or illustrations
   - b. research results
   - (c.) expert opinion

4. Circle one or more of the appropriate letters to indicate the presence or absence of errors in the author's argument.
   - a. irrelevant reasons
   - b. circular reasoning
   - c. hasty generalizations
   - d. unidentified or inappropriate experts
   - e. unidentified or dated research
   - (f.) no errors

EXPLANATION The two reasons given are both relevant to the author's point that China does not deserve MFN status. In addition, the author uses examples to clarify her claim that political repression continues. She also uses the opinion of an expert—Wei Jingsheng—whose credentials are clearly identified.

1. Who Really Benefits from the Lottery?

1 On the editorial page of this newspaper, an argument recently was put forth in favor of a state-run lottery. According to the article, there are many benefits to a state-run lottery and apparently no drawbacks. The writer of that article may honestly believe that a lottery would be a boon to everyone in the state, but I believe that legalized gambling is a disaster waiting to happen.

2 Knowingly or unknowingly—and it doesn't matter which—state governments encourage addictive gambling when they promote lotteries. According to the American Psychiatric Association, ad-

dictive or problem gambling is a mental illness. It's treatable, but it's still an illness, one that can lead to a host of social problems such as bankruptcy, theft, domestic violence, and job loss. Needless to say, these social problems can prove costly to the states who hoped to benefit from lottery revenues. In promoting lotteries, the state, in essence, collects money from gambling with one hand and pays out double that amount in social services with the other hand. Advocates of state-run lotteries should consider that fact when they justify the lotteries by claiming they are a source of revenue for social programs. That logic may sound good, but it doesn't add up on paper when the costs of addictive gambling are accounted for.

3   In 1995, for example, a study by the Wisconsin Policy Research Institute estimated that each problem gambler cost the state around $9,500 per year in social services and business losses. The total loss to the state was about $307 million dollars per year.[4]

4   Another study indicates that around one in four problem gamblers has a history of substance abuse. This is yet another reason why state governments should not encourage gambling.

5   As Dr. Benjamin Martino has pointed out, legalized gambling also blurs an important moral distinction, the distinction between money that has been honestly earned and "ill-gotten" gains. Money from gambling is ill-gotten because it is not connected with any honest labor that benefits society. When we approve of legalized gambling, we approve of bestowing wealth on people who have not worked for it.

1. What is the author's point?

_____

_____

2. What four reasons does the author give in support of that point?

a. _____

_____

b. _____

_____

---

[4]Chester Hartman, "Lotteries Victimize the Poor and Minorities," *New Haven Register*, August 3, 1998, p. 176.

c. _____

_____

d. _____

_____

3. Circle one or more of the appropriate letters to indicate the presence or absence of errors in the author's argument.

a. irrelevant reasons

b. circular reasoning

c. hasty generalizations

d. unidentified or inappropriate experts

e. unidentified or dated research

f. no errors

2. Grading Teachers

Unfortunately, many students believe they cannot control the quality of the instruction they receive at their university. They think that their only option is to complain privately but say nothing in public. There is, however, an alternative to being silently miserable and dissatisfied. Students would have a lot more control over the quality of their instruction if they would consider using a public rating system for their professors. With such a system, teachers would be rated on everything from willingness to hold office hours to clarity of lectures, and the results would be published and distributed schoolwide.

On an immediate level, such a rating system could help students choose courses. For the most part, students, particularly new students, have no idea who does the most effective job teaching a particular subject. They do not know, for example, that Professor X does not keep office hours or return papers, and they register for his course. Equally important, they do not know that Professor Y, who teaches the same subject, returns every paper and regularly meets with students. If they did, they would probably have the good sense to choose Professor Y's course instead of Professor X's.

Such a system of public rating would have long-term effects as well. Professors who could not infer from their decreasing enrollment that their methods were inadequate would still have to face the results of the public rating. Given consistently negative evaluations, the majority of instructors would seek to change their style of instruction. It is hard to imagine an instructor who would receive low ratings year after year and still continue to do exactly the same thing he or she did before. As one might expect, studies show that student evaluations have a profound effect on teacher performance and behavior.

1. What is the author's point?

   _____

   _____

2. What two reasons does the author give in support of that point?

   a. _____

   _____

   b. _____

   _____

3. Circle one or more of the appropriate letters to indicate the presence or absence of errors in the author's argument.

   a. irrelevant reasons

   b. circular reasoning

   c. hasty generalizations

   d. unidentified or inappropriate experts

   e. unidentified or dated research

   f. no errors

3. Restricting Pesticide Use

1 No one can deny that pesticides have helped farmers bring more crops to market. Thanks to pesticides, farmers no longer have to worry that they will lose an entire crop to an army of cutworms or fruit flies. As a result, Americans can rely on a large and varied food supply.

2 However, we Americans need to become more informed about the effects of those pesticides on our food. More specifically, we need to think about what new legislation is necessary to protect ourselves from a diet too rich in pesticide residue.* If we don't demand greater restrictions on pesticide use, we may be surprised, dismayed, and ultimately horrified by the consequences of its use.

3 On the most obvious level, farm workers who continue to use the pesticides at their present rate will be stricken with serious dis-

---

*residue: remains, leftovers.

eases. In one study, farmers exposed to herbicides had a six times greater risk of getting cancer. In addition, children who lived in homes where pesticides were used had an increased chance of getting childhood leukemia.[5]

4   But the farmers are not the only ones at risk. Consumers may also suffer serious side effects from daily consumption of foods tainted by pesticides. Although scientists have yet to prove the link conclusively, they are concerned that pesticide use may be one reason for the startling increase in various forms of cancer like breast and colon cancers.

5   We need new legislation that adopts stricter standards governing pesticide residues in food. Much of the current legislation is based on ignorance. Simply put, we allow high levels of carcinogens in our food because we don't know for sure that they do cause cancer in humans. Yet, why should we take the risk? If there's a chance that a pesticide causes cancer, then it should be banned from use.

1. What is the author's point?

_____

_____

2. What three reasons does the author give in support of that point?

    a. _____

    _____

    b. _____

    _____

    c. _____

    _____

3. Circle one or more of the appropriate letters to indicate the presence or absence of errors in the author's argument.

    a. irrelevant reasons

    b. circular reasoning

    c. hasty generalizations

    d. unidentified or inappropriate experts

    e. unidentified or dated research

    f. no errors

_____

[5]Al Meyerhoff, "No More Pesticides for Dinner," *New York Times,* September 19, 1993, p. 20.

4. Protecting the Sharks

1 Studies show that millions of sharks are killed each year by humans, and much of this killing is sparked by fear of these mysterious creatures. Yet the number of humans killed annually by sharks is in the single digits; your chances are greater of being killed by falling airplane wreckage or by bee stings than by a shark.

2 Instead of hunting these marvelous creatures, we should protect them. Sharks help maintain the ocean's natural system of checks and balances. Because sharks kill weak, wounded, or diseased fish (all of which would be too slow to evade a shark), they function as a "clean-up crew" for the oceans. They also help keep fish populations down, just as land predators such as wolves help regulate deer and other animal populations.

3 According to Dr. Ellen Erlich, sharks can also help scientists tackle one of the worst diseases known—cancer. As Dr. Erlich points out, scientists know that sharks don't get cancer; however, they do not fully understand the reason for sharks' immunity to this terrible disease. Researchers hope that by studying sharks, they will find a cure for cancer. Unfortunately, this will become more difficult as the shark populations dwindle.

1. What is the author's point?

   _____

   _____

2. What two reasons does the author give in support of that point?

   a. _____

   _____

   b. _____

   _____

3. Circle one or more of the appropriate letters to indicate the presence or absence of errors in the author's argument.

   a. irrelevant reasons

   b. circular reasoning

   c. hasty generalizations

   d. unidentified or inappropriate experts

   e. unidentified or dated research

   f. no errors

EXERCISE 9

> **DIRECTIONS** Look over the draft you wrote for Exercise 7. Check to see where the addition of research results or expert opinions might help convince your readers. Revise the draft accordingly. Wait one full day before you write the final draft.

Are There Any Objections?

Arguments are guaranteed to include a point of view or position and some type of support. However, some arguments contain an additional element. Written arguments often include an objection or opposing point of view along with the author's response. Look, for example, at a longer version of the argument against war introduced on pages 385–386. Note how the author anticipates and answers potential objections:

1   How is it that anyone can be jubilant or joyous during wartime? For both winners and losers, war is a curse. It brings nothing but death and destruction. It destroys feelings of compassion and understanding, and it encourages aggression and brutality. Horrified by a human being who takes the life of another during peacetime, we pin medals on those who do it during wartime.

2   To those who argue that war is not a curse but a reasonable and rational way to defend property and prestige, I can only shake my head in sorrow. Losing control of overseas markets, maintaining face before the rest of the world—these are not adequate reasons for war and all its attendant evils. Nothing but the necessity of self-defense is an adequate justification for war, the most terrible of human tragedies.

Notice that in addition to providing reasons for her conclusion, the author also answers readers who might disagree with her and claim that war is not a curse but a necessary defense of government interests. She responds to the opposition by insisting that because war brings with it such horrors, self-defense is the only possible justification. No other reason is acceptable, at least from her point of view.

Not all writers mention and respond to opposing points of view. But enough do so that it's worth your while to be alert to any statements that counter or respond to an opposing point of view. Here is an expanded version of the argument on page 382 in favor of banning swimsuit competitions. What objection does the author choose to answer?

Banning Bathing Suits

1   After far too many years, critical attention has finally been paid to the portion of the Miss America pageant called the swimsuit competition. Thankfully, people are beginning to complain about this event. In 1996, a telephone poll was conducted on the night of the pageant to determine if the swimsuit competition should remain. Although the majority of callers voted to retain it, a good portion were critical and argued that the swimsuit segment should be eliminated. The question will undoubtedly be raised again, and this time the answer may well be different. Let's hope so, because the swimsuit competition only serves to demean the women who participate in it.

2   It should be clear to everyone that there are women whose appearance and intellect make them likely candidates for the crown. Yet these same women might well be eliminated from the competition for some minor physical flaw, like bulging thighs. A woman who has the appropriate appearance and intellect should not be eliminated because she bulges in a bathing suit. Beauty and brains are infinitely more important criteria for choosing Miss America than are ten extra pounds of body fat.

3   Many who insist on retaining the swimsuit competition will argue that it is a tradition. Yet, as everyone knows, traditions change. In particular, they change with the times. Nowadays, who really believes it's improper for women to play sports with men? But in the nineteenth century, a woman who did so would have challenged the traditional view of femininity. Once again, the times are ripe for a change.

In this case, the author challenges those who believe traditions are sacred and not subject to change. Her answer is that traditions have changed before and they need to do so again.

EXERCISE 10

DIRECTIONS Read each argument. Then answer the questions that follow.

EXAMPLE

Home Schooling Just Isn't School

1 As a teacher in a public school, I have to admit I cringe every time I hear the phrase "home schooling." I know that many parents believe they are helping their children by teaching them at home.

But in my experience, home schooling does more harm than good.

2   Children who enter my class after a long period of home schooling usually have huge gaps in their education. True, they often read and write better than the average fifth grader, and their spelling is good. But they know little about the social sciences, and science itself is a foreign word.

3   In addition, children who have gone to school at home frequently have difficulty working with other children. They are unused to the give-and-take of group interactions and are quick to show their discomfort or displeasure. This is understandable since they have spent years being schooled at home in a class of one or two at most.

4   I know that many parents believe that home schooling protects their children from ideas and experiences of which they disapprove. They are probably correct in that assumption. Unfortunately, the protection they provide comes at too great an intellectual price. Most parents simply do not have the necessary training or background to give their children the wide-ranging and up-to-date education they need.

1. What is the point of the author's argument?

   Home schooling does more harm than good.

2. What two reasons does the author give in support of that point?

   a. *The children end up with huge gaps in their education.*

   b. *Children schooled at home usually have difficulty working in groups.*

3. To what objection or opposing point of view does the author respond?

   Parents believe that they are protecting their children from bad experiences and inappropriate ideas.

4. Paraphrase the author's response.

   The protection costs too much intellectually.

EXPLANATION As is typical, the author states the point of the argument at the beginning of the reading—home schooling does more harm than good—and then follows with two reasons for that position. Although the answer to a possible objection appears at the end, this is not necessarily standard. Answers to objections can just as easily be sprinkled throughout.

1. The Benefits of Home Schooling

1 Although it has been harshly criticized by many—often by those who have a vested interest* in supporting the status quo*—home schooling just may be the answer to our current crisis in education.

2   At home, children learn one-on-one or in small groups. If they need some additional explanation or instruction, the home tutor can easily supply it. In public schools, in contrast, children often sit in classrooms of thirty or more students, making it impossible for teachers to give students the kind of individual attention they frequently require. There are so many competing voices and questions, a teacher can't possibly respond to all of them, and someone has to go unattended.

3   Home schooling also allows children to learn in an environment that is comforting, familiar, and, above all, lacking in distractions. Any parent who has ever delivered a weeping child to the door of his or her classroom knows all too well how terrifying some children find the classroom atmosphere with its noisy hubbub. Children who learn at home aren't distracted by their surroundings, nor are they inhibited by the presence of other children who might unthinkingly laugh at their mistakes.

4   Critics who claim that home schooling can't provide children with the breadth of knowledge they need always assume that the parents don't have the necessary qualifications. Yet, of the parents I know personally who teach their children at home, two have a master's degree in physics, another a doctorate in psychology, and still another is a former elementary teacher with ten years of teaching experience to her credit. Parents who take on the responsibility of home schooling do not do so lightly. They know full well that they must provide their children with an education that prepares them for the world they will eventually enter.

1. What is the point of the author's argument?

    _____

    _____

---

*vested interest: having a special interest in promoting or protecting that which gives one a personal advantage.
*status quo: existing state of affairs.

2. What two reasons does the author give in support of that point?

a. _____

_____

b. _____

_____

3. To what objection or opposing point of view does the author respond?

_____

_____

4. Paraphrase the author's response.

_____

_____

2. Community Service and Graduation

1 In 1997, the Chicago public schools made community service a condition of graduation for high school seniors. In order to get their diploma, students will now have to complete sixty hours of volunteer work in the community. Among other duties, they may help children learn to read, assist patients at a local hospital, or spend time with the elderly in a nursing home. They will be able to choose from a variety of social programs. What they won't be able to choose is *not* to participate—not if they want to graduate.

2 As one might expect, some students are grumbling that they won't learn anything from doing community service. But is that even possible? After all, if you teach a child how to read, you have to learn a good deal about effective teaching and learning, and that is not exactly useless information. Spend time with the elderly and you are bound to learn about aging and what it entails, physically, mentally, and financially. In fact, students who feel that life is forever, that doors never close, and that choices will always be available could probably benefit mightily from time spent with people who know for sure that choices made or not made in youth often have lasting consequences. Put another way, community service can teach students lessons they need to learn about life's limits.

3 It can also give students career ideas. A young person who spends some time working in a hospital might decide to be an

X-ray technician or a cardiologist. For that matter, a student who volunteers to work in the library might become a researcher or a librarian. Volunteering to work in the community puts students in contact with career choices they never knew they had.

4   Then, too, in a society where the word "values" is constantly bandied about, why shouldn't schools teach the young that giving something back to the community is an essential part of community membership. It's a straightforward lesson in civics.* Sometimes your community helps you; sometimes you help the community. This is the kind of lesson textbooks don't teach, but it's one that needs to be learned. The Chicago public schools are doing the right thing by making community service a graduation requirement.

1. What is the point of the author's argument?

   _____

   _____

2. What three reasons does the author give in support of that point?

   a. _____

   _____

   b. _____

   _____

   c. _____

   _____

3. To what objection or opposing point of view does the author respond?

   _____

   _____

4. Paraphrase the author's response.

   _____

   _____

———————————
*civics: the branch of political science that deals with the rights and duties of citizens.

3. Reducing the Deer Population

1 According to the National Forest Service, there are currently around 27 million deer roaming the woodlands of the United States. They damage seedlings in new growth forests, destroy habitats of smaller animals, and ravage suburban gardens. In 1996, more than one hundred people were killed when their cars collided with deer. Clearly, the deer population must be reduced in order to avoid the continuation of these problems.

2 However, lengthening the hunting season, as some have suggested, is not the answer. After all, deer often roam in highly populated areas, and how could we guarantee that a family pet or, even worse, a child wouldn't be hit by a hunter's bullet? Clearly, a safer, more humane method of reducing the deer population must be found.

3 An experiment at Fire Island National Seashore suggests that a safer solution to deer overpopulation is already in existence. Since 1993, female deer on Fire Island have been injected with what amounts to a birth control pill. The injection is given either after the animal has been tranquilized or by means of a blow dart. A few weeks after the first injection, the doe gets a booster shot, and from then on, she is revaccinated once a year.

4 This experiment proves that the problem of deer overpopulation can be solved. We just need to expand the Fire Island experiment to include woodland areas all across the nation.

1. What is the point of the author's argument?

   _____

   _____

2. What reason does the author give in support of that point?

   _____

   _____

3. To what objection or opposing point of view does the author respond?

   _____

   _____

4. Paraphrase the author's response.

   _____

   _____

4. Casey Martin's Big Win

1   In 1998 golfer Casey Martin won a big victory. Judge Thomas Coffin ruled in Martin's favor in his suit against the PGA Tour. Only twenty-five-years old, Martin suffers from a rare disease called Klippel-Trenauney-Weber syndrome, a rare circulatory ailment that affects his right leg and severely limits his ability to walk long distances. Thanks to Judge Coffin's ruling, Martin's painful disability will no longer keep him out of the PGA Tour; the young man can now use a golf cart.

2   Martin's big win is not just good news for him; it's good news for all Americans with disabilities. As Bobby Silverstein, director of the Center for the Study and Advancement of Disability Policy at George Washington University Medical Center aptly expressed it, Martin's legal victory is all "about empowering people with disabilities."

3   With his lawsuit, Martin proved that the Americans with Disabilities Act (ADA) has real teeth. Backed by the ADA, Americans with disabilities no longer have to suffer in silence when they are shut out of activities or events freely open to others who are not disabled. As Martin's case shows, the disabled truly have a weapon with which to fight back. Ruling that the cart did not give Martin an unfair advantage, Judge Coffin argued that refusing to allow the disabled golfer a cart was an infringement of his civil rights. As long as Martin could physically compete when it came time to tee off or putt, the PGA had no right to deny him access to the green by denying him access to a motorized cart. Martin didn't want special treatment; he just wanted a chance to compete, and the courts have given it to him.

4   Arguments criticizing Martin's win just don't hold up under scrutiny. The claim, for example, that as a result of the ruling, players are going to be banging on the PGA commissioner's door demanding golf carts because they have stubbed toes is just silly. Casey Martin had to prove that he had a debilitating illness to get a golf cart; players with similar requests would have to do the same. It's unlikely that any player would actually be willing to get up in court and claim that a bruised toe or ripped cuticle could be classified as a debilitating disease.

5   Then there's the claim that walking eighteen holes over a period of five hours is actually a test of stamina and an essential part of playing the game. Aware of this objection, Judge Coffin rightfully dismissed it, saying that the five hour walk is "not significantly taxing" to qualify as an essential part of the competition. Given the fact that golfers don't generally walk at a particularly brisk pace, it's hard to take seriously the claim that strolling

along the green is a crucial ingredient in a player's game. What counts are talent, courage, and determination, and Casey Martin scores high on all three.

1. What is the point of the author's argument?

_____

_____

2. What reason does the author give in support of that point?

_____

_____

3. To what objections does the author respond?

_____

_____

_____

_____

4. Paraphrase the author's response.

_____

_____

_____

_____

WORD NOTES

Page 398 introduced the verb *sanction,* meaning "to approve." Similarly, the noun *sanction* can mean "permission" or "approval." However, the noun *sanction* has an additional definition, one you should be aware of because it often turns up in the news. In its plural form, the word refers to penalties or actions used to bring about a change in a nation's behavior. For example, there are economic *sanctions* in place against the country of Iraq; the goal of those penalties is to exact more responsible behavior from Iraqi leader Saddam Hussein.

The following sentences use the word *sanction* in different ways. For each sentence, give the correct meaning.

1. How can you *sanction* such obviously unethical practices?

   _____

2. The economic *sanctions* against the government of South Africa were harshly criticized by the corporations who had a vested interest in free trade.

   _____

Now it's your turn to create two different sentences, each one illustrating a different use of the word *sanction*.

1. _____

   _____

2. _____

   _____

Summing Up

Listed below are the most important points in Chapter 11. Put a check mark in the box if you think the point is clear in your mind. Leave the box blank if you need to review the material one more time. The page numbers in parentheses tell you where to look to review each point on the list.

☐ **1.** Whenever you encounter an argument in your reading, the first thing to do is discover the author's point. This will be easier if you are familiar with the three kinds of statements that form the core of most arguments: (1) statement of condition, (2) statement of value, and (3) statement of policy. (pp. 377–379)

☐ **2.** Authors who want to be taken seriously know they have to provide the appropriate support. Four types of support are likely to be used in an argument: (1) reasons, (2) examples and illustrations, (3) expert opinion, and (4) research results from studies, questionnaires, and polls. (pp. 385–388)

☐ **3.** In their haste to support and prove their point, authors sometimes provide irrelevant or circular reasons. They may also support a broad generalization with too few examples and produce a hasty generalization. Expert opinion is a fine source of support, but only if the expert's qualifications are identified. Research results are a common source of support, but they need attribution and should be current. (pp. 393–397)

☐ **4.** Every argument you encounter will include a point and support. But some will also present and respond to an opposing point of view. (pp. 405–406)

TEST YOUR UNDERSTANDING

To see how well you have understood the chapter, take the following review quiz. Then correct it using the answer key provided by your instructor. If you score 80 percent or above, you're ready to take the end-of-chapter exam. However, if you score below 80 percent, look over the quiz carefully to see what kinds of questions you missed. Then use the **Summing Up** section to find out which pages you should review before taking the chapter exam.

Chapter 11: Review Quiz

DIRECTIONS Read each argument and answer the questions that follow. *Note:* The author may or may not respond to opposition.

1. TV Coverage Leaves Opening for the Internet

1 By the time the Summer Olympics roll around again in the year 2004, those who want to watch the games may be spending more time on the Internet than they do in front of the television set. After all, why would viewers choose to watch hours-old videos of athletes winning the gold, when they can watch them winning live on the Internet? Sure, they won't have the pleasure of listening to highly paid anchors shoot the breeze. And yes, they will be denied the dubious delight of all those biographical short features the networks are so fond of running. You know the ones I mean. They have lots of closeups of the athletes doing the fun things they enjoy in their everyday lives like going on family picnics and dancing in nightclubs. Yet does it really matter to anyone that skater Tara Lipinski is a diehard shopper when she is not on the ice?

2 Although the networks don't seem to know it, most fans of the Olympics don't care about getting up close and personal with the athletes. What they care about is seeing the people they root for win gold—silver or bronze will do, too—medals. And they want to see them win live. They don't want to see them triumph a day later, after the results of the games have already been announced in the newspaper.

3 In the Atlanta games in 1996, a camera was set up at every venue. It was called the Sneak Peak Cam, and every 15 seconds it took a picture of a sports event and sent it to the Olympic Internet site. In this way, fans of the high jump, for example, could get a stop-and-go version of what was happening in Atlanta almost at the very moment that the athletes sprang into the air. Now that's entertainment. It's also precisely what television cannot, and in some cases will not, provide.

4 Armando Garcia of IBM, the company in charge of building the Internet site for the Olympics, says there is no reason why the Internet won't be able to bring "near-TV" quality viewing to a mass audience. According to Garcia, "there are debates about when it will happen, but it will happen."[6]

5 Let's hope it happens by 2004, and those of us who are diehard fans of the Olympics, summer or winter, will never again have to endure boring commercials, newscaster chatter, or those tedious, of-

---

[6]Kevin Maney, "Olympics TV Coverage Leaves Opening for the Internet." *USA Today*, February 12, 1998, p. 2B.

ten saccharine,* biographical sketches before we are allowed to see our favorite sprinter or weight lifter go for the gold.

1. What is the author's point?

    _____

    _____

2. What two reasons does the author give to support his point of view?

    a. _____

    _____

    b. _____

    _____

3. In addition to those two reasons, does the author include any of the following?

    a. examples or illustrations

    b. research results

    c. expert opinion

4. Does the author respond to any opposing point of view? _____ If so, fill in the blanks that follow.

Opposition   _____

    _____

Response   _____

    _____

5. Circle one or more of the appropriate letters to indicate the presence or absence of errors in the author's argument.

    a. irrelevant reasons

    b. circular reasoning

    c. hasty generalizations

    d. unidentified or inappropriate experts

    e. unidentified or dated research

    f. no errors

    _____

    *saccharine: overly sweet and sentimental.

2. Kids and Sports

1   For many parents, competitive team sports like Little League Baseball and Peewee Football are an essential part of childhood. Thus, they are anxious for their kids to try out and "make the team." Supposedly, competitive sports build physical strength. Even more important—or so the argument goes—playing competitive sports early on in childhood builds character. Still, parents intent on making sure their kids learn how to compete might want to rethink the notion that sports in which somebody has to win or lose are important to a young child's development. Competitive sports for pre-teen kids have some important disadvantages; these disadvantages need to be considered before parents push those kids onto a playing field where the winner takes all.

2   One thing that has to be considered is the physical effect of a sport on a child's still developing body. Football, basketball, baseball, and even tennis are physically demanding; they put a strain on the body, particulary at an early age when muscles or bones are still developing. Now a ten-year-old who is just playing for the fun of it will probably not repeat a movement or motion that hurts, but what if that same child is playing to win a trophy? Is he or she going to stop throwing that tough-to-hit curve ball just because there is a little pain involved? It's not likely. The end result can be lifelong damage to a shoulder or an arm. Thomas Tutko, author of the book *Winning Is Everything and Other Myths*, argues that kids should not be playing physically demanding sports before the age of fourteen. From Tutko's perspective playing demanding competitive sports before that age is simply too "traumatic," both physically and psychologically.

3   In his book *No Contest: The Case Against Competition*, author and researcher Alfie Kohn emphasizes that the psychological effects of competitive sports on those still too young to play them may be worse than the physical injuries that can ensue. Kohn's book summarizes the results of several hundred studies focusing on the effects of competition both on and off the playing field. Whether in the context of sports or the classrooms, Kohn contends that competition "undermines self esteem, poisons our relationships, and holds us back from doing our best."[7] Clearly, Kohn would not support the notion of competition as a character builder for children. If anything, he sees it as a character destroyer, even when those competing are grown-ups.

4   To be fair to those who insist there's no point to playing basketball, football, or baseball unless you keep score, these are games

---

[7]A. Kohn, "No Win Situations," *Women's Sports and Fitness*, July/August 1990, pp. 56–58.

where the score counts. However, the position argued here is not that competitive sports should be abandoned but that they should be postponed until the child is ready to be not just a winner, but a loser as well. A fifteen-year-old is probably ready to accept the simple fact that, at some time in life, everyone loses at something. But does a nine-year-old have to learn this lesson? In their early years, kids should concentrate on achieving their personal best. Are they running faster, jumping higher, or throwing faster than they did the last time around? Those are the questions they should be asking themselves, not who won and who lost.

1. What is the author's point?

   _____

   _____

2. What two reasons does the author give in support of that point?

   a. _____

   _____

   b. _____

   _____

3. In addition to those two reasons, does the author include any of the following?

   a. examples or illustrations

   b. research results

   c. expert opinion

4. Does the author respond to any opposing point of view? _____
   If so, fill in the blanks that follow.

   Opposition   _____

   _____

   Response   _____

   _____

5. Circle one or more of the appropriate letters to indicate the presence or absence of errors in the author's argument.

   a. irrelevant reasons

   b. circular reasoning

   c. hasty generalizations

d. unidentified or inappropriate experts

e. unidentified or dated research

f. no errors

3. **Opening Adoption Files**

1 In some states, people who have been adopted are not allowed to have access to their files. They have no idea who their real parents are or why they were put up for adoption, and all their attempts to discover this information are met with firm bureaucratic resistance. In short, adoption officials will tell them nothing.

2 However, in the past decade, many adoptees have publicly protested this situation, and some states have changed their policies. What I want to argue here is that this change in adoption policy should take place nationwide. Adopted children need to know about both their parents and their past, and those who do not care can simply refuse access to their files.

3 Although they make the search much harder, restrictions against opening adoption files do not necessarily deter those adoptees who want to discover who their biological parents are. Those men and women desperate to find their biological parents will, if they can afford it, hire a detective to find out what they want to know. If they cannot afford it, some are willing to devote all their time and energy to learning more about their origins. What this shows is just how important it is for adoptees to recover their past, and the state should not place obstacles in their path.

4 Adoptees frequently feel guilty because they were put up for adoption. They tend to assume that they did something wrong, something that made them unlovable and forced their parents to give them up. These men and women need to know the real causes for their adoption. It helps the adoptee to know, for example, that his mother gave him up for adoption because she was too young to support him, not because she didn't love him. This knowledge helps relieve the painful burden of guilt some adoptees carry around all their lives.

5 There are also physical—rather than psychological—reasons why adoptees need access to their files. To take proper care of their health, they need to know what diseases they might be prone to inheriting. In more extreme cases, knowledge about the biological parents can make the difference between life and death. Sometimes adoptees need to have an organ that comes from a natural relative, but if all their relatives are unknown, they are at a terrible disadvantage—one that could cost them their life.

6 Many parents who have given up their children for adoption re-

sent the idea of opening up adoption files. They feel that their right to privacy will be threatened. Yet this objection is based on the assumption that adopted children want to hunt down their parents and intrude on their lives. But, at most, what adoptees want is to know who their biological parents are. In some cases, they may even want to meet them, but they do not want to push their way into the lives of people who will not accept them. Giving the adopted person access to files does not mean that the parent or parents forsake all rights to privacy. It only means that the adopted child can attempt to make contact if he or she wishes, and the parents can refuse or accept.

1. What is the author's point?

   _____

   _____

2. What three reasons does the author give in support of that point?

   a. _____

   _____

   b. _____

   _____

   c. _____

   _____

3. In addition to those three reasons, does the author include any of the following?

   a. examples or illustrations

   b. research results

   c. expert opinion

4. Does the author respond to any opposing point of view? _____ If so, fill in the blanks that follow.

Opposition   _____

   _____

Response   _____

   _____

5. Circle one or more of the appropriate letters to indicate the presence or absence of errors in the author's argument.

   a. irrelevant reasons

   b. circular reasoning

   c. hasty generalizations

   d. unidentified or inappropriate experts

   e. unidentified or dated research

   f. no errors

4. The Death Penalty: Legal Murder

1 I am opposed to the death penalty, and current state efforts to reinstate it across the country sadden and anger me. The death penalty should be abolished, not reinstated. It is not just morally reprehensible*; it is also not even an effective deterrent* to murder.

2 When we support the death penalty we support the very act we claim to abhor*—the taking of human life. We stoop to the level of the killers we mean to punish and make it even harder for them to understand why what they have done was morally wrong. If, as a society, we truly believe in the value of human life, then the taking of it—whether justified by law or not—is an immoral act. Legalized murder is still just that—murder.

3 To those who claim that the death penalty acts as a deterrent to crime, I can only say that the research is not on your side. When William Bowers analyzed the murder rate in New York State from 1907 to 1973, he found that the number of murders rose by an average of two following an execution. As a result of his research, Bowers now believes that executions only encourage acts of murder by legitimizing violence. His research results and his conclusions have been reaffirmed by similar state-funded studies in Utah and California. After more than a century of international research, the American Civil Liberties Union has also come to the conclusion that the death penalty does not act as a deterrent to murder.

1. What is the author's point?

   _____

   _____

---

*reprehensible: wrong.
*deterrent: means of discouragement.
*abhor: hate, detest.

2. What two reasons does the author give in support of that point?

    a. _____

    _____

    b. _____

    _____

3. In addition to those two reasons, does the author include any of the following?

    a. examples or illustrations

    b. research results

    c. expert opinion

4. Does the author respond to any opposing point of view? _____ If so, fill in the blanks that follow.

    Opposition   _____

    _____

    Response   _____

    _____

5. Circle one or more of the appropriate letters to indicate the presence or absence of errors in the author's argument.

    a. irrelevant reasons

    b. circular reasoning

    c. hasty generalizations

    d. unidentified or inappropriate experts

    e. unidentified or dated research

    f. no errors

> Correct your quiz using the answer key provided by your instructor. If you score 80 percent or above, you are ready for the chapter exam. If you score below 80 percent, look carefully at the questions you answered incorrectly. Then use the **Summing Up** section to decide which pages you need to review.

Chapter Test 11

DIRECTIONS Read each paragraph and answer the questions that follow.

1. Banning Peanuts

1 There was a time when the peanut butter and jelly sandwich was a staple of the school lunchbox. Often it was the one food that fussy children would willingly eat, and parents were grateful it existed, even if they personally found the combination distasteful. The popularity of peanut butter and jelly sandwiches, however, is a thing of the past as schools from New York to California have stopped serving them in the cafeteria. Many school officials have also asked parents not to put peanut products of any kind into their kids' lunches.

2 If the ban on peanuts sounds silly to you, then you obviously don't know an important fact: Around 5 percent of children under the age of 6 have food allergies, and many of those same childen are violently allergic to peanuts in any form. The ban on peanuts in the school may sound trivial, but it's not. On the contrary, it's a matter of life or death, particularly since studies indicate that allergies to peanuts are on the rise.

3 In November of 1998, seventeen-year-old Mariya Spektor of Niskayuna, New York, died after she unknowingly ate some cereal that had peanut oil in it. In the very same month, twelve-year-old Kristine Kastner of Mercer Island, Washington, died after she ate a chocolate chip cookie that had finely minced peanuts in it. The reality is that children can and do die if they unwittingly ingest peanut products, and neither parents nor educators can afford to take the chance that this might happen.

4 Opponents of the ban, among them members of The Food Allergy Network, an advocacy group for people with allergies, argue that it pits parents against parents and avoids the real issue: teaching children with allergies how to manage them. As a spokesperson for the group has pointed out, no medical studies indicate that sitting next to someone else eating peanuts can cause an allergic reaction, so why tell parents they can't put peanut products into school lunches?

5 This criticism, however, seems to miss a crucial point. Kids sit together at lunch and trade food all the time. Thus if schools allow kids to bring peanut products from home to school, there's every possibility that a child with an allergy will ingest a snack

that might prove deadly. Naturally a child allergic to peanuts is not going to bite into a peanut butter and jelly sandwich, but that same child might well munch on a chocolate chip cookie containing peanuts, not realizing that nuts are in the cookie.

6   Parents of children allergic to peanuts are aware that many do not want peanut products banned from schools. One of those parents is Mark LoPresti of Grand Island, New York. LoPresti has a three-year-old son who is severely allergic to peanuts, and the father acknowledges the ban can create problems. Still he is fiercely determined that peanuts must be banned when his son is ready to go to school. As LoPresti puts it, "I'm not going to sacrifice my son's life for the right to have a peanut butter sandwich."[8] It's hard not to sympathize with LoPresti's point of view. When it comes to the ban on peanut products in schools, an old adage seems to apply: "It's better to be safe than sorry."

1. What is the author's point?

   _____

   _____

2. What reason does the author give in support of that point?

   _____

   _____

3. Does the author include any of the following?
   a. examples or illustrations
   b. research results
   c. expert opinion

4. Does the author respond to any opposing point of view? _____ If so, fill in the blanks that follow.

Opposition   _____

   _____

Response   _____

   _____

----

[8]Carrie Hodges, "Peanut Ban Spreads to Cafeteria." *USA Today*, December 3, 1998, p. 17a.

5. Circle one or more of the appropriate letters to indicate the presence or absence of errors in the author's argument.

   a. irrelevant reasons

   b. circular reasoning

   c. hasty generalizations

   d. unidentified or inappropriate experts

   e. unidentified or dated research

   f. no errors

2. Keep Our Libraries Free of Pornography

1 In November of 1998, a federal judge in Loudon County, Virginia, ordered the town's library to remove the software called *X-Stop* from its computers. Up until that ruling, *X-Stop* had effectively prevented hard-core pornography from entering the library's computer terminals. The software filter had been put in place after the library's board sensibly decided that underage patrons should not be allowed to log on to Web sites that featured rape, torture, and mutilation. The court's view, however, was that the filter was an unfair restriction on freedom of speech.

2 Yet in 1996, Congress granted immunity to the users of software filters if the filters were put in place to restrict objectionable pornography, even if that pornography was otherwise protected under the law. One wonders, then, why the federal judge in Virginia did not consider the Loudon County libraries to be under the jurisdiction of the Communications Decency Act. To do so would have been to avoid making a ruling that is obviously dangerous to the health and well-being of children. As long as libraries attract underage patrons—and may they always do so—computer access to X-rated sites has to be strictly controlled.

3 More than 70 percent of the nation's public libraries offer Internet access. Thanks to that access, any twelve-year-old—unless filters are in place—can contact Web sites that feature hard-core sex scenes. Even worse, kids can get into chat rooms where they might make contact with sex offenders or child molesters. Children should not be exposed to such Web sites or chat rooms. Yet how many children, knowing that the sites exist, would not seek them out, drawn as kids are by the lure of the forbidden?

4 Opponents of filters claim that it's the job of parents, not libraries, to control what children view on the Internet. But parents can't rely on even the most obedient children to censor themselves. After all they are children; they don't realize the consequences of their actions. Since parents can't accompany their children on every visit to the library, it is up to the libraries to control what their younger patrons can view.

5   Libraries routinely enact the role of censor when they **refuse to** stock their shelves with pornographic books, magazines, or **videos,** and you won't find copies of *Hustler* or *Penthouse* tucked away in the magazine rack of your local library. Nor for that matter will you find a copy of *Deep Throat* in the video department. Yet no one claims that this act of censorship infringes on the right to free speech. Why shouldn't the same principle apply to the Internet? Libraries don't stock pornography; therefore, they have a right to exclude pornographic sites from their offerings to the public.

6   Our libraries need to be open to everyone. But as long as children can get onto X-rated sites simply by typing in the word *sex,* they can't be. By allowing children access to any Web site available on the Internet, we are turning our libraries into adult bookstores and doing what real adult bookstores cannot do for fear of legal retribution—exposing vulnerable children to pornographic material that might well do them terrible harm.

1. What is the author's point?

    _____

    _____

2. What three reasons does the author give in support of that point?

    a. _____

    _____

    b. _____

    _____

    c. _____

    _____

3. Does the author include any of the following?
    a. examples or illustrations
    b. research results
    c. expert opinion

4. Does the author respond to any opposing point of view? _____
    If so, fill in the blanks that follow.

Opposition   _____

    _____

Response _____

_____

5. Circle one or more of the appropriate letters to indicate the presence or absence of errors in the author's argument.

   a. irrelevant reasons

   b. circular reasoning

   c. hasty generalizations

   d. unidentified or inappropriate experts

   e. unidentified or dated research

   f. no errors

3. Dangerous Self-Esteem

1   For years now, we have heard that high self-esteem is a prerequisite for achievement. As a result, many students work in classrooms where posters proclaim "we applaud ourselves." Exactly for what isn't always made clear. In elementary school, students complete sentences that begin "I am special because. . . ."[9] According to what has become established educational wisdom, children who are praised, even for their mistakes, will become confident, successful adults. In response to that wisdom, some states (California for one) have established educational task forces on—you guessed it—promoting self-esteem. Yet now there is some evidence that self-esteem, if it's not backed by real achievements, might be dangerous.

2   As psychologist Brad Bushman of Iowa State University puts it, kids who develop unrealistically high opinions of themselves can, when brought face to face with a more realistic version of who they are, become "potentially dangerous."[10] Bushman, along with Ray Baumeister of Case Western Reserve University, conducted a study of unrealistic self-esteem and found that students inflated by self-esteem not based on real achievement were likely to react with hostility or aggression when confronted by a world that did not mirror their sense of importance.

3   The findings of Bushman and Baumeister have also been echoed by James Gilligan of Howard Medical School. Gilligan, a long-time researcher into the causes of violence, agrees that inflated self-esteem with no basis in fact can be dangerous. Clinical psychologist Robert Brooks of Harvard concurs as well. According

---

[9]Sharon Begley, "You're OK, I'm Terrific," *Newsweek*, July 13, 1998, p. 69.
[10]Begley, p. 69.

to Brooks, if teaching self-esteem is done wrong, "you can raise a generation of kids who cannot tolerate frustration."[11]

4   Those who argue that the failure to teach self-esteem can cause a generation of children to grow up feeling worthless are missing the point. Schools and parents should continue to praise children for a job or task well done. No one is saying that they shouldn't. But self-esteem has to be based on real achievement, not on empty praise that encourages a child to believe everything he or she does is perfect. In the end, inflated self-esteem not based on any real accomplishment may well do more harm than good. Unfortunately, this tendency for young people to become aggressive whenever the world does not reflect their own inflated sense of self-importance is proof positive that an entire generation of young people will never amount to anything. Raised by self-indulgent parents who threw traditional values out the window because they had to "do their own thing," these kids never had a chance to become responsible adults, and one can only fear for our society once it is in their hands.

1. What is the author's point?

   _____

   _____

2. What reason does the author give in support of that point?

   _____

   _____

3. Does the author include any of the following?

   a. examples or illustrations

   b. research results

   c. expert opinion

4. Does the author respond to any opposing point of view? _____ If so, fill in the blanks that follow.

Opposition   _____

               _____

Response   _____

               _____

_____
[11]Begley, p. 69.

5. Circle one or more of the appropriate letters to indicate the presence or absence of errors in the author's argument.

   a. irrelevant reasons

   b. circular reasoning

   c. hasty generalizations

   d. unidentified or inappropriate experts

   e. unidentified or dated research

   f. no errors

4. In Praise of Bilingualism

1 Lack of English skills is the main reason why minority students fall behind in school. For those who care about the education of America's young people, that should be reason enough to promote bilingual education. But for those who are still not convinced, let me offer the results of some significant research and lay to rest commonly expressed worries about the effect of bilingual education on the acquisition of English.

2 Research on the effects of bilingual education shows that bilingualism does not interfere with performance in either language (Hakata & Garera, 1989). Thus, it makes no sense to argue that non-native speakers should not have bilingual instruction because it will interfere with their acquisition of English. This claim is not grounded in any factual evidence.

3 Instead of discouraging bilingual education by trying to eliminate funding for it, we should encourage it because research suggests that the ability to speak two languages improves cognitive flexibility* and the ability to think creatively (Diaz, 1983). This may be one reason why most other industrialized countries insist that their students master *at least* one other language. They know what we in the United States ignore: Bilingualism enlarges a person's capacity for understanding the world by giving him or her two different languages of interpretation. As linguist Benjamin Whorf established decades ago in his now classic article "Science and Linguistics," "We dissect nature along lines laid down by one native language. . . . The world's presented in a kaleidoscopic* flux* of impression which has to be organized by our minds—and this means largely by the linguistic systems in our minds."[12]

*cognitive flexibility: ease and quickness of thinking.
*kaleidoscopic: like a child's toy that constantly changes patterns and colors.
*flux: change, movement.
[12]Edward T. Hall, *The Silent Language.* New York: Anchor Books, 1973, p. 123.

4   The child—or for that matter, the adult—who can speak two languages has more tools for understanding the world than we who are limited solely to English.

1. What is the author's point?

   _____

   _____

2. What two reasons does the author give in support of that point?

   a. _____

   _____

   b. _____

   _____

3. Does the author include any of the following?
   a. examples or illustrations
   b. research results
   c. expert opinion

4. Does the author respond to any opposing point of view? _____
   If so, fill in the blanks that follow.

Opposition   _____

   _____

Response   _____

   _____

5. Circle one or more of the appropriate letters to indicate the presence or absence of errors in the author's argument.
   a. irrelevant reasons
   b. circular reasoning
   c. hasty generalizations
   d. unidentified or inappropriate experts
   e. unidentified or dated research
   f. no errors

C H A P T E R   1 2

Reading and Responding to Essay Questions

 In this chapter, you'll learn

- how to analyze essay questions.

- how to recognize key words in essay questions.

- how to write focused and complete answers.

Like many students, you're probably anxious about essay exams. You may assume that you have a fighting chance with multiple-choice questions, but essay questions strike fear into your heart. If that's how you feel, take a deep breath and relax. In working your way through *Reading for Thinking*, you've already mastered the skills you need to do well on essay exams. You already know how to identify topics, draw inferences, distinguish between fact and opinion, and evaluate arguments. Chapter 12 shows you how to put together all these skills and use them to take and pass essay exams.

The Three *Rs* of Passing Exams: Review, Review, Review

Chapter 1 encouraged you to review a chapter section right after you finish reading it. Chapter 3 talked about reviewing for exams by answering potential test questions you jotted in the margins. Chapter 5 suggested you summarize and synthesize your notes until you had only a few pages to review the night before the exam. Got the message? The reading and writing strategies outlined here will definitely help you do well on essay exams, but even they can't take the place of systematic reviews before the test.

Reading Essay Questions

Nervous about the exam and anxious to get started, many inexperienced test takers skim the question and plunge into writing the answer. That's a mistake. Essay questions demand the kind of close and careful reading described in the pages that follow.

Identifying the Topic and Requirements

Your goal in analyzing an essay question is to discover the two essential elements of every essay question: the topic and the requirement or requirements. The topic is like the topic of a paragraph. It's the subject you need to discuss. The requirements tell you how to approach or handle the topic.

Defining the Topic

Look at the following essay question. As you read it, ask yourself "What word or phrase most effectively sums up the topic?"

On occasion, Mark Twain's novel *Huckleberry Finn* has been criticized for its supposed racism. Yet according to Twain expert Mark

Fischer, Twain's novel is actually an attack on the institution of slavery, and the true hero of the novel is *not* Huck, but Jim. Begin your essay by summarizing Professor Fischer's argument. Then explain why you do or do not agree with it. Be sure to use evidence from the text to argue your position.

What is the topic of the question: (1) Mark Twain's novel *Huckleberry Finn*, (2) Mark Fischer's view of *Huckleberry Finn*, or (3) racism in the work of Mark Twain? If you chose topic 2, you're absolutely right. The sample essay question does not ask for a general discussion of the novel—its setting, characters, and themes. Nor does it ask you to go beyond *Huckleberry Finn* and look for evidence of racism in Twain's other works. The topic of the question is narrower than that. It focuses on Mark Fischer's defense of *Huckleberry Finn*. Your answer to the question should do the same.

Understanding the Requirements

Every essay question has one or more requirements, or tasks, that your answer must fulfill. Let's look again at that sample essay question about Mark Twain. How many requirements does it have? In other words, how many tasks must you complete in your answer in order to get full credit: one, two, or three?

On occasion, Mark Twain's novel *Huckleberry Finn* has been criticized for its supposed racism. Yet according to Twain expert Mark Fischer, Twain's novel is actually an attack on the institution of slavery, and the true hero of the novel is *not* Huck, but Jim. Begin your essay by summarizing Professor Fischer's argument. Then explain why you do or do not agree with it. Be sure to use evidence from the text to argue your position.

This essay question has three requirements: (1) summarize Professor Fischer's position, (2) explain why you agree or disagree, and (3) use evidence from the text. If you failed to do any one of these, your exam score would suffer. That's why reading closely to determine all the requirements of an essay question is so important.

Key Words Help Identify Requirements

To determine exactly how many requirements you need to fulfill, pay close attention to words like *who, where, why, when, which,* and *how.* They frequently introduce a specific requirement of the essay question, often one that asks you to recall an important fact before you express an opinion or take a stand.

However, you should also familiarize yourself with the words listed below. Words like *argue, describe,* and *summarize* frequently introduce the individual requirements in an essay question.

Key Words on Essay Exams

Analyze	Divide or break a large whole into parts and comment on one or more of the parts, showing how it relates to the whole or reveals an underlying meaning.	*Analyze* the following excerpt from James Madison's *Federalist Papers* and show how it reveals his bias in favor of the wealthy.
Apply	Show how a principle or theory is illustrated in a particular instance or process.	*Apply* the Doppler effect to the behavior of light and sound waves.
Argue	Express a definite point of view and make it convincing through specific reasons, illustrations, and studies.	*Argue* the positive or negative effect of the *Miranda* decision on the American legal system.
Compare and Contrast	Describe how two topics are both similar and different. *Note:* Some essay questions may only use the word *compare,* but that almost always means point out similarities *and* differences.	*Compare and contrast* the leadership roles played by Grant and Lee during the Civil War.
Criticize	Explain the positive and negative effects of a particular decision, argument, or stand. *Note:* Sometimes instructors use the word *criticize* to ask for a summation of negative effects. If the meaning is not clear from the context, clarify it with your instructor.	*Criticize* the current regulations governing the use of pesticides in agriculture.
Define	Give a full and complete meaning, preferably one that includes an example or two and some history of how the term came into being.	*Define* Manifest Destiny and explain its effect on the American West.

Describe	Tell how something looks or happens. Supply specific details.	*Describe* how Benjamin Franklin came to develop his theory of positive and negative charges.
Discuss	Give the details of a situation, stand, or decision. Then explain the consequences.	*Discuss* the role of California governor Earl Warren in the government's decision to intern Japanese Americans during World War II.
Evaluate	Explain the pros and cons of a situation or point of view and take a stand based on your evaluation.	*Evaluate* Richard Nixon's role in the shaping of U.S. policy toward China.
Illustrate	Give examples that clarify a point or show how something works.	*Illustrate* the different ways in which lasers have revolutionized the treatment of heart disease.
Interpret	Explain the meaning of a statement and give examples.	*Interpret* Edward L. Bernays's claim that "propaganda is only another word for education."
Show	Give examples. *Note:* This verb is usually used in combination with one of the other words listed here.	*Trace* the highlights of Lenny Bruce's career and *show* how he affected the next generation of American comedians.
Summarize	Cover the most essential points of a theory, discovery, or event.	*Summarize* the results of the Kefauver hearings on organized crime.
Trace	Step-by-step, explain how something happened (or happens) over a period of time.	*Trace* the chain of events that led to the Clear Air and Water Act.

What If the Question's Not a Question?

In the best of all possible worlds, essay requirements would always be neatly and clearly stated, as they are in the following example.

Define the term "republicanism"* and explain why the framers of the Constitution chose it over "direct democracy."

*republicanism: form of government in which decisions are made by elected officials.

This question asks you to do two things: (1) define the term "republicanism" and (2) explain why the framers of the Constitution chose republicanism over "direct democracy." For an essay question, the requirements are pretty clear-cut. But what about this next question: Does it also neatly spell out its requirements?

> Compare the use of participant and nonparticipant observation in sociological research.[1]

This kind of vaguely formulated essay question really benefits from a critical reading that teases out its hidden questions: (1) What do the terms *participant* and *nonparticipant observation* mean? (2) In what ways are they different or similar?

If an essay question is vague, don't just run with it and hope for the best. Instead, do a critical reading to infer the questions it implies.

CHECK YOUR UNDERSTANDING

What two key elements should you look for in every essay question?

_____

◼ EXERCISE 1

DIRECTIONS Read each essay question. When you finish, answer the questions by filling in the blanks or circling the correct answer.

EXAMPLE In the 1952 election, Dwight D. Eisenhower was the first presidential candidate to make effective use of television as part of his campaign. In your essay, identify the media adviser Ike relied upon and explain how and why he needed television to promote his candidacy.

1. The topic of this essay question is
   a. Dwight D. Eisenhower.
   (b.) Dwight D. Eisenhower's use of television in the 1952 campaign.
   c. the media's role in the shaping of presidential candidates.

---

[1]Example comes from Gregory S. Galica, *The Blue Book*. New York: Harcourt, Brace, 1991, p. 40.

2. How many requirements are there? _3_

3. List each one separately, paraphrasing where possible.

   a. *Identify Ike's media adviser*

   b. *Explain how he used television*

   c. *Explain why Ike needed television*

   _____

EXPLANATION In this case, you are not being asked to discuss the life and times of Dwight D. Eisenhower or the role of the media in presenting candidates to the public. The focus of the question is a good deal more specific. You're being asked to discuss Dwight D. Eisenhower's use of television in the 1952 campaign—topic *b*.

1. Who was Edward L. Bernays and why was he nicknamed the "Father of Spin"?

   1. The topic of this essay question is
      a. the life and times of Edward L. Bernays.
      b. Edward L. Bernays.
      c. spin.

   2. How many requirements are there? _____
   3. List each one separately.

   _____

   _____

   _____

   _____

2. What was the Seneca Falls Convention,* who attended it, and what consequences did it have for American women?

   1. The topic of this essay question is
      a. American women.
      b. the Seneca Falls Convention.
      c. attendance at the Seneca Falls Convention.

   ――――――――――

   *Seneca Falls Convention: held in 1848, the Seneca Falls Convention gave official status to the feminist movement.

2. How many requirements are there? _____

3. List each one separately.

_____

_____

_____

_____

3. Writer Gabriel García Márquez has been called a *magical realist.* Define that term and provide at least three examples of it from Márquez's most famous work, *One Hundred Years of Solitude.*

1. The topic of this essay question is

   a. Gabriel García Márquez's effect on Latin American literature.

   b. Latin American literature in the twentieth century.

   c. magical realism in the work of Gabriel García Márquez.

2. How many requirements are there? _____

3. List each one separately.

_____

_____

_____

_____

4. Summarize Marcus Garvey's* contribution to the early movement for civil rights and contrast his position on civil rights to that of W. E. B. Du Bois. End your essay by explaining who in the modern civil rights movement followed in Garvey's footsteps. (Be sure to explain why you think this person or group was influenced by Garvey.)

1. The topic of this essay question is

   a. the early civil rights movement.

   b. Marcus Garvey's position on civil rights.

   c. W. E. B. Du Bois.

2. How many requirements are there? _____

_____

*Marcus Garvey: less well known than civil rights leader W. E. B. Du Bois, Marcus Garvey (1887–1940) favored racial separation and a return to Africa.

3. List each one separately.

_____

_____

_____

_____

5. Describe William James's theory of the "twice-born soul" and apply that theory to James's own life experience.

1. The topic of this essay question is

   a. the life of William James.

   b. the life and work of William James.

   c. William James's theory of the "twice-born soul."

2. How many requirements are there? _____

3. List each one separately.

_____

_____

_____

_____

─■ EXERCISE 2

DIRECTIONS Read the following excerpts. For each one, write an essay question that you think would test a reader's understanding of the material.

EXAMPLE

1. Developing an Ego Ideal

1 In his book *Fire in the Belly,* author and activist Sam Keen offers an intriguing theory of how men and women develop their *ego ideal,* the heroic being they aspire to be even if they never quite achieve their goal. For Keen, the mind of each person contains a mental Hall of Fame in which live the heroes and heroines of the moment. Our personal Hall of Fame may contain people in the news because of heroic achievements, but it can also contain people we know personally and admire because of their talent, wit, beauty, or

character. One's internal Hall of Fame might include figures as diverse as the singer Queen Latifah, the runner Jesse Owens, and the director John Sayles, lined up right along side your mother and favorite aunt. In his own Hall of Fame, Keen includes people such as the philosopher Soren Kierkegaard and his wife, Jan.

2   But our ego ideal is not based solely on who lives in our Hall of Fame. According to Keen, we also compile, as the years go on, an internal Hall of Exemplars.* The people in this hall have nothing to do with current events. Nor are they there because of some personal relationship to us. The Hall of Exemplars contains men and women who have been or will be honored throughout the ages because of their contributions to humanity. In Keen's case, the Hall of Exemplars contains figures like Jesus, Gandhi, Buddha, and Mother Teresa.

3   From Keen's point of view, the Hall of Exemplars and the Hall of Fame work together to help shape who we are and what we hope to be. The internalized* images living in the Hall of Fame help guide particular aspects of behavior. We decide, for example, that we want to be talented like Queen Latifah and determined like Aunt Betty, and we strive as much as possible to be like them. Members of the Hall of Exemplars, in contrast, act as our moral compass. They tell us what we could or should do to make the world a better place. They remind us that there is, indeed, a world beyond the self, one that deserves and requires our attention.

Essay Question   *Summarize Sam Keen's theory of how we define our ego ideal, making sure to explain the difference between the Hall of Fame and the Hall of Exemplars.*

EXPLANATION This is a good essay question because it tests the reader's understanding of Keen's theory. If you can summarize Keen's theory, then you've understood it. The question also picks up on and reflects a key point of the passage: the difference between the Hall of Fame and the Hall of Exemplars.

1. The Advent of Polio as an Epidemic

1   Poliomyelitis, more commonly known as polio, is an infectious disease caused by a virus that usually enters through the mouth and takes up residence in the throat and intestinal tract. Actually, there are three different forms of polio, each caused by a sep-

---

*exemplars: people worthy of imitation, role models.
*internalized: taken within, made part of the self.

arate virus. However, only one of those three viruses can destroy nerve cells and cause lasting paralysis. Tragically, this was the virus that spread through the United States in the 1940s and '50s, leaving in its wake around 650,000 paralyzed children.

2   Ironically, the advent of polio as a treacherous, and sometimes deadly, disease was caused by advances in hygiene. Prior to the turn of the century, open sewers were everywhere and children were exposed to the polio viruses early on. As a result, they developed an immunity to the disease, usually by the age of six. Once the sewers were closed, the early exposure was gone and so was the childhood immunity. In 1916, the first polio epidemic hit the United States, and after that, not a year went by without another epidemic. By 1957, a vaccine was finally available—thanks to the work of Jonas Salk—and the threat of polio, while it didn't disappear altogether, was seriously diminished. In 1952, the disease had taken its toll on 52,000 victims, most of them children. By 1960, there were only 3,000 reported cases.

Essay Question _____

_____

_____

2. **Three Types of Conversations**

1 There are three types of conversations we have with others: monologues, technical dialogues, and dialogues (Buber, 1958). *Monologues* are self-centered conversations in which other people are treated as objects. When we engage in monologues, we do *not* see others as unique people or take their needs into consideration. We are engaging in monologues any time we focus on ourselves and do *not* take the other person into consideration or adjust what we say and do to what the other person says and does.

2   Often when we engage in monologues we are being conversational narcissists. *Conversational narcissism* is the "way conversationalists turn the topics of ordinary conversations to themselves without sustained interest in others' topics" (Derber, 1979, p. 5).

3   Narcissistic communication occurs when we emphasize our self-importance by boasting or using terms others do not understand, when we exploit others by shifting responses to ourselves or talking for long periods, when we engage in exhibitionism by using exaggerated facial expressions or making ourselves the focal point of conversations, and when we are nonresponsive to others by "glazing over" or being impatient when they are talking (Vangelisti, Knapp, & Daly, 1990).

4   *Technical dialogues* are information-centered conversations. The purpose of the conversation is to exchange information with the other person, *not* make a connection with the other person. Monologues and technical dialogues are necessary and appropriate at times, but problems emerge when they are used too frequently, because this leads to a lack of connection between the participants.

5   In *dialogues,* other people are not treated as objects. Rather, they are seen as unique humans. The goal of dialogue is *not* to use or change other people, but to understand them. In a dialogue, there is a search for mutuality (Buber, 1958). Goals and expectations do not come between the two people. Rather, what goes on between the two people is the focus. Participants in a dialogue adjust their goals and messages depending on what is taking place in the conversation. Each participant's feeling of control and ownership is minimized. Each participant confirms the other, even when conflict occurs. It is this mutual confirmation that allows us to be human (Buber, 1958). (Gudykunst et al., *Building Bridges: Personal Skills for a Changing World,* pp. 96–97.)

Essay Question _____

_____

_____

▟◣◥◖ Responding to Essay Questions: Getting Organized

Once you've analyzed and paraphrased the question, technically you're ready to start writing. But hold on a moment; this is the time to take a minute and get your thoughts organized.

Start with an Outline

Making a rough outline is one of the best ways to make sure your answer is complete and focused. Remember the question about Dwight D. Eisenhower's use of television in the 1952 campaign? Here's an informal outline listing the *absolutely essential* points— the ones that need to be fleshed out in the answer. Notice how each part of the outline is labeled to indicate which part of the question it answers. Annotations like these are a good way to get your thoughts organized before you begin writing.

who—1. Rosser Reeves was Ike's main media consultant.

why—2. Everyone horrified by how old and bland Eisenhower was coming across in campaign

how—3. Television spots with USP (Unique Selling Proposition)—based on Rosser's commercial experience

4. Reeves polled *Reader's Digest* for best image—Ike "Man of Peace" won

5. Flooded states where Eisenhower not doing well with TV spots

6. Transformed Ike into a statesman and he won the election

With an outline like the one above to guide you, you can be assured that you'll write an essay that focuses on the question and doesn't ramble away from the topic.

Watch the Time

Essential as it is to outline your answer, don't let it take up too much time. Your outline should take no more than a few minutes, so keep an eye on the clock.

◼ EXERCISE 3

DIRECTIONS Take one of the essay questions you created for Exercise 2 and make a rough outline of the key points a good answer would cover. To illustrate, here's a rough outline for an answer to the essay question on page 441.

EXAMPLE

1. *We are defined by the people we admire.*

   —who you admire says who you want to be

2. *"Hall of Fame": people who are heroes for the moment.*

   —leaders, friends, achievers, heroes of the moment

3. *"Hall of Exemplars": people who expand our sense of what it means to be human, like Jesus and Gandhi.*

Writing to the Point

With some modification, you can apply to essay exams everything you've learned about writing to inform or persuade. Only this time, you're the writer who has to take your instructor-reader into account, making sure that you present your information effectively and argue your point convincingly.

Skip the Introduction

In your writing courses, you may have been encouraged to write creative introductions designed to stimulate your reader's interest. That instruction, however, does not apply to essay exams where you need to get right to the point and show your instructor that you have mastered the material on the exam.

Open with a General Answer to the Essay Question

The first sentence or two of your answer should generally outline how you intend to answer the question. To make sure your teacher understands that your answer will address the question asked, try to restate a portion of the question at the very beginning of your essay. Imagine, for example, that you were answering this question: "Describe the methods television news programs utilize in an effort to make current events visually exciting." Your answer could begin with a statement like this:

> Television news programs use three different methods to make their news coverage visually exciting: staging, tape doctoring, and ambush interviewing.

In effect, this is the thesis statement of your essay answer, and it does two things. First, by restating the topic—"methods used to make current events visually exciting"—it tells your instructor that you've understood the focus of the question and are going to respond appropriately. Second, it gives your instructor a mental blueprint to follow. That blueprint says your answer will have three parts to it, with each part addressed according to the order indicated in your opening thesis statement.

EXERCISE 4

DIRECTIONS Read each essay question. Then look at the opening statements that follow. Circle the letter of the statement that seems to respond most directly to the essay question.

Essay Question **EXAMPLE** The view that "news" is simply what happens doesn't fit the reality. No form of mass media can carry every newsworthy event. It's up to reporters, editors, and publishers to decide what is news. In your essay, describe and illustrate the criteria used to select newsworthy stories.

Opening Statements a. Unfortunately, most local news programs are committed to the old saying, "If it bleeds, it leads." In other words, if there's a lot of blood and gore in a local story, that story will get the most air time. The sad truth, then, is that local news programs spend less and less time on political issues. Politics, unless there's a scandal involved, isn't bloody enough.

(b.) Reporters, editors, and publishers are in a position to "make" news because they are the ones who decide which events are worthy of being reported, and they make their decisions on the basis of how these three questions are answered: (1) Is it timely or novel? (2) Is there any violence, conflict, or scandal? and (3) Are the people involved familiar to the public?

EXPLANATION Answer *b* is correct because it restates part of the essay question and lays out in general terms what the answer will accomplish. Answer *a* goes off in the wrong direction, focusing strictly on local news when the question addresses news on a broader scale.

Essay Question **1.** By the 1920s, the Ku Klux Klan, formerly restricted to rural areas, had made inroads into several of America's biggest cities. What city was the exception to the Klan's invasion and why did it escape Klan influence?

Opening Statements a. In the 1920s, New York City was the only racially diverse metropolis* to escape the influence of the Ku Klux Klan. Klan groups, called "Klaverns," were founded in New York City, but the opposition to them—from both the media and the local government—was so strong that the Klan eventually gave up hope of taking hold in New York City.

b. How did the Ku Klux Klan become an urban phenomenon?* According to Kenneth Jackson, the author of *The Ku Klux Klan in the*

---

*metropolis: big city.
*phenomenon: an occurrence or event that is observable to the senses.

City, 1915–1930, the Klan claimed two to five million members in the 1920s, and many of these members lived in big cities. The Klan found a foothold in the cities because it had expanded its circle of hatred to include immigrants as well as African Americans.

Essay Question 2. The American mass media are relatively free of government restrictions. Nevertheless, the government does exercise some control over radio and television. In your essay, identify and describe the two ways in which the government monitors and, to some degree, controls these two media.

Opening Statements
    a. In 1934, Congress created the Federal Communications Commission (FCC); that agency has the power to monitor and regulate the use of the airwaves. For that very reason, the FCC has often been the target of lobbyists who want the FCC to exercise greater or lesser control.

    b. Government licensing and the equal time rule are the two primary ways in which the Federal Communications Commission, founded by Congress in 1934, regulates both radio and television.

Don't Skimp on Details

When you take an essay exam, you need to keep in mind your relationship to your instructor-reader. Of course, your instructor already knows the answer to the question posed on the exam, but that doesn't mean you are free to skimp on supporting details. Instructors give exams to test *your* knowledge of their subject matter. Therefore, you need to answer exam questions as fully and completely as possible. A detailed answer is your way of saying, "I have mastered and am in command of the material covered by this question."

Give Partial Answers When Necessary

Unfortunately, there may well be a time or two when you look at an essay question and just aren't sure how to answer all of the parts. If that should happen, don't freeze and give up. Instead, figure out what parts of the question you can answer and concentrate on those. When it comes to an essay exam, a partial answer is always better than none. In fact, if you run out of time while you're answering an essay question, include your outline when you turn in your test booklet. The purpose of turning in the outline is to show your instructor that you do know the answer, even if you didn't have time to get it down on paper.

 ## Become a Critical Reader

Imagine you've still got ten or fifteen minutes before the exam comes to an end. Do you get up, turn in your blue book, and trot out the door, happy the exam is over? Not on your life. This is the time to assume the role of critical reader—someone who objectively evaluates both content and style. The key word is *objectively*. The fact that it's your own writing you are evaluating does not mean you should relax your critical standards. If you think the opinion you expressed comes up short on evidence, spend a few minutes thinking about another example or study you might add. The need to add last-minute additions is why it's always a good idea to write on every other line of your exam booklet. When you have to add something, there's space available.

In evaluating the language of your essay answer, the key word is *clarity.* Check your sentences to make sure they say what you want them to. If you need to, add transitions to make sure that your reader can move smoothly from one sentence to the next. Here again, don't rely on the instructor to fill in the gaps. That task is yours, not your instructor's.

In the last minute or two, check for errors in punctuation and grammar. Make sure, too, that your writing is legible. Cross out any words that are scribbled or scrawled and rewrite them right over the space where you have crossed them out.

EXERCISE 5

DIRECTIONS Read the following selection and the essay question that accompanies it. Then look over the two possible answers to that question. Circle the letter of the answer you think more effectively meets the guidelines outlined in this chapter.

EXAMPLE

Silence on the Supreme Court

1 Often the cases that the Supreme Court doesn't decide are just as important as the ones it does decide. Here are some cases involving claims of religious freedom that were decided by lower courts.

Since the Supreme Court refused to hear an appeal of these decisions, the lower court decisions, at least for now, are the law.

2   **Reading the Bible**   In a Colorado public school, classrooms occasionally have a silent reading period during which the students and teachers can read various books. One teacher silently read his Bible during this period. There is no evidence his students knew what he was reading; however, the principal of the school told the teacher he could not read the Bible because *if* the students found out it might influence them to read the Bible also. A federal court upheld the principal.

3   **Mentioning God**   A professor of physiology at the University of Alabama occasionally mentioned in class the importance to him of his Christian faith. He also gave an after-class lecture on "Evidences of God in Human Physiology." Attendance was optional. The university ordered him not to present any comments from a Christian perspective in class. A federal court upheld the university.

4   **Spouse Abuse and Religion**   The New Orleans Baptist Theological Seminary expelled a student when it learned from the police that he had abused his wife. The state courts ordered him reinstated because spouse abuse did not bear on his academic qualifications for a degree. The seminary argued that giving him a degree would entitle him to be a Baptist minister, and that spouse abuse was incompatible with a religious vocation. The seminary lost. (Information drawn from Michael McConnell, "Freedom from Religion?" *The American Enterprise*, January/February 1993, pp. 32–43. In Wilson and DiIulio Jr., *American Government*, p. 558.)

Essay Question

> According to the authors of your textbook, some of the cases that the Supreme Court does *not* decide are as important as those they do. Summarize three cases that the Supreme Court refused to hear and identify the issue or topic that connected all three.

Answers a. The Supreme Court has repeatedly had to respond to what is a fact of American life: Religion plays a key role in it. Thus, over the years, the Supreme Court has been confronted by numerous church-state issues. In one key case, the New Orleans Baptist Theological Seminary expelled a student when it learned of the student's arrest for domestic violence. According to the seminary administration, spousal abuse was incompatible with the life and work of a minister.

The Louisiana state courts disagreed, arguing that abusing his wife had nothing to do with the man's academic qualifications. When the seminary appealed the courts' decision, the Supreme Court refused to hear the appeal.

In my opinion, this was a grave mistake on the part of the Supreme Court. Domestic violence is a crime, and a criminal should not be allowed to become a minister. The Louisiana courts were wrong to reinstate him, and the Supreme Court should have taken a stand and rectified that injustice.

(b.) In at least three separate cases involving religious freedom, the Supreme Court has let stand the decisions of lower courts. In one case, for example, a teacher in a Colorado public school read his Bible during a silent reading period. However, he was forbidden to do so by the principal on the grounds that the teacher might influence his students to do the same. A federal court sided with the principal and the Supreme Court refused to hear an appeal.

In a second instance, a professor of physiology at the University of Alabama mentioned in class how important his Christian faith was to his life. He also lectured after class on the "Evidence of God in Human Physiology" and invited his students to attend. In response, the university forbade him to comment on Christianity in the classroom, and the university's decision was upheld by a federal court. Here again the Supreme Court did not intervene.

In a third case, the New Orleans Theological Seminary expelled a student who had abused his wife. The seminary administration insisted that a man who abused his wife should not be allowed to become a minister. The State of Louisiana, however, disagreed. According to the state, spousal abuse had no bearing on the man's academic performance and ordered him reinstated. The Supreme Court refused to hear an appeal, and the seminary had to abide by the state's ruling.

EXPLANATION Answer *b* is a better answer because it stays focused on the question, which has two requirements: (1) summarize three cases rejected by the Supreme Court and (2) identify the issue that connects them. Answer *a* summarizes only one case and therefore can't possibly identify the connecting thread asked for in the question.

Answer *a* also assumes information not specified in either the reading or the question—that the man was convicted of domestic violence against his wife and could, therefore, be legally considered a criminal. The writer of the answer has, in short, drawn an inappropriate inference.

1. **The Rights of the Disabled**

1 In 1990 the federal government passed the Americans with Disabilities Act (ADA), a sweeping law that extended many of the protections enjoyed by women and racial minorities to disabled persons.

Who Is a Disabled Person?

2 Anyone who *has* a physical or mental impairment that substantially limits one or more major life activities (for example, holding a job), anyone who has a *record* of such impairment, or anyone who is *regarded* as having such an impairment is considered disabled.

What Rights Do the Disabled Have?

3 **Employment**   The disabled may not be denied employment or promotion if, with "reasonable accommodation,"* they can perform the duties of that job. (Excluded from this protection are people who currently use illegal drugs, gamble compulsively, or are homosexual or bisexual.) Reasonable accommodation need not be made if this would cause "undue hardship" on the employer.

4 **Government Programs and Transportation**   Disabled persons may not be denied access to government programs or benefits. New buses, taxis, and trains must be accessible to disabled persons, including those in wheelchairs.

5 **Public Accommodations**   The disabled must enjoy "full and equal" access to hotels, restaurants, stores, schools, parks, museums, auditoriums, and the like. To achieve equal access, owners of existing facilities must alter them "to the maximum extent feasible"; builders of new facilities must ensure that they are readily accessible to disabled persons, unless this is structurally impossible.

6 **Telephones**   The ADA directs the Federal Communications Commission to issue regulations to ensure that telecommunications devices for hearing- and speech-impaired people are available "to the extent possible and in the most efficient manner."

7 **Congress**   The rights under this law apply to employees of Congress.

8 **Rights Compared**   The ADA does not enforce the rights of the disabled in the same way as the Civil Rights Act enforces the rights of blacks and women. Racial or gender discrimination must end *regardless of cost;* denial of access to the disabled must end unless "undue hardship" or excessive costs would result. (Wilson and DiIulio Jr., *American Government*, p. 598.)

---

*accommodation: consideration.

Essay Question

> The 1990 Americans with Disabilities Act guaranteed certain rights to disabled Americans. In your essay, describe who would benefit from this act and summarize the rights they would be accorded.

Answers a. The 1990 Americans with Disabilities Act guaranteed certain rights to disabled Americans. This group was defined as people who possessed a physical or mental impairment serious enough to limit a major life activity, such as holding a job, as well as those who had a record of such an impairment and those regarded as having such an impairment.

Anyone who fell into one of these three categories was guaranteed the following rights. They could, for example, not be denied either employment or a promotion if, "with reasonable accommodation," they could do the job. Disabled persons could also not be denied access to government programs or benefits, and new buses, trains, and taxis had to be wheelchair accessible.

In the area of public accommodations like hotels, parks, schools, and restaurants, access for the disabled had to be made available. This meant old buildings had to be altered to make them accessible to the disabled, while new buildings had to be created with the disabled in mind.

According to the ADA, the Federal Communications Commission had to make sure that telecommunications devices for hearing- and speech-impaired people were available "to the extent possible."

Modeled on civil rights legislation, the ADA still took the cost of change into account. Whereas the law says that racial and gender discrimination must end no matter what the cost, the ADA applied the yardstick of "undue hardship" in demanding change. Thus, for example, an employer could deny employment to a disabled person who could only do the job if very special and very expensive provisions were made.

b. In 1973, Congress passed the Rehabilitation Act, which forbids discrimination against disabled persons in any program receiving federal aid. A disabled person is defined as anyone who has a physical or mental impairment that substantially limits one or more of life's major activities.

Once the act passed, federal agencies, under pressure from organizations representing the disabled, decided on a broad interpretation that would bring about sweeping changes.

For example, city transit systems receiving federal aid had to make sure that buses and subways were accessible to the disabled. While disabled people were pleased with this interpretation of the act, some state and city officials took a dim view of it.

New York City's mayor at the time, Edward Koch, protested that the expenses would be too great. Koch estimated that making all buses and subways accessible was going to cost the city billions, but his protests were ignored until 1981, when the Reagan administration relaxed the requirements that buses be able to lift wheelchairs aboard.

WORD NOTES

Page 446 introduced the word *phenomenon,* meaning "an occurrence or event observable to the senses." But like many other words, this word has more than one meaning. The word *phenomenon* can refer to "an unusual or unaccountable fact," as in "The comet was a once-in-a-century phenomenon." It can also refer to a person who is remarkable or outstanding," as in "He was already a musical phenomenon at the age of nine." When *phenomenon* is used to identify someone or something remarkable, its plural form is *phenomenons.* Otherwise, the plural form is *phenomena.*

Use the correct plural form of *phenomenon* to fill in the blanks.

1. The brothers were literary _____ who had both published first novels at the age of twenty.

2. Shooting stars are natural _____ in this part of the country.

Now it's your turn to use each plural in a sentence.

1. phenomena: _____

_____

2. phenomenons: _____

_____

Summing Up

Listed below are the most important points in Chapter 12. Put a check mark in the box if you think the point is clear in your mind. Leave the box blank if you need to review the material one more time. The page numbers in parentheses tell you where to look to review each point on the list.

☐ **1.** To sift out the key elements of an essay question, test takers need to do a close and careful reading. They need to read every single sentence in order to discover (1) the topic and (2) the requirements. (pp. 433–435)

☐ **2.** Key words like *who, where, why, when, which,* and *how* are clues to the number of requirements in an essay question. So, too, are words like *define, trace,* and *summarize.* (pp. 434–436)

☐ **3.** If essay questions are not phrased as actual questions, it helps to infer the implicit question or questions suggested by the statement on the exam. (pp. 436–437)

☐ **4.** Making a rough outline of your answer *before* you start writing is one of the best ways to ensure that an answer is complete, coherent, and focused. (pp. 443–444)

☐ **5.** When answering an essay question, skip the introduction and start with a general answer to the question asked. Whenever possible, use a portion of the question in your answer. (pp. 445–447)

☐ **6.** Before you turn in your test booklet, assume the role of critical reader and check your answer carefully, looking for places where you might need stronger reasons or better examples to be convincing. (p. 448)

TEST YOUR UNDERSTANDING

To see how well you have understood this chapter, take the following review quiz. Then use the answer key provided by your instructor to correct it. If you score 80 percent or above, you're ready to take the end-of-chapter exam. However, if you score below 80 percent, look over the quiz carefully to see what kinds of questions you missed. Use the **Summing Up** pages of the chapter to find out which pages you should review before taking the chapter exam.

Chapter 12: Review Quiz

Part A

DIRECTIONS Answer the following questions by filling in the blanks or circling the letter of the correct answer.

1. When you analyze an essay question, what is your main goal?

_____

2. Which of the following is *not* a key word in essay questions?

   a. who

   b. why

   c. trace

   d. show

   e. circle

3. Once you've carefully read the essay question, what is the next step you should take?

_____

4. What should the first sentence in your answer to an essay question do?

_____

5. Once you've finished writing your answer to an essay question, it's time for you to

_____

Part B

DIRECTIONS Circle the letter of the correct answer.

6. In 1535, English scholar and statesman Sir Thomas More was beheaded for refusing to comply with the Act of Supremacy. What was the Act of Supremacy and why was More willing to die rather than uphold it?

The topic of this question is

   a. political controversy in sixteenth-century England.

   b. Thomas More's refusal to comply with the Act of Supremacy.

   c. Thomas More's political career in the court of Henry VIII.

The question has

a. one requirement.

b. two requirements.

c. three requirements.

d. four requirements.

7. Writer Budd Schulberg has called boxer Muhammad Ali "America's Paul Bunyan." Summarize the myth of Paul Bunyan. Then trace the highlights of Ali's career and show why the allusion to Paul Bunyan is an appropriate one.

The topic of this question is

a. Budd Schulberg's career as a critic of boxing.

b. Paul Bunyan.

c. Paul Bunyan and Muhammad Ali.

The question has

a. one requirement.

b. two requirements.

c. three requirements.

d. four requirements.

8. What three antitrust acts were passed between 1890 and 1914,* and what specific effects did they have on existing business practices?

The topic of this question is

a. American corporations in the late nineteenth century.

b. antitrust legislation in the late nineteenth and early twentieth centuries.

c. antitrust legislation in the late nineteenth century.

The question has

a. one requirement.

b. two requirements.

c. three requirements.

d. four requirements.

---

*The Sherman Act (1890), the Federal Trade Commission Act (1914), and the Clayton Act (1914).

9. Describe the Supreme Court controversy known as *Marbury v. Madison,* making sure to explain the roles of John Marshall and James Madison. How was this case resolved and what effect did it have on the government of Thomas Jefferson?

The topic of this question is

a. James Madison.

b. *Marbury v. Madison.*

c. Thomas Jefferson.

The question has

a. one requirement.

b. two requirements.

c. three requirements.

d. four requirements.

10. Who was Charles Katz and how did the case *Katz v. the United States* affect the role of privacy in search and seizure cases?

The topic of this question is

a. the American justice system.

b. *Katz v. the United States.*

c. the role of private property in search and seizure cases.

The question has

a. one requirement.

b. two requirements.

c. three requirements.

d. four requirements.

Use the answer key provided by your instructor to correct your quiz. If you score 80 percent or above, you are ready for the chapter exam. If you score below 80 percent, look carefully at the questions you answered incorrectly. Then use the **Summing Up** section to decide which pages you need to review.

Chapter Test 12

Part A

DIRECTIONS Answer the following questions by filling in the blanks or circling the letter of the correct answer.

1. In analyzing an essay question, what two elements should you be looking for?

   _____

2. Which one of the following is *not* a key word in essay questions?

   a. why

   b. describe

   c. false

   d. summarize

   e. trace

3. After reading an essay question, what should you do to make sure your answer has a clear focus?

   _____

4. How should you begin your essay answer?

   _____

5. Once you finish writing your answer to an essay question, what should you do?

   _____

Part B

DIRECTIONS Circle the letter of the correct answer.

6. Summarize both sides of the controversy over the use of animals in scientific research. Then state your own position on this topic and give specific reasons for your point of view.

   The topic of this question is

   a. the animal rights movement.

   b. the role of animals in scientific research.

   c. the controversy over the use of animals in research.

The question has

a. one requirement.

b. two requirements.

c. three requirements.

d. four requirements.

7. In her book *Without Lying Down*, author Cari Beauchamp argues that Hollywood between 1915 and 1925 was a place where women were equal in power to men; women flourished* not just as actresses but as writers, directors, producers, and editors. In your essay, identify at least three of the women Beauchamp uses to make her point. Be sure to explain not just who they were but what they accomplished as well. Then describe the changes in studio management that pushed these same women into the background and deprived them of their former power.

The topic of this question is

a. Cari Beauchamp.

b. Hollywood's failure to enlarge the role of women.

c. the role of women in Hollywood between 1915 and 1925.

The question has

a. one requirement.

b. two requirements.

c. three requirements.

d. four requirements.

8. Since its discovery, Antarctica has been the source of competing national claims, but only once has there been actual fighting over the territory. What nations were involved in that fight and what was the outcome?

The topic of this question is

a. the Arctic circle.

b. the fight over claims to Antarctica.

c. the riches of Antarctica and the greed those riches inspire.

_____

*flourished: did well, were successful.

The question has

a. one requirement.

b. two requirements.

c. three requirements.

d. four requirements.

9. Throughout the 1970s, the Mexican-American group *La Raza Unida* was a powerful force in the Southwest. Who were the leaders of this group and what were its goals? Once you have outlined the goals of the group, evaluate the group's success as a political force in the Southwest.

The topic of this question is

a. Mexican Americans in the Southwest.

b. Southwestern politics.

c. *La Raza Unida.*

The question has

a. one requirement.

b. two requirements.

c. three requirements.

d. four requirements.

10. Summarize the reasons for the United States's withdrawal from Vietnam and describe the public's reaction to that withdrawal.

The topic of this question is

a. the causes of the Vietnam War.

b. reasons for the U.S. withdrawal from Vietnam.

c. American foreign policy in Southeast Asia.

The question has

a. one requirement.

b. two requirements.

c. three requirements.

d. four requirements.

PART III

Putting It All Together

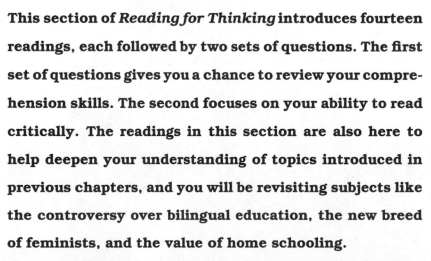

This section of *Reading for Thinking* introduces fourteen readings, each followed by two sets of questions. The first set of questions gives you a chance to review your comprehension skills. The second focuses on your ability to read critically. The readings in this section are also here to help deepen your understanding of topics introduced in previous chapters, and you will be revisiting subjects like the controversy over bilingual education, the new breed of feminists, and the value of home schooling.

In addition, this section of *Reading for Thinking* includes numerous writing assignments, many of which ask you to do what, up till now, you've seen others do—argue a point of view. In truth, *Reading for Thinking* is not solely concerned with teaching you to understand and evaluate the ideas of others. Ultimately, its goal is to encourage you to express and argue with confidence your own particular point of view.

■ **READING 1**

THE PATERSON PUBLIC LIBRARY

LOOKING AHEAD Almost all of the readings in this section are linked to specific topics already introduced in previous chapters. This reading is the one exception. Its connection to *Reading for Thinking* is more subtle. It is connected less by topic and more by point of view. Like the author of "The Paterson Public Library," I also believe that reading is a way to both escape and discover the world.

GETTING FOCUSED Read the first and last paragraphs. Then read the first sentence of the remaining paragraphs and all the words in **Word Watch.** Based on your survey, why do you think the author titled this essay "The Paterson Public Library"? Is, in fact, the library the topic of her writing?

_____

_____

As you read, consider your own relationship to books. Are they important to your life? Why or why not?

WORD WATCH Some of the more difficult words in the reading are defined in this section. Watch for these words as you read. They are marked with an asterisk. When you finish the reading, review the words in **Word Watch** by covering up the definitions and checking to see if you now know all the meanings. Record any words you still don't know in a notebook or on index cards. Review them periodically until they are part of your vocabulary.

archeological site: place where digging is done in an effort to locate remnants of the past

incongruous: not fitting; inappropriate to the setting

façade: outer surface of a building

astigmatism: a problem with the lens of the eye

supplicants: people who are worshipping or pleading

fait accompli: already accomplished

sanctuary: place of safety

organic: growing naturally out of the earth

insatiable: incapable of being satisfied

adept: skillful

obsessiveness: state of being overly focused on an idea

1   IT WAS A GREEK TEMPLE IN THE RUINS OF AN AMERICAN CITY.
To get to it I had to walk through neighborhoods where not even
the carcasses of rusted cars on blocks or the death traps of dis-
carded appliances were parted with, so that the yards of the bor-
derline poor, people who lived not in a huge building, as I did, but
in their own decrepit little houses, looked like a reversed archeological site,* incongruous* next to the pillared palace of the Paterson Public Library.

2   The library must have been built during Paterson, New Jersey's, boom years as the model industrial city of the North.
Enough marble was used in its construction to have kept several
Michelangelos busily satisfied for a lifetime. Two roaring lions,
taller than a grammar school girl, greeted those brave enough to
seek answers there. Another memorable detail about the façade*
of this most important place to me were the phrases carved
deeply into the walls—perhaps the immortal words of Greek philosophers—I could not tell since I was developing an astigmatism*
at that time and could only make out the lovely geometric designs
they made.

3   All during the school week I both anticipated and feared the
long walk to the library because it took me through enemy territory. The black girl Lorraine, who had chosen me to hate and ter-
rorize with threats at school, lived in one of the gloomy little
houses that circled the library like sackclothed supplicants.* Lorraine would eventually carry out her violence against me by beating me up in a confrontation formally announced through the
school grapevine so that for days I lived with a panic that has
rarely been equaled in my adult life, since now I can get grown-
ups to listen to me, and at that time disasters had to be a fait accompli* for a teacher or a parent to get involved.

4   Why did Lorraine hate me? For reasons neither one of us fully
understood at the time. All I remember was that our sixth-grade
teacher seemed to favor me, and her way of showing it was by having me tutor "slow" students in spelling and grammar. Lorraine,
older and bigger than myself since she was repeating the grade,
was subjected to this ritual humiliation, which involved sitting
in the hallway, obviously separated from the class—one of us
for being smart, the other for the opposite reason. Lorraine resisted my efforts to teach her the basic rules of spelling. She
would hiss her threats at me, addressing me as *You little Spic.*"
Her hostility sent shudders through me. But baffling as it was,
I also accepted it as inevitable. She would beat me up. I told
my mother and the teacher, and they both reassured me in

vague adult terms that a girl like Lorraine would not dare get in trouble again. She had a history of problems that made her a likely candidate for reform school. But Lorraine and I knew that the violence she harbored had found a target: me—the skinny Puerto Rican girl whose father was away with the navy most of the time and whose mother did not speak English; I was the perfect choice.

5   Thoughts like these occupied my mind as I walked to the library on Saturday mornings. But my need for books was strong enough to propel me down the dreary streets with their slush-covered sidewalks and the skinny trees of winter looking like dark figures from a distance: angry black girls waiting to attack me.

6   But the sight of the building was enough to reassure me that sanctuary* was within reach. Inside the glass doors was the inexhaustible treasure of books, and I made my way through the stacks like the beggar invited to the wedding feast. I remember the musty, organic* smell of the library, so different from the air outside. It was the smell of an ancient forest, and since the first books that I read for pleasure were fairy tales, the aroma of transforming wood suited me as a prop.

7   With my pink library card I was allowed to check out two books from the first floor—the children's section. I would take the full hour my mother had given me (generously adding fifteen minutes to get home before she sent my brother after me) to choose the books I would take home for the week. I made my way first through the world's fairy tales. Here I discovered that there is a Cinderella in every culture, that she didn't necessarily have the white skin and rosy cheeks Walt Disney had given her, and that the prince they all waited for could appear in any color, shape, or form. The prince didn't even have to be a man.

8   It was the way I absorbed fantasy in those days that gave me the sense of inner freedom, a feeling of power and the ability to fly that is the main reward of the writer. As I read those stories I became not only the characters but their creator. I am still fascinated by the idea that fairy tales and fables are part of humankind's collective unconscious—a familiar theory that acquires concreteness in my own writing today, when I discover over and over that the character I create or the themes that recur in my poems and in my fiction are my own versions of the "types" I learned to recognize very early in my life in fairy tales.

9   There was also violence in these stories: villains decapitated in honorable battle, goblins and witches pursued, beaten, and

burned at the stake by heroes with magic weapons possessing the supernatural strength granted to the self-righteous in folklore. I understood those black-and-white duels between evil and justice. But Lorraine's blind hatred of my person and my knee-liquefying fear of her were not so clear to me at that time. It would be many years before I learned about the politics of race, before I internalized* the awful reality of the struggle for territory that underscored the lives of blacks and Puerto Ricans in Paterson during my childhood.

10   Each job given to a light-skinned Hispanic was one less job for a black man; every apartment leased to a Puerto Rican family was one less place available to them. Worst of all, though the Puerto Rican children had to master a new language in the schools and were often subjected to the scorn and impatience of teachers burdened with too many students making too many demands in a classroom, the blacks were obviously the ones singled out for "special" treatment. In other words, whenever possible they were assigned to special education classes in order to relieve the teacher's workload, mainly because their black English dialect sounded "ungrammatical" and "illiterate" to our white Seton Hall University and City College–educated instructors.

11   I have on occasion become angry at being treated like I'm mentally deficient by persons who make that prejudgment upon hearing an unfamiliar accent. I can only imagine what it must have been like for children like Lorraine, whose skin color alone put her in a pigeonhole she felt she had to fight her way out of every day of her life.

12   I was one of the lucky ones; as an insatiable* reader I quickly became more than adept* at the use of the English language. My life as a navy brat, moving with my family from Paterson to Puerto Rico every few months as my father's tours of duty demanded, taught me to depend on knowledge as my main source of security. What I learned from books borrowed from the Greek temple among the ruins of the city, I carried with me as the lightest of carry-on luggage. My teachers in both countries treated me well in general. The easiest way to become a teacher's pet, or *la favorita*, is to ask the teacher for books to read—and I was always looking for reading material; even my mother's romantic novels by Corin Tellado and her *Buenhogar* (Spanish *Good Housekeeping* magazine) were not safe from my insatiable word hunger.

13   Since the days when I was stalked by Lorraine, libraries have always been an adventure for me. Fear of an ambush is no longer the reason why I feel my pulse quicken a little when I approach a

library building, when I enter the stacks and inhale the familiar smell of old leather and paper. It may be the memory of the danger that heightens my senses, but it is really the expectation that I felt then and that I still feel now about books.

14   I gained confidence in my intelligence by reading books. They contained most of the information I needed to survive in two languages and in two worlds. When adults were too busy to answer my endless questions, I could always look it up; when I felt unbearably lonely, as I often did during those early gypsy years traveling with my family, I read to escape, and also to connect: You can come back to a book as you cannot always to a person or place you miss. I read and reread favorite books until the characters seemed like relatives or friends I could see when I wanted or needed to see them.

15   I still feel that way about books. They represent my spiritual life. A library is my sanctuary, and I am always at home in one. It is not surprising that in recalling my first library, the Paterson Public Library, I have always described it as a temple.

16   Lorraine carried out her threat. One day after school, as several of our classmates, Puerto Rican and black, circled us to watch, Lorraine grabbed a handful of my long hair and forced me to my knees. Then she slapped my face hard enough that the sound echoed off the brick walls of the school building and ran off while I screamed at the sight of blood on my white knee socks and felt the throbbing on my scalp where I would have a bald spot advertising my shame for weeks to come.

17   No one intervened. To this crowd, it was one of many such violent scenes taking place among the adults and the children of people fighting over a rapidly shrinking territory. It happens in the jungle and it happens in the city. But another course of action other than "fight or flight" is open to those of us lucky enough to discover it and that is channeling one's anger and energy into the development of a mental life. It requires something like obsessiveness* for a young person growing up in an environment where physical labor and physical endurance are the marks of a survivor—as is the case with minority peoples living in large cities. But many of us do manage to discover books. In my case, it may have been what anthropologists call a cultural adaptation. Being physically small, non–English-speaking, and always the new kid on the block, I was forced to look for an alternate mode to survival in Paterson. Reading books empowered me.

18   Even now, a visit to the library recharges the batteries in my brain. Looking through the card catalog reassures me that there is no subject I cannot investigate, no world I cannot explore.

Everything that is, is mine for the asking. Because I can read
about it.

Judith Ortiz Cofer, "The Paterson Public Library,"
from *The Latin Deli: Prose & Poetry* by Judith Ortiz
Cofer. The University of Georgia Press, pp. 28–33.

CHECKING YOUR COMPREHENSION | **DIRECTIONS** Answer the following questions by circling the letter of the correct response.

1. Which statement more effectively paraphrases the main idea of the entire reading?

    a. For much of my life, books have provided me with both safety and comfort.

    b. For much of my life, books have given me an outlet for my anger.

2. In the library, the author discovered that

    a. Little Red Riding Hood appears in fairy tales from many different cultures.

    b. fairy tales can be frightening to children.

    c. there is a Cinderella story in every culture.

3. As a little girl, the author was often afraid to walk the streets near her home. What helped her overcome her fear?

    a. her personal courage

    b. her father's encouragement

    c. her need for books

4. According to the author, what is the writer's main reward?

    a. the feeling of being all powerful

    b. the feeling of being a creator

    c. the feeling of being powerful and capable of flight

5. According to the author, the girl named Lorraine hated her

    a. because she is Puerto Rican.

    b. for reasons neither really understood.

    c. for being such a smart and pretty little girl.

6. The author began to understand why Lorraine hated her when she

    a. grew old enough to forget her fear.

    b. understood the politics of race.

    c. moved out of her old neighborhood.

7. In paragraph 3, the topic sentence is

    a. sentence 1.

    b. sentence 2.

    c. sentence 3.

8. Which inference follows from the reading?

    a. Even as an adult, the author still hates her childhood enemy, Lorraine.

    b. As an adult, the author feels sympathy for Lorraine's situation.

    c. As an adult, the author just wants to forget her past.

9. What pattern of organization is at work in paragraph 12?

    a. cause and effect

    b. comparison and contrast

    c. process

10. Based on the reading, which question would you predict might appear on an exam?

    a. Explain what the author means by the phrase "the politics of race."

    b. Trace the history of the Paterson Public Library.

SHARPENING YOUR CRITICAL SKILLS

DIRECTIONS Answer the following questions by filling in the blanks or circling the letter of the correct response.

1. Which statement most effectively describes the author's purpose?

    a. The author wants to tell her readers about the Paterson Public Library.

    b. The author wants to describe the racism she encountered as a child.

    c. The author wants to tell her readers about the role that reading played in her life.

2. The title of the reading suggests the author's goal is

    a. to inform.

    b. to persuade.

3. Based on the reading, which inference do you think is appropriate?

   a. The author firmly believes in the importance of bilingual education programs.

   b. The author firmly believes that children should start reading at an early age.

4. How would you describe the author's use of language?

   a. She relies mainly on words that are more denotative than connotative.

   b. She relies heavily on connotative language to make her ideas clear and compelling.

5. In paragraph 6, the author says, "I made my way through the stacks like the beggar invited to the wedding feast." That figure of speech is a

   a. simile.

   b. metaphor.

6. The figure of speech about the beggar and the wedding feast helps the author make what point?

   _____

7. In paragraph 9, the author talks about her "knee-liquefying fear." That phrase illustrates which figure of speech?

   a. metaphor

   b. allusion

   c. simile

8. What does the author hope to communicate through the phrase "knee-liquefying fear"?

   _____

   _____

9. Which inference follows from the author's statements in paragraphs 10 and 11?

   a. Because their mostly white instructors were unfamiliar with black dialect, African Americans were unfairly singled out for special classes.

   b. The author thinks that Puerto Rican students spoke better English than did African-American students.

10. How would you describe the author's tone?

   a. emotionally neutral

   b. arrogant and angry

   c. strong and passionate

DRAWING YOUR OWN CONCLUSIONS Do you think the author makes a strong case for encouraging children to read? Why or why not?

WRITING SUGGESTION Describe your first experience with being read to or with learning to read. In either the introduction or conclusion of your paper, be sure to tell your readers how the experience has affected you as an adult. Like the author of "The Paterson Public Library," re-create your experience with vivid, concrete detail and figurative language.

■ READING 2

BILINGUAL EDUCATION

LOOKING AHEAD Chapter 11 introduced the sometimes controversial topic of bilingual education. Reading 2 adds to that discussion by giving you some background about the origins and methods of bilingual education in the United States.

GETTING FOCUSED Read the first and last paragraphs, the headings, marginal annotations, and the words in **Word Watch.** Based on your survey, what prediction would you make about the marginal note *Lau v. Nichols*?

_____

_____

Based on the headings "The Government Response," "Bilingual Education Models," and "Controversies," what questions will you use to guide your reading?

_____

_____

As you read, think about how you feel about bilingual education. Do you or do you not support the presence of bilingual education programs in our schools?

WORD WATCH Some of the more difficult words in the reading are defined in this section. Watch for these words as you read. They are marked with an asterisk. When you finish the reading, review the words in **Word Watch** by covering up the definitions and checking to see if you now know all the meanings. Record any words you still don't know in a notebook or on index cards. Review them periodically until they are part of your vocabulary.

constitute: make up, consist of

proficient: skilled

amended: changed, modified

class-action suit: a lawsuit in which one person or group goes to court on behalf of themselves and a much larger group of people who

foreclosed: excluded, shut out

mandate: order into law

interim: temporary

fluency: ease, skill

implications: consequences, results

are making the same claim of wrongdoing

immersion: to be completely involved; to be submerged in water

1 STUDENTS WHOSE NATIVE LANGUAGE IS NOT ENGLISH CONSTItute* one of the most at-risk groups in the American educational system. Because of their difficulty in speaking, writing, and understanding English, many of these limited English proficient* (LEP) students fall further and further behind in school, and overwhelming numbers drop out before finishing high school.

2 **The Government Response**

To cope with this problem, Congress passed the Bilingual Education Act in 1968, and subsequently amended* it five times, to provide federal funds to develop bilingual programs. Much of the expansion of bilingual programs in the 1970s can be attributed to a series of court cases, the most notable of which was the 1974 *Lau v. Nichols* U.S. Supreme Court case of *Lau v. Nichols.* The case involved a class-action suit on behalf of Chinese-speaking students in San Francisco, but it had implications* for all the nation's non–English-speaking children. The Court found "that there is no equality of treatment merely by providing students with the same facilities, textbooks, teachers, and curriculum; for students who do not understand English are effectively foreclosed* from any meaningful education." Basing its ruling on the Civil Rights Act of 1964, the Court held that the San Francisco school system unlawfully discriminated on the basis of national origin when it failed to cope with the children's language problems.

3 Although the *Lau* case did not mandate* bilingual education as the means to solve the problem, subsequent state cases did order bilingual programs. With the advice of an expert panel, the U.S. Office of Civil Rights suggested guidelines for school districts to follow, the so-called Lau Remedies. The guidelines "specified that language minority students should be taught academics in their primary home language until they could effectively benefit from English language instruction."

4 *Bilingual Education Models*

different models There are several types or models of bilingual education programs. The *transitional model* uses the child's native tongue only as an interim* medium of instruction until the child develops fluency* in English. Students move on to regular all-English classes as quickly as possible. The *immersion* model* requires students to learn English by being in a classroom of LEP students where the teacher understands their first language but speaks only in English. In *submersion model* classes, students attend all-English classes; they must "sink or swim" until they learn English. The *English as a second language (ESL) model* consists of regular classroom instruction for most of the day combined with a special pullout program of English-language instruction for one or more periods a day.

5 *Controversies*

Considerable controversy surrounds the whole issue of bilingual education. Whereas ethnic groups lobby strongly for expanded support for bilingual programs, others charge that bilingual pro

research evidence grams prevent minority groups from learning English. One major study examined over 300 bilingual program evaluations and concluded that the evidence supports a "structured immersion" approach where instruction is in English at a level the students can understand in a self-contained classroom consisting entirely of LEP students. Others conclude that a variety of programs for helping LEP students can be effective, and that the specific model of instruction should be chosen at the local level.

6 Despite this controversy, many school districts are in desperate

need for bilingual need of bilingual teachers, particularly those who speak Spanish
teachers and Asian languages. If you speak a second language or still have time to include learning a language in your college program, you could help meet a serious educational need and at the same time greatly enhance your employment opportunities.

Adapted from Kevin Ryan and James M. Cooper,
Those Who Can, Teach.
Boston: Houghton Mifflin, 1998, pp. 93–95.

CHECKING YOUR   **DIRECTIONS** Answer the following questions by circling the letter
COMPREHENSION of the correct response.

1. Which statement more effectively sums up the main idea of the entire reading?

a. The 1974 U.S. Supreme Court case *Lau v. Nichols* changed the face of American education, and the controversy surrounding that case continues to this day; in fact, there are signs that the controversy is heating up rather than cooling down.

b. Non–native speakers are at risk of failure in America's schools. In response to that problem, Congress passed the Bilingual Education Act in 1968, but it was the *Lau v. Nichols* case that had the most profound effect on bilingual education.

2. The *Lau v. Nichols* case involved

    a. Spanish-speaking students.

    b. Chinese-speaking students.

    c. Arabic-speaking students.

3. Although the author does not say it directly, you can infer that the students in the *Lau* case filed their suit against the

    a. federal government.

    b. San Francisco school system.

    c. U.S. Office of Civil Rights.

4. Which of the following statements more effectively paraphrases the Supreme Court's view on equality of treatment?

    a. Students who have not mastered English are required by law to attend bilingual classes until they pass an exam that indicates their English mastery.

    b. If students have not mastered English, giving them the same books, classrooms, teachers, and course work cannot be considered equal treatment.

5. What was the basis for the Court's ruling?

    a. the right to freedom of speech

    b. Title IX

    c. the Civil Rights Act of 1964

6. The Lau Remedies are

    a. court cases that followed in the wake of *Lau v. Nichols*.

    b. guidelines for school districts to follow.

    c. countersuits that challenged the ruling in *Lau v. Nichols*.

7. How many times was the Bilingual Education Act amended?

    a. twice

    b. three times

    c. five times

8. In paragraph 2, which sentence is the topic sentence?

   a. sentence 1

   b. sentence 2

   c. sentence 3

9. What pattern of organization can you see at work in paragraph 2?

   a. cause and effect

   b. classification

   c. process

10. If you were to take an exam on this reading, which of the following questions would you *not* expect to appear on the exam?

    a. Describe the effect of *Lau v. Nichols* on American education.

    b. What does the existing research tell us about the effects of speaking two languages?

    c. Name and describe each of the models for bilingual education.

SHARPENING YOUR CRITICAL SKILLS **DIRECTIONS** Answer the following questions by filling in the blanks or circling the letter of the correct response.

1. How would you describe the purpose of this reading?

   a. to inform

   b. to persuade

2. What are some of the clues that helped you identify the author's purpose?

   _____

   _____

   _____

3. Do you think the authors of this reading and the author of the reading "In Praise of Bilingualism" on page 430 of Chapter 11 share the same purpose?

   _____

   Please explain your answer.

   _____

4. Which of the following statements more effectively synthesizes the reading on page 430 with the reading you just finished?

a. Unlike the author of "In Praise of Bilingualism," the authors of this reading provide background on bilingual education and let the readers come to their own conclusions.

b. Although the authors of "Bilingual Education" do not say it as directly, they too, like the author of "In Praise of Bilingualism," recognize the importance of bilingual education.

5. The Bilingual Education Act was amended five different times. What inference could safely be drawn from this fact?

a. Because the act addressed a complicated and controversial issue, it needed to be modified more than once.

b. The American public did not support the bill.

c. Some members of the Congress did not want the bill to succeed.

6. In paragraph 5, the authors sum up the controversy over bilingual education. Then they cite several pieces of research. That research offers support for which side of the controversy?

_____

7. One of the models for bilingual education is called the *immersion method*. Look back at the meaning of the word *immersion*. This method of teaching a second language is implicitly being compared to what physical action?

_____

This is an example of what kind of figurative language?

a. simile

b. metaphor

c. analogy

8. What statement more effectively describes the authors' use of language?

a. The authors' language is factual and denotative.

b. The language is highly connotative and thick with opinion.

9. In the last paragraph of the reading, the authors make a suggestion to readers. Based on that suggestion, it would be safe to draw what inference concerning the authors' personal feelings?

a. The authors strongly support bilingual education.

b. The authors believe that bilingual education is not going to disappear in the near future.

10. How would you describe the authors' tone?

_____

■ **DRAWING YOUR OWN CONCLUSIONS**   What is your position on bilingual education? Are you for or against it?

■ **WRITING SUGGESTIONS**

1. Summarize paragraphs 1 through 3, reducing them to one clear, concise paragraph.

2. Write an essay question that you think would effectively test someone's understanding of this reading.

■ **READING 3**

THE EFFECTS OF BILINGUALISM

LOOKING AHEAD Here's another perspective on bilingualism. This reading is less concerned with bilingual education and more concerned with how speaking two languages affects the way we think.

GETTING FOCUSED Read the first and last paragraphs, along with the headings. Then read the first sentence of the remaining paragraphs and all the words in **Word Watch.** Based on your survey, what do you predict: Do the authors think that speaking two languages has a positive or negative effect? Or is it a little bit of both?

_____

_____

This reading is somewhat technical in places, so take your time and paraphrase to monitor your comprehension. Mark paragraphs for a second reading or even a third if you think it's necessary. It's a well-kept secret but even the most experienced readers frequently reread to understand the meaning of a paragraph or passage.

WORD WATCH Some of the more difficult words in the reading are defined in this section. Watch for these words as you read. They are marked with an asterisk. When you finish the reading, review the words in **Word Watch** by covering up the definitions and checking to see if you now know all the meanings. Record any words you still don't know in a notebook or on index cards. Review them periodically until they are part of your vocabulary.

---

monolinguals: people who speak only one language

cognitive: related to thinking

arbitrary: not planned

presumably: assuming without testing or proving

facilitate: ease or aid

---

1 ALTHOUGH MOST MONOLINGUALS* MAY NOT REALIZE IT, A MAjority of children around the world are able to speak two languages and therefore are bilingual (Paulston, 1988). Bilingualism is common in the United States even though the nation is officially monolingual; somewhere between 30 million and 75 million

individuals (about 10 to 15 percent) regularly use another language in addition to English (United States Bureau of the Census, 1993). Does this skill benefit their cognitive* development? Research suggests that it does, but primarily when they acquire both languages equally well and when both languages are treated with respect by teachers and other representatives of the community (Bialystok & Hakuta, 1994). Language specialists call such children **balanced bilinguals.**

Cognitive Effects of Bilingualism

2 For one thing, balanced bilingual children show greater cognitive flexibility—skill at detecting multiple meanings of words and alternative orientations of objects—than monolingual children do. Bilingual children can substitute arbitrary* words for normally occurring words relatively easily without changing any other features of the sentence. If asked to substitute *spaghetti* for *I* in the sentence "I am cold," bilingual children more often produce the exact substitution "Spaghetti am cold" and resist the temptation to correct the grammar ("Spaghetti is cold"), thereby violating the instructions for the task. Presumably* such a skill stems from bilinguals' special experience with the arbitrary, conventional nature of words and language.

3   In part, such flexibility shows **metalinguistic awareness,** the knowledge that language can be an object of thought. Metalinguistic awareness develops because bilingual experiences often challenge children to think consciously about what to say and how to say it (Jimenez et al., 1995). A question such as "What if a dog were called a cat?" therefore poses fewer problems for bilinguals. So do follow-up questions such as "Would this 'cat' meow?" or "Would it purr?"

4   However, all of these cognitive advantages apply primarily to balanced bilingual children, those with equal skill in both languages. What about the unbalanced bilinguals, those with more skill in one language than in the other? Does knowledge of a second language help, even if it is limited? Evidence is scarce, but what there is suggests that unbalanced bilingualism has mixed effects on children's thinking skills, largely because of the interplay of social attitudes surrounding language differences in society (Pease-Alvarez, 1993).

Social Effects of Bilingualism

5 When children acquire two languages, one language usually has more prestige than the other. In the United States, the "best," or most important, language almost always is English. Its prestige results not only from its widespread use but also from its association with success and power: all the important people in

American society, it seems, speak English fluently. These circumstances create negative attitudes or stereotypes about people who speak other languages and challenge educators to overcome social prejudices at the same time they facilitate* learning new grammar, vocabulary, and usage.

6   The influence of language on attitudes has been well documented through experiments using the *matched guise technique* (Giles & Coupland, 1991). In this type of experiment, perfectly balanced and fluent bilinguals tape record standard messages in each of their two languages, and the messages are interspersed among other tape-recorded messages to disguise the identities of the bilingual speakers. Then listeners evaluate the competence and social attractiveness of each speaker. Time after time, two consistent trends occur in studies of this type. First, speakers of English are rated more highly than speakers of other languages. Second, listeners from non–English-speaking cultural groups rate the English speakers more highly than they do speakers of their own language. The prestige of English, in other words, comes from sources in addition to English speakers themselves.

7   Negative attitudes toward non-English languages reduce children's school performance by making them less willing to use their primary, or first, language in public and reducing their self-confidence about linguistic skills in general. Fortunately, however, educational programs exist that can counteract these effects by treating children's first language as an educational resource rather than a liability.

8   Overall, research favors *additive bilingual education,* programs that develop language skills in *both* of a child's languages rather than attempting to replace a first language with English (Perez & Torres-Guzman, 1992). As a practical matter, such programs usually are conducted partly in each language, depending on children's current language skills, but they do not confine either language to isolated "lessons" lasting only short periods each day. The challenge is a double one: to foster new language skills while also promoting respect for a child's original language and culture. In countries where language is less strongly associated with economic or social status (for example, Canada, where about 25 percent of the population speaks French as a first language), bilingual education often does not include this double agenda. Therefore, successful bilingual programs more often emphasize simple immersion in a second language and tend to ignore a child's first language without negative educational effects (Lambert et al., 1993).

Kelvin L. Seifert and Robert J. Hoffnung, *Child and Adolescent Development,* 4/e. Boston: Houghton Mifflin, 1997, pp. 380–381.

CHECKING
YOUR
COMPREHENSION

DIRECTIONS Answer the following questions by circling the letter of the correct response.

1. Which of the following statements more effectively paraphrases the main idea of this reading?

   a. Being bilingual has a powerful effect on the way we think. Those who are bilingual tend to be more flexible in their thinking and are more comfortable with complex ideas that do not readily lend themselves to easy answers.

   b. Research suggests that bilingualism is beneficial if both languages have been mastered equally well and are treated with equal respect in the culture.

2. According to the authors, what portion of the population is bilingual?

   a. about 12 to 14 percent of the population is bilingual.

   b. about 10 to 15 percent of the population is bilingual.

   c. about 20 to 25 percent of the population is bilingual.

3. The term *metalinguistic awareness* means that language

   a. can be an object of thought.

   b. shapes how we see the world.

   c. is bound to distort how we see the world.

4. According to the authors, children who acquire two languages usually discover that

   a. the quality of their thinking improves.

   b. they enjoy comparing the way two different languages express the same ideas.

   c. one language has more prestige than the other.

5. According to the authors, balanced bilinguals

   a. speak two languages equally well and switch back and forth between them almost without thinking.

   b. are psychologically more stable.

   c. speak two languages equally well and sense that both languages are equally respected in their culture.

6. In paragraph 2, the topic sentence is

   a. sentence 1.

   b. sentence 2.

   c. sentence 3.

7. The phrase "spaghetti am cold" is a supporting detail that illustrates which main idea?

    a. To be skillful users of two languages, children need to know that both of those languages are of equal value in their culture.

    b. Being bilingual can increase one's ability to be a flexible thinker.

    c. If monolingual children are asked to use nonsense words in sentences, they are likely to distort the original meaning of the sentence.

8. Which statement more effectively paraphrases the topic sentence of paragraph 6?

    a. There is a good deal of research suggesting that bilingual children have better social skills.

    b. There is a good deal of evidence suggesting that language affects attitude.

9. Paragraph 4 opens with a transition that signals

    a. cause and effect.

    b. contrast.

    c. classification.

10. Based on this reading, which test question do you think would *not* appear on an exam?

    a. Define and illustrate the term *metalinguistic awareness*.

    b. What technique has been used to document the influence of language on attitude?

    c. Given the benefits of being bilingual, why have bilingual education programs come under attack?

SHARPENING YOUR CRITICAL SKILLS **DIRECTIONS** Answer the following questions by filling in the blanks or circling the letter of the correct response.

1. How would you describe the author's purpose?

    _____

2. How did you arrive at your answer? What clues to purpose did you use?

    _____

    _____

3. Paragraph 5 offers what opinion about bilingualism?

_____

4. What kind of evidence do the authors offer in support of that opinion?

_____

5. What generalization opens paragraph 8?

_____

Why might critical readers think twice about that generalization?

_____

6. What word in paragraph 7 reveals something about the authors'

point of view? _____

7. Who would be more likely to use the research cited in this reading as evidence for their position?

    a. those who support bilingual programs

    b. those who want to do away with bilingual programs

Please explain your inference. _____

_____

8. In paragraph 5, the authors suggest that in countries all over the world "when children acquire two languages, one language usually has more prestige than the other." What evidence in the reading seems to suggest that this statement may be true about the United States but not necessarily true of other countries?

_____

_____

9. This reading offers support for a point made by Judith Ortiz Cofer in reading 1. What is that point?

_____

_____

10. Which statement accurately describes the authors' bias?

    a. Under the right conditions, the authors think bilingualism should be encouraged.

    b. The authors think that bilingualism may actually do more harm than good.

    c. It's impossible to determine the authors' personal feelings.

DRAWING YOUR OWN CONCLUSIONS Did the reading you just completed in any way affect your position on bilingual education? Please explain why or why not.

Do you speak more than one language? If you do, describe the advantages or the disadvantages of being bilingual.

WRITING SUGGESTION Write an essay in which you begin by taking a stand for or against bilingual education. Make sure to argue your position with sound reasons and specific illustrations. Feel free to cite as part of your argument either of the readings you have just completed.

■ **READING 4**

CONVERSATIONAL BALLGAMES

LOOKING AHEAD   Nancy Masterson Sakamoto, the author of the following reading, speaks her second language—in this case, Japanese—just fine. The problem is she doesn't fully understand the conversational rules of her host country. An American overseas, she thinks the rules of talk are the same everywhere. In this instance, at least, she couldn't be more wrong.

GETTING FOCUSED   Read the first and last paragraphs. Then read all the words in **Word Watch.** Based on your survey, make a prediction: Will the author figure out the rules of Japanese conversation?

_____

_____

As your read, see if you can determine the various ways in which a conversation can be like a ballgame, and don't be afraid to pick up your pace with this reading. Much less technical than the last two readings, it probably will not require the same level of concentration, so relax and enjoy the author's sense of humor.

WORD WATCH   Some of the more difficult words in the reading are defined in this section. Watch for these words as you read. They are marked with an asterisk. When you finish the reading, review the words in **Word Watch** by covering up the definitions and checking to see if you now know all the meanings. Record any words you still don't know in a notebook or on index cards. Review them periodically until they are part of your vocabulary.

vigorous: strong, forceful	**instinctively:** without thinking
parallel: being an equal distance apart at every point	**indispensable:** absolutely necessary
belatedly: not on time	**etiquette:** rules for correct behavior

1 AFTER I WAS MARRIED AND HAD LIVED IN JAPAN FOR A WHILE, my Japanese gradually improved to the point where I could take part in simple conversations with my husband and his friends and family. And I began to notice that often, when I joined in, the others would look startled, and the conversational topic would come to a halt. After this happened several times, it became clear to me that I was doing something wrong. But for a long time, I didn't know what it was.

2 Finally, after listening carefully to many Japanese conversations, I discovered what my problem was. Even though I was speaking Japanese, I was handling the conversation in a western way.

3 Japanese-style conversations develop quite differently from western-style conversations. And the difference isn't only in the languages. I realized that just as I kept trying to hold western-style conversations even when I was speaking Japanese, so my English students kept trying to hold Japanese-style conversations even when they were speaking English. We were unconsciously playing entirely different conversational ballgames.

4 A western-style conversation between two people is like a game of tennis. If I introduce a topic, a conversational ball, I expect you to hit it back. If you agree with me, I don't expect you simply to agree and do nothing more. I expect you to add something—a reason for agreeing, another example, or an elaboration to carry the idea further. But I don't expect you always to agree. I am just as happy if you question me or challenge me, or completely disagree with me. Whether you agree or disagree, your response will return the ball to me.

5 And then it is my turn again. I don't serve a new ball from my original starting line. I hit your ball back again from where it has bounced. I carry your idea further, or answer your questions or objections, or challenge or question you. And so the ball goes back and forth, with each of us doing our best to give it a new twist, an original spin, or a powerful smash.

6 And the more vigorous* the action, the more interesting and exciting the game. Of course, if one of us gets angry, it spoils the conversation, just as it spoils a tennis game. But getting excited is not at all the same as getting angry. After all, we are not trying to hit each other. We are trying to hit the ball. So long as we attack only each other's opinions, and do not attack each other personally, we don't expect anyone to get hurt. A good conversation is supposed to be interesting and exciting.

7 If there are more than two people in the conversation, then it is like doubles in tennis, or like volleyball. There's no waiting in line.

Whoever is nearest and quickest hits the ball, and if you step back, someone else will hit it. No one stops the game to give you a turn. You're responsible for taking your own turn. But whether it's two players or a group, everyone does his best to keep the ball going, and no one person has the ball for very long.

8   A Japanese-style conversation, however, is not at all like tennis or volleyball. It's like bowling. You wait for your turn. And you always know your place in line. It depends on such things as whether you are older or younger, a close friend or a relative stranger to the previous speaker, in a senior or junior position, and so on. When your turn comes, you step up to the starting line with your bowling ball, and carefully bowl it. Everyone else stands back and watches politely, murmuring encouragement. Everyone waits until the ball has reached the end of the alley, and watches to see if it knocks down all the pins, or only some of them, or none of them. There is a pause, while everyone registers your score. Then, after everyone is sure that you have completely finished your turn, the next person in line steps up to the same starting line, with a different ball. He doesn't return your ball, and he does not begin from where your ball stopped. There is no back and forth at all. All the balls run parallel.* And there is always a suitable pause between turns. There is no rush, no excitement, no scramble for the ball.

9   No wonder everyone looked startled when I took part in Japanese conversations. I paid no attention to whose turn it was, and kept snatching the ball halfway down the alley and throwing it back at the bowler. Of course the conversation died. I was playing the wrong game.

10   This explains why it is almost impossible to get a western-style conversation or discussion going with English students in Japan. I used to think that the problem was their lack of English language ability. But I finally came to realize that the biggest problem is that they, too, are playing the wrong game. Whenever I serve a volleyball, everyone just stands back and watches it fall, with occasional murmurs of encouragement. No one hits it back. Everyone waits until I call on someone to take a turn. And when that person speaks, he doesn't hit my ball back. He serves a new ball. Again, everyone just watches it fall. So I call on someone else. This person does not refer to what the previous speaker has said. He also serves a new ball. Nobody seems to have paid any attention to what anyone else has said. Everyone begins again from the same starting line, and all the balls run parallel. There is never any back and forth. Everyone is trying to bowl with a volleyball.

11   And if I try a simpler conversation, with only two of us, then the other person tries to bowl with my tennis ball. No wonder foreign English teachers in Japan get discouraged.

12   Now that you know about the difference in the conversational ballgames, you may think that all your troubles are over. But if you have been trained all your life to play one game, it is no simple matter to switch to another, even if you know the rules. Knowing the rules is not at all the same thing as playing the game. Even now, during a conversation in Japanese I will notice a startled reaction, and belatedly* realize that once again I have rudely interrupted by instinctively* trying to hit back the other person's bowling ball. It is no easier for me to "just listen" during a conversation, than it is for my Japanese students to "just relax" when speaking with foreigners. Now I can truly sympathize with how hard they must find it to try to carry on a western-style conversation.

13   If I have not yet learned to do conversational bowling in Japanese, at least I have figured out one thing that puzzled me for a long time. After his first trip to America, my husband complained that Americans asked him so many questions and made him talk so much at the dinner table that he never had a chance to eat. When I asked him why he couldn't talk and eat at the same time, he said that Japanese do not customarily think that dinner, especially on fairly formal occasions, is a suitable time for extended conversation.

14   Since westerners think that conversation is an indispensable* part of dining, and indeed would consider it impolite not to converse with one's dinner partner, I found this Japanese custom rather strange. Still, I could accept it as a cultural difference even though I didn't really understand it. But when my husband added, in explanation, that Japanese consider it extremely rude to talk with one's mouth full, I got confused. Talking with one's mouth full is certainly not an American custom. We think it very rude, too. Yet we still manage to talk a lot and eat at the same time. How do we do it?

15   For a long time, I couldn't explain it, and it bothered me. But after I discovered the conversational ballgames, I finally found the answer. Of course! In a western-style conversation, you hit the ball, and while someone else is hitting it back, you take a bite, chew, and swallow. Then you hit the ball again, and then eat some more. The more people there are in the conversation, the more chances you have to eat. But even with only two of you talking, you still have plenty of chances to eat. Maybe that's why polite conversation at the dinner table has never been a traditional

part of Japanese etiquette.* Your turn to talk would last so long without interruption that you'd never get a chance to eat.

Nancy Masterson Sakamoto,
"Conversational Ballgames," in Polite Fictions,
Kinseido, Ltd., 1982.

CHECKING YOUR COMPREHENSION **DIRECTIONS** Answer the following questions by circling the letter of the correct response.

1. Which statement more effectively paraphrases the main idea of the entire reading?

   a. Speaking Japanese fluently doesn't necessarily mean one knows how to play by Japan's polite conversational rules.

   b. Americans may learn how to speak Japanese, but they will never learn the Japanese code of polite behavior.

2. According to the author, a western-style conversation between the two people is like a game of

   a. volleyball.

   b. stickball.

   c. tennis.

3. A Japanese-style conversation, in contrast, is like

   a. poker.

   b. chess.

   c. bowling.

4. Although the author does not volunteer the information, you can infer that she learned to speak Japanese because

   a. she had a scholarship to study in Japan.

   b. she married a man from Japan.

   c. her grandmother was born in Japan.

5. Which statement more effectively paraphrases the two-step topic sentence in paragraph 8?

   a. Japanese conversations are more like bowling than they are like tennis.

   b. In a Japanese conversation, you wait your turn.

6. In paragraph 12, the author describes the "startled reaction" of her Japanese conversational partner. Which main idea does this supporting detail serve to develop?

a. Once you learn the rules of Japanese conversation, you can transform your behavior and take your conversational hosts by surprise.

b. Knowing the rules of Japanese conversation does not mean that you can automatically abandon western-style conversational techniques.

7. Paragraph 8 relies on transitions that help the reader

a. link cause and effect.

b. follow events in time.

c. compare and contrast two topics.

8. The reading as a whole relies on which pattern?

a. cause and effect

b. definition

c. comparison and contrast

9. Paragraph 14 contains three different transitions. All three of those transitions signal

a. contrast.

b. similarity.

c. cause and effect.

10. According to the author, conversation at the Japanese dinner table is not a tradition because

a. the Japanese think food should be eaten in silence to show appreciation for the cook.

b. the Japanese rules of conversation would never give the person speaking a chance to eat.

SHARPENING YOUR CRITICAL SKILLS **DIRECTIONS** Answer the following questions by filling in the blanks or circling the letter of the correct response.

1. How would you describe the purpose of this reading?

a. This essay was written solely to entertain.

b. Meant to be entertaining, this essay also informs.

c. Meant to be entertaining, the essay also tries to persuade readers that western-style conversations are more satisfying than Japanese-style conversations.

2. Based on the reading, which inference do you think is appropriate?

    a. The chances are good that with the passage of time, the author will no longer have trouble following the conversational rules of her adopted country.

    b. Even with the passage of time, it is doubtful that the author will be able to completely abandon the conversational habits of her native tongue.

3. The author says "a western-style conversation between two people is like a game of tennis." Is that a simile or metaphor?

_____

4. Explain how a conversation can be like a game of tennis.

_____

5. Throughout the reading the author refers to the topic of the conversation as a _____. Is she speaking literally or figuratively? _____

6. If more than two people take part in a conversation, the author compares the conversation to what? _____.
Does she use a simile or a metaphor to make that comparison? _____

7. What comparison does the author make in order to describe a Japanese-style conversation?

_____

This comparison helps make the point that in a Japanese conversation you always have to _____

8. How would you describe the author's tone?

    a. lighthearted

    b. angry

    c. emotionally neutral

9. Which of the following does *not* contribute to the author's tone?

    a. figurative language

    b. references to her personal life

    c. highly charged language

10. Which statement most effectively sums up the author's bias?

    a. The author does not favor one set of conversational rules over the other.

    b. The author clearly thinks that the Japanese rules of conversation are silly.

    c. The author clearly thinks that Americans could learn a lot from the Japanese.

DRAWING YOUR OWN CONCLUSIONS Do you think the author's account of conversational differences between cultures rings true? Why or why not? Do you have any experience carrying on a conversation in a foreign language? If so, did you ever sense that the other person might be playing by different conversational rules? If your answer is yes, please describe what you noticed.

WRITING SUGGESTION Try your hand at creating similes that help make the following situations more vivid for readers.

1. The two friends were wildly happy to see one another. They were like _____

_____.

2. Everyone was getting a bit bored by the happy couple's endless displays of affection, which were like _____

_____.

■ **READING 5**

Television's Influence on America at War

LOOKING AHEAD This reading returns to a topic briefly discussed in Chapters 2 and 3—how television shapes our perception, or understanding, of events, particularly during times of war and following acts of terrorism.

GETTING FOCUSED Read the first and last paragraph, all the headings and the first sentence of every paragraph following those headings. Then read all the words listed in **Word Watch.** Based on your survey, do you think the authors believe that television has had a powerful effect on our attitudes toward war and how it is conducted?

_____

_____

This is certainly a reading where you can apply your own background knowledge to the subject under discussion. How do you feel about the role of television in wartime? Do you think television should be allowed to bring war into your living room? In contrast to the previous reading, this reading is rather technical, so adjust your pace accordingly. Remember to check your comprehension regularly by posing and answering test questions for each section of the reading.

WORD WATCH Some of the more difficult words in the reading are defined in this section. Watch for these words as you read. They are marked with an asterisk. When you finish the reading, review the words in **Word Watch** by covering up the definitions and checking to see if you now know all the meanings. Record any words you still don't know in a notebook or on index cards. Review them periodically until they are part of your vocabulary.

---

morale: attitude

sanitized: made acceptable by removing what is unpleasant or disturbing

gore: blood, often from a wound

blatant: obvious

icons: images, symbols

> **untenable:** incapable of being held
>
> **alleging:** claiming without proof
>
> **subsequent:** following
>
> **aura:** atmosphere
>
> **disquieting:** disturbing
>
> **paradoxically:** having the opposite effect of what one would expect, seeming to be a contradiction but actually making sense upon more thought
>
> **manipulation:** trickery

1 DURING WORLD WAR II (1939–1945), BROADCAST RADIO'S FIRST war, network news and entertainment played a highly supportive role in building both civilian and military morale.* In the years that followed, however, television played a more complicated role in the conduct of war.

Vietnam

2 Television's first war coverage came with the Vietnam conflict (the Korean War of 1950–1953 occurred during the formative years of television news, when live coverage from such a remote distance was impossible). Television coverage for the 1965–1975 decade made Vietnam a "living room war," in the words of *New Yorker* critic Michael Arlen (1969).

3 In total, this longest war in U.S. history played in living rooms for 15 years. CBS sent its first combat news team to Vietnam in 1961, and news photography of the final evacuation of Saigon, showing desperate pro-American Vietnamese being beaten back as helicopters lifted off the landing pad atop the U.S. embassy, came in 1975.

4 At first, Vietnam coverage tended to be "sanitized,"* stressing U.S. efficiency and military might, and playing down the gore* and suffering of actual combat. Although little direct military censorship was imposed, as had been the case in previous wars, in this undeclared war generals and presidents had public relations uppermost in their minds. Thus control of access to events could serve the same end as more blatant* censorship.

5 A more violent phase of news coverage came as a result of the early 1968 Tet offensive, which brought fighting to the very doors of the Saigon hotels where correspondents stayed. Broadcast news from a host of network and local-station reporters turned increasingly to combat realities, and Vietnam became a real war in American living rooms, not the sanitized version of military public relations.

6   Following the Tet offensive by the North Vietnamese, several events combined to turn U.S. opinion against the war. Television's leading journalist, CBS's Walter Cronkite, gave a sharply negative assessment of the war after a visit to Vietnam. Loss of Cronkite's support for the war was said to have solidified President Lyndon Johnson's decision not to run for reelection. At about the same time, vivid photographic images from the battlefields became icons* of American disillusionment.

More Wars

7 Television's effect on public perception of the Vietnam conflict raised troublesome questions about future war reporting. Could a nation at war afford to allow television freely to bring home the horror of combat night after night?

8   In 1983 terrorist bombing that killed some 240 Americans in a U.S. Marine barracks in Beirut seemed a case in point. Television coverage of the bombing's aftermath undermined public support for the "peacekeeping" role of the Marines in Lebanon, making the venture politically untenable.* American troops pulled out shortly thereafter.

9   On the other hand, would the public support a war that was made temporarily invisible by rigid military censorship? To the dismay of journalists, a U.S. invasion of the tiny Caribbean island of Grenada in 1984 suggested that it might. Alleging* security concerns, the military barred all media access to the initial assault. For the first forty-eight hours the world knew what happened only from military press releases. Subsequent* press disclosures of military bumbling in the invasion and apparent official misrepresentation of circumstances leading to the attack came too late to dispel entirely the aura* of success and righteousness surrounding the Grenada "rescue" of American civilians allegedly endangered by the volatile political situation on the island.

10   The public largely supported the action and applauded the administration's decision to limit media access—and impact. Strong media criticism of this abrupt departure from prior practice, however, led to agreement that in future actions the military would set up a news pool to cover events from the outset.

11   In the 1980s, Reagan administration efforts to bring down the Sandinista regime in Nicaragua and related guerrilla fighting in several Central American countries served as testing grounds for television journalism's post-Grenada maturity. Controversy surrounded coverage of these conflicts. New Right politicians claimed that television weakened efforts to gain public support for "freedom fighters"; others, remembering Vietnam, said that aggressive

television coverage might serve to keep American soldiers out of another prolonged, undeclared conflict.

12   When President Bush sent troops to Panama to help remove President Manuel Noriega from power, the media were critical of the press pools set up by the military. According to many correspondents covering that action, media personnel once again were not allowed to accompany the combat troops and were admitted to battle areas only after most of the fighting had ceased.

Persian Gulf Crisis

13 Lessons learned in all these events heavily influenced television's coverage of and impact on the 1990–1991 Gulf War, when the United States led a successful UN effort to throw Iraqi troops out of occupied Kuwait. The Pentagon invoked strong censorship and pooling of reporters, making it almost impossible for the media to report from troop sites during the months-long build-up unless a military public-affairs officer was present (SGAC, 1991).

14   An intense war began in mid-January 1991 and was seen live on American East Coast television screens in prime time as CNN cameras in Baghdad focused on falling bombs and anti-aircraft fire. Reporters Peter Arnett and Bernard Shaw continued live *voice*casts from Baghdad by means of a high-tech satellite telephone.

15   When reporters questioned Pentagon officials the next day as to the impact of initial bombing runs, officers made clear that much of what they knew had come from the same CNN reports seen by everyone else. That pattern was evident in the first few days of the air war, when (as shown by research) 44 percent of those turning to television watched CNN coverage while 41 percent turned to one of the three traditional broadcast networks (Birch Scarborough, 1991: 9). Later analyses often attributed CNN's "arrival" as an accepted news source to its stellar role in reporting all aspects of the Gulf conflict.

16   Even more than had been the case with Vietnam, Operation Desert Storm—thanks to time-zone differences and satellite relays, as well as around-the-clock reporting—was a "living room war" in American prime time. But it was a far more *controlled* television war than Vietnam had been, the result of tight Pentagon limits on media access to troops and events—and of censorship, often directed more at the possible political impact of negative coverage than at any military security need.

17   Only months after the war was over did disquieting* television reports about Iraqi civilian losses, allied soldiers killed by "friendly fire," and attempted cover-ups of other military mistakes become widely reported—but by then few were paying attention.

Pentagon and administration officials called the Gulf War press pools a model for future conflict coverage, while reporters argued the opposite—that censorship had prevented their usual multifaceted job of reporting.

18   Most public-opinion surveys found that viewers were generally satisfied with what they had seen and believed military controls to have been justified. The controversy arose again when television images of starving women and children pressured the United States to send troops to Somalia to help stabilize that country. Military personnel attempting to disembark on the beaches of Somalia under cover of darkness were met by the bright lights of the television cameras, recording their every action. Public opinion turned against U.S. participation after several of the troops were killed and their bodies were shown being abused by their killers. It seemed likely the contest of wills over the "proper" role of news media in wartime would continue into the *next* war.

Terrorism

19 News media problems took a vicious turn when terrorist organizations began committing crimes to gain news coverage. In the 1980s small and desperate political or religious groups seeking world attention increasingly employed violence against usually innocent third parties. Such *publicity crimes* paradoxically* transform pseudoevents into real events.

20   Bombings of airport terminals and subway stations, hijackings, and kidnappings, the most common kinds of terrorist stories, pose difficult ethical dilemmas for all news media. The very act of reporting a publicity crime transforms media into accomplices, and the eagerness with which the public awaits news about it makes all of us inadvertent accomplices as well.

21   Observers complain that television's massive coverage encourages future terrorists by providing them with an international forum. Criticism focuses especially on coverage of news conferences staged and controlled by terrorists, whereby media appear captive to terrorist manipulation.* Cable and broadcast news people often counter that they are merely accommodating the public's insatiable demand for more coverage. And surely these criticisms do not apply to terrorist acts such as the Oklahoma City or Olympic Park bombings, where no terrorist group came forward to claim "credit" for the actions.

Sydney W. Head, Christopher H. Sterling, and
Lemuel B. Schofield, *Broadcasting in America*, 8/e.
Boston: Houghton Mifflin,
1998, pp. 311–314.

CHECKING YOUR COMPREHENSION

DIRECTIONS Answer the following questions by circling the letter of the correct response.

1. Which statement most effectively sums up the main idea of the entire reading?

   a. Since World War II, television has assumed an increasingly important role in how we view both war and terrorism.

   b. Because of the way the war in Vietnam was televised, the American military lost public support and was forced to withdraw.

   c. On the whole, the American public strongly supports censorship of the press during wartime and following acts of terrorism.

2. According to the reading, televised coverage of the Vietnam War became more violent after

   a. Dien Bien Phu.

   b. the Tet offensive.

   c. the shootings at Kent State.

3. According to the reading, strict press censorship was enforced

   a. during the Vietnam War.

   b. after the bombing of the Marine barracks in Beirut.

   c. during the Gulf War.

4. When the military strictly limited media access during the war in Grenada, the public

   a. didn't care.

   b. was outraged.

   c. supported the military's position.

5. Which sentence more effectively paraphrases the topic sentence in paragraph 6?

   a. Several different events contributed to Walter Cronkite's decision to publicly criticize the Vietnam War.

   b. There is more than one reason why public support of the Vietnam War changed so dramatically.

6. Which statement more effectively paraphrases the two-step topic sentence in paragraph 9?

   a. Generally speaking, the American public supports censorship during wartime.

    b. The U.S. invasion of Grenada suggested that the public would accept censorship during wartime.

7. Which sentence more effectively synthesizes the main ideas of the sections titled "Vietnam" and "Persian Gulf Crisis"?

    a. Having learned during the war in Vietnam that television could have a powerful effect on public support, the American military kept a tight rein on the press throughout the Gulf War.

    b. During the Vietnam War, the American military learned how to control the press's access to information, and they used that knowledge very effectively during the Gulf War.

8. Overall, the reading combines which two patterns of organization?

    a. process and classification

    b. cause and effect and sequence of dates and events

    c. comparison and contrast and definition

9. In paragraph 16, what type of transition is essential to following the writers' train of thought?

    a. a transition signaling cause and effect

    b. a transition signaling contrast

    c. a transition signaling dates and events

10. Based on this reading, what do you think is a likely test question?

    a. Compare and contrast the press coverage of the wars in Vietnam and the Persian Gulf.

    b. Describe how radio created and maintained support for World War II.

    c. Trace the chain of events that led the United States to go to war with Grenada.

SHARPENING YOUR CRITICAL SKILLS | DIRECTIONS Answer the following questions by filling in the blanks or circling the letter of the correct response.

1. How would you describe the purpose of this reading?

    a. The authors want to inform their readers about the influence of television on war and describe efforts made to control that influence.

    b. The authors want to persuade their readers that television has had too much influence on American military policy and ultimately done more harm than good.

2. What elements or characteristics of the reading helped you determine its purpose?

_____

_____

3. In paragraph 2, the authors say "television's first war coverage came with the Vietnam conflict." Is that a fact or an opinion?

_____

Please explain. _____

4. In paragraph 4, the authors say that during the Vietnam War, "generals and presidents had public relations uppermost in their minds."

Is that a fact or an opinion? _____

Please explain. _____

5. In paragraphs 4 and 5, the authors say that initially the Vietnam War coverage was "sanitized." Used in the context of medicine, objects are made sanitary by removing all elements, such as bacteria, that might injure health, but what do the authors have in mind when they use the word _sanitized_ in this context?

_____

Are they using the word literally or figuratively? _____

6. When the authors call the war in Vietnam a "living room war" (paragraph 2), what do they mean?

_____

Are they speaking literally or figuratively? _____

7. In paragraph 9, the authors say that the military were "alleging security concerns." By using the word _alleging_, the authors suggest what about those security concerns? (If you need to, refer to **Word Watch** to refresh your memory about the meaning of _alleging_.)

a. Those concerns were ridiculous.

b. They may not have had a basis in reality.

c. The military was lying to the American public.

8. How would you describe the authors' tone? _____

9. How would you describe the authors' personal feelings?

   a. They approve of military censorship of the media during wartime.

   b. They disapprove of military censorship of the media during wartime.

   c. It's impossible to determine the authors' personal feelings.

10. In paragraph 21, the authors describe the position of observers who "complain that television's massive coverage encourages future terrorists." Do you think the authors agree with that position? _____

   Please explain. _____

   _____

DRAWING YOUR OWN CONCLUSIONS What is television's responsibility during wartime? Should it concentrate on keeping morale high or on telling the American public what is really happening at the scene of battle? Whatever your position, please explain your reasoning.

WRITING SUGGESTION Write a paper in which you argue for or against the need to sanitize the news during wartime. Begin your paper by summarizing the shift in television coverage described in the reading under the heading "Vietnam"—from a sanitized version of the war to a no-holds-barred version that revealed the war's gore and suffering. Then explain why you think the shift was or was not necessary. Was it beneficial to the American public or not? Remember to give specific reasons for your opinion. Complete the paper by identifying and responding to objections that might be raised about your position.

■ **READING 6**

THE TRAGEDY OF JAPANESE INTERNMENT

LOOKING AHEAD Like "Conversational Ballgames," this reading also focuses on Japanese-American relations, but from a much more somber point of view. In 1942, Franklin Delano Roosevelt—over the protests of his wife, Eleanor—signed Executive Order 9066. The selection that follows describes the misery and suffering Roosevelt's decision inflicted on Japanese Americans when they were rounded up, forced to sell their possessions, and herded into makeshift camps, where they either froze or sweltered.

GETTING FOCUSED Read the first and last paragraphs along with the headings. Then read all the words in **Word Watch.** What event would you predict played a key role in the creation of the internment camps?

As you read, ask yourself how it was possible that innocent people could be so badly treated without any public outcry.

WORD WATCH Some of the more difficult words in the reading are defined in this section. Watch for these words as you read. They are marked with an asterisk. When you finish the reading, review the words in **Word Watch** by covering up the definitions and checking to see if you now know all the meanings. Record any words you still don't know in a notebook or on index cards. Review them periodically until they are part of your vocabulary.

euphemisms: words that hide a harsh or disturbing reality

refuge: place of safety

unscrupulous: lacking any moral or ethical sense

affiliation: connection

foremost: most important

fervor: intense emotional feelings

dereliction: neglect, abandonment

reticent: shy, withdrawn

rebuff: rejection

unsubstantiated: unproven, lacking in evidence

reparations: repayments for injury

1 ON THE MORNING OF DECEMBER 7, 1941, JAPANESE SUB-
marines and carrier planes launched an attack on the U.S. Pacific
Fleet at Pearl Harbor. Two hundred American aircraft were destroyed, eight battleships were sunk, and approximately eight
thousand naval and military personnel were killed or wounded.
This savage attack and its horrifying consequences propelled the
United States into World War II.

2 For people of Japanese descent living in the United States—
both the American born *Nissei* and the Japanese born *Issei*—the
attack on Pearl Harbor was doubly catastrophic. It was tragic
enough that their adopted country was going to war with the land
of their ancestors. But the attack on Pearl Harbor also unleashed
a storm of fury and outrage against America's Japanese citizens.
The result was *Executive Order 9066,* issued in February 1942.
Signed by the president of the United States, Franklin Delano Roosevelt, the order condemned 120,000 Japanese Americans—two-
thirds of them native born—to be evacuated from their homes
and interned in camps for the duration of the war. Even some
Japanese Americans who had volunteered to fight for the United
States were viewed as potential spies. They were stripped of their
uniforms and sent to relocation camps because they were considered too dangerous to go free.

The Reality of the Camps

3 In discussing the camps, government administrators favored euphemisms.* The camps were temporary "resettlement communities"—"havens of refuge"* designed to protect the Japanese Americans from those who did not trust them (Weglyn, 89). Comforted
by words like *community* and *refuge,* few Americans were confronted by the reality of camp life. If they had been, there probably would have been a groundswell of public outrage.

4 Erected at breakneck speed, the camps were crude and flimsy.
The "family apartments," as they were called, were tarpaper
shacks surrounded by barbed wire. They usually measured
twenty by twenty-four feet and housed anywhere from five to
eight people. Furniture, except for that brought by residents, was
almost nonexistent. The apartments contained cots, blankets,
mattresses, and a light fixture—nothing more.

5 Because the buildings were shoddy, the weather created hardships. In the summer, residents of the Manazar Camp in California sweltered. The sun beating down on tarpaper roofs turned
rooms into ovens. Occasionally, the asphalt floors melted (Weglyn, 80). Those living in colder climates like the Gila Relocation
Center in Arizona or the Granada Center in Colorado fared little

better. They were exposed to freezing temperatures that turned their "homes" into iceboxes.

6   There were other hardships as well. Because walls would have added to building expenses, there were few of them. Camp residents had almost no privacy. They ate and showered together. Even the toilet facilities were communal, and there was no way to be alone.

Economic Losses

7   Japanese Americans also suffered terrible economic losses. Forced by the government to settle their affairs in a matter of days, they fell victim to unscrupulous* people who bought their property at the lowest possible prices. The property and possessions they couldn't sell were stored, but no one seemed concerned with protecting what the Japanese Americans left behind. Much of it was stolen or vandalized (Conrat, 22). In the end, the Japanese who were interned lost property valued at more than $500 million; they lost as well their leading position in the truck-garden, floral, and fishing industries.

Psychological Loss

8   But the tragedy of relocation was not limited to physical hardship and economic loss. For Japanese Americans, the worst hardship was psychological. They had lost face in their adopted country. They had suffered the embarrassment and humiliation of being herded together and forced to live in poverty. For a proud people, it was a spiritual death sentence (Girdner and Loftis, 238). Their family life was disrupted, and they felt themselves powerless. Although the young were able to bear up under such indignity, some of the old could not. One elderly man committed suicide and was found holding an Honorary Citizenship Certificate in his hand (Weglyn, 78).

No Evidence of Espionage

9   Although many people seemed convinced that only a network of Japanese-American spies could account for the success of Japan's attack on Pearl Harbor, there was no evidence of such spying. On the contrary, there was a great deal of evidence affirming the loyalty of America's Japanese residents.

10   Two months prior to the attack on Pearl Harbor, Curtis B. Munson, a special representative of the U.S. State Department, conducted a study of Japanese Americans. His objective was to find the degree of their loyalty to America. The results of Munson's research suggested that Japanese Americans were deeply loyal to

their adopted country. Their deepest affiliation* was to America rather than to the land of their birth. From Munson's perspective, they showed a "patriotic eagerness" to be Americans. There was, in fact, no Japanese-American threat: "There is no Japanese problem on the coast. There will be no armed uprising of Japanese" (Weglyn, 47).

11   Unfortunately, the Munson report became one of the war's best-kept secrets. As Eugene Rostow, one of America's foremost* authorities on constitutional law, expressed it, "One hundred thousand persons were sent to concentration camps on a record which wouldn't support a conviction for stealing a dog" (Weglyn, 53).

How Could It Happen Here?

12 Given the lack of evidence against Japanese Americans, given the suffering they endured, the question must be raised: How could it happen? How could a country famous for its democratic fervor* allow loyal citizens to be imprisoned?

13 *The Humiliation of Pearl Harbor.*   Japan's attack on Pearl Harbor was extraordinarily swift and successful. Later investigations laid most of the blame at the feet of the two men in charge of the area, Rear Admiral Husband E. Kimmel and General Walter C. Short.[1] They were found guilty of errors in judgment and dereliction* of duty. Initially, however, Americans found it hard to blame their own military commanders. It was easier to believe rumors about a network of Japanese-American spies operating on the West Coast of the United States.

14 *A History of Prejudice.*   Then, too, as historians Donald Pike and Roger Olmstead point out, "a century of anti-Orientalism stood back of the relocation order" (Conrat, 16). Prejudice against Asians had first been ignited when the Chinese arrived during the gold rush of the 1850s. As the number of gold seekers increased, it was clear that there simply wasn't enough gold to go around. American miners retaliated by demanding restrictions on Chinese miners, who were seen as intruders on American soil. When the Japanese began arriving in the 1890s, they inherited the anger and distrust originally directed at the Chinese.

15   Throughout the beginning of the twentieth century, anti-Japa-

---

[1]The subject of who was to blame for Japan's success is still being debated today. Some historians believe Kimmel and Short were forced to take all the blame even though others were at fault as well.

nese sentiment tended to swell and ebb with the economy. In times of economic expansion, evidence of prejudice diminished. But in times of recession, the Japanese were singled out for restriction and ostracism. Prevented by labor unions from working in the city, they moved to agricultural areas, where they became successful farmers. Their thrift and industry made them significant competitors, able to purchase several hundred thousand acres of land. But their success backfired when California passed the Alien Land Law preventing Japanese from purchasing land or leasing it for more than three years.

16   Japan's entry into World War I on the side of the United States temporarily curbed anti-Japanese sentiment in America. But it flared up again following the war, when Japan invaded Manchuria and China, withdrew from the League of Nations, and refused to limit naval arms. A threat to her neighbors, Japan was also perceived as a threat to America. As a result, the United States passed the Japanese Exclusion Act of 1924, which specifically limited Japanese immigration. By the time Pearl Harbor exploded, the country was psychologically prepared to mistrust Japanese Americans.

17   *Fear of the Unknown.*   Following their internment, Japanese Americans tended to take the blame for their misfortunes. They blamed themselves for being too clannish, for trying to preserve Japanese customs, for being reticent* and reclusive when they should have been forward and open. Tragically, they had a point. "Because little was known about the minority which had long kept itself withdrawn from the larger community in fear of rebuff,* it was possible to make the public believe anything" (Weglyn, 36). Fed on vicious stereotypes about Oriental cunning and largely ignorant of Japanese customs, far too many Americans found it easy to believe the myth of Japanese conspiracy and sabotage.

18   *Government Secrecy.*   The decision to relocate the Japanese Americans was hardly a public one. It was made by a few government officials who justified their actions in various ways. When General John L. DeWitt was questioned about evidence of Japanese-American treachery, he offered this logic: "The very fact that no sabotage has taken place to date is a disturbing and confirming indication that such action will take place" (Weglyn, 39). According to this argument, Japanese Americans had to be imprisoned because they hadn't *yet* done anything wrong. From DeWitt's perspective, their failure to engage in any spying activi-

ties was proof that they would do so any day. Viewed this way, internment was a form of preventive medicine.

19   When members of humanitarian, religious, and civil liberties groups protested the internment, they were given another explanation. They were told that the camps were nothing more than "protective custody." The government allegedly needed to protect its Japanese-American citizens because Pearl Harbor had aroused so much anti-Japanese sentiment.

20   If friends and neighbors of Japanese-American citizens protested the relocation policy, yet another reason was proposed. Military officials insisted that Japanese Americans were in possession of evidence that made internment a necessity. What this evidence was, however, had to be kept top secret—government security was involved.

The Final Verdict

21   Initially, the U.S. Supreme Court upheld the government's internment policy. In 1943, the Court claimed that "residents having ethnic affiliations with an invading enemy may be a greater source of danger than those of different ancestry" (Norton et al., 801). Similarly, in the 1944 Korematsu case, the Court approved the removal of Japanese Americans from the West Coast. However, Justice Frank Murphy called the decision the "legalization of racism." In his anger, he echoed Circuit Court Judge William Denman, who had compared Japanese-American internment to the policies of the Nazis: "The identity of this doctrine with that of the Hitler generals . . . justifying the gas chambers of Dachau is unmistakable" (Norton et al., 802).

22   Thirty-eight years after these Supreme Court decisions, the government formed a special Commission on Wartime Relocation and Internment of Civilians. Not surprisingly, that commission did not share the earlier view of the Supreme Court justices. On the contrary, it recommended that victims of the internment policy be compensated for their suffering. In the view of the commission, they had been victimized by "race prejudice, war hysteria, and a failure of political leadership" (Norton et al., 802).

23   A year later, in 1983, the Korematsu case was overturned in a federal district court. The court ruled that Fred Korematsu had been the victim of "unsubstantiated* facts, distortions, and misrepresentations" (Norton et al., 802). In clearing Fred Korematsu, the court also implicitly cleared the other men, women, and children who had shared his fate.

24   Currently, reparations* are being paid to Japanese Americans who suffered from the policy of internment. Although money can

never make up for the humiliation and hardship they suffered, the reparations are a much needed form of public apology.

Sources

Conrat, Maisie, and Richard Conrat. *Executive Order 9066.* California: Historical Society, 1972.

Girdner, Audrie, and Anne Loftis. *The Great Betrayal.* London: Collier-Macmillan, 1969.

Norton, Mary Beth, et al. *A People and a Nation.* Boston: Houghton Mifflin, 1986, pp. 801–802.

Weglyn, Michi. *Years of Infamy.* New York: William Morrow, 1976.

CHECKING YOUR COMPREHENSION

DIRECTIONS Answer the following questions by circling the letter of the correct response.

1. Which of the following more accurately paraphrases the thesis statement?

   a. The attack on Pearl Harbor shocked the United States and ended any indecision about the country's entry into World War II.

   b. The attack on Pearl Harbor caused a storm of outrage against people of Japanese descent living in the United States.

2. In discussing the camps, government administrators

   a. were not ashamed to describe them.

   b. refused to discuss them.

   c. favored euphemisms.

3. For Japanese Americans, the worst hardship was

   a. physical.

   b. economic.

   c. psychological.

4. According to the reading, there was a good deal of evidence indicating that America's Japanese residents

   a. supported Japan.

   b. were loyal to the United States.

   c. engaged in espionage.

5. Following their internment, Japanese Americans

   a. tended to be resentful of their treatment.

   b. tended to blame themselves.

   c. refused to talk about their suffering.

6. Which sentence paraphrases the topic sentence in paragraph 5?

   a. During the summer months, residents of the camps in California suffered terribly from the heat.

   b. Because the buildings in the camps were cheaply built, the weather added to the suffering of the camp's residents.

7. In paragraph 7, which sentence is the topic sentence?

   a. sentence 1

   b. sentence 2

   c. sentence 3

8. What's the main idea of paragraph 13?

   a. Because Americans were reluctant to blame the bombing of Pearl Harbor on their own commanders, they found it easier to believe rumors about a Japanese-American spy ring.

   b. Even today, no one really knows for sure how the Japanese were able to launch their surprise attack on Pearl Harbor.

9. What's the implied main idea of paragraph 21?

   a. Most Americans believed that the U.S. Supreme Court's decision to uphold the policy of internment was unjust.

   b. Although initially the U.S. Supreme Court upheld the policy of internment, there were those who strongly criticized the judges' decision.

10. Paragraphs 14 through 16 rely on which two patterns of organization?

    a. classification

    b. cause and effect

    c. process

    d. sequence of dates and events

SHARPENING YOUR CRITICAL SKILLS **DIRECTIONS** Answer the following questions by filling in the blanks or circling the letter of the correct response.

1. The title of the reading suggests that the author's purpose is

   a. to inform readers about the internment of Japanese Americans.

   b. to persuade readers that Japanese Americans were badly treated during the years of internment.

2. In paragraph 3, the author describes some of the euphemisms government administrators used to describe the camps. Why do you think the administrators favored euphemisms?

_____

_____

_____

3. The author says that words like *community* and *refuge* "comforted" Americans. Given what they represented, how could those words possibly provide comfort?

_____

_____

_____

4. Label each of the following statements fact (*F*), opinion (*O*), or a blend of both (*B*).

_____ a. *Executive Order 9066* "condemned 120,000 Japanese Americans . . . to be evacuated from their homes."

_____ b. If Americans had been "confronted by the reality of camp life, . . . there probably would have been a groundswell of public outrage."

_____ c. "Although money can never make up for the humiliation and hardship [Japanese Americans] suffered, the reparations are a much needed form of public apology."

5. Summarize the argument offered by General John L. DeWitt.

_____

_____

_____

_____

6. Do you think General DeWitt had a convincing reason for his conclusion?

_____

Please explain. _____

_____

_____

7. In paragraph 16, the author says that anti-Japanese sentiment flared up following World War I. What evidence does the author offer for this conclusion?

_____

_____

_____

_____

8. In paragraph 17, the author describes the stereotypes that fed anti-Japanese sentiment. How do you think the author views those stereotypes?

_____

_____

What words reveal her personal bias?

_____

9. How would you describe the author's tone?
   a. serious
   b. outraged
   c. emotionally neutral

10. In paragraph 24, what personal point of view does the author reveal?

_____

_____

_____

_____

DRAWING YOUR OWN CONCLUSIONS Think back to the reading about television's effect during wartime after World War II. Do you think television might have made a difference to the government's internment policy? Explain your answer.

WRITING SUGGESTION Write a paper arguing that Americans do or do not need to know about such shameful incidents in the past as the internment of Japanese Americans. While some believe that we as a nation have to know about past injustices in order to avoid repeating them, others argue that there is no point in raking up a past better left forgotten. Begin your paper by stating your position and giving reasons for it. Then show how that position could be put into practice in the context of a high school history course.

■ **READING 7**

WORLD WAR II: THE FIGHT AGAINST RACISM

LOOKING AHEAD Unlike Japanese Americans whose lives were tragically altered for the worse by World War II, African Americans saw the wall of discrimination begin to crack when America went to war against Hitler and his allies.

GETTING FOCUSED Read the first and last paragraphs. Then read the first sentence of the remaining paragraph and the words in **Word Watch.** Predict at least one reason why World War II helped diminish racism in the United States.

_____

_____

Use the title to pose a question that will help guide your reading.

_____

Consider whether you already possess some knowledge about the effect of World War II on African Americans. Have you read any books or articles that dealt with this subject? Perhaps you have seen films that focused on this topic.

WORD WATCH Some of the more difficult words in the reading are defined in this section. Watch for these words as you read. They are marked with an asterisk. When you finish the reading, review the words in **Word Watch** by covering up the definitions and checking to see if you now know all the meanings. Record any words you still don't know in a notebook or on index cards. Review them periodically until they are part of your vocabulary.

> **rationalized:** gave reasons that were really excuses
>
> **sophistry:** argument based on faulty logic
>
> **induction:** admission to military service
>
> **Jim Crow:** policies of strict separation on the basis of race

> **abridged:** condensed, abbreviated, reduced
>
> **integration:** the process of opening an institution to all races on an equal basis
>
> **exacerbated:** worsened
>
> **smoldering:** burning
>
> **disenfranchised:** denied the right to vote
>
> **doctrines:** body of principles or rules that organize a group
>
> **obsolete:** outmoded, no longer of any use
>
> **plasticity:** ability to be shaped or molded

1 DURING WORLD WAR II (1939–1945), 1.15 MILLION AFRICAN Americans entered the armed services and many fought overseas. However, the armed forces were totally segregated and the African-American press continued to emphasize similarities between persecution of the Jews in Europe and racial segregation in the United States. Throughout the war, the Red Cross kept "white blood" and "black blood" in separate containers.

2 Although chiefs of staff would have preferred to think that the armed services were immune from racial conflict, they came under increasing pressure to abandon their ironclad segregation code of 1941. By the terms of this code, African Americans could not enlist in the Marine or Air Corps. In the navy, they could serve only in menial tasks. The army did admit African Americans but maintained segregated training facilities and units and retained African-American troops primarily in a supportive capacity rather than in combat. African-American officers were assigned to so-called Negro units and had to serve under white superiors. No African-American officer could ever become superior to a white in the same unit.

3 The army rationalized* this policy, partly on the sophistry* that African Americans were poor fighters, partly on the grounds that the army was not a suitable laboratory for social experiments, and partly in the belief that integration would destroy the morale of white soldiers. The War Department insisted that it could not "ignore the social relationships between negroes and whites which have been established by the American people through custom and habit." However, as the numbers of African-American soldiers increased sevenfold, from one hundred thousand in 1941 to seven hundred thousand in 1944, so did their dissatisfaction with military segregation.

4 African-American recruits came primarily from the North be-

cause those from the South were usually neither sufficiently healthy nor well enough educated to pass induction* tests. African Americans from the North were less likely to accept Jim Crow.* One African-American leader, Edgar Brown, advised Roosevelt in a letter of May 20, 1942, how "many of these young people have lived all their lives in New York, Detroit, Philadelphia, Chicago and other metropolitan areas where their civil rights have never before been abridged."* Thus, gradually (and reluctantly) chiefs of staff came to accept that military segregation was wasteful of manpower, that it was exposing the armed services to liberal criticisms, and that it was depressing the morale of an ever larger section of the army. Somewhat shamefaced, the army began to use African Americans in combat and the navy introduced a program of cautious integration.* Nevertheless, the army remained totally segregated. The agitation for integration led Army Chief of Staff George C. Marshall to declare, "My God! My God! . . . I don't know what to do about this race question in the army. I tell you frankly, it is the worst thing that we have to deal with. . . . We are getting a situation on our hands that may explode right in our faces."

5   Thus, the war exacerbated* racial difference. As Richard Polenberg says in *One Nation Divisible* (1980), "From the black perspective, the lowering of some barriers made those remaining seem more intolerable. To many whites, however, the remaining barriers seemed even more desirable than before." A student quoted by Mary F. Berry and John W. Blassingame in *Long Memory: The Black Experience in America* (1982) expressed smoldering* resentment among African Americans: "The Army Jim Crows us. The Navy lets us serve only as mess men. The Red Cross refuses our blood. We are disenfranchised,* Jim Crowed, spat upon. What more could Hitler do than that?" However, in contrast to their position in World War I, groups of African Americans and their political leaders were now a political force to be reckoned with.

6   Nazi emphasis on racism helped discredit racial doctrines* in the United States. For several decades, progressive anthropologists such as Franz Boas and Otto Kleinberg had challenged the idea that some races were superior to others. During the war, their successors argued these points for a mass audience. Ruth Benedict in *Race: Science and Politics* (1940), Gunnar Dahlberg in *Race, Reason and Rubbish* (1942), and Ashley Montagu in *Man's Most Dangerous Myth: The Fallacy of Race* (1942), all emphasized how much all human beings have in common; that individual differences are more important than racial averages; that so-called racial traits are really determined by culture and environment;

and that the notion of racial purity was, at best, obsolete,* especially given increasing migration and intermarriage.

7   In short, such authors argued for the plasticity* rather than the permanence of human nature. Thus, Ashley Montagu in *Man's Most Dangerous Myth* declared how the rise of fascism "shows us today where we end up if we think the shape of the nose or the color of the skin has anything to do with human values and culture."

> Sean Dennis Cashman, *African-Americans and the Quest for Civil Rights, 1900–1990*. New York: New York University Press, 1991, pp. 74, 75, 79.

CHECKING YOUR COMPREHENSION

DIRECTIONS Answer the following questions by circling the letter of the correct response.

1. Which implied main idea more effectively sums up the main idea of the reading?

a. World War II revealed a harsh fact about life in America: Even the military was not immune to racism.

b. Despite the military's policy of racial segregation, World War II actually helped strike a blow against racism in America.

2. Prior to World War II, the Joint Chiefs of Staff liked to think that

a. the armed services were in the forefront of the fight against racism.

b. the armed services were immune to racial conflict.

c. racism in the military had been eliminated during World War I.

3. Which of the following was *not* one of the terms of the military segregation code in 1941?

a. African Americans were not permitted to enlist in either the Marine or Air Corps.

b. African Americans were barred from enlisting in the U.S. Army.

c. African-American officers could not be ranked higher than white officers in the same unit.

d. African Americans in the navy were restricted to serving in menial positions.

4. Based on what the author says about the Red Cross, which inference is more appropriate?

a. Like the military, the Red Cross helped enforce Jim Crow.

b. The Red Cross openly challenged the military's Jim Crow laws.

5. Which statement paraphrases the topic sentence of paragraph 5?

    a. World War II tended to increase racial tension in America.

    b. The military's treatment of African Americans during World War II created racial solidarity.

6. Who was worried that the racial tensions in the army were about to explode?

    a. Harry Truman

    b. Dwight D. Eisenhower

    c. George C. Marshall

7. For decades before the war, anthropologists like Franz Boas and Otto Kleinberg argued

    a. that some races were superior to others.

    b. against the idea that some races were superior to others.

    c. that anthropologists should have no opinions on racial relations.

8. Choose the better paraphrase of the following statement: "During World War II, authors like Ruth Benedict, Gunnar Dahlberg, and Ashley Montagu argued for the plasticity rather than the permanence of human nature."

    a. During the war, some intellectuals set forth their theories about human nature: For people like Ruth Benedict, Gunnar Dahlberg, and Ashley Montagu, the human race was constantly improving.

    b. During World War II, writers like Ruth Benedict, Gunnar Dahlberg, and Ashley Montagu argued that human nature was not rigidly fixed but subject to growth and change.

9. In books like *Race: Science and Politics, Race, Reason and Rubbish,* and *Man's Most Dangerous Myth: The Fallacy of Race,* the authors argued which of the following points?

    a. Racism will one day simply disappear.

    b. Fascism and racism had nothing in common.

    c. The notion of racial purity was out of date.

10. According to the author, Nazi emphasis on the importance of racial purity

    a. helped encourage racism in America.

    b. helped discredit racism in America.

    c. had no effect on racism in America.

SHARPENING YOUR CRITICAL SKILLS

DIRECTIONS Answer the following questions by filling in the blanks or circling the letter of the correct response.

1. Label the following statements *F* (fact), *O* (opinion), or *B* (both).

_____ a. "During World War II (1939–1945), 1.15 million African Americans entered the armed services."

_____ b. "Although chiefs of staff would have preferred to think that the armed services were immune from racial conflict, they came under increasing pressure to abandon their ironclad segregation code of 1941."

2. What reasons did the army put forth in support of segregation?

_____

_____

_____

3. Do you think the author considers the Army's argument in favor of segregation solidly grounded in logic and reason?

_____

Please explain. _____

_____

_____

4. In paragraph 2, the author refers to the "ironclad segregation code of 1941." Is this an example of a simile or a metaphor?

_____

What is the point of the author's comparison? _____

_____

_____

5. In paragraph 4, the author points out that the chiefs of staff "reluctantly" came to accept that military segregation was wasteful of manpower. Why does the author include the word *reluctantly*? What does he want to imply?

_____

_____

_____

6. How would you describe the author's tone?

    a. angry

    b. casual

    c. emotionally neutral

7. Overall, which of the following statements best describes the author's personal bias?

    a. The author thinks the military's position was understandable for that time and should not be judged too harshly.

    b. The author considers the military's position to be an embarrassing error in judgment that cannot be defended.

    c. The author does not reveal how he feels about the military's policy of segregation.

8. How did the anthropologists who criticized the notion of racial superiority argue their claims? What four reasons did they give to convince their audience?

    _____

    _____

    _____

    _____

    _____

    _____

    _____

9. How is it possible that the Nazi emphasis on racism helped discredit racial doctrines in the United States?

    _____

    _____

    _____

10. What do you think is the author's primary purpose in writing?

    a. The author wants to inform readers about the effect World War II had on racism in the military.

    b. The author wants to persuade readers that the military's segregationist policies toward African Americans undermined the war effort.

DRAWING YOUR OWN CONCLUSIONS In his best-selling book *Citizen Soldiers*, author Stephen Ambrose describes the "outstanding" platoons of African Americans whose performance during World War II "led many officers who served with them to reject segregation in the Army in the future." What do you think motivated these soldiers to perform so splendidly after the American military had treated them with the disrespect described in "World War II: The Fight Against Racism"?

WRITING SUGGESTION One of the most controversial questions haunting the military today is the role of women in combat. Write a paper in which you argue for or against the presence of women on the battlefield. Be sure to give reasons for your position and answer at least one objection.

■ **READING 8**

HUNKS AND HANDMAIDENS

LOOKING AHEAD Reading 8 revisits a topic introduced in Chapter 6, where one writer suggested that the Spice Girls probably have more of an impact on young women today than do an earlier generation of feminists like Gloria Steinem and bell hooks. In "Hunks and Handmaidens," author Victoria Register-Freeman suggests that her brand of feminism doesn't seem to have been passed on to the girls of her son's generation. If her sons are ready to be liberated, their girlfriends, it seems, are not.

GETTING FOCUSED Read the first sentence of every paragraph. Then read all the words in **Word Watch.** Based on your survey, why do you think the author titled her essay "Hunks and Handmaidens"?

_____

_____

As you read, ask yourself if it's true that young women today aren't terribly interested in the feminist goals of the previous generation.

WORD WATCH Some of the more difficult words in the reading are defined in this section. Watch for these words as you read. They are marked with an asterisk. When you finish the reading, review the words in **Word Watch** by covering up the definitions and checking to see if you now know all the meanings. Record any words you still don't know in a notebook or on index cards. Review them periodically until they are part of your vocabulary.

flaxen-haired: blonde	**en masse:** in a large group
metamorphosis: change, transformation	**cum laude:** with honors
spawned: produced	**disorient:** confuse
manifesto: statement of rights or beliefs	**cohorts:** companions
atrophied: died, lost strength	**subterranean:** underground

1 RHETT, MY NINETEEN-YEAR-OLD SON, WENT FROM TOM SAWyer to Tom Cruise around fifteen, about the time his voice changed. Suddenly, the family phone recorder began to fill up with breathless messages from what his older brother referred to as "Rhett's Gidgets," flaxen-haired* surfer girls from a nearby beach. Like fruit flies they appeared in dense buzzing masses with exotic names like Shaunna, Tiffany, Kendra, and Kimberly.

2 I was prepared for this metamorphosis* because it had happened to Rhett's older brother Robert at about the same age. My first inkling of the change came in a pizza parlor during a post-basketball-game dinner. Since I could not decide between black olives and anchovies, Robert gave his order first. The waitress, an attractive Madonna clone, went into great detail with him concerning salad dressings, crust types, cheese consistencies, toppings, whether he wanted ice with his Coke, did he live in the neighborhood, was there *anything* else he might want. When he smiled and shook his head, she floated off toward the kitchen, totally forgetting to take my order. Next to my son, I had become invisible.

3 I was stunned. Like most American moms, I had been so blinded by the sight of my offspring in ripped jeans and SAVE THE MANATEE T-shirts, and so deafened by numerous arguments over the acceptable decibel level of Beastie Boys CDs, that I was slow to recognize my firstborn had become heartthrob material.

4 Nevertheless, it was true, and it became equally true for his younger brother. Through some quirks of DNA, my ex-husband and I—two average-appearing adults—spawned* genetic celebrities: square-jawed, pearly-toothed, mahogany-haired, six-foot-five-inch slabs of guy flesh whose casual glance seems to turn many otherwise articulate young women into babbling Barbies.

5 I'm not proud of this. Wasn't the motherhood manifesto* for women of my generation to abolish stereotypes? Weren't nineties men supposed to be fully functioning members of a newly designed home team, a mutually supportive, multiskilled unit? I thought so. Many of my friends thought so too. We've done our part to raise our sons as full-fledged "new" team members—competent, caring individuals who can do more around the house than crush cans for the recycling bin and put a new plastic liner in the garbage pail. Both of my sons learned early to make an edible lasagna, toss a salad, sew on buttons, grocery-shop and separate the whites from the darks at laundry time. They could iron a shirt as well as rebound a basketball or kick a soccer goal. Growing up in a single-mom household for much of their lives, they really had to carry their weight domestically. And they did—for a while.

6 Then came puberty and hunkhood. Over the last few years, the

boys' domestic skills have atrophied* because handmaidens have appeared en masse.* The damsels have driven by, beeped, phoned, and faxed. Some appeared so frequently outside the front door they began to remind me of the suction-footed Garfields spread-eagled on car windows. While the girls varied according to height, hair color, and basic body type, they shared one characteristic. They were ever eager to help the guys out.

7   For example, Robert's freshman year at college, I arrived home from work one day to hear the sound of a vacuum. The sound intrigued me because Robert, home on spring break, was sprawled on the sofa reading the swimsuit edition of Sports Illustrated and Rhett was at crew practice. I daydreamed briefly that my fantasy had been realized and the dust wads under the bed had generated a cleaning lady. I strode back to the bedroom, briefcase in hand, but there was no one there but Bonnie, Robert's current girlfriend. Yes, it was cum laude* Bonnie of the Titian curls and the Always on Time Term Paper. Bonnie was vacuuming Robert's room—known in our family as The Room From Hell. This meant she had been on this project for most of the afternoon, because there hadn't been any visible floor in Robert's room for more than a year.

8   I pulled the plug on the Kenmore. "What are you doing, Bonnie?" I inquired gently. She replied that she was cleaning Robert's room for him. She did not see the broader implications.* I sat down slowly on the unwrinkled bed, my entire life as a postmodern woman passing before my eyes. It was a psychic near-death experience; I felt I was on the Disorient* Express for good this time. I explained to her that Robert held the high school record for rebounds in a single basketball game. His motor skills were intact. He could clean his own room. It was his choice. He chose not to do so. He chose instead to lounge in the living room and undress Kathy Ireland with his eyes.

9   Bonnie, despite her 140 IQ, seemed perplexed. Her green eyes widened. Her brow furrowed. After all, Robert had mentioned his room was a mess and it seemed so natural to . . . This is the frightening thing I've noticed about my homegrown hunks. Females don't require enough "real" help from them. My sons do not have to employ many of the skills I've so painstakingly taught them during our time together. Young women take one look at the guys and stand in line to become the chosen one to clean rooms, pick up laundry, fry chicken, lend money, drop dates with girlfriends, rent videos, treat for drinks.

10   This is not the way it was supposed to be—the reason I read fifty books on raising males in the new world order. This is not the payoff I would like for spending years in a support group for

single moms with sons. But I'm realistic. I've done my part. It's up to the others—the girlfriends, cohabitants, main squeezes, or wives—to insist that the hunks carry their fair share of the domestic load. Despite catchy commercials to the contrary, bringing home the bacon *and* frying it can get irksome. Besides, the hunks—like many of their cohorts*—have seen their moms work hard to survive economically. They know what women can do; they respect that ability and—at some subterranean* level— they're hard-wired to help. We, the Elvis-era moms, have done the best we can. It's now up to Tiffany, Kendra, and Kimberly.

Victoria Register-Freeman, "Hunks and Handmaidens," *Newsweek,* November 4, 1996, p. 16.

CHECKING YOUR COMPREHENSION

DIRECTIONS Answer the following questions by circling the letter of the correct response.

1. Which statement more effectively paraphrases the main idea of the entire reading?

   a. Now that my sons have grown up, they are following in the footsteps of their father and leaving housework to the women in their lives.

   b. My sons have been trained to do their fair share of housework, but the girls in their lives encourage them to treat housework as women's work.

2. According to the author, her sons went through a startling metamorphosis around the age of

   a. thirteen.

   b. fourteen.

   c. fifteen.

3. According to the author's account, when she discovered her sons were heartthrob material, she was

   a. happy.

   b. stunned.

   c. proud.

4. The author says that all the girls in her sons' lives shared one essential characteristic. What was that characteristic?

   a. They were all attractive.

   b. They were all smart.

   c. They all wanted to make her boys' lives easier.

5. In paragraph 2, the topic sentence is

   a. sentence 1.

   b. sentence 2.

   c. sentence 3.

6. When the author visits a pizza parlor and the waitress treats her as if she were invisible, the author correctly infers that

   a. the young girl doesn't like her.

   b. her young son has turned into a handsome man.

   c. the young girl is too busy to pay her any attention.

7. The author uses a visit to the pizza parlor to illustrate what main idea?

   a. Teenage girls spend too much time on their appearance and not enough time thinking about becoming independent.

   b. Until the visit to the pizza parlor, the author had not noticed that her son Robert had undergone a stunning transformation.

   c. To the young, the middle-aged are not worthy of notice.

8. What pattern of organization do you recognize in paragraph 6?

   a. comparison and contrast

   b. cause and effect

   c. process

9. Paragraph 7 is a supporting detail used to illustrate which main idea?

   a. Young girls today can't do enough to help others, but they need to remember that charity begins at home.

   b. Because girls are so willing to clean up after the author's sons, the boys have stopped taking care of themselves.

   c. Give men of any age a chance to avoid housework, and that's what they will do.

10. Which statement most effectively paraphrases the topic sentence in paragraph 10?

   a. My sons have given up on housework, and the chances are good that they will not rediscover their domestic skills anytime soon.

   b. I've taught my sons to help out; now it's up to the women in their lives to do the same.

   c. Young girls today think they can do it all—keep house and bring home a paycheck—but they will learn otherwise.

SHARPENING YOUR CRITICAL SKILLS DIRECTIONS Answer the following questions by filling in the blanks or circling the letter of the correct response.

1. Which statement more effectively describes the author's purpose?

   a. She wants to tell readers about her experience as a feminist whose efforts to raise sons with a feminist consciousness have been stymied, not by them, but by the girls in their lives.

   b. She wants to convince her younger female readers that they should stop volunteering to do housework for her handsome sons.

2. In the opening paragraph, to indicate just how many girls began turning up when her boys turned into hunks, the author compares

   the girls to _____.

   This is an example of what figure of speech?

   _____

3. Which statement more effectively describes the author's use of language?

   a. The author's language is factual and denotative.

   b. The author's language is highly connotative and rich in opinion.

4. In the opening, the author says that her son went from Tom Sawyer to Tom Cruise at the age of fifteen. What does she mean to express by means of these two allusions?

   _____

5. According to the author, her sons' casual glances turned many young women into "babbling Barbies." What does she imply with that metaphor?

   _____

   What connotations does the phrase "babbling Barbies" carry with

   it, positive or negative? _____

6. In paragraph 6, what does the author imply by means of an allusion to the cartoon cat Garfield, whose likeness is often used in car ornaments that have suction cups for feet?

   _____

7. In discussing Robert's girlfriend Bonnie in paragraph 7, why does the author tell her readers that Bonnie had graduated from high

school cum laude and had always turned in her term papers on time. What does she imply by including those details?

_____

_____

8. When the author finds her son's girlfriend Bonnie cleaning his room, she feels as if she were on the Disorient Express. Are readers meant to take this statement literally or figuratively?

_____

What does the author want to communicate to her readers?

_____

9. How would you describe the author's tone?

a. angry and annoyed

b. humorous but still serious

c. emotionally neutral

10. In paragraph 10, the author says her sons and his cohorts have, at some "subterranean level," been "hard-wired to help." Both of these metaphors combine to suggest what inference?

a. Like it or not, men like the author's sons have been programmed to see themselves as the stronger sex, needing to care for and protect the women in their lives.

b. On some unconscious level, men who have been raised by working women like the author know that keeping house is not women's work. Given half a chance, they will share household responsibilities.

DRAWING YOUR OWN CONCLUSIONS Have you seen young women behave as the author describes? Does her description ring true to you? Why or why not?

WRITING SUGGESTION Write a paper that summarizes and responds to the reading by Victoria Register-Freeman. Begin by summarizing the article; then explain why her description does or does not fit your experience. Do most of the young men you know refuse to let women clean up after them or do they prefer it? Similarly, do you think women behaving like "babbling Barbies" is a thing of the past or very much part of the present?

■ **READING 9**

THE WOMEN'S MOVEMENT: A HISTORICAL PERSPECTIVE

LOOKING AHEAD In the previous reading, Victoria Register-Freeman made it clear that the girls her sons knew didn't seem to have much interest in the feminist goals of a previous generation. For those of you not quite sure what those goals were, the following reading discusses the women's movement past and present.

GETTING FOCUSED Read the first and last paragraph. Then read the first sentence of the remaining paragraphs and all the words in **Word Watch.** On the basis of your survey, can you predict the underlying pattern of organization in this reading? Do you think the current women's movement, if viewed from a historical perspective as the title suggests, will have much in common with the movements of the past?

_____

_____

As you read, consider what you might already know or think about feminism. For example, do you consider yourself a feminist?

WORD WATCH Some of the more difficult words in the reading are defined in this section. Watch for these words as you read. They are marked with an asterisk. When you finish the reading, review the words in **Word Watch** by covering up the definitions and checking to see if you now know all the meanings. Record any words you still don't know in a notebook or on index cards. Review them periodically until they are part of your vocabulary.

abolitionist: a person who fought to put an end to slavery	**ritual:** traditional
eradicate: eliminate	**radical:** demanding deep-rooted changes
oppressed: people who have been held down or treated badly by those more powerful	**discrimination:** the act of treating one group better than another
concubine: mistress	**affirmative-action guide-lines:** guidelines designed to make up for previous discrimina-
professed: claimed	

tion in schools and in the workplace	**inclusive:** open, not restrictive
paucity: small amount or number	

1 THE WOMEN'S MOVEMENT FOR GENDER EQUALITY IN THE United States can be divided historically into three waves. *The first wave* began in the middle of the last century, developing out of the larger social movement to abolish slavery. The women who participated in the abolitionist* movement came to realize that they themselves also lacked freedom. Initially, they attempted to eradicate* all forms of sexual discrimination, but gradually focused their attention on winning the right for women to vote. When women's suffrage finally became a reality in 1920, the feminist movement came to a complete halt (Flexner and Fitzpatrick, 1996).

2 In the mid-1960s, the women's movement was put back into action, and thus began *the second wave* of feminism. Two factors seem to have brought it on. First, after the end of World War II, more and more women were going to college. After receiving so much education, the women were unhappy to be mere housewives or to hold low-status, low-paying jobs outside the home. Second, many young women participating in various social movements (including the civil rights movement, the student movement, and the anti–Vietnam War movement), supposedly fighting for the freedom of the oppressed,* found themselves oppressed by the male freedom fighters. These women, wrote Annie Gottlieb (1971), "found themselves *serving* as secretary, mother and concubine,* while men did all the speaking, writing, and negotiating—and these were men who professed* to reject the 'oppressive' ritual* machinery of their society."

3 Out of this background emerged a number of women-only organizations. Some might be considered radical* because they hated men, rejected marriage, and vowed to tear down the whole gender-role system. They gave their organizations such names as SCUM (Society for Cutting Men) or WITCH (Women's International Terrorist Conspiracy from Hell). Other feminist groups were more moderate, the most well-known being NOW (National Organization for Women). NOW has been the most successful feminist organization and continues to have a strong influence on women's positions today. NOW's aim is to end sexual discrimination* in ed-

ucation, work, politics, religion, and all other social institutions. Consequently, many states have passed laws requiring equal pay for equal work, and government departments have issued affirmative-action guidelines* to force universities and businesses to hire more women. Also, in many cases, court decisions have supported women's charges of sexual discrimination in hiring, pay, and promotion (Flexner and Fitzpatrick, 1996; Whittier, 1995).

4   Now, in the 1990s, a new generation of young women in their teens and twenties have started *the third wave* of feminism. These women have grown up taking equality for granted, because of their mothers' victories for women's rights. A series of events in the early 1990s awakened them to the fact that the fight for equality is not over. The most jolting event was probably the spectacle of an all-male Senate committee questioning Anita Hill on her charges of sexual harassment against Supreme Court nominee Clarence Thomas. The hearings, broadcast widely, revealed how political institutions still grossly disadvantage women with their paucity* of female members and their old-boy connections. The negative reaction against women's progress, detailed in Susan Faludi's controversial 1992 book, *Backlash*, has further demonstrated that equality is far from being attained.

5   But the "third wavers" are different from their mothers. The young feminists today are more inclusive,* welcoming men to join them in addressing not only women's concerns but also problems that affect both sexes, such as racism, pollution, and poverty (Schrof, 1993). By being inclusive in organization and concern, these young feminists can achieve goals that the older generation has largely ignored. Made up largely of highly educated white women, the older feminists made great strides for women in college education, professional schools, and white-collar jobs. But less attention has been paid to the plight of poor and minority women, and these issues remain to be addressed by the third wavers (Whittier, 1995; Guttman, 1994).

Alex Thio, *Sociology*, 5/e. New York:
Addison Wesley Educational Publishing, 1998,
pp. 285–286.

CHECKING
YOUR
COMPREHENSION
 DIRECTIONS Answer the following questions by circling the letter of the correct response.

1. Which statement most effectively paraphrases the main idea of the entire reading?

   a. Unlike the first wave of feminism, the third wave is more accepting of men.

    b. If you look at it from a historical point of view, the American women's movement has had three separate stages.

    c. If you look at the American women's movement from a historical point of view, it is clear that only the first wave made a real difference in the lives of women.

2. The first wave of feminism began around

    a. 1750.

    b. 1850.

    c. 1950.

3. The first wave of feminism was concerned mainly with

    a. ending slavery.

    b. winning the vote.

    c. improving working conditions for women.

4. The second wave of feminism began

    a. right after women won the right to vote.

    b. in the mid-1940s.

    c. in the mid-1960s.

5. Which statement most effectively paraphrases the main idea of paragraph 2?

    a. At least three different factors contributed to the second wave of feminism.

    b. Two different factors contributed to the second wave of feminism.

    c. World War II was the most important contributor to feminism's second wave.

6. The reference to Anita Hill is a supporting detail that serves to develop which main idea?

    a. Many of the women's organizations that formed during the second wave of feminism were hostile to men.

    b. Several events in the 1990s encouraged a new generation of women to initiate a new wave of feminism.

7. What pattern do you see at work in paragraph 2?

    a. classification

    b. cause and effect

    c. process

8. What pattern do you see at work in the reading overall?

    a. classification

    b. cause and effect

    c. sequence of dates and events

9. Which statement more effectively synthesizes this reading with the previous one, "Hunks and Handmaidens"?

    a. Like Victoria Register-Freeman, Alex Thio is aware that there are some crucial differences between younger and older feminists, and both are equally pessimistic as to what the younger crop of feminists will accomplish.

    b. From Victoria Register-Freeman's perspective, feminism seems to have been all but forgotten by the young women who pursue her handsome sons, but Alex Thio suggests that the spirit of feminism lives on in today's young women—it just wears a different face.

10. Based on this reading, which test question does *not* seem likely?

    a. Date and describe the three waves of feminism outlined by Alex Thio in the reading "The Women's Movement: A Historical Perspective."

    b. How does the third wave of feminism differ from the second?

    c. Summarize and evaluate the criticisms that women of color have leveled against the mainstream feminist movement.

SHARPENING YOUR CRITICAL SKILLS

DIRECTIONS Answer the following questions by filling in the blanks or circling the letter of the correct response.

1. How would you describe the author's purpose?

    a. The author wants to describe the three waves of feminism in the United States.

    b. The author wants to persuade readers that the third wave of feminism does not match the first two in importance.

2. In the opening paragraph, the author says, "The women's movement for gender equality in the United States can be divided historically into three waves." That statement is

    a. a fact.

    b. an opinion.

Please explain. _____

3. In the second paragraph, the author says, "In the mid-1960s, the women's movement was put back into action. . . . Two factors seem to have brought it on." What word in that statement reveals that it is more opinion than fact?

_____

4. In paragraph 4, the author says, "In the 1990s, a new generation of young women in their teens and twenties have started the third wave of feminism. These women have grown up taking equality for granted, because of their mothers' victories for women's rights." This statement is

a. a fact.

b. an opinion.

c. a blend of fact and opinion.

Please explain. _____

_____

5. Which statement more accurately describes the reading?

a. Although the author supplies some factual evidence, it is heavily laced with opinions.

b. Overall, the author relies more heavily on fact than on opinion.

6. When it appeared, Susan Faludi's book *Backlash* (paragraph 4) was criticized by some who claimed Faludi was grossly exaggerating the alleged attacks on women's progress. What's your inference? Did the author agree or disagree with this complaint?

_____

Please explain. _____

_____

7. How does the author feel about the U.S. Congress? Does he think it serves the interests of women as well as men?

_____

Please explain. _____

_____

8. Based on what the author says in paragraph 5, is it appropriate to infer that he believes the "third wavers" will address the needs of poor and minority women?

_____

Please explain. _____

9. How would you describe the author's language?

   a. The author's language is highly charged throughout.

   b. The author relies strictly on denotative language.

   c. The author effectively balances connotative and denotative language.

10. Which statement sums up your sense of the author's bias?

   a. The author is strongly in favor of feminist goals and women's rights.

   b. The author is subtly critical of the women's movement.

   c. It's impossible to determine the author's personal feelings.

DRAWING YOUR OWN CONCLUSIONS

1. The author says that the current generation of young women takes equality for granted. Do you think he is right about that? Why or why not?

2. Are women the only ones who can be feminists? Please explain.

WRITING SUGGESTION

Write a paper explaining what the word *feminism* means to you. Try to illustrate your definition with specific examples.

READING 10

WHAT MAKES A HERO?

LOOKING AHEAD   In Chapter 12, you learned about how our heroes can affect and mold our ego ideal. In a much lighter vein, author Ted Tollefson also turns to the subject of heroes. From Tollefson's point of view, heroes need to possess some special characteristics that distinguish them from ordinary celebrities.

GETTING FOCUSED   Read the first paragraph and all of the italicized statements. Then read all the words in **Word Watch.** Based on your survey, make one or two predictions. What points do you expect the author to develop?

_____

_____

_____

_____

In addition to making predictions, jot down one or two questions you will try to answer as you read.

_____

_____

_____

_____

As you read, keep asking yourself how you would define a hero if you were to write an essay similar to this one. List some key traits of a hero in the margins of the reading. Think, too, about people who do or do not match Tollefson's description.

WORD WATCH   Some of the more difficult words in the reading are defined in this section. Watch for these words as you read. They are marked with an asterisk. When you finish the reading, review the words in **Word Watch** by covering up the definitions and checking to see if you now know all the meanings. Record any words you still don't know in a notebook or on index cards. Review them periodically until they are part of your vocabulary.

orator: speaker

transformers: devices used to transform electricity from one circuit to another

zest: excitement, enthusiasm

abundant: rich, full, varied

catalyst: someone or something that causes another event

charismatic: possessed of personal magnetism or charm

universal: common to all people

tutelage: teaching, education

disdained: disliked, disregarded

unbridled: uncontrolled

purveyors: people who hand out or give out something

grandiose: grand, great

pious: saintly

collage: a picture created out of pieces from other pictures

1 FOR SEVERAL YEARS, A PICTURE OF WARREN SPAHN OF THE Milwaukee Braves hung on my closet door, one leg poised in midair before he delivered a smoking fastball. Time passed and Spahn's picture gave way to others: Elvis, John F. Kennedy, Carl Jung, Joseph Campbell, Ben Hogan. These heroic images have reflected back to me what I hoped to become: a man with good moves, a sex symbol, an electrifying orator,* a plumber of depths, a teller of tales, a graceful golfer. Like serpents, we keep shedding the skins of our heroes as we move toward new phases in our lives.

2 Like many of my generation, I have a weakness for hero worship. At some point, however, we all begin to question our heroes and our need for them. This leads us to ask: What is a hero?

3 Despite immense differences in cultures, heroes around the world generally share a number of traits that instruct and inspire people.

4 *A hero does something worth talking about.* A hero has a story of adventure to tell and a community who will listen. But a hero goes beyond mere fame or celebrity.

5 *Heroes serve powers or principles larger than themselves.* Like high-voltage transformers,* heroes take the energy of higher powers and step it down so that it can be used by ordinary mortals.

6 *The hero lives a life worthy of imitation.* Those who imitate a

genuine hero experience life with new depth, zest,* and meaning. A sure test for would-be heroes is what or whom do they serve? What are they willing to live and die for? If the answer or evidence suggests they serve only their own fame, they may be celebrities but not heroes. Madonna and Michael Jackson are famous, but who would claim that their adoring fans find life more abundant?*

7   *Heroes are catalysts* for change.* They have a vision from the mountaintop. They have the skill and the charm to move the masses. They create new possibilities. Without Gandhi,† India might still be part of the British Empire. Without Rosa Parks† and Martin Luther King Jr., we might still have segregated buses, restaurants, and parks. It may be possible for large-scale change to occur without charismatic* leaders, but the pace of change would be glacial, the vision uncertain, and the committee meetings endless.

8   Though heroes aspire to universal* values, most are bound to the culture from which they came. The heroes of the Homeric Greeks wept loudly for their lost comrades and exhibited their grief publicly. A later generation of Greeks under the tutelage* of Plato disdained* this display of grief as "unmanly."

9   Though the heroic tradition of white Americans is barely three hundred years old, it already shows some unique and unnerving features. While most traditional heroes leave home, have an adventure, and return home to tell the story, American heroes are often homeless. They come out of nowhere, right what is wrong, and then disappear into the wilderness. Throughout most of the world, it is acknowledged that heroes need a community as much as a community needs them.

10   And most Americans seem to prefer their heroes flawless, innocent, forever wearing a white hat or airbrushed features. Character flaws—unbridled* lust, political incorrectness—are held as proof that our heroes aren't really heroes. Several heroes on my own list have provided easy targets for the purveyors* of heroic perfectionism.

11   The ancient Greeks and Hebrews were wiser on this count. They chose for their heroes men and women with visible, tragic flaws. Oedipus'† fierce curiosity raised him to be king but also

---

†Mahatma Gandhi: Indian leader who used nonviolent disobedience to gain India's independence from Great Britain.
†Rosa Parks: When, in 1955, African-American Rosa Parks refused to give up her bus seat to a white man, she helped ignite the civil rights movement.
†Oedipus: the hero of a Greek tragedy who was determined to know the secret of his birth. When he found it out, he was so horrified that he blinded himself.

lured him to his mother's bed. King David's unbounded passion made him dance naked before the Ark *and* led him to betray Uriah so he could take Bathsheba for his wife.

12   American heroes lack a sense of home that might limit and ground their grandiose* ambitions. American heroes avoid acknowledging their own vices, which makes them more likely to look for somebody else to blame when things go wrong. Our national heroes seem to be stuck somewhere between Billy Budd† and the Lone Ranger: pious,* armed cowboys who are full of energy, hope, and dangerous naïveté.

13   Here are some exercises to give you insights into your own ideas about heroes and villains:

1. Draw a time line with markings every five years in your life. For each era, name an important hero (male or female). Identify three core qualities each stands for. Look at the overall list for recurring qualities. Who or what do your heroes serve?

2. Make a list of enemies, the people who really push your buttons. For each, specify three qualities that make your blood boil. Now look for recurring qualities. What emerges is your "shadow," parts of yourself that you fear, loathe, and therefore loan to others. What does your shadow know that you don't?

3. Make a collage* of your heroes, leaving room for their tragic flaws and holy vices. Hang it opposite a large mirror.

Ted Tollefson, "Is a Hero
Really Nothing but a Sandwich?"
Utne Reader, May/June 1993, pp. 102–103.

CHECKING YOUR COMPREHENSION   **DIRECTIONS** Answer each question by circling the letter of the correct response.

1. Which paragraph introduces the thesis statement?

    a. paragraph 1

    b. paragraph 2

    c. paragraph 3

2. Which of the following accurately paraphrases the thesis statement?

    a. In different stages of our lives, we need different heroes on whom to model ourselves.

    b. It doesn't matter where they come from; heroes are likely to share similar traits that are admired and imitated by others.

---

†Billy Budd: a character from a short story by Herman Melville. Billy is so innocent he arouses the hatred of his ship's captain.

3. Based on the reading, which of the following is *not* a characteristic of a hero?

    a. Heroes bring about change.

    b. Heroes do something worth talking about.

    c. Heroes are worthy of being imitated.

    d. Heroes have more self-confidence than ordinary people do.

4. According to the author, what is the question that helps identify heroes?

    a. How much fame do they have?

    b. How many people imitate them?

    c. What are they willing to live or die for?

5. Based on what the author says in paragraph 6, which inference is appropriate?

    a. He thinks heroes and celebrities are two words that mean the same thing.

    b. He thinks heroes should not be confused with celebrities.

6. In paragraph 6, which of the following sentences does *not* provide an essential detail?

    a. "Those who imitate a genuine hero experience life with new depth, zest, and meaning."

    b. "Madonna and Michael Jackson are famous, but who would claim that their adoring fans find life more abundant?"

7. Gandhi, Rosa Parks, and Martin Luther King Jr. are illustrations of which main idea?

    a. Heroes always suffer for their beliefs.

    b. Heroes bring about change in the world.

8. According to the author, heroes are influenced by the

    a. disapproval of others.

    b. culture in which they live.

    c. heroic behavior of previous generations.

9. According to the author, heroes in American culture are likely to be

    a. fearless.

    b. violent.

    c. homeless.

10. Which pattern do you recognize in paragraphs 10 and 11?

    a. sequence of steps

    b. comparison and contrast

    c. cause and effect

SHARPENING YOUR CRITICAL SKILLS

DIRECTIONS Answer the following questions by filling in the blanks or circling the letter of the correct response.

1. Label the following statements *F* (fact), *O* (opinion), or *B* (both).

_____ a. "At some point, we all begin to question our heroes and our need for them."

_____ b. "Most Americans seem to prefer their heroes flawless."

_____ c. "Heroes are catalysts for change."

2. Compare paragraphs 4 and 7. Each paragraph offers a different opinion on what makes a hero. Which paragraph does a better job of arguing the author's opinion?

_____

Explain the basis for your choice.

_____

_____

_____

3. In paragraph 9, the author tells us that the American heroic tradition has some unique features. To support that opinion, the author offers a reason: Unlike heroes of other cultures, American heroes have no connection to their communities. Do you find the author's argument convincing? Why or why not?

_____

_____

_____

4. In paragraph 10, the author tells readers that "most Americans seem to prefer their heroes flawless." How effectively does the author argue his opinion?

_____

_____

_____

5. Based on what the author says, which inference is more appropriate?

    a. The author is disturbed by the idea that America's heroes tend to be homeless.

    b. From the author's perspective, it's quite natural for heroes to be homeless.

6. In this reading, the allusions to Billy Budd and the Lone Ranger help to make what opinion convincing?

_____

_____

_____

7. What kind of tone does the author of this essay assume?

    a. friendly and informal

    b. solemn and serious

    c. emotionally neutral

8. In the first sentence of paragraph 9, the author tells us that the heroic tradition in America has some unique features. What word in that sentence reveals the author's attitude toward that tradition?

_____

9. How would you describe the author's feelings about the American tradition of heroism?

    a. The author disapproves of the American tradition.

    b. The author admires the American tradition.

    c. It's impossible to determine the author's personal feelings.

10. With which of the following statements do you agree?

    a. The author's purpose is to tell readers about the characteristics that typically define heroes in American fiction.

    b. The author's purpose is to define the heroic character and celebrate the American hero in particular.

    c. The author's purpose is to tell readers about the characteristics that typically define heroes and persuade them that the American ideal of a hero may be going in the wrong direction.

DRAWING YOUR OWN CONCLUSIONS The author lists his heroes. Who are your heroes? Do they fit the author's description? How are they similar or different? Do you think you are capable of being a hero? Why or why not?

WRITING SUGGESTION Write an essay in which you define the characteristics of a hero. Begin with a brief description of someone you consider heroic—it doesn't have to be a famous person; it just has to be someone you admire—then describe the characteristics that make that person a hero to you.

■ READING 11

RAOUL WALLENBERG: A LOST HERO

LOOKING AHEAD Raoul Wallenberg unquestionably embodied all of the characteristics Ted Tollefson cites in his essay. Unfortunately, Wallenberg's heroic spirit couldn't save him from what most believe was a lonely death in a Russian prison camp.

GETTING FOCUSED Read all the headings and the first sentence of every paragraph. Then read all the words in **Word Watch.** When you finish, see if you can predict what Wallenberg did to become one of the great heroes of World War II.

_____

_____

As you read, imagine yourself in Wallenberg's place. Would you have been willing to do what he did for people who were neither friends nor family?

WORD WATCH Some of the more difficult words in the reading are defined in this section. Watch for these words as you read. They are marked with an asterisk. When you finish the reading, review the words in **Word Watch** by covering up the definitions and checking to see if you now know all the meanings. Record any words you still don't know in a notebook or on index cards. Review them periodically until they are part of your vocabulary.

---

cultivated: refined by training and education

atrocities: acts of cruelty and violence

callously: without feeling or pity

unorthodox: untraditional

dismantled: taken apart

---

1   IN 1937, RAOUL WALLENBERG WAS A YOUNG MAN WHO SEEMED to have everything. Born into one of Sweden's richest and most respected families, he was cultivated,* handsome, and charming. His future seemed assured. After a few years spent learning the family business, he would follow in his grandfather's footsteps and become a banker.

2   But the young Wallenberg was not content. In a letter to his grandfather, he made it clear that something was missing: "To tell the truth, I don't feel especially bankish. . . . I think it is more in my nature to work positively for something" (Lester, 26).

3   Wallenberg's words were prophetic. By 1944, he was indeed working positively for something. He was risking his life to save the Jews of Budapest, Hungary. Members of the last large Jewish community in Europe, the Jews of Budapest had been targeted for extinction. Without their death, Nazi Germany could not claim that the "Final Solution," their plan to eliminate all the Jews in Europe, was a success. And, as the world now knows, the Nazis were determined to be successful.

4   Adolf Eichmann, one of the architects of Hitler's Final Solution, openly proclaimed his enthusiasm for the Hungarian "project." He personally organized the transportation of Jews to Auschwitz and insisted that the job be completed as swiftly as possible (Lester, 69). But Eichmann had reckoned without the arrival of Raoul Wallenberg. Almost single-handedly, Wallenberg saved over 100,000 Hungarian Jews. Then, in one of the great mysteries of all time, he vanished. To this day, his disappearance remains shrouded in mystery and his whereabouts, alive or dead, are still in question.

Wallenberg's American Connection

5 By late 1942, most of the world's leaders knew that the German government was determined to make all of Europe *judenrein,* or free of Jews. Although reports of atrocities* had been circulating for months, government officials had viewed them as isolated events. As 1942 drew to a close, however, both the American State Department and the British Foreign Office had to confront the terrible truth hidden behind the euphemism *Final Solution.* The Nazis were systematically killing, or, in their words "exterminating," the Jews of Europe.

6   By 1944, the American government had decided to organize the War Refugee Board. Its goal was to block "Nazi plans to exterminate all the Jews" (Lester, 61). This goal clearly required intervention in Hungarian affairs, because Hungary was the only remaining country with a large Jewish population. The country was also under German occupation.

7   As a result, Iver C. Olsen, a member of the U.S. Treasury Department, was sent to neutral Sweden. His task was to find a Swedish representative who could enter Hungary and somehow stop deportations to the concentration camps. Within days of meeting Olsen, Raoul Wallenberg was ready to travel.

A Powerful Piece of Paper

8 Raoul Wallenberg arrived in Budapest on July 9, 1944. When he entered the Swedish embassy, he saw a long line of people wearing the yellow Star of David that proclaimed their status as Jews. Word had gotten out that the Swedes were giving travel documents or citizenship papers to Hungarian Jews who were planning to become Swedish citizens or residents. In several cases, those documents had offered protection against deportation and death.

9 One Jewish businessman had even gone to court, claiming his Swedish citizenship protected him from deportation. To everyone's surprise, he had won his case. Another man had escaped deportation to Auschwitz, the most dreaded of all concentration camps, by showing a Swedish document. The German officer in charge had simply let him go, obviously intimidated by the sight of an official document.

10 Quick to infer a valuable lesson from these incidents, Wallenberg realized immediately that the same people who could callously* inflict suffering and death could also be intimidated by a piece of paper. Inhumanity did not disturb them, but failure to follow the rules did. Inspired by that knowledge, Wallenberg designed an impressive looking document, bearing the symbol of the Swedish government. More important, it announced that anyone carrying the document was under the protection, or *Schutz,* of the Swedish government. The document was signed by Raoul Wallenberg.

11 Wallenberg's next step was to set up a small network for the distribution of the *Schutz* passes. He then visited members of the Hungarian government and showed them a letter from King Gustav of Sweden. He made it clear to all present that Sweden was committed to protecting the Jews against further aggression. Other Swedish diplomats were a bit taken aback by Wallenberg's unorthodox* efforts, citing questions of procedure and legality. But Wallenberg managed to brush all such considerations aside with one answer: "It will save lives" (Lester, 89).

12 By October of 1944, Wallenberg had been in Budapest just three short months. During that time, he had purchased a number of houses with the money provided by Olsen. Draping them with Swedish flags, Wallenberg claimed the houses were Swedish property and therefore not subject to German or Hungarian law. In effect, they became "safe houses," places of sanctuary for Jewish refugees.

13 When, on one occasion, Hungarian troops tried to force their way into one of Wallenberg's safe houses, he blocked their way,

saying, "No one leaves this place as long as I live" (Stanglin et al., 36). The troops withdrew.

14   On October 15, 1944, Hungarian radio announced that the war was lost, and the announcer openly blamed the Germans for dragging Hungary into a losing battle. In the Jewish quarter, there was dancing in the streets. Unfortunately, the dancing was premature. Shortly after the first announcement came another more ominous broadcast. The Hungarian Nazi Party, the hated and feared Arrow Cross, had taken over. Along with the German Nazis still in Hungary, members of the Arrow Cross would continue to be loyal to Adolf Hitler. Above all, they would continue to work toward the Final Solution.

The Arrow Cross's Reign of Terror

15   The notorious Adolf Eichmann was again in Budapest, and fifteen members of the Arrow Cross roamed the streets hunting down and shooting Jews on sight. At one point, a small band of Jewish laborers and a handful of Communists got hold of arms, and they fought back. Immediately the German SS† and the Hungarian police were at the scene of the fighting. They rounded up hundreds of suspected sympathizers and executed them where they stood (Lester, 105). A nightmare world prior to October 15, Budapest had now become a living hell.

16   As Soviet tanks drew closer, the Nazis became more violent and more vicious. They barged into Wallenberg's "safe" houses and dragged out the "protected" Jews. They tortured their victims, shot them, and then threw their bodies into the Danube River.

17   Eichmann, however, was furious that his plans for exterminating the Hungarian Jews were being interrupted. Nazi officials had become anxious about what was going to happen when the war ended. With good reason, they were afraid of being tried as war criminals. Auschwitz was being dismantled,* and orders had been given to stop the extermination program. But Eichmann was not to be stopped; he devised yet another scheme.

18   Jews now were to be rounded up to work on the "East Wall" in Vienna. The wall would supposedly be protection against the advance of the Russians. But, more important, Eichmann knew that most of the Jews who would be marched on foot to Vienna would not survive. The cold and hunger would do their work.

19   Wallenberg also knew that the "labor march," as it was called,

---

†SS: *Schutzstaffel* (protective units); the elite guard of the Nazi party, notorious for their brutal tactics.

was bound to be a death march. He tried to have the march postponed but succeeded only in getting exemptions for those Jews bearing *Schutz* passes. On November 9, the march began.

20   Shivering for lack of clothing and starving for food, the Jews were marched toward the Austrian border. Anyone who stumbled or fell out of line was shot. The marchers were without hope. But then Wallenberg miraculously began to turn up at points along the way. Susan Tabor, a survivor of the march, described lying on the floor of a shed so crowded she could neither stand up nor move. Suddenly she saw Wallenberg stride in, carrying a briefcase. Through a megaphone he announced that food and medical supplies would soon arrive. When he left, the marchers had new hope. As Susan Tabor was to say long after the march was over, "He made me feel human again. For the first time I had hope" (Werbell & Clarke, 91).

21   As always, true to his word, Wallenberg returned the next day with food and medicine. He also brought a stack of protective passes. Within minutes, he had created chaos by telling the marchers to assemble in various lines:

> The Jews ran helter-skelter around the brick factory. They changed lines and jostled one another to get a good place as Wallenberg backed his trucks into the yard. The *Arrow Cross* guards lost control. . . . In the confusion many Jews simply walked away or bribed individual guards to let them escape. (Werbell & Clarke, 91)

This scene was repeated many times as Wallenberg worked tirelessly to save as many Jews as he could.

The Russians Arrive

22   By January of 1945, the Russians were closing in on Budapest, and it was clear to everyone that the war was truly coming to an end. On January 13, 1945, a small group of Russian soldiers broke through the wall of a house where Wallenberg was staying. He explained who he was, and the soldiers examined his documents. But something about Wallenberg or his papers seemed to make them suspicious. A few hours later, some high-ranking Soviet officials arrived to question him, in the first of several interrogations by the Russian secret police. Nevertheless, Wallenberg was permitted to move freely through the now-liberated city of Budapest.

23   On January 17, Wallenberg dropped in on friends before leaving to visit Soviet headquarters. He was in high spirits, convinced that the Soviets wanted his advice on postwar relief and recon-

struction: "The Russians are certain to respect the suggestions of a Swedish diplomat" (Werbell & Clarke, 157).

24   Shortly after the visit, Wallenberg left Budapest under Russian escort. As he looked at the soldiers who were to accompany him, he made a cruelly prophetic joke: "I still don't know if they're coming along to protect me or guard me. Am I a guest, or a prisoner?" (Werbell & Clarke, 158).

25   Even today, no one is really sure what happened to Raoul Wallenberg after he left with his Soviet escorts. When he failed to return to Budapest as planned, the Swedish Foreign Office sent the Russians a series of messages asking for an investigation. There was no reply. After repeated refusals of requests for information, the Soviets claimed to have no knowledge of his whereabouts. Then, in 1957, Andrei Gromyko, the Soviet deputy foreign minister, claimed Wallenberg had died in 1947. According to Gromyko, Wallenberg had suffered a heart attack at the age of thirty-four. Despite Soviet claims, however, rumors persist to this day that Raoul Wallenberg is still alive.

26   Whatever Wallenberg's fate, his name must be remembered and honored. As Frederick E. Werbell and Thurston Clarke have pointed out, Wallenberg's life is an important source of inspiration: "If the Holocaust is to be taken as evidence that human nature is essentially evil, then Wallenberg's life must be considered as evidence that it is not" (p. 256).

Sources

Lester, Elenore. *Wallenberg: The Man in the Iron Web.* Englewood Cliffs, N.J.: Prentice-Hall, 1982.

Stanglin, Douglas, Mortimer B. Zuckerman, Jeff Trimble, and David Bartal. "A Lost Prisoner of the Gulag Still Holds Moscow Hostage." *U.S. News and World Report,* June 26, 1989, pp. 34–36.

"Wallenberg Reported Shot in '47." *New York Times,* October 18, 1990, A14.

Werbell, Frederick E., and Thurston Clarke. *Lost Hero: The Mystery of Raoul Wallenberg.* New York: McGraw-Hill, 1982.

CHECKING YOUR COMPREHENSION

DIRECTIONS Answer the following questions by circling the letter of the correct response.

1. Which of the following accurately paraphrases the thesis statement?

    a. To this day, no one knows for sure what happened to Raoul Wallenberg.

    b. After risking his life to save thousands of Hungarian Jews, Raoul Wallenberg mysteriously vanished, and, to this day, no one knows what happened to him.

2. Which of the following details is *not* essential to developing the main idea of the reading?

    a. "In 1937, Raoul Wallenberg was a young man who seemed to have everything."

    b. "Raoul Wallenberg arrived in Budapest on July 9, 1944."

    c. "Wallenberg's next step was to set up a small network for the distribution of *Schutz* passes."

3. Which statement sums up the main idea in paragraph 5?

    a. The euphemism "Final Solution" helped to hide a horrifying truth.

    b. By 1942, it was clear that the German government was prepared to murder all the Jews in Europe.

4. What inference did Wallenberg draw from the stories about people who had escaped deportation and death?

    a. People willing to commit murder could still be frightened by the sight of an official-looking document.

    b. The Germans really were determined to kill all the Jews in Europe.

5. According to the author, other Swedish diplomats

    a. admired Wallenberg.

    b. were taken aback by Wallenberg's unorthodox efforts.

    c. criticized Wallenberg's behavior.

6. Based on paragraph 11, which inference is appropriate?

    a. Wallenberg held other Swedish diplomats in contempt.

    b. Wallenberg was impatient with questions of procedure and legality when they concerned human lives.

7. In paragraph 13, which inference does the author expect readers to supply?

    a. The troops withdrew because they had been called back to combat.

    b. The troops withdrew because they were intimidated by Wallenberg.

8. The following sentence appears in paragraph 14: "Unfortunately, the dancing was premature." Which statement most accurately describes the function of that sentence?

    a. It helps to introduce the topic sentence.

    b. It sums up the main idea.

    c. It functions as a transition.

9. When the Russians first arrived, Wallenberg was convinced that

    a. they would kill him.

    b. they wanted his advice.

    c. they would leave him alone.

10. Which two patterns help organize the supporting details in this reading?

    a. sequence of dates and events

    b. process

    c. comparison and contrast

    d. cause and effect

SHARPENING YOUR CRITICAL SKILLS

DIRECTIONS Answer the following questions by filling in the blanks or circling the letter of the correct response.

1. Which word or words in the following sentence suggest that it's an opinion: "In 1937, Raoul Wallenberg was a young man who seemed to have everything."

_____

2. Label each of the following statements *F* (fact), *O* (opinion), or *B* (both).

_____ a. "By 1944, the American government had decided to organize the War Refugee Board."

_____ b. "Raoul Wallenberg arrived in Budapest on July 9, 1944."

_____ c. "Whatever Wallenberg's fate, his name must be remembered and honored."

3. In paragraph 15, what are some of the words with strong connotations the author uses to suggest for readers the horror of the situation she describes?

_____

_____

_____

4. In paragraph 16, why does the author use the word *barged* rather than *entered*?

_____

_____

_____

5. During World War II, the followers of Adolf Hitler openly proclaimed their hatred and contempt for Jews. Yet, they still used a euphemism, "the Final Solution," to describe their plans for murdering all the Jews in Europe. What does that suggest to you?

_____

_____

_____

6. How would you describe the author's tone?

   a. angry

   b. admiring

   c. emotionally neutral

7. Many people now believe that the United States did not act quickly enough to help those being persecuted during World War II. Reread paragraphs 5, 6, and 7. Then decide which statement you think is accurate.

   a. The author leans toward the belief that the United States did not act quickly enough.

   b. The author is inclined to believe that the United States acted as quickly as possible.

   c. It's impossible to determine the author's personal feelings on this subject.

8. The author insists that Wallenberg must be remembered and honored. What reason does she give for her opinion?

_____

_____

_____

9. Paraphrase the quotation that ends the reading. In your own words, what does it mean?

_____

_____

_____

How do you think someone who disagrees with the point of the quotation might respond to it?

_____

_____

_____

10. How would you describe the author's purpose?

a. The author wants to tell readers about Wallenberg's exploits during World War II.

b. The author wants to tell readers about Wallenberg's exploits and convince them that his name must be remembered.

DRAWING YOUR OWN CONCLUSIONS

1. Why do you think Raoul Wallenberg was willing to risk his life for people he did not know? What do you think motivated him? Do you think you could be capable of that kind of heroism?

2. Do you think Raoul Wallenberg has all the traits described in "What Makes a Hero?" by Ted Tollefson? Does he have additional traits not mentioned by Tollefson?

WRITING SUGGESTION

Write a paper arguing for or against the importance of heroes as role models. Do you think we do or do not need heroic figures to guide our present-day actions?

READING 12

TAYLOR'S MIRACLE

LOOKING AHEAD Taylor Touchstone was ten years old when he got lost for four days in the Florida swamp near his home. Up until Taylor's miraculous journey, it was generally thought that no one could survive four days in the dark and deadly swamp waters, home to hungry alligators and poisonous snakes. But to everyone's astonishment, Taylor Touchstone did just that.

GETTING FOCUSED Read the first and last paragraphs along with the headings. Then read the first paragraph following each heading and all the words in **Word Watch.** Based on your survey, can you answer the question, What was it that helped Taylor to survive?

_____

_____

As you read, imagine yourself in Taylor's position. Do you think you would figure out how to survive, or would you panic and end up a meal for the alligators?

WORD WATCH Some of the more difficult words in the reading are defined in this section. Watch for these words as you read. They are marked with an asterisk. When you finish the reading, review the words in **Word Watch** by covering up the definitions and checking to see if you now know all the meanings. Record any words you still don't know in a notebook or on index cards. Review them periodically until they are part of your vocabulary.

> **autistic:** to be the victim of a mysterious disease that imprisons a person in his or her own private world where reality cannot enter
>
> **glints:** small flashes of light
>
> **neurological:** having to do with the brain and nervous system
>
> **manifests:** reveals, shows
>
> **coddling:** spoiling; treating like a baby
>
> **redundant:** repetitious
>
> **hypothermia:** abnormally low body temperature

1 TAYLOR TOUCHSTONE, A TEN-YEAR-OLD AUTISTIC* BOY WHO takes along a stuffed leopard and pink blanket when he goes to visit his grandmother, somehow survived for four days lost and alone in a swamp acrawl with poisonous snakes and alligators.

2 He swam, floated, crawled and limped about fourteen miles, his feet, legs, and stomach covered with cuts from brush and briars that rescuers believed to be impassable, his journey lighted at night by thunderstorms that stabbed the swamp with lightning.

3 People in this resort town on the Gulf of Mexico say they believe that Taylor's survival is a miracle, and that may be as good an explanation as they will ever have. The answer, the key to the mystery that baffles rescue workers who have seen this swamp kill grown, tough men, may be forever lost behind the boy's calm blue eyes. "I see fish, lots of fish," was all Taylor told his mother, Suzanne Touchstone, when she gently asked him what he remembered from his ordeal in the remote reservation on Eglin Air Force Base.

4 Over years, Taylor may tell her more, but most likely it will come in glints* and glimmers of information, a peek into a journey that ended on Sunday when a fisherman found Taylor floating naked in the East Bay River, bloody, hungry but very much alive. He may turn loose a few words as he sits in the living room, munching on the junk food that is about the only thing his mother can coax him to eat, or when they go for one of their drives to look at cows. He likes the cows, sometimes. Sometimes he does not see them at all, and they just ride, quiet.

5 Taylor's form of autism is considered moderate. The neurological* disorder is characterized by speech and learning impairment, and manifests* itself in unusual responses to people and surroundings.

6 "I've heard stories of autistic people who suddenly just remember, and begin to talk" of something in the far past, Mrs. Touchstone said. "But we may never know" what he lived through, or how he lived through it, she said. His father, Ray, added, "I don't know that it matters." Like his wife and their twelve-year-old daughter, Jayne, Mr. Touchstone can live with the mystery. It is the ending of the story that matters.

7 Still, they have their theories. They say they believe that it is possible that he survived the horrors of the swamp not in spite of his autism, but because of it. "He doesn't know how to panic," Jayne said. "He doesn't know what fear is." Her brother is focused, she said. Mrs. Touchstone says Taylor will focus all his attention and energy on a simple thing—he will fixate on a knot in

a bathing suit's draw string—and not be concerned about the broader realm of his life.

8   If that focus helped him survive, Mrs. Touchstone said, then "it is a miracle" that it was her son and not some otherwise normal child who went for a four-day swim in the black water of a region in which Army Rangers and sheriff's deputies could not fully penetrate. He may have paddled with the gators, and worried more about losing his trunks.

9   "Bullheaded," said Mrs. Touchstone, who is more prone to say what is on her mind than grope for pat answers. Instead of coddling* and being overly protective of her child, she tried to let him enjoy a life as close to normal as common sense allowed.

10   Taylor has been swimming most of his life. In the water, his autism seems to disappear. He swims like a dolphin, untiring.

The Journey

11   His journey began about 4 P.M. on August 7, a Wednesday, while he and his mother and sister were swimming with friends in Turtle Creek on the reservation lands of the Air Force base. Taylor walked into the water and floated downstream, disappearing from sight. He did not answer his mother's calls. An extensive air, water, and ground search followed. It involved Army Rangers, Green Berets, Marines, deputies with the Okaloosa County Sheriff's Department, and volunteers, who conducted arm-to-arm searches in water that was at times neck-deep, making noises to scare off the alligators and rattlesnakes and water moccasins, and shouting Taylor's name.

12   He is only moderately autistic, Mrs. Touchstone said, but it is possible that he may not have responded to the calls of the searchers. At night when it was nearly useless to search on foot, AC-130 helicopters crisscrossed the swamp, searching for Taylor with heat-seeking, infrared tracking systems. In all, the air and ground searchers covered 36 square miles, but Taylor, barefoot, had somehow moved outside their range. "The search area encompassed as much area as we could cover," said Rick Hord of the Sheriff's Department. "He went farther."

13   It was not just the distance that surprised the searchers. Taylor somehow went under, around or through brush that the searchers saw as impassable. Yet there is no evidence that anyone else was involved in his journey, or of foul play, investigators said.

14   Apparently, Taylor just felt compelled to keep moving. Members of his family say they believe that he spent a good part of his time swimming, which may have kept him away from snakes on land.

The nights brought pitch blackness to the swamp, and on two nights there were violent thunderstorms. Lightning would have penetrated his shell, Mrs. Touchstone said. "I think it may have kept him moving," she said, and that might have been a blessing. Certainly, said his mother and doctors who treated the boy, he was exhausted. "Do you really think God would strike him with lightning?" she asked. "Wouldn't that be redundant?"*

15   Somewhere, somehow, he lost his bathing trunks. His parents said he might have torn them, and, concentrating on a single blemish, found them unacceptable. Mrs. Touchstone compared it to a talk she once heard by an autistic woman who had escaped her shell, who told the audience that most people in a forest see the vastness of trees, but she might fixate on a spider web.

16   On the third day of Taylor's journey, Mrs. Touchstone realized that her son might be dead. For reasons she could not fully explain, she did not want to see his body recovered. It would have been too hard to see him that way. Even though Taylor is physically fit and strong, friends and relatives knew that this was the same terrain that in February 1995 claimed the lives of four Rangers who died of hypothermia* while training in swampland near here.

17   Instead, about 7 A.M. last Sunday, a fisherman named Jimmy Potts spotted what seemed to be a child bobbing in the waters of the East Bay River. He hauled him into his small motorboat. Later that day, Taylor told his momma that he really liked the boat ride. In the hospital, he sang, "Row, Row, Row Your Boat."

Independence

18 Mrs. Touchstone lost Taylor at a Wal-Mart, once. "That was bad," she said. He ran out of Cheetos once and hiked a few blocks, alone, to get some. The police found him and brought him home. He decided once that the floor in the grocery store needed "dusting"—he likes to dust—and he got down on the floor and began dusting the grimy floor with his fingers.

19   But he has never lived in a prison of overprotectiveness. Even though his mother says there are limits to how much freedom he can realistically have and how much so-called normal behavior she can expect from him, she decided years ago that the only way he could have anything approaching a normal life—in some ways, the only way she herself could have one—was to let him go swimming, visit neighbors, take some normal, childlike risks.

20   He is prone, now and then, to just walk into a neighbor's house. Once, he went into the kitchen of a neighbor, opened the refrigerator, took out a carton of milk, slammed it down on the

counter and stood there, expectantly. The woman called Mrs.
Touchstone. "What should I do?" the woman asked. "Well," Mrs.
Touchstone said, "I'd pour him a glass of milk."

21   The fact that he is not completely dependent on his parents,
that he is not treated like an overgrown infant, that he is allowed
to swim on his own and roam the aisles of the Wal-Mart and raid
the neighbors' refrigerators, may have helped him survive when
he was all alone in the swamp, his family believes. "That's all his
mom," said Mr. Touchstone. "I was overly protective."

22   The phenomenon of his journey has prompted teachers at his
school to consider changes in the study plan for autistic or handi-
capped students. One teacher told Mrs. Touchstone that they
would stress more self-reliance.

23   Mrs. Touchstone, who jokingly calls herself "Treasurer for Life"
for the Fort Walton chapter of the Autism Society of America, said
her son's journey should clarify, in some people's minds, what
autism is. "I want every inch of that swamp he crossed to count
for something," she said. For now, life is back to normal. He
screamed when he was forced to take his medicine, which is not
so unusual for a ten-year-old. "We've got a little autism in all of
us," Mrs. Touchstone said.

24   Taylor has always been something of a celebrity in his neighborhood, so his mother does not expect much to change after his ordeal. There was a sign outside his school that just said, "Welcome
Home," and many people have called or written to tell her how relieved they are. One elderly neighbor wrote to tell Mrs. Touchstone how relieved she was that "our child" was home safe.

25   Mrs. Touchstone will not waste time wondering, at least not
too much, about her son's strange trip. She can live with the notion of a miracle. "I guess God was looking for something to do,"
she said. "I guess he looked down and said, 'Let's fix things up a
little bit.'"

Rick Bragg, "Boy's Autism No Handicap,
Boy Defies Swamp," *New York Times*,
August 17, 1996, pp. 1, 7.

CHECKING YOUR COMPREHENSION | DIRECTIONS Answer the following questions by circling the letter of the correct response.

1. Which statement more effectively paraphrases the main idea of the
    entire reading?

    a. Taylor Touchstone's experience in a deadly swamp is a perfect
        illustration of an everyday miracle that proves the existence
        of God.

b. Ironically, being autistic may well have saved **Taylor** Touchstone's life when he was lost for four days in a dangerous swamp.

2. According to the reading, Taylor's form of autism is

   a. incurable.

   b. severe.

   c. moderate.

3. Taylor's parents believe that Taylor survived his ordeal because

   a. he has always been lucky.

   b. God was watching out for him.

   c. his autism kept him from panicking.

4. Mrs. Touchstone thought Taylor might be dead because

   a. he was a poor swimmer.

   b. four Rangers had died in the swamp.

   c. he had been gone for so long.

5. Which statement more effectively paraphrases the topic sentence in paragraph 3?

   a. For Taylor's neighbors, calling his experience a **miracle** may be the only way they will ever be able to explain what **happened.**

   b. Taylor's neighbors are convinced that what happened to the boy is a miracle, and they may be right.

6. Which statement more effectively paraphrases the topic sentence in paragraph 7?

   a. Taylor's parents believe that their son's stubborn **nature is what** helped him survive.

   b. Taylor's parents don't actually know what happened to him, but they and their daughter have a theory about his **survival.**

7. The quotation from Rick Hord in paragraph 12 is a supporting detail that develops what main idea?

   a. Right after he floated away, every effort was made to find Taylor, but somehow the boy still managed to swim deeper and deeper into the swamp.

   b. Immediately after he floated away, efforts were made to find Taylor, but because the searchers did not try hard enough, the boy managed to get away.

8. In paragraph 14, Mrs. Taylor asks "Do you really think God would strike him with lightning?" How would you label that supporting detail?

    a. major

    b. minor

9. Paragraphs 16 and 17 are linked together by transitions that signal

    a. contrast.

    b. time order.

    c. cause and effect.

10. Paragraph 22 relies on what pattern of organization?

    a. process

    b. classification

    c. cause and effect

SHARPENING YOUR CRITICAL SKILLS **DIRECTIONS** Answer the following questions by filling in the blanks or circling the letter of the correct response.

1. Which of the following statements more effectively describes the author's purpose?

    a. The author wants to tell readers about Taylor Touchstone's extraordinary adventure.

    b. The author wants to convince readers that autistic children can lead perfectly normal lives.

2. What elements or characteristics of the reading helped you make your decision?

_____

3. How would you label the following statement—*fact, opinion,* or a *blend* of both? "People in this resort town on the Gulf of Mexico say they believe Taylor's survival is a miracle and that may be as good an explanation as they will ever have."

_____

Explain the basis for your answer.

_____

4. How would you label the following statement—*fact, opinion,* or a *blend* of both? "Apparently, Taylor just felt compelled to keep moving."

_____

Explain the basis for your answer.

_____

5. In paragraph 14, Mrs. Touchstone is quoted as saying "Do you really think God would strike him with lightning? Wouldn't that be redundant?" What is she implying with those questions?

_____

_____

6. How would you describe the tone of the quotations from Mrs. Touchstone?

    a. scared and angry

    b. down-to-earth

    c. emotionally neutral

7. Do you think her tone is similar or different from the author's?

_____

Please explain.

_____

8. Mrs. Touchstone calls her son "bullheaded." Is that a metaphor or a simile?

_____

What does she want to communicate about her son by means of this particular figure of speech?

_____

9. The Touchstone family argues that Taylor's autism may have helped him survive. What reasons do they give to support their point of view?

_____

_____

10. What statement most effectively sums up the author's personal feelings about Taylor?

    a. The author doesn't think the boy did anything special.

    b. The author also thinks the boy's experience is extraordinary.

    c. It's impossible to determine the author's personal feelings.

■ **DRAWING YOUR OWN CONCLUSIONS** Do you think Ted Tollefson, the author of the reading on heroes, would consider Taylor a hero? Why or why not?

■ **WRITING SUGGESTION** Write a paper in which you explain why you think Taylor Touchstone would or would not qualify as a hero. Begin by summarizing the highlights of his journey, and follow your summary with a thesis statement that clearly identifies your position. Conclude by answering a possible objection from those who might not agree with your point of view.

■ **READING 13**

RESEARCHING THE EFFECTS OF PORNOGRAPHY

LOOKING AHEAD   Chapter 4 pointed out that some feminists believe pornography needs to be strictly controlled and censored because it is dangerous to women. The authors of the following reading sum up some significant research studying the link between pornography and violence.

GETTING FOCUSED   Read the first and last paragraphs. Then read the first sentence of the remaining paragraphs and all the words in **Word Watch.** Based on your survey, how do you think the authors will answer this question: Does reading or viewing pornography contribute to violence against women?

_____

_____

This is rather technical reading, so don't rush through it. Take your time. If you need to, read the more difficult paragraphs twice. The more technical a reading, the slower your reading rate should be. As you read, ask yourself if the authors would or would not support the position of feminists who believe pornography must be censored.

WORD WATCH   Some of the more difficult words in the reading are defined in this section. Watch for these words as you read. They are marked with an asterisk. When you finish the reading, review the words in **Word Watch** by covering up the definitions and checking to see if you now know all the meanings. Record any words you still don't know in a notebook or on index cards. Review them periodically until they are part of your vocabulary.

coercive: characterized by the use of force or might

consensual: agreed upon by all parties

rendition: version

hypothesis: theory

confederate: companion, colleague

simulated: pretended

erotica: sexually explicit material

debriefed: questioned and instructed

terminating: ending

replicated: repeated

depictions: descriptions

eroticized: arousing sexual love and desire

1 TO EXAMINE THE EFFECT OF EXPOSURE TO VIOLENT POR-
nography, two of the most active researchers on the topic, Malamuth and Donnerstein (1984), exposed men to a series of slides
and tapes of women reading stories that included coercive* or consensual* sexual interaction. Before participating in the studies,
volunteers were asked to indicate the likelihood that they would
commit rape, if they could be sure of not getting caught. Those
who revealed that they thought they might engage in coercive sexual acts were classified as *force oriented.*

2 Although the designs of these studies varied, the stimuli usually consisted of a story of an attractive woman wandering along a
deserted road. A man finds her there, but when he approaches
her, she faints. He carries her to his car, and when she awakens
they engage in sex. In one version of this basic story, the woman
is tied up and forced to have sex in the car. In other variations,
she clearly consents to the act. Regardless of which rendition*
they saw, male volunteers found this story arousing. . . . This
finding is consistent with others showing that certain rape portrayals elicit relatively high sexual arousal in nonrapists (Malamuth, 1984; Malamuth & Check, 1983).

3 What about the kind of violent pornography that depicts a positive reaction on the part of the victim? As Donnerstein (1984)
pointed out, pornographic media quite often portray victims of assault as responding favorably to a rape. Further, in real life, convicted rapists often fail to perceive their assaults as coercive, believing that their victims desired intercourse and enjoyed their
sexual attentions (Gage & Schurr, 1976). Because exposure to violent pornography has been shown to heighten sexual arousal, promote acceptance of rape-supportive attitudes, and foster negative
attitudes toward women (Donnerstein & Linz, 1986; Malamuth,
1984), Donnerstein reasoned that such exposure would also increase aggressive behavior against women, particularly when a
woman is depicted as having a positive reaction to sexual assault.

4 To test this hypothesis,* each male volunteer was paired with a
female confederate,* who either angered the man or treated him
in a neutral manner. Each man then watched one of four films—
a neutral version, a variation that involved consensual interaction, a version in which the victim had a negative reaction to
forced sex, or a variation in which the victim's reaction to forced
sex was positive.

5 After viewing one of these films, the volunteer was given an opportunity to administer simulated* electric shocks to the female
confederate. Of the volunteers who had been angered prior to

watching the movie, those who had viewed either of the forced-sex films chose to give higher levels of electric shock to the female confederate than did those who viewed either of the other films. Even the nonangered men, however, became more aggressive (as measured by electric-shock level) following exposure to the version of the film showing a positive reaction to forced sex. When a male confederate angered a male volunteer prior to the latter's exposure to the film, the versions of the film did not affect aggression toward the male confederate (Donnerstein, 1984).

6   Even a rape portrayal emphasizing the victim's pain and distress may, under certain conditions, stimulate high levels of sexual arousal in viewers. But this effect appears to vary as a function of whether the viewer describes himself as force oriented or not (Malamuth, 1981). Force-oriented volunteers reported having more arousal fantasies after exposure to the rape version than after exposure to the mutual-consent version. Non–force-oriented men, however, reported having more arousing fantasies in response to the variations of the story involving mutual consent than in response to the rape variation. . . .

7   One criticism of laboratory-based studies of aggressive behavior in response to portrayals of erotica* involves the limited response alternatives that have been provided to respondents (Fisher & Grenier, 1994). To determine if the limited range of responses provided by previous experimenters had affected the findings, Fisher and Grenier provided a broader range of alternatives for volunteers. That is, after being angered by the female confederate and shown sexual material containing violent content, men in Fisher and Grenier's research could select shock, verbal feedback, or the alternative of simply being debriefed,* receiving their experimental credit, and terminating* their participation in the study.

8   Almost all participants selected the last alternative. This research is preliminary and needs to be replicated* by other researchers to see if the findings hold up, but by providing the option of allowing participants to leave without displaying aggression against the confederate, Fisher and Grenier (1994) provided a more realistic range of responses in the well-controlled environment of the laboratory.

9   What is the effect of violent pornography on women's arousal? To investigate this question, Stock (1982) presented college women with variations in rape depictions* while measuring their . . . responses and their subjective reports of arousal. Stock also compared the effect on their arousal levels of highly eroticized versus more realistic rape depictions because Malamuth and

Check's depictions had focused on erotic aspects of the interaction rather than on the victims' negative response.

10   Accordingly, Stock's volunteers were exposed to either eroticized* or realistic rape depictions, as well as to other variations. Based on the women's responses, Stock concluded that "women are not aroused by rape when described in a realistic manner, but only to a distorted misrepresentation of rape in which the victim does not suffer and no harm is done. This is far from the experience of victims of rape" (1982, p. 9).

11   In their investigations of the effects of violent pornography, it is the romanticized portrayals of rape that concern Malamuth and his colleagues. Stock's finding that women, too, can be aroused by such eroticized rape depictions, but not by realistic rape depictions, also adds to our knowledge about the effects of violent pornography. The belief of some rapists and members of the general public that women secretly enjoy rape is not supported by Stock's conclusions, and her work suggests that society should be concerned about rape representations that lead viewers to perceive sexual assault as an erotic experience. In the context of films and videos portraying sexual assault, how would you work in the message that rape is a frightening and traumatizing experience for its victims?

12   Further research is needed on the effects of violent pornography. . . . Our present knowledge does not permit us to determine whether men who report strong arousal to rape depictions and who are aroused by their own rape fantasies will actually commit rape.

Albert Richard Allgeier and Elizabeth Rice Allgeier,
Sexual Interactions. Boston:
Houghton Mifflin, 1995, pp. 534–536.

CHECKING YOUR COMPREHENSION   **DIRECTIONS** Answer the following questions by circling the letter of the correct response.

1. Which of these statements do you think most effectively sums up the contents of the reading?

   a. Studies on the effects of pornography all show the same results: Men who read or watch pornography are more likely to commit acts of violence against women, and there is a clear cause and effect relationship.

   b. Although some studies suggest a connection between violent pornography and violence against women, there is still not enough evidence to be absolutely sure, particularly given the artificial nature of the laboratory setting.

   c. Because of the overwhelming evidence connecting violent pornography to violence against women, stricter measures must be
taken to censor the publishing of pornographic books and the
filming of pornographic movies.

2. Before participating in the study, volunteers were asked if they

   a. watched or read pornography on a regular basis.

   b. would commit rape if they knew they would not get caught.

   c. had ever had rape fantasies.

3. According to the reading, subjects characterized as *force oriented*
were those who

   a. had been in the armed forces.

   b. said they would commit rape if they knew they would not get
caught.

   c. believed that using force was appropriate in sexual relations.

4. According to the authors of the reading, the belief that women secretly enjoy rape

   a. is supported by research.

   b. is not supported by research.

   c. has not been the subject of research.

5. There is a good deal of research cited in this study, but the names
of the most important researchers are

   a. Gage and Schurr.

   b. Check and Linz.

   c. Malamuth and Donnerstein.

6. In paragraph 2, the main idea appears in

   a. sentence 1.

   b. sentence 2.

   c. sentence 3.

7. Which sentence more effectively paraphrases the topic sentence in
paragraph 6?

   a. The effect of rape portrayals emphasizing the victim's pain and
humiliation varies with the individual viewer.

   b. Rape portrayals emphasizing the pain and humiliation suffered
by victims stimulated sexual arousal in viewers.

8. Together, paragraphs 4 and 5 rely on what two organizational patterns?

   a. comparison and contrast and classification

   b. cause and effect and process

   c. process and definition

9. The two transitions used in paragraph 6 signal

   a. cause and effect.

   b. contrast.

   c. dates and events.

10. Based on this reading, which of the following test questions would you be *least* likely to predict?

    a. Summarize the findings of Malamuth and Donnerstein.

    b. Describe the research study conducted by Gage and Schurr.

    c. Describe how Donnerstein went about testing his hypothesis that exposure to violent pornography would increase violence against women.

SHARPENING YOUR CRITICAL SKILLS

DIRECTIONS Answer the following questions by filling in the blanks or circling the letter of the correct response.

1. Which statement more effectively describes the authors' purpose?

   a. The authors want to inform their readers about current research on the connection between viewing violent pornography and carrying out acts of violence against women.

   b. The authors want to persuade readers that there is no solid connection between viewing violent pornography and carrying out acts of violence against women.

2. Explain the basis for your answer to question number 1.

   _____

   _____

3. What inference can be drawn from the research cited in paragraph 6?

   a. It's not that easy to generalize about the effects of pornography on men.

   b. Force-oriented individuals are likely to commit rape if they watch violent pornography.

4. Label the following statement *F* (fact), *O* (opinion), or *B* (both).

Pornographic media often portray victims of assault as responding favorably to rape.

_____

Explain the basis for your answer: _____

_____

5. Label the following statement *F* (fact), *O* (opinion), or *B* (both).

Further research is needed on the effects of violent pornography.

_____

Explain the basis for your answer: _____

_____

6. The 1994 study by Fisher and Grenier lends support to what claim?
   a. There is a direct link between watching violent pornography and violence against women.
   b. A direct link between watching violent pornography and violence against women has not yet been firmly established.

7. In paragraph 11, the authors say that the work of Stock (1982) should make society "concerned about rape representations that lead viewers to perceive sexual assault as an erotic experience." However, they don't say exactly why society should be concerned. What reason can you infer?

_____

_____

8. On the controversy over the censorship of pornography, do you think the authors would or would not side with those who want to see strict censorship enforced?

_____

Please explain. _____

_____

9. How would you describe the authors' tone?

_____

10. Which statement most effectively describes the authors' personal bias?

    a. The authors do not believe that there is a connection between violent pornography and violence against women.

    b. The authors believe that there is a direct link between violent pornography and violence against women.

    c. The authors believe more research needs to be done before a decision can be made about the relationship between violent pornography and violence against women.

■ **DRAWING YOUR OWN CONCLUSIONS** What do you think: Does pornography lead to violence? Can you explain the basis for your opinion?

■ **WRITING SUGGESTION** Write a paper in which you argue for or against the censorship of pornography. Should it be protected under the right to free speech or not? State your position clearly in the opening of your paper. Then give at least two reasons that support your point of view. Conclude by answering what you think might be an objection to your stand.

■ **READING 14**

LEARNING AT HOME: DOES IT PASS THE TEST?

LOOKING AHEAD   Chapter 11 debated the subject of home schooling. The following reading suggests that home schooling, despite some controversy over its effectiveness, is here to stay.

GETTING FOCUSED   Read the first and last paragraphs. Then read the first sentence of the remaining paragraphs and all the words in **Word Watch.** When you finish, predict how you think the authors will answer the question posed in the title.

_____

_____

As you read, consider how you feel about home schooling. Would you consider taking your children out of school and teaching them at home?

WORD WATCH   Some of the more difficult words in the reading are defined in this section. Watch for these words as you read. They are marked with an asterisk. When you finish the reading, review the words in **Word Watch** by covering up the definitions and checking to see if you now know all the meanings. Record any words you still don't know in a notebook or on index cards. Review them periodically until they are part of your vocabulary.

habitat: the place in which a person, plant, or creature is most likely to be found

province: area or location of control

fundamentalists: people who insist on strict adherence to biblical writings

unsavory: disagreeable, morally offensive

inundated: flooded

statutes: laws, rules

advocates: supporters

Pollyanna: a person who is foolishly optimistic; from the main character of the novel by the same name

1 THIS FALL, AS MOST KIDS MADE THEIR ANNUAL TREK BACK TO the classroom, a small but growing army of parents just said no to school. Some, like Jean Forbes of Alexandria, Virginia, thought their children needed extra attention. Forbes is a former actress whose current career is teaching her two sons, Aaron, fourteen, and Jesse, seven, and running a theater group for forty other kids who are taught in their homes. She and her husband, Jan, pulled Aaron, who is dyslexic, out of public school six years ago because they felt teachers weren't helping him enough. Other parents want to give their kids the chance to follow their interests rather than a textbook. Outside Los Angeles, Marcy Kinsey, a mother of three kids—ages eleven, nine, and seven—calls herself an "un-schooler." Right now her kids are studying bats, everything from their diet to their wingspan to the specifics of their natural habi-tat.* They've even built a bat house in the backyard, which re-quired many hours of practical math problems.

2 Still other parents pull their kids out of school to solve what they think is a short-term problem—and find long-term chal-lenges. Eric and Joyce Burges, who live outside Baton Rouge, Lou-isiana, began home schooling nearly a decade ago after their old-est son, Eric Jr., had a disastrous year at a selective magnet high school. It was a struggle at first; neither is a professional teacher. But as Eric Jr.'s confidence rose at home, so did Joyce's, and she now teaches her four other kids, ages fifteen to three, at home as well. School begins every morning at 7 and lasts until lunch. Joyce says home schooling has been a test of her strengths and weaknesses. Accepting the latter, she hired music and algebra tu-tors. "I know what I want them to learn, and I know what they want to learn," she says. "I don't have to do it all."

3 Just a few years ago, home schooling was the province* of re-ligious fundamentalists* who wanted to instill their values in their children and back-to-the-earth types who rejected the insti-tutional nature of public schools. Now it's edging ever closer to the mainstream. In 1993—after years of court battles—it became legal in all fifty states for parents to take charge of their kids' edu-cation from kindergarten to college. While there are no national statistics, researchers who study home schooling estimate that as many as 1.5 million youngsters are currently being taught primar-ily by their mothers or fathers. That's five times the estimated number of home schoolers just a decade ago and bigger than the nation's largest public-school system, New York City's. The in-crease is especially remarkable in an era of two-income families, since it pretty much requires one parent to stay home (generally the mother), at some financial sacrifice. In a recent Newsweek

poll, 59 percent of those surveyed said home-schooled kids were at least as well educated as students in traditional schools. "Home schoolers' image is not wacko, fringe, lunatic-type people anymore," says Brian Ray, president of the Home Education Research Institute in Salem, Oregon, a nonprofit group. "Today almost everyone knows a home schooler, so it's more socially acceptable."

4   Some of the new home-schooling parents are looking for a way to reclaim family closeness in an increasingly fast-paced society. Others have kids with special needs, perhaps because they're highly gifted or have learning disabilities or emotional problems. Still other parents worry about unsavory* influences in school— drugs, alcohol, sex, violence. Florida education officials report that in the last few years, the number one reason parents gave for home schooling was "safety." Some intend to teach at home all the way through twelfth grade. Others see home schooling as a way to get through a bad patch in a kid's school life.

5   Their lesson plans are as diverse as their reasons for dropping out of the system, but what unites all these parents is a belief that they can do a better job at home than trained educators in a conventional school. That would have been an outrageous notion a generation ago, when far fewer parents had college degrees and most people regarded teachers and schools with more respect and even awe. Today parents are much better educated, hooked up to a world of information via the Internet and inundated* with headlines about problems plaguing public schools. They see home schooling as one more step in the evolution of parent power that has given birth to school-choice programs, vouchers, and charter schools. "Americans are becoming fussy consumers rather than trusting captives of a state monopoly," says Chester Finn, a senior fellow at the Hudson Institute, a Washington, D.C., think tank. "They've declared their independence and are taking matters into their own hands."

6   But while home schooling is winning converts, it still has plenty of critics who worry that millions of youngsters will grow up without adequate academic or social skills. "Kids need to be successful in three overlapping spheres—at home, at school, and with peers," says Phoenix pediatrician Daniel Kessler, a member of the American Academy of Pediatrics developmental-behavior group. "Home schooling compresses all that into a single setting that can be very difficult for kids." The National Education Association, the nation's biggest teachers' union, backs much more rigorous regulation.

7   Only thirty-seven states now have statutes* that set standards

for home schooling, says Christopher Klicka, executive director of the National Center for Home Education, an advocacy group. About half of those demand some kind of annual testing or evaluation; the rest require only that certain subjects be covered within a specified time frame. Many educators say it's the government's responsibility to make sure kids get what they need to become productive citizens. "After all, if home schooling fails," says Ronald Areglado of the National Association of Elementary School Principals, "we pay the freight" when a person ends up on public assistance or in jail. Areglado has good reason for his concern; as a principal, he saw a home-schooled kid who got no instruction at all from his parents.

8   But home-schooling parents say they are better equipped than ever before to give kids what they need. "What they're doing is reinventing the idea of school," says Patricia Lines, a senior research analyst for the U.S. Department of Education. The Internet and sophisticated new educational software help fill in academic gaps. If they need more inspiration, they can browse through bookstore shelves filled with how-to books and subscribe to dozens of newsletters and magazines with titles like *Growing Without Schooling* that are packed with ads for home-schooling textbooks, videos and software, and seminars. "There are much better, more sophisticated curriculum materials available," says Kathi Kearney, an expert in the home schooling of gifted students at Iowa State University.

9   These tools have transformed the conventional image of a home-schooling family: a couple of kids with workbooks open on the kitchen table under the supervision of Mom or Dad. Not only have the new generation of home schoolers moved beyond workbooks, they've also moved well out of the kitchen and often join home-schooling cooperatives, where parents take turns teaching different subjects and get together for group field trips. Jean Forbes's home-schooling theater group in Virginia is more than just a chance for kids to enjoy center stage. History and even science lessons are part of the program. When the girls put on hoop skirts for *Little Women*, they talked about how children played a century ago. When they used dry ice onstage in a play, they talked about the science behind the special effects.

10   Home-schooling parents are also turning to a surprising source for help: public schools. In the wake of lawsuits in many states by home-schooling parents, more communities are opening the doors to school libraries or computer rooms. Some districts have "part time" options that allow kids to sign up for a few courses or participate in extracurricular activities like the football team or

the band. Oregon even allows students to register for courses at different schools, so that a teenager could take advanced biology at one high school and art at another. Almost every state now has a home-schooling coordinator, and some, such as Washington and Iowa, have established resource centers for parents—giving families a chance to get something in return for their taxes.

11   In California—where the troubled public schools have pushed thousands of parents into home schooling—many families sign up for the independent study program at their local public schools to get books and other materials. A teacher monitors the child's progress, usually through monthly visits. Jon Shemitz, a computer-programming consultant, enrolled his son, Sam, ten, in independent study through his district near Santa Cruz. During the teacher's monthly visits, Shemitz says, she "fills out the paperwork, sits around and chats, and allows us to participate in a few programs like field trips."

12   Despite these new resources, no one really knows how this new generation of home schoolers will turn out. There are no reliable long-term studies, but advocates* say home schoolers generally do as well as other kids on standardized tests, and some are accepted into the most elite colleges. Harvard has even assigned an admissions officer, David Illingsworth, to review applications from home schoolers. "Ten years ago, if you didn't have a diploma we didn't want you," he says. "Today we're always willing to look at different kinds of credentials." Other colleges have mixed views of home-schooled students. In one recent survey of admissions officers, only 20 percent thought that parents were better able to motivate their children than teachers. But 83 percent agreed that high-school students could be adequately taught at home.

13   At every age, a strong parent-child relationship is far more important than any particular curriculum, experts say. Those bonds can be stretched when the whole family is together 24-7. Kids have to respect parents as teachers and still love them as Mom and Dad—a difficult task. Parents don't even have the luxury of time off while their children are in the classroom; they are always on duty. It's so tough that some parents give up after only a year or two. "I've seen it tear families apart," says William Coleman, associate professor of pediatrics at the University of North Carolina.

14   Kids with special needs—gifted or learning disabled—are more likely than most to benefit from home schooling, researchers say, but only if their parents have the right training and resources. Ryan Abradi, a ten-year-old who lives in central Maine, started multiplying when he was just two and a half, and even then understood the concept of negative numbers. "From the beginning,

he seemed hard-wired for math," says his mother, Valerie, a mechanical engineer. When he reached school age, she checked out the local gifted program and could tell right away that Ryan was already well beyond it. "He had no patience," she says. "He was intolerant of the questions other kids would ask." Ryan is now happily at home, working his way through second-semester college calculus.

15   Home-schooling parents reject critics' claims that their kids aren't well socialized. Many of them say they've overcome the isolation by getting kids involved in Scouts, 4-H or sports teams. "Ninety percent of these kids play with people outside their families," says Brian Ray of the National Home Education Research Institute. But home-schooled kids themselves say they are different—in both good and bad ways. They're probably more likely to be independent and self-motivated, but group activities can be a struggle. Eighteen-year-old Jon Williams of Missoula, Montana, is clearly outgoing and confident: he's a Republican candidate for his state's legislature. But Williams, who has been home schooled since ninth grade, credits the eight years he spent in Christian school with helping him hone his basic social skills. . . .

16   Social isolation can be especially damaging in the middle-school years, says Coleman of the University of North Carolina. "Parents have this Pollyanna* view that they're going to keep their kids away from bad influences," he says, "when kids biologically and psychosocially are going to want to push away" from their families.

17   At some point, of course, home-schooled kids will move out on their own. What lessons will serve them best? The ultimate goal of any educational path is to inspire love of learning, a passion that lasts a lifetime.

Barbara Kantrowitz and Pat Winger,
"Learning at Home: Does It Pass the Test?"
Newsweek, October 5, 1998, pp. 66–70.

CHECKING YOUR COMPREHENSION

DIRECTIONS Answer the following questions by circling the letter of the correct response.

1. Which statement more effectively sums up the main idea of the entire reading?

a. The idea of teaching your children at home is becoming part of the mainstream and is catching on all over the country.

b. Home schooling, once the province of religious fundamentalists, has become so successful that children are leaving public schools in droves and threatening the future of public education.

2. According to the authors, estimates about the number of children being taught at home are as high as

a. one million.

b. one and a half million.

c. two million.

3. Parents who teach their children at home are quite diverse, but what idea unites them?

a. Home-schooling parents all believe that religion should be part of the school curriculum.

b. Home-schooling parents are worried about the sexual freedom they believe is encouraged in public schools.

c. Home-schooling parents are convinced that they can do a better job than the more traditional schools are doing.

4. How many states currently have statutes that set standards for home schooling?

a. twenty-four

b. thirty-seven

c. forty

5. Home-schooling parents are getting help from

a. the government.

b. local churches.

c. public schools.

6. Which sentence more effectively paraphrases the two-step topic sentence in paragraph 3?

a. There are no national statistics about home schooling, but estimates suggest that nearly 1.5 million children are being taught at home, usually by their mothers.

b. Not too long ago, religious fundamentalists were just about the only ones championing home schooling, but now it is becoming a widely accepted alternative to public schools.

7. What's the implied topic sentence of paragraph 4?

a. Parents who choose home schooling are hoping that it will encourage family unity.

b. There are several different reasons why parents choose to school their children at home.

8. Paragraph 3 ends with which type of supporting detail?

   a. major

   b. minor

9. Paragraph 9 relies on which pattern?

   a. process

   b. cause and effect

   c. classification

10. On the basis of the reading, which test question is likely to turn up on an exam?

    a. Identify at least three famous people who were taught at home.

    b. What are some of the reasons some parents are teaching their children at home?

    c. Trace the history of home schooling from the nineteenth century until now.

SHARPENING YOUR CRITICAL SKILLS

DIRECTIONS Answer the following questions by filling in the blanks or circling the letter of the correct response.

1. Which statement more accurately expresses the purpose of this reading?

   a. The authors want to describe for their readers the current status of the home-schooling movement.

   b. The authors want to convince their readers that home schooling is a wise choice.

2. How did you determine the author's purpose? What clues did you use?

   _____

   _____

3. Label the following statement *F* (fact), *O* (opinion), or *B* (both).

   In 1993 . . . it became legal in all fifty states for parents to take charge of their kids' education from kindergarten to college.

   _____

   Please explain. _____

   _____

4. Label the following statement *F* (fact), *O* (opinion), or *B* (both).

Kids need to be successful in three overlapping spheres—at home, at school, and with peers.

_____

Please explain. _____

_____

5. In paragraph 3, Brian Ray is quoted in support of home schooling. With what organization is he affiliated?

_____

What does that organization suggest to you about Mr. Ray's possible bias?

_____

6. In paragraph 6, Daniel Kessler criticizes the home schooling movement. What are his qualifications as a source of expert opinion?

_____

What do those qualifications suggest about Mr. Kessler's possible bias?

_____

_____

7. Based on what the authors say about Ronald Areglado, would you expect Mr. Areglado to be biased in favor of or against home schooling?

_____

Please explain. _____

_____

8. Based on the quotation from Patricia Lines in paragraph 8, you would infer that she

   a. supports home schooling.

   b. does not support home schooling.

   Lines's background suggests that she is

   a. likely to be biased in favor of home schooling.

   b. likely to be biased against home schooling.

   c. unlikely to be biased either way.

9. In paragraph 8, the author tells us that Kathi Kearney is an "expert." In response, what question might critical readers pose about her qualifications?

_____

10. Which statement most effectively describes the authors' personal feelings?

a. The authors favor home schooling.

b. The authors are critical of home schooling.

c. It's impossible to determine the authors' personal feelings.

DRAWING YOUR OWN CONCLUSIONS In the reading you just finished, both sides of the home-schooling debate argue their positions. Which side do you think offered the more effective argument and why?

WRITING SUGGESTION Write a paper in which you argue for or against home schooling. Give at least two reasons for your position, and be sure to respond to at least one objection.

Memory

Memory The mental
system for receiving,
storing, organizing, altering,
and recovering information.

This chapter discusses memory and forgetting. As an inquiring person, you should find the information interesting. Also included is a large section on improving memory skills. As a student, you should find this discussion particularly helpful. Almost anyone (including you) can learn to use memory more effectively.

Survey Questions

- How do we store information in memory?
- Is there more than one type of memory?
- What are the features of each type of memory?
- How is memory measured?
- What are "photographic" memories?
- What causes forgetting?
- How accurate are everyday memories?
- What happens in the brain when memories are formed?
- How can memory be improved?

Stages of Memory—Do You Have a Mind Like a Steel Trap? Or a Sieve?

- **Survey Question**
  How do we store information in memory?

Encoding Converting information into a form in which it will be retained in memory.

Storage Holding information in memory for later use.

Retrieval Recovering information from storage in memory.

"A dusty storehouse of facts." That's how many people think of memory. In reality, **memory** is an *active system* that receives, stores, organizes, alters, and recovers information (Baddeley, 1990). In some ways memory acts like a computer. Information to be recorded is first **encoded,** or changed into a usable form. This step is like typing data into a computer. Next, information is **stored,** or held in the system. (As we will see in a moment, human memory actually has three separate storage systems.) Finally, memories must be **retrieved,** or taken out of storage, to be useful. To remember something, encoding, storage, and retrieval all must take place. Psychologists have identified three stages of memory. To be stored for a long time, information must pass through all three.

Sensory Memory

• **Survey Question**
Is there more than one type of memory?

Icon A mental image or representation.

Echo A brief continuation of sensory activity in the auditory system after a sound is heard.

Let's say a friend asks you to pick up several things at a market. How do you remember them? Incoming information first enters **sensory memory.** Sensory memory holds an exact copy of what is seen or heard for a few seconds or less. For instance, if you look at an object and then close your eyes, an **icon** (EYE-kon), or fleeting image, will persist for about one-half second afterward. Similarly, information you hear is held as a brief **echo** in sensory memory for up to 2 seconds (Klatzky, 1980). An ability to mentally "play back" what someone else just said is based on echoic memory (Eysenck & Keane, 1990).

In general, sensory memory holds information just long enough to transfer it to the second memory system.

Short-Term Memory

Selective attention Voluntarily focusing on a selected portion of sensory input, most likely by rerouting messages within the brain.

Short-term memory (STM) The memory system used to hold small amounts of information for relatively brief time periods.

Not everything seen or heard is kept in memory. Let's say a radio is playing in the background as your friend reads you her shopping list. Do you remember what the announcer says too? Probably not, because **selective attention** controls what information moves on to **short-term memory (STM).** Short-term memories are also brief, but longer lasting than sensory memories. Paying attention to your friend's words will place the shopping list in short-term memory (while allowing you to ignore the voice on the radio saying, "Buy Burpo Butter").

Short-term memories can be stored as images. But more often they are stored by *sound,* especially when you recall words and letters (Anderson, 1990). If you are introduced to Tim at a party and you forget his name, you are more likely to call him by a name that *sounds like* Tim (Jim, for instance) than a name that sounds different, such as Bob or Tod. Your friend with the shopping list will be lucky if you don't bring home peas instead of cheese and soap instead of soup!

Working memory Another name for short-term memory, especially as it is used for thinking and problem solving.

Short-term memory acts as a *temporary* storehouse for *small amounts* of information. Unless the information is important, it is quickly "dumped" from STM and forever lost. Short-term memory prevents our minds from collecting useless names, dates, telephone numbers, and other trivia. At the same time, it provides a **working memory** where we do much of our thinking. Dialing a phone number, doing mental arithmetic, remembering a shopping list, and the like, all rely on STM (Atkinson & Shiffrin, 1971).

Long-Term Memory

Long-term memory (LTM)
The memory system used for relatively permanent storage of meaningful information.

Information that is important or *meaningful* is transferred to the third memory system, called long-term memory. In contrast to STM, **long-term memory (LTM)** acts as a permanent storehouse for information. LTM contains everything you know about the world—from aardvark to zucchini, math to Monopoly, facts to fantasy. And yet, there appears to be no danger of running out of room in LTM. LTM has a nearly limitless storage capacity. In fact, the more you know, the easier it becomes to add new information to memory. This is the reverse of what we would expect if LTM could be "filled up" (Eysenck & Keane, 1990). It is also one of many powerful reasons for getting an education.

Information in LTM is stored on the basis of *meaning* and importance, not by sound. If you make an error in LTM, it will probably be related to meaning. For example, if you are trying to recall the word BARN from a memorized list, you are more likely to mistakenly say SHED or FARM than BORN.

When new information enters STM, it is related to knowledge stored in LTM. This gives the new information meaning and makes it easier to store in LTM. As an example, try to memorize this story:

> With hocked gems financing him, our brave hero bravely defied all scornful laughter. "Your eyes deceive," he had said, "An egg, not a table, correctly typifies this unexplored planet." Now three sturdy sisters sought proof. Forging along, days became weeks as many doubters spread fearful rumors about the edge. At last from nowhere welcome winged creatures appeared, signifying momentous success. (Adapted from Dooling & Lachman, 1971)

This odd story emphasizes the impact of meaning on memory. People given the title of the story were able to remember it far better than those not given a title. See if the title helps you as much as it did them. The title is "Columbus Discovers America."

Short-Term Memory—Do You Know the Magic Number?

Do you know how much information can be held in short-term memory? For an answer, read the following numbers once. Then close the book and write as many as you can in the correct order.

8 5 1 7 4 9 3

This is called a **digit-span test.** If you were able to correctly repeat this series of seven digits, you have an average short-term memory. Now try to memorize the following list of digits, reading them only once.

| 7 | 1 | 8 | 3 | 5 | 4 | 2 | 9 | 1 | 6 | 3 |

This series was probably beyond your short-term memory capacity. Psychologist George Miller has shown that short-term memory is limited to what he calls the "magic number" **seven** (plus or minus two) **bits** of information (Miller, 1956). A *bit* is a single "piece" of information—a single digit, for example. It is as if short-term memory has seven "slots" or "bins" into which separate items can be placed.

When all of the "slots" in STM are filled, there is no room for new information. Picture how this works at a party: Let's say your hostess begins introducing everyone who is there, "Ted, Barbara, Donna, Roseanna, Wayne, Shawn, Linda. . . ." "Stop," you think to yourself. But she continues, "Eddie, Jay, Gordon, Frank, Marietta, Dan, Patty, Glen, Ricky." The hostess leaves, satisfied that you have met everyone. And you spend the evening talking with Ted, Barbara, and Ricky, the only people whose names you remember!

Recoding

Before we continue, try your short-term memory again, this time on letters. Read the following letters once, then look away and try to write them in the proper order.

| TVI | BMUS | NY | MCA |

Notice that there are twelve letters, or "bits" of information. This should be beyond the seven-item limit of STM. However, since the letters are presented as four groups, or **chunks** of information, many students are able to memorize them.

Chunking **recodes** information into larger units. Most often, it does so by taking advantage of units already in LTM. For example, you may have noticed that NY is the abbreviation for New York.

● **Survey Question**
What is chunking?

If so, the two bits N and Y became one chunk. In a memory experiment that used lists like this one, subjects remembered best when the letters were read as familiar meaningful chunks: TV, IBM, USN, YMCA (Bower & Springston, 1970). If you recoded the letters this way, you undoubtedly remembered the entire list.

Chunking suggests that STM holds about seven of whatever units we are using, be they numbers, letters, words, phrases, or familiar sentences (Klatzky, 1980). Picture STM as a small desk again. Through chunking, we combine several items into one "stack" of information. This allows us to place seven stacks on the desk, where before there was only room for seven separate items.

Rehearsal

Rehearsal Silently repeating or mentally reviewing information to hold it in short-term memory or aid its long-term storage.

Short-term memories appear to weaken and disappear very rapidly. However, a short-term memory can be prolonged by silently repeating it until it is needed. Remembering a telephone number you intend to use only once is often done this way.

Keeping a short-term memory alive by silently repeating it is called **rehearsal**. The longer a short-term memory is rehearsed, the greater its chances of being stored in LTM. What if rehearsal is prevented, so a memory cannot be recycled or moved to LTM? Without rehearsal, STM is incredibly short.

In one experiment, subjects heard meaningless syllables like XAR followed by a number like 67. As soon as subjects heard the number, they began counting backward by threes (to prevent them from repeating the syllable). After only 18 seconds of delay, memory scores fell to zero. (Peterson & Peterson, 1959)

After *18 seconds* without rehearsal, the short-term memories were gone forever! Keep this in mind when you get only one chance to hear information you want to remember. For example, if you are introduced to someone, and his or her name slips out of STM, there is no way to retrieve it. To escape this awkward situation you might try saying something like, "I'm curious, how do you spell your name?" But unfortunately, the response is often an icy reply like, "B-O-B S-M-I-T-H, it's really not too difficult." To avoid embarrassment, pay careful attention to the name, repeat it to yourself several times, and try to use it in the next sentence or two—before you lose it.

Long-Term Memory—Where the Past Lives

An electrode was placed at location number 11 on the patient's brain. She immediately said, "Yes, sir, I think I heard a mother calling her little boy somewhere. It seemed to be something happening years ago. It was somebody in the neighborhood where I live." A short time later the electrode was applied to the same spot. Again the patient said, "Yes, I hear the same familiar sounds, it seems to be a woman calling, the same lady" (Penfield, 1958). These statements were made by a woman undergoing brain surgery for epilepsy. Only local anesthetics were used (there are no pain receptors in the brain), so the patient was awake as her brain was electrically stimulated. When activated, some brain areas seemed to produce vivid memories of long-forgotten events.

Permanence   Results like those described led neurosurgeon Wilder Penfield to claim that the brain records the past like a "continuous strip of movie film, complete with sound track" (Penfield, 1957). But as you now know, this is an exaggeration. Many events never get past short-term memory. More importantly, in only about 3 percent of cases does brain stimulation produce memory-like experiences. Most reports resemble dreams more than memories, and many are clearly fictional. Memory experts Elizabeth and Geoffrey Loftus have carefully examined Penfield's work as well as research on "truth serums" and hypnosis. They conclude that there is little evidence that long-term memories are absolutely permanent (Loftus & Loftus, 1980). It is probably more accurate to say that long-term memories are relatively permanent, or long lasting.

Constructing Memories

There is another reason to doubt Penfield's claim. As new long-term memories are formed, older memories are often updated, changed, lost, or *revised* (Baddeley, 1990). To illustrate this point, Loftus and Palmer (1974) showed subjects a filmed automobile accident. Afterward, some subjects were asked to estimate how fast the cars were going when they "smashed" into each other. For others the words "bumped," "contacted," or "hit" replaced "smashed." One week later, subjects were asked, "Did you see any broken glass?" Those asked earlier about the cars that "smashed" into each other were more likely to say yes. (No broken glass was shown in the film.)

The new information ("smashed") was included in subjects' memories and altered them.

Updating memories is called **constructive processing.** Research shows that gaps in memory, which are common, may be filled in by logic, guesses, or new information (Loftus, 1977, 1980). Indeed, it is possible to have "memories" for things that never happened (such as remembering broken glass at an accident when there was none). People in Elizabeth Loftus's experiments who had these **pseudo-memories** (false memories) were often quite upset to learn they had given false "testimony" (Loftus & Ketcham, 1991). Other research has shown that being confident about a memory tells little about the actual accuracy of the memory (Smith, Kassin, & Ellsworth, 1989).

Organization

Long-term memory may record one quadrillion separate bits of information in a lifetime. How is it possible, then, to quickly find specific memories? The answer is that each person's "memory index" is highly organized.

The arrangement of information in LTM may be based on rules, images, categories, symbols, similarity, formal meaning, or personal meaning (Baddeley, 1990). In recent years, psychologists have begun to develop a picture of the **structure,** or arrangement, of memories. One example will serve to illustrate this research.

You are given the following two statements, to which you must answer yes or no: *A canary is an animal. A canary is a bird.* Which do you answer more quickly? Collins and Quillian (1969) found that *A canary is a bird* produced a faster yes than *A canary is an animal.* Why should this be so? Many psychologists believe that a **network model** of memory explains why. According to them, LTM is organized as a network of linked ideas. When ideas are "farther" apart, it takes a longer chain of associations to connect them. The more two items are separated, the longer it takes to answer. In other words, *canary* is probably close to *bird* in your "memory files." *Animal* and *canary* are farther apart. Remember though, this has nothing to do with alphabetical order. We are talking about organization based on related meanings.

Types of Long-term Memory

As we have seen, *memory* is an umbrella term that includes both short-term and long-term memory. Beyond this, it is becoming clear

Constructive processing Reorganizing or updating memories on the basis of logic, reasoning, or the addition of new information.

Pseudo-memories False memories that a person believes are real or accurate.

Memory structure Patterns of associations among bits of information stored in memory.

Network model A model of memory that views it as an organized system of linked information.

that more than one type of long-term memory exists. Let's probe a little further into the mysteries of memory.

Skill Memory and Fact Memory   A curious thing happens to many people who develop amnesia. Amnesic patients may be unable to learn a telephone number, an address, or a person's name. And yet, the same patients may learn to solve complex puzzles in the same amount of time as normal subjects (Squire & Zola-Morgan, 1988). These and other observations have led many psychologists to conclude that long-term memories fall into at least two categories. One of these might be called **procedural memory** (or skill memory). The other is called **fact memory.**

Procedural memory includes basic conditioned responses and learned actions like those involved in typing, solving a puzzle, or swinging a golf club. Memories such as these can be fully expressed only as actions. It is likely that skill memories register in "lower" brain areas, especially the cerebellum, and that they appeared early in the evolution of the brain (Tulving, 1985). They appear to represent the more basic "automatic" elements of conditioning, learning, and memory.

Fact memory involves remembering specific information, such as names, faces, words, dates, and ideas. This is the memory that a person with amnesia lacks and that most of us take for granted. Some psychologists believe that fact memory can be further divided into two other types, called semantic and episodic memory (Tulving, 1989).

Semantic Memory   Most of our basic factual *knowledge* about the world is almost totally immune to forgetting. The names of objects, the days of the week or months of the year, simple math skills, the seasons, words and language, and other general facts are all quite lasting. Such facts make up a part of LTM called **semantic memory.** Semantic memory serves as a mental dictionary or encyclopedia of basic knowledge.

Episodic Memory   Semantic memory has no connection to times or places. It would be rare, for instance, to remember when and where you first learned the names of the seasons. In contrast, **episodic memory** (ep-ih-SOD-ik) is an "autobiographical" record of personal experiences. It stores life events (or "episodes") day after day, year after year. Can you remember your seventh birthday?

Procedural memory That part of long-term memory made up of conditioned responses and learned skills.

Fact memory That part of long-term memory containing factual information.

Semantic memory A subpart of fact memory that records impersonal knowledge about the world.

Episodic memory A subpart of fact memory that records personal experiences that are linked with specific times and places.

Your first date? An accident you witnessed? The first day of college? What you had for breakfast three days ago? All are episodic memories.

In general, episodic memories are more easily forgotten than semantic memories. This is because new information constantly pours into episodic memory. Stop for a moment and remember what you did last summer. That was an episodic memory. Notice that you now remember that you just remembered something. You have a new episodic memory in which you remember that you remembered while reading this text! It's easy to see how much we ask of our memory system.

Measuring Memory—The Answer Is on the Tip of My Tongue

- **Survey Question**
  How is memory measured?

Because memory is not an all-or-nothing event, there are several ways of measuring it. Three commonly used **memory tasks** are *recall, recognition,* and *relearning.* Let's see how they differ.

Recall

Memory task Any task designed to test or assess memory.

Recall To supply or reproduce memorized information with a minimum of external cues.

What is the name of the first song on your favorite record album? Who won the World Series last year? Who wrote the *Gettysburg Address?* If you can answer these questions you are demonstrating recall. To **recall** means to supply or reproduce facts or information. Tests of recall often require *verbatim* (word-for-word) memory. If you study a poem or a speech until you can recite it without looking, you are recalling it. If you complete a fill-in-the-blank question, you are using recall. When you take an *essay* exam and provide facts and ideas without prompting you are also using recall, even though you didn't learn your essay verbatim. Essay tests tend to be difficult because they offer few cues to aid memory.

The order in which information is memorized has an interesting effect on recall. To experience it, try to memorize the following list, reading it only once:

> BREAD, APPLES, SODA, HAM, COOKIES, RICE, LETTUCE, BEETS, MUSTARD, CHEESE, ORANGES, ICE CREAM, CRACKERS, FLOUR, EGGS.

Serial position effect The tendency to make the most errors in remembering the middle items of an ordered list of information.

If you are like most people, you had the most difficulty recalling items from the middle of the list. This is called the **serial position effect.** The last items on a list appear to be remembered best because they are still in STM. The first items are also remembered because they entered an "empty" short-term memory where they could be rehearsed and moved to long-term memory (Medin & Ross, 1992). The middle items are neither held in STM nor moved to LTM, so they are often lost.

Recognition

Recognition Memory in which previously learned material is correctly identified as that which was seen before.

If you tried to write down all the facts you could remember from a class taken last year, you might conclude that you learned very little. However, a more sensitive test based on **recognition** could be used. For instance, you could be given a *multiple-choice* test on facts and ideas from the course. Since multiple-choice tests only require you to recognize the correct answer, we would probably find evidence of considerable learning.

Recognition memory can be amazingly accurate for pictures, photographs, or other visual input. One investigator showed subjects 2560 photographs at a rate of one every ten seconds. Subjects were then shown 280 pairs of photographs. One in each pair was from the first set of photos and the other was similar but new. Subjects could tell with 85 to 95 percent accuracy which photograph they had seen before (Haber, 1970). This finding may explain why people so often say, "I may forget a name, but I never forget a face."

Recognition is usually superior to recall. This is why police departments use photographs or a lineup to identify criminal suspects. Witnesses who disagree in their recall of a suspect's height, weight, age, or eye color often agree completely when recognition is all that is required. Identification is even more accurate when witnesses are allowed to hear suspects' voices as well as see them (Melara, DeWitt-Rickards, & O'Brien, 1989).

Distractors False items included with a correct item to form a test of recognition memory (for example, the wrong answers on a multiple-choice test).

False positive A false sense of recognition.

Question: Is recognition always superior? It depends greatly on the kind of **distractors** used. These are false items included with an item to be recognized. If the distractors are very similar to the correct item, memory may be poor. A reverse problem sometimes occurs when only one choice looks like it could be correct. This can produce a **false positive,** or false sense of recognition. For example, there have been instances in which witnesses described a criminal as black, tall, or young. Then a lineup was held in which a suspect was the only African American among whites, the only tall suspect, or the only young person (Loftus, 1980). Under such circumstances a false identification is very likely.

Relearning

In a classic experiment on memory, a psychologist read a short passage in Greek to his son. This was done daily when the boy was between fifteen months and three years of age. At age eight, the boy was asked if he remembered the Greek passage. He showed no evidence of recall. He was then given selections from the passage he heard and selections from other Greek passages. Could he recognize the one he heard as an infant? "It's all Greek to me!" he said, indicating no recognition (and drawing a frown from everyone in the room).

Had the psychologist stopped, he might have concluded that no memory of the Greek remained. However, the child was then asked to memorize the original quotation and others of equal difficulty. This time his earlier learning became evident. The boy memorized the passage he had heard in childhood 25 percent faster than the others (Burtt, 1941). As this experiment suggests, relearning is typically the most sensitive measure of memory.

When a person is tested by **relearning,** how do we know a memory still exists? As with the boy described, relearning is measured by a **savings score.** Let's say it takes you one hour to memorize all the names in a telephone book. (It's a small town.) Two years later you relearn them in forty-five minutes. Because you "saved" fifteen minutes, your savings score would be 25 percent (15 divided by 60 times 100). Savings like this are a good reason for studying a wide range of subjects. It may seem that it's a waste to learn algebra, history, or a foreign language because so much is lost within a year or two. But if you ever need such information, you will find you can relearn it in far less time.

Relearning Learning again something that was previously learned. Used to measure memory of prior learning.

Savings score If relearning takes less time than original learning, the amount of time saved (expressed as a percentage) is a savings score.

Forgetting—Why We, Uh, Let's See; Why We, Uh . . . Forget!

● **Survey Question**
What causes forgetting?

Generally speaking, most forgetting occurs immediately after memorization. In a famous set of experiments, **Herman Ebbinghaus** (1885) tested his own memory at various times after learning. Ebbinghaus wanted to be sure he would not be swayed by prior learn-

Nonsense syllables
Invented three-letter words used to test learning and memory.

ing, so he memorized **nonsense syllables.** These are meaningless three-letter words such as LAZ, CEF, and WOL. The importance of using meaningless words is shown by the fact that VEL, FAB, and DUZ are no longer used on memory tests. Subjects who recognize these words as detergent names find them very easy to remember.

By waiting various lengths of time before testing himself, Ebbinghaus plotted a **curve of forgetting** and his findings remain valid today. Forgetting is rapid at first and is then followed by a slow decline. As a student, you should know that forgetting is minimized when there is little delay between review and taking a test. However, don't take this as a reason for cramming. The error most students make is to cram *only.* If you cram, you don't have to remember for very long, but you may not learn enough in the first place. If you use short, daily study sessions and, in addition, review intensely before a test, you will get the benefit of good preparation and a minimum time lapse.

Curve of forgetting A graph that shows the amount of memorized information remembered after varying lengths of time.

Encoding Failure

Whose head is on a U.S. penny? Which way is it facing? What is written at the top of a penny? Can you accurately draw and label a penny? In an interesting experiment, Nickerson and Adams (1979) asked a large group of students to draw a penny. Few could. Well then, could the students at least recognize a drawing of a real penny among fakes? (See the figure.) Again, few could.

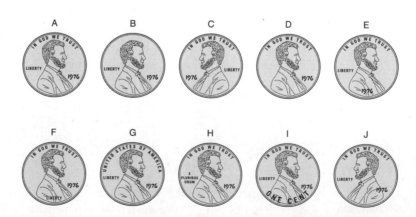

Some of the distractor items used in a study of recognition memory and encoding failure. Penny A is correct but was seldom recognized. Pennies G and J were popular wrong answers. (Adapted from Nickerson & Adams, 1979.)

The most obvious reason for forgetting is also the most commonly overlooked. In many cases we "forget" because of **encoding failure.** That is, a memory was never formed in the first place. Obviously, few of us ever encode the details of a penny. If you are bothered by frequent forgetting, it is wise to ask yourself, "Have I been storing the information in the first place?" When 140 college professors were asked what strategies they use to improve their memory, the most frequently recommended technique was to write things down (Park, Smith, & Cavanaugh, 1990). Making notes ensures that information will not be lost from short-term memory before it can be stored more permanently.

Decay

One view of forgetting holds that **memory traces** (changes in nerve cells or brain activity) fade, weaken, or **decay,** over time. Decay appears definitely to be a factor in the loss of sensory memories. Such fading also applies to short-term memory. Information stored in STM seems to initiate a brief flurry of activity in the brain that quickly dies out (Shiffrin & Cook, 1978). Short-term memory therefore operates like a "leaky bucket": New information constantly pours in, but it rapidly fades away and is replaced by still newer information.

Disuse Theory that attributes forgetting to a weakening of memory traces that occurs when the memories are not periodically used or retrieved.

Disuse Is it possible that the decay of memory traces also explains long-term forgetting? That is, could long-term memory traces fade from **disuse** and finally become so weak they cannot be retrieved? As tempting as this theory may be, there are reasons to doubt it. One reason already mentioned is the recovery of seemingly forgotten memories. Another is that disuse fails to explain why some unused memories fade, while others are carried for life. A third contradiction will be recognized by anyone who has spent time with the elderly. People growing senile may become so forgetful that they can't remember what happened a week ago. Yet at the same time your Uncle Oscar's recent memories are fading, he may have vivid memories of trivial and long-forgotten events from the past. "Why, I remember it as clearly as if it were yesterday," he will say, forgetting that the story he is about to tell is one he told earlier the same day. In short, disuse alone does not adequately explain long-term forgetting.

Cue-Dependent Forgetting

Often, memories appear to be *available,* but not accessible. An example is having an answer on the "tip of your tongue." You know the answer is there, but it remains just "out of reach." This situation indicates that many memories are "forgotten" because **cues** present at the time of learning are absent when the time comes to retrieve information. For example, if you were asked, "What were you doing on Monday afternoon of the third week in September two years ago?" your reply might be, "Come on. How should I know?" However, if you were reminded, "That was the day the courthouse burned," or "That was the day Mary had her automobile accident," you might remember immediately. The presence of such cues almost always enhances memory.

Memory cue Any stimulus associated with a particular memory. The presence of such cues usually enhances memory retrieval.

State-Dependent Learning   Nearly everyone has heard the story about the drunk who misplaced his wallet and had to get drunk again to find it. Although this tale is often told as a joke, it is not too farfetched. The *bodily state* that exists during learning can be a strong cue for later memory (Overton, 1985). Being very thirsty, for instance, might make you remember events that took place on another occasion when you were thirsty. Because of such effects, information learned under the influence of a drug is best remembered when the drugged state occurs again. This is known as **state-dependent learning.**

A similar effect may apply to emotional states. For instance, Gordon Bower (1981) found that people who learned a list of words while in a happy mood recalled them better when they were again happy. People who learned while they felt sad remembered best when they were sad. Similarly, if you are in a happy mood you are more likely to remember recent happy events (Salovey & Singer, 1989). If you are in a bad mood you will tend to have unpleasant memories (Eich, Rachman, & Lopatka, 1990). Such links between emotional cues and memory could explain why couples who quarrel often end up remembering—and rehashing—old arguments.

State-dependent learning Memory influenced by one's bodily state at the time of learning and at the time of retrieval. Improved memory occurs when the bodily states match.

Interference

Further understanding of forgetting comes from an experiment in which college students learned lists of nonsense syllables. After studying, students in one group slept for eight hours and were then tested for memory of the lists. A second group remained awake for eight hours and went about business as usual. When members of the second group were tested, they remembered *less* than the group that slept. This difference is based on the fact that new learning can *interfere* with previous learning (Shiffrin, 1970). **Interference** refers to the tendency for new memories to impair retrieval of older memories, and the reverse. It seems to apply to both short-term and long-term memories.

It is not completely clear if new memories alter existing memory traces or if they make it harder to "locate" (retrieve) earlier memories. In any case, there is no doubt that interference is a major cause of forgetting (Johnson & Hasher, 1987). College students who memorized twenty lists of words (one list each day) were able to recall only 15 percent of the last list. Students who learned only one list remembered 80 percent (Underwood, 1957).

Interference The tendency for new memories to impair retrieval of older memories, and the reverse.

● **Survey Question**
How accurate are everyday memories?

Repression

Take a moment from reading and scan over the events of the last few years of your life. What kinds of things most easily come to mind? Many people find that they tend to remember happy, positive events better than disappointments and irritations (Linton, 1979). A clinical psychologist would call this tendency **repression,** or motivated forgetting. Through repression, painful, threatening, or embarrassing memories are held out of consciousness by forces within one's personality. The forgetting of past failures, upsetting childhood events, the names of persons you dislike, or appointments you don't want to keep may reveal repression.

Adults who were sexually abused as children may repress all memory of their mistreatment. Some are startled when their repressed memories are brought to the surface by psychotherapy or other events.

Repression can be distinguished from **suppression,** an active, conscious attempt to put something out of one's mind. By not thinking about the test, you have merely suppressed a memory. If you choose to, you can remember the test. Clinicians consider true repression an *unconscious* event. When a memory is repressed we are unaware that forgetting has even occurred.

Highlight 1   The False Memory Syndrome

The idea that early traumatic memories are often deeply repressed is gaining wide acceptance. Perhaps too wide. The pursuit of "repressed memories of sexual abuse" as an explanation for adult emotional problems may be turning into a witch-hunt. Certainly, some memories that return to awareness are genuine. Sexual abuse is so tragically common that many adults could have repressed memories. However, there is no way to distinguish real memories of childhood abuse from false memories.

Question: Why would anyone have a false memory about such disturbing events?

Several popular books and some therapists actively encourage people to find repressed memories of abuse. This is, in fact, something of a fad. Some therapists state that abuse *must have* taken place and insist that their patients produce memories. Such practices can lead people to produce fantasies and mistake them for real memories.

Clearly there is a need to strike a balance between uncovering and treating real repressed trauma and doing damage by fabricating memories. False allegations of sexual abuse create a living nightmare for the accused. There is almost no way they can prove their innocence. If large numbers of people are persuaded to create memories of abuse, many families will be needlessly torn apart. (Sources: Loftus, 1993; Gardner, 1993.)

Improving Memory—Keys to the Memory Bank

- **Survey Question**
How can memory be improved?

While you're waiting around for the development of a memory pill, let's focus on some ways of improving your memory skills right now.

Knowledge of results
During learning, feedback about the correctness of responses or other aspects of performance.

Knowledge of Results   Learning proceeds best when feedback, or knowledge of results, allows you to check to see if you are learning. Feedback also helps you identify ideas that need extra practice. In addition, knowing that you have remembered or answered correctly can be rewarding. A prime means of providing feedback for yourself when studying is *recitation*.

Recitation As a memory aid, repeating aloud information one wishes to retain.

Recitation   Recitation means repeating to yourself what you have learned. If you are going to remember something, eventually you will have to retrieve it. Recitation forces you to practice retrieving information as you are learning. When you are reading a text, you should stop frequently and try to remember what you have just read by summarizing it aloud. In one experiment, the best memory score of all was earned by a group of students who spent 80 percent of their time reciting and only 20 percent reading (Gates, 1958). Maybe students who talk to themselves aren't crazy after all.

Rehearsal Silently repeating or mentally reviewing information to improve memory.

Rehearsal The more you rehearse information as you read, the better you will remember it (Muth, et al., 1988). Rehearsal refers to mentally repeating, paraphrasing, and summarizing information. Rehearsal is similar to recitation, but it can be done privately. It's also helpful to frequently ask yourself "why" questions about what you read. For example, you could ask about this paragraph, "Why would it make sense that rehearsal improves memory?" (Woloshyn et al., 1990). Thinking about facts helps link them together in memory.

Selection The Dutch scholar Erasmus said that a good memory should be like a fish net: It should keep all the big fish and let the little ones escape. If you boil down the paragraphs in most textbooks to one or two important terms or ideas, your memory chores will be more manageable. Practice very selective marking in your texts and use marginal notes to further summarize ideas. Most students mark their texts too much instead of too little. If everything is underlined, you haven't been selective. And, very likely, you didn't actually pay much attention to what you read (Peterson, 1992).

Organization Assume that you must memorize the following list of words: *north, man, red, spring, woman, east, autumn, yellow, summer, boy, blue, west, winter, girl, green, south.* This rather difficult list could be reorganized into *chunks* as follows: *north-east-south-west, spring-summer-autumn-winter, red-yellow-green-blue, man-woman-boy-girl.* This simple reordering made the second list much easier to learn when college students were tested on both lists (Deese & Hulse, 1967). In another experiment, students who made up stories using long lists of words to be memorized learned the lists better than those who didn't (Bower & Clark, 1969). Organizing class notes and outlining chapters can be helpful when studying (Dickinson & O'Connell, 1990). It may even be helpful to outline your outlines, so that the overall organization of ideas becomes clearer and simpler.

Whole learning Studying an entire package of information (such as a complete poem) at once.

Part learning Separately studying subparts of a larger body of information (such as sections of a textbook chapter).

Whole versus Part Learning If you had to memorize a speech, would it be better to try to learn it from beginning to end or in smaller parts like paragraphs? Generally it is better to practice whole packages of information rather than smaller parts. This is especially true for fairly short, organized information. An exception is that learning parts may be better for extremely long, complicated information. Try to study the largest *meaningful* amount of information possible at one time.

For very long or complex material, try the *progressive part method.* In this approach, you break a learning task into short sections. At first, you study part A until it is mastered. Next, you study parts A and B; then A, B, and C; and so forth. This is a good way to learn the lines of a play, a long piece of music, or a poem (Ash & Holding, 1990). After the material is learned, you should also practice it by starting at points other than A (at C, D, or B, for example). This helps prevent getting "lost" or going blank in the middle of a performance.

Serial position effect The tendency for the greatest number of memory errors to occur in the middle portion of an ordered list.

Serial Position   Whenever you must learn something in *order,* be aware of the *serial position effect.* This is the tendency to make the most errors in remembering the middle of a list. If you are introduced to a long line of people, the names you are likely to forget will be those in the middle, so you should make an extra effort to attend to them. The middle of a list, poem, or speech should also be given special attention and extra practice.

Cues   The best cues for remembering are those that were present during encoding (Reed, 1988). For example, students in one study had to recall a list of 600 words. As they read the list (which they did not know they would be tested on), the students gave three other words closely related in meaning to each listed word. In a test given later, the words each student supplied were used as cues to jog his or her memory. The students recalled an astounding 90 percent of the original word list (Mantyla, 1986). This shows why it often helps to *elaborate* information as you learn. When you study, try to use new names, ideas, or terms in several sentences. Also, form images that include the new information, and relate it to knowledge you already have (Pressley et al., 1988). Your goals should be to knit meaningful cues into your memory to help you retrieve information when you need it.

Overlearning Study or learning that continues after initial mastery of skills or information.

Overlearning   Numerous studies have shown that memory is greatly improved when study is continued beyond bare mastery. In other words, after you have learned material well enough to remember it once without error, you should continue studying. Overlearning is your best insurance against going blank on a test because of nervousness.

Spaced practice A practice schedule that alternates study periods with brief rests.

Massed practice A practice schedule in which studying continues for long periods, without interruption.

Spaced Practice   To keep boredom and fatigue to a minimum, try alternating short study sessions with brief rest periods. This pattern, called **spaced practice,** is generally superior to **massed practice,** in which little or no rest is given between learning sessions (Naveh-Benjamin, 1990). By improving attention and consolidation, three 20-minute study sessions can produce more learning than one hour of continuous study. Perhaps the best way to make use of this principle is to *schedule* your time. If most students were to keep a totally honest record of their weekly activities, they would probably find that very few hours were spent really studying. To make an effective schedule, designate times during the week before, after, and between classes when you will study particular subjects. Then treat these times just as if they were classes you had to attend.

Sleep   Remember that sleeping after study reduces interference. Since you obviously can't sleep after every study session or study everything just before you sleep, your study schedule (see Spaced Practice) should include ample breaks between subjects. Using your breaks and free time in a schedule is as important as living up to your study periods.

Review   If you have spaced your practice and overlearned, review will be like icing on your study cake. Reviewing shortly before an exam cuts down the time during which you must remember details that may be important for the test. When reviewing, hold the amount of new information you try to memorize to a minimum. It may be realistic to take what you have actually learned and add a little more to it at the last minute by cramming. But remember that more than a little new learning may interfere with what you already know.

Using a Strategy to Aid Recall   Successful recall is usually the result of a planned *search* of memory (Reed, 1988). For example, one study found that students were most likely to recall names that eluded them if they made use of partial information (Reed & Bruce, 1982). The students were trying to answer questions such as, "He is best remembered as the scarecrow in the Judy Garland movie *The Wizard of Oz.*" (The answer is Ray Bolger.) Partial information that helped students remember included impressions about the length of the name, letter sounds within the name, similar names, and related information (such as the names of other characters in the movie). A similar helpful strategy is to go through the alphabet, trying each letter as the first sound of a name or word you are seeking.

Using a variety of cues, even partial ones, opens more paths to a memory. After that, the Applications section covers some of the most powerful memory techniques of all.

A Look Ahead   Psychologists still have much to learn about the nature of memory and how to improve it. For now, one thing stands out clearly: People who have good memories excel at organizing information and making it meaningful. With this in mind, the **Applications** for this chapter tells how you can combine organization and meaning into a powerful method for improving memory.

Highlight 2   Memory Detectives

You may not think of yourself as a "memory detective," but active probing often helps improve recall. A case in point is the *cognitive interview,* a technique used to jog the memory of eyewitnesses. The cognitive interview was created by R. Edward Geiselman and Ron Fisher to help police detectives. When used properly, it produces 35 percent more correct information than standard questioning (Geiselman et al., 1986).

By following four simple steps, you can apply cognitive principles to your own memory. The next time you are searching for a "lost" memory—one that you know is in there somewhere—try the following search strategies.

1.   Say or write down *everything* you can remember that relates to the information you are seeking. Don't worry about how trivial any of it seems; each bit of information you remember can serve as a cue to bring back others.

2.   Try to recall events or information in different orders. Let your memories flow out backward or out of order, or start with whatever impressed you the most.

3.   Recall from different viewpoints. Review events by mentally standing in a different place. Or try to view information as another person would remember it. When taking a test, for instance, ask yourself what other students or your professor would remember about the topic.

4.   Mentally put yourself back in the situation where you learned the information. Try to mentally re-create the learning environment or relive the event. As you do, include sounds, smells, details of weather, nearby objects, other people present, what you said or thought, and how you felt as you learned the information (Fisher & Geiselman, 1987).

These strategies help re-create the context in which information was learned, and they provide multiple memory cues. If you think of remembering as a sort of "treasure hunt," you might even learn to enjoy the detective work.

Applications

Various "memory experts" entertain by giving demonstrations in which they memorize the names of everyone at a banquet, the order of all the cards in a deck, long lists of words, or other seemingly impossible amounts of information. Such feats may seem like magic, but if they are, you can have a magic memory too. These tricks are performed through the use of **mnemonics** (nee-MON-iks). A mnemonic is any kind of memory system or aid. In some cases, mnemonic strategies increase recall ten-fold (Patten, 1990).

Some mnemonic systems have become so common that almost everyone knows them. If you are trying to remember how many days there are in a month, you may find the answer by reciting, "Thirty days hath September. . . ." Physics teachers often help their students remember the colors of the spectrum by giving them the mnemonic "Roy G. Biv": **R**ed, **O**range, **Y**ellow, **G**reen, **B**lue, **I**ndigo, **V**iolet. The budding sailor who has trouble telling port from starboard may remember that port and left both have four letters or may remind himself, "I *left* port." And what beginning musician hasn't remembered the notes represented by the lines and spaces of the musical staff by learning "F-A-C-E" and "Every Good Boy Does Fine."

Mnemonic techniques are ways of avoiding *rote* learning (learning by simple repetition). The superiority of mnemonic learning as opposed to rote learning has been demonstrated many times. For example, Bower (1973) asked college students to study five different lists of twenty unrelated words. At the end of a short study session,

subjects were asked to recall all one-hundred items. Subjects using mnemonics remembered an average of seventy-two items, whereas a control group using simple, or rote, learning remembered an average of twenty-eight.

Stage performers rarely have a naturally superior memory. Instead, they make extensive use of memory systems to perform their feats. Few of these systems are of practical value to you as a student, but the principles underlying mnemonics are. By practicing mnemonics you should be able to greatly improve your memory with little effort.

Here, then, are the basic principles of mnemonics.

1. **Use mental pictures.** There are at least two kinds of memory, *visual* and *verbal*. Visual pictures, or images, are generally easier to remember than words. Turning information into mental pictures is therefore very helpful (Kroll et al., 1986).

2. **Make things meaningful.** Transferring information from short-term to long-term memory is aided by making it meaningful. If you encounter technical terms that have little or no immediate meaning for you, *give* them meaning, even if you have to stretch the term to do so.

3. **Make information familiar.** Connect it to what you already know. Another way to get information into long-term memory is to connect it to information already stored there. If some facts or ideas in a chapter seem to stay in your memory easily, associate other more difficult facts with them.

4. Form bizarre, unusual, or exaggerated mental associations. Forming images that make sense is better in most situations (Reed, 1988). However, when associating two ideas, terms, or especially mental images, you may sometimes find that the more outrageous and exaggerated the association, the more likely you are to remember it later (Iaccino & Sowa, 1989). Bizarre images can make stored information more *distinctive* and therefore easier to retrieve (Riefer & Rouder, 1992).

Chapter Summary

How Do We Store Information in Memory?

- **Memory** is an active, computer-like system that **encodes, stores,** and **retrieves** information.

Is There More Than One Type of Memory?

- Humans appear to have three interrelated memory systems. These are **sensory memory, short-term memory** (STM, also called **working memory**), and **long-term memory** (LTM).

What Are the Features of Each Type of Memory?

- Sensory memory is exact, but very brief. Through **selective attention,** some information is transferred to STM.

- STM has a capacity of about **seven bits** of information, but this can be extended by **chunking,** or **recoding.** Short-term memories are brief and very sensitive to **interruption,** or **interference;** however, they can be prolonged by **rehearsal.**

- LTM functions as a general storehouse of information, especially *meaningful* information. Long-term memories are relatively *permanent,* or lasting. LTM seems to have an almost *unlimited storage* capacity.

- LTM is subject to **constructive processing,** or ongoing revision and updating. LTM is highly *organized* to allow retrieval of needed information. The pattern, or **structure,** of memory **networks** is the subject of current memory research.

- Within long-term memory, **fact memories** seem to differ from **procedural memories.** Fact memories may be further categorized as **semantic memories** or **episodic memories.**

How Is Memory Measured?

- The **tip-of-the-tongue state** shows that memory is not an all-or-nothing event. Memories may therefore be revealed by **recall, recognition,** or **relearning.**

- In recall, memory proceeds without *explicit cues* for an *essay* exam. Recall of listed information often has a **serial position effect** (middle items on the list are most subject to errors). A common test of remembering is the *multiple-choice* question. In relearning, forgotten material is learned again, and memory is indicated by a **savings score.**

- Recall, recognition, and relearning mainly measure explicit memories.

What Causes Forgetting?

- Forgetting and memory were extensively studied by **Herman Ebbinghaus,** whose **curve of forgetting** shows that forgetting is most rapid immediately after learning.

- **Failure to encode** information is a common cause of "forgetting." Forgetting in sensory memory and STM probably reflects **decay** of **memory traces** in the nervous system. Decay or **disuse** of memories may also account for some LTM loss, but much forgetting cannot be explained in this way.

- Often, forgetting is **cue dependent.** The power of cues to trigger memories is revealed by **state-dependent learning** and the link between moods and memory.

- Much forgetting in both STM and LTM can be attributed to **interference** of memories with one another.

How Accurate Are Everyday Memories?

- **Repression** is the forgetting of painful, embarrassing, or traumatic memories. Repression is thought to be unconscious, in contrast to **suppression,** which is a conscious attempt to avoid thinking about something.

How Can Memory Be Improved?

- Memory can be improved by using **feedback, recitation,** and **rehearsal,** by selecting and **organizing** information, and by using the **progressive part method, spaced practice, overlearning,** and active **search strategies.** Effects of **serial position, sleep, review, cues,** and **elaboration** should also be kept in mind when studying or memorizing.

- **Mnemonic systems** use mental images and unusual associations to link new information with familiar memories already stored in LTM. Such strategies give information personal meaning and make it easier to recall.

Dennis Coon, *Essentials of Psychology: Exploration and Application,* 6th ed. St. Paul, Minn.: West Publishing Co. 1994, pp. 301–332.

Acknowledgments

Diane Ackerman, from *A Natural History of Love* by Diane Ackerman. Copyright © 1994 by Diane Ackerman. Reprinted by permission of Random House, Inc. **Simon Adams and Lesley Riley**, reprinted from *Facts & Fallacies*, copyright © 1988 by The Reader's Digest Association, Inc. Used by permission of The Reader's Digest Association, Inc. **Freda Adler, Gerhard O.W. Mueller, and William Laufer**, from *Criminal Justice*. Copyright © 1994. Reproduced with permission of The McGraw-Hill Companies. **Albert Richard Allgeier and Elizabeth Rice Allgeier**, *Sexual Interactions*, 5/e. © 1995 by Houghton Mifflin Company. Reprinted by permission. **Billy Allstetter**. Adapted with permission from *American Health*, November 1991, p. 27. **Patricia Barnes-Svarney**. Reprinted with the permission of Macmillan General Reference USA, a division of Ahsuog, Inc. from *The New York Public Library Desk Reference*, edited by Patricia Barnes-Svarney. Copyright © 1993 by New York Public Library and the Stonesong Press, Inc. **Carol Berkin et al.**, from *Making America: A History of the United States*. Copyright © 1995 by Houghton Mifflin Company. Used by permission. **Roy Berko, Andrew Wolvin, and Karlyn Wolvin**, from *Communicating*. Copyright © 1995 by Houghton Mifflin Company. Used by permission. **Rick Bragg**, Copyright © 1996 by the New York Times Co. Reprinted by permission. **Sharon S. Brehm and Saul M. Kassin**. From *Social Psychology*. Copyright © 1997 by Houghton Mifflin Company. Used by permission. **Sean Dennis Cashman**, from *African-Americans and the Quest for Civil Rights, 1900-1990*. Copyright © 1991. Reprinted by permission of New York University Press. **Judith Ortiz Cofer**, "The Paterson Public Library" from *The Latin Deli: Prose & Poetry* by Judith Ortiz Cofer. Reprinted by permission of The University of Georgia Press. **Dennis Coon**, from *Essentials of Psychology: Exploration and Application*, 6th ed., pp. 139, 222, 228, 256, 301-333, 419, 484. Copyright © 1994 West Publishing Co. Reprinted by permission of Wadsworth Publishing Co. **James West Davidson and Mark Hamilton Lytle**. From *After the Fact*. Copyright © 1982 by Alfred A. Knopf, Inc. Reprinted by permission of the publisher. **Andrew DuBrin**. From *Leadership*. Copyright © 1998 by Houghton Mifflin Company. Used by permission. **Ashley Dunn**, Copyright © 1995 by the New York Times Co. Reprinted by permission. **Howard W. French**, copyright © 1997 by The New York Times Co. Reprinted by permission. **Alan Gitelson, Robert L. Dudley, and Melvin J. Dubrick**, from *American Government*, 5/e. © 1998 by Houghton Mifflin Company. Reprinted by permission. **William B. Gudykunst et al.**, from *Building Bridges: Personal Skills for a Changing World*, © 1995 by Houghton Mifflin Company. Reprinted by permission. **Sydney W. Head, Christopher H. Sterling, and Lemuel B. Schofield**, *Broadcasting in America*, 8/e. Copyright © 1998 by Houghton Mifflin Company. Reprinted by permission. **Wayne D. Hoyer and Deborah J. MacInnis**, from *Consumer Behavior*, © 1997 by Houghton Mifflin Company. Reprinted by permission. **Kenneth Janda, Jeffrey M. Berry, and Jerry Goldman**, from *The Challenge of Democracy*. Copyright © 1995 by Houghton Mifflin Company. Used by permission. **Paul E. Johnson et al.**, from *American Government*, © 1994 by Houghton Mifflin Company. Used by permission. **Kantrowitz and Winger**, from *Newsweek*, October 5, 1998. © 1998 Newsweek, Inc. All rights reserved. Reprinted by permission. **Saul Kassin**, from *Psychology*. Copyright © 1995 by Houghton Mifflin Company. Used by permission. **Kaufman and Franz**, Adapted from *Biosphere 2000*, © 1996. Used by permission of Kendall/Hunt Publishing Company. **Ron Kline**, "A Scientist: I Am the Enemy," *Newsweek*, December 18, 1991, pp. 77-78. Ron Kline is Director of Pediatric Hematology/Oncology/BMT at Atlantic Health System, NJ. Reprinted by permission of the author. **D. Knox**. From *Choices in Relationships: An Introduction to Marriage and the Family*. © 1985. Reprinted with permission of Wadsworth Publishing, a division of International Thomson Publishing. Fax 800-730-2215. **Robert MacNeil**, from *Wordstruck* by Robert MacNeil. Copyright © 1989 by Neely Productions, Ltd. Used by permission of Viking Penguin, a division of Penguin Putnam, Inc. **Kevin Maney**. "Olympics TV Coverage Leaves Opening for the Net," *USA Today*. February 12, 1998. Copyright 1998, USA TODAY. Reprinted with permission. **Michael Mason**. From *Newsweek*, May 20, 1991. © 1991 Newsweek, Inc. All rights reserved. Reprinted by permission. **Kathleen D. Mullen et al.**, from *Connections for Health*. Copyright © 1997. Reproduced with permission of The McGraw-Hill Companies. **Mary Beth Norton et al.**, from *A People and a Nation*. Copyright © 1986, 1993, 1994, 1998 by Houghton Mifflin Company. Used by permission. **Ted Nugent**, from "Hunters Are Wildlife's Best Friends," *USA Today*, October 3, 1991. Reprinted by permission of the author. **Lynette Padwa**. From *Everything You Pretend to Know and Are Afraid Someone Will Ask*. Copyright © 1996 by Affinity Publishing, Inc. Used by permission of Viking Penguin, a division of Penguin Putnam, Inc. **PETA excerpts**. From fact sheet from "People for the Ethical Treatment of Animals." Used by permission of PETA. **Barry L. Reece and Rhonda Brandt**, *Effective Human Relations in Organizations*, © 1996 by Houghton Mifflin Company. Reprinted by permission. **Register-Freeman**, From *Newsweek*, November 4, 1996. All rights reserved. Reprinted by permission. **Andrew C. Revkin**, copyright © 1995 by the New York Times Co. Reprinted by permission. **Zick Rubin, Letita Anne Peplau, and Peter Salovey**, from *Psychology*. Copyright © 1993, 1990 by Houghton Mifflin Company. Used by permission. **Kevin Ryan and James M. Cooper**, from *Those Who Can, Teach*, 8/e. Copyright © 1998 by Houghton Mifflin Company. Reprinted by permission. **Nancy Masterson Sakamoto**, from "Conversational Ballgames," in *Polite Fictions*, Kinseido, Ltd., 1982, by Nancy Masterson Sakamoto. Reprinted by permission of the author. **John Santrock**, from *Life-Span Development*, 5th ed. Copyright © 1995 by William C. Brown Communications, Inc. Reprinted by permission of Times Mirror Higher Education Group, Inc., Dubuque, Iowa. All rights reserved. **Kelvin Seifert**, from *Educational Psychology*. Copyright © 1991 by Houghton Mifflin Company. Used by permission. **Kelvin Seifert and Robert J. Hoffnung**, from *Child and Adolescent Development*, 4/e. Copyright © 1997 by Houghton Mifflin Company. Reprinted by permission. **Kelvin L. Seifert, Robert J. Hoffnung, and Michelle Hoffnung**, from *Lifespan Development*. © 1997 by Houghton Mifflin Company. Reprinted by permission. **Alex Thio**, from *Sociology*, 5/e by Alex Thio. Copyright © 1998 by Addison-Wesley Educational Publishers, Inc. Reprinted by permission. **Ted Tollefson,** from "Is a Hero Really Nothing but a Sandwich?," *Utne Reader*, May/June 1993. Reprinted by permission of the author. Ted Tollefson, a Unitarian Universalist Minister, is co-founder of Mytaos Institute in Minnesota. **James Q. Wilson and John DiIulio**, from *American Government*, 7/e. © 1998 by Houghton Mifflin Company. Reprinted by permission.

INDEX